Anthropology

A general introduction

THE DORSEY SERIES IN ANTHROPOLOGY

VICTOR BARNOUW

Professor of Anthropology
University of Wisconsin–Milwaukee

Anthropology
A general introduction

1979 **THE DORSEY PRESS** Homewood, Illinois 60430
IRWIN-DORSEY LIMITED Georgetown, Ontario L7G 4B3

Cover: Fishermen on poles, Ceylon (Sri Lanka)
Photo by Robert Frerck, DIMENSIONS—visual productions

ISBN 0-256-02113-9
Library of Congress Catalog Card No. 78–59220
Printed in the United States of America

1 2 3 4 5 6 7 8 9 0 K 6 5 4 3 2 1 0 9

Learning Systems Company—
a division of Richard D. Irwin, Inc.—has developed a
Programmed Learning AID
to accompany texts in this subject area.
Copies can be purchased through your bookstore
or by writing PLAIDS,
1818 Ridge Road, Homewood, Illinois 60430.

This book is dedicated to my wife
SACHIKO

PREFACE

In this book I have synthesized and condensed in one volume the material presented in my two-volume work, *An Introduction to Anthropology,* which was first published in 1971, with revisions in 1975 and 1978.

Anthropology has to do with humans at all times and places; it is not limited to the study of early people and "primitive" non-Western cultures, as it was sometimes held to be. It deals with both the physical and cultural evolution of human beings and with their adaptations to different environments in different periods of time, including our own.

In general, my approach to this broad field has been eclectic. When controversies occur I have presented the contending viewpoints, as, for example, in interpretations about the australopithecines and their bearing on the course of human evolution, the different theories about the origin of the state, or the conflicting explanations for the development of incest taboos.

Courses in Introduction to Anthropology are often given in two semesters, the first usually dealing with physical anthropology and archaeology and the second with ethnology or sociocultural anthropology. My earlier two separate volumes were primarily intended for a two-semester sequence of this sort. But introductory anthropology courses are also often given in a single semester which covers the whole field, and it was for such courses that the present one-volume text was designed. The basic information offered in both volumes has been retained in this one-volume work.

The proposed outline for this text was sent to the following anthropologists, who offered critical comments and suggestions: Stanley D. Bussey, New Mexico State University; Thomas P. Templeton, Mesa Community College; and Joseph R. Walsh, Buck County Community College. The manuscript for the book was then reviewed by Stanley D. Bussey, William Madsen of the University of California at Santa Barbara, and J. Anthony Paredes of Florida State University. I am grateful to them all for their comments and criticisms.

December 1978   VICTOR BARNOUW

CONTENTS

1

INTRODUCTION: THE FIELD
OF ANTHROPOLOGY

The purpose of this introductory chapter is to explain what anthropology is and what anthropologists do. It will also sketch the historical background of this field, for anthropology as a separate professional discipline came into being in a particular historical period; we need to have some understanding of why that happened. The research methods of anthropology's subdisciplines will be briefly described. Finally, the point will be made that, despite these separate subdisciplines, anthropologists tend to think of anthropology as a unified, holistic field of research.

Anthropology is the study of human beings (from Greek *anthropos,* man, and *logia,* study). It is concerned mainly with a single species, *Homo sapiens* (the zoological term for our species), rather than with many diverse organisms, as in the cases of botany and zoology. Our objective is to learn all we can about our species, how we have become what we are, what we have accomplished, and what our potentialities are.

In such a many-sided investigation as this, there must be some division of labor, so anthropology is broadly divided into physical anthropology and cultural anthropology. Cultural anthropology, in turn, may be divided into three main branches: linguistics, archaeology, and ethnology. The significance of the main two-fold division of the field is that humans are always both biological and cultural beings. Our species has a particular kind of physical structure, physiology, and biochemistry, and all human beings also have a particular *culture.* This is a crucial term which requires definition.

Culture refers to learned behavior shared by the members of a society. It is acquired by experience, as opposed to being inborn, genetically determined behavior. This use of the term must be distinguished from older colloquial meanings expressed in phrases like "a man of culture." In the anthropological sense, all humans have culture. **Culture**

1

Although anthropologists sometimes use the word *culture* in a broad generic sense, they also speak about *a culture,* like Eskimo culture or Hopi culture. Here is a definition of culture in this sense: *A culture is the way of life of a group of people, the configuration of all of the more or less stereotyped patterns of learned behavior handed down from one generation to the next through the means of language and imitation.*

The nub of this definition is "the way of life of a group of people." This way of life has some integration and cohesion to it—hence the term *configuration.* It consists of patterns of learned behavior transmitted through language and imitation—not through instinct or any direct action of the genes, although the *capacity* for culture is determined by heredity. These patterns are only relatively fixed and are amenable to change; hence, they are said to be "more or less stereotyped."

Examples of patterns of learned behavior are: speaking English, Chinese, Bantu, or Hindi; wearing trousers in our society, kilts in Scotland, or togas in ancient Rome; sitting on chairs in the Western world or sitting cross-legged on the ground in many societies; eating at set mealtimes—breakfast, lunch, and dinner, or twice a day in some societies, or four times, as when the English add afternoon tea; using knife, fork, and spoon to eat with in the Western world, chopsticks in China and Japan, or the fingers of the right hand in India; believing in the tenets of Jesus Christ, Confucius, Mohammed, or Buddha; consulting the medicine man, the priest, the doctor, or the psychiatrist; making a Navaho sand painting, a Kwakiutl totem pole, or an abstract painting. A person is destined to learn the patterns of behavior prevalent in the society in which he or she grows up. A person does not necessarily learn them all, for there may be cultural differences appropriate to persons of different age, sex, status, and occupation, and there may also be genetically determined differences in learning ability. Moreover, the culture patterns of a society may change with the appearance of new inventions or through contact with other ways of life.

Some knowledge of the diversity of human cultures is a useful antidote to ethnocentrism. *Ethnocentrism* is the tendency to judge and evaluate other ways of life in terms of one's own culture, with the assumption that one's own culture is the best. This is a common human tendency, found in other cultures besides our own. Generalizations about human nature should always be checked to see if they are applicable to societies other than our own, for we are often led to assume that some characteristic of our own way of life is true of all mankind.

Patterns of culture require *language* for their transmission. That is why linguistics is one of the branches of anthropology.

Linguistics, archaeology, and ethnology

Linguistics is the study of languages. Although other animals besides human beings have communication systems, and although the cries of apes and monkeys seem to have communicative functions, no other organism

Taking notes and measurements in an archaeological site.

is known to have as elaborate a system of symbolic communication as *Homo sapiens.* The transmission of culture from generation to generation is made possible by language, which enables humans to preserve the traditions of the past and to make provisions for the future.

Not all linguists are anthropologists, but some anthropologists specialize in the study of languages. Ethnologists (anthropologists who study contemporary cultures) often learn the language of the people whom they are studying in the field. It is possible to do ethnological fieldwork with bilingual interpreters, but it is much better if the anthropologist understands the local speech. All kinds of subtleties may be lost in translation, for example, in a discussion of religious concepts.

Archaeology is the study of extinct cultures, as distinguished from ethnology, which is the study of living ones. Anthropological archaeologists are usually, although not always, concerned with what are called *prehistoric cultures,* those that existed before the development of written records. Archaeologists willingly make use of written records if they are available, as in

Mesopotamia, Egypt, and Guatemala, but often they have nothing to work with but such relics and remains of bygone peoples as potsherds, arrowheads, clay figurines, and tools of bone, stone, or other durable materials.

Since systems of writing developed only about 5,000 years ago, while there were ancestors of ours who were able to make tools about 2.6 million years ago, it is evident that the period of prehistory is immensely long. We depend upon the archaeologist, working with the paleontologist, geologist, physical anthropologist, and other specialists, to reconstruct what happened during these hundreds of thousands of years. In many parts of the world—Australia, Melanesia, Polynesia, most of the New World, and Africa— writing had only a relatively recent introduction. Here, again, the archaeologist works to uncover the past.

The archaeologist seeks to reconstruct culture history and the lifeways of peoples of the past. He also tries to understand cultural processes insofar as they may be inferred from archaeological remains and other evidence.

Ethnology is the study of contemporary cultures. Ethnologists go to a particular society, let us say an Eskimo group; they get to know the people, learn something of their language, and keep a record of observations and interviews. A detailed written description of a particular culture is known as an *ethnography*. Ethnologists have varied interests and objectives, but all of them try to delineate some of the characteristic culture patterns of the group they study. An ethnologist may, for example, be particularly interested in how kinship is reckoned in an Eskimo community, what religious beliefs the people have, or how the religion is related to other aspects of the culture. An ethnologist may also study techniques of food getting, such as seal hunting, and the material equipment used in the process: methods of making dogsleds, harpoons, warm clothing. Also of interest might be how children are brought up and what personality traits are fostered in the society under study, how people get along with one another, how men acquire their wives and how many they may have.

An ethnologist usually studies a particular society, or at least one at a time. But it should be pointed out that ethnological works are not limited to descriptions of particular cultures or to comparisons of two or three of them. Efforts are also made to generalize on a broad scale about cultures in general, for example about societies with a hunting-gathering basis of subsistence, peasant societies, matrilineal societies, and so on.

Physical anthropology

The biological aspects of *Homo sapiens* and the evolution of our species are studied by physical anthropologists. Human beings are members of the Primate order of mammals, which also includes the apes and monkeys. Physical anthropologists have pursued the following kinds of research with regard to primates: (1) the analysis of primate fossils, with an attempt to place them in a geological, temporal sequence; (2) comparative anatomical study of living primates; (3) observation of living primates in the field, with an emphasis on their patterns of social interaction; and (4) laboratory experimentation with apes, monkeys, and other animals.

Physical anthropologists also study human variation. All human beings today belong to a single species and are capable of breeding with members of other human groups and of producing fertile offspring. Within this single species, however, there is a good deal of variation. Physical anthropologists not only analyze the distribution of such observable traits as hair form and skin color, which may differ widely in human groups, but they are also interested in the distribution of blood types, such as A, B, AB, O, Rh, M, N, and other biochemical factors. They also study the incidence of ailments determined by heredity, such as sickle-cell anemia and hemophilia, and the relative susceptibility or immunity of different human populations to certain diseases. They have made studies of patterns of human growth and nutrition, climatic adaptation, and body composition.

One final subdivision of anthropology may be singled out: *applied anthropology.* Anthropologists have worked in community-development projects in different countries where a knowledge of local culture patterns may help the authorities to understand why there is resistance to certain programs. Why are members of a highland Peruvian community reluctant to boil their drinking water, despite lectures and explanations to the effect that boiling the water greatly decreases the incidence of dysentery? The value of compost pits is explained to the members of a small town in India; some pits are dug, but they are not maintained. A small, low-priced clinic is established in a Mexican town, but nobody patronizes it. Anthropologists have investigated problems of this sort and tried to suggest ways of surmounting the difficulties involved. Work in the field of public health requires some knowledge of cultural anthropology.

Applied anthropology

Curiosity about the effects of different cultures upon human attitudes and behavior can develop only in a society which has contacts with other societies with contrasting ways of life. It is understandable, then, that the earliest ethnographic accounts we have come from the mercantile Greeks of classic times. Herodotus (484–25 B.C.) was a great traveler who visited Macedonia, Thrace, Babylon, Palestine, and Egypt, and wrote an extensive description of Egyptian culture. The later Roman historian Tacitus (*circa* A.D. 55–after A.D. 117) similarly wrote a lengthy account about the barbarians of northern Europe.

The historical background of anthropology

After the fall of the Roman Empire, there was an apparent decline of curiosity, or at least of ethnographic descriptions, about other cultures. But this kind of interest strongly revived with the discovery of the New World and reports of its varying cultures, ranging from hunting-gathering bands to the advanced civilizations of Mexico and Peru. That shook Europeans out of their provinciality and stimulated the imaginations of scholars. These discoveries were accompanied by the new intellectual currents of the Renaissance which had uncovered the past glories of ancient Greece and Rome.

Since the invention of printing coincided with the discoveries in the New World, it was possible to publish the early accounts about American Indians by soldiers and missionaries; there was an eager market for such reports.

The Pacific voyages of Captain Cook in the 18th century brought more large areas of the world, formerly unknown to Europeans, to their attention. Increasing familiarity with information about non-Western peoples made intellectuals aware of the influence of culture upon human behavior, even though they did not use the term *culture*. (It was first used in the anthropological sense by Edward B. Tylor in 1871.)

While knowledge about different continents and cultures grew during the 18th century, there was also an increase in knowledge about the time depth of our species, and there began to be some speculation about human physical and cultural evolution. Even down to the 19th century, most Europeans believed that the creation of the world and of man had taken place only a few thousand years in the past. The orthodox view, as set forth by St. Augustine (A.D. 354–430), was that all human beings were descended from Adam and Eve, who had been created by God about 6,000 years before. In the 17th century a date of 4004 B.C. was widely accepted as the date of Adam and Eve's creation.

Early drawing
of Polynesian
outrigger canoe.

At that time little was known about geology. But a systematic comparative study of plants and animals began in the 18th century. The voyages of exploration brought back to Europe many varieties of plants and animals, which led to an interest in the classification and comparison of organisms. The Swedish botanist Linnaeus (Carl von Linné, 1707–78) designed a binomial system whereby each plant and animal is assigned a genus name and a species name. In the 10th edition of his work *Systema naturae* ("System of Nature"), Linnaeus classified man with the apes under the term *Primates.*

By grouping man with the apes, Linnaeus showed his awareness of the close physical similarity between them, but this did not lead him to speculate about their common ancestry or evolution. The very process of labeling species may have tended to freeze them into separate compartments, so to speak, so that the species currently known were assumed to be the same as those brought into being by the Creator at the beginning of time. But there were other 18th-century naturalists who did offer speculations about evolution, including the French naturalists Georges Buffon (1707–88) and Jean Lamarck (1744–1829), and Erasmus Darwin (1731–1802), grandfather of Charles Darwin.

Knowledge about geology developed in the 18th century, as the Industrial Revolution led to the digging of mines and canals and the building of railways. An engineer who was involved in such work, William Smith (1769–1839), announced that geological strata could be identified by the fossils they contained and that the lower strata generally were older than those above them. This principle is known as the law of *superposition.*

Another principle, the idea of *uniformitarianism,* is that the earth has been shaped, and still is being shaped, by natural forces, such as wind, water, heating, cooling, erosion, and organic decay, operating over long periods of time. The classic expression of this view appeared in Charles Lyell's *Principles of Geology* (3 vols., 1830–33), a work that greatly influenced Charles Darwin.

Speculation about evolution and greater knowledge about the past were spurred by discoveries of fossil forms. A fossil is the remains of an ancient form of life, often mineralized.

During the 18th century many fossil remains of strange extinct animals were found in Europe. In some cases they seemed to be associated with human remains. In 1715 the skeleton of an elephant-like creature was reported to have been recovered from gravel deposits near London, and next to it was a worked flint tool. In 1771 human bones were found in association with extinct cave-bear remains in a site in Germany. In 1797 hand axes were found along with the remains of extinct animals at Hoxne, England.

A Frenchman, Boucher de Perthes (1788–1868), found hand axes in such deep geological strata that he declared them to be tools made by "antediluvian man," or man before the flood. This claim met with much skepticism but led others to search in similar deposits, where like finds sometimes were made.

Charles Darwin.

In 1848 a primitive-looking human skull was found in Gibraltar. A similar one turned up in 1856 in the Neander valley in Germany, which gave us the name of Neandertal or Neanderthal man. But the significance of these finds was not realized at the time. A leading German scientist, Rudolf Virchow, dismissed the Neanderthal skull as pathological, a view which made it difficult for many scholars to consider Neanderthal man as a possible ancestor of ours. Neanderthal man is now classified as a form of *Homo sapiens* that lived between approximately 100,000 and 35,000 years ago.

In 1859 Charles Darwin published *On the Origin of Species by Means of Natural Selection* in which he not only presented evidence that evolution had occurred among many organic forms but also proposed a concept, that of natural selection, to help account for evolutionary change. This concept is discussed in the following chapter, along with the contributions of Gregor Mendel, who founded the science of genetics. *Origin of Species* was about evolution in general, not human evolution, but Darwin turned to the latter topic in a later work, *The Descent of Man* (1871). Darwin's work represented a turning point in the history of science.

In 1891 Eugène Dubois, a Dutch doctor, discovered a thick-boned and rather apelike skullcap near the Solo River in Java. Later he found a human left thighbone and two molar teeth nearby. Concluding that the skullcap and thighbone belonged to the same organism, Dubois gave it the name of *Pithecanthropus erectus,* or erect ape-man, a creature whose cranial capacity was judged to be intermediate between that of African apes and modern man. In the late 1920s some very similar skeletal material was found near Peking, China. Like the Java find, these are now classified as *Homo erectus,* a stage of human evolution preceding Neanderthal man and living between approximately 1 million and 300,000 years ago.

In the 1920s still earlier forms were also found, the australopithecines of South Africa, dating back to more than a million years ago. But there was already good evidence in the 19th century that the human species must have come into existence much earlier than 4004 B.C.

Besides tracing the physical evolution of our species, 19th-century scholars were also interested in reconstructing our cultural evolution, and for this a new terminology had to be developed to distinguish between different cultural stages. It was a museum curator, Christian Thomsen (1788–1865), who, being obligated to systematize the artifacts in the Danish National Museum early in the 19th century, came up with the Three Ages classification of Stone, Bronze, and Iron. These were in chronological sequence: a long Stone Age preceded an age in which bronze was used, which in turn gave way to an Iron Age. This simple scheme proved to be a very useful framework, later elaborated upon and subdivided.

The term *prehistory,* first coined in 1857, was popularized by John Lubbock (1834–1913) in a book called *Prehistoric Times* (1865), in which a distinction was made between two subdivisions of the Stone Age: Paleolithic (Old Stone Age) and Neolithic (New Stone Age). Lubbock knew that during the Paleolithic there were animals living in Europe that later became extinct, such as the mammoth, cave bear, and woolly rhinoceros. He also knew that there were characteristic differences in the making of Paleolithic and Neolithic stone tools.

An interest in European prehistory was spurred by the discovery and excavation of well-preserved Swiss Lake Dwelling settlements during the 1850s and 1860s. Some of these were Neolithic, while others dated from the Bronze and Iron Ages. Stratification helped to establish culture sequences. Meanwhile, excavations were also being made in Paleolithic cave sites, particularly in the Dordogne region of France, where several sites became famous for their yields of skulls, skeletons, and artifacts, giving names to particular periods or types of early humans: Le Moustier, La Madeleine, Aurignac, Cro-Magnon, and others.

In 1879 impressive Paleolithic cave paintings were discovered at Altamira, in Spain, although their authenticity was generally doubted for many years. In the following decades, much Upper Paleolithic art in bone, ivory, and clay was discovered, as well as more examples of cave painting.

During the 19th century, work was done also in the advanced Bronze Age civilizations of the past: in Persia by Henry C. Rawlinson, in Assyria by Paul Émile Botta and Austen Henry Layard, at Troy and Mycenae by

Heinrich Schliemann, and in the Maya area of the New World by John Lloyd Stephens. This archaeological research was accompanied by linguistic achievements in the deciphering of inscriptions in Egypt, Persia, and elsewhere. A linguistic genius, Jean François Champollion (1788–1867), deciphered Egyptian hieroglyphs from the Rosetta Stone, while Rawlinson and others worked on Old Persian, Akkadian, and Elamite.

Through his archaeological work, Schliemann had shown that an earlier civilization lay behind that of classical Greece. Layard, Botta, and Schliemann had uncovered hitherto unknown centers of Bronze Age civilization. Beginning in 1899, Arthur Evans carried this search into the past a step further by excavating at Knossos in Crete and bringing to light the elegant civilization of the ancient Minoans. Another formerly unknown civilization was revealed by John Marshall in his archaeological work in the Indus Valley between 1922 and 1927. Still older than either the Cretan or Indus Valley civilizations was that of Sumer. Although excavations in Sumer began in the 19th century, the most revealing finds were made by Charles Leonard Woolley in the late 1920s.

Thus, gradually, archaeologists opened up more and more forgotten centers of early civilization.

Toward the end of the 19th century, some writers such as Edward B. Tylor (1832–1917) and Lewis Henry Morgan (1818–81) began to synthesize the knowledge then available about human cultural development and to make generalizations about cultural evolution. They divided up the past into the stages of *savagery, barbarism,* and *civilization,* which would roughly correspond to Paleolithic, Neolithic, and Bronze Age. According to Tylor, the earliest religions were polytheistic, monotheism being a late development in the evolution of religion. Morgan held that the earliest family organization, following a stage of promiscuity, was based on matrilineal descent (reckoning descent through the mother), while patrilineal descent, reckoned through the father, came later.

A reaction against the speculations of 19th-century theorists developed among the first professional anthropologists under the leadership of Franz Boas (1858–1942) in the United States. Boas held that global reconstructions of human cultural evolution were premature. What was needed now was intensive field work and the collection of detailed ethnographies in different parts of the world. The emphasis in American ethnology, then, was on field research.

In time some specialization developed. Some ethnologists worked in the field of social anthropology, concerned with the social structures of particular societies, especially kinship systems. Some were drawn to the study of psychological anthropology or culture-and-personality, which overlaps with the field of psychology, especially the psychology of personality. Others specialized in political organization or the study of folklore, religion, art, or ethnomusicology. Cultural evolutionary speculation, first rejected by the Boasians, underwent a revival beginning in the 1930s. There was also a new interest in human ecology, concerning human adaptation to the environment, and in schools of thought known as functionalism and structuralism which are discussed later in Chapter 24.

The different branches of anthropology—ethnology, linguistics, archaeology, and physical anthropology—have necessarily used different methods of research. Let us briefly consider each field in turn.

Research methods in anthropology

Participant observation is a term used for an ethnographer's immersion in the life of a society he or she is studying, involving attendance at weddings, funerals, and the daily round of events. The ethnographer gets to know the people by living with them but must also take notes in the process. In cases where a detailed ethnographic account is being prepared, the ethnologist describes the geographical environment and indicates how the local community under investigation is related to other communities and the outside world. A census of the local population may be compiled. An ethnologist generally has certain key informants and should try to assess how representative they are of the larger community. The information they give should be checked against the reports of others, and what people say they do should be compared with what they do in actuality.

Behavior may be observed and recorded either informally or, in some cases, with the use of prearranged behavioral charts, as in some studies of child behavior in different cultures. Interviews may also be carried out informally or by making use of standardized questionnaires. For example, mothers in several cultures have been asked a range of standardized questions about their methods of child rearing.

The use of film is a valuable resource, if the budget can afford it. Some early films made in the course of field work have become classics, such as *Trance and Dance in Bali* by Margaret Mead and Gregory Bateson. Some films are of professional caliber, such as *The Hunters,* which follows a group of Kalahari Bushmen in their pursuit of a wounded giraffe. Film is particularly valuable for recording material like dances, which are hard to convey through written descriptions. Techniques in making things, such as house building, may also be conveyed with special clarity in films. But not all ethnographers can afford such equipment. They generally can, at any rate, take still photographs. Tape recording is often used, especially for the recording of music and the narration of myths and tales in the native language. This method saves time in note taking, and the tapes can later be replayed, transcribed, and translated when the ethnographer or linguist returns home.

Anthropologists interested in psychological anthropology have sometimes given projective personality tests such as the Rorschach (ink blot) Test and modified forms of the Thematic Apperception Test adapted to particular cultures. Cross-cultural testing of cognition has been carried out through the use of such instruments as the Müller-Lyer illusion, Embedded Figures Test, and other devices.

Two research options are available in ethnography which have been termed *etic* and *emic*. The *etic* option involves the recording and analysis of behavior from the viewpoint of an outside observer or community of observers. In the *emic* approach an effort is made to understand how things are seen and experienced by members of the society being studied. Both approaches can be followed during field work, but some ethnologists and linguists have emphasized the emic approach. *Cognitive anthropologists* believe that language provides a key to the thinking processes and underlying assumptions in a particular culture. Hence they seek to learn the local terminology and to discover the ways in which the world is classified and ordered in that language.

Anthropologists often study languages that have not been previously described and for which there is no published grammar or vocabulary. The sound units in such languages are often different from our own. Therefore, when recording native terms, anthropologists use standardized phonetic symbols like those adopted by the International Phonetic Association. They must also analyze word sequences to discover the grammatical principles of the language, which are often different from those of English grammar.

Archaeologists follow quite different sets of procedures in their work, which involves the reconstruction of past cultures from the analyses of excavated sites. There are different types of sites: *living sites,* where people lived; *butchering sites,* where animals were cut up; *workshop sites,* or "floors,"

Excavation at
Cahokia, Illinois.

where tools were made; *quarry sites,* where flint or minerals were extracted; *ceremonial sites;* and *burial sites,* such as graves and tombs.

Different kinds of information may be derived from these different kinds of sites. From a living site one may be able to make a rough assessment of the size of a settlement's population on the basis of the number and size of the dwellings and the general size of the settlement. If there is an adjacent cemetery, the number of burials may also provide clues, although one would have to determine how long the cemetery had been in use and estimate the characteristic life span. Of course, one could not be sure that all the people who lived in that community were buried there, but at least a rough approximation of the population could be made.

Caves, or parts of them, were sometimes living sites, such as those of Neanderthals in Europe and the Near East. From a living site one may also determine the basis of subsistence, whether hunting-gathering or agriculture. Animal bones and plant remains may be examined. There may be storage rooms, silos, or storage pits for grain. The impressions of grain on clay bricks or pottery are sometimes as clear evidence as the grains themselves. But ancient plant remains are often preserved, both in very dry environments, as in Peru and the American Southwest, and in damp peat bogs, as in Scandinavia.

A living site may give some evidence of the nature of social organization. There may be evidence of planned settlement—large communal dwellings, a grid layout of streets, and walls enclosing the settlement—or else small, dispersed units may indicate a more atomistic social order. A living site may also provide evidence of class stratification, implied by striking differences in the size of dwellings or by the concentration of valued objects, such as jade, in limited areas. Implications of trade are suggested by objects such as sea shells or obsidian that must have come from considerable distances.

Workshop sites and quarry sites yield information about technology, the making of tools. Ceremonial sites give an indication of the importance of religion in the life of the people. If there are representations of deities, some ideas may be gleaned about the kinds of gods worshiped. There may be archaeological evidence of sacrifice or of the existence of a priesthood. Burial sites not only yield skeletal material but very often grave goods as well, and indications of relative status may be deduced from the kinds of such associated material. They may testify to the existence of class stratification. Collective burials, as in the Neolithic passage graves of Europe, may indicate the importance of lineages or clans. There are also sites where petroglyphs and pictographs are found.

After a site has been chosen for excavation, the usual procedure is to stake it out in a grid plan, with the area divided into numbered squares. Before excavation, a scale map is made of the area. A fixed point, known as the *datum point,* is established on or near the site, marked by an object of steel, cement, or other durable material. This is the reference point for the excavations. If work is done on the site in later years, it can be determined where the earlier excavations were made. A grid may be dispensed with if a structure such as a house with different rooms is being excavated. The rooms may then become convenient units, rather than grid squares.

Preliminary test pits or trenches may be dug first. As the excavation proceeds, photographs are taken from different vantage points. When an artifact is uncovered, its position is recorded in its particular square and also in depth; it is numbered, cataloged, and listed in a register. Objects are placed in strong paper or cloth bags, labeled with identifying numbers.

Sites are often stratified. Objects found in lower strata are generally older than those nearer the surface, although this stratification may be disturbed and sometimes reversed. For example, the former inhabitants may have dug a large hole and piled up the dirt from it nearby. Animal burrowings, frost heaving, and other natural forces may cause disturbances in strata. Another possible source of confusion is that members of a community may have started a new settlement next to the old one. The second site may not overlap the older one and may seem to be on the same level. Thus time sequences may be difficult to interpret.

Objects found together presumably come from the same time period, although there may be exceptions, as in the preservation of heirlooms. It is necessary to have records of the spatial location of all the material found if one is to make an adequate interpretation of the remains.

The associated material found in a site, known as an archaeological *assemblage,* consists of *artifacts,* which are man-made objects; *features,* which are man-made but are usually not removed from the site, such as storage pits; and objects that are not made by man, such as animal bones, plant seeds, shells, and ashes.

Animal bones and remains of plants and pollen are preserved for analysis by specialists to determine the types of animals and plants collected or domesticated. These remains may also help to date the site. If the dig is in an area suitable for the application of tree-ring analysis, logs or beams are preserved. These may require special treatment to prevent decay and decomposition. Bits of charcoal are also collected for dating purposes, as will be explained later. Shells found in the site may give an indication of climatic conditions. It may be determined if they are of local origin or brought or traded from a distance. The sources of pieces of stone or metal may also be deduced, as well as techniques of manufacture of artifacts made from stone, bone, metal, or other materials. Casts and molds are sometimes made of valuable objects, particularly perishable ones, and tracings or rubbings may be made of rock carvings or of bas-reliefs if they are present, as has been done in the Camonica Valley in Italy and in Maya sites in Guatemala.

Field methods in archaeology have become progressively more painstaking and detailed. This is partly because of recent advances in dating methods, which have shown the value of preserving and analyzing organic materials, pollen, logs, and other objects that formerly received little attention. But the great care taken with excavations nowadays is also due to the realization that a site can properly be excavated only once, for to excavate a site is to destroy it.

After work in the field, the material found is analyzed in the laboratory. The first step in laboratory work is to identify and classify artifacts and to determine what they were used for. This may be relatively simple in the case of an arrowhead, but some stone tools require closer examination.

A Russian investigator, S. A. Semenov, was a pioneer in making microscopic analyses of wear patterns, striations on stone tools, in order to get a better idea of their possible functions. Some striations run parallel with the sides of a blade, for example, whereas others are at right angles. By analyzing the type of wear, one may deduce whether the tool was apt to have been used for cutting, scraping, or piercing.

Differences in tool kits may reflect a division of labor. In some European Neanderthal sites, for example, it has been deduced that notched tools made from local flint were probably used by women in processing food at the base camp, while men ranged further afield while hunting and made use of more distant flint, worked in a somewhat different fashion.

In living sites, tools used in food preparation, such as metates, manos, cooking pots, and butcher knives, give evidence of the kinds of foods eaten. Direct evidence of what people have eaten has come from the intestines of corpses preserved in peat bogs in northern Europe and also from *coprolites* (human feces fossils) found in dry caves. Analyses of coprolites may tell not only what was eaten but also how the food was prepared.

It is in the laboratory that investigations are made of the animal bones and plant remains recovered from a site. These may be turned over to specialists such as botanists and zoologists. Botanists can identify plant remains, including pollen, and can also distinguish between wild and domesticated plants.

Zoologists can identify animal remains, which sometimes, like plants, give evidence of domestication. They may also suggest the extent to which people at a given site depended on hunting and what animals were hunted. Animal bones also provide clues to chronology, particularly in the case of extinct animals when the date of their disappearance is approximately known. Different kinds of animals flourish in warm and cold periods. During warmer periods there were animals like elephants and hippopotami in Europe; during cold periods of glacial advance there were reindeer and cave bears, although the "tropical" hippopotamus survived in Italy until near the end of the Mousterian period. Small animals may be particularly useful for clues to climatic conditions, for rodents, birds, and especially mollusks are very sensitive to changes in climate.

One reason for the care given to laboratory analyses is that new questions are now asked about archaeological sites. The old aims of reconstructing culture history and past lifeways are still primary goals in archaeology, but some contemporary archaeologists now emphasize the need to study cultural processes. They are interested in such matters as ecological adaptation, demography, settlement patterns, and the analysis of cultural systems in connection with the sites they analyze. For members of this school, known as the *new archaeology,* the ultimate question is not where or when a particular cultural development took place, but why. Processual theorists try to formulate hypotheses, construct behavioral models, and make predictions about what sorts of patterns may be found in particular sites.

Since physical anthropologists study human beings as biological organisms, their work is more closely related to that of zoologists and biologists. Those who are interested in problems concerning human evolution specialize in osteology, the study of bones, which includes the study of teeth.

Teeth, which are so subject to decay in the living human mouth, tenaciously outlast all other parts of the body after death and, compared to other body parts, are relatively well preserved in the fossil record. For the earlier primates particularly, teeth are about all physical anthropologists have to work with. It is fortunate if they know the geological stratum in which these teeth were found and the climatic and environmental conditions it suggests.

The teeth give some indication of the size of the animal, and they may suggest the type of diet to which it was accustomed. Physical anthropologists study living primates as well as fossil forms. A knowledge of the anatomy and physiology of different apes and monkeys helps the physical anthropologist to interpret the skeletal material of extinct species. Where there is much similarity between a living form and a fossil find, some relationship may be inferred.

If limb bones and parts of the vertebral column are present, the animal's form of locomotion may be deduced, whether it went on all fours or with upright posture, whether it was used to swinging from branch to branch through the trees by brachiation. Some inferences may also be made about the animal's musculature:

We can make deductions about the size and form of the nerves and muscles with which they formed a single functional unit. Muscles leave marks where they are attached to bones, and from such marks we can assess the size of the muscles. At the same time, such parts of the skeleton as the cranium give us considerable evidence of the size and form of the brain and spinal cord (Campbell 1974:2).

One of the determinations made by physical anthropologists is the cranial capacity of skulls, which has a clear relation to brain size, although it is larger, since the braincase also contains membranes, a layer known as dura mater, and cerebrospinal fluid. Cranial capacity is determined by first plugging up the holes in a cranium to prevent leakage and then filling the inverted skull with seeds, water, or small shot, which are then poured into a graduated container.

Hominid evolution has been marked by an increase in brain size and cranial capacity. African apes have a cranial capacity of about 500 cubic centimeters. Australopithecine cranial capacity was about the same. *Homo erectus* skulls ranged between 900 and 1,225 cubic centimeters, while modern skulls have a capacity of about 1,400 cubic centimeters. But the evolution of the brain has involved not only increases in size but also changes in shape and organization, with an enlargement of parietal and temporal cortex. An idea of such morphological features may be obtained by making endocasts of fossil skulls, another method used by some physical anthropologists. Laboratory studies of living primates also contribute to our knowledge of brain anatomy and neural organization.

The field of physical anthropology has expanded greatly in the past 30 years. Physical anthropologists were formerly concerned mainly with body measurements and the classification of human types. Their training is now more diversified and exhaustive, with an emphasis on genetics, blood chemistry, and the acquisition of specialized laboratory techniques. These emphases have brought physical anthropology closer to the other biological sciences than to the cultural branches of anthropology. At the same time, the growing specialization of physical anthropology has made it difficult for cultural anthropologists to keep abreast of new developments in physical anthropology. Despite this specialization, physical and cultural anthropologists generally share a desire to see humans as a whole, as products of both physical and cultural evolution.

In contrast to our closest relatives, the apes, whose geographical distri-

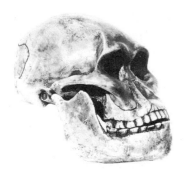
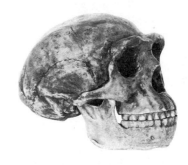

Reconstructed plaster casts of skulls of (*top, from left*) *Australopithecus africanus* and Peking man, (*left*) "Classic" Neanderthal man.

butions are much more restricted and localized, human beings have spread out all over the world and have come to adjust to many different environments. The adjustment of an organism to its environment is known as *adaptation*. In the case of human beings, adaptation has been both somatic and cultural. The fur coat of the polar bear represents biological, somatic adaptation to the cold climate of the Arctic, while the igloo and the blubber lamp are cultural adaptations made by the Eskimo to the same conditions. Both kinds of adaptation make survival possible. Somatic adaptations are the result of genetic changes and natural selection, while cultural adaptations depend upon the invention and diffusion of ideas, communicated by language and imitation. In studying how human beings have adapted physically to different environments such as the Arctic, dry deserts, and high altitudes, physical anthropologists have focused on body build and other biological features, while ethnologists are interested in the cultural means by which people cope with the world. As a result, the physical anthropologist and the ethnologist pursue divergent lines of work, and the reports they produce are quite different from one another. But both deal with the same general problem, the adaptation of human beings to their environments. Besides, physical anthropologists often do concern themselves with aspects of culture and their effects upon human physiology. Sometimes the understanding of a particular ailment requires knowledge of both fields. For example, the spread of a degenerative disease leading to paralysis, known as *kuru,* prevalent among the Fore of New Guinea, was shown to be borne by a latent virus which had probably been spread by cannibalism involving the consumption of human brains which had been infected by the *kuru* virus.

Chapter 7 contains a discussion of falciparum malaria in Africa and genetic factors leading to human immunity or susceptibility to that disease. The spread of falciparum malaria in Africa is intimately related to cultural factors, particularly to yam cultivation, forest clearing, and village settlement. The forests could not have been cut down until iron tools were introduced for that purpose. Therefore, ethnologists and archaeologists can provide an understanding of the historical background of present ecological conditions in Africa.

Physical anthropology and archaeology join forces in the study of human evolution. An early primate or human skull may be excavated by an archaeologist and analyzed by a physical anthropologist. Each specialist values the contribution of the other. Similarly, an ethnologist's knowledge of the life of present-day hunting-gathering peoples, like the Bushmen of South Africa, may help to clarify an archaeologist's analysis of an early hunting site. It is for such reasons that anthropologists tend to think of their field as a unified, holistic discipline.

Summary

Anthropology is the study of human beings. One way in which it differs from other fields that study humans (such as sociology, economics, political science, and history) is that it contains a main division, physical anthropology, which is concerned with *Homo sapiens* as a physical organism and with our evolution from simpler forms of life.

The other main division, cultural anthropology, is subdivided into the three branches of linguistics, archaeology, and ethnology, all of which deal with aspects of human culture, the shared behavior learned by members of a society. Linguistics deals with language, the principal medium through which culture patterns are transmitted. Archaeology is the study of extinct cultures; ethnology is the study of contemporary cultures. Although each field involves specialization, anthropologists tend to think of their field as a unified discipline. Advances in any one branch often depend upon contributions from one or more of the others.

Anthropology is relatively recent as an organized discipline, but it is important for our understanding of human behavior. Without the work of physical anthropologists and archaeologists, we would have little knowledge of the place of *Homo sapiens* in nature and the long process of human evolution. Without the work of ethnologists we would have little awareness of the great variety of human cultures.

Suggestions for further reading

For a work on the development of early speculation about man, see Stanley Casson, *The Discovery of Man: The Story of the Inquiry into Human Origins* (New York: Harper & Bros., 1939). A selection of texts on anthropological subjects dating from the 14th to the 18th century is available in J. S. Slotkin, ed., *Readings in Early Anthropology*, Viking Fund Publications in Anthropology no. 40 (Chicago: Aldine Publishing Co., 1965). See also Phyllis Dolhinow and Vincent M. Sarich, eds., *Background for Man: Readings in Physical Anthropology* (Boston: Little, Brown & Co., 1971).

In the field of archaeology three successful works of popularization can be recommended: C. W. Ceram, *Gods, Graves and Scholars: The Story of Archaeology,* trans. from the German by E. B. Garside (New York: Alfred A. Knopf, 1951); Geoffrey Bibby, *The Testimony of the Spade* (New York: Alfred A. Knopf, 1956); Glyn Daniel, *The Idea of Prehistory* (Baltimore: Penguin Books, 1964).

For good statements about methods in ethnological field work see the "Introduction" in Bronislaw Malinowski, *Argonauts of the Western Pacific* (New York: E. P. Dutton & Co, 1961, pp. 1–25; first published in 1922) and Hortense Powdermaker, *Stranger and Friend: The Way of an Anthropologist* (New York: W. W. Norton & Co., Inc., 1966). On methods in archaeology, see James B. Griffin, "The Study of Early Cultures," in *Man, Culture, and Society,* ed. Harry L. Shapiro (New York: Oxford University Press, 1960), pp. 22–48; and James Deetz, *Invitation to Archaeology* (New York: Natural History Press, 1967). On methods in physical anthropology, see Gabriel Ward Lasker, *Physical Anthropology* (New York: Holt, Rinehart & Winston, 1973), chap. 1. On linguistics, see Dwight Bolinger, *Aspects of Language* (New York: Harcourt, Brace & World, 1968).

part one
Primate evolution

2

MECHANISMS OF
EVOLUTIONARY CHANGE

E volution is the development of more complex forms of life from simpler forms. Most of what we know about evolutionary processes is very recent, dating back to little more than 100 years ago. Even after people became convinced that evolutionary changes had taken place, they still found it hard to understand how a species could change in form over time. An early naturalistic theory to account for this was proposed by Jean Lamarck (1744–1829). Lamarck suggested that organs are strengthened through use and come to atrophy through disuse. He interpreted the long neck and long forelegs of giraffes as due to their stretching up to browse in the upper leaves of trees over long periods of time. Blind cave fishes have been found in both Europe and America; Lamarck would explain their blindness as being caused by the atrophy of organs that have ceased to be used in the dark.

The difficulty with these views is that they assume the inheritance of characteristics acquired in the lifetime of an organism. Most scientists today do not accept the notion that such acquired characteristics are inherited, although that was, until not long ago, a dogma in Soviet biological science.

Our present understanding of the mechanisms involved in evolution has been derived largely from the work of two men: Charles Darwin (1809–82) and Gregor Mendel (1822–84). Darwin provided the concept of natural selection and synthesized data bearing on the theories of evolution; Mendel founded the science of genetics.

Natural selection

Darwin's *Origin of Species* (1859) opens with a discussion of variation among cultivated plants and animals. Darwin drew attention to the great changes that breeders have been able to develop in domesticated species through artificial selection by isolating and breeding strains of organisms characterized by a variation in a particular desired direction, such as length

23

of legs and speed in race-horses or increased weight and early maturity in cattle. But changes also take place in nature through the operation of natural selection. Everywhere in nature there is a struggle for survival—for resources of food and sunlight and the other needs of life. Plants and animals reproduce many more of their kind than can survive, and most of them perish.

The principle of natural selection is stated as follows:

Owing to this struggle, variations, however slight and from whatever cause proceeding, if they be in any degree profitable to the individuals of a species, in their infinitely complex relations to other organic beings and to the physical conditions of life, will tend to the preservation of such individuals, and will generally be inherited by the offspring (Darwin 1859:51–52).

Darwin pointed out that organisms, if unchecked, tend to increase in geometrical ratio. The elephant is the slowest-breeding animal known; but Darwin calculated that if an elephant pair were to give birth to six young in a lifetime of 100 years and if this rate continued, in a period of 740–750 years there would be almost 19 million elephants alive, descended from the first pair. Darwin cited some actual instances of "population explosion" among species under favorable environmental conditions, when natural enemies or other checks had been removed.

However, in spite of the tendency to multiply, species generally have fairly constant populations. Their numbers are, in fact, held in check by the universal struggle for life and by the fact that, while a species may multiply, its available food supply is apt to remain constant. Since many individuals in every species perish, favorable variations of any sort must greatly enhance an organism's chances of survival and reproduction. Thus, Darwin would explain the long necks and forelegs of giraffes, not in terms of their straining up to nibble lofty leaves for many generations, but in a quite different manner, reasoning that if some members of the species were born with longer necks and forelegs than others, this might be a favorable selective difference, which would give them a greater chance to survive and propagate than their shorter-necked contemporaries. Over a period of time, the long-necked variety would therefore increase at the expense of the short necks, culminating, as an evolutionary end product, in the giraffe we know today.

Darwin was struck by the fact that most beetles on the island of Madeira are unable to fly. He saw this as a selective advantage, since beetles that could take to flight would often be blown out to sea and destroyed. Darwin also considered a Lamarckian explanation for the wingless beetles; perhaps disuse of wings led to their atrophy. In any case, he argued, wingless beetles would be more apt to survive in Madeira than those with fully developed wings. This, then, would be an example of natural selection.

To take another example, consider the advantages of protective coloration. There are both brown and green mantises. Scientists have performed some experiments with them, tethering both types of mantis in both brown and green grass. In an environment of green grass, the brown insects were soon destroyed by natural enemies, while the green mantises survived. In brown grass, it was the other way around; there the brown mantises were favored and continued to live, while the green ones perished. Thus the protective coloring became an instrument of natural selection.

Adaptations of this sort are complicated by the fact that organisms may move to new environments or there may be seasonal changes, as in the turning of leaves in autumn. Hence, what-was formerly protective may become highly unfavorable under changed conditions and what was unfavorable may become beneficial. Both dark- and light-colored moths are found in the English countryside, but the light moths predominate because they have more protection from their enemies. But during the last 100 years, dark, almost black, moths have become much more numerous than light ones in the sooty industrial cities of England. The dark moths are hardier, but they had formerly been exposed to their enemies when seen against light-colored tree bark covered by lichens. Now, in a new environment of gray towns and factories, as well as in rural areas with soot-covered tree bark, they have flourished.

Darwin did not know how new variations arise in an organism; that was later to be shown by geneticists. But he argued that once a new feature such as a change in color or size appears, it may either help or hinder the organism in its adaptation to the environment. If it hinders that adaptation, the organism will be less apt to survive and reproduce, and the new feature will not be perpetuated. But if it enhances the organism's chances of survival and reproduction, the new feature will be maintained, and organisms possessing the trait will flourish at the expense of those not having it. In this way, changes gradually take place in the appearance and structure of an organism. Since organic forms have been living for many millions of years, there has been plenty of opportunity for plants and animals to adapt to many different environments, progressively deviating from parental forms as they establish more appropriate adjustments to their surroundings.

After the publication of *Origin of Species,* the work was criticized on various grounds. Darwin and his supporters were able to answer most of his critics. But there was one criticism that shook Darwin's faith in his own theories. The question was raised: If an organism appears with a new trait that has survival value, how can it be maintained? If it is to reproduce, the organism must mate with other members of its species which are apt to lack the new variation. Within a few generations the new trait will be swamped and should disappear. It could only be maintained if several organisms were to simultaneously vary in the same direction. But acceptance of this possibility would involve an orthogenetic view of evolution lacking the fortuitous character of natural selection.

To cope with this objection Darwin developed a complex theory of inheritance, which has since been shown to be inadequate. Darwin might have solved the problem if he had known about the work of his contemporary,

Gregor Mendel. But, although Mendel gave two reports dealing with his findings before the Brünn Society for the Study of Natural Science in 1865 and he published his paper the following year in the *Proceedings* of that society, Mendel's work was, for all practical purposes, unknown in the Europe of his day. The few people who heard or read his report in 1865 and 1866 evidently did not understand it or grasp its significance. It was not until 1900, 16 years after Mendel's death, that his forgotten treatise was simultaneously discovered by three scholars in three different European countries. And then the science of genetics was born.

Gregor Mendel's experiments

Gregor Mendel was an Austrian monk who, over a period of eight years, performed some careful experiments with plants in a patch of garden beside his monastery. His most important work was done with garden peas. One reason for his success in these experiments was that he crossed strains of peas that differed from each other in one definite character. Some had round seeds; others had wrinkled ones. Some were yellow; others, green. Some of the plants were tall; others, short. Mendel took pollen from a plant that regularly produced round seeds and placed it on the stigma of a plant that produced wrinkled ones. In the same way he crossed the yellow with the green plants and the tall with the short. He did this with seven pairs of contrasting characters.

Another reason for Mendel's success in these experiments is that he kept quantitative records of the appearance of his plants in each generation. Moreover, he kept records of large numbers of plants so that accidental variations present in groups of small numbers did not significantly influence his findings. After crossing the peas with the round and wrinkled seeds, Mendel found that the peas of the offspring were all round; none were wrinkled. In the yellow-green cross, the peas of the offspring were all yellow. In the tall-short cross, the offspring were all tall. These results were surprising, for one might have expected to find some blending of the contrasting traits. Instead, in each case, one factor appeared to be dominant over the other. However, the submerged (recessive) factor did not disappear. This was shown when Mendel next cross-pollinated his hybrid plants. This time the round-wrinkled hybrids produced about three round peas to every wrinkled one; apparently the wrinkled factor of one of the grandparents had not been lost. The same 3-to-1 ratio was found for the other factors as well. The recessive traits for greenness of the pea, for shortness of the plant, and the other recessive traits were all preserved.

Mendel found that when the peas were allowed to reproduce by self-fertilization, the wrinkled-seed plants always had wrinkled peas and pure strains of the round-seed type always produced round peas. But the hybrids produced three round seeds to one wrinkled one. We shall return later to the question of why this 3-to-1 ratio appeared.

The term *genotype* has come to be used for the genetic constitution of an organism, while *phenotype* denotes its observable appearance. Phenotypically, members of the first generation of Mendel's round-wrinkled hybrids were all alike; all their peas were round. But the underlying genetic makeup of the hybrids was different, as was shown by the reappearance of the recessive factor in the following generation.

Mendel concluded that heredity is determined by discrete units that retain their original character for generation after generation. Nowadays we call these units *genes.*

Since Mendel did not work with a microscope, he could not observe the inner structure of cells. His conclusions were drawn from observation and mathematics. Later, microscopes with great power and efficiency became available, and today we know a great deal about the composition of cells that was unknown in Mendel's day. In the nucleus of a cell, there are some rod-shaped bodies that can be seen much more clearly through the microscope if they are stained. Hence, they have been called *chromosomes,* or

Genes and chromosomes

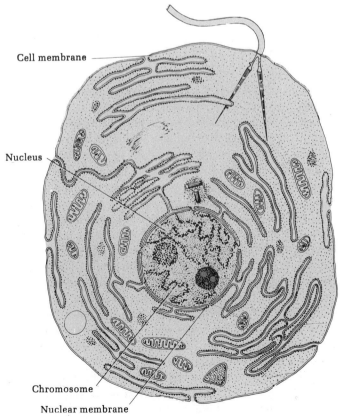

Diagram of a "typical" animal cell.

Cell membrane

Nucleus

Chromosome

Nuclear membrane

colored bodies. These structures cannot be the genes themselves, because there are too few of them. There is an intestinal worm that has only two chromosomes. The fruit fly, *Drosophila melanogaster,* has eight, but it has been roughly estimated that *Drosophila* has 10,000 genes. So there are thousands of times as many genes as chromosomes. It was concluded that perhaps the genes are located on the chromosomes.

Drosophila melanogaster has very large chromosomes in its salivary glands during the larval stage. Through observation on the effects of radiation, the scientists who have worked with the fruit fly have been able to make detailed chromosome maps showing at exactly which part of a chromosome a particular gene is to be found. The genes themselves, however, are too small to be seen through a microscope. It is perhaps best to think of them as positions on a chromosome.

The genes on the chromosome are formed in pairs, which may be either of the same or of contrasting type. These partner genes are called *alleles.* When the alleles are of the same type, the organism is said to be *homozygous* for that trait. For example, if both alleles cause roundness in peas or if both cause wrinkledness, they are homozygous. But, if one allele causes roundness and its partner causes wrinkledness, they are *heterozygous.*

All cells undergo the process of cell division, or *mitosis,* which creates new cells. In this process the chromosome divides so that each cell has the same number of chromosomes with the same genes. The new cells are exactly like the parent cells. A somewhat different process takes place in the reproductive cells that develop into the egg and sperm. In their cell division, called *meiosis,* the daughter cells have only half the traditional species number of chromosomes. There is one member present from each chromosome pair, not just any half. The alleles, or gene pairs, separate, with one going to each daughter cell. The maternally and paternally derived chromosomes assort randomly, making a great number of combinations possible. Thus, when the egg and sperm unite in fertilization, each brings half the normal number of chromosomes, and in their fusion the full number of chromosomes characteristic of the species is provided for the embryo.

The combination of genes that takes place at fertilization is a matter of chance. This can be shown if we return to Mendel's experiment with the round and wrinkled peas. We are now in a better position to understand the 3-to-1 ratio that Mendel discovered in his third generation of plants. The following paragraphs may be clarified by reference to the accompanying chart. Mendel began with a pure round strain, containing two alleles for roundness, and a pure wrinkled strain, with two alleles for wrinkledness. Every offspring of this cross must contain both a round and a wrinkled gene; they are all heterozygous. Phenotypically, their peas are all round, since roundness is the dominant trait.

Consider now what happens when two of these heterozygotes are crossed. At fertilization the dominant round gene of the first pair of alleles could join either with the dominant round gene or with the recessive wrinkled

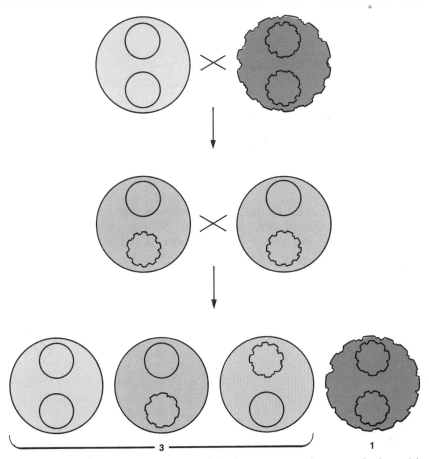

3   1   Mendel's 3-to-1 ratio.

This chart shows three generations of peas, with the first generation on the top row. On the top left there is a pure round pea having two genes for roundness, represented by the two smaller circles inside. On the top right there is a pure wrinkled pea having two genes for wrinkledness. When these two peas are crossed, each member of the next generation (second row) is heterozygous, having received one of the two genes for roundness-wrinkledness from each parent. Although they each have a gene for wrinkledness, they all look round, since roundness is a dominant trait. When members of this second generation are crossed, there are four possible combinations in the third generation (third row). Since the first three peas all have a gene for roundness, they all look round. The fourth, being pure wrinkled, looks wrinkled.

one of the other pair. The recessive wrinkled allele of the first pair could join either with the dominant round gene or with the recessive wrinkled one of the other pair. We thus have four possibilities: round-round, round-wrinkled, wrinkled-round, and wrinkled-wrinkled. Since the first three combinations all contain a round allele, these will all appear round. Phenotypically, then, we have a 3-to-1 ratio.

It should be noted that a 3-to-1 ratio is not always obtained in the crossing of heterozygotes, for traits are not always clearly dominant or recessive, and genes that are dominant under some conditions may be recessive in others. There are cases where a kind of blending takes place, as in the skin color of mulattos.

Another qualification that needs to be made about Mendel's findings has to do with the implication that a single gene always affects a single trait, such as the roundness or yellowness of peas. We now know that a particular trait may be influenced by several genes and that linkages may occur among genes, as among those found on the same chromosome. For example, hemophilia and color blindness are called sex-linked traits, because the genes responsible for them are located on the X chromosome, one of the two chromosomes that determine sex.

In the preceding paragraphs, we have been considering processes involved in sexual reproduction, which is characteristic of the majority of plants and animals. But not all plants and animals have sexual reproduction; many reproduce asexually by mitotic cell division. The more common and more complex processes of sexual reproduction must have been favored by natural selection. Their advantage evidently lies in the variety made possible by the genetic recombination in sexual reproduction. In mitosis each new cell gets a set of chromosomes just like the parental set; thus asexual reproduction provides little opportunity for variation and for evolutionary change. Genetic recombination, however, does provide variety in the raw material upon which natural selection acts.

Mutation

Genes seem to be remarkably stable. They are always making faithful copies of themselves and so continue for generation after generation. But sometimes an inheritable change takes place in the structure or the chemistry of a gene. This is called a *mutation*. A new gene, in effect, has appeared, which may result in a difference in coloring, size, or other attributes of the organism. Most such changes are harmful to the organism and may lessen its adaptability. This is because every organism has established a *modus vivendi;* it has acquired successful means of coping with the world. An innovation is more apt to be harmful to it than helpful. Harmful genes tend to disappear before long, since the carriers may either die out or fail to reproduce.

Sometimes mutations occur that have no apparent effect for generations. New recessive traits may be masked for decades and only become manifest if mating takes place between two carriers of the trait. To give an example of a recessive trait resulting from mutation, in 1931 a Wisconsin mink rancher found a light-furred female in a batch of otherwise normally dark-furred offspring. The light color was a recessive characteristic due to mutation. The rancher crossed the female with one of her offspring. In this way, a homozygous strain was developed which bred true—a kind of homogenized mink. In the wild state such a mutation might not have had much survival value. Under domestication it was profitable, at least to the mink rancher, who introduced platinum mink to the world. Naturally, it was preserved and perpetuated.

Not all types of mutations are possible, and there are some that no doubt recur again and again. Very likely, light-furred mink have often been born in the past, but they were not favored by natural selection. Mutations leading to blindness are, of course, harmful to the organisms affected and tend to be weeded out, but in cave fish living in the dark, such mutations make no difference and may therefore accumulate—an interpretation to be contrasted with Lamarck's notion of atrophy through disuse.

Mutations occur with some regularity, although with relative rarity, in all species. The rates of mutation may be increased by exposure to X-ray or cosmic radiation and by exposure to some chemicals or to heat. Although most mutations are harmful, it sometimes does happen that a favorable mutation occurs—one that enhances the survival and breeding potentialities of the organism. An example was given earlier of the dark-colored moths in the industrial areas of England. Mutations toward dark pigmentation must often have occurred among these moths in the past, but they did not prove to be useful until parts of England became sooty enough to favor their selection.

Isolation and species formation

Evolutionary change is fostered by geographic and reproductive isolation, resulting in the formation of new species. A species may be defined as an interbreeding population of organisms reproductivity isolated from other such groups. Within a species, fertile offspring are produced. While mating may take place across species lines, the offspring that may result usually are infertile or sterile.

Let us consider an imaginary animal species that has spread out across an island. In this process some groups of the species have become geographically isolated from others due to the formation of barriers, such as streams. Each group then begins to adapt to somewhat different environmental conditions and, in time, assumes some different physical traits, such as contrasts in pigmentation. We may call these groups *subspecies,* groups that are potentially capable of becoming separate species. If the ecological barriers now are withdrawn or surmounted and if the groups are allowed to mingle with one another and produce fertile offspring, it is evident that they still belong to the same species, even though the subspecies have developed contrasting traits in color, size, or other attributes.

Let us now allow more time for our imaginary animal species, so that each group within it continues to adapt to its own environmental settings, with the development of still more variation. Such variation may reach the point where the former subspecies can no longer interbreed, or they may have sterile offspring, or else their hybrid offspring may be at a disadvantage of some kind. In the latter case, those animals that mate with members of their own kind are apt to leave more offspring than those that interbreed with the other subspecies. Hence, even if interbreeding is possible, the separation between the two subspecies will widen.

The subspecies that have been isolated from one another may develop incompatible features. For example, differences in size prevent interbreeding between the small oak toad and the much larger Gulf Coast toad. A feature such as this, which prevents an exchange of genes, is known as an *isolating mechanism*. There are various kinds of isolating mechanisms. Mating or flowering periods may come at different seasons; there may be noncorrespondence of genitalia or floral parts; there may be contrasting courtship movements or other patterns leading to copulation. If two former subspecies reach the point of reproductive isolation through some such mechanism, *speciation* has taken place. There are now two separate species where formerly there was one. Even if these groups are allowed to intermingle, they will not interbreed; or if they should succeed in doing so, their offspring will be sterile. If a male donkey copulates with a female horse, the mare may give birth to a mule, but mules are sterile and cannot reproduce. Obviously, the two species of horse and donkey are related; they belong to the same genus, *Equus*. Technically, the horse is called *Equus caballus* and the donkey, *Equus asinus*. A lion and tiger may also mate but have infertile offspring. These two species belong to the genus *Felis;* the lion is called *Felis leo* and the tiger, *Felis tigris.* Thus, genus, species, and subspecies represent progressive differentiations. The species is a reproductively isolated group in which fertile offspring are produced.

The study of populations

Evolution does not concern an individual alone but a whole population of organisms. An individual changes in appearance from birth to death but does not evolve. Evolution takes place within an interbreeding population. Natural selection affects differential fertility within a species and brings about changes in gene frequencies. Evolution takes place through changes in the *gene pool* of a population, a gene pool being the total collection of genes of the members of the breeding population. Despite changes, there is a tendency for the proportions of genotypes to remain constant from one generation to the next. If random mating occurs in a population, there should be genetic equilibrium without evolutionary change. Random mating means that mating occurs without bias and that every member of the population has an equal chance of mating with any mature member of the opposite sex. A bias would occur, for example, if people of the same height or skin color were preferred partners. In practice, preferential mating patterns are common in human societies. In some societies, for example, it is the accepted practice for cousins to marry one another. In random mating, on the other hand, there is no such tendency in mate selection. Although the assumption of random mating in a population is somewhat artificial, the assumption has been useful in the development of calculations of gene frequencies in populations. The field of research concerned with such matters is known as *population genetics*.

One of the mechanisms involved in changes in the gene frequencies of a population is *genetic drift*. This is the result of a chance sampling "error" such as might result from the migration of a small subgroup from a larger population. For example, a large human population contains both blue-eyed and brown-eyed persons, with a somewhat larger percentage of the latter. A small migrant group from this stock contains only blue-eyed persons, as the result of chance, just as one might draw a handful of blue marbles from a sack containing equal numbers of blues and browns. If the migrants land on an island and start to interbreed, their descendants will deviate genetically from the parent stock in having only blue eyes. A similar effect could be brought about by drastic population reduction resulting from a war, famine, or epidemic. Either through migration or through population reduction, then, there is a *founder population,* a new breeding population in which the genetic frequencies differ from those of their parent stock, a condition known as the *founder effect.*

Genetic isolation like that of our hypothetical blue-eyed islanders may also come about through sociocultural mechanisms, such as rules of *endogamy* requiring members of a particular caste or religion to marry only members of that group. For example, the Jews of Rome, confined to a ghetto area for many generations, now have a higher frequency of blood group B than do other Jewish groups and a much higher frequency of B than that of the general Italian population.

Opposed to isolation is *gene flow* or *hybridization,* which involves an exchange of genes between populations. The resultant genetic diversity may lead to an improved strain. Animal and plant breeders, when crossing distinct varieties, have sometimes produced a population superior to either parental strain. This phenomenon is known as *heterosis* or *hybrid vigor.* Some examples of studies of population genetics relating to humans, including a discussion of blood groups, will be found in Chapter 7.

The field of molecular biology has provided much information about the structure and chemistry of genetic material. As a result, we are hearing a bit less about genes and a good deal more about "coding." Chromosomes consist partly of chains of DNA (deoxyribonucleic acid) molecules and partly of protein. A DNA molecule is believed to consist of two intertwined sugar-phosphate strands, shaped like a spiral staircase. The nitrogenous bases—adenine, guanine, cytosine, and thymine—form internal links like steps in the staircase. The DNA of all plants and animals seems to have this structure and chemical composition, but variety is made possible by variations in the four kinds of "steps." A thread of DNA has been compared with a recording tape that codes instructions. These instructions are issued in the form of chemicals. A gene may be considered as a position on the tape that issues a particular kind of message.

In addition to DNA, all plant and animal cells contain a similar substance called RNA (ribonucleic acid), which contains a sugar called ribose. (The ribose of DNA has one less oxygen atom; hence the "deoxy" in its name.)

DNA

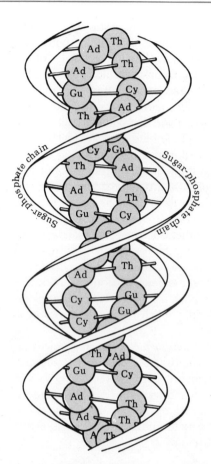

The double helix, or
Watson-Crick, model
of a DNA molecule.

DNA is always found in the nuclei of cells; RNA is usually found in the cytoplasm. Within the nucleus, DNA transmits messages concerning protein manufacture to various forms of RNA called *messenger RNA*. The essential business of life, the determination of heredity and the manufacture of proteins necessary for life, is therefore carried out by these minute molecules.

A failure in the coding process may result in a mutation. An example is sickle-cell anemia, which results from the failure of the organism to produce a particular amino acid. This ailment will be discussed in Chapter 7.

Summary

This chapter has dealt with the problem of how evolutionary changes are brought about in plants and animals.

Darwin's concept of natural selection, when combined with modern knowledge of genetics, gives an understanding of how evolutionary changes have come about. Genetic variability is provided by genetic recombination, genetic drift, genetic hybridization, changes in chromosome structure and number, and gene mutation. Geographic or reproductive isolation allows for the operation of natural selection upon a particular species in different environmental settings, leading to species differentiation.

Knowledge of genetics has helped to solve some problems Darwin could not answer and to explain why a new variant form need not be "swamped" through matings with organisms that do not have the trait in question.

Charles Darwin's *Origin of Species* (1859) still makes interesting reading. It is available in a Modern Library edition, along with Darwin's *The Descent of Man* (1871). For a history of evolutionary theory, see Loren Eiseley, *Darwin's Century: Evolution and the Men Who Discovered It* (New York: Doubleday & Co., Inc., 1958); and John C. Greene, *The Death of Adam: Evolution and Its Impact on Western Thought* (Ames: Iowa State University Press, 1959). See also George Gaylord Simpson, *The Meaning of Evolution* (New Haven, Conn.: Yale University Press, 1967).

Suggestions for further reading

For readable works on genetics and related topics, see Ashley Montagu, *Human Heredity* (New York: New American Library, 1960); Hampton L. Carson, *Heredity and Human Life* (New York: Columbia University Press, 1963); and Ruth Moore, *The Coil of Life: The Story of the Great Discoveries in the Life Sciences* (New York: Alfred A. Knopf, Inc., 1961). For a recent introduction to human genetics, see Daniel L. Hartl, *Our Uncertain Heritage: Genetics and Human Diversity* (Philadelphia: J. B. Lippincott Co., 1977).

3

HOW HUMAN BEINGS
ARE CLASSIFIED:
CHARACTERISTICS
OF *HOMO SAPIENS*

A human being is a vertebrate, a mammal, and a primate. In this chapter we will examine these progressively narrower classifications and consider how human beings resemble and differ from other forms of life. To begin with, *vertebrates* (including all fishes, amphibians, reptiles, birds, and mammals) are bilaterally symmetrical animals that have segmented backbones. Running through the backbone is a spinal cord connected with the brain, which is usually enclosed in a skull. Thus the brain and central nervous system are well protected. The backbone is flexible, since it is made up of a series of bony rings. The head of the animal contains sense organs, such as nose, eyes, and ears, and a mouth, sometimes equipped with teeth. Vertebrates are generally able to move about quickly and can readily mobilize energy, giving them some advantages over invertebrates such as worms, mollusks, insects, starfishes, and octopuses, all of which lack an internal skeleton.

The first vertebrates, which appeared about 480 million years ago, were water dwelling, for life originated in the waters of the earth, and it was only gradually that first plants, and later animals, appeared on land and made their ways inland. The first such animals were *amphibians*, which retained the method of reproduction of most fishes, laying their eggs in water. But unlike fishes they developed lungs to breathe air and two sets of limbs to pull themselves along on dry land. These limbs had three segments each: first a single bone like our upper arm or thighbone, then two parallel bones, and then the bones that make up the "hands" and "feet" with their separate digits. Our limbs are based on the same plan as that of the early amphibian limbs. In this respect *Homo sapiens* has remained very conservative, while animals such as horses and cows have limbs that deviate a great deal from the early amphibian type of limb. The structure of the human hand must be very ancient; it remarkably resembles that of some tortoises.

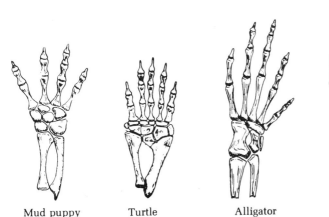

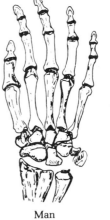

Mud puppy   Turtle   Alligator   Man

Right hands of mud
puppy, turtle,
alligator, and man,
from dorsal view.

An explanation for this conservatism will be presented shortly (page 38).

The later emerging stage of *reptiles* (beginning about 260 million years ago) was characterized by improved adaptations to life on land, including stronger limbs which, in some cases, raised the body off the ground. A new method of reproduction, associated with copulation, involved the laying of eggs encased in a hard shell.

Mammals

About 160 million years ago archaic mammals appeared. *Mammals* are warm-blooded creatures that are able to maintain a consistent high body temperature. They are thus less at the mercy of the environment than are the cold-blooded amphibians and reptiles and are able to live in different parts of the world with different climates, even in the Arctic. Mammals, except for the duckbill platypus and the spiny anteater, or echidna, which are noneutherian mammals, do not lay eggs.

Human beings belong to the infraorder of *eutherian mammals* which have a *placenta* and do not lay eggs. The embryo growing in the maternal uterus derives nourishment from the placenta, allowing it to stay for a long time in the mother's body. When the offspring is born it suckles from the mother's breasts (*mammae*) from which the class gets its name. This establishes a mother-child relationship which is of particular importance among the higher primates (especially humans), among whom the infant is born in a relatively helpless condition.

Mammals have an efficient circulatory system powered by a four-chambered heart. They generally have a covering of hair or fur and a skin equipped with sweat glands. All of these features have to do with regulating the temperature of the body. They also have a diaphragm that separates the thoracic from the abdominal parts of the body and helps to draw air into the lungs. The lower jaws of reptiles consist of several bones, but in mammals there is only one bone on either side; it articulates directly with the skull.

Mammalian dentition is said to be *heterodont,* having different kinds of teeth with different shapes and functions, as opposed to the *homodont* dentition of reptiles. Reptile teeth, which are often incurved, serve to grasp or trap food and all have the same general appearance and function. The mammalian jaw became stronger in the course of evolution, and teeth became specialized for different functions, with incisors for cutting, canines for grasping and piercing, premolars and molars for crushing and grinding.

The eutherian mammals have two sets of teeth. In the young animal there is a temporary milk set of teeth. When the jaw is more fully formed, the permanent teeth appear. The ancestral mammals are believed to have had 44 teeth, but present-day species have lost some of them in the course of evolution. Human beings usually have 32 teeth, which is more than most mammals have. (Many people, however, have only 28 teeth, and many have impacted third molars.)

Within the grouping of eutherian mammals, human beings belong to the order of *Primates,* which also includes the lemurs, tarsiers, monkeys, and apes.

Primate traits   The outstanding characteristic of primates is their prehensile (grasping) five-digited hands and feet.

The hands and feet of many primates have opposable digits in the thumb and big toe. The thumb can touch the other digits. When you grasp a branch, the thumb goes around one side, while the other four fingers wrap around the other. We cannot do this with our toes because our feet have become specialized for support and locomotion. Our big toes are in line with the other toes and not set apart from them as the thumb is set apart in the hand. The other primates, however, can generally grasp as well with their feet as with their hands, and their big toes are opposable.

Another feature of primate hands and feet is the presence of flat or slightly curved nails on the digits. Some of the lower primates have claws on some of their digits, but not the higher primates.

How have the primates been able to retain the early amphibian-reptilian type of hand? The answer must be that our early mammalian ancestors did not take to quadrupedal terrestrial life as did the ancestors of the ungulates, or hoofed mammals. It is believed that the first mammals were arboreal, or tree dwelling. Most of the primates of the present day still live in trees. Only a few, such as the baboon, gorilla, and humans, move about on the ground. The grasping hands and feet of the primates are admirably suited to life in the trees, and it must have been their adaptation to such an environment that preserved the mobility and flexibility of the limbs and maintained their original structure with so little change.

Another important function of the grasping hand and foot is seen in the clinging of a monkey infant to its mother. All monkeys are born with a clinging reflex; the infant hangs onto its mother's fur. The mother must often be very active, moving about through the trees, with hands and feet occupied in locomotion and exploration. If the infant could not hang onto its mother, it would die. The grasping primate hand is therefore essential to survival in such species.

Another feature of the primate skeleton, useful in an arboreal habitat, is the clavicle, or collarbone. This, again, is an early structure found in some amphibians but missing in many terrestrial mammals. It serves as a strut to keep each forelimb at the side of the body, thus allowing more space in which a primate can move.

Most primates, then, became adapted to life in the trees, and this adaptation enabled these mammals to maintain some features of the early amphibian-reptilian skeleton that have been lost by mammals that became adapted to other environments.

The teeth of primates are less specialized than those of most other mammals. Their jaws are generally rather short, and they have short faces, in contrast to the long-snouted terrestrial quadrupeds.

Life in the trees demands good eyesight, but a sharp sense of smell is not so important. For ground-dwelling nocturnal animals, on the other hand, a keen sense of smell may be more important than good vision. It is not surprising to find the sense of smell deficient in primates, especially among the higher ones, in contrast to most terrestrial animals. Many terrestrial animals have eyes set on either side of a snout so that they do not have overlapping stereoscopic vision. But most of the primates, whose eyes are set close together on the frontal plane, do have this feature. It may have developed originally as a response to the insect-catching diet of the simpler primates. At any rate, stereoscopic vision gives the primates a better conception of depth, so important for life in the trees. Moreover, the higher primates also have color vision.

An arboreal habitat is demanding. Leaping from branch to branch requires agility and good timing. The primates, therefore, are generally rather intelligent, high-strung creatures, and their brains are relatively large in proportion to body size. Most of the primates are quite small. Bulk is not suitable for life in the trees. *Homo sapiens* seems to have acquired large size after adjusting to life on the ground. The gorilla, a large and heavy primate, also spends much of the time on the ground.

Although most primates are quadrupedal, they are capable of sitting or standing in an upright position. When climbing, their bodies are vertical. Their forelimbs and hindlimbs have become differentiated, with the forelimbs being used for exploration and the lower limbs for support. Monkeys pick up objects with their hands and examine them. They also feed themselves with their hands, unlike long-snouted terrestrial animals that have to close in on food with their large jaws. Primates have flatter faces than such animals.

ERA	SYSTEM AND PERIOD	SERIES AND EPOCH	YEARS BEFORE PRESENT
CENOZOIC	Quaternary	Recent	11 thousand
CENOZOIC	Quaternary	Pleistocene	0.5 to 2 million
CENOZOIC	Tertiary	Pliocene	3.5±1 million
CENOZOIC	Tertiary	Miocene	14±2 million
CENOZOIC	Tertiary	Oligocene	28±2 million
CENOZOIC	Tertiary	Eocene	47±2 million
CENOZOIC	Tertiary	Paleocene	61±2 million
MESOZOIC	Cretaceous		
MESOZOIC			135±5 million
MESOZOIC	Jurassic		
MESOZOIC			180±5 million
MESOZOIC	Triassic		
MESOZOIC			230±10 million
PALEOZOIC	Permian		
PALEOZOIC			280±10 million
PALEOZOIC	Carboniferous	Pennsylvanian	
PALEOZOIC	Carboniferous		310±10 million
PALEOZOIC	Carboniferous	Mississippian	
PALEOZOIC			345±10 million
PALEOZOIC	Devonian		
PALEOZOIC			405±10 million
PALEOZOIC	Silurian		425±10 million
PALEOZOIC	Ordovician		
PALEOZOIC			500±10 million
PALEOZOIC	Cambrian		
PALEOZOIC			600±50 million
	Precambrian		

Chart showing appearance of different forms of life on earth at different periods.

Tarsier.

Primates usually bear only one offspring at a time, and the females usually have only one pair of breasts, although there are some exceptions among the lower primates.

The order of Primates is subdivided into two suborders: the Prosimii, or prosimians, and the Anthropoidea. The Prosimii include the lower primates, such as the lemurs and the tarsiers. Sometimes tree shrews are included in this group. Lemurs, found only on the island of Madagascar, have rather long snouts, heavy coats of fur, and bushy tails. The small tarsier, found in parts of Indonesia and the Philippines, is somewhat more advanced, having a large head and brain in proportion to its body, large ears, and very large eyes.

The higher primates

The Primate suborder to which we belong is the Anthropoidea, which also includes the Old World and New World monkeys and the apes. These animals tend to be larger than the prosimians, a feature which also involves larger brains, greater strength, and greater longevity. Members of this suborder have eyes set on the frontal plane, so, unlike some prosimians, they have stereoscopic vision. Both eyes can focus on the same object in front of the face, and since each eye sees it from a slightly different angle, there is a heightened sense of depth. The higher primates have the best-developed color vision in the class of mammals. Among the Anthropoidea there is a back wall to the eye socket. Brains are larger and more highly developed than those of the Prosimii, with the occipital lobes overhanging the cerebellum. There is only one pair of breasts, set high up on the chest.

The Anthropoidea may be divided into three superfamilies: Ceboidea (New World monkeys), Cercopithecoidea (Old World monkeys), and Hominoidea (apes and humans).

New World and Old World monkeys

The Ceboidea, or New World monkeys, which are found in Central and South America, evolved from a prosimian base in the New World. They have nostrils separated by a broad nasal septum. Some of these primates, including the howler and spider monkeys, have prehensile tails. They can wrap the tail around a branch and hang from it. None of the Old World monkeys have developed this feature.

The New World primates have a different dental formula from that of the Old World monkeys, apes, and humans. Among the latter, the characteristic dental formula is

$$I\frac{2}{2} \, C\frac{1}{1} \, P\frac{2}{2} \, M\frac{3}{3} \times 2 = 32.$$

This means that, in the jaws of either side, above and below, one will find two incisor teeth, one canine, two premolars, and three molars. Among lemurs and New World monkeys there are three premolars instead of two.

A notable feature of the Old World monkeys is the presence of *ischial callosities*—bare patches of calloused skin on the buttocks. These are thought to provide some protection for the monkeys when they spend the night sleeping in a sitting position in the fork of a tree. Old World monkeys may also have a sexual skin that sometimes becomes brilliantly colored. Some of these monkeys, like the baboons, have cheek pouches that can be stuffed with food to be subsequently digested.

Most monkeys, both Old and New World, have an essentially quadrupedal manner of locomotion, making their ways along the tops of branches or on the ground. They have long, narrow trunks like those of dogs and cats.

There are about 150 species of monkeys in the world, as compared with only one species of *Homo sapiens*. And monkeys are very numerous, outnumbering human beings in many parts of the world. Some monkeys, such as vervets, have a population density that humans came to equal only after they had acquired a knowledge of agriculture. The apes, who are more closely related to us, have not been so successful, and their numbers are dwindling.

The great variation among monkey species is best explained by their adaptations to different environments. Arboreal monkeys tend to be divided into more species than terrestrial ones.

The superfamily within the Anthropoidea to which we belong is that of the Hominoidea. Its other members are the apes—gibbon, orangutan, chimpanzee, and gorilla—who differ from the monkeys in lacking external tails and cheek pouches.

The apes

The apes all have long arms and relatively short legs. The apes do not have erect posture as we do, except for brief periods. When they stand supported by arms and legs, the spine is not parallel to the ground as in regularly quadrupedal animals, since their arms are longer than their legs. This gives them a semierect posture. When a chimpanzee or gorilla is in motion, its long arms serve to bear its weight, a method of locomotion known as *knuckle-walking*. In keeping with this semierect posture, the pelvises of apes are broader and more basin shaped than those of monkeys and more like those of humans.

Gibbons and orangutans are east Asiatic apes, while the chimpanzee and gorilla both live in Africa. The gibbons are the smallest, lightest, and most acrobatic of the apes, with very long arms adapted to *brachiation,* swinging from limb to limb through the trees, their usual habitat. Orangutans are larger, more sluggish, barrel-chested animals with rather high-domed foreheads and less of a brow ridge than any other ape. Anyone who has

Lowland gorilla in knuckle-walking position.

been to the zoo knows that chimpanzees are noisy, sociable, and boisterous animals. Among the apes they seem to be unique in having some tool-using capacities.

This ability with tools has its foreshadowings in the wild state. Jane van Lawick-Goodall, who studied free-ranging chimpanzees in Tanzania, East Africa, over a period of four years, has observed chimpanzees poking sticks into ant and termite nests. When they pull them out, the sticks are covered with termites, which the chimps lick off and eat. The sticks have to be the right length and shape. If they are too long, the chimpanzees break off part. If there are leaves on the stick, they strip them off. One chimp was seen to carry a stick for half a mile to where some termite nests were located. Chimpanzees also use leaves as a sponge to soak up water for drinking and show their young how to do it. Gorillas have not been seen to use tools in this way. Nor is there any evidence that gorillas eat meat in the wild state. Chimpanzees, however, sometimes eat meat, although fruit constitutes their main diet. They have been known to eat colobus monkeys, juvenile baboons, bush pigs, small antelopes, and infant chimpanzees.

Their most common prey seems to be baboons, probably because these two species are so often together in the same environment. Chimpanzee hunting behavior is mainly an adult activity and almost exclusively male. This hunting is sometimes coordinated. Geza Teleki once saw five males working together to surround three baboons which had taken shelter in trees (Teleki 1975:92–93). When a chimpanzee has made a kill, other chimps may move in to eat the carcass, and there seems to be little squabbling over the meat, although Teleki states that he never saw an ape yield the brain or any part of it to another. Both Teleki and Adriaan Kortlandt have described the "requesting" behavior of chimpanzees who hold out hands as if begging for a handout. Of 395 requests observed by Teleki, 114 were rewarded. "In the total of 43 hours of meat-sharing that I observed not once did two chimpanzees fight over possession of meat" (Teleki 1975:100).

The gorillas are the largest and strongest of the apes. In the wild state, adult males weigh between 300 and 450 pounds, while adult females weigh between 150 and 250 pounds. They weigh much more in zoos, where they have nothing to do but sit around and eat and therefore sometimes attain weights of 500 or 600 pounds. Gorillas have powerful, long arms and barrel chests, which they beat with their hands to frighten intruders. Their hands and feet are quite humanlike, although the fingers and toes are webbed nearly to the first joint. The foot has something of a heel bone. Another humanlike feature is the presence of mastoid processes at the base of the skull. The adult male gorilla has massive brow ridges and crests on the top and sides of his skull; these sagittal crests serve to anchor his heavy chewing muscles. Gorillas have large interlocking canine teeth. They live on vegetable food, and eat for six to eight hours a day. Although gorillas do not eat meat in the wild, they have sometimes become accustomed to eating it in captivity.

Let us now consider how human beings differ from the apes and other primates. The most important distinguishing features of *Homo sapiens* are upright posture, highly developed central nervous system, and large brain. The human brain is more than twice as large as that of the gorilla, who has the next largest brain among the primates. Compared with the brains of most primates, which have a small size, the human brain is enormous. But this is a relatively recent development in evolution, preceded by the assumption of upright posture. We infer this because the brains of the australopithecines, who had bipedal locomotion, were little larger than those of apes.

Distinctive traits of *Homo sapiens*

Several of the distinctions between man and other primates have to do with the assumption of upright posture. For example, in the lumbar region in *Homo sapiens,* there is a curvature of the spine that is not found among other primates. A human being has an S-shaped spinal column adapted to upright posture, while other primates have a more bow-shaped spine. The human pelvis has *ilia* (blades), which are much shorter than those of the larger apes and have been bent backward in the course of time. The pelvis is broad and basin shaped, particularly in females. The *gluteus maximus* muscles of the hip are well developed. Like apes, but unlike the monkeys, we lack external tails and have no ischial callosities. In contrast to the ape, our straight and heavily muscled legs are much longer than our arms. Humans are walkers, not brachiators.

Classification of *Homo sapiens*

	Members
Kingdom ..... Animalia	All animals
Phylum ...... Chordata	Animals having a notochord at some stage of development, constituting an internal skeleton
Subphylum ... Vertebrata	Animals having a vertebral column
Class .... Mammalia	Warm-blooded animals that suckle their young
Infraorder .... Eutheria	Placental mammals
Order .... Primates	Lemurs, tarsiers, monkeys, apes, humans
Suborder ..... Anthropoidea	Monkeys, apes, humans
Superfamily ... Hominoidea	Apes and humans
Family .... Hominidae	*Australopithecus, Homo erectus,* and modern humans
Genus .... *Homo*	*Homo erectus,* Neanderthals, and modern humans
Species .... *Sapiens*	Neanderthals and modern humans
Variety .... *Sapiens*	All modern human beings, including all living races

Human feet show a number of specializations resulting from their functions of support and bipedal locomotion. The foot is arched from front to back and from side to side and is equipped with a heel. The big toe is not set apart from the other toes, like a thumb, but is lined up with the others, and it is not opposable.

The human face also shows some modifications from an earlier form. *Homo sapiens* does not have heavy brow ridges and crests on the skull

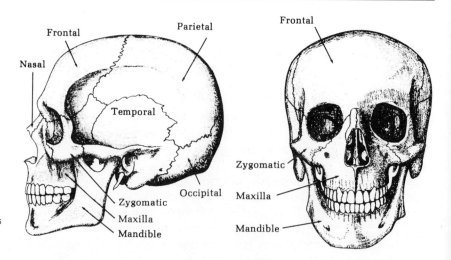

Side and front views of human skull.

as some of the apes do. Humans have a bony nose bridge with an extension of cartilage, which gives a more prominent nose than other primates (except for the proboscis monkey). Beneath the nose there is a groove in the upper lip called the *philtrum,* which is peculiar to humans. On either side of the nose, below the eye sockets, is a depression known as the *canine fossa.* The human face is relatively lacking in *prognathism,* or facial protrusion.

The mouth and jaws of humans have various distinctive characteristics. Our lips are outrolled, with the membranous red portion showing, in contrast to the thin lips of other primates in which the membranous portion is not easily seen. Modern humans have a chin that juts forward, in contrast to the sloping jaw of the ape. There is no *simian shelf* (a bar of bone that binds together the lower jawbones of apes). The canine teeth do not interlock, so there is no *diastema,* or gap in the upper row of teeth to receive the lower canine. The jaws flare out and are parabolic, in contrast to the long, narrow, U-shaped jaws of the apes.

At the bottom of the skull there is a large hole called the *foramen magnum,* through which the spinal cord connects with the brain. This is located at the rear of the skull in quadrupedal animals. At birth it is in the center of the base of the skull in all primates, but ends up being further back in the course of growth. In humans, however, the *foramen magnum* remains in the center of the base of the skull, for the skull is balanced on the spinal column. Since it is balanced in this way, we do not need a lot of neck muscles, like those of the gorilla. Our necks are longer than those of the apes.

The human body is relatively hairless, in comparison with the bodies of other primates, although there are some hairy individuals. But we usually have a lot of hair on our heads. (Again, there are exceptions.) These human patterns are particularly manifest in women, whose head hair is particularly

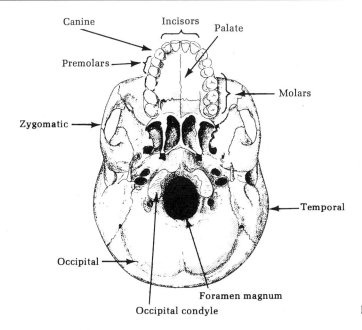

Base of human skull.

abundant while their body hair is scanty. The form of human hair shows some specializations; kinky or tightly curled hair is not found among the other primates.

One final point of difference between humans and the other primates: We mature more slowly than do the other primates, making necessary a longer period of dependency in childhood. This also makes possible a much longer period of learning, which is important in the transmission of culture from one generation to the next. The acquisition of culture is the crucial distinction between humans and the other primates, more important than the morphological differences between ourselves and the apes. But morphological features such as the greater size and complexity of the human brain and the development of upright posture made possible the acquisition of culture. Through culture human beings came to occupy a new ecological niche and a partially artificial environment of their own making. Through their acquisition of language, human beings became "time-binding" creatures; speech made it possible for them to talk about things that happened in the past and to make plans for the future.

In reviewing the distinctive traits of *Homo sapiens,* the ways in which we differ physically from other primates, it will be seen that many of these features, such as the lumbar curve, the characteristics of the pelvis, the long legs, and the specialization of the feet, represent adaptations to upright posture and bipedalism. Some of the differences are matters of degree—larger brains, less body hair. Some of the features mentioned have been acquired rather recently by *Homo sapiens* and were not characteristic of early hominids such as the australopithecines, Java man, and Peking man, who did not have chins or high nose bridges.

The differences that separate us from the pongids are not numerous. The striking thing, perhaps, is the extent of the resemblance between the apes and ourselves. This resemblance extends to matters of body chemistry. A number of biochemical studies show that *Homo sapiens* has more in common with the apes than *Homo sapiens* has with other primates. This is true of such features of the blood as purine metabolism, MN blood groups, and gamma globulin. The ABO blood groups are found in the Old World monkeys and the apes, as well as in *Homo sapiens*. The albumins of chimpanzees, gorillas, and humans are closely similar. Apes and human beings suffer from some of the same diseases, with similar symptoms, and they harbor some of the same parasites.

The extent of the similarities between apes and ourselves suggests that we share a common ancestry with them. There are many similarities between human beings and apes in biochemical features and molecular biology, particularly between humans and the African apes. Strands of chimpanzee DNA may be fitted to human DNA strands in the laboratory with only a 2.5 percent difference in fit, but monkey DNA shows a difference of 10 percent. Comparisons of hemoglobin chains in humans and other primates demonstrate that humans and chimpanzees have no differences at all, whereas gorillas have two differences and monkeys 12 differences from humans. There is similar evidence of the close relationship between humans and apes, particularly the chimpanzee, in the formation of antibodies and in aspects of albumin and transferrin (Washburn and Moore 1974:3–29).

Summary

Proceeding from broader to narrower classifications, human beings are vertebrates, eutherian mammals, and primates; we belong to the suborder Anthropoidea, the superfamily Hominoidea (along with the apes), and the family Hominidae, genus *Homo,* and species *sapiens.* As vertebrates we are bilaterally symmetrical animals with segmented backbones and brains enclosed in a skull. By virtue of being eutherian mammals we are warm blooded, maintain a constant high body temperature, and spend considerable time in the mother's body before birth, receiving nourishment from a placenta. Along with the other primates we have prehensile five-digited hands with opposable thumbs, and like other members of the Anthropoidea we have eyes set on the frontal plane, with stereoscopic and color vision.

Human beings differ from the other primates mainly in having upright posture, a larger brain, and a more highly developed central nervous system. Various anatomical features are related to the assumption of upright posture, such as a lumbar curve in the spine, a broad basin-shaped pelvis, and feet which have arches and a heel.

Human beings mature more slowly than do other primates, which results in a longer period of dependency in childhood. This also facilitates learning and the acquisition of culture, the crucial distinction between human beings and the apes, our closest relatives, who otherwise resemble us in many details of biochemistry and molecular biology.

A well-illustrated general discussion of the primates is *The Primates* by Sarel Eimerl and Irven De Vore (New York: Life Nature Library, 1965). See also George Schaller, *The Mountain Gorilla: Ecology and Behavior* (Chicago: University of Chicago Press, 1963). On human anatomy and physiology, see Richard J. Harrison and William Montagna, *Man* (New York: Appleton-Century-Crofts, 1969). For the food habits of chimpanzees and baboons, see Geza Teleki, "The Omnivorous Chimpanzee," in Solomon H. Katz, ed., *Biological Anthropology* (San Francisco: W. H. Freeman & Co., 1975), pp. 91–102. For a well-executed blend of lyricism and science concerning evolution, see Loren Eiseley, *The Immense Journey* (New York: Random House, Modern Library, 1957).

Suggestions for further reading

4

THE SOCIAL LIFE
OF PRIMATES

An examination of primate social relations may give us some insights into the biological and cultural evolution of our species. The australopithecines, who will be discussed in Chapter 5, were small-brained hominids with upright posture who inhabited African savannas 2 million years ago. We can make some deductions about their ways of life and the survival problems they faced by seeing how savanna-dwelling primates like baboons live today. Comparisons with chimpanzee social groups are also instructive. The sociological emphasis of the present chapter is thus not a detour; it should be seen as an integral part of the study of primate and human evolution.

It is important to note that, with the exception of some prosimian species, the primates are social animals that live in groups the year round. This is not true of all animals. Among the lower vertebrates, which lay eggs, there may be no continuing tie between mother and offspring. This is not the case among birds, which nest and feed their young, but reptiles, after laying their eggs, usually go off and forget about them. The baby reptile that survives steps out of the shell into a world that has no family structure. A baby primate, however, whether a lemur, a baboon, or a human being, is born into a social world.

Mother-child relations

It must be kept in mind that primates are mammals. The mammalian pattern of suckling provides for a continuing tie between mother and offspring. While this is true of all mammals, the mother-child relationship is stronger and longer lasting among primates than it is among most of the others. This is because the complex nervous system and brain development of primates requires a longer time to become coordinated. Although the gestation period is longer among more advanced mammals, the young are born in a relatively helpless condition, which increases their dependence upon the mother. There is a great contrast in this respect between primates and ungulates. On the day of birth, a baby deer or antelope can walk about; within a week it can run with great speed. It thus becomes self-sufficient much more quickly than a baby primate. Rodents and carnivores are more helpless at birth than ungulates, but rats and rabbits reach maturity at five or six months and can shift for themselves after a month or so. Baby primates, on the other hand, cling to the mother's body for the first weeks or months of life. Gibbon babies do so for about seven months.

Male-female relations

Primate social groups contain adult males who remain with the females and offspring the year round. Again, this is not true of all mammals. Among many mammals, the males remain with the females only during a rutting or mating season. Among most of the higher primates, there is no special mating season; females are sexually receptive throughout the year and pregnancies may occur at any time.

Among monkey groups that have special breeding seasons, the males continue to remain with the females throughout the year. It cannot be sexual attraction that keeps the primate males together with the females in this way. Another function of the continuing social bond is the protection afforded by the social group. There is safety in numbers. Monkeys that stay within

Hamadryas baboon group.

a group are more likely to survive. Loners may be picked off by predators. Thus, natural selection must have favored a genetic capacity for group life.

Adult male-young relations

Adult males in most primate groups are either tolerant or helpful in their attitudes toward the young. In many species, especially the more terrestrial ones, protective behavior has been reported, and there have been many observations of adult males rescuing or carrying away young animals from danger. Adult male baboons sometimes seem to supervise juvenile play groups and to intervene if the fighting gets too rough. The arboreal langurs are somewhat different in these respects; the males are more aloof and disinterested in the young. Their protective function is not so vital as it is for the ground-dwelling baboons.

Young peer relations

Among the Japanese macaques and similar monkeys whose offspring tend to be born within a particular season of the year, there are "age sets"; that is to say, there will be many infants of the same age. As they become older, the juveniles form play groups, chase each other, wrestle, and engage in vigorous play. This is also done among primates that have no breeding seasons. Some juveniles of similar age range are generally available to form play groups of this sort. As the young primates gradually lessen their dependence upon the mothers, they spend more and more time with peers. This shift may be accelerated by the weaning process and maternal rebuffs, particularly after the birth of a younger sibling. But the shift to the play group seems to be a natural transition. In play groups among macaques and baboons there are usually more males than females, and the juvenile females often remain with the adult females. Through active play with others, the juvenile not only acquires physical skills but also learns to interact with others. In groups where dominant-submissive relations are important, the relative status of individuals may be worked out in the course of rough-and-tumble play.

Variations in composition of primate social groups

We find, then, that most primates live in social groups containing males, females, and offspring. The size and composition of such groups, however, vary a great deal. In a general way, there has been an increase in group size from prosimian to more advanced forms. Insectivorous, nocturnal forest primates are sometimes solitary or have small family units consisting of a male, female, and offspring. Terrestrial primates that occupy forest fringes and savannas tend to have fairly large groups which contain several adult males. Savanna baboon troops commonly number between 30 and 50 individuals, with 5 to 10 adult males and 10 to 20 adult females.

There is much variation in social organization among the apes. Gibbons live in small, monogamous family groups consisting of a male, female, and offspring. The monogamous nature of the gibbon family is perpetuated by the aggressive behavior of the male when another male approaches the group, or by that of the female when another female approaches. Moreover, as offspring mature, they leave the family unit.

Orangutans are relatively asocial. They rarely form groups of more than three or four. Sometimes lone adult males are encountered in the jungle; they often leave the female and offspring and wander off by themselves.

Gorilla groups vary from 2 to 30 members, with an average of 6 to 17. Their social groups are more compact and consistent than those of chimpanzees. A dominant male usually determines the movements of the group, leading the way. Gorillas are normally quiet and make few vocalizations, in contrast to the noisy gibbons and chimpanzees.

The social life of chimpanzees is complex and variable. The composition of groups frequently changes. Some bands consist of mothers and young, some have adults of both sexes with some adolescents, and others consist of adult males only. Such groups may merge, split, or regroup. Subgroups number between two and 30. Adult males seem to do more traveling than mothers with offspring, whose ranges are more restricted. Chimpanzee mothers are extremely solicitous of their young. According to Adriaan Kortlandt, who studied chimpanzees in the Congo, they carry them around for the first four years of life. The young do not learn to be independent, although they show great curiosity about the environment. Indeed, Kortlandt considered them to be retarded in comparison to chimpanzees raised in captivity. Chimpanzees that inhabit the forest sometimes make a great deal of noise, hooting, screaming, and drumming on trees. This hullabaloo does not seem to function as a spacing mechanism, like the calls of howler monkeys. Instead, it may be a means of summoning other chimpanzees to an area where there are ripe fruit trees.

It is significant that there are not only contrasts in group size and composition in different species of primates but there may also be differences within a species among groups that have adapted to different environments. It was mentioned above that savanna baboon troops containing both adult males and females and offspring number between 30 and 50 individuals. In these groups the adult males have access to all the females. Such multimale groups are stable social units. Forest groups of baboons are smaller; they are also more fluid, often changing in composition. Females and their offspring form the core of a group; males come and go. In dry areas of Somalia and Ethiopia, on the other hand, hamadryas baboons form groups in which one male dominates a small harem of females and their offspring, making sure that they all keep together. These one-male groups join large congregations of hamadryas baboons at night, when they sleep on the walls of cliffs. Each group goes off by itself the next day, and there is little interaction between the one-male bands.

The occurrence of variation of social organization within a species shows that such organization is determined not only be genetic factors but also by the animals' responses to particular ecological conditions. Primates are **Learned primate behavior** animals that learn from one another and that may change their patterns of behavior in different settings. The long period of childhood dependence facilitates social learning among primates.

Reference was made earlier to the chimpanzee practice of poking sticks into termite nests and then licking them off. This is something young chimpanzees learn by watching and imitating older ones. The practice is not found in all chimpanzee groups.

Another example of learned behavior is the custom of washing sweet potatoes, which developed in a group of macaques living on an island off the coast of Kyushu, Japan. This began when a 16-month-old female washed a sweet potato in a brook to get rid of adhering sand. Other monkeys imitated her practice, and it caught on. After four years about half the macaques were doing it, and after nine years, 71 percent. Some monkeys began to carry their sweet potatoes to wash in the sea, rather than in the nearby brook, perhaps because of the salty taste. Wading into the sea and carrying their sweet potatoes, the monkeys assumed an erect posture, which they continued to carry on land more frequently than before. Here is a whole complex of learned behavior traits not shared by other monkeys of the same species.

It is interesting that new patterns of learned behavior like these often are initiated by the more plastic and playful youngsters and later taken up by older members of the group. It was adult females rather than males who imitated the innovative youngsters. Since the young ones feed together, they imitate one another. Females interact with the young and hence may pick up the new pattern, but the males feed separately from the females and young and do not learn the innovation.

If primates can learn so much, why don't they learn still more? For example, why have primates never learned to store food, which is done by many lower animals? Chimpanzees and gorillas build nests to sleep in, but not shelters. Despite the presence of learning ability, there are evidently limitations to it. For example, Jane van Lawick-Goodall observed baboons watching chimpanzees eat termites by poking sticks into termite nests and licking the sticks. Baboons also like to eat termites, but although they could see what the chimps were doing, they did not pick up the practice from them.

Dominance-submission

Different species of primates vary with regard to the degree of dominance and submission manifest within the group. Something like the pecking order of birds is found in many animal species. Dominant animals are those that display more aggression, win most of the fights, appropriate most of the food if there is a limited amount, and have priority in sexual relations. Dominant animals are the focus of attention of other members of the group. Where dominant-submissive polarities are found among primates, males are generally dominant over females, and some males are dominant over others.

The dominance of males over females is associated with sexual dimor-

Order of march in savanna baboons, with the dominant males, females, and infants occupying the center of the band and the young males the periphery.

phism, or the appearance of striking differences in size and strength between males and females. Sexual dimorphism is more marked among terrestrial primates like baboons and gorillas than among arboreal ones like the gibbon. In general, dominant-submissive patterns seem to be associated with terrestrial activity and the defensive functions of the males who, as among baboons and macaques, have developed an aggressive sort of temperament, which helps them to face predators in defense of the group.

The existence of dominant-submissive patterns does not mean that a lot of fighting is always going on among the adult males. On the contrary, fighting tends to be inhibited in such groups, since everyone's position in the hierarchy is relatively fixed and recognized. A threatened individual in a baboon troop may run toward a dominant male for help as a frightened baboon infant runs to its mother. Dominant male baboons will not let others fight and may dash to the scene of a quarrel to prevent it. There is not much fighting over food resources among baboons in the wild, since the troop is usually spread out over a fairly wide area with each individual seeking its own food.

Among monkey troops that move about, foraging as they go, there may be some structure to the group. At least this is the case among baboons and Japanese macaques. Dominant males and mothers and infants are usually found in the center of the band and young males on the periphery. Dominance-submission patterns may therefore contribute to order and stability in the group.

We tend to think of monkey behavior as being largely instinctual. But it is important to remember that monkeys behave differently in different situational contexts. Indian rhesus monkeys who live in temple compounds

Significance of the social matrix

display more aggression that those who live in the forest. Baboons studied in the London Zoo showed more aggression than those observed in the wild state. When C. R. Carpenter transported more than 100 rhesus mothers and infants from India to Puerto Rico, he found that the mothers, cramped in small cages and sparingly fed, fought their own offspring away from the food, and about nine mothers killed their infants. This sort of behavior would not be apt to occur under normal conditions.

What is still more striking is that a rhesus monkey who has been brought up in caged isolation from birth and later, after about a year and a half, introduced to the company of other members of its species, does not know how to interact with them. Mature male rhesus monkeys who have been socially deprived in this way cannot even perform the sexual act. Mature female rhesus monkeys who have been raised in isolation from birth and later impregnated by normal males do not behave in a maternal manner toward their offspring. Indeed, they are quite indifferent toward them, reject them, and often treat them with unfeeling cruelty.

These experiments suggest the enormous importance of adequate maternal care for the normal development of primates. Other such experiments, performed by Harry Harlow and his colleagues at the University of Wisconsin, suggest the equally great importance of peer relations. Infant monkeys who have been deprived of their mothers but allowed to play with other young members of their species for 20 minutes a day seem to develop normally with regard to social and sexual interaction. These experiments show that sexual behavior, which we might have assumed to be instinctive among monkeys, depends upon the development of adequate patterns of social interaction with other members of the species.

Temperament, instinct, and behavior

Some observers have commented on differences in the characteristic temperaments found in different primate species: the phlegmatic gorilla, the lively chimpanzee, the aggressive male savanna baboon. John O. Ellefson (1968:137) has suggested that: "The modal or normative personalities of species have adaptive significance; that is, norms of personality are the result of an adaptive process, an interplay between natural selection and the genetic variation intrinsic to sexual reproduction and mutation through time in populations." Thus, the aggressive temperament of male savanna baboons may have developed as an adaptive response to a terrestrial environment in which there are many predators.

This raises the question of what sort of temperamental traits were fostered in the course of *human* evolution. A number of writers have claimed that human beings are particularly aggressive animals and that this aggressiveness is related to the adoption of hunting and a carnivorous diet on the part of our ancestors and also due to a human territorial instinct—the urge to defend a particular range of territory against intruders. The writings of Konrad Lorenz, Robert Ardrey, Desmond Morris, Robin Fox, and Lionel Tiger, as well as other writers, along these lines have become popular during the past decade. In rebuttal against this school of thought there have also appeared some books and articles, by writers such as Ashley Montagu, Alexander Alland, and others, attacking these assumptions.

The idea that man is basically a nasty, aggressive creature is at least as old as the doctrine of Original Sin. It was expressed by the 17th century philosopher Thomas Hobbes and more recently by Sigmund Freud, among others. It is, therefore, a view of man that many people have been ready to accept. It is admittedly one way of making sense out of today's headlines and the long, bloody history of the human species. But the reader who has come this far in this chapter should be able to see some of the weaknesses in this view of humans. The animals most often cited by Ardrey, Tiger, and Fox for insights into the behavior of our protohominid ancestors are the baboons. This may be partly because baboons have been studied more than other nonhuman primates. It also may be because savanna baboons occupy territory similar to that presumably inhabited by our ancestors. But human beings are not as closely related to the baboons as they are to the gorillas and chimpanzees, whose social organization, temperament, and behavior patterns differ in various ways from those of baboons. We have noted, moreover, that differences in social organization and troop size may appear within a species such as baboons, among groups that have adapted to different environments, and that this plasticity is related to the learning abilities of primates, which are thus not totally at the mercy of instinctual drives.

Our ancestors of 4 million or 5 million years ago must have been more adaptable than baboons, since they developed a culture, a way of life dependent upon learning and the use of language. Moreover, human beings have adapted to a great range of environments. To derive present-day human behavior from instincts fostered during mankind's early hunting stage seems at least oversimplified. The importance of aggression also may have been exaggerated by Lorenz, Ardrey et al., not only as far as human behavior is concerned but also in relation to other animal species. "When Lorenz says that 'fighting is an ever-present process' in nature, he must be forgetting all the moles, hedgehogs, raccoons, opossums, woodchucks, otters, chipmunks, squirrels of several kinds, rabbits, lemmings, moles, muskrats and beavers. . . ." (Carrighar 1968:48). Among these animal species there is little show of aggression. In relation to territoriality also, there may have been an overemphasis on the part of Lorenz, Ardrey, and others.

Territoriality

In all classes of vertebrates there are species characterized by *territoriality,* that is, the pattern of defending a particular range of territory, principally against other members of the same species. This concern may be confined to a particular period, especially the breeding season, or it may be a more permanent preoccupation. Generally, small animals have small territories and large animals have big ones, although carnivorous animals tend to have larger territories than herbivores. A kind of territoriality has been found among many, but not all, primate species. Among some prosimians, urination and defecation help to demarcate the territory, providing boundary stakes, so to speak. Among some of the higher primates, such as the howler monkey and the gibbon, vocalization helps to indicate which group belongs in which part of the forest. Gibbons and howlers both make a lot of noise. Aggressive gestures and cries greet invaders of the territory, who usually retreat. But according to Paul E. Simonds (1974:75), most wild primates that have been studied do not defend territories.

Terrestrial primates are apt to wander over a wider range of territory than arboreal ones. Baboons seem to stay within a particular range of land, but they do not fight other baboon groups to defend their territory. Similarly, gorillas do not try to defend particular areas. While the gibbons do exhibit territorial behavior, this is not true of the gorilla and chimpanzee, the animals most closely related to humans. The clearest cases of primate territoriality occur among leaf-eating forest dwellers, who are much more distantly related to us.

Summary

An examination of primate social life is helpful for insights into primate and human evolution. Except for some prosimian species, the primates are social animals that live in groups the year around. Suckling provides for a continuing bond between mother and dependent offspring. Males and females also tend to remain together thoughout the year. Adult males in most primate groups are either tolerant or helpful in their attitudes toward the young and may play a protective role, especially in terrestrial species.

The size and composition of primate groups varies widely. In general there has been an increase in group size from prosimian to more advanced forms. Terrestrial primates tend to have fairly large multi-male groups, but there may be differences in group size and composition within a species among groups that have adapted to different environments. This suggests that social organization is not determined by genetic factors alone but also by learning and adaptation to changing conditions.

Some writers have argued that human beings have inherited aggressive tendencies related to hunting and territorial defense. But territoriality is not characteristic of all primate species; the gorilla and chimpanzee, our closest relatives, do not show territorial behavior.

Suggestions for further reading

Studies about various primates—lemurs, baboons, rhesus monkeys, langurs, macaques, gorillas, and chimpanzees—may be found in Irven De Vore, ed., *Primate Behavior: Field Studies of Monkeys and Apes* (New York: Holt, Rinehart & Winston, 1965). A very readable work is Jane van Lawick-Goodall, *In the Shadow of Man*

(Boston: Houghton Mifflin Co., 1971). For interesting observations on baboon groups, see Hans Kummer, *Primate Societies: Group Techniques of Ecological Adaptation* (Chicago: Aldine and Atherton, 1971). An excellent general survey is Alison Jolly, *The Evolution of Primate Behavior* (New York: Macmillan Co., 1972).

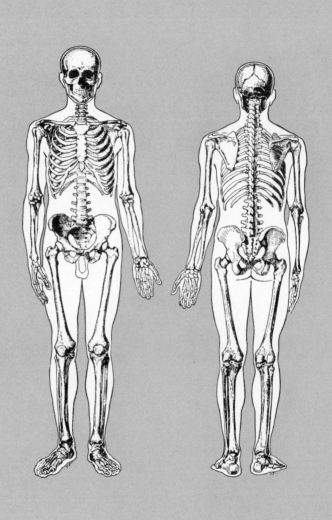

part two
Human physical and cultural evolution

5

EVOLUTION OF THE PRIMATES TO THE AUSTRALOPITHECINES

The earliest primates we know anything about were small prosimians resembling modern tree shrews or lemurs, dating back to the Paleocene epoch, about 60 million years ago. Lemurs and tarsiers of various kinds had become abundant by the Eocene epoch, about 57 million years ago, when they spread across North America and parts of Eurasia. Then their numbers declined. They continued to exist in parts of the Old World, but by the end of the Eocene they appear to have become extinct in Europe and North America, where their once-abundant fossil record comes to an end. This debacle may have been due to the development of competing mammals, such as rodents and carnivores, and in the Old World to the appearance of higher primates that had evolved from prosimian forms. Increasingly colder weather conditions may also have played a role. Whatever the reasons, the range of prosimians contracted. Although more than 20 different fossil types of Eocene tarsioids have been identified, there is now only one living genus, *Tarsius,* with three living species.

While the term *hominid* refers to members of the family Hominidae, to which we belong, *hominoid* refers to members of the super-family Hominoidea, which includes both apes and human beings. So the latter term, Hominoidea, is the broader classification. Hominid, human being, and *Homo sapiens* are not interchangeable terms in a strict sense. The human beings of the present day are all of one species, *Homo sapiens.* We are the only living hominids. But there were formerly other types of hominids in existence, like the australopithecines, which, although not human beings, had more in common with us than with the apes.

The best candidates for the earliest hominoid fossil finds come from Oligocene deposits in the Fayum, Egypt, dating from about 35 million years

Early hominoids

63

ago. The Fayum was then a wet tropical region containing land tortoises, turtles, and crocodiles. In those days the Mediterranean reached about 100 miles inland in this area, which was then a border region between sea and jungle. More than 100 specimens of primate finds have been recovered in the Fayum, including the remains of *Oligopithecus savagei,* a foot-high creature on or near the ancestral line of the Old World monkeys. *Oligopithecus* is the oldest known primate having 32 teeth of the catarrhine type. It has been dated at about 32 million years ago. *Aegyptopithecus zeuxis,* dated at around 28 million years ago, was another Fayum primate, which is represented by an almost complete skull and other skeletal material. This early hominoid, which is sometimes called the first true ape, is believed to have lived an arboreal life and to have been about the size of a modern gibbon, almost twice as large as the other Oligocene primates from the Fayum. *Aegyptopithecus* may have developed from the earlier *Propliopithecus* and may have been in the line of descent of the later East African apes of Miocene times. Unlike the apes of the present day, *Aegyptopithecus* had a tail. *Pithecus,* which appears in these names, means ape.

More hominoid fossils have been recovered from deposits of the Miocene epoch, dating between approximately 5 million and 23.5 million years ago.

Time scale for the evolution of the primates

Epoch	Approximate years B.P. (before the present)	Some important representative primate species
Pleistocene	10,000–1,800,000	Homo sapiens, Homo erectus, Australopithecus
Pliocene	1,800,000–5,000,000	Australopithecus
Miocene	5,000,000–23,500,000	Ramapithecus, Dryopithecus
Oligocene	23,500,000–35,000,000	Aegyptopithecus, Propliopithecus, Oligopithecus
Eocene	35,000,000–58,000,000	Tarsiers, lemurs
Paleocene	58,000,000–65,000,000	Prosimians like tree shrews or lemurs

Various kinds of Miocene apes, generally classified as *Dryopithecus* ("forest ape") have been found in Europe, Africa, the USSR, India, and China. The lower molar teeth have what has been called the Y-5, or *dryopithecus, pattern,* a pattern found also in humans but not among Old World monkeys. The crowns of monkey molars have a cusp at each corner, while the crowns of chimpanzee, gorilla, and human lower molars usually have five cusps. In between the cusps there is a groove that looks like the letter *Y.* This tooth pattern is found only in the lower molars of chimpanzees, gorillas, and humans and in some of their precursors.

More complete than the remains of other early hominoid fossils are those

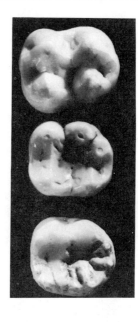

Molars of a monkey (*top*), ape (*center*), and human (*bottom*), showing the Y-5 or dryopithecus pattern in ape and human.

of *Dryopithecus africanus,* sometimes called *Proconsul,* a dryopithecine ape dating from the early Miocene in East Africa. Here we have not only jaws and teeth, but also skull and limb bones. At least three species have been identified, one of which is as small as a gibbon, another as large as a gorilla. *Dryopithecus africanus* did not have heavy brow ridges like those of present-day apes, nor did their lower jaws have a simian shelf. Their teeth had the Y-5 pattern. Their canines were large. Their arms and legs were rather humanlike in appearance, and they do not seem to have been brachiators like the gibbon. It is thought that the advanced kind of brachiation

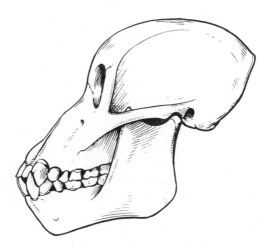

Dryopithecus africanus (20–10 million years ago).

of modern apes was a late development in their evolution, perhaps occurring in later Pliocene times. The fossil record seems to show that the apes of the present day are less humanlike than some of their ancestors, and we are less apelike than our ancestors. Apes and humans have adapted to different environments and have evolved in different directions. The ancestral apes had more humanlike limb proportions, lighter brow ridges, and less pronounced canine teeth than their descendants. Like our assumption of upright posture, the long arms of the apes may have been a relatively recent development in primate evolution.

The ramapithecines

From some widely separated Miocene sites in northwestern India, East Africa, Europe, and China come the fossil remains of jaws and teeth that are different from those of *Dryopithecus* and have been thought to be human-like in some respects. These finds have been dated between 8 million and 14 million years ago.

The teeth and jaws of *Ramapithecus* lack some apelike features. Apes have large, interlocking canine teeth that require the presence of a *diastema,* a gap in the tooth series for reception of the canine tooth from the other jaw. Large, interlocking canine teeth are not found in *Ramapithecus,* and the incisors are also small. It is assumed that a foreshortened face went with such a jaw. Early descriptions of the *Ramapithecus* jaws gave them a parabolic appearance, like those of modern humans, instead of the long, narrow, U-shaped jaws of apes. A recent reconstruction of *Ramapithecus wickeri,* however, presents a more primitive picture. The palate now is de-scribed as being long and narrow and not rounded or parabolic (Andrews and Walker 1976:289).

It has been speculated that *Ramapithecus* may have had upright posture and may have been a true hominid; but there are no limb bones or other skeletal material to demonstrate upright posture.

Still, it seems likely that a differentiation took place at around this time with regard to habitat and locomotion, with the apes adjusting to a more arboreal habitat with an emphasis on brachiation, while our ancestors, per-haps the ramapithecines, became more terrestrial and developed bipedalism. In bipedalism the burden of locomotion is on the feet, thus freeing the hands for carrying things and using tools. Upright locomotion, then, would be a valuable preadaptation to the regular use and manufacture of tools. It also would enable the females to carry their dependent young. Moreover, the assumption of upright posture results in an increased range of vision. We cannot be sure when bipedalism originated, but it was already well established among the australopithecines by the beginning of the Pleistocene, about 1.8 million years ago. The fact that the hipbones of the australopithe-cines were already similar to modern hipbones suggests hundreds of thou-sands of years of prior adaptation to erect posture. Moreover, australopithe-cine foot bones found at Olduvai Gorge in Tanzania differ in only minor details from those of modern feet.

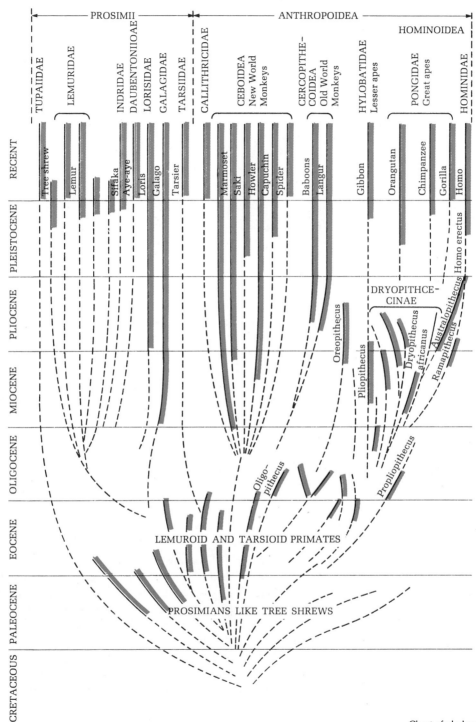

Chart of phylogeny of
the primates.

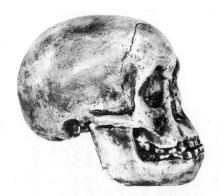

Reconstructed plaster cast of the Taung child fossil, labeled *Australopithecus africanus* by Raymond Dart.

Australopithecus africanus

In 1924, Raymond Dart, an anatomist at the University of the Witwatersrand, acquired a well-preserved fossil skull that seemed to be that of an immature ape. It came from some limestone bluffs at Taung, South Africa. The skull was evidently that of a five- or six-year-old juvenile, since its milk teeth were intact. The first four permanent molar teeth were also present. Although somewhat apelike in appearance, the juvenile's braincase was as large as that of an adult chimpanzee. Dart gave this find the name of *Australopithecus africanus,* or South African ape, but he drew attention to many humanlike features in the skull. There were no heavy brow ridges or projecting canine teeth. The appearance of the teeth was more human than apelike. The face was quite flat and the skull a bit rounded on top. There were implications of upright posture in the central position of the *foramen magnum.* As critics pointed out after Dart published his findings, most of these features are not unusual in immature apes, which have flatter faces, smaller brow ridges, less projecting canines, and higher foreheads than adult apes. But what was unusual, in any case, was the location of this find. The present-day African apes, the gorilla and chimpanzee, live in tropical forests 2,000 miles farther north. Taung is in a dry, savannalike environment, and Dart estimated that climatic conditions were not very much different a million years ago, when the Taung child was thought to have lived. Its diet must have been quite different from those of chimpanzees and gorillas. Perhaps, like the baboons who now live in such terrain, it ate berries, grubs, lizards, and birds' eggs. It was probably more of a meat eater than most primates, but such shifts of diet are not uncommon in the different orders of mammals. The panda, for example, although classed among the carnivores, has become a strict vegetarian.

About ten years after Dart's discovery, a number of fossils of similar type were found in South Africa; they have come to be known as australopithecines. Their skeletal material, now abundant, consists not only of skulls, jaws, and teeth but also of limbs and pelvic bones. A nearly complete australopithecine foot was found at Olduvai Gorge in Tanzania. Most of a vertebral column and pelvis come from Sterkfontein in South Africa. Many hundreds of fossil finds have been made. A total of 1,022 bones have come from the South African sites alone. From this material it has been judged that the australopithecines had upright posture and either partial or complete bipedal locomotion. At the same time, they had small brains, which suggests that our ancestors assumed upright posture before developing a large brain. The cranial capacity was about 500 cubic centimeters, no larger than that of African apes. But their brains were larger in proportion to body size than those of the great apes.

The australopithecines had large, chinless jaws, with canine teeth that were relatively small. There was no diastema. Mastoid processes like those of modern humans appear on the skulls. Some had a good deal of facial protrusion, with heavy brow ridges and crests on top of the skull. These are apelike features, but there is general agreement that the australopithecines

An outline map of Africa, showing location of australopithecine sites.

should be classed as hominids; they had more in common with us than with the apes.

Dating
techniques

A number of dates, usually in the millions of years, have been given so far for particular time periods. These dates are often tentative, based on geological and paleontological evidence, but we are now coming to a period when more specific dating techniques are possible. For example, a site at Olduvai Gorge in Tanzania, East Africa, associated with australopithecine remains, has been dated about 1,750,000 years ago by the potassium-argon method. This method is similar to the radiocarbon system applicable to more recent sites. A review of these methods may help to show how our chronological picture of the past is pieced together.

The most widely used archaeological dating technique is radiocarbon dating. This method is based on the discovery that all living things, both plants and animals, contain a radioactive carbon (radiocarbon) known as carbon-14 (C^{14}). Plants absorb this carbon from the atmosphere. Animals acquire it by eating plants or by eating animals that have eaten plants. The amount of C^{14} normally present in a living plant or animal species is known. Although some disintegration of radiocarbon may take place during the life of an organism, it is balanced by the intake of C^{14}; so, in a living organism, the amount of radiocarbon remains fairly constant. After death, however, no more C^{14} is taken in, and disintegration of C^{14} proceeds at a steady rate. In 5,730 years, half of the C^{14} in the organism has decayed; this is known as the half-life of carbon.

Since the rate at which C^{14} disintegrates is known, it is possible to date the time of death of some organic material by determining how much radiocarbon remains in it. Charcoal is among the most suitable such material for analysis. Shells are less reliable. Carbon-14 dates derived from marine mollusks may have to be corrected by the addition of several hundred years, since shellfish take in carbonates from seawater.

The date yielded by the radiocarbon method is not a definite, specific date but one plus or minus a certain number of years, giving a standard deviation. Thus, instead of 15,300 B.P., the date would be given as 15,300 B.P. $\pm$ 300, which means that there is a 67 percent chance that the correct figure will fall between 15,000 and 15,600 B.P. It does not mean that the correct figure *must* fall between these two extremes. Note that B.P. (before present) is used instead of B.C. (before Christ). The B.P. date refers to the number of years before A.D. 1950.

This technique was tried out by testing it with various objects whose ages were known through historical records or other sources, such as linen from the Dead Sea Scrolls and wood from an Egyptian tomb known to be dated between 4,700 and 5,100 years ago. The radiocarbon dates met these tests very well. Since then the method has been applied to archaeological sites all over the world.

YEARS AGO (X 1000)	GLACIATIONS (ALPS)	GEOLOGICAL DIVISIONS	ARCHAEOLOGICAL DIVISIONS
	Postglacial	Holocene	Neolithic Mesolithic
10			
			Upper Paleolithic
35	Würm	Upper Pleistocene	
			Middle Paleolithic
75			
100			
	Riss		
200		Middle Pleistocene	
275			
	Mindel		
		Lower Pleistocene	
500			
	Günz		Lower Paleolithic
		Basal Pleistocene	
	Donau and Earlier Stages		
2000			

Geological and archaeological divisions of time, with subdivisions of the Pleistocene epoch and the Paleolithic correlated with periods of glaciation.

Despite its many advantages, there have been some difficulties in using C^{14} for dating purposes. One of the assumptions underlying its original application was that the carbon-14 content in the atmosphere has always been constant. This has now been shown to be untrue. There was much more radiocarbon in the atmosphere 6,000 years ago than there is today.

Changes in the earth's magnetic field and solar radiation may account for such differences. New calibration charts for radiocarbon dates have been drawn up to correct for this situation. The C^{14} method is mainly useful for sites dating up to 20,000 years and so cannot be applied to the australopithecine material.

In potassium-argon dating, a radioactive form of potassium decays at a known rate to form argon. The ages of some rocks can be dated by measuring the potassium-argon ratios. One advantage of this technique is that it can be used to date older sites than those within the range of C^{14} dating. But most archaeological sites cannot be dated by the potassium-argon method. It is mainly useful for sites dating to 500,000 years or more ago, and it is applicable to only rocks or sediments rich in potassium, such as volcanic ash. Intense heat is needed to drive off excess argon. Potassium-argon dating has not been possible in nonvolcanic areas such as South Africa.

For much more recent sites, up to 2,000 years ago, dendrochronology, or tree-ring dating, supplies a specific date in terms of years.

A tree adds a new growth ring each year. By counting the annual layers one can find out just how old the tree was when it was cut down. The rings on a tree are sometimes thick and sometimes thin, depending upon the amount of rainfall during the year. When plenty of moisture is available, they are wide; in times of drought, they are narrow. In subarctic regions, warmth is the critical factor. Since all the trees within a particular area are

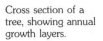

Cross section of a tree, showing annual growth layers.

affected by the same weather conditions, their tree-ring sequences show the same patterns. Let us say that we have three thin layers, then a fat one, then two thin ones, then three fat ones, and so on. By comparing the tree-ring sequences of many trees in a particular area, a master chart may be drawn up to show the characteristic tree-ring sequence for that area. This chart can be extended far back in time, as progressively older trees are found whose later tree-ring sequences overlap those of younger trees.

The technique of dendrochronology has been used in the southwestern United States, where a master chart of tree-ring sequences goes back almost to the time of Christ. If a Pueblo ruin is excavated in Arizona, let us say, a cross section of a beam is analyzed to see how its tree-ring sequences fit into the master chart. In this way it is possible to say in which year the beam was cut, which may also give the year in which the Pueblo structure was built. There is a minor catch, however, for the beam might have been used in an earlier house and later transferred to the Pueblo structure; it might have been added to the house sometime after it was built. Despite such ambiguities, tree-ring analysis has been very helpful in dating sites in the American Southwest.

Dendrochronology cannot be applied to all kinds of trees or in all kinds of environments. Apparently it will not work in New Zealand, and it cannot be used in areas where there is little annual variation in rainfall. However, tree-ring analysis has been practiced with some success in England, Germany, Norway, Turkey, Egypt, and various parts of the United States, including Alaska.

These dating techniques have added much precision to the archaeologist's reconstruction of the past. There are often problems, however, concerning the ages of specific finds, especially in the early time range of the australopithecines. One of the issues discussed later in this chapter is whether more advanced forms of *Homo* coexisted with australopithecines. In such a case it is crucial to have convincing evidence for the age of the more advanced forms.

Evidence of hunting

The presence of animal bones at australopithecine sites suggests that the australopithecines ate meat. Mary Leakey, the wife of Louis S. B. Leakey, mapped a 3,400-square-foot "living floor" at Olduvai Gorge, a site that has been dated by the potassium-argon method at about 1.75 million years ago. Within the Olduvai site there is an area with a 15-foot diameter littered with smashed animal bones, which were evidently broken to get at the marrow. Stone tools were also found. The evidence suggests that the Olduvai hominids were both tool users and meat eaters.

Some of the animals whose meat was eaten were very large, including an elephant and an extinct *Deinotherium*. Their remains were found at butchering sites, not on the living floor. These animals may have died of natural causes or else been trapped and butchered in a swampy area. In any case, as many as 123 stone-cutting tools were found with the elephant remains; there were 39 associated artifacts with the *Deinotherium* remains.

If they were hunters, the australopithecines risked encounters with dangerous predators, such as lions and hyenas. But the two latter species are mainly nocturnal, and the australopithecines could have avoided them by hunting in open savannas during the day, thus entering a new ecological niche.

Home base

The Leakeys uncovered a semicircular wall at Olduvai, which may have served as a windbreak and has been dated at around 2 million years old ± 280,000 years—the oldest man-made structure known (Pfeiffer 1969:79).

The windbreak and the living floor with its bone collection suggest the presence of a home base. A home base is a pattern associated with carnivores rather than with primates, but the smashed animal bones at Oldowan sites show that at least some of the australopithecines were meat eaters and thus qualified as both primates and carnivores, if not in zoological classification. Something like a home base is foreshadowed in some other primate species. Baboons require nesting places for sleeping that keep them out of reach of predators. These are usually trees, but in arid regions in Ethiopia hamadryas baboons occupy cliffs at night. Reliance on a particular refuge area is not so different from a home base. Simonds (1974:74) notes: "Females with newborn infants tend to remain closest to the core areas since they are the safest part of the home range." A home base serves the same functions among human hunters; it provides a refuge for the old and sick as well as for females with young.

A study of the eruption rates of australopithecine teeth suggests that their young were as dependent upon adults as children are today. A long period of maturation facilitates learning, and this may have made possible a reliance upon culture among the hominids of that time.

It seems likely that the inhabitants of such a site shared their meat. After all, chimpanzees do so (see p. 44). The more advanced australopithecines had only to carry the practice a step further by bringing meat back to the home base. Being bipedal or partially bipedal walkers, with hands freed, they could have carried both weapons and meat in their hands.

The use of tools

The stone tools at Olduvai consist mostly of pieces of lava and quartz, which must have been brought to the site from about three miles or more away; they do not occur naturally at the site itself. Crude, rounded pebble tools called choppers are among the artifacts.

Because of the relative absence of tools of other materials, we must learn what we can from the imperishable remains of stone tools dating from the australopithecine period. It is not always easy to determine whether

Plaster casts of choppers used by Peking man. These are similar to African Oldowan tools.

a particular piece of stone was deliberately fashioned. Early humans made much use of flint, which fractures easily when given a blow. But stone can be flaked by natural agencies—by rapid changes in temperature, frost, glacial action, and other causes. However, a close examination of the stone may reveal whether man-made blows dislodged a flake. As a leading authority on the subject has written: ". . . the surface of a fracture due to a sharp external blow appears clean-cut, and shows a definite bulb of percussion with faint radial fissures and ripples originating at a point on the edge of the flake or flake-scar" (Oakley 1964:17).

The earliest stone tools showing deliberate flaking were choppers, pebble tools with a jagged cutting edge formed by striking off a few flakes. Choppers were the most common tools found in Bed I in Olduvai Gorge; they have come to be known as Oldowan tools. Such tools, sometimes flaked on both sides or in two directions, have been found from the Cape in South Africa to the Transvaal, Kenya, Morocco, Algeria, and Ethiopia. There were hominids early in the Pleistocene using Oldowan choppers in most parts of Africa before stone tools first appeared in Europe. Later, simple choppers were used by Peking man and have been found in many parts of eastern Asia, including China, Burma, Indonesia, and India. Some early European sites also have yielded tools similar to the Oldowan and Peking choppers, notably Clacton-on-Sea and Swanscombe in southeastern England, Vértesszöllös in Hungary, near Menton in southern France, and a couple of sites in Romania. In Africa the Oldowan chopper gradually gave rise to a more advanced tool, the hand axe, which is discussed in the following chapter.

Although the chopper is the most common and most characteristic tool in the lower strata at Olduvai Gorge, it is not the only type of stone tool. There were also stone balls and scrapers, burins for chiseling, awls, anvils, and hammerstones. The round stone balls may have been used as bolas, such as were used on the pampas of South America. Two or three stones tied with thongs are thrown to entangle an animal's legs. There are also indications that australopithecines may have used tools of bone and horn.

John T. Robinson, one of the leading students of the South African finds, suggested that the australopithecines should be divided into two groups. He first proposed that one genus was *Australopithecus;* the second was *Paranthropus.* More recently Robinson has promoted *Australopithecus* to the genus *Homo* and christened him *Homo africanus.* This terminology has not been adopted by most anthropologists. Species terms more generally used for the two subdivisions are *Australopithecus africanus* for the first type and *Australopithecus robustus* for the second, which was first called *Paranthropus.* To simplify matters, let us call them, as is commonly done, *A. africanus* and *A. robustus.*

According to Robinson, these types were found in different sites and differed markedly in size and weight. *A. robustus* had about the height of present-day human beings and weighed betwen 100 and 200 pounds. *A. africanus* was much shorter and weighed less than 100 pounds. *A robustus* had a round, low skull, while *A. africanus* had a narrow, slightly domed one and the brow ridges were less prominent. In contrast to *A. africanus,* *A. robustus* had crests on the top of the skull, like those of an adult male gorilla, although less pronounced. *A. robustus* had heavy cheekbones that protruded further forward than the flat nose, but *A. africanus* had more facial protrusion. *A. robustus* had much larger molar teeth but smaller canines and incisors than *A. africanus.* The contrasts in dentition and in the framework of the skull suggest to Robinson that *A. robustus* depended more on a vegetarian diet, which required a great deal of chewing and grinding of food, whereas *A. africanus* is presumed to have been more carnivorous or omnivorous. Robinson believes that *A. africanus* evolved into *Homo erectus,* while *A. robustus* was only an aberrant form that finally became extinct (Robinson 1963).

Some authorities deny that there were different hominid species at this time. Milford Wolpoff (1971b) claims that the differences between *A. africanus* and *A. robustus* were no greater than those found in present-day human groups or among gorillas and chimpanzees. In Africa today there are very tall people like the Watussi and very short ones like the Pygmies of the Congo, just as there are both large and pygmy forms of chimpanzee. Variation in size need not prevent gene flow. If the early hominids had adapted through the means of culture, they would all have occupied the same general niche. Some authorities believe that the larger types classified as *A. robustus* were the males of a single species, while the more gracile *A. africanus* types were the females.

Phillip V. Tobias and John R. Napier have proposed the establishment of a new genus, *Homo habilis,* to represent a hominid stage of evolution between *Australopithecus* and *Homo erectus.* Most authorities seem to re-gard *Homo habilis* as a relatively progressive *A. africanus.* Again, Louis S. B. Leakey and some of his colleagues have assigned a separate genus (while some have assigned a separate species label) to the most primitive form found at Olduvai Gorge, which Leakey named *Zinjanthropus boisei* and others call *Australopithecus boisei.* Many physical anthropologists con-sider the latter to be simply a form of *A. robustus.* Others, however, consider the distinction between *A. boisei* and *A. robustus* to be significant, since the North African *A. boisei* is described as being a "super-robust" type, even more rugged than the South African *A. robustus.*

In 1976 Richard Leakey reported the discovery of a complete skull in northern Kenya which closely resembles that of Peking man, a form of *Homo erectus.* But the latter lived 500,000 years ago, whereas Leakey dates his 1976 find at 1.5 million years ago, contemporary with the australopithe-cines. Moreover, Mary Leakey found fossil jaws and teeth of eight adults and three children at Laetolil, Tanzania, in 1975, which have been dated at between 3.35 million and 3.75 million years ago, and which she places in the genus *Homo;* they are not australopithecine.

Indications of contempora-neity of australopithe-cines and more advanced hominids

A complete upper jaw containing all its teeth, found in 1974 by Karl Johanson and Maurice Taieb in the Awash Valley in Ethiopia, together with other skeletal material, dating between 3 million and 4 million years ago, has been tentatively assigned to the genus *Homo.*

In keeping with this picture is a recent tendency to see the australopithe-cines as being less humanlike than has hitherto been assumed. After applying a multivariate statistical approach to australopithecine postcranial bones, Charles E. Oxnard (1975:67) has taken issue with some generally held as-sumptions about australopithecine locomotion. His findings are based prima-rily on studies of shoulder, pelvis, and foot bones. Oxnard believes that *Australopithecus* was not truly bipedal, as are modern humans; nor were the australopithecines knuckle-walkers like present-day African apes. They may have been able to move quadrupedally and also climb trees acrobatically in ways impossible for modern humans. At any rate, according to Oxnard, human bipedal striding is not indicated by the australopithecine pelvis.

A possible implication of these findings, together with the relatively ad-vanced fossils assigned to the genus *Homo* dating back 3 million or 4 million years, is that our ancestors coexisted with australopithecines, who were an offshoot, not in our line of descent. But, as is often the case, the authorities are not in agreement about the reconstruction of australopithecine locomotion. Lovejoy, Heiple, and Burstein (1973:778) state that it was "as fully commensurate with erect striding as that of modern man." And Milford Wolpoff (1973:382) concludes that ". . . australopithecines were striding hominids, fully adapted to the upright posture and striding gait characteristic of modern man." John T. Robinson's position is in between Oxnard's and those just cited. In keeping with his views about the more advanced evolution-ary status of *Homo africanus* (or *Australopithecus africanus*), Robinson be-lieves that the latter had a fully human type of locomotor adaptation, whereas *Paranthropus* (or *A. robustus*) had a partly bipedal, partly quadrupedal-climbing adaptation (Robinson 1972:250–53). Since Robinson classifies *A. africanus* as *Homo,* the early finds of *Homo* made by Richard Leakey, Mary Leakey, Johanson, and Taieb are not so surprising from his perspective. But the general situation remains full of uncertainty and complexity.

Another confusing consideration is the possibility that the main develop-ment in human evolution did not occur in Africa, as the foregoing discussion might lead one to assume, but may have taken place elsewhere. A very large-jawed hominid found in Java known as *Meganthropus palaeojavanicus* (large man of old Java) is held by some authorities to have been an australo-pithecine of robust type. The lowest part of the Djetis bed in Java, in which it was found, is now dated by potassium-argon at 1.9 million years ± 0.4 million years. So, relatively advanced hominids existed as far away from Africa as Indonesia, well over a million years ago. Richard Leakey's Lake

Skull found in 1972 by Richard Leakey near Lake Rudolf in Kenya, dated about 2.8 million years ago. Gaps are filled in with plastic.

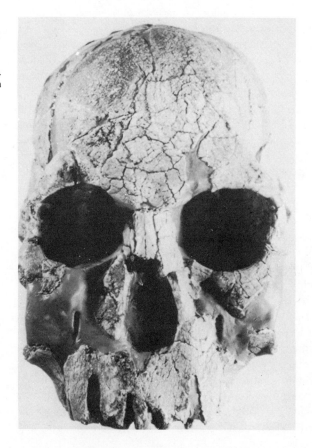

Rudolf find is, of course, much older still, but we do not know what kinds of contemporaries there may have been between Kenya and Java.

The earliest primates in the fossil record were small prosimians dating **Summary** back to about 60 million years ago. They were abundant in North America and Eurasia during the Eocene epoch, but then their numbers declined. The earliest hominoid fossils that have been recovered come from Oligocene deposits in the Fayum, Egypt, dating from about 35 million years ago, including one that has been called the first true ape. There are more widespread apelike forms in the Miocene epoch, dating between around 23.5 million and 5 million years ago. Some of these finds have humanlike features in some respects, suggesting that apes and humans evolved in different directions. The ancestral apes had more humanlike limb proportions, lighter brow ridges, and smaller canine teeth than their descendants.

Between 8 and 14 million years ago there were creatures termed ramapithecines which some authorities consider to have had hominid-like features, including perhaps upright posture and bipedalism. They may have given rise to the australopithecines which flourished between 5 million and 1 million years ago.

The australopithecines have been classified as hominids; they had upright posture combined with a small cranial capacity like that of present-day African apes. There is evidence that these hominids were hunters, used tools, and had home bases. Some authorities divide the australopithecines into different species such as *A. africanus, A. robustus,* and *A. boisei,* although other authorities prefer a single species hypothesis, one version of which holds that the more gracile forms were females and the more rugged ones males. The australopithecines apparently coexisted with more advanced forms resembling *Homo erectus,* represented by skeletal material dating back from 1.5 million years ago to more than 3.3 million years ago. There are many uncertainties in unraveling the picture of human evolution presented by these finds.

For a recent roundup of data about the australopithecines, much of it very techni- **Suggestions** cal, see Glynn Ll. Isaac and Elizabeth R. McCown, eds., *Human Origins: Louis* **for further** *Leakey and the East African Evidence* (Menlo Park, Calif.: W. A. Benjamin, Inc., **reading** 1977).

Excellent drawings of an artist's reconstructions of *Australopithecus africanus* and *A. robustus* and other early hominids may be found in F. Clark Howell and the Editors of Life, *Early Man* (New York: Life Nature Library, 1965).

On the role of culture in human evolution, see M. F. Ashley Montagu, ed., *Culture and the Evolution of Man* (New York: Oxford University Press, 1962). See also Charles F. Hockett and Robert Ascher, "The Human Revolution," *Current Anthropology,* vol. 5, 1964, pp. 135–68.

An article which shows the relevance of carnivore behavior to an understanding of the australopithecines is George B. Schaller and Gordon R. Lowther, "The Relevance of Carnivore Behavior to the Study of Early Hominids," *Southwestern Journal of Anthropology,* vol. 25, 1969, pp. 307–41.

A stimulating but overly sensational work is Robert Ardrey's *African Genesis: A Personal Investigation into the Animal Origins and Nature of Man* (New York: Atheneum Publishers, 1961).

6

FROM *HOMO ERECTUS* TO THE NEANDERTHALS

Homo erectus was a form of hominid, more advanced than *Australopithecus,* dating back to between 1 million and about 300,000 years ago. Fossil discoveries that fall under the heading of *Homo erectus* have been made in Africa, China, and Indonesia. The principal advance at this level of hominid development was an increase in height and cranial capacity. *Homo erectus,* of course, used tools and probably had a language. The remains of fire have been found in association with some skeletal remains in China. From the neck down, *Homo erectus* seems to have been much like ourselves, although with thicker bones. Other characteristics were thick skull, no chin, heavy brow ridges, and relatively small cranial capacity. The proportion of arms to legs was greater than for present-day humans.

Hunting-gathering peoples tend to have larger ranges than nonhuman primates, whose ranges are generally small, with the exception of some, such as baboons, chimpanzees, and gorillas. Mankind's hunting effectiveness must have increased greatly during this period and led to wider dispersal. Aided by the use of fire, some representatives of the *Homo erectus* group were now able to make their way up into cold northerly areas, such as northern China.

The first *Homo erectus* fossil to be found was Eugène Dubois' discovery of what he called *Pithecanthropus erectus,* or erect apeman. His principal discovery was a thick-boned fossil skullcap, the part of the skull above the ears. This find was made near the Solo River in 1891. In the following year, Dubois resumed digging near the same spot and this time uncovered a left human thighbone about 40 or 50 feet from where he had found the skullcap. Nearby, Dubois also found two molar teeth. The thighbone

Java man

was a straight femur of modern human type with a ridge (*linea aspera*) to which were once attached muscles used in upright locomotion. This, then, was a creature with upright posture, about five feet, eight inches in height. The skullcap was very primitive in comparison. It was low, had heavy brow ridges, and a cranial capacity of about 900 cubic centimeters. The brain of Java man, as this fossil form came to be known, was therefore intermediate in size between those of the African apes (having about 500 cubic centimeters) and modern man (with about 1,400 cubic centimeters).

Publication of Dubois' findings set off a lot of controversy. This was the first discovery of so early a hominid. *Australopithecus africanus* was not known until 1925; the discoveries of Peking man were announced in the late 1920s. Since this was the first reported find of a type more primitive than Neanderthal man, it is understandable that there was much skepticism. How, it was asked, could so small a brain go with such a modern femur? Why not assume that the femur was that of a modern human and the skullcap that of a large ape? Perhaps they even came from different time periods.

These were sensible enough objections at the time, but there are now many australopithecine and *Homo erectus* fossils available for study. There

An outline map of the Old World showing where sites of *Homo erectus* have been found.

is no longer any incongruity in finding upright posture associated with a small brain. The australopithecines, who lived long before *Pithecanthropus,* combined these features and had even smaller brains. Besides, eight more skulls of the same type as Dubois' find have since been found in Java; and near Peking in China the remains of a closely related hominid have been found which show essentially the same characteristics. This was a widespread type of early human.

The more recently discovered skulls from Java show the same traits: thick skull walls, heavy brow ridges, and low elevation.

No tools or evidence of fire have been found in association with *Pithecanthropus erectus,* but it is likely that these hominids used tools and had a culture, for tools have been found in association with several other forms of *Homo erectus.*

Lan-t'ien man

The oldest hominid skull discovered in China is that of Lan-t'ien man, found in 1963 in Shensi Province and dated at more than 600,000 years old. The skull has low elevation, thick walls, heavy brow ridges, and a cranial capacity of about 780 cubic centimeters. It looks much like the Javanese skulls. The skull was found in association with stegodont elephant, ancient small bear, saber-toothed cat, Sanmen horse, tapir, giant deer, and bison.

Peking man

In the late 1920s, the contents of some limestone caves were excavated at Choukoutien near Peking. This rich site yielded the remains of about 40 *Homo erectus* individuals. Their bones were splintered and fragmented but some fairly complete skulls could be assembled, and limb bones and other skeletal parts were recovered. The individuals were of both sexes and different ages. The cave seems to have been occupied off and on over a

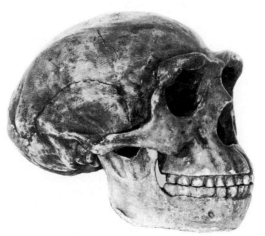

Reconstructed plaster cast of skull of Peking man.

period of thousands of years, so the 40 or so persons were not necessarily members of the same family or band.

The physical type represented in this collection was very similar to that of Java man, though with a higher cranial capacity, ranging from about 925 cubic centimeters (in the immature skull of an eight- or nine-year-old boy) to 1,225 cubic centimeters. The larger skulls are within the modern human range. The Peking skulls are low and thick walled, with a slight ridge along the top and heavy brow ridges over the eyes. The jaws and teeth are large, and the jaw has no chin.

Peking man was definitely a toolmaker and user of tools. Stone choppers were found in the cave at Choukoutien. Although their workmanship was rough, they were deliberately flaked. There were also thousands of quartz flakes that show no sign of retouching but must have been used as tools. These pieces of quartz must have been brought to the cave from elsewhere, for no quartz is found within two miles of the site. Worked bits of bone were also found.

Charred hearths in the cave provide the earliest evidence in Asia of mankind's use of fire—perhaps around 500,000 or more years ago. The discovery of the uses for fire may have made it possible for humans to live so far north. It seems likely that Peking man cooked the animals he hunted, although the animal bones in the cave show no evidence of charring. In any case, fire would have provided protection againt predators at night, as well as warmth and visibility. Without fire, cave habitation would be dangerous.

The use of fire must have had some important psychological consequences for early humans. A fire provides a rallying point, a center, a circle of warmth in the dark night. Fire must have given early humans a greater sense of security and perhaps heightened the feeling of solidarity of those grouped around it. It may also have had aesthetic and religious connotations; for fire, with its warmth and mysterious beauty and its potentialities for both destruction and protection, has always been a source of awe for human beings.

Fire also made possible an extension of working hours. People could now sit up late, staring into the embers as we now stare into a television set, perhaps continuing to chip away at some piece of stonework in the artificial light. Animals tend to have built-in time clocks that regulate their sleeping hours. Humans have moved away from strict biological controls of this sort. Perhaps this break was encouraged by the regular use of fire with its artificial extension of daytime.

Another use of fire was in the making of tools: splitting stones by heating and sudden cooling and hardening the tips of wooden shafts. Three fourths of the animal bones found at Choukoutien were of deer; so the favorite food of these hunters was venison. Other animal bones found in the cave deposits included boar, sheep, mammoth, water buffalo, bison, camel, ostrich, and otter. Seeds of fruits were also found.

Contemporaneously with Java and Peking men there were hominids **Early** living in Europe. Remains of a pebble-tool culture in a cave on the French **hominids in** Riviera, dated at about 1 million years ago, were reported in April 1974 **Europe** by Henry de Lumley. There was no evidence of fire in the cave. However, the earliest evidence of fire from Europe is even older than that from Peking, dating from as far back as 750,000 years ago at the Escale Cave in the Durance Valley, not far from Marseilles in southern France; hearths of charcoal and ash have been found in the cave, along with the remains of primitive wolves and saber-toothed cats. Another site of about the same age is the Vallonet Cave in southeastern France on the Mediterranean, which contains tools dating from between 750,000 and 1 million years ago. Two choppers like those of Olduvai Gorge were found, along with a few other worked stone tools and the fossil bones of such animals as rhinoceros, elephant, horse, and whale.

At Vértesszöllös in western Hungary an occupation site roughly contemporaneous with Peking man has been found that shows many parallels with Choukoutien. First of all, the Oldowan-like chopping tools are similar; second, there is evidence of the use of fire. In this case it is clear that the animals eaten were cooked; many bones show traces of charring, although there were also many unburned bones. Finally, there is some skeletal material, of which the three teeth of an immature child show similarities to immature teeth found at Choukoutien. On the other hand, there is also an occipital bone (rear part of the skull) that seems more advanced than that of Peking man, although the ridge for muscle attachment is a primitive feature of the skull. One estimate of the cranial capacity of the Vértesszöllös skull is about 1,500 cubic centimeters, which is much higher than that of either Java or Peking man or any other representative of *Homo erectus.*

Some interesting archaeological finds relating to the activities of early humans have been made at two sites in north central Spain, Torralba and Ambrona. Here there is evidence that elephants were deliberately trapped in bogs by setting fire to surrounding grass and driving the animals into the marsh where they could be attacked when they floundered and sank. There are indications that elephant bones were hacked off and removed. Many artifacts have been recovered from these Spanish sites, which have been dated at about 300,000 years ago. There are no human skeletal remains. Work here has been done by F. Clark Howell (1965:85–99).

Another site dated at about 300,000 or 400,000 years ago is at Terra Amata, part of Nice on the Riviera in France, where remains have been found of some apparently oval-shaped dwellings about 50 feet long and 12–18 feet wide, containing fireplaces. Holes about one foot in diameter are believed to have held upright beams. The site was near a stream running into the sea. Remains of rhinoceros, *Elephas antiquus,* rabbit, deer, and wild boar have been found.

Although the sites of Escale, Vértesszöllös, Torralba, Ambrona, and Nice are roughly contemporaneous with the eastern Asiatic *Homo erectus,* it cannot be asserted that the humans at these places had the same physical characteristics, although it would not be at all surprising if they had.

Homo erectus in Africa

In 1954 and 1955 the French paleontologist Camille Arambourg excavated three hominid mandibles, together with many teeth and a right parietal bone, at Ternifine in Algeria, North Africa. The appearance of these bones is like those of the eastern pithecanthropines: thick parietals, no chin, broad ascending ramus of the jaw, and big molars with enlarged pulp cavities. Associated with the bones were some roughly made hand axes, a tool type discussed in the following section.

An incomplete cranium in Bed II at Olduvai Gorge also has been classified by some authorities as *Homo erectus*. Hand axes were found in association with the skeletal remains.

The hand axe

A *hand axe* is a pear-shaped core tool of some stone, like flint, that can be fractured. Here we must distinguish between *core* and *flake* tools. Suppose you grasp a rough piece of flint and give it a blow on the top or side with another stone. If you keep banging away at it effectively enough, you will knock off some flakes or slivers of stone. If you can dislodge these flakes so as to shape the original piece of stone into the kind of tool you want, you end up with a *core* tool, so called because it consists of the core of the stone that has been trimmed.

It might happen that one of the flakes struck off from the core has a sharp cutting edge. It might make a good knife or scraper. If you use it as a tool, you have a *flake* tool. Both core and flake tools were used in the Lower Paleolithic. The hand axe, also known as a core-biface (because trimmed on both sides) and as a *coup de poing* (from the French "blow

Some Lower
Paleolithic hand axes.

of the fist"), was the characteristic tool of the Acheulean period of the Lower Paleolithic dating back more than 1 million years ago. In the Upper Paleolithic, the hand axe ceased to be used. The Paleolithic is marked by a gradual increase in the number and kinds of flake tools, which became particularly prominent in the Upper Paleolithic.

Hand axes were fashioned so as to have a continuous cutting edge all around the bottom part. They were not hafted to handles but held in the hand. They may have been all-purpose tools, used for cutting, banging, scraping, and digging. The hand axe had a wide distribution throughout Africa, western Europe, and India. The appearance of hand axes was very stable throughout this vast area, so that one found in Madras looks just like one that comes from South Africa or France.

In Africa, hand axes have been found in association with skeletal remains of *Homo erectus.* It seems likely that the use of this tool spread northward into Europe during the Lower Pleistocene and eastward to India. But the hand axe did not extend into China and other parts of eastern Asia, where the chopper remained the characteristic stone tool of the Lower Paleolithic.[1]

The distribution of the hand axe in Europe is rather puzzling. It is found in Spain, Italy, England, and France, but not east of the Rhine.

During the Acheulean period a new technique, called *Levallois,* was developed for making flake tools. This involved trimming and preparing a core before dislodging flakes. Flakes detached from such specially prepared "striking platforms" were larger and more symmetrical than flakes knocked off in the hit-and-miss fashion of earlier times. With this invention flake tools became more important and there was more control over their production.

The Levallois technique was widely used in Africa, western Europe, the Near East, and India, but, like the hand axe, it did not spread as far east as China in Middle Pleistocene times. The invention, however, may have been independently arrived at in several different areas where humans habitually worked flint.

The culture of *Homo erectus*

At the stage of *Homo erectus,* there must have been some division of labor, with men specializing as hunters and women as collectors and perhaps preparers of food. No doubt the women looked after the children, fetched wood and water, and kept the fire going. Such groups would be apt to split up during the day but have some agreed-upon place to return to in the late afternoon or evening.

Planning of this sort requires a language. Primitive though they may have appeared, with their heavy brow ridges, low skulls, and large chinless jaws, these people had relatively large brains, which were often within the range of modern humans. It seems likely that their brains had become sufficiently developed for language to be possible.

---

[1] Hand axes did, however, appear in Java, perhaps as an independent invention, according to François Bordes (1968:81, 136, 139).

Instruction in toolmaking and the use of fire would certainly be facilitated by the use of language, although perhaps conceivable without it. The tools used by *Homo erectus* had become more elaborate than those of the australopithecines, and *Homo erectus* hunted large mammals, which probably demanded planning and collective action.

One of the earliest expressions of aesthetic interest is what has been described as an engraved "ox" rib found at Pech de l'Azé in France and dated at around 300,000 B.C. It seems to be the earliest example of intentional engraving known so far. This engraved piece of bone falls within the time period of *Homo erectus* and Acheulean stone technology. While it provides no direct evidence of language ability, the engraved bone does suggest emergent faculties of a symbolic sort. No apes make such engravings, nor did the australopithecines. Here we have something altogether new (Marshack 1976).

Between *Homo erectus* and the Neanderthals

In between *Homo erectus* and Neanderthal finds there are a few fossil skulls of early humans, some of which were thought to show quite modern features. For example, at Steinheim in Germany an almost complete skull, thought to be female, was found, dated from the second interglacial period about 250,000 years ago. Some authorities, notably Carleton Coon, see modern features in the appearance of the skull, although it has thick brow ridges, little elevation, and a cranial capacity of around 1,150 cubic centimeters. Coon says that, except for some taurodontism, the teeth are like those of a modern European woman (Coon 1962:495).

The back part of a young adult skull found at Swanscombe, England, along with some Acheulean stone tools, was also dated through associated animal bones at around 250,000 years ago. The bones of the skull are thick and the vault is rather low, but some physical anthropologists consider the skull to tend in the modern direction. It cannot be known whether thick brow ridges were present or what the facial region looked like, since these parts are missing.

A more complete and even more robust skull has been recovered from a cave at Arago in the Pyrenees in the south of France, dated at around 200,000 years ago. It is judged to be that of a man of about 20 years of age. Skeletal material has also been recovered from Vértesszöllös, Hungary, and Montmaurin and Fontéchevade in France. These finds seem to represent a population intermediate between *Homo erectus* and *Homo sapiens.*

The Neanderthals

From around 100,000 to 35,000 years ago there were hominids whom we call Neanderthal living in Europe, North Africa, the Near East, and parts of Asia. Neanderthal man was long considered to be a species distinct from modern man and was labeled *Homo neanderthalensis.* Now, however, he is classified as a subspecies, *Homo sapiens neanderthalensis.* Fossil remains of this type have been found in Spain, France, Belgium, Germany, Italy, Czechoslovakia, Hungary, Yugoslavia, the Crimea, Uzbekistan, Israel, Lebanon, Iraq, Libya, and Morocco.

The period of the Neanderthals covers the Middle Paleolithic, in contrast to the preceding Lower Paleolithic associated with the australopithecines and *Homo erectus* and the succeeding Upper Paleolithic associated with humans of modern physical type, *Homo sapiens sapiens.*

The principal evolutionary change between *Homo erectus* and Neanderthal man was an increase in brain size. Peking man had a cranial capacity of about 1,100 cubic centimeters. Europeans of the second interglacial period also seem to have had relatively small skulls. The Steinheim skull had a capacity of 1,150 cubic centimeters. Two skulls from Saccopastore near Rome had 1,200 to 1,300 cubic centimeters. But the Monte Circeo (Italy) Neanderthal skull had 1,550 cubic centimeters; the man of La Chapelle aux Saints in France had 1,620 cubic centimeters; a man from Shanidar, Iraq, had over 1,700 cubic centimeters; and a skull from Amud, Israel, had 1,740 cubic centimeters.

Neanderthals generally retained various characteristics of *Homo erectus*— thick skull walls and brow ridges, heavy chinless jaws and teeth, and some prognathism, or facial protrusion, but the Neanderthal facial region was larger. The skull often had low elevation. This may seem paradoxical, since a large cranial capacity has just been cited as a characteristic Neanderthal feature. The explanation is that Neanderthal skulls were often very long, compared to those of modern humans, which are rounder and more highly domed, and the Neanderthal skull broadened out behind the ears. The frontal part of the skull was not so fully developed as in modern humans. Neanderthals often had a broad nose, large eye sockets, and a forwardly projecting upper jaw. Frequently there was no *canine fossa* on either side of the nose, as in modern humans; instead there was a slight puffing out of bone in this region. The mouth was very broad, and the neck was thick and heavily muscled. Neanderthal men were barrel chested and had powerfully muscled arms and legs. They were about five feet tall, or a little taller.

Our relation to the Neanderthals

There has been much argument among anthropologists about the relationship between *Homo sapiens sapiens* and the Neanderthals. Fossil remains of the latter seem to disappear from Europe after the retreat of the last glaciation. In place of Neanderthals we now find humans of modern physical type, equipped with a high-domed skull, a chin, and other characteristics of present-day *Homo sapiens.* What became of the Neanderthals, then? There are at least three possible answers: (1) Modern humans evolved from Neanderthals. (2) Neanderthals became extinct in Europe as humans of modern physical type moved in after the retreat of the glaciers. Perhaps the modern types wiped out the Neanderthals or displaced them by being more efficient hunters. (3) Humans of modern physical type interbred with

Neanderthals. At least some modern Europeans would then be descendants of the resultant hybrid stock.

Many writers on the subject of our evolution seem to have been reluctant to think that we could have evolved from such brutish characters as Neanderthals. They have argued that humans of modern physical type already existed at the time of Neanderthals; hence, we need not be descended from the latter. Moreover, the disappearance of Neanderthals and the associated Mousterian culture was rather sudden. There would not have been enough time, it has been argued, for modern humans to have evolved from the European Neanderthals. Modern types of humans must have been living elsewhere, developing the Upper Paleolithic culture they brought into Europe.

The variability of Neanderthals

There are many problems involved in the issues just raised. One problem is what constitutes the Neanderthal type. What do we mean when we speak of "Neanderthal man"? In the general description of physical traits given earlier, the terms *often* and *frequently* were used when referring to particular traits, such as heavy brow ridges. That is because such traits are not invariable; there seems to have been much variation in the Neanderthal population. Most of the traits listed are common in what have been called the "Classic" Neanderthal skeletons found in western Europe: Spain, France, Belgium, Germany, and Italy. The complex of traits is less evident in many of the Near Eastern Neanderthals found in Israel and Lebanon, which have been called "Progressive." The latter often had rounder, more highly domed skulls with less continuous brow ridges, and they often differed in other respects from the Classical type. For example, the skull of a seven-year-old boy found near Beirut, Lebanon, with one radiocarbon date of about 43,750 years

Reconstructed plaster cast of skull of a "Classic" Neanderthal man (La Chapelle aux Saints).

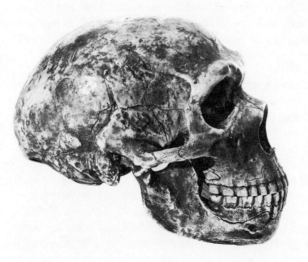

ago, lacked brow ridges, although such ridges have been found in the skulls of other Neanderthal children of about the same age. The boy's forehead was vertical, the profile straight, and his jaw had a chin.

Some authorities consider the Classic Neanderthals to have been a specialized stock adapted to the cold weather conditions of glacial times. Neanderthals occupied southern Europe at at time when most of Europe was covered by ice. They lived in caves and used fire. There were also warmer times during the last interglacial period. During the cold period, there were many mammals with heavy coats of fur, such as the mammoth, woolly rhinoceros, and cave bear. Neanderthals were able to kill these large animals, whose bones have been found in their caves. During the last, or Würm, glaciation, the European Neanderthals became confined to the southern parts of Europe. Escape was blocked by the Mediterranean to the south and by glaciers to the north and east, although there was a narrow corridor through central Europe. One interpretation, then, is that Classic Neanderthals represented a physical type that developed in response to the prolonged cold weather in Europe. The thickset body build, like that of the Eskimo, should have helped to conserve body heat. The puffed-out bone in the region where the modern human *canine fossa* is found may have helped to warm the air breathed in. But it is hard to account for the wide nasal aperture in such Darwinian terms; Eskimos have a narrow one. It has been argued, however, that a large projecting nose may have adaptive advantages in a cold climate (Howells 1973:107–9). If the Classic Neanderthals were specially adapted to particular climatic conditions, they may have been a "dead-end" stock which became extinct when the weather got warmer and more advanced humans with Upper Paleolithic cultural traditions moved into the area. Those who hold this view derive the modern type of *Homo sapiens* from Progressive Neanderthals who originally lived farther east.

One difficulty with this interpretation is that Classic Neanderthals were not limited to western Europe and must often have lived beyond the confines of the glaciers, as shown by a skull found at Casablanca in 1962 and by the skeletal material at Shanidar. Between 1953 and 1960, archaeologist Ralph Solecki found seven Neanderthal skeletons with Classic features in a large cave at Shanidar, Iraq. The deposits have been dated between approximately 60,000 and 45,000 years ago. One male of about 40 years of age was taller than the European Neanderthals, being about 5 feet, 8 inches; he also had an enormous cranial capacity—over 1,700 cubic centimeters. His face resembles that of the man of La Chapelle aux Saints in its length and thick brow ridges. There is no *canine fossa* but some appearance of a chin.

Problems are also presented by the apparent coexistence of Neanderthaloid and more modern types of humans at Mt. Carmel in Israel, where a great range of variation appears in the skeletal material. Remains of about a dozen individuals have been recovered from two caves at Mount Carmel, showing a combination of Neanderthal and modern human traits. Although all have heavy brow ridges, some individuals have fairly high-domed skulls and some have chins. The caves date from around 40,000 to 35,000 years ago. There seem to be three ways of accounting for the variability of the Mt. Carmel population: (1) This was an area where Neanderthal types were evolving into the modern form of *Homo Sapiens.* (2) This was an area where two types of humans, Neanderthal and *Homo sapiens sapiens,* came together and interbred. (3) The population was simply characterized by a great deal of variability.

Geneticists are said to disfavor the first view. The second view has the advantage of a certain dramatic appeal and is supported by some authorities. But the third view seems to present a sufficient explanation. Moreover, the only other Neanderthal population that has remains of more than ten individuals (at Krapina in Yugoslavia) shows the same kind of variability as that found in Israel. It may be that anthropologists have been led to expect too much uniformity in the fossil record and to expect all Neanderthals to look like the man of La Chapelle aux Saints. Evolution in the direction of modern humans did, after all, take place. It should not be surprising, then, to find a variable Neanderthal population in which some persons had chins, high-domed skulls, and other modern features. The division of Neanderthals into Classic and Progressive types may be a premature ordering of the fossil material, for there must have been a good deal of variation in western Europe, even in areas where the Classic type was prominent (Brace 1962a).

It may be concluded, then, that modern humans are descended from Neanderthals and that there is no reason to rule out the western European Neanderthals from the human line. The transition of physical type and culture after the Würm glaciation, the last of the four Pleistocene glaciations, is not necessarily abrupt. At any rate, there is no direct evidence of any clash between Neanderthals and more modern types of humans.[2]

Outside the range of Neanderthals some skulls have been found that have been dubbed "Neanderthaloid" or Neanderthal-like but not necessarily of the same species. One example is Rhodesian man. Remains of two individuals were found in a quarry at what was then Broken Hill, Northern Rhodesia (now Kabwe, Zambia) The skull of the first and more complete find has a very primitive appearance in its low elevation, huge brow ridges, large eye sockets, wide mouth, and long face. The cranial capacity is about 1,300 cubic centimeters. A skullcap similar to that of Rhodesian man was found at Saldanha Bay, about 90 miles north of Capetown; it also resembles a skull from Olduvai Gorge. Apparently this was a widespread type of early human found in southern and eastern Africa. Rhodesian man was formerly assigned a relatively late Upper Pleistocene date, but recent dating techniques

---

[2] Evidence for the lack of abruptness and for a gradual transition from Middle Paleolithic to Upper Paleolithic cultures in Europe is presented in Brose and Wolpoff 1971.

A plaster cast of the skull of a Rhodesian man, a Neanderthaloid type of man dating from the late Middle Pleistocene in Rhodesia, South Africa, with a cranial capacity of about 1,300 cubic centimeters, huge brow ridges, large eye sockets, and long face.

have now given an earlier date of more than 125,000 years ago in the later part of the Middle Pleistocene (Klein 1973:311–12).

Another fossil find that has been called "Neanderthaloid" is the skulls of Solo man. Twelve skulls and two tibia were found together near the Solo River in Java, dated at perhaps around 100,000 years ago. The skulls were resting on their tops, bases facing upward. Since only skulls were found, without other skeletal material besides the tibia, and since all of the bases, except two, were broken or partly removed, it looks as though cannibalism was practiced. These skulls are thick walled and seem more primitive than Neanderthal skulls. Carleton Coon classifies them as *Homo erectus,* but the more common practice has been to characterize them as "Neanderthaloid."

Human facial structure underwent an evolution from the large facial region with prominent teeth and heavy brow ridges of Classic Neanderthal and Neanderthaloid types to a reduction of these features. C. L. Brace has argued that early humans up to the time of Neanderthals must have used their front teeth as tools for cutting meat or for softening leather as Eskimos do. Such teeth always show considerable wear. Brace believes that with the invention and diffusion of more effective cutting tools in the Upper Paleolithic, it was no longer necessary for people to have such large teeth and powerful jaws. Their reduction could therefore take place without selective disadvantage; mutations in that direction could occur without detriment. The development of cooking and the use of fire to soften meat would also make massive jaws and teeth less necessary. This seems to be a convincing explanation for the modifications in Neanderthal facial structure in the course of evolution leading to modern humans (Brace 1962b; Brose and Wolpoff 1971).

**Technology
of the
Neanderthals**

Mousterian tools, associated with Neanderthals, have been found north of the Sahara, from Europe to China, in the Middle Paleolithic period, dating from about 80,000 to 32,000 B.C. During this period the Levallois flaking tradition continued. Although hand axes were still in use, their numbers declined, and the main emphasis was on flake tools. The first known projectile points, evidently used on hand-thrown spears, appeared at a site at Ehringdorf, Germany, near the edge of the northern Eurasiatic plains, which humans were beginning to occupy.

Some use was made in Mousterian times of bone, but only in a rudimentary way, in contrast to the Upper Paleolithic, when bone tools become prominent.

Mousterian tools are characterized by great variety, marking a considerable advance over the period of *Homo erectus.* French archaeologist François Bordes distinguished about 60 different types of stone tools.

Although the stone tools were well made, the culture of Neanderthals was still primitive, when compared with that of the Upper Paleolithic. There is not much evidence of art, ornament, and decorative design. However, there is at least some such material, which shows that the Neanderthals did have potentialities that are more dramatically in evidence during the Upper Paleolithic. From Neanderthal sites have come pendants made from a reindeer phalanx and a fox canine; a bovid shoulder blade covered with fine parallel lines; and a carved mammoth molar, dated by radiocarbon at around 50,000 B.C. The latter piece, which is quite beautiful, shows skilled workmanship. It is reproduced in color in Marshack 1976:143. Also reproduced in color by Marshack is a remarkably elegant statuette of a horse carved in mammoth ivory found at Vogelherd in South Germany in 1931

Map showing the distribution of the Mousterian stone tool tradition.

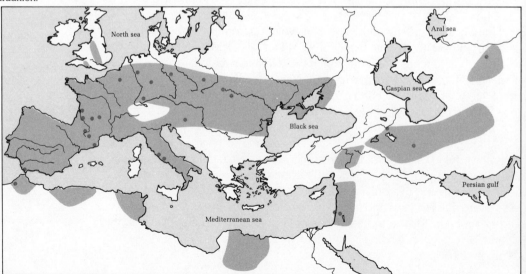

and dated at more than 30,000 B.C., near the end of the Mousterian period. This work of art is 10,000 years or more older than the cave paintings of Lascaux and Altamira.

Neanderthals were the first people known to bury the dead. They did not always do so—sometimes their bones, mixed up with those of animals, appear in disorder in the backs of caves. But sometimes graves were dug in the dirt floors of their caves. The limbs were often flexed, perhaps to save space, although there may have been other reasons for this practice. In these burials we see the beginnings of a practice that became more elaborate in later periods—the placing of grave goods with the dead. At Le Moustier in the Dordogne region of France, a youth was buried with his head resting on a pile of flint fragments, with the charred and split bones of wild cattle around him and a fist axe near his hand. In a burial at La Chapelle aux Saints, also in the Dordogne, were a number of shells, some Mousterian flints, and various animal bones. At Mt. Carmel, some large animal jawbones were included in the burial. At Teshik-Tash in Uzbekistan, a child's corpse was surrounded by six pairs of goats' horns, whose points were pushed into the ground. **Evidence of religious beliefs**

Where grave goods are buried with the dead among present-day peoples, the practice is usually associated with the idea of an after-life and with the notion that the spirit of the dead person will use the object in the other world. Neanderthals may have had such ideas, which are certainly very old, to judge by their universality among primitive peoples. To be sure, there may be other explanations for these burial practices.

A remarkable discovery was made in the excavation of the Shanidar cave. Ralph Solecki collected samples of pollen from a grave for botanical analysis. It turned out that they came from flowers of a bright-colored species that had apparently been heaped on the dead body, the earliest record of honoring the dead in such a fashion.

There are other implications of religious beliefs held by Neanderthals in the collections of bear skulls found in their caves. The mere preservation of skulls need not suggest anything religious, but in some cases special attention was given to their placement. In one cave, five bear skulls were found in niches in the cave wall. The skulls of several cave bears in a group have been found surrounded by built-up stone walls, with some skulls having little stones placed around them, while others were set out on slabs.

All this suggests some kind of bear cult, like that practiced until quite recently by the Chippewa and other North American Indians. After a Chippewa hunter had killed a bear, he would cut off the head, which was then decorated with beads and ribbons (in the period after contact with Europeans). Some tobacco was placed before its nose. The hunter would then make a little speech, apologizing to the bear for having had to kill it. Bear skulls were preserved and hung up on trees so that dogs and wolves could not get at them. Bear ceremonialism had a wide circumpolar distribution—from the Great Lakes to the northwestern coast of North America in the New World and from the Ainu of northern Japan through various Siberian tribes, such as the Ostyaks and the Orochi, to the Finns and Lapps of Scandinavia. So wide a distribution of this trait, associated as it was with other apparently very early circumpolar traits, suggests great age. It is possible, therefore, that some aspects of this bear ceremonialism go back to Middle Paleolithic times.

Summary

Homo erectus flourished in Africa, China, and Indonesia between a million and about 300,000 years ago. These hominids were thick skulled, had heavy brow ridges, and lacked a chin, but they were taller and had larger brains than did the australopithecines. At least some bands of *Homo erectus* had the use of fire, and they employed a variable technology, some groups using crude choppers and others hand axes. It seems likely that they had a language.

The Neanderthals were a later, more advanced form, now classified within our species as *Homo sapiens neanderthalensis.* They lived in Europe, North Africa, the Near East, and parts of Asia between around 100,000 to 35,000 years ago. The principal evolutionary change between *Homo erectus* and the Neanderthals was an increase in brain size, although the skull still had low elevation. Like *Homo erectus,* the Neanderthals had thick skull walls and brow ridges and heavy chinless jaws, although these traits were variable.

The Mousterian tools associated with the Neanderthals are well made and marked by great variety, but there is not much evidence of art, when compared with the later culture of the Upper Paleolithic. The Neanderthals, however, were the first people known to bury the dead and to include grave goods with the corpse, which suggests possible belief in an afterlife. Their preserved collections of bear skulls also give evidence of bear ceremonialism. Thus the Neanderthals showed the first indications of religious beliefs and practices.

Suggestions for further reading

The following are recommended: Grahame Clark and Stuart Piggott, *Prehistoric Societies* (New York: Alfred A. Knopf, 1965), and *Early Man* by F. Clark Howell and the Editors of Life (New York: Time, Inc., 1965). The latter (pp. 85–89) contains pictures of the excavation at Ambrona, with a map of the site divided up into squares, showing location of artifacts and bone material.

For a brief review of the Neanderthals, see Kenneth A. R. Kennedy, *Neanderthal Man* (Minneapolis, Minn.: Burgess Publishing Co., 1975). A well-illustrated survey is George Constable and the Editors of Time-Life Books, *The Neanderthals* (New York: Time-Life Books, 1973). Detailed descriptions of particular Neanderthal finds appear in Carleton S. Coon, *The Origin of Races* (New York: Alfred A. Knopf, 1962). For a description of the Shanidar excavation, see Ralph S. Solecki, *Shanidar: The First Flower People* (New York: Alfred A. Knopf, 1971).

On the stone technology of early man, see Kenneth P. Oakley, *Man the Tool-

Maker (Chicago: University of Chicago Press, Phoenix Books, 1964); S. A. Semenov, *Prehistoric Technology,* trans. from the Russian by M. W. Thompson (New York: Barnes & Noble, 1964); Robert J. Braidwood, *Prehistoric Men,* 8th ed. (Glenview, Ill.: Scott, Foresman and Co. 1975); François Bordes, trans. from the French by J. E. Anderson, *The Old Stone Age* (New York: McGraw-Hill Book Co., 1968); Jacques Bordaz, *Tools of the Old and New Stone Age* (New York: Natural History Press, 1970).

7

BIOLOGICAL VARIATION IN
THE HUMAN SPECIES

Approximately 40,000 years ago, *Homo sapiens sapiens* appeared—humans of modern physical type, represented by such early examples as Cro-Magnon man found in the Dordogne region of France. Other such finds in France were made at the sites of Combe-Capelle, Chancelade, and Grotte des Enfants on the Riviera. But *Homo sapiens sapiens* was not limited to the European scene at this time, for a contemporary skull of modern type was found in Niah cave in Malaysian Borneo. There are skulls of an earlier date (45,000–55,000 years ago) in the caves of Skhul, Israel, which have been labeled *Homo sapiens sapiens.* A still earlier skull from Omo, Ethiopia, has been compared with those from Skhul and seems to be essentially modern in general form. These people were like ourselves but more ruggedly built. The Europeans of the Upper Paleolithic had relatively narrow heads, rather short from front to back, with higher foreheads and smaller, more divided brow ridges, in contrast to the more continuous ridges of earlier forms. Their skulls were more domed or vaulted than those of *Homo erectus* and the Classic Neanderthals. The cranial capacity was that of present-day humans. The facial region was less protrusive than in earlier forms. Their jaws had prominent chins.

Homo sapiens sapiens is now the only type of hominid in existence. We all belong to the same species and subspecies. However, there is a good deal of biological variation within our species. The present chapter deals with this topic, after which we will return to the subject of cultural evolution and the advances in technology and the arts and the geographical expansion of our species that took place during the Upper Paleolithic and Mesolithic.

Human populations in different parts of the world display many differences in skin color, hair form, and other observable features. These are often referred to as race differences. What, then, is a race? What, if anything, do race differences signify?

Watussi and white
man.

A race may be defined as a human population whose members have **Race defined**
in common some hereditary biological characteristics that differentiate them **and**
from other human groups. Putting it in more genetic terms, a race is a **questioned**
breeding population that differs from others in the frequency of certain
genes. Membership in a race is determined only by hereditary biological
traits and has no necessary connection with language, nationality, or religion,
although language, nationality, and religion often act as isolating mechanisms
that may maintain to some extent the distinctiveness of a racial group.
There is no such thing as an Aryan race, a French race, or a Muslim race.

Some anthropologists even argue that there is no such thing as race at
all; races, in their view, are merely products of human imagination and
reason that correspond to no reality in the world of nature. This extreme
opinion has long been advocated by Ashley Montagu (1964); but it has
been adopted by a number of other physical anthropologists, including Frank
Livingstone, Jean Hiernaux, and C. Loring Brace.

One reason these writers reject the race concept is that there is no agreement among physical anthropologists about how many races there are.

Racial classifications

Many anthropology textbooks in recent years list three major racial stocks: Caucasoid, Negroid, and Mongoloid. The Caucasoids are the so-called whites, who seem to have originated in western Europe and who specialized

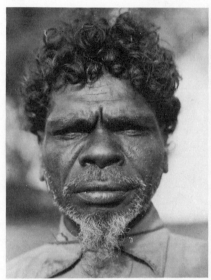

Racial types:
Australian aborigine;
Mongoloid, Siberian;
Mongoloid, Eskimo;
African Negro
(Swaziland).

Samoan man;
Caucasian woman
(India); Papuan
Negro; and White
man (Ireland).

in light pigmentation, so that some of the more northerly Europeans have light skin, blue eyes, and blond hair, although Mediterranean Caucasoids, found on both sides of the Mediterranean and extending eastward through the Near East into India, have dark hair and dark eyes.

The Negroids include the African Negroes; some writers have grouped the dark-skinned peoples of Melanesia with them as Oceanic Negroes. Ne-

groes generally have dark pigmentation; dark hair and eyes; a broad, low-bridged nose; thick, everted lips; and kinky or curly hair.

The Mongoloids include the Japanese, Chinese, and other peoples of eastern Asia, the Eskimos, and all the American Indians down to the tip of South America. They are therefore grouped around the Pacific Ocean. Mongoloids generally have straight black hair and dark eyes, with yellowish skin pigmentation. They often have broad cheekbones, low nose bridges, and eyes characterized by an epicanthic fold, a flap of skin that covers the inner pink margin of the eye near the nose. Facial and body hair are usually sparse.

In addition to the three large categories of Caucasoids, Negroids, and Mongoloids, various other groups can be distinguished that have some distinctive physical characteristics. The Bushmen of South Africa are lighter skinned than the Negroes, although they have tightly curled hair of Negroid type, which in their case is often clustered in little clumps on the skull—"peppercorn" hair. They have short stature. Women sometimes have the condition known as *steatopygia,* a marked enlargement of the buttocks.

The Ainu of northern Japan differ from Japan's Mongoloid majority in having a lot of body and facial hair of a wavy type and large brow ridges.

The Australian aborigines have dark brown skin, abundant body and facial hair, large jaws, and heavy brow ridges. The Vedda of Ceylon and some of the dark-skinned peoples of southern India resemble the Australian aborigines in many respects.

The Polynesians are rather large brown-skinned people who seem hard to classify under any of the three major racial groupings.

In some racial classifications, the groups just mentioned are listed as separate races, apart from the three major ones. Other authorities lump some of them together as subdivisions of the larger ones. For example, Ralph Beals and Harry Hoijer (1965:218) characterize the Ainu, the Vedda, "Dravidian" Indians, and the Australian aborigines as possible Archaic Caucasoids.

The Melanesians and Papuans used to be classified with the Negroes of Africa, since they have dark skin, dark eyes, and, often, kinky hair. But they are a long way from Africa, although there are some intermediate Negroid or Negrito peoples, the Andaman Islanders of the Indian Ocean, who have short stature, like the Pygmies of the Congo. There are also many dark-skinned, but not Negroid, peoples in southern India, and there are Negritos in the Malay Peninsula.

The question arises: Do the African Negroes and the Melanesians have a common ancestry? Was there once a dark-skinned population somewhere in South Asia that split into two wings, with one moving down into Africa and the other toward New Guinea? Or were there simply two distinct groups of human beings that developed in some ways along parallel lines? We will later consider the hypothesis that dark pigmentation confers some benefits in tropical areas. This might also be true of kinky or curly hair and broad nostrils. If these features have survival value in the tropics, it is understandable that they could develop in different tropical areas of the world through the operation of natural selection.

A similar question of classification concerns the African Pygmies and Southeast Asiatic Negritos. The Pygmies of the Congo are short-statured Negroes. There are also short people of Negroid appearance in the Andaman Islands, in the Malay Peninsula, and in parts of New Guinea and the Philippines. Do these scattered groups represent surviving members of an early, short-statured Negro population? Or are they different populations that have developed along similar lines? Coon (1962:4n) has argued that the Melanesians and Africans are not genetically related since they differ completely in the composition of their blood groups. Blood-group studies also would seem to show that there is no genetic relationship between the African Pygmies and the Papuan Negritos. However, J. B. Birdsell claims that blood-group similarities or differences cannot indicate genetic relationships or lack of them; blood groups are influenced by natural selection. Particular blood types may have adaptive value in particular environments. Birdsell believes that the Oceanic Negritos are, after all, genetically related to the African rainforest people (Birdsell 1972:444–45; see also Giles 1973:239).

These, at any rate, are the problems of lumping or splitting—of grouping together or separating—that face racial taxonomists. Hence the disparity in the numbers of races listed in different texts.

Another reason why opponents of the race concept criticize current racial categories is that the latter are based primarily on observable and measurable phenotypic traits that give little indication of underlying genotypes. Even so, there are often greater physical differences within a given race than between any two. For example, the world's tallest and shortest peoples are both classified as Negroid.

Europe has been the scene of recurrent invasions and migrations. This makes it hard to postulate a "pure" Nordic or other racial stock in Europe. In the United States, there has been much interbreeding between blacks and whites. Bentley Glass and C. C. Li (1953; Glass 1955) have calculated from blood-group distributions that North American Negroes have about 31 percent white ancestry. In a later publication, Glass reduced this figure to about 28 percent. In any case, the percentage is substantial. On the basis of a genetic probability table, Robert P. Stuckert (1976) has concluded that over 36 million whites in the United States are descendants of persons of African origin and that the majority of persons with African ancestry are classified as white.

To review some of the points made so far: A race was defined as a human population whose members have in common some hereditary biological characteristics that differentiate them from other groups. Some anthropologists deny the validity and usefulness of the race concept, partly because there is no agreement among physical anthropologists as to how many races there are. Moreover, there is much overlapping, and there has been much interbreeding among human populations.

It is undeniable, however, that a blonde Swede, an African Negro, and a Chinese Mongoloid look quite different from one another. How can we explain the development of such observable differences?

Pigmentation and environment

There has been much speculation to account for the extremes of pigmentation found in human beings. Such extremes are also found in some wild animals, such as black bears and white polar bears. They are more common, however, in domesticated forms of cows, horses, pigs, sheep, dogs, and so on. Since humans domesticated themselves before they domesticated other animals, Franz Boas suggested that such variations in pigmentation, as well as other "racial" differences, may in some way be due to domestication or the experience of living in an artificially protected environment (Boas 1938:99). It may be argued that black and white forms of animals would be too noticeable for safety in many environments and that mutations in these directions would be disfavored, but under the protection of domestication, such mutations could occur without penalty.

A more widely held view among physical anthropologists is that degree of pigmentation is related to climate. Those who advance this view sometimes cite Gloger's rule, which holds that races of birds and mammals living in warm, humid regions have more melanin pigmentation than races of the same species living in cooler, drier regions. This rule was at first meant to account for the color of fur and feathers and had more to do with the effects of humidity than of temperature. But dark-skinned human beings are also found in warm, humid regions, although not all occupants of such regions have dark skins. Dark pigmentation occurs mainly among people who live within 20 degrees of the equator. It may therefore provide some selective advantage in tropical regions. What advantages can it have?

It is somewhat paradoxical to note that black skin absorbs more heat than white skin. It has been shown that "black Yoruba skin reflects only 24 percent of incident light whereas untanned European skin reflects as much as 64 percent" (Loomis 1973:259). Black skin in the tropics must therefore possess some advantages that more than offset the disadvantage of absorbing more heat than white skin.

Negroes and whites differ in the amount of melanin in the skin. The melanin serves to absorb ultraviolet rays. People with very light skin not only suffer more from sunburn than dark-skinned persons but they also have a higher incidence of skin cancer, especially in sunny southerly areas. Humans were originally naked tropical animals. Mutations in the direction of dark pigmentation would evidently have been favorable for human beings living in the tropical zone where solar radiation is most intense and subject to little seasonal change.

There are some difficulties with this theory, although they are not necessarily damaging to the basic principle. One difficulty is that many African Negroes live in jungle areas where they are not much exposed to sunlight. Another difficulty is that the American Indian inhabitants of tropical South America and most of the peoples of Indonesia and Southeast Asia are relatively light skinned. The first objection has been met by a historical reconstruction that has not been exactly demonstrated but that seems plausible: that is, the African Negroes are relative newcomers to the jungle area, having formerly lived in more open savanna country. Coon (1954) has argued that the African Negroes cannot have made their homes in the forest much before the time of Christ. If the ancestors of the modern Negroes lived in grasslands south of the Sahara during Pleistocene times, dark pigmentation would have been advantageous for them. He also points out that there are other bare-skinned animals living in the same environment that are either black or dark gray in color, such as the elephant, rhinoceros, hippopotamus, and buffalo.

There are two ways of accounting for the relatively light pigmentation of American Indians in tropical South America. One is that they are relatively late arrivals in this region. The other is that those who live in the tropical forest area are not exposed to much sunlight, while those who live in the highlands wear much clothing and broad-brimmed hats. The light-skinned inhabitants of Indonesia and Southeast Asia are also believed to be relatively recent immigrants of post-Neolithic times (Brace 1964:118–19).

The solar-radiation theory seems plausible. But we must also try to account for the development of light pigmentation. It has been suggested that light pigmentation is favorable in clouded northerly areas, since it allows more ultraviolet rays to penetrate the skin and build up vitamin D. Dark-skinned persons in northerly areas run the risk of rickets. Negroes suffer more from rickets than do members of other races. Not enough vitamin D is absorbed through the skin from exposure to sunlight. One experimenter, A. F. Hess, took six white and six black rats and placed them on a rickets-inducing diet, low in phosphorus. When he exposed the rats to a critical amount of ultraviolet light, all the white rats remained healthy, while the black rats developed rickets. The farther north one goes, the less the availability of ultraviolet radiation in wintertime. Light pigmentation would thus seem to be adaptive in a northern environment and dark pigmentation less adaptive (Loomis 1973:253–55). This argument seems convincing. C. Loring Brace, however, has another suggestion; he believes that the use of clothing originated in western Europe. Neanderthals and their successors had to wear clothes to stay alive during the periods of intense cold weather in Europe. The abundance of scrapers dating from the beginning of the Würm glaciation suggests that animal skins were prepared for clothing, and we know from the presence of bone needles that Upper Paleolithic Europeans made clothes. Once this pattern began, the presence or absence of melanin in the skin became relatively immaterial (although some parts of the body were still exposed to ultraviolet rays), and mutations in the direction of pigment loss could occur without ill effects. We may assume that this development would be apt to occur whenever human beings wear clothing, but clothes have been worn longest in the area where the lightest-skinned people are found (Brace 1964:115–17). These speculations seem reasonable, although the absence of proof gives them a tentative character.

Body build and environment

Another rule, like that of Gloger's, referred to in zoology is Bergmann's rule, which holds that the smaller-sized races of a species are found in the warmer parts of its range, while the larger races are found in the cooler parts. Julian Huxley has written that most small or moderate-sized species of birds and mammals vary in size with latitude and become larger the nearer they are found to the poles. He writes:

Thus, for each degree of north latitude, the linear dimensions of puffins increase by over 1 percent; with the result that puffins from their furthest north in Spitzbergen have nearly doubled the bulk of puffins from their furthest south on the coast of Brittany. The biological reason for this is that absolutely larger bodies have a relatively smaller surface, and so lose heat less readily (Huxley 1957:43–44).

Another such rule is Allen's rule, which holds that animals in colder regions tend to have shorter protruding body parts and limbs than those in warmer regions, thus exposing less body surface to heat loss.

How well do these rules apply to humans? In some ways not so well, since humans have a culture with which they modify their environment. They may wear clothes, build a shelter, or crouch beside a fire. Climatic forces do not bear upon human beings as directly and inexorably as they do upon puffins. Nevertheless, Coon, Garn, Birdsell, and others have argued a case for the influence of climate on body build among humans.

The Eskimos are short, not tall, and Coon, Garn, and Birdsell point out that they have chunky bodies, thick chests, short legs, and short fingers and toes. Their bodies are thus well constructed to preserve heat. In contrast, the Nilotic Negroes of the Sudan are tall and lanky; they have long, narrow chests and long arms and legs. Such a body build would be unfortunate in the Arctic, but is well suited to a hot, dry environment where it is well adapted to shed heat. Not all Negroes have this type of body build. The so-called Forest Negroes are more rugged and stockily built and have shorter legs, and the Pygmies of the Congo are, of course, very short in stature. The Nilotic Negroes, however, are generally long and slender. Caucasoids who have lived for many generations in the same environment as these Negroes have a similar body build. Moreover, many of the mammals that inhabit hot, dry deserts and savannas, such as giraffes, camels, and cheetahs, are also built along lean lines. The Australian aborigines who live in the hot, dry desert regions of northern and central Australia, as pointed out by Coon, Garn, and Birdsell (1950:37), have slender body builds.

Eskimos have a short, squat body build adaptable to a cold climate.

Here one begins to wonder, however. The Australian aborigines, until recently, never wore clothing. Perhaps their slenderness might be appropriate to the heat of the day, but how would it protect them from the coldness of the night? The aborigines sleep naked on the ground, between fires, under conditions that cause extreme discomfort to Europeans.

It must be said that Bergmann's rule has been criticized, not only in its applicability to humans but also in application to animals in general. To quote one critic, Charles G. Wilber:

The barren ground caribou is given as larger than the more southern forest species. The extensive migrations back and forth of these animals should not be ignored and the greater severity of cold in the subarctic forests is a pertinent factor. The penguins of the extreme south are said to be larger than those nearer the equator. But, large and small penguins are found together in some antarctic areas. In all these examples when one examines the basic data, the differences in size and weight are relatively trivial. . . . (Wilber 1960:108).

These Nilotic African Negroes have a tall, lanky body build adapted to a hot, dry climate.

Besides, asks Wilber, what about the roly-poly hippopotamus, rhinoceros, and elephant in the tropics?

These criticisms seem to place the burden of further proof on the climatic determinists.

Intelligence testing

Although racial differences may be seen as adaptations to different environments, it is a common attitude for people to have a marked preference for their own racial type. This may take the form of racist assumptions about the superiority and inferiority of particular groups. Unfortunately, there is a lot of literature in which authors try to demonstrate the superiority of their own racial stock. In some of the recent literature much has been made of the fact that whites generally do better than blacks in intelligence tests given in the United States. This fact has long been known, but the most generally held interpretation among psychologists and other social scientists is that the poorer performance of blacks on such tests reflects poorer educational facilities for blacks and a more generally depressing, inhibiting social environment. IQ scores do not reflect native intelligence. Many studies have shown that when children are moved from orphanages to satisfactory foster homes their IQ scores often shoot up. And IQ scores may also drop if the individual's environment is restrictive and unrewarding.

Otto Klineberg has shown that an individual's performance on intelligence tests is affected by many factors besides intelligence, such as familiarity with the language in which the test is given, motivation, rapport with the investigator, and level of education. He showed that northern blacks did better than southern blacks in intelligence tests given to army recruits in World War I. For that matter, northern whites also did better than southern whites. Evidently these differences reflect more adequate educational facilities in the North. What is more, some groups of northern blacks did better than southern whites. Indeed, on the Beta tests, the blacks of Ohio did better than the whites of 27 other states (Montagu 1963:111).

In a much-debated article, "How Much Can We Boost I.Q. and Scholastic Achievement?", Arthur R. Jensen (1969) claims that efforts in compensatory education such as the Head Start program have failed to raise the level of scholastic performance among blacks; their inability must therefore be due to a genetic deficiency in intelligence. Some of Jensen's critics have replied that most programs in compensatory education have not been effectively administered; their alleged failure need not imply any genetic inadequacy on the part of blacks.

Jensen and other writers with a racist orientation assert that when blacks and whites of comparable status and educational level are tested, whites still come out ahead. But in what sense is status comparable? Negroes were slaves little more than 100 years ago, and in the intervening years they have faced barriers of poverty and prejudice.

To understand the low IQ scores and the high rates of divorce, delinquency, and crime among American blacks, often cited by racists, we must look at the social environment and past history of the American black. One need hardly invoke race to account for such phenomena.

It is striking that despite the prejudices they have encountered, American blacks have often been outstanding in the fields where they have been accepted, especially in literature, music, the entertainment world, and athletics.

Frank B. Livingstone (1964:47) has written, "There are no races, there are only clines." A *cline* is a geographical transition from higher to lower incidence of a biological trait, a gradient in the frequency of a trait over a geographical range. Julian Huxley's example of the size of puffins, cited earlier, would be an example. One can follow a gradient in size from large to small as one goes from pole to equator. To take a human illustration: As one moves from northern to southern Europe, one notices a decrease

The concept of cline

in the frequency of blue eyes and blond hair among the inhabitants. If one took blood samples from the people in the same area, one would find different frequencies of certain blood groups, but cline maps of their distributions would not resemble those for eye color or hair color. For example, gene *b,* the gene for blood group B, progressively increases in frequency from west to east. (See the map below.)

There is a tendency in present-day physical anthropology to study the distribution of genetically determined single traits. When these are plotted, they often do not coincide very well with traditional racial groupings. Serological studies provide some of the best examples. Knowledge of the different blood groups has great practical importance in relation to blood transfusion. For this reason, abundant records about blood groups are available from populations all over the world. We can therefore trace the distribution of blood factors A, B, O, Rh, and others in different human populations. Let us consider some of these distributions.

The ABO blood groups

The blood types A, B, AB, and O are the earliest known and most fully studied. Blood with the chemical factor A is said to belong to blood group A. If the blood has another chemical factor called B, it is assigned to blood group B. If blood has both factors, it belongs to blood group AB. If blood has neither A nor B, it belongs to blood group O. An individual inherits one blood-group gene from each parent, so there are six possible genotypic combinations: OO, AA, AO, BB, BO, and AB. Since neither A nor B is dominant over the other, their combination results in the blood group AB. But O is recessive to both A and B. Thus both AA and AO result in the phenotypic blood group A, and both BB and BO result in the phenotypic blood group B, making four main blood types.

Distribution
frequency of gene *b.*

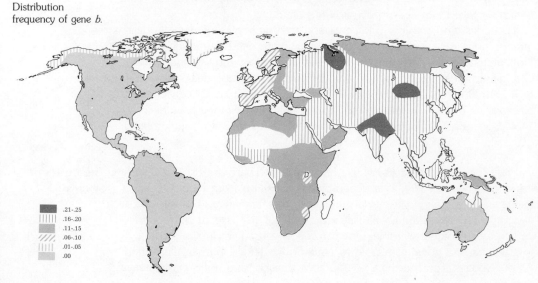

.21-.25
.16-.20
.11-.15
.06-.10
.01-.05
.00

These blood groups have been distinguished because they may not be compatible in blood transfusions. Transfusion of A blood into a person of blood group B, or vice versa, may result in the clumping or disintegration of blood cells. This also happens if an O recipient receives blood of another type. It used to be thought that persons of blood group O were "universal donors" who could give blood to patients of any type, while AB individuals were "universal recipients" who could receive blood of other types without injury. This is not always the case, however; so blood given in transfusions is usually of the same type as that of the person receiving the blood.

Turning now to the anthropological significance of the blood groups, it has been shown that they are not evenly distributed throughout mankind. Although the gene for O is recessive, blood group O has the highest frequency in human populations. Most American Indians belong to blood group O. There is very little B among North and South American Indians, but some northern tribes, the Blackfoot and Flathead Indians of Montana, have surprisingly high percentages of A.

There is a high incidence of A in western Europe and high concentrations of B in northwestern India, Pakistan, and northern China and Manchuria. These distributions do not accord very well with traditional racial classifications. The Caucasoids of northwestern India and Pakistan have blood types like those of the Chinese and unlike those of western Europe, while the Mongoloids of eastern Asia have a different blood type from that of most American Indians.

The significance of these distributions is not yet understood. The factors for A and B have not been brought about by recent mutations, since the apes also have them, or substances very similar to them, and it is likely that the blood groups are older than *Homo sapiens.* Natural selection may

Distribution frequency of gene *a.*

.51-.60
.41-.50
.31-.40
.21-.30
.11-.20
.01-.10
.00

have influenced their distribution. It has been shown that there is some association between blood group O and susceptibility to duodenal and gastric ulcers, and between blood group A and susceptibility to stomach cancer. It is also possible that the different blood groups have been selectively affected by plagues and epidemics.

The Rh factor

The chemical factor known as Rh is present in the blood of about 85 percent of Caucasoids. Those who have it are said to be Rh positive. The 15 percent who lack this chemical substance are said to be Rh negative. The significance of the Rh factor lies in the damage to embryos that may occur during prenatal development in Rh-negative women married to Rh-positive men. Mother and fetus have separate circulatory systems, but it sometimes happens that some of the fetus' blood filters through into the mother's bloodstream. Since the fetus manufactures the Rh substance derived from its father's genetic combination (the Rh-positive condition being dominant over the negative), the mother's blood produces antibodies that may subsequently filter into the fetus' body and damage its blood cells. The danger is greater in the case of third, fourth, or later pregnancies, by which time the mother may have produced more antibodies, which may then attack the fetus at an earlier stage of development, when it is more vulnerable. This resulting ailment is known as *erythroblastosis fetalis.* Fortunately, it is relatively rare and may be controlled by a vaccine if it is given to the mother within a few days after her first delivery.

It is interesting that American Indians have no Rh-negative genes; hence, they do not suffer from *erythroblastosis fetalis.* Rh negative is also absent among Polynesians, Melanesians, and Australian aborigines. Its incidence is apparently low among peoples of the Far East. African Negroes and American Negroes have about half the incidence found among whites. The highest known concentrations of Rh negative are among the Basques of northern Spain and southern France and among some isolated village communities in Switzerland. It may be that Rh negative originally developed as a mutation in Europe and subsequently spread to other areas of the world.

Much work is currently being done in the analysis of blood chemistry. Various other blood factors have been discovered, such as the MNSU system, the Duffy system, the Diego system, and others. Mapping of the frequencies of these systems will throw more light on the genetic relationships of different human populations.

The sickle-cell gene

Sicklemia is a condition in which a person's red blood cells, when deprived of oxygen, assume a crescent or sickle-shaped appearance instead of the usual round form. This may be seen when a drop of the person's blood is left to stand on a glass slide. The condition of sicklemia is determined by genetic factors and may exist in either a homozygous or heterozygous form.

In the former case, the individual produces only the sickle-cell type of hemoglobin in which oxygen is transported to the various cells of the body. Such individuals suffer from anemia and usually die before maturity. Heterozygotes have both a sickle-cell gene and a normal gene. Since such persons have a fair amount of normal hemoglobin, they may not suffer from anemia, although they sometimes do. In a population in which the sickle-cell allele is present, there are also "normal" homozygous persons who do not have the gene.

Since anemic homozygous individuals usually die without reproducing, one would expect the incidence of the sickling gene to diminish through natural selection; but there are parts of Africa where the gene has an incidence of over 20 percent. Although it has not been found among the Bushmen of South Africa, the sickle cell is present in most African Negro populations and in about 10 percent of American Negroes. The sickling gene is also

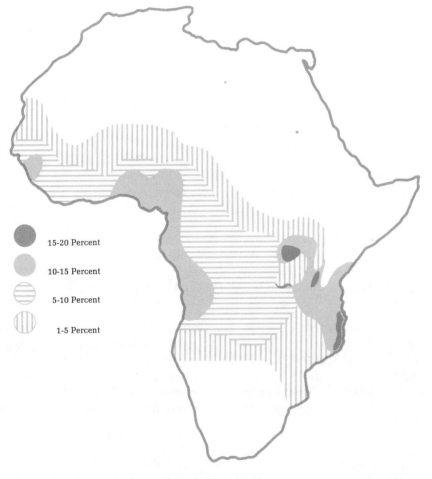

Distribution of sickle-cell gene. Frequency of the sickle-cell gene is plotted in percent on the map of Africa. High frequencies are confined to a broad belt in which malignant tertian malaria is an important cause of death.

15-20 Percent

10-15 Percent

5-10 Percent

1-5 Percent

found in parts of Sicily, Italy, Greece, Turkey, Arabia, and India, but it is not known to be present in the peoples of eastern Asia, Melanesia, Polynesia, Australia, or the American Indians.

The wide distribution and the sometimes high incidence of the sickling gene suggest that it has some selective advantage. The gene is generally found in malarious tropical regions; apparently the sickle-cell trait provides some protection against falciparum malaria. Just how it does so is not understood, but investigations in Africa have shown that heterozygous persons have much more resistance to the disease than do normal homozygous ones. Anemic homozygous persons die out; normal homozygous ones get malaria. It is the heterozygous persons, therefore, who are favored by natural selection in malarial areas.

This accounts for the persisting incidence of the sickle-cell gene, despite the selective pressures against it. One would expect the incidence of the gene to decline among American blacks who do not live in malarial regions. One would also expect it to decline in Old World regions where DDT campaigns have helped to eradicate malaria. Meanwhile, it has some survival value in the tropics, although it also poses the threat of anemia.

Livingstone (1958) has shown how humans have fostered the spread of malaria in Africa through their own cultural advance. Here we have an intricate network of factors involving technology, population increase, mosquitoes, and genes. Livingstone points out that the cline in the frequency of the sickle-cell trait coincides with the spread of yam cultivation. Such cultivation is relatively recent in West Africa, having had to wait for the introduction of iron tools for clearing the forest.

The major local carrier of malaria, *Anopheles gambiae,* cannot breed in water that is brackish, shaded, polluted, or has a swift current. In former times there were relatively few favorable breeding places in the forest for this mosquito, since the trees provided shade and there were few stagnant pools. But, when people began to cut down the forest and establish farming settlements, swamps were formed, the shade cover was removed, and villages, ponds, and garbage dumps provided attractive breeding grounds. Population increase also favored the spread of malaria. It was in this setting, then, that the sickle-cell mutation became favored by natural selection.

Thalassemia

A type of anemia known as *thalassemia* is also common in malarious regions. In this case, the areas involved are the Mediterranean region, Asia Minor, India, Thailand, and Indonesia. Here, again, individuals who are homozygous for the gene that causes the anemia are apt to die young, but those who are heterozygous seem to receive some protection from malaria, although the evidence for such protection is not so clear as it is for the sickling gene.

Lactase deficiency

Mammals suckle their young, whose first food is milk. Some human infants, however, cannot digest milk, since they do not have enough lactase, the enzyme that breaks down lactose. Lactose is the milk sugar which provides about 40 percent of the caloric value in human milk.

In the United States many adults drink milk, which we consider to be a natural, healthful drink for human beings. But in the past dozen years or so it has become evident that this is not a general human trait. In most parts of the world people lack the lactase enzyme after four years of age. If they drink milk, such persons suffer from flatulence, belching, cramps, or diarrhea. Since this lactose intolerance is also characteristic of most adult mammals, it is evidently the normal human condition, while milk drinking among adults is the exception.

Lactose tolerance among adults has been found in about 90 percent of northern Europeans. Lactase deficiency, or lactose intolerance, has been reported for more than 75 percent of Thais, Koreans, and Chinese tested and for more than 75 percent of such West African tribes as the Hausa, Yoruba, and Ibo. Australian aborigines, Greenland Eskimos, and many American Indian groups have also been rated high in lactase deficiency. The problem for investigation, then, is not why some people cannot digest milk but, rather, why so many Europeans and Americans are able to. This ability is evidently related to the domestication of cattle, which took place by around 7000 B.C. in both Europe and the Near East, while goats were domesticated in the Near East around 7500 B.C. It is not known when such animals began to be milked, or when adults began to drink the milk, but it has been hypothesized that in such human populations mutations may have occurred which served to prolong the production of lactase into the adult state. Through natural selection, such individuals and their offspring would have benefited from the increased nutrition thus provided. Lactose tolerance seems to be transmitted genetically and is dominant.

In support of this hypothesis is the distribution of lactase deficiency found in Africa. Two northern pastoral tribes, the Fulani of Nigeria and the Tussi of Uganda, have a rate of 78 or 80 percent lactose tolerance and in this respect resemble northern Europeans. But, as noted earlier, the Hausa, Yoruba, and Ibo of Nigeria have more than 75 percent lactose intolerance. The Yoruba and Ibo never acquired cattle, since they inhabit an area infested with tsetse flies. The Fulani live farther north in an area free of the tsetse fly, where they have raised cattle for hundreds of years. The Fulani drink the fresh milk of their cattle and sell a kind of yogurt in local markets, which can be digested by lactase-deficient persons.

Most of the slaves taken to America were West Africans like the Yoruba and Ibo, who were lactose intolerant. American blacks have about 70 percent lactose intolerance, which is lower than that of West Africans, probably because of gene flow from whites (McCracken 1971; Kretschmer 1972).

Summary

The contrasting concepts of race and cline were discussed in this chapter. A race may be defined as a human population whose members have in common some hereditary biological characteristics that differentiate them from other human groups. A problem with this concept is lack of agreement about how many races there are. There are differences of opinion about splitting or lumping racial groups in the case of the Negroid peoples of Africa and Melanesia or the African Pygmies and southeast Asiatic Negritos. Moreover, there has been a good deal of interbreeding among the world's racial stocks.

Some theories to account for group differences in pigmentation and body build were examined. Since dark pigmentation occurs mainly among people who live with 20 degrees of the equator, it may have some selective advantage in tropical regions, especially in providing protection against solar radiation. Bergmann's rule and Allen's rule may help to account for differences in body build between squat, compact Eskimos and tall, slender Nilotic Negroes. But these hypotheses, although plausible, have received cogent criticisms.

A cline is a gradient in the frequency of a biological trait over a geographical range. Maps may be made to illustrate such gradients, as in the frequency of gene *a* or gene *b* or the sickling gene. Many physical anthropologists believe that the concept of cline is more useful than the race concept for research purposes.

Suggestions for further reading

The case for the climatic determinism of racial features in man is best set forth in Carleton S. Coon, Stanley M. Garn, and Joseph B. Birdsell, *Races: A Study of the Problem of Race Formation in Man* (Springfield, Ill.: Charles C Thomas, Publisher, 1950.) For a criticism of such theories, see Weston La Barre, *The Human Animal* (Chicago: University of Chicago Press, 1954), chap. 8.

For some stimulating hypotheses about the development of diversity in man, see C. Loring Brace, "A Nonracial Approach towards the Understanding of Human Diversity," in *The Concept of Race,* ed. Ashley Montagu (London: Free Press of Glencoe, Collier-Macmillan, Ltd., 1964), pp. 103–52. The latter book presents the views of those who are critical of the race concept.

On the general subject of race and ability, see Franz Boas, *The Mind of Primitive Man,* rev. ed. (New York: Macmillan Co., 1938); Otto Klineberg, *Race Differences* (New York: Harper & Bros., 1935).

On the Jensen article, see Martin Deutsch, "Happenings on the Way Back to the Forum: Social Science, I.Q., and Race Differences," *Harvard Educational Review,* vol. 39, no. 3 (1969), pp. 523–57, and other articles in the same issue. See also C. Loring Brace and Frank B. Livingstone, "On Creeping Jensenism," pp. 426–37; Lee Willerman, Alfred F. Naylor, and Ntinos C. Myrianthopoulos, "Intellectual Development of Children from Interracial Matings," pp. 438–42; Sandra Scarr-Salapatek, "Book Reviews: Unknowns in the I.Q. Equation," pp. 458–67, in *Man in Evolutionary Perspective,* ed. C. Loring Brace and James Metress (New York: John Wiley and Sons, 1973).

For historical background on British and white American attitudes toward the Negro, see Winthrop D. Jordan, *White over Black: American Attitudes toward the Negro, 1550–1812* (Chapel Hill: University of North Carolina Press, 1968); William Stanton, *The Leopard's Spots: Scientific Attitudes toward Race in America, 1815–59* (Chicago: University of Chicago Press, 1960). See also Chapter 4, "Rise of

Racial Determinism," in Marvin Harris, *The Rise of Anthropological Theory: A History of Theories of Culture* (New York: Thomas Y. Crowell Co., 1968), pp. 80–107.

Two articles by Frank B. Livingstone are recommended: "On the Nonexistence of Human Races," in *The Concept of Race,* ed. Ashley Montagu (London: Free Press of Glencoe, Collier-Macmillan, Ltd., 1964), pp. 46–60; and "Anthropological Implications of Sickle Cell Gene Distribution in West Africa," *American Anthropologist,* vol. 60, no. 3 (1958), pp. 533–62.

On the human blood groups, see William C. Boyd, *Genetics and the Races of Man* (Boston: Little, Brown & Co., 1950); "Four Achievements of the Genetical Method in Physical Anthropology," *American Anthropologist,* vol. 65, no. 2 (1963), pp. 243–52.

On lactase deficiency, see Norman Kretschmer, "Lactose and Lactase," *Scientific American,* vol. 227 (1972), pp. 70–78.

8

THE UPPER PALEOLITHIC
AND MESOLITHIC

When the glaciers began to retreat in Europe during the last interglacial period, 50,000 years ago, they left behind a relatively treeless
tundra, across which blew loess, the yellowish brown dust deposited
by the glaciers. In warmer, moister weather, loess was gradually converted
into loam. During the warm summer months, grasses and other vegetation
sprang from this soil, providing admirable grazing grounds for the four-
footed, herbivorous ungulates that flourished in Europe at that time. Wild
horses, reindeer, mammoths, bison, rhinoceroses, and other animals moved
across the open plains, providing splendid opportunities for human hunters.

The human skeletal remains of this period in Europe are much more
common than those of their predecessors, suggesting that a steady population increase was taking place at this time, due partly to the abundance of
game. But we must also credit human ingenuity in devising new hunting
tools, for this was a period that saw many cultural innovations, despite
the fact that the Upper Paleolithic covered only a fraction of the whole
Paleolithic period.

**Upper
Paleolithic
inventions**

One of the new inventions was the spear-thrower, or throwing-board.
Spears had been in use for a long time before this, but the new device
gave them greater impetus. Instead of being thrown directly by hand, the
spear was now propelled from a grooved board, gripped near the front
end. The butt of the shaft was held by a projection at the back of the
board. With a twist of the wrist, a spearsman could send a shaft through
the air with much greater force than with the unaided arm. This invention
is probably earlier than that of the bow and arrow. The throwing-board
was used by early American Indians, the Eskimos, and the Australian aborigines. The widespread use by hunting peoples of different continents sug-

gests great age. The Aztec name for spear-thrower, *atlatl,* is sometimes used for this device in anthropological literature.

In Europe the bow and arrow is known to have been in use in the later Mesolithic period but was possibly also used in the Upper Paleolithic. One bit of early evidence is a collection of about 100 wooden arrows found near Hamburg, which may be dated at about 10,500 years ago. What look like representations of feathered arrows (although they may have been darts) appear in the cave paintings of Lascaux.

Harpoons with detachable heads were used by Upper Paleolithic hunters, as they have been used by Eskimos. It may be noted that these hunting devices—spear-thrower and harpoon—are not only ingenious, far from obvious inventions, but they also required a good deal of training and practice to be effective. Moreover, they are composite tools consisting of different parts, often of different materials. Instead of having fire-hardened tips, spears and harpoons now had separate heads made of antler, bone, ivory, and flint. The harpoon consisted of three parts: head, shaft, and line.

Another hunting device was the *leister,* a trident-shaped spear with a point flanked by two prongs of bone that could hold a speared fish.

The characteristic stone tools of the Upper Paleolithic were blade tools. A blade is a sharp-edged flake with long parallel sides at least twice as long as they are wide. It is made from a carefully prepared core of flint or obsidian from which the flakes are knocked off. Blades were used as knives and scrapers. Burins are also found in Upper Paleolithic assemblages. A *burin* is a chisel-like stone tool that may be made from a blade and is used as a graver. Burins were used for working bone, antler, ivory, and wood.

More use was made of materials other than stone. Bone was used for chisels, gouges, and arrow-straighteners. The presence of bone needles and

Upper Paleolithic tools (*left to right*): blade with sharp cutting edge; blade core from which blades are struck off; borer, or drill; blade; burin, or graver.

ivory pins suggests that skin clothing was worn. Various materials were used for decoration. In Upper Paleolithic burials necklaces have been found made of shells, fish vertebrae, deer teeth, and pieces of bone and ivory.

Decorative art

Decorations and animal figures were often engraved on the shafts of spear-throwers, shaft-straighteners, and other objects. Some of this artwork is quite beautiful.

An implement of bone or horn, looking somewhat like a monkey wrench, is called a *pierced staff.* Such staffs are often decorated, particularly with the figures of horses. Since much artistic elaboration had been devoted to these objects, it was formerly thought that they were scepters, or *bâtons de commandement,* as they were called. More recently it has been decided that they were thong-stroppers or else shaft-straighteners, similar to objects used by Eskimos and Indians for straightening arrows and spears.

Other decorated tools included bone spatulas, half-rounded horn rods, and objects (perhaps pendants) evidently meant to be suspended since they had holes for the insertion of cords.

With the exceptions noted on page 94, the people of the Upper Paleolithic are the first artists whose work has been preserved. One might expect that the first known artwork of early humans would be rather crude, but the art of the Upper Paleolithic is not at all crude; it is vigorous and well executed. This art was produced in various media: clay sculpture, engraving in antler and ivory, and paintings on the walls of caves. The major subject matter of the representational art consisted of the animals hunted by Upper Paleolithic people, such as reindeer and deer, mammoths, wild horses and cows, bison, and rhinoceroses.

Cave paintings

The most impressive Upper Paleolithic artworks are the cave paintings of Spain and southern France, where walls were covered with the forms of animals, some small, some as large as 20 feet in length. These were painted with mineral oxide pigments, the main colors being black, red, and yellow. At Lascaux Cave, dated between 35,000 and 17,000 years ago, large bulls were painted, outlined in black, but there were also filled-in, shaded figures with more subtle colors, such as lavender and mauve.

The animals are not depicted in settings or landscape. Earlier observers were struck by the seeming absence of composition. For example, a later animal figure is sometimes superimposed over an earlier one. But there is some degree of composition, as in some of the groupings at Lascaux.

The animals are drawn with skill, showing good anatomical observation. There is no doubt about which animals were meant to be shown. However, the drawings are not always complete. Legs and belly lines were sometimes left out. Sometimes natural features of the rock were utilized in the painting, so that an outward bulge of rock, for example, was turned into a horse's flank.

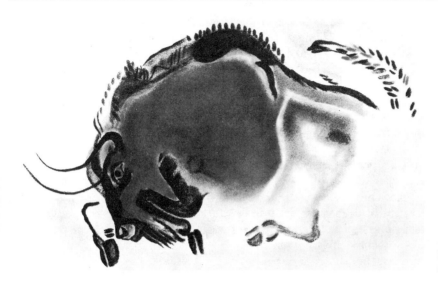

Cave painting of bison, Altamira, Spain.

Human figures are seldom shown in the cave art. When they appear, they are sometimes stick figures, lacking the close observation and accuracy of the animal drawings. When humans are depicted, they often wear animal masks or have animal heads.

Some of the large animal figures, such as the bulls of Lascaux, 13 and 16 feet long, must have involved a lot of work and perhaps the cooperation of several people. Some figures on the ceilings of caves suggest that scaffolding was erected. So these must have been serious projects involving some group planning and cooperation.

Why did Upper Paleolithic people make the numerous animal paintings? We do not know for certain. A commonly accepted explanation has been that the paintings had magico-religious functions and were designed to increase the number of game animals or to win control over them. It was pointed out that the main motive cannot have been aesthetic; it was not a question of art for art's sake. This is suggested by the fact that many of the paintings are found in deep recesses, in pitch darkness, a long way from the entrance. Some cave art at Niaux in the Dordogne is over two thirds of a mile from the mouth of the cave. Sometimes, in order to reach the paintings, one has to crawl through narrow tunnels. The difficulty of access, remoteness, and darkness are testimony to the serious, religious nature of cave art.

The hunting-magic hypothesis seems reasonable, but there are other possible ways of interpreting Upper Paleolithic cave art. A recent line of inquiry has been pursued by Annette Laming-Emperaire and André Leroi-Gourhan. They have made statistical analyses of the different kinds of animals painted and the locations of the paintings on the cave walls. Their findings suggest that certain animals had symbolic significance for the artists.

Not all animals known to the Paleolithic hunters were painted on the cave walls. The number of species depicted is smaller than that known to have existed at the time. In Leroi-Gourhan's analysis of 2,188 animals figures from 66 caves and rock shelters, the following species are the most common: 610 horses, 510 bison, 205 mammoths, 176 ibexes, 137 "oxen," 135 hinds, 112 stags, 84 reindeer, 36 bears, 29 lions, and 16 rhinoceroses.

These animals tend to appear in particular parts of caves; they are not distributed at random. Some species tend to be found in the central portions of caves: 91 percent of bison, 92 percent of "oxen," 86 percent of horses, and 58 percent of mammoths. Remaining species have a percentage of less than 10.

Stags and ibexes are found at the entrances and backs of caves. Twelve percent of the horses are found with the stags and ibexes. Stags, ibexes, and horses seem to have been associated symbolically, for these form the overwhelming majority of animals depicted on spears, harpoons, spear-throwers, and handles of pierced staffs. Partly because of their association with men's weapons, Leroi-Gourhan classifies stags, ibexes, and horses as "male" animals, while the bison, "oxen," and hinds are classified as "female." Human female figures are often found in the center along with the large herbivores, while male figures are found at the backs of caves or on the peripheries of central compositions.

Various signs or symbols commonly appear in the caves, such as dots, strokes, ovals, and triangles, Although a dubious Freudian projection may be involved here, Leroi-Gourhan has divided these into male and female signs. Dots, strokes, and barbed signs are held to be male, while enclosed signs, such as ovals, triangles, and rectangles, are considered female. It is consistent with Leroi-Gourhan's analysis that male signs usually occur at entrances and backs of caves, although sometimes also in the center, while female signs, like bison and "oxen," do not occur at entrances and backs of caves but are concentrated in the center, where they are matched with male signs.

Upper Paleolithic *bâton de commandement.*

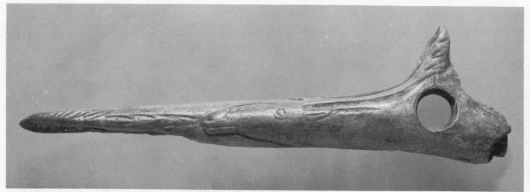

While some of this analysis may be doubtful, the work of Laming-Emperaire and Leroi-Gourhan has brought to light a hitherto unsuspected order and pattern that applies to many caves and rock shelters. There is evidently more sophistication and symbolism in Upper Paleolithic art than was formerly believed.

Following the herds of wild game and aided by their new inventions, *Homo sapiens sapiens* explored new territories during the Upper Paleolithic period. One of the Upper Paleolithic cultures known as the *Gravettian* ranged from southern Russia to Spain, but centered mainly in central and eastern Europe. Gravettian tools included flint points and knife blades. The Gravettians in central and eastern Europe and in southern Russia were mammoth hunters, and they made use of mammoth ivory for weapons, implements such as spoons, necklaces, and pins, and artwork. Shovels or scoops were made of mammoth ribs. Mammoth bones seem also to have been used as fuel.

Expansion during the Upper Paleolithic

The Gravettians were skilled artists. In Czechoslovakia they made figurines of animals in clay, which were fired like pottery: mammoths, cave bears, bison, horses, rhinoceroses, and other animals. Figurines were also carved from bone, ivory, limestone, and steatite. It was the Gravettians who made the Venus figurines, found in Upper Paleolithic sites from Russia to France. These female figures often have a pregnant appearance; at any rate, the secondary sexual characteristics are exaggerated: broad hips, large breasts and abdomen, but spindly arms and stunted legs. No facial features are shown, although the hairdo may be indicated.

The Gravettians also made elaborate decorative carvings in ivory and antler with meanders, chevrons, and other patterns. Cave paintings of mammoths, cave bears, and horses in Russia resemble those of southern France.

In parts of Europe where caves were available, the Gravettians occupied them, but in the Russian plains they seem to have built dwellings. It is hard to reconstruct such shelters, but they may have been skin tents with poles, the corners being held down by stones and mammoth bones. Burials were more elaborate than they had been in the Middle Paleolithic periods. Corpses, with knees flexed, were sprinkled with red ocher and sometimes sheltered by large stones or bones. Radiocarbon dates for the Gravettian culture in Europe range from $26,000 \pm 225$ to $20,830 \pm 140$ years ago.

Some bands in Upper Paleolithic times also pushed their way across Siberia. In the middle of Siberia is the site of Mal'ta, containing bones of more than 200 killed reindeer, seven mammoths, and many tools, such as scrapers, burins, and needles, and figurines. The site has been given a radiocarbon date of $14,750 \pm 120$ B.P., but humans must have passed through Siberia long before this, for, by this time, there were already people in the New World, whose ancestors must have crossed the land bridge that connected eastern Siberia with Alaska.

The Venus of
Willendorf.

The population increase and the dispersal of human beings in Upper
Paleolithic times show that human adaptations at this time were very successful. Humans had not yet reached the Pacific islands of Micronesia and
Polynesia, but otherwise they were spreading rapidly across the world. By
about 30,000 years ago, human beings had arrived in Australia; some entered
Japan around 24,000 years ago, while the continent of North America was
being explored.

By the end of the Pleistocene, blade tools like those of Europe were
being made in Siberia, China, and Japan.

Siberia and Alaska are not far apart. On a clear day one can see the Siberian shore from the heights of Cape Prince of Wales, Alaska. St. Lawrence Island, Big Diomede Island (USSR), and Little Diomede Island (U.S.) form stepping stones in between. During a large part of the Pleistocene, this area was dry land. With water being locked up in glaciers, there came a lowering of sea levels. When the Wisconsin glacier reached its maximum, the sea level is estimated to have dropped more than 300 feet, leaving a corridor about 1,000 miles wide. With some interruptions, this corridor was available for thousands of years, during which many animals and plants moved from Siberia to Alaska, while others passed in the reverse direction. Among the animals to move from Asia to America were moose, caribou, yak, bison, antelope, bighorn sheep, and musk-ox. The human beings who unwittingly entered a new continent must have been hunting these animals. It seems likely that the movements of the new migrants into the interior of the continent were sometimes held up by ice sheets; if so, they still had about 200,000 square miles of hunting land in Alaska in which to roam about. Some ice-free corridors to the south appeared during the latter part of the last period of glaciation. Thus, the newcomers were able to make their way southward, some probably following the eastern flanks of the Rocky Mountains, while others traveled between the Rocky and Cascade Mountains to the Pacific Coast, to California and Mexico. Some groups moved eastward, fanning out across North America. Others continued to head south through Mexico, the Isthmus of Panama, and into South America.

The Bering Straits land bridge

Some early skeletal material comes from California. There is a cranium dated through the analysis of amino acids in bone protein at about 23,600 years old. Skeletal material at Laguna Beach has been given a radiocarbon date of 17,150 ± 1,470 years old. There are also human bones from the La Brea tar pit dated at more than 23,600 years old.

The first migrants from Asia must have brought with them a rather simple Paleolithic material culture, perhaps including scrapers and chopping tools like those used in eastern Asia. They probably knew how to make fire and may have woven mats and made baskets.

These early Americans spoke many different languages, or else their languages eventually became very differentiated through isolation, for it has been estimated that by 1492 there were about 2,000 mutually unintelligible languages spoken in the Americas. There seem to be no clear-cut relationships between any of these languages and the languages spoken in the Old World. This linguistic differentiation suggests a very long time span for the occupation of the New World.

Richard S. MacNeish (1976) has reviewed data from about 50 sites in the New World yielding radiocarbon dates earlier than 12,000 B.P. He suggests dividing Paleoindian prehistory into four stages and has tried to fit particular sites into this framework. MacNeish would date Stage I as far back as 70,000 ± 30,000 B.P. in North America but later, of course, in

MacNeish's stages of Paleoindian prehistory

South America. Artifacts associated with this stage include bifacial chopper tools, cleavers, and hammers. At Pikimachay Cave, Ayacucho, in highland Peru, about 80 artifacts were found in association with extinct giant sloth, horse, deer, and giant cat. MacNeish speculates that hunters probably attacked the sloths (over ten feet tall!) in their den and then stayed to butcher and eat the kill. Choppers, cleavers, hammers, and flake tools were among the artifacts found. This site provides the best evidence for the existence of MacNeish's Stage I. The radiocarbon dates are between 14,700 ± 1,400 and 20,200 ± 1,000 years ago.

Another site assigned to Stage I is at Lewisville, Texas, where a chopper, hammer, flakes, and burned bone were found along with hearths and remains of extinct animals. Charcoal from the hearths has been radiocarbon dated at more than 37,000 years old.

Stage II is dated between 40,000 and around 25,000 B.P. in North America. The dates in Central America range between 25,000 and 15,000 B.P., and in South America from 16,000 to 12,000 B.P. The stone tools in this stage include projectile points, scrapers, and burins. Bone tools are also found.

Stage III dates between approximately 25,000 and 13,000 B.P. in North America, and between 15,000 and 11,000 B.P. in Mesoamerica and South America. At this time humans were specialized hunters of big-game animals, using an advanced stone technology with large well-made bifacial projectile points, blades, and burins. As in the case of Stages I and II, the best evidence for this stage comes from South America. At three sites in Venezuela, Stage III artifacts have been found along with various extinct animals, including mastodon and horse, dated between approximately 15,000 and 12,000 years ago.

The big-game hunters

Stage IV dates between approximately 13,000 and 8,500 years ago and includes the first clearly distinguishable culture in North America: that of the big-game hunters, which was organized around the hunting of herding animals, particularly in the western plains. The characteristic tools were projectile points of the Clovis, Sandia, Folsom, and Plano types, Clovis, Sandia, and Folsom are sites in New Mexico where the characteristic projectile points were discovered. These points usually have been found at kill sites, sometimes imbedded in the bones of extinct animals. Most radiocarbon tests for such sites give a date of around 10,000 or 9000 B.C. The tradition seems to have declined after 8000 B.C. with the advent of warmer, drier weather.

Clovis points were used to tip spears, not arrows. They are associated with mammoths, while the later and smaller Folsom fluted points have been found in association with extinct forms of bison. Other extinct animals hunted by the big-game hunters included mastodon, camel, and horse. Although most of the sites have been found in the Great Plains and Southwest areas, fluted points have also turned up in many parts of eastern North

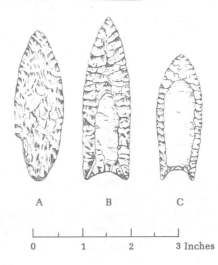

A   B   C

|____|____|____|____|
0   1   2   3 Inches

Projectile points:
A. Sandia point.
B. Clovis fluted point.
C. Folsom fluted point.

America. Fluted points are characteristic New World artifacts; they are not found in Eurasia and must have been developed here.

A site in Colorado, dated at about 10,000 years ago, gives an indication of how some of the early hunters went about their work. There was organized group hunting in this case, with people driving long-horned bison into a stampede into a ravine, where the animals piled up, trampling one another. Some of the bison were speared, and their huge carcasses were then hauled out of the ravine, butchered, and skinned. Archaeologists found the skulls of 190 bison at this site (Wheat 1972). Similar techniques of killing buffalos were used by Plains Indians in historic times.

The long-horned bison found in the Colorado site are an extinct species. Many other animals hunted by the big-game hunters also became extinct in the New World between 6,000 and 12,000 years ago, including the mammoth, mastodon, horse, camel, and ground sloth. Did the wholesale killing techniques of the big-game hunters bring about this extinction? Some authorities think so, although there were species of animals, like the modern bison, that managed to survive down to the present. Perhaps a change in climatic conditions was responsible, or a combination of factors.

The Mesolithic

About 12,000 years ago, with the withdrawal of the ice sheets from Europe, changes in climate and vegetation began to take place, which brought about some modifications in human culture. The weather became warmer. Forests began to appear—first birch, then pine, and later mixed oak forests. As the open plains of Upper Paleolithic times were gradually replaced by woods, the fauna necessarily changed. The herds of grazing animals, such as buffalos, wild horses, and cattle, began to disappear; the mammoths were gone and reindeer made their way up to the north. At the same time, animal figures vanished from the walls of caves. The Azilians, a European

Mesolithic people who occupied some of the same caves, had a more abstract kind of art, painting pebbles with mysterious symbols, the significance of which is still unknown.

Climatic changes also took place in the Near East, which later became a center of plant and animal domestication. During the late Pleistocene much of the area consisted of steppes having a cool, dry climate, but around 11,000 B.C. the region became warmer, and there were savannas having scattered oak and pistachios.

In northern China, after the glaciers receded, forests of longleafed trees spread out over the former plains, and animals like the woolly rhinoceros and mammoth died out, to be replaced by mammals adapted to warmer environments.

In North America similar changes took place. Forests spread out into the plains, and the large grazing herd animals of the Pleistocene began to disappear. In these different areas, then, people had to find new sources of food and new ways of life to come to terms with changed ecological conditions.

The Mesolithic in Europe

One important new development in the Mesolithic period, from around 11,000 to 5000 B.C. in Europe,[1] was the increased attention given to fish and seafood. Mesolithic settlements in northern Europe were found along the coast from England to Russia. (The coasts in those days did not follow the same outlines as the seacoast today, for the North Sea area was mostly dry and the Baltic was a lake.) The northerly coastal culture has been called *Maglemosian,* from a Danish phrase meaning "big bog," for remains of this culture have been found in swampy areas near lakes and streams. The Maglemosians had various devices for catching fish: hook, line, and sinker; spears or harpoons; and seine nets. Humans of the Upper Paleolithic ate fish, too, but this source of food seems to have become much more important in Mesolithic times, as the fishhooks and other implements suggest. Dugout canoes were invented at this time; animal skins were also used for boats, stretched over a framework, like the watercraft of the Eskimos.

Particularly toward the end of the Mesolithic period, the northern Europeans ate shellfish and left discarded shells in large heaps known as kitchen middens. Seals, which then were found in coastal waters, were also killed.

Inland, Mesolithic people hunted forest animals, which had replaced the fauna of Upper Paleolithic times—aurochs, moose, deer and elk, beavers, wild pigs, and other animals. They used bows and arrows, remains of which have been found preserved in bogs. Their bows were notched at both ends for the bowstrings. Spears were used, with heads of bone or antler.

---

[1] In parts of England and Scandinavia, Mesolithic cultures persisted until around 2500 B.C. or later.

A characteristic stone tool of the Mesolithic period was the *microlith,* a small stone tool made from a blade that had been split up into fragments. One kind of microlith was an arrowhead held in place by resin. Microliths were also set in handles of bone or antler as cutting or scraping tools.

One consequence of the growth of forests was an increased use of wood. For the first time, axes of stone, bone, or antler were hafted to handles. Crude but apparently effective axes and adzes were used for chopping down trees, making dugout canoes, paddles, and, perhaps, house construction. Wooden runners found in peat bogs show that sleds were used in wintertime. Wood could also be used in the construction of shelters. The large heaps of shellfish show that some settlements were long lasting.

In contrast to major dependence on a single source of food, such as big game, the Mesolithic peoples developed what Kent Flannery has called a *broad-spectrum* pattern of subsistence, which involves exploiting many aspects of a given region, both plant and animal resources (Flannery 1969). If such a program is successfully carried out, sedentism, more permanent settlement, is made possible, and this facilitates better care for the old, the very young, and the sick than is possible in nomadic hunting-gathering societies.

The Near East

Around 8500 B.C. there were some people with a Mesolithic culture, called Natufian, living in various parts of Israel. They usually lived in the mouths of caves, but there are also some open sites. Their stone technology included blades, burins, microliths, grinding and polishing stones, net stones, net weights, and hammer stones; they used bone for making skewers, needles, awls, harpoons, and fishhooks. Microliths constituted about 80 percent of their chipped flint work. There is evidence of hunting, principally of gazelle, which outnumber remains of deer, implying a dry climate like that of today. There are also remains of hyena, bear, wild boar, and leopard. The dog was present, but there is no other evidence of domestication. There is some evidence of harvesting of grain from the flint blades mounted on bone handles. Surviving examples of these implements have a sheen that seems to have been acquired by reaping, and well-made stone pestles and mortars attest to the preparation of plant food, although the plants that were harvested do not seem to have been domesticated.

It was evidently possible in Mesolithic times for hunting-gathering peoples to live very well on stands of wild grain. In 1966 Jack R. Harlan, an agronomist from the University of Oklahoma, found a field of wild wheat on a mountain slope in eastern Turkey. Harlan stripped the grain from the stalks until his hands got sore. Later he experimented with using a 9,000-year-old flint sickle blade to reap the grain. After removal of the chaff, Harlan found that he had reaped more than two pounds of grain per hour, and he calculated that in three weeks a family of reapers with flint sickles could harvest more grain than they could consume in a year. The Natufians, then, might have lived very well on grain without domesticating it, and might have lived in such a region for a considerable time.

Ten major Natufian sites have been found so far. Some of them give evidence not only of extended occupation but also of population growth. One Natufian cemetery had 87 burials; another, more than 700. Walls and paved platforms were sometimes built, and at one site circular stone houses were constructed with plastered bell-shaped pits.

A similar broad-spectrum subsistence pattern developed in Nubia and Upper Egypt between approximately 15,000 and 9000 B.C. The people along the Nile were then collecting wild grains and seeds and killing birds and fish, as well as larger animals. Around 12,000 B.C. there is evidence of population increase and also of warfare. A solution in such situations, at least for the weaker contestants, is escape through migration. But the Nile Valley is a relatively enclosed zone, and escape to the desert is not a favorable outcome. This situation would give further impetus to intensive exploitation of resources within a limited area on the part of each local group along the Nile. Like the Natufians, the Nubians had much equipment that could be used for grinding seeds and grain. They made use of local grains, which were superseded when more suitable domesticated grains from Asia were introduced in the fifth millennium B.C. But, even after that, the local grains continued to be grown as minor crops (J. D. Clark 1971).

Mesolithic patterns in eastern Asia

Developments comparable to those in the Nile Valley and the Near East also occurred in southern China in the lake region of Yunnan Province, where there were small settlements of people subsisting on shellfish before the introduction or full adoption of wheat cultivation. It has been suggested that people who engaged in this form of subsistence must have practiced some form of animal and plant conservation (Treistman 1972:39–40).

The term *Hoabinhian* has been applied to widespread Mesolithic assemblages in Southeast Asia, which include adzes and ground-stone knives. Reference will be made in the following chapter to early evidence of plant domestication in a Hoabinhian site in northern Thailand dated at about 7000 B.C.

Kwang-chih Chang has pointed to similarities between the Hoabinhian culture of Thailand and contemporaneous traditions in both northern China and Japan. The Japanese culture known as Jomon has been dated at about 9,000 to 500 years ago. It lacked agriculture but did have cord-marked pottery, which is also found in northern China in the valleys of the Weishu and Yellow Rivers. The Jomon culture stretched from Hokkaido, Japan's northernmost island, to Kyushu, its most southerly. In the north, trout, salmon, and shellfish were collected, along with roots, nuts, and berries. Mounds of shellfish characterize Jomon sites, as in the coastal settlements of Mesolithic Europe.

In North America, around 8000 B.C., the Big-Game Hunting tradition gave way to the Archaic, which has many interesting parallels with the European Mesolithic. In both cases, because of the climatic changes, man-made decimation of fauna, or both, broad-spectrum food exploitation replaced an earlier dependence on big-game hunting. Subsistence became based on small-game hunting, fishing, and the collection of wild plants. Polished stone tools such as grooved axes and adzes were used for working wood. There were also tools for grinding wild seeds, including manos and metates, mortars and pestles. Carved and polished bone ornaments were made and stone vessels used. The Archaic cultures show a greater variety of tools and more sophistication than those of the earlier big-game hunters. Around 5000 B.C., people who lived along the rivers of Alabama, Tennessee, and Kentucky were subsisting on freshwater mussels, wild plants, and small game. In some cases there were permanent or semipermanent residences indicated by large shell middens. The earliest southeastern pottery is most often found on such shell heaps. Some local plants such as sunflowers may have been cultivated in Archaic settlements, later to be replaced by maize, when it was introduced.

The Eva site in Tennessee, near a river bank, is characteristic of Archaic

The North American Archaic tradition

Excavation of Coxatlan cave, Tehuacán valley, Mexico. Twenty-eight occupation levels were unearthed, of which the three lowest were of hunting-gathering groups.

settlements in the area, dated by radiocarbon at around 5200 B.C. Freshwater clams were abundant, as testified by clam shell heaps which also contained other garbage, such as the bones of animals hunted: deer, elk, bear, wolf, and other forest animals. The Eva people also ate nuts, fruits, and roots. They had tools of chipped flint, but also fashioned stone tools by pecking and grinding. Mortars and hammerstones were used to grind seeds and nuts. Fishhooks were found and also bone awls and needles. Dogs were domesticated and buried, either along with human skeletons or in separate graves of their own (Lewis and Kneberg 1958).

Contemporary with the Archaic tradition and having some parallel features was the Desert tradition, dating from around 8000 B.C. and persisting in some groups down to historic times. This tradition was adapted to arid regions in the Great Basin, the Southwest, and Mesoamerica. Social units in these areas were small. A pattern of cyclic wandering was common, depending on the ripening of plants or the availability of animals in different valleys and uplands.

On different continents, then, small groups of hunting-gathering peoples made remarkably similar adjustments in the process of staying alive. They were discovering the nutritive properties of similar foods, such as seeds, grains, fish, and shellfish, and often fashioning similar tools, such as milling stones for grinding seeds. In all of these areas these hunting-gathering peoples were laying the groundwork for the domestication of plants, a turning point in the evolution of human culture.

Summary

By around 40,000 years ago there were humans of modern physical type in Europe, Israel, Ethiopia, Borneo, and no doubt many other regions. These people had relatively narrow heads with high foreheads, domed skulls, divided brow ridges, and prominent chins.

In Upper Paleolithic times the grassy plains of Europe provided fine grazing grounds for many species of animals, such as wild horses, reindeer, mammoths, and bison, all of which were hunted by the people of that time. New hunting inventions were devised: spear-thrower, harpoon, and leister. Antler, bone, and ivory were used in Upper Paleolithic technology. The characteristic stone tools included blades, burins, and gravers. There was a new development of decorative art and of cave paintings.

New regions of the earth were explored as population increased. By about 30,000 years ago there were human beings in Australia. People reached Japan around 24,000 years ago. If Richard MacNeish is right, the New World was entered long before that, perhaps as far back as 70,000 years ago. Some human skeletal material in California has been dated at more than 23,000 years old. The most likely route of entry into the New World was across a land bridge in the region of the Bering Straits which once connected Siberia and Alaska.

Climatic changes in both the Old World and the New World ushered in new adaptations to altered environments during the Mesolithic period that succeeded the Upper Paleolithic about 10,000 years ago. With warmer weather and increased forestation, the herding animals of the former grassy plains of Europe began to disappear. Human settlements proliferated along the coasts of northern Europe, and increased attention was given to fish and seafood. In technology an increased use was made of wood. Axes and adzes were hafted to handles. The bow-and-arrow was in use, and dugout canoes were made.

A widespread response to the changed ecological conditions was development of a broad-spectrum pattern of subsistence which involved exploiting the varied plant and animal resources of a region. Often included in this pattern was the harvesting of wild grain, such as was done by the Natufians of Israel around 8500 B.C. Mortars and pestles were used to prepare such plant foods. This dependence on wild grain helped to prepare the way for the ultimate domestication of plants.

Chester S. Chard's *Man in Prehistory* (New York: McGraw-Hill Book Co., 1969) presents a good world survey. For its analysis of Upper Paleolithic cave art, see the beautifully produced book by André Leroi-Gourhan, *Treasures of Prehistoric Art* (New York: Harry N. Abrams, 1967). Another handsome book, with a stimulating thesis about possible lunar notations made by Paleolithic people, is Alexander Marshack, *The Roots of Civilization* (New York: McGraw-Hill Book Co., 1972). Also recommended is Jacquetta Hawkes, *Prehistory: History of Mankind, Cultural and Scientific Development* (New York: Mentor, in cooperation with UNESCO, 1963), Vol. 1, pt. 1.

Suggestions for further reading

The best general treatment of New World archaeology is Gordon R. Willey, *An Introduction to American Archaeology,* 2 vols. (Englewood Cliffs, N.J.: Prentice-Hall, Inc., 1966 and 1971). Two books deal with the early phases of man in the New World: Robert Claiborne and the Editors of Time-Life Books, *The First Americans* (New York: Time-Life Books, 1973), and Richard S. MacNeish, ed., *Early Man in America* (San Francisco: W. H. Freeman & Co., 1973). For the stages of Paleoindian prehistory, see Richard S. MacNeish, "Early Man in the New World," *American Scientist,* vol. 64 (1976) pp. 316–27.

On the Mesolithic, see Lewis R. Binford, "Post-Pleistocene Adaptations," in *New Perspectives in Archaeology,* ed. Sally R. Binford and Lewis R. Binford (Chicago: Aldine Publishing Co., 1968), pp. 313–41. This article is recommended for its analytic approach. For a more popular style of writing, see Book Two, "The Retreat of the Ice," in Geoffrey Bibby, *The Testimony of the Spade* (New York: Alfred A. Knopf, 1956), pp. 113–97.

9

THE NEOLITHIC

The term *Neolithic* has been applied to the period of plant and animal domestication in the Near East between around 8000 and 3500 B.C. Neolithic means new stone, for this period in the Old World was characterized by the use of ground-stone tools, along with weaving, pottery, and other aspects of culture. But the most significant feature of Neolithic life was the domestication of plants and animals, which made possible the development of settled village life on a larger scale than formerly.

Plant domestication in the Near East

Plants may be said to be domesticated when their seeds, roots, or shoots are planted by human beings who keep them from one season to the next for this purpose. Plant domestication may facilitate certain kinds of mutations, for example, in the direction of the retention of seeds. In the wild state such mutations would not be favored by natural selection. Some cultivated plants are characterized by gigantism in certain organs. Human beings sometimes have found such alterations useful and, either consciously or unconsciously, have preserved and encouraged their development. Domestication is promoted, then, when people take organisms to niches for which they are not adapted, protect them from the hazards of natural selection, and select for traits that normally are not advantageous under natural conditions.

The domestication of plants seems to have developed in more than one center: in the Near East, in Southeast Asia or China, in Mesoamerica, and perhaps also in North Africa. Perhaps "center" is not the right word. We must conceive of plant domestication as a very gradual process engaged in to a greater or lesser extent by many hunting-gathering peoples in these different regions. Important domesticated crops in the Old World were wheat and barley. The wild ancestors of these plants grew in upland regions in altitudes of 750–1,000 meters above sea level. Some of these wild prototypes still grow in the uplands of Iraq.

Two types of wheat were grown in the Neolithic period: einkorn and emmer. Wild forms of einkorn ranged from the Balkans to western Iran. Emmer was found in northern Mesopotamia, eastern Turkey, Iraq, Syria, Israel, and Jordan. Barley occurred in the same area, although wild barley has a wider range, from central Asia to the Atlantic. However, early farming was not based on barley alone but on a combination of barley and wheat. Barley was domesticated by 7000 B.C. Emmer also was domesticated by at least 7000 B.C., and the earliest domesticated einkorn wheat has been dated at around 6500 B.C.

It seems likely that such crops were collected by hunting-gathering peoples who gradually depended more and more on this source of food and began to plant their seeds and cultivate them, pulling up weeds and driving away birds and foraging animals.

Kent V. Flannery has pointed out that plants and animals sought by Mesolithic collectors in the Near East were available at different seasons in different regions and altitudes. There were dates in the lowlands; acorns, almonds, and pistachios in the foothills; and grapes, apples, and pears in the northern mountains. Even in preagricultural times, some items were exchanged in trade, such as obsidian, used in flaked tools, and asphalt for setting and hafting flints. Some regional specialization seems evident. This made possible the removal of wild seeds from mountain slopes to lowlands, to niches where they did not naturally grow. Artificial selection was now possible, since people could select for characters that were not beneficial to the plant under normal conditions. In other words, plant domestication was now under way (Flannery 1965).

Flannery (1969:81) writes: "It is possible . . . that cultivation began as an attempt to grow artificially, around the *margins* of the 'optimum' zone, some stands of cereals as dense as those in the *heart* of the 'optimum' zone."

How were these cereals first prepared for food? Carleton S. Coon believes that porridge of some kind preceded the making of bread, which required a communal oven. Porridge is easier to prepare than bread and is eaten throughout the Middle East. A maize porridge was eaten by the Indians of South and Central America. The California Indians, who gathered wild seeds, also made porridge.

Early farming was a form of simple horticulture; its principal tool was the digging stick. More advanced horticultural societies had hoes and made use of terracing and techniques of fertilization. At a still more advanced level, that of agriculture, Old World farmers had animal-drawn plows and dug irrigation channels to fertilize their fields.

Animals are domesticated when they can breed successfully while being dependent on human beings. People had to have rather assured control over their environment and food supply to forego killing off such animals. **Domestication of animals**

The most important animals to be domesticated by Neolithic people—sheep, goats, cattle, and pigs—inhabited the same upland regions of the Near East where wild barley and wheat were found.

The domestication of sheep and other animals may have developed independently in several places in Asia Minor and Europe, for the idea of domesticating seems to have spread faster than the domesticated animals themselves. Both in the Baltic area and in Iraq there are gradual transitions from wild to domesticated forms of pigs. Similarly, cattle apparently developed from wild aurochs, both on the southern shore of the Bosphorus and in Schleswig-Holstein (Herre 1963:242).

On the basis of calibrated radiocarbon dates, cattle and pigs are said to have been domesticated in both Greece and the Near East by around 7000 B.C. Sheep were first domesticated in the Near East or Turkey at about 7500 B.C. The earliest evidence of goat domestication is at Asiab in the Near East around 8000 B.C. There is later evidence of domesticated goats at Jarmo, Ali Kosh, and Sarab in the Near East at around 7000 B.C. and of domesticated onagers at Jarmo around 7000 B.C. Dogs were domesticated earlier in Mesolithic times, both in Europe and in the Near East. The horse was not domesticated until around 4000 B.C. in the steppes of the Ukraine, while asses were domesticated in Lower Egypt in the fourth millennium B.C. (Protsch and Berger 1973).

How can archaeologists tell whether some animal bones were from wild or domesticated forms? Sometimes size is an indication. Domesticated animals tend to be smaller than wild ones. Moreover, the bone structure tends to be less solid. Polarized light may reveal features of bone structure that distinguish domesticated from wild forms. The horns of domesticated goats often differ in appearance and in cross section from those of wild goats. The corkscrew shapes of Near Eastern goat horns are not found in wild forms. There are also distinguishing features in the horns of wild and domesticated sheep.

The most likely purpose of most animal domestication was to keep a ready supply of meat around. At any rate, sheep were not domesticated for their wool, since wild forms have little of it; wool developed in the course of domestication. Similarly, cows were not domesticated for their milk, since wild forms do not produce much milk. One hypothesis is that cows were first corraled and kept on hand for sacrificial purposes, since cows often have been regarded as sacred animals. While there may have been some such nonutilitarian purposes in animal domestication, the practical advantages evidently became recognized, at least in the Near East.

Apart from milk, meat, hides, and wool, domesticated animals transported plant nutrients to the village through their manure and helped to fertilize the fields.

Plant domestication in eastern Asia   In the preceding chapter, reference was made to a Mesolithic stone assemblage known as Hoabinhian, found in all parts of mainlaind Southeast Asia. Hoabinhian tools such as adzes and ground-stone knives were found in

Spirit Cave in northern Thailand, excavated by Chester F. Gorman of the University of Hawaii. The cave has also yielded remains of domesticated plants dated by radiocarbon at about 7000 B.C., contemporary with early plant domestication in the Near East. The plants from Spirit Cave are quite different, however, including leguminous beans, bottle gourds, and cucumbers. Pepper, betel, and water chestnut also were found. Cord-marked pottery appeared soon after the domesticated plants. A similar Mesolithic culture with cord-marked pottery seems to have existed around 8000 B.C. in northern China, Taiwan, and Japan, where pottery existed long before it appeared in the Near East. Kwang-chih Chang believes that the early plant domesticators in eastern Asia were probably fishermen who had a settled way of life. He suggests that the first domesticated plants were used mainly for containers, such as bamboo trunks and bottle gourds. Plants also were used for cordage in making fishing nets and lines. Bamboo, bottle gourds, and tubers such as yam and taro probably played a minor role in subsistence at first, supplementing a diet consisting mainly of fish, shellfish, and wild animals (Chang 1970). Rice was not domesticated until much later. There is evidence that rice was cultivated in Thailand prior to 3500 B.C., before it was grown in either India or China.

Domestication of plants in the New World

Mesoamerica may be said to include the territory from northern Mexico to northwestern Costa Rica. In this area, between approximately 7000 and 2000 B.C., there were many groups with variants of the Desert tradition who hunted small game and collected wild plants. Very gradually plant collection was transformed into cultivation. Two archaeological sites involving cave deposits best document this transition: one in the mountains of Tamaulipas on the northeastern fringe of Mesoamerica and the other in the Tehuacán Valley of southern Puebla in the heart of Mesoamerica. The two regions are about 400 miles apart. Metates and manos for grinding seeds were found at both sites. These became standard equipment used in grinding corn for tortillas.

It is interesting that the same plants do not appear to have been domesticated in the same periods at these two sites. There was wild maize (Indian corn) at Puebla in 5000 B.C.; but there was no maize in Tamaulipas until around 2500 B.C. Pumpkins were cultivated at Tamaulipas between 7000 and 5000 B.C. but do not appear at Puebla until 3000 B.C. Squash was known in Puebla in 6000 B.C. but not until 2000 B.C. at Tamaulipas. It seems likely that different plants began to be cultivated by different groups. Later, with the development of Mesoamerican culture and increased interaction between communities, there was an interchange of cultivated plant species. Finally, a complex of plants became widely diffused, particularly maize, pumpkins, squash, beans, chili peppers, tobacco, and bottle gourds. Cotton appeared at both Puebla and Tamaulipas around 1700 B.C.

The principal plants developed in Neolithic times in the Old World—barley, wheat, millet, and rice—did not appear in the New World, where

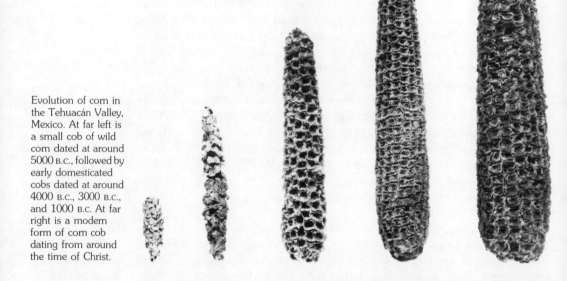

Evolution of corn in the Tehuacán Valley, Mexico. At far left is a small cob of wild corn dated at around 5000 B.C., followed by early domesticated cobs dated at around 4000 B.C., 3000 B.C., and 1000 B.C. At far right is a modern form of corn cob dating from around the time of Christ.

the main crops, instead, were maize, beans, and squash. These plants and the techniques of their cultivation were quite different from the plants and methods of cultivation in the Old World.

This shows that plant domestication was discovered by the American Indians, not taught to them by some superior invaders from abroad.

It is true that three New World plants are found also in the Old World: cotton, the sweet potato, and the gourd. Some proponents of trans-Pacific diffusion have argued that cotton must have been brought across the sea to the Americas in pre-Columbian times. This cannot be ruled out as a possibility, but it has not been proven.

Sweet potatoes were grown in Polynesia and Melanesia, as well as in the New World. Some authorities believe that the plant originated in the New World and spread to the Pacific Islands; others claim that the diffusion worked the other way around.

The early date of the gourd at Tamaulipas would seem to rule out the possibility of trans-Pacific diffusion. Gourds may have drifted across the ocean in pre-Columbian times.

Mesoamerica was not the only center of New World domestication. Domesticated beans from Peru have been dated by radiocarbon as far back as between 8500 and 5500 B.C. In 1970 a cave near Ayacucho in the Andes of Peru yielded corncobs that have been dated between 4300 and 2800 B.C. It has also been shown that maize agriculture was present in Ecuador about 5,000 years ago. Bitter manioc was cultivated in tropical Venezuela and adjacent regions. Its consumption depended upon techniques for squeezing poisonous prussic acid from the roots—another original American Indian invention. In the Andean highlands, potatoes were grown. It is possible that corn was first domesticated in Peru. But Mesoamerica was the center from which the important maize-beans-squash complex diffused to North America. Maize had spread to the North American Southwest by around 2500 B.C. Within 2,000 years, maize was being cultivated from Canada to Florida in the eastern half of North America, as well as in the Southwest, and along the western coast of South America as far south as northwestern Argentina.

An important difference between Old World and New World agriculture is that it was not accompanied in the New World by much domestication of animals. A few animals were domesticated in the Americas: guinea pigs and muscovy ducks in Peru, turkeys and bees in Mexico. Llamas were employed as pack animals in Peru; their wool and that of the vicuña and alpaca were used for textiles. Dogs had probably been brought over by emigrants from Asia.

There were no indigenous wild horses or cows to be domesticated in the New World. The horses of Pleistocene times had become extinct; these animals were not known to American Indians until their introduction by Europeans. American buffalos do not seem to be amenable to domestication. As a result, the Indians had no animals to serve for traction, and they developed no wheeled vehicles or plows. Fortunately, the American crops were of a sort that did not require plow cultivation; digging sticks usually were sufficient.

Village life

The development of horticulture led to various alterations in the way of life in both the Old World and the New, but these changes came about gradually. Long after farming was first begun, hunting and gathering must have continued to be the main sources of subsistence, with horticulture only a sideline. Even after farming became a major source of food, seminomadic conditions persisted when soil resources were depleted, forcing a shift to new quarters. For example, a Neolithic settlement in the Rhineland consisting of 21 households is estimated to have been occupied seven times during a 450-year period. Sites like this were inhabited for about ten years and then abandoned to give the soil time to regenerate itself. Nevertheless, the potential for permanent settlement based on food production was strengthened in the Neolithic period.

Horticulture also facilitated the preservation of food. Grain could now be stored for the future. Hunters have no special problem if their region is rich in game, but if it is not and if they have no techniques for salting, drying, or preserving meat, they are out of luck. Perhaps the Eskimos were fortunate to live in a natural icebox in winter; their food could be cached out of reach of dogs and wolves for later consumption. The Blackfoot and other Indian tribes of the plains pounded dried lean meat, sometimes mixed with berries and bone marrow, to make pemmican, which they stored in buffalo skin containers. Although hunting peoples such as these devised various ways of preserving meat, it is a common practice for hunters to divide their game right after the kill and eat it within a short time. Then, the hunters must be off again for more. The addition of easily stored grain to peoples' diets added to their security.

There also were hazards in increased sedentary life, however. In preagricultural times, no epidemic-forming parasites could have had man as their only host. Human populations were small and scattered. Congregation in villages, however, meant that garbage dumps and human feces provided new sources of infection, as did the domesticated animals that were often carriers of the human types of salmonella, ascaris worms, hookworm, and other parasites that spread through fecal matter (Polgar 1964:204–5).

Although humans thus became exposed to new diseases, the developments of Neolithic times seem to have favored their survival, since there was a population explosion in the Old World during the Neolithic. Skeletal

Mesolithic and Neolithic sites in the Near East.

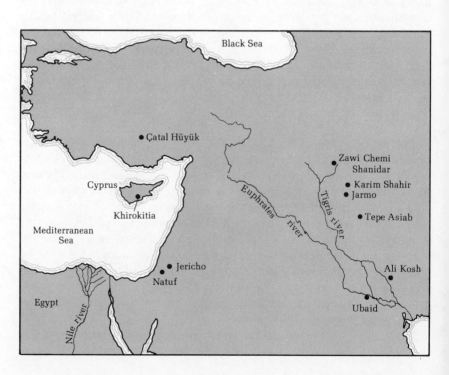

remains from Neolithic burial sites greatly outnumber those of preceding periods, despite the relatively short duration of the Neolithic.

We need not assume from the foregoing contrast of nomadism and village life that hunters are necessarily more anxious about food supplies or less well fed than village farmers. A conference of anthropologists who had worked with present-day hunting-gathering groups was held at the University of Chicago in 1966. Their findings were presented in a published volume (Lee and De Vore 1968). One of their conclusions was that meat generally plays a minor role in the diet of such peoples, constituting from 20 to 40 percent. Vegetable foods, fish, and shellfish make up the bulk of the diet. (Exceptions occur among peoples such as the Eskimos who lack vegetable foods.) Even though they live in poorly favored marginal regions, the hunting-gathering peoples of the present day do not seem to suffer from food shortages. They know where available roots, berries, or nuts are apt to be found and usually do not have much anxiety about where their next meal is coming from. Two or three hours of work may suffice to provide the day's food. (Again, there are exceptions, as among Eskimos or northern Algonquians, especially in wintertime.)

Hunting-gathering peoples often live longer than one might expect. In a Bushman group numbering 466, there were 46 persons over 60 years of age (Lee and DeVore 1968:36). The ways of life of hunting-gathering peoples of the present day who live in the most ill-favored parts of the world cannot be representative of the pre-Neolithic hunting-gathering life. The Old World hunters lived in much more favorable environments, and they must have been better fed than the hunters of today.

Still, when all this is acknowledged, the settled life of Neolithic times must nevertheless have had distinct advantages. This is clearly indicated by the enormous population increase and by the burst of new inventions characteristic of the period.

Neolithic housing in the Old World

When sedentary life was made more feasible, people could begin to give more attention to their dwellings, building more substantial houses than hunting-gathering peoples are usually apt to do. The material used depended on what was locally available and on the climatic conditions. In the Near East, for example, at the Turkish site of Çatal Hüyük, which is described in more detail later, houses were often made of rectangular, sun-dried mud bricks, reeds, and plaster. There was little use of stone at Çatal Hüyük, for it is not found locally in the alluvial plain. The houses were closely huddled together, perhaps for defense. Çatal Hüyük rather resembles a Southwest American Indian pueblo, including the feature that entrance to a house was made by ladder from the roof.

The houses of Khirokitia in Cyprus were large, domed, circular dwellings, like beehives, with stone foundations and mud-brick walls. Entrance was through wooden framed doors sunk slightly below ground level. Some of these houses had a second story resting on square limestone pillars.

Apart from dwellings, Neolithic villages also contained grain storage pits or granaries and ovens. Ovens were not only important for the baking of bread but they also served as prototypes for the pottery kiln and later the smelting furnace.

It is understandable that in the wooded regions of Europe much of the Neolithic housing was made of wood. The Danubian farmers built long houses with gabled roofs. Somewhat similar wooden structures were built by the Swiss Lake Dwellers.

Housing in the New World

Permanent housing also became practical in the New World with the development of horticulture, and we find some understandable parallels to Old World architecture, based on the limitation of possibilities. Only certain kinds of materials are useful in building construction, and there is a limited number of functionally effective ways in which they can be put together. Such features as doors and lintels in stone and adobe houses are understandable from this point of view. Inca houses were generally rectangular, thatched, and gable-roofed. They usually had no windows, but some late Inca buidings had them. The Pueblo Indians of the North American Southwest built closely massed apartment-house-like structures of adobe, stone, and wood, which resembled the houses of Çatal Hüyük, while the Iroquois Indians of the eastern woodlands of North America constructed longhouses, which bore some similarities to those of the Neolithic Danubian peasants of eastern Europe. As in the Old World, the builders in each area were limited by the materials at hand. Rectangular adobe bricks were units of building construction in coastal Peru. The only people to use lime mortar were the Maya of Mesoamerica.

Later, we shall see that still more parallels to Old World architecture appeared in the higher centers of civilization in Mesoamerica and Peru, where city life developed.

Stonework

The term *Neolithic,* or *new stone,* refers to the fact that the stone tools used during this period were different from those found in the Paleolithic. Neolithic tools included ground-stone axes and adzes, hafted to handles. Similar tools were used in Mesolithic Europe. Axes and adzes made possible the carpentry involved in the construction of Danubian longhouses, doors, beds, and other furniture. Such tools could be made of granular stone instead of flint and were fashioned by rubbing and grinding. This is a more laborious, time-consuming process than flaking, but the resulting tool is more durable and effective. Axes and adzes were sometimes drilled to provide for a shaft or handle. In early Neolithic times, this was probably done with a bow drill, drilling from both sides. Querns, rubbing stones, mortars, and pestles are common Neolithic tools used for preparing cereals. Sickles and polished

Neolithic axes.

stone bowls are also commonly found. Ground-stone tools came into use in the New World at comparable cultural levels.

Weaving was a by-product of the domestication of plants and animals, **Weaving** utilizing the fibers of plants such as flax or of animals such as sheep wool. The making of basketry and matting must have preceded weaving; it is sometimes hard to distinguish between them in archaeological remains. Woven textiles, characterized by being made from spun or twisted threads, depend upon some spinning technique. An old and widespread device for this purpose is the spindle, a thin rod usually made of wood, equipped with a weighted whorl of wood or clay. Some twisted fiber is fastened to the spindle, which is then dropped toward the ground, rotating, while the spinner draws out the thread and adds more fiber.

Weaving can be done without a loom in a way similar to making woven baskets, but finger weaving is a slow process. The invention of a loom in the Neolithic period greatly facilitated the making of textiles. Woven garments thenceforth supplemented or replaced animal skins for clothing. There is abundant evidence of woven clothing at Çatal Hüyük, where fur and animal skins (especially leopard skins) were also worn. Neolithic Egyptian graves have yielded textiles. The material most often occurring in early Neolithic

Zapotec women in Mexico weaving with belt looms.

sites is flax. Domestication of cotton evidently came later, first attested to in the Indus Valley civilization of the third millennium B.C.

Weaving also developed in the New World. Domesticated cotton was used for textiles in Peru by 2000 B.C. The preceramic site of Huaca Prieta, dated at around that time, gives evidence of finger weaving; the loom was not yet known. By about 1,000 years later, mantles uncovered at Paracas show that the loom had been invented. Looms and spindle whorls for spinning were also used throughout Mesoamerica. The most widespread form of New World loom was a belt or backstrap loom in which the horizontal or slightly tilted loom was attached to the weaver by a belt around her back while the other end was tied to a post or a tree.

The textiles of the Aztecs and Maya have not remained down to the present, but judging from paintings on pottery and murals and from contemporary descriptions by Spanish conquistadores, they must have been beautiful.

Because of the dryness of the climate, much Peruvian weaving has been preserved and may be seen in museums throughout the world. Peruvian textiles show impressive workmanship of great variety. The Peruvians had one advantage over all other American Indians: the use of wool obtained from llamas, alpacas, and vicuñas. The highlanders in the Andes, where the weather can be very cold, had a practical motivation to prepare warm clothing. As already noted, cotton was also known from early times. Both men and women wove in Peru, but the finest weaving was made by "Chosen Women" who were specialists in this art (see p. 168). Among the Aztecs and Maya, spinning, dyeing, and weaving were all women's work.

The use of the loom spread through the areas of higher civilization in the New World—to Bolivia and Ecuador and even to some of the tropical forest peoples, such as the Jivaro. Weaving also diffused to the Pueblo area in the North American Southwest. Apparently as an independent invention, weaving developed among the tribes of the northwestern coast of North America, who devised a suspended-warp upright loom. Textiles were made from spruce roots, wild hemp, and cedar bark. So-called Chilkat blankets were made of mountain-goat wool, spun and twined over a core of cedar-bark string.

Pottery is not always found in Neolithic sites. It is absent, for example, **Pottery** from the lower strata of excavations at Jarmo and Jericho. It occurs in some nonagricultural sites. Some of the oldest-dated pottery, estimated at about 12,600 years old, comes from Kyushu in southern Japan, before agriculture was introduced.

Some nomadic hunting-gathering peoples, such as the Bushmen and the Eskimos, have pottery. Generally, however, pottery is inappropriate for such people, being rather heavy, bulky, and breakable, and skin or basketry containers are more suitable. With settled village life, however, pottery can be very useful. Large jars can then be used to store grain; dishes, mugs, cooking pots, and other vessels can be made. Thus, pottery is usually found in abundance in later Neolithic sites.

The properties of clay were known before the Neolithic period. Clay figurines, sometimes fired, were made by Upper Paleolithic hunters. Clay generally requires some treatment before it can be worked. If it is too dry, water must be added. If it is too sticky, it may be tempered by adding grit, sand, shell, or other material. Such tempering also helps to prevent cracking when the vessel is fired. Clay is usually mixed and kneaded before working to ensure uniform texture or composition.

Neolithic pottery was not made on the potter's wheel but was built up of coils or strips of clay, one above the other. Making a large pot in this manner may take two or three days. The clay must always be kept at an appropriate degree of dampness, not too wet and not too dry.

Firing involves exposing the vessel to heat long enough (above 500°C) to drive out its water content. This was first done in open fires, but later kilns or ovens were built for the purpose.

Since pottery is porous, water kept in a jar may seep through. Glazing was invented in the Near East to give the ware a smooth, waterproof finish.

The earliest Neolithic pottery was not decorated, but in the late Neolithic period, vessels were painted in southern Turkey. Red-on-cream ware is dated at around 5500 B.C. Finely made, dark burnished ware comes from Çatal

(*Above*) Caddoan style jars from Arkansas.

(*Right*) Plate from Cocle, Panama.

(*Below, left*) Nazca B pottery, Peru; (*right*) coast Tiahuanaco pottery, Peru.

Hüyük. Pots of various sizes and shapes, including anthropomorphic types, and painted with various designs, including imitations of basketry, have been found at Hacilar in southern Turkey, dated at around 5200 B.C. The practice of painting pottery extended from Iran to the Balkans in the sixth millennium B.C.

What may be the oldest known pottery in the New World comes from Valdivia, Ecuador. Gordon Willey gives it a radiocarbon date of 3000 to 2500 B.C. Pottery from Puerto Hormigas on the Caribbean coast of Colombia is dated at around 2900 B.C. The earliest pottery in Mesoamerica is from 2300–1500 B.C., while, in Peru, pottery appears at some sites at around 1200 B.C.

It used to be thought that there was little trade in Neolithic times, since **Trade** each community was apt to be self-sufficient—able to meet its own needs for food, clothing, and other necessities. Whatever trade was engaged in was apt to concern only luxuries, nonessentials (Childe 1953:74). However, there is now evidence that trade began early in Neolithic times and covered considerable distances. Obsidian was traded in the eighth century B.C., and in Neolithic times there was trade in other substances, such as salt and sulfur. Most of the raw materials used at Çatal Hüyük, apart from clay, reeds, and wood, seem not to have been available locally. Timber had to be brought down from the hills, obsidian from volcanoes, marble from western Anatolia, stalactites from caves in the Taurus Mountains, and shells from the Mediterranean. This was evidently a society depending heavily on trade from many different sources. Çatal Hüyük also seems to have been characterized by considerable specialization and division of labor. In these respects Çatal Hüyük anticipated the stage of civilization.

In the preceding pages we have reviewed some general features in both the Old World and the New of cultural patterns commonly found in societies at the Neolithic level: plant and animal domestication, housing, ground-stone tools, weaving, pottery, and trade. To get a more integrated conception of some particular Neolithic communities, let us consider in more detail two Old World Neolithic settlements: Çatal Hüyük in Turkey, and Pan-p'o-ts'un in northern China.

Çatal Hüyük, Turkey

A remarkably sophisticated Neolithic settlement, dating from around 6500 to 5700 B.C., has been found at Çatal Hüyük on the plateau of Anatolia in Turkey. The settlement covered 32 acres. The people here raised crops (barley, wheat, peas) and had sheep and cattle. Pottery was made. The plastered, mud-brick houses were laid out in a rather orderly manner, rectangular in shape and grouped around courtyards. Some of the houses, which

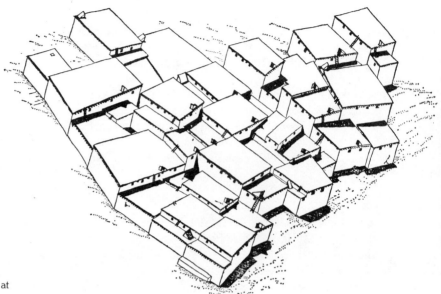

Schematic
reconstruction of a
section of Level VI at
Çatal Hüyük.

may have been shrines or temples, contain the earliest murals found on
man-made walls.

A large bull, six feet long, rather reminiscent of the big bulls at Lascaux
Cave, covers one of the walls. It is surrounded by very small human figures.
(Many pairs of bulls' horns, some set in plaster, have also been found at
Çatal Hüyük, suggesting the existence of a cult of the bull, like that which
developed later at Crete.) Deer are also depicted in the murals, together
with human hunters holding bows. The most impressive of the murals shows
about a dozen men grouped in three rows performing a dance. Some hold
bows, one beats a drum, and some are jumping. This is a lively scene,
well executed. These paintings were applied with a brush on white plaster,
the colors including red, pink, mauve, black, and yellow. There are also
wall paintings of giant vultures attacking human bodies. This may imply a
practice of exposure of corpses to vultures, as is done by the present-day
Parsis of India. The defleshed bones were assembled for secondary burial
beneath the floors of the houses.

Handicrafts were varied, including, among other things, beautifully made
wooden bowls and boxes, basketry, pins, knives, and obsidian mirrors.

There is a good deal of sculpture, including many seated goddesses,
sometimes depicted giving birth. They tend to be rather fat, like Upper
Paleolithic Venuses. Similar statuettes came from other Neolithic sites in
the Near East, including Hacilar and Jarmo (Mellaart 1967).

Pan-p'o-ts'un, China

Wheat and barley were domesticated in northern China in Neolithic times. The use of wheat and barley must have diffused eastward from southwestern Asia, moving along the southern edge of the steppes. But the grain that became most popular in northern China was millet, which may have been domesticated locally. Cattle also were introduced, although the Chinese never took to drinking milk.

Neolithic settlements developed in a region in northern China where three great rivers come together—the Huangho, Fenho, and Weishu—and where three modern Chinese provinces adjoin—Honan, Shansi, and Shensi. In these three provinces two early Neolithic cultures flourished: Yangshao and, somewhat later, Lungshan. More than 1,000 Yangshao sites have been found, dating between approximately 6000 and 4000 B.C. There are over 400 of these sites in the Wei valley.

The following are some of the characteristic traits of the Chinese Neolithic: cultivation of millet and rice; domestication of pigs, cattle, sheep, dogs, and chickens; construction of stamped-earth and wattle-and-daub structures; domestication of silkworms and possible loom weaving of silk and hemp; cord-marked pottery and ceremonial ware; use of jade; and scapulimancy (divination by means of cracks in shoulder blades) (Chang 1968:86–87).

An extensively excavated Yangshao settlement is Pan-p'o-ts'un in Shensi Province, dated by radiocarbon from around 5000 to 4000 B.C. During the early period about 600 people lived there, in about 200 houses. There were over 200 deep storage pits in the village. Millet was the staple crop. Only dogs and pigs seem to have been domesticated; deer hunting evidently provided the bulk of the meat consumed. Most of the dwellings were round or oblong semisubterranean houses with thatched roofs. Clay was used to

Yangshao Neolithic pottery.

make cupboards, benches, and ovens. In the center of the village was a plaza with a large communal structure, around which the smaller houses were ranged in a circle, with the doors facing the center. North of the dwelling area was a village cemetery. Six pottery kilns have been found on the outskirts. Most of the ware was coarse household pottery, but finer painted vessels used for funerary purposes were buried with the dead. The potter's wheel does not seem to have been used.

The planned layout of Pan-p'o-ts'un, the communal building and the common cemetery, suggest a consciousness of community, perhaps along clan or lineage lines. The Chinese ancestor cult may have had its origin in this early period, although there is more definite evidence of such a cult in the later Lungshan stage. This tightly knit community seems to have been largely self-sufficient, but there is evidence of trade in the remains of seashells and stone materials, such as jade, from distant regions.

Although it shared some of the same domesticated plants, animals, and other features as the Southwest Asiatic Neolithic, the Chinese Neolithic seems to have had its own characteristic style from early times.

Diffusion of Neolithic patterns

There were Neolithic communities in eastern Europe by the sixth millennium B.C.; in central Europe, by the fifth; and in England, by the fourth.

Meanwhile, Neolithic cultures also spread across North Africa. In climate and in culture, the African Mediterranean coast resembled that of Europe. Racially, too, there was much similarity. The Berbers, ancient peoples of North Africa, are Caucasoids. Some of their more isolated groups in the Atlas Mountains have retained an essentially Neolithic way of life down to recent times.

Much of North Africa today, particularly the deserts of Libya and the great Sahara Desert, is bleak and inhospitable. But, before 2000 B.C., the land was well watered. This is indicated by the presence of bones of many animals that could not live there now: giraffe, hippopotamus, elephant, antelope, and others. (Ancient isolated trees still survive in soil where seeds no longer grow, and stunted crocodiles inhabit desert pools they could not have reached by waddling overland.)

Neolithic pastoralists once lived in the Tassili Plateau in the central Sahara in Algeria, where they painted beautiful frescoes on rock walls. The first settlers brought sheep and goats; a later wave had herds of cattle, which are depicted with realism and elegance on the rock. Also shown are scenes of men hunting rhinoceros and hippopotamus, girls of Ethiopian type with sugarloaf hair style and white robes, and a woman with a row of pots, cooking food.

Pastoralism

Pastoralism is a way of life that developed in semiarid grasslands, deserts, and steppes in which dependence on animal husbandry became the main basis of the economy and plant cultivation of lesser or little importance.

Different kinds of animals have been herded by pastoralists in different parts of the Old World: reindeer by the Lapps of northern Europe, cattle in Africa, camels in Arabia and the Sahara Dessert, and herds of mixed composition in many areas.

Pastoralists often engage in some agriculture as a sideline. This is true, for example, of the Marri Baluch of Baluchistan, among whom there are groups that may temporarily abandon farming if their herds grow large enough. Robert Pehrson (1966:14) writes:

Once the herd reaches about 100 animals, its value is so great that other considerations become secondary compared with the welfare of the herd, and unless very favorably situated the camp then breaks loose from its village nucleus, migrating widely in search of pasture and water.

The migrations of pastoral tribes, however, are not usually erratic and random. Nomads often follow traditional routes in cycles that may require several years to complete. Or else an annual cycle, known as *transhumance,* may be observed, which involves having different winter and summer camps. Thus, pastoralists in the western part of the Indian subcontinent drive their herds up to the mountains in summer, down to the plains in winter. Cattle herders in the Upper Nile Valley have different grazing grounds in dry and wet seasons.

Cattle-herding pastoralists often engage in fighting and raiding. This has been noted for various African cattle-raising groups and for such peoples as the ancient Aryans.

Occupation of the Pacific islands

One of the most remarkable and dramatic phases of mankind's advance across the globe was the peopling of the Pacific islands. This was a relatively late migration by people with a Southeast Asiatic Neolithic culture. It had to depend upon the development of adequate means of navigation, the outrigger canoe, and other seaworthy craft. (Some Polynesian canoes were over 100 feet long and six or more feet wide). The migration had to proceed in easy stages, since the ocean is vast and islands are often hundreds or thousands of miles apart. Some, like New Zealand or Easter Island, were from 1,000 to 1,800 miles away from the nearest other inhabited island.

One authority, Andrew Sharp, believes that the long voyages of the Polynesians must have been largely accidental, made in canoes blown off course. Without instruments of navigation, the Polynesians had to steer by the sun by day and by the stars at night; but the heavenly bodies were often hidden by clouds. Sea currents were changeable. The early voyagers cannot have set out on deliberate expeditions to distant, unknown islands; they must have been blown there by unexpected storms and then been unable to find their way home again. Sharp gives an example of a late 17th-century canoe that was lost at sea for 70 days and traveled for 1,000 miles. The people in the canoe had no idea where they were (Sharp 1957:15).

This seems to be a minority view among anthropologists. Those who disagree with Sharp concede that accidental, storm-driven voyages must have often occurred, but they believe that deliberate expeditions also took place. This is suggested by the fact that dogs, pigs, and the various domesticated plants used for food by the Polynesians were transported to distant

Map showing routes in the peopling of the Pacific.

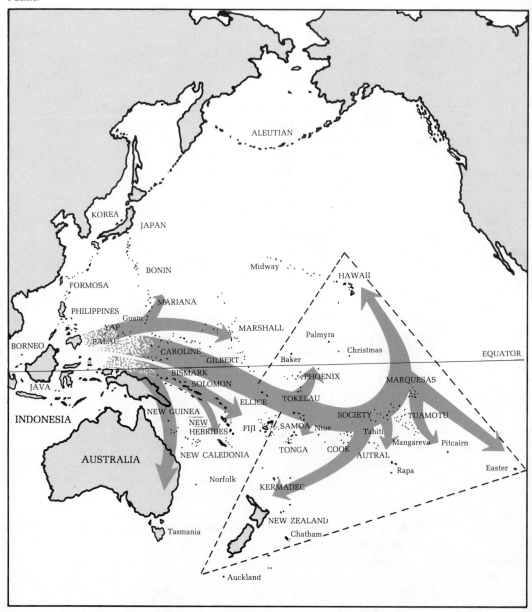

islands. The men and women who made these trips had all the necessities for beginning life over again in a new setting. Some of these voyagers were exiles, either going voluntarily or else being driven off by a more powerful faction. While many such parties must have disappeared, some did land on distant islands such as Hawaii and Easter Island.

In contrast to the views of Thor Heyerdahl, who thought that the Pacific islands were peopled by migrants from the New World, most anthropologists see their origins in Southeast Asia.

Several botanists have claimed an Old World origin for the sweet potato, as for most other Polynesian plants. The breadfruit, pandanus, yam, and sugarcane all came from Southeast Asia, while the taro may have originated in southern Asia. (Suggs 1960:23). The few domesticated animals of Polynesia, the dog, pig, and jungle fowl, also have an Old World origin.

The Malayo-Polynesian language has ties with the Old World, not with the New. It is spoken as far west as the large island of Madagascar, near the southeastern coast of Africa, and as far east as Easter Island, 2,000 miles from the coast of Peru. The Malayo-Polynesian language stock includes the languages of Polynesia, Micronesia, Melanesia, Indonesia, and the Philippines; and it is related to some languages spoken in Thailand and Taiwan. Thus, the evidence of botany, biology, and linguistics seems to point to Southeast Asia as a point of origin for the Polynesians. There is similar evidence in material culture. For example, a type of adze used in southern China in Neolithic times, and not found elsewhere in Asia, is very similar to the Polynesian adze.

Robert C. Suggs believes that the expansion of the Shang state in northern China some time before 1600 B.C. was a catalyst that resulted in emigration among coastal peoples in southern China who had a Neolithic horticultural and maritime culture. These emigrants are believed to have settled first in the Philippines, later moving through Melanesia and Papua. The Mariana Islands are thought to have been settled by migrations from the Philippines. The Society Islands in the heart of Polynesia may have been the point from which Hawaii, New Zealand, and other islands were settled. Hawaii became inhabited around the second century A.D.; Easter Island, in the fourth century; and New Zealand, not until around A.D. 1000.

The culture carried through these islands was a Neolithic one based on root-crop horticulture, breadfruit, and fishing. Bark-cloth clothing was made from the paper mulberry. Evidently this culture was well adapted to its tropical island environment, since population generally built up in the islands. But this led to warfare and sometimes emigration. There was much fighting in Polynesia; the natives of Tonga built forts with moats, walls, and lookout towers, while the Samoans had fortified villages. Chiefs acquired high status. Rules of primogeniture determined relative rank. Some chiefs gave expression to their status by directing the building of large ceremonial structures. Megalithic architecture appeared in Tahiti, the Marquesas, Hawaii, and Easter Island.

Summary

   The principal new development in the Neolithic period was the domestication of plants and animals, which facilitated sedentary village life. Plant domestication developed in several places in the Near East, eastern Asia, Mesoamerica, and Peru. Barley, wheat, and millet were leading crops in the Old World, and corn, beans, and squash in the New. Sedentary village life made it possible to store and preserve food. More permanent housing appeared. There were new methods for making stone tools. Axes and adzes were made of granular stone instead of flint and were ground rather than flaked. Weaving was a by-product of the domestication of plants and animals, making use of plant fibers and sheep's wool. Looms were invented in both the Old World and the New. Pottery is also a common feature of Neolithic sites, although missing in some of the earlier levels. This pottery is not made on the potter's wheel but slowly built up with coils or strips of clay. Some trade took place between villages. There is evidence that Neolithic patterns of culture diffused from the Near East across North Africa and into Europe. A pastoral economy often developed in grasslands, deserts, and steppes, in areas not suitable for farming. It was from Southeast Asia that peoples with a Neolithic culture emigrated to populate the islands of the Pacific.

Suggestions for further reading

   A valuable collection of articles is assembled in Stuart Struever, ed., *Prehistoric Agriculture* (New York: The Natural History Press, 1971); see especially the papers by Binford and Flannery. See also Peter J. Ucko and G. W. Dimbleby, eds., *The Domestication and Exploitation of Plants and Animals* (Chicago: Aldine Publishing Co., 1969).

   Although some of its findings have been shown to be wrong, V. Gordon Childe's *Man Makes Himself* (New York: Mentor Books, 1936, 1953) is recommended. It is a stimulating work.

   Also recommended are: Ralph Linton, *The Tree of Culture* (New York: Alfred A. Knopf, 1955), especially Chapters 13–18; James Mellaart, "Roots in the Soil," in *The Dawn of Civilization: The First World Survey of Human Cultures in Early Times,* ed. Stuart Piggott (New York: McGraw-Hill Book Co., 1961), pp. 41–64, and *Çatal Hüyük: A Neolithic Town in Anatolia* (New York: McGraw-Hill Book Co., 1967).

   On early China see Kwang-chih Chang, *The Archaeology of Ancient China* (New Haven, Conn.: Yale University Press, 1968).

10

THE DEVELOPMENT OF CIVILIZATIONS

We have seen that some Neolithic communities, such as Çatal Hüyük, developed some rather sophisticated culture traits and had sizable populations. Pottery was made; in Çatal Hüyük and probably elsewhere fresco paintings were executed. These communities were moving in the direction of what has vaguely been called *civilization*. Perhaps they could be said to have already reached that level, but that would depend on one's definition of the term.

Civilization has sometimes been equated with urbanism or city life, though with the added implication of a more polished way of life—civil, urbane behavior, in contrast with the roughness and naïveté of rural yokels.

Criteria of civilization

A difficulty with using city life as a criterion for civilization is that it is hard to determine at just what point a town becomes a city. During the Predynastic period and much of its early history, Egypt seems to have been a country of villages and market towns with no cities except for temporary capitals. John A. Wilson (1951:34) writes: "Probably one would have to come far down into history—possibly down to the Eighteenth Egyptian Dynasty before one could be sure of a city in the modern sense." Minoan Crete, also, did not represent a true city culture.

The presence of a writing system has also been suggested as the distinguishing mark of civilization. It is true that Sumer, Egypt, the Indus Valley, and Crete all had writing systems in the Bronze Age period, but the pre-Columbian Inca of Peru possessed no writing, although they did have city life, metallurgy, and other features commonly associated with civilization.

Since the advanced cultures of the Old World developed in what has been called the Bronze Age, between approximately 3500 and 1500 B.C., it is tempting to use bronze metallurgy as an indicator of civilization; but such metallurgy was unknown to the Aztecs of Mexico, although they knew how to work copper and gold.

Another yardstick for civilization is the presence of a state, a ruling governmental body. A state and city life seem to be related. In a tribal society, kinship units provide agencies for social control; but, in a city, many people are strangers and informal social sanctions are harder to apply. A superordinate governmental agency becomes necessary if social order is to be maintained.

We need not insist on a single criterion for the level of civilization. In addition to those already cited, some other common features of civilizations may be mentioned: the building of monumental constructions with mass labor, class stratification, division of labor and craft specialization, development of trade and communications, development of warfare, and advances in knowledge in such fields as mathematics, astronomy, and calendrical calculations. These topics, among others, will be elaborated upon further in this chapter.

Courses toward civilization have probably differed greatly in different regions. Yet there have often been striking parallels in such cultural advances, so that the civilizations of Mexico and Peru, although largely independent in their development, not only showed many similarities to one another

Centers of Old World civilization.

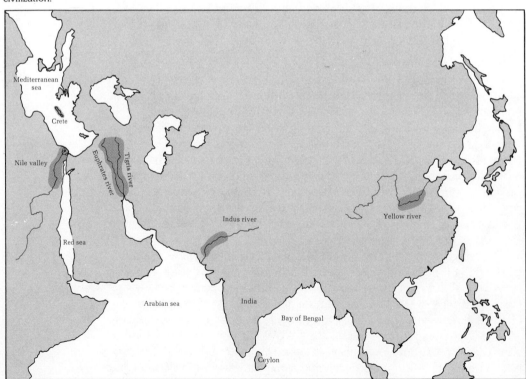

but both resembled the Bronze Age civilizations of the Old World in many respects as well.

One important precondition of civilization is the productivity of agriculture, which makes large concentrations of population possible. Some new inventions facilitated increased agricultural production.

Agricultural productivity

Early farming was of the type known as *swidden cultivation* or slash-and-burn horticulture. This process involves clearing a patch of land by burning, planting crops and tending them for a year or more, and then abandoning the plot so that its fertility may be renewed. New plots are opened up in the same way; earlier ones, once abandoned, may be reopened once their fertility is restored. This kind of cultivation must have developed independently in many forested regions. It is still widely practiced in different parts of the world today among tribal groups in India, the Congo, the Amazon, and Oceania and among peasants in Mexico and Southeast Asia.

Swidden cultivation is usually done on a small scale, often with plots of an acre or less. The population density in societies practicing this type of cultivation tends to be low; settlements are small, seldom with more than 250 persons. This type of horticulture does not encourage political unification, although it may occur.

New farming techniques

Some new developments in Bronze Age times increased agricultural productivity. One was the invention of the ox-drawn plow, which was used in Mesopotamia by 3000 B.C. The ox-drawn plow appeared in Egypt and the Indus Valley at about the same time, perhaps due to diffusion of the idea from Mesopotamia. With a plow drawn by oxen, people could put a much greater area of land under cultivation than before, with less time and effort involved.

Oxen also pulled carts with solid wooden wheels in Bronze Age centers and were sometimes used for trampling grain as a form of winnowing.

Another aid to agriculture was the use of metal sickles for reaping, which were in evidence by 3000 B.C. Another was the pickax, a prominent tool in Sumer, where a seeder plow that dropped seeds into newly plowed land through a kind of funnel was also developed.

Large granaries have been found in the remains of Old World centers of civilization, which show that a sizable surplus of grain could be stored. These granaries provide direct evidence of the enhanced productivity of agriculture in the Bronze Age.

Irrigation

Still another contribution in this direction was the development of irrigation. It may be noted that the civilizations of Mesopotamia, Egypt, and the Indus Valley are developed in rather dry regions through which rivers run.[1]

In Mesopotamia, there are the Tigris and Euphrates Rivers; in Egypt, the Nile; and in the Indus Valley, in what is now Pakistan, there are the Indus River and its tributaries. The dryness of the climate in these regions would naturally encourage the development of irrigation networks to tap the river waters. In northern China, where the Bronze Age Shang dynasty civilization developed, the climate has been described as semiarid. Here, too, irrigation was resorted to on a large scale.

The earliest of these civilizations dependent upon irrigation developed in Mesopotamia, a flat, treeless plain, where irrigation had to be employed if farm communities were to survive. But only one of the two great rivers in this region lent itself well to irrigation. The Tigris had too deep a bed to be easily tapped by canals. The Euphrates, however, had a high bed and was flanked by banks that rose high above the surrounding plains. The high level of this river made it well suited for irrigation.

The first settlements beside the Euphrates must have had relatively simple canals, but as the riverside communities expanded, an increasingly complex irrigation network developed with various smaller channels leading off from the larger ones and reaching fields progressively farther away from the river. This system of irrigation greatly enhanced the productivity of agriculture and made it possible for the Mesopotamian farmers to harvest two crops a year. They were no longer dependent on rainfall as the upland Neolithic farmers had been or as were the swidden agriculturalists of central Europe. Their settlements also were more permanent; the Mesopotamian farmers no longer had to move their villages or fields from time to time.

There were similar developments in parts of the New World. Irrigation systems were developed in coastal Peru about 2,000 years ago, making it possible for farmers to raise two or more crops a year. Peruvian farmers also made use of guano—bird droppings—for fertilizer. In the highlands, terraces with strong retaining walls were built to provide level fields and to prevent erosion. This more productive kind of cultivation can be called agriculture rather than horticulture.

Irrigation was also practiced in the Valley of Mexico and in the North American Southwest in pre-Columbian times. A device used by the Aztecs to increase food productivity was the *chinampa,* a man-made islet composed of reeds, mud, and rotting vegetation that supported beds of topsoil. Although *chinampas* have been called *floating gardens,* they were anchored by willow trees planted at their edges. *Chinampas* provided excellent soil, allowing for three harvests a year.

Through such devices as irrigation, terracing, and *chinampas,* agricultural productivity increased, allowing for greater concentrations of population.

---

[1] The Indus Valley, however, is thought to have been more fertile and better watered at the time of Harappa and Mohenjo-daro than it is at present.

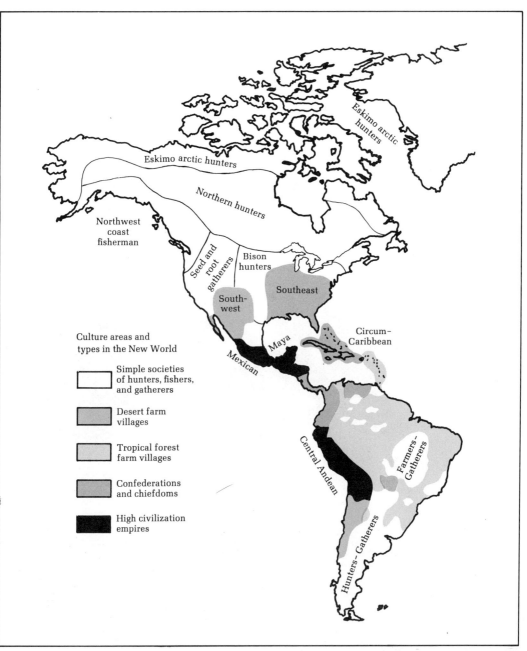

Eskimo arctic hunters

Eskimo arctic hunters

Northern hunters

Northwest coast fisherman

Seed and root gatherers

Bison hunters

Southeast

South-west

Circum-Caribbean

Maya

Mexican

Central Andean

Farmers-Gatherers

Hunters-Gatherers

Culture areas and types in the New World

Simple societies of hunters, fishers, and gatherers

Desert farm villages

Tropical forest farm villages

Confederations and chiefdoms

High civilization empires

Map showing culture areas and types of society in pre-Columbian North and South America.

Social control   An irrigation network requires some centralized supervision to prevent the outbreak of quarrels over access to the water. This may have been one of the reasons for the development of political organization in the early city-states of Sumer. Moreover, large cooperative undertakings were required to build, maintain, clean, and repair the canals and to combat the danger of floods to which Mesopotamia was subject. Such efforts had to have some direction, and this may have been one of the functions of the nascent city government.

Monumental constructions and mass labor

In each of the earliest centers of Old World civilization, one finds massive structures that must have required the organization and direction of large work gangs. In Egypt there are the pyramids; in Mesopotamia, the ziggurats; and in the Indus Valley cities, the large mounds, or citadels, as they have been called. The purpose and significance of these great structures differed

Pyramids of Giza, Egypt.

in the respective societies, but they all attest to the ability of a centralized power to exact hard labor from large numbers of people. Some authorities have argued that this labor need not have been particularly burdensome and that it may have been done in small doses during spare times after the harvest. Be that as it may, these huge constructions embody many man-hours of work. Herodotus was told that 100,000 men worked on the Great Pyramid. Even if we grant this to be an exaggeration,[2] it is clear that a great labor force was required. About 2.3 million stones went into the making of the Great Pyramid (completed about 2600 B.C.), with an average weight of 2.5 tons, although some weigh 15 tons and there are also some granite slabs that weigh nearly 50 tons.

The ziggurats of Mesopotamia and the mounds of the Indus Valley cities were made of piles of sun-dried brick; so they are less awesome constructions as far as their logistics is concerned. Yet they are impressive structures, too. The ziggurat at Ur was 68 feet high, topped with a shrine to the moon god. It could be seen 15 miles away across the flat plain. A ziggurat at Uruk has been estimated to have required a full-time labor force of 1,500 men working for five years. The walled citadel at Mohenjo-daro in the Indus Valley was up to 50 feet high and contained several public buildings. Here, again, a large labor force under the supervision of overseers must be assumed.

It may be that collective work on the irrigation canals provided the model for later large-scale enterprises. The needs of defense were involved in some cases, glorification of the state or its religion in others. Palaces and royal tombs were built to honor kings or pharaohs and to emphasize their power and wealth.

Comparable phenomena took place in the New World. Great pyramids appeared in Mesoamerica and Peru. The massive Inca fortifications at Sacsahuamán are reminiscent of Old World defense works.

Class stratification

There is archaeological evidence to show that the Old World centers of civilization had class stratification. There are considerable differences, for example, in the size of Indus Valley homes, some being large, with many rooms, while there are also cramped rows of what have been called working-men's quarters. Sumerian cities also had class stratification. S. N. Kramer (1963:77, 89) states that the population consisted of four categories: nobles, commoners, clients, and slaves. Nobles owned large estates; the poor lived in humble quarters.

A similar situation appears at the later 14th century B.C. Egyptian site of Tell el-Amarna, where there were royal palaces, lavish homes of court nobility, well-appointed middle-class dwellings, and also the cramped quarters of the poor.

---

[2] A recent estimate is that only about 4,000 men were employed at a time.

Slavery was a recognized institution in both Egypt and Sumer. Some Egyptian rulers from the 15th century B.C. on brought large numbers of Asiatic captives back from their wars. Many were employed in quarries and mines; others became house slaves.

There were special laws in Mesopotamia regarding the treatment of slaves. The latter were usually captured prisoners of war, but in Mesopotamia one might also become a slave through failure to pay debts, or one might sell a wife or child into slavery to avoid bankruptcy. But freemen who became slaves in this way could be ransomed and freed, and their period of slavery was meant to be temporary, limited by law to three years. It can be seen from this that slavery in Mesopotamia was a somewhat different institution from slavery in the United States before the end of the Civil War, where slavery was usually a lifelong inherited condition associated with a particular racial group.

In Peru, in the New World, the emperor, called the Inca, was regarded as the son of the Sun, a divine being. His tribesmen, especially his closest

Machu Picchu, late Inca settlement.

relatives, made up the nobility, just below which came the *curaca,* or provincial nobles, who provided the lesser officials of the government.

The common people were distinguished from the nobles by dress. They were not allowed to wear the finer wool of alpaca and vicuña, but only llama wool. They could not wear gold and silver ornaments. In matters of food and drink they were also restricted, and they were not allowed to hunt. The commoners tilled the soil for the upper classes and for the state religion as well as for themselves, providing grain and other produce; they were liable to military and corvée service—working on roads, irrigation ditches, terraces, fortifications, and other public-works projects. The nobles, who generally lived in the capital at Cuzco, were exempt from such work and service. The nobles were allowed to hold landed estates, to receive formal education, and to marry more than one wife—privileges not granted the common people.

Each Maya city-state was ruled by a man who was believed to be divine and was supported by councilors and various other officials. These men were of the upper class, not subject to taxation. The common people provided tribute of such items as vegetable produce, cotton cloth, game fowls, fish, cacao, copal for incense, honey and wax, and strings of jade, coral beads, and shells (Morley 1956:158). There was also class stratification among the Aztecs at Tenochtitlán, with a class of nobles at the top and one of slaves at the bottom.

Division of labor

The civilizations of Mesopotamia, Egypt, the Indus Valley, Mexico, and Peru were characterized by the development of division of labor. During the Neolithic period there seems to have been relatively little division of labor. Men did the hunting and worked in the fields, while women wove cloth and made pottery. There was relatively little craft specialization.

V. Gordon Childe's explanation for the proliferation of specialties during Bronze Age times in the Old World was that the heightened productivity of agriculture ensured a grain surplus and thus allowed some segments of the population to engage in specialized nonagricultural tasks. It was no longer necessary for all able-bodied workers to till the fields. New technological advances also spurred the division of labor. Another way of looking at these phenomena is to stress the growing social inequality and political centralization as causative factors. A ruling class could exert pressures in the formation of a surplus and also in the direction of craft specialization. Among the Inca of Peru, for example, the grain and produce provided by the commoners were placed in government storehouses from which the state could withdraw goods as needed. In times of famine, grain could be transported from areas having a surplus. Very strict punishments were applied to criminal offenses, particularly those against the state. Particular specialists, such as female weavers, were state-supported.

Some different theoretical approaches to the development of civilization will be discussed later, after we have finished our review of the common characteristics of civilizations.

Metallurgy

One of the new specialists was the metallurgist, whose complex craft involved technical knowledge, which was often kept secret. The smelting of ores under high temperatures, the preparation of casts, hammering, and annealing all required extensive training. Widely regarded as a kind of miracle

Bronze vessel from China, Shang Dynasty (1523–1028 B.C.)

worker, skilled in magic, it was to the smith's own interest to maintain this reputation.

The making of bronze tools was an important development in what has come to be known as the Bronze Age. Bronze is an alloy of copper and tin, which is harder than copper alone. Mineral resources of copper and tin are not usually found together. It has been suggested, therefore, that people learned to work copper before they made bronze tools and that a Copper Age should be interposed between the Neolithic and the Bronze Age.

The oldest known work in bronze comes from Ban Chiang in northeastern Thailand, where bronze spearheads, anklets, and bracelets were found which have been dated at around 3600 B.C. In the Near East, bronze came a little later, and in China about 1,000 years later than in Thailand.

Metallurgy also developed in the New World. As far back as around 3000 B.C. there were Indians in northern Wisconsin making spear points, knives, and other objects from cold-hammered copper; but this was not metallurgy, for the metal was not smelted.

The first true metallurgy in the New World was developed in Peru by around 700 B.C. In the Chavín period, various gold ornaments were made, including pendants, tweezers, crowns, pins, and spoons. The Peruvians learned how to make bronze, something not attained by the Aztecs, although knowledge of metallurgy diffused from South America to Mesoamerica. Platinum, which was not worked in Europe until A.D. 1730, was made into ornaments by the Indians of Colombia and Ecuador. The American Indians did not have an Iron Age.

The lost-wax process of casting, which was known in Mesopotamia, was practiced in Peru, Central America, and Mexico. This is a relatively complex invention, since it depends upon a prior knowledge of the properties of wax, fired clay, and molten metal. Let us say that you wish to make a dagger; first, you make a dagger of wax and then coat it with clay, leaving a hole to the outside. The clay is then fired and turned into pottery; the wax melts and pours out through the hole, leaving a dagger-shaped hollow in the interior. Molten metal is then poured in through the aperture. It fills up all the available space and takes on the dagger shape. After the metal has cooled and hardened, the pottery mold is broken; the dagger may then be filed and polished.

The Inca were able to make remarkable objects of gold and silver, including life-sized gold statues of their rulers and replicas of local plants and animals in gold. Unfortunately, the Spaniards melted most of this artwork down into gold bullion.

Pottery

Another new specialist in the Old World Bronze Age was the potter. It is probable that in the preceding Neolithic period the womenfolk of a particular household usually made their own pots and jars, building up the walls by hand with strips or coils of clay. In the Bronze Age, however, there were professional potters who exchanged their wares for other goods.

This specialized trade resulted from yet another technological innovation: the potter's wheel, which first appeared in Mesopotamia in the fourth millennium B.C. In this technique, the potter centers a damp lump of clay on a horizontal revolving wheel that may be rotated either by hand or by pumping a foot pedal. A rim of clay is formed by holding the hands steadily together on the circumference of the clay lump and quickly raising up the side walls as the wheel revolves.

Mastery of the potter's wheel is not easy; training and practice are required to learn this art. But, once the knack has been acquired, a potter can produce pottery vessels on the wheel much more quickly than by the old coil-strip method. Moreover, wheel-made ware is more finished in appearance, being more perfectly round and smooth.

Priesthood

Priests were also specialists. In Egypt there were various classifications of priests whose services at the temple were complemented by other specialized personnel: singers, musicians, astrologers, interpreters of dreams. Although Egyptian and Sumerian religions differed considerably in content, both saw a great expansion of the priesthood and the development of huge temple complexes during the Bronze Age. In both areas, temples owned

Olmec head.

land. It has been estimated that at one point temple lands amounted to about one fifth of all Egypt. The temples of Sumer were not only places of worship but also elaborate centers of production, with workshops for weavers, tailors, sculptors, goldsmiths, carpenters, and other specialists. The temples also provided formal education (although there were private secular schools as well in Sumer), and the priests formed the principal group of the educated, often skilled in writing, mathematics, and medicine, as well as in ritual. Some of the Egyptian priests were similarly learned.

The priesthood was also an important institution in the higher civilizations of the New World.

Most hunting-gathering societies in North and South America had shamans or medicine men rather than priests. Shamans are generally concerned with individual crises, such as sickness; they attempt to make contact with the supernatural world through trance, magic, divination, or other means. Priests, who are engaged in rituals of a more collective, organized variety, are officials of a cult or church from which their authority derives.

In Mesoamerica the emergence of the priest has been dated at 900 B.C., when the first large-scale religious structures were built. Ultimately, ceremonial centers appeared throughout Mesoamerica, all under the supervision of priest-intellectuals who were set apart from the rest of the people by distinctive dress and special knowledge. Part of this special knowledge was a system of writing first developed by the Olmecs or Zapotecs, ancestral to the Maya script. Ceremonial centers were associated with trade; they were also market centers. Priests were involved in economic affairs in another respect; as specialists in calendrical knowledge they could advise farmers when to plant crops. And, of course, they led the rituals and sacrifices that persuaded the gods to bring rainfall, fertility, and success in war. The priests were thus high-ranking specialists whose services became indispensable and who were able to maintain a dominant position in the societies of Mesoamerica for many hundreds of years.

The pattern of human sacrifice was particularly developed in the Aztec area. The Aztecs believed their gods had to be offered human hearts in order to keep the universe going. This provided motivation for wars and raids on neighboring tribes; captured warriors were sacrificed. Sometimes thousands of victims were killed at a time. This practice understandably made the Aztecs unpopular with their neighbors, who were quite willing to ally themselves with Hernando Cortés when the Spaniards appeared on the scene.

The Inca religion in Peru was state-supported. The priests were fed by the labor of the common people; special storehouses were set apart to supply the religious order. The priesthood formed a hierarchy, at the top of which was a High Priest, who was always a brother, uncle, or other close relative of the emperor. As in Mesoamerica, church and state were closely interlinked.

There were priestesses as well as priests. Government officials visited each village from time to time to select some of the more attractive girls of about ten years of age for special training and government service. Known as "Chosen Women," these girls filled various roles. Some became concubines of the emperor or were given by him to members of the nobility as secondary wives. Some became priestesses of the Sun cult and weavers attached to temples, and some were killed in sacrifice. The Inca, however, did not indulge in large-scale human sacrifice as the Aztecs did. They took it out on the llamas instead. A white llama was offered every morning at the Temple of the Sun in Cuzco. On special ceremonial occasions hundreds or thousands of llamas were killed. One form of Inca divination was based on the examination of the entrails of sacrificed llamas.

A curious parallel with Christian practices was the Inca custom of confession of sins to priests, who exacted penance, usually a period of fasting or prayer. After penance was completed, the sinner washed in a stream to be purified.

Peasantry

We do not usually think of the peasant as a kind of specialist, but they are now coming to be seen as dependent on urban life, in which respect they differ from tribal groups that practice agriculture.

There were no peasants before the development of civilization. George M. Foster has written:

When settled rural peoples subject to the jural control of outsiders exchange a part of what they produce for items they cannot themselves make, in a market setting transcending local transactions, then they are peasants. We see peasants as a peripheral but essential part of civilization, producing the food that makes urban life possible, supporting (and subject to) the specialized classes of political and religious rulers and the other members of the educated elite (Foster 1967:6).

Other specialties

With the development of writing systems, scribes appeared in Egypt and Sumer, having knowledge and training that gave them relatively high status. This is reflected in an Egyptian text dating from perhaps the Eleventh Dynasty (late third millennium B.C.) in which a father urges his son to study hard to enter this profession. The father contrasts the easy and prestigious work of the scribe with the demanding, unpleasant labors of the smith, stonemason, barber, and farmer.

We learn from this text that the barber was another specialist, one low in the hierarchy:

The barber shaves from morning till night; he never sits down except to meals. He hurries from house to house looking for business. He wears out his arms to fill his stomach, like bees eating their own honey (Woolley 1965:170).

Weaving was a hereditary specialty in Mesopotamia, where guilds and workshops developed. Indeed, there were separate guilds for spinners, dyers, and fullers.

Other specialists referred to in early texts include brickmakers, carpenters, goldsmiths, and jewelers.

Not only were there many kinds of specialists, some of a hereditary nature, but these occupations were often ranked high or low in relationship to others. Some, like the higher scribes and priests, had high status; others, like barbers and sweepers, ranked low. Here we see the development of class or caste differentiation.

Trade and communication

Since Bronze Age specialists were now producing various kinds of goods, it is evident that trade was concomitantly increasing. Trade was both local and far-ranging. Mesopotamia, Egypt, and the Indus Valley all had to import copper and other metals from elsewhere. Egypt and Mesopotamia both imported wood, and Sumer and the Indus Valley imported stone. Since these were all commodities of basic importance, foreign trade was clearly a necessity. Improved means of transport had to be developed to meet such needs.

Although wheeled vehicles such as the ox cart existed, they were not suitable for long journeys, and there were few roads in Bronze Age times. The light, two-wheeled chariot drawn by asses or horses was geared to the uses of warfare rather than trade. It was not known to the Egyptians until the invasion of the Hyksos in 1730 B.C. Pack asses were relied upon mainly for overland transport, although camels were also used. Water transport, however, was much preferred in the valleys of the Nile and the Tigris and Euphrates. Sailing ships also plied the Mediterranean, bringing luxury goods such as silver, lapis lazuli, and other precious stones, as well as oil, myrrh, and resin. Ships that carried such cargo over long distances had to be larger and more strongly built than the simpler craft of Neolithic times. The Bronze Age, then, saw various advances in communication—improvements in shipping and navigation and the domestication of animals used in transportation, such as the donkey, camel, and horse.

Abundant evidence of contact between distant communities appears in the archaeological record. Seals made in the Indus Valley have turned up in Sumer, and Egyptian beads, palettes, and stone tools have been found in the Syrian port of Byblos. Texts are available of treaties made between the Egyptian Pharaoh and the King of the Hittites in the 15th century B.C. Despite much trade and communication, however, these different societies remained distinct in culture, each with its own writing system and its characteristic styles of art and architecture.

The original form of trade exchange in the early Bronze Age must have been barter, but, in time, a medium of exchange became established, first in grain and later in metal. As early as 2400 B.C., silver was a recognized medium of exchange in Mesopotamia, with a fixed ratio to grain, one *mina* of silver equaling 60 *gur* of grain in value. The development of such a standard further facilitated international trade. In Mesopotamia both internal and international trade ultimately became protected by legislation relating to rates of interest, debt, safe conduct for merchants in foreign countries, and related matters.

It should not be assumed that all these merchants were free agents concerned only with profits for themselves. Polanyi (1957c) has presented evidence that Babylonia in Hammurabi's time had a "marketless" economy in which prices were fixed.

In Egypt, where trade was dominated by the pharaoh, merchants seem to have had even less freedom of action.

Trade and communications also developed in the New World. Compared with Mesoamerica, however, there was relatively little trade in Peru, despite the Inca's excellent system of roads. The roads were built for military purposes so that the army could strike quickly. The main road from north to south served no economic purpose; most of the trade was between coast and highland. Cotton and fish from the coast were exchanged for llama wool and potatoes from the highlands. But private travel and trade were restricted under the Inca. There was no standard medium of exchange, and most of the barter that took place was in regional markets.

Although movement and trade were limited, some systems of communication were highly developed in Peru. Relay runners were stationed at intervals along the highways so that the rulers at Cuzco could be quickly informed of any disturbance in the provinces. Watch-fire signals were also used.

Mesoamerica did not have road systems as good as those of Peru, but there was more trade, partly because of the great ecological diversity of the region. Different valleys, mountains, and lowlands produced different kinds of products.

Much Mesoamerican trade took place in connection with temples. There was trade in shells, feathers, cotton, rubber, and other goods from different parts of Mexico.

Temple centers were also marketplaces. Some, like the market at Tenochtitlán, the Aztec capital, were very large; the latter was judged by Cortés to serve 60,000 buyers and sellers daily. Since produce sold at the market was taxed, one was not allowed to buy and sell apart from the marketplace. The market had judges to decide disputes. There were separate sections or streets for different wares: pottery, herbs, game birds, textiles, and jewelry. Slaves were also sold. As in Peru, there was no money, and most exchange was by barter. But cacao (chocolate) beans were used to some extent as a medium of exchange, as were lengths of cloth. In the Maya area a slave was worth 100 cacao beans.

Among the Aztecs, merchants known as *pochteca* formed a special favored class. They lived in a separate quarter of the city and worshiped a god of their own. The Maya had a similar merchant class, not subject to taxation and having other special privileges. They were not concerned with the trade of the marketplace but with long-distance trade in luxury goods, slaves, and valued raw materials, such as animal skins, precious stones, and the feathers of wild birds.

The Aztecs at Tenochtitlán made much use of dugout canoes for transportation, since the capital city was a kind of Venice, built out on the lake with canals taking the place of streets. "Not a wheel turned or a pack animal neighed; transport was on the backs of men or in the bottoms of boats" (Vaillant 1956:218).

The Aztecs had no use for boats larger than dugouts, for they were not seafaring people. Like the Inca, the Aztecs had a courier system. Through their reports, Montezuma was able to receive a steady stream of information about the Spaniards who landed on the coast, long before Cortés' men arrived at Tenochtitlán.

One by-product of the development of civilization was a steady increase in the scale of warfare. With larger concentrations of population, the number of persons involved in a siege increased. More people could be drawn into battle. The Bronze Age workers who were conscripted to build pyramids or ziggurats could also be conscripted to fight. Meanwhile, metal weapons—spears, swords, helmets, shields, and other accouterments—increased the efficiency of war. **Warfare**

The Sumerians seem to have been the first to organize drilled armies in which there were different types of soldiers—infantry, spearmen, and charioteers. These are depicted in the Royal Standard of Ur (circa 2700 B.C.). Most of the early fighting among the Sumerian city-states seems to have been over possession of water and land resources; later, there was fighting for control of trade routes. The Royal Standard shows orderly phalanxes of helmeted foot soldiers and chariots with solid wheels drawn by onagers. To be effective the Sumerian phalanxes must have been drilled to act in unison. Phalanxes were named and had special insignia. No doubt efforts were made to establish *esprit de corps* in such units.

Drilled armies of increasing size became a common institution in Mesopotamia. Akkadian troops waged distant campaigns, with Sargon (2872–17 B.C.) leading a standing army of 5,400 men.

Being protected by natural boundaries of desert and sea, Egypt was relatively well protected from outside attack, but around 1730 B.C. it was invaded by the Hyksos, nomadic warriors who ruled the country until around 1570 B.C. The Hyksos had the advantage of a secret weapon unfamiliar to the Egyptians, the horse and chariot, which had long been used in Mesopotamia. They also had a composite bow built up of layers of wood, sinew, and horn glued together, which was more effective than the bows used in Egypt. The Hyksos wore body armor and had new types of swords and daggers. All these factors gave them the upper hand over the almost naked and

Section of Royal
Standard of Ur.

poorly armed Egyptians, from whom the Hyksos proceeded to exact tribute, while living apart in fortified camps.

After the Egyptians had acquired the use of the new military devices, they succeeded in driving out the Hyksos. Not content with that, a new imperial spirit developed in the ruling dynasty. Under Thutmose III (1490–36 B.C.) Egyptian armies invaded Palestine and Syria. This resulted in changes in the composition of troops. Although conscription had been practiced formerly, the Egyptian farmers had always been needed on the land to produce their crops; but now a standing army was required in Syria. The problem was solved by forming foreign mercenary troops. In Syria, the Egyptian forces came up against the Hittites, who were said to have had 3,500 chariots at the battle of Carchemish, although this may have been an exaggeration. Thus, warfare raged back and forth through the Near East, with different nations rising and falling—Hittites, Assyrians, Persians, and others.

There was also large-scale fighting in the New World. The city of Teotihuacán, 30 miles northwest of present-day Mexico City, is estimated to have had a population of 50,000 or more, but it collapsed and was looted and burned around A.D. 700. Another city, Casas Grandes, in the present-day north Mexican state of Chihuahua, was sacked and burned by unknown enemies between A.D. 1300 and 1340. The Aztecs were originally a marauding tribe that settled at Tenochtitlán in 1325 and demanded tribute from neighboring peoples. Like the Aztecs, the Inca were a tribe that had overrun and dominated their neighbors.

Writing

Advances in knowledge

The earliest Sumerian and Egyptian written texts date from the last quarter of the fourth millennium B.C. Since writing of quite different types appears in the two societies at about the same time, one conclusion could be that the invention of writing was made independently in both Mesopotamia and Egypt. Some authorities, however, hold that the Mesopotamians were the first to develop a writing system and that the *idea* of writing, if not the specific system, spread from Sumer to Egypt. The people of the Indus Valley also had a distinctive writing system at the time they had trade relations with Sumer. Here, again, it is possible that the idea of writing was derived from Mesopotamia. The Cretan writing systems, which date from the first half of the second millennium B.C., are also different from those of the other Bronze Age centers and so is that of ancient China, dating from about the same period. It is known that various culture patterns diffused from Egypt to Crete and from the Near East to China; so the idea of writing may have diffused as well. At any rate, each of these Bronze Age centers had its own form of writing. Evidently, the way of living had come to require some system of keeping records and transmitting information in relatively permanent form.

Writing at Sumer was done on clay tablets. The cuneiform (wedge-shaped) inscriptions were made by a stylus, often a reed, while the clay was still damp. The earliest clay tablets at Sumer contain lists of things stored at the temple and give the number of cows, sheep, and other items owned. From this concern for bookkeeping, it has been held, a writing system ultimately developed. In early Egyptian writing, however, the underlying need seems to have been the communication of orders and the recording of royal accomplishments. In ancient Mesopotamia, where merchants played an active role, most of the clay tablets were business contracts; in Egypt, on the other hand, writing mainly recorded the commands and achievements of the pharaoh and preserved valued spells and magical formulae. Large numbers of texts have been preserved in both Mesopotamia and Egypt. The Mesopotamians baked important clay-tablet contracts; the firing process made them practically indestructible. But many unfired, sun-dried clay tablets also have been unearthed in good condition, still legible. The Egyptians sometimes carved inscriptions in stone, which, of course, survived; but so did many writings on papyrus, the Egyptian paper made from the papyrus reed. Rolls of papyrus have often remained well preserved because of the dryness of the Egyptian climate.

Not all the ancient writing systems have been deciphered. Scholars can read Egyptian hieroglyphics, Mesopotamian cuneiform tablets, and the ancient Chinese script, but the Indus Valley writing remains largely indecipherable. One of the Cretan writing systems, known as Linear B, was decoded in 1952; its language proved to be Greek. Another Cretan script, Linear A, has not yet been deciphered.

The earliest writing systems are pictographic in character, consisting of a series of pictures or pictograms. The pictures stand for concepts, not specific sounds; so, if they are clear enough, they may be understood by people speaking different languages. A weakness of such a system is that abstract ideas are hard to convey in this form of writing.

A later stage of writing is ideographic, in which the individual symbols are called ideograms. One symbol may stand for various things; a round disk is not only the sun but may also represent heat, light, day, and other concepts. When seen in context, the right meaning may be understood, just as we immediately know what is meant when we see a skull and crossbones on the label of a bottle. This system may express abstract ideas, but it may also lead to confusion. Should the picture of a foot be interpreted to mean foot, walking, standing, or what? One way of coping with such ambiguities was the insertion of classifying signs, indicating the category of objects to which the word belonged—birds, gods, or whatnot. Sumerian scribes placed such markers before or after the more ambiguous symbols; such signs are known as *determinatives.*

The oldest known Mesopotamian and Egyptian scripts are not purely ideographic, although they may have been so in earlier stages of their development. The first writings known already contain phonetic elements and so are referred to as mixed or transitional—presumably on their way to becoming phonetic scripts, although some of the early transitional scripts lasted for 3,000 years or more.

When concepts were hard to represent in pictograms, a phonetic principle might be employed. To express *I,* one might draw an eye; they sound alike. The Sumerian word *ti* meant both arrow and life. The latter, more abstract term could be expressed by the picture of an arrow.

Phonetic writing, the last stage, may be either syllabic or alphabetic. The most important form in the development of the modern world has been alphabetic writing, in which letters represent single sounds. This is the most simplified, efficient writing system. The alphabet has between 22 and 26 signs, in contrast to about 460 Egyptian hieroglyphs, 600 Babylonian characters, and 400 in the Indus Valley script. A. L. Kroeber has drawn attention to the fact that the alphabet was invented only once. Although there are many alphabets in the world today that look quite different from one another, all are traceable to a single source, some Semitic people, perhaps the Phoenicians in southwestern Asia before 1000 B.C. (Kroeber 1948:313, 514).

In Mesoamerica, in the New World, the Olmecs, Mixtecs, Zapotecs, Aztecs, Totonacs, and Maya had writing systems. That of the Maya, which may have developed from the Olmec system of writing, was the most advanced. It was an ideographic script. Only about one fourth of the Maya glyphs have been deciphered.

Zapotecs, Totonacs, Aztecs, Mixtecs, and Maya made a kind of paper from beaten bark, strips of which, covered with writing, could be fashioned into a book folded in an accordianlike fashion. Only three of these books, or codices, remain from the Maya region, of which one, the Dresden Codex, concerns mathematics, astronomy, and calendrical matters, among other things.

It is curious that the Inca did not develop a system of writing, since in some respects, such as metallurgy and political organization, their civilization was more advanced than those of Mesoamerica. So complex a society with such tight political control demanded some system of record keeping. In the case of the Inca, this need was met by strings of knotted cords called *quipus.* A quipu had a main cord, from a few inches to over a yard in length, to which were attached smaller colored strings knotted at intervals. Knots and colors had particular ascribed meanings. The knots could stand for numbers counted in a decimal system. The color may have indicated the category of items to be counted. In this way, a census was kept. At Cuzco, where the quipus were stored, it could be known how many families or how many men of fighting age lived in such-and-such community. The number of llamas, sandals, and other items could be quickly ascertained for particular regions.

A group of specialists memorized these quipu records, including historical accounts. Unfortunately, the system by which they worked has not been preserved.

Mathematics

Besides developing writing systems, the civilizations of the Bronze Age also increased knowledge of mathematics, although this advance was uneven. In Mesopotamia much was known about algebra, geometry, and arithmetic. (The Babylonians were familiar with the "Pythagorean theorem," squares, cube roots, and multiplication tables.) But in Egypt there was relatively little knowledge of these subjects, despite the very accurate calculations involved in the construction of the pyramids. The Egyptians had a decimal system of numeration, while the Mesopotamians had a sexagesimal system, with units of 60. This applied to weights, so that 180 grains made a shekel, 60 shekels equaled a *mina,* and 60 *mina* were a talent.

Both decimal and sexagesimal systems have influenced our modern ways of reckoning. The Mesopotamian system survives in our way of dividing the circle into 360 degrees, the hour into 60 minutes, and the minute into 60 seconds.

The Dresden Codex shows that the Maya had developed much astronomical knowledge and a remarkable mathematical system. The latter was a vigesimal system, based on the number 20. The number 1 was indicated by a single dot; 2, by two dots; 3, by three; and 4, by four. The number 5 was indicated by a bar; 6, by a bar with a dot above it; 7, by a bar with two dots; and so on. Ten was indicated by two bars, one above the other; 11, by two bars with a dot above them. Fifteen was indicated by three bars. Twenty was symbolized by a shell (the symbol for zero) with a dot above it.

The invention of zero and position numbering was an independent invention of the Maya, paralleling the invention of the zero in India but dated even earlier in time. This, of course, weakens the possible significance of diffusion from the Old World as a source of higher civilization in Mesoamerica.

Astronomical and calendrical calculations

Some knowledge about the yearly cycle is useful to farmers who have to plan ahead, sow seed at a propitious time, and harvest their crops at the right moment. In the Bronze Age, astronomical and calendrical calculations were facilitated by the development of writing and mathematics, which made it possible to keep records of astronomical phenomena, to note the lengthening and shortening of days, and to record other cyclic manifestations. Such calculations could be made by educated priests in Egypt and Mesopotamia, who not only used the information for immediate agricultural purposes but also had to determine fixed dates for the celebration of annual festivals, which generally had some relationship to the agricultural cycle.

The astronomical knowledge of the time was mixed up with astrological notions about the influence of gods and planets on human life. Nevertheless, many accurate observations were made and recorded. Because of their superiority in mathematics, the Babylonians had greater knowledge of astronomy than the Egyptians. They studied the risings and settings of the moon and of Venus, and the lengths of day and night in different seasons. The Babylonians do not seem to have developed any scientific theory about these phenomena, but they did embark on a preliminary phase of scientific investigation: the systematic recording of observations.

The Babylonians had a calendar of 12 lunar months of 29 or 30 days each. The months were divided into four seven-day weeks, with one or two additional feast days thrown in. The Babylonian calendar was thus like ours in some respects, although there was some awkwardness in the fact that the lunar calendar did not jibe with the yearly solar one; hence it was necessary to insert an intercalary month now and then to reestablish uniformity.

The ancient Egyptian calendar was the forerunner of the one in use today, since their year consisted of 365 days with 12 months of 30 days plus five additional days. This was the time usually involved from one inundation of the Nile to the next. The year was divided into three seasons of four months each. The early Egyptians did not insert an intercalary day every four years as we do today; so their calendar, like that of the ancient Mesopotamians, became more inaccurate with time. Egyptians of a later period, however, found a fixed astronomical peg for their calendar in the heliacal rising of Sirius, which used to occur just before the annual flooding of the Nile. It was the Egyptians who first broke up the day into 24 hours, dividing day and night into 12 segments each. They invented a water clock, which remained the best timing device until the medieval European invention of the mechanical clock.

In the New World the Maya had an accurate calendrical system, but

Maya astronomical observatory at Chichén Itzá, Yucatán, Mexico.

one involving elaborate astrological concepts of the relationships between gods and divisions of time. There were auspicious and inauspicious periods, just as in the astrological systems of the Old World. Both the Maya and the Aztecs distinguished a 52-year cycle. The Aztecs believed that the world might come to an end after such a cycle was finished. When this proved not to be the case, there was much celebration.

The priests had to keep track of the calendrical round and its astrological concomitants in order to perform the correct rituals and to offer appropriate sacrifices to the right god at the right time. It seems likely that this calendrical knowledge, together with the knowledge of writing and mathematics, was largely limited to the priesthood.

The development of ironworking

The development of iron metallurgy had many consequences for the civilizations of the Old World, in some ways quickening, in others destructive. Iron objects have been found in Bronze Age sites; but iron was not used much until around 1400 B.C., when some tribesmen in Armenia learned how to work the metal more effectively. About 200 years later the knowledge of ironworking began to diffuse rather quickly, so that iron tools finally came to be used not only by agriculturalists but also by many pastoral nomads and hunting-gathering peoples, who often acquired them through trade. The knowledge of ironworking was introduced to Egypt from Asia Minor in the first millennium B.C. and diffused south of the Sahara to tribes in both West and East Africa. But this knowledge never reached Australia, Polynesia, or the New World until the coming of Europeans.

Although the furnaces of early times were unable to liquefy iron, the ore could be reduced to a spongy mass filled with slag, which had to be pounded out while the metal was white-hot. Early metallurgists also found that the hardness and flexibility of the metal could be increased by heating it with wood and repeatedly hammering and bending it. Bellows were used to keep the fire at a high temperature.

Once these techniques were mastered, the resulting iron tools proved to be tougher and more useful than those made of bronze. Moreover, iron was much more abundant and readily available. Its use is often said to have had a democratizing effect, for copper and bronze were for the upper classes but iron was used by the common people. There were iron hoe blades, plowshares, sickles, and knives in Palestine before 1000 B.C. From around 700 B.C., iron axes were used to clear forests in Europe. Greek and Roman farmers had iron shovels and spades, scythes, hooks, and other implements. Iron shears for shearing sheep and iron saws, tongs, hammers, and chisels were known from around 500 B.C. Pulleys and lathes were also known in the early Iron Age.

All these useful inventions aided the common people and greatly raised their standard of living. Unfortunately, however, iron was also used for improved weaponry—swords, daggers, and spears. Barbarous tribes thus equipped were able to assault the centers of former Bronze Age civilizations. The Dorian invasion led to Greece's Dark Age (circa 1100–750 B.C.), during which communities reverted to a self-sufficient agrarian and pastoral economy, trade relations were broken, and traditions of literacy lost. During the centuries that followed, new states rose and fell in various parts of the Old World.

Cross-cultural regularities in the development of civilizations

In this chapter some general attributes of civilizations have been discussed. These civilizations all developed from a Neolithic level of cultural development but represent something quite different from the Neolithic way of life. There seem to be no marked indications of social inequality in Neolithic settlements, even in such advanced ones as at Çatal Hüyük. In the Chinese Neolithic site of Pan-p'o-ts'un there are communal buildings and cemeteries and evidence of an apparently egalitarian, tightly knit community. These two communities may not be representative of all Neolithic settlements, and there must have been much variation, but, generally, they seem to differ from the higher civilizations in the ways mentioned. With the development of urban life there may have been a deemphasis of kinship ties accompanied by greater class stratification and political centralization.

Some writers see the formation of a state as the crucial integrating factor in these developments, since the state is the warmaking unit that levies taxes and corvée labor and builds fortifications and monumental constructions. But how did the state come into being?

Different explanations have been offered. Karl A. Wittfogel's view is that political centralization was related to the practice of irrigation. He calls the ancient civilizations of Mesopotamia, Egypt, India, China, and Peru "hydraulic societies." Wittfogel (1957) holds that control over the irrigation network in these societies gave the state a despotic domination unchallenged by other centers of power. The monumental constructions raised in each of these "oriental despotisms" testify to the power of the state and the religion associated with it.

Although Wittfogel's ideas seem convincing, some criticisms have been made of the hydraulic theory. There are despotic societies that have had no connection with irrigation and there are societies that make much use of irrigation but have not become despotic. The ancient Hohokam society of the American Southwest built an elaborate irrigation system, but there is no evidence of a ruling class. There were also large irrigation works in ancient Ceylon but no evidence for the hypothesized hydraulic bureaucracy.

Wolfram Eberhard (1958, 1965) does not agree with the assertion that there were no other important sources of power besides the state in China and India. He refers to secret societies, the Buddhist church, organized artisan groups, federations of landowning gentry in China and castes in India. He does not agree that the governments were always so powerful or effective in these countries.

Colossal stone figures
of Toltec culture,
Tula, Mexico,
between 8th and 12th
centuries A.D.

Eberhard claims that the impetus to construct irrigation works in China, from Sung times on (and, thus, perhaps earlier), often came from individuals rather than from the state, as Wittfogel's theory would assume. Religious organizations and village assemblies also undertook such projects. In northern china, where the Shang Dynasty developed and where wheat and millet were raised, irrigation was not really vital. It became more important, after Chinese civilization had already developed, in the later rice culture of the south.

A similar criticism has been made by Robert McCormick Adams (1966:66–69), who argues that irrigation developed on a large scale in Mesopotamia only *after* the appearance of strongly centralized state systems. This criticism has in turn been challenged by William Sanders and Barbara Price (1968:177–88), who have argued for the importance of irrigation in both Mesopotamia and Mesoamerica. They point to the fact that in societies using irrigation there are frequent conflicts over water rights, such as between upstream and downstream communities. This conflict stimulates a need for central authority to supervise the irrigation network, as Wittfogel suggested. There are thus both critics and defenders of the hydraulic theory. It would seem, at any rate, that irrigation was an important concomitant of most of the first Bronze Age civilizations and that most of these societies had strong political centralization.

Robert L. Carneiro (1970) has argued that a state system develops most readily in a geographically circumscribed area, hemmed in by desert or mountain walls. In a developing agricultural society, population expands. In more open, uncircumscribed settlements, groups can bud off and exploit more distant land resources, but this cannot be done in a circumscribed setting. What happens, then, is that conflict over the limited land resources takes place, and one group finally becomes dominant over the others. It is then able to exact tribute or taxes from the defeated groups, which cannot escape. Thus, class stratification and political centralization develop simultaneously.

D. E. Dumond (1965) has pointed out some exceptions to Carneiro's thesis. There are societies, such as the Ifugao of the Philippines and the Chimbu of the New Guinea highlands, that had high population densities and also presumably had circumscribed boundaries but did not develop political integration. Conversely, the Maya lowland area lacks circumscribed boundaries, but city-states developed there.

According to Leslie A. White (1959) the distinguishing feature of cultural evolution from one stage to another, such as from the Neolithic level to that of civilization, is the increase in energy made available. Hunters and gatherers rely on their own human power. Animal domestication in Old World Neolithic communities added animal power as a source of energy for human exploitation, but still more sources of energy were available for human use in Bronze Age civilizations. This does not explain how or why particular Neolithic communities developed into urban centers of civilization while others did not, but it provides an index of cultural evolution: increase in available energy resources.

The many parallels in the development of Old World and New World civilizations give an impression of orderly sequences in cultural evolution, of cross-cultural regularities. Julian H. Steward (1955b) has presented a scheme for conceptualizing the development of complex societies, subdivided into certain stages: Pre-Agricultural Era, Incipient Agriculture, Formative Era, Era of Regional Development and Florescence, and Period of Cyclical Conquests. Thus, the *Formative Era* is one in which basketry, pottery, weaving, metallurgy, and construction are developed and in which there is a growth of population, relative peace, and wide diffusion of culture between centers of civilization. In the *Era of Regional Development and Florescence* there are theocratic states with a priestly intelligentsia and class stratification. The *Period of Cyclical Conquests* is marked by increasing militarism, urbanization, and building of fortifications.

Despite such recurrent patterns, it should be noted that each of the Bronze Age civilizations of the Old World retained some distinctive features and maintained its own culture and style of life. The languages and writing systems of Sumer, Harappa, Egypt, Crete, and China were all different from one another. Egyptian architecture was not like that of Mesopotamia or Crete, despite the communication between these centers. Greeks visited Egypt, but they did not borrow or imitate the pylon, pyramid, or obelisk, nor did they start to mummify the dead. Some of these centers of civilization were ahead of their contemporaries in some respects, behind in others. The metalwork and handicrafts of the Indus Valley cities were not so good as those of Sumer, but their city planning and concern with sanitation were far advanced. Egyptian knowledge of medicine was superior to that of Mesopotamia, but the Mesopotamians were ahead in mathematics and astronomy. The advance of civilization was thus not uniform. Besides, the significance of a particular invention may have differed from one society to another. We have noted that the earliest use of writing in Mesopotamia was in connection with bookkeeping, while in Egypt it was used for the transmission of orders and the recording of royal achievements.

Summary

A culmination of Neolithic sedentary life based on farming was the development of urbanism. City life is one of the principal criteria of civilization. Among the others are a writing system, bronze metallurgy, division of labor, class stratification, and the formation of a state. Most of these components appeared in the advanced Old World centers of culture in the Bronze Age, between around 3500 and 1500 B.C. in Sumer, Harappa, and Egypt and also, a little later, in China of the Shang dynasty. There were parallel developments in the advanced cultures of the New World among the Maya, Aztecs, and Inca.

City life depends upon increased agricultural productivity, which resulted from such farming techniques as the ox-drawn plow, metal sickles for reaping, the pickax, and use of irrigation.

Political centralization characterized the Bronze Age civilizations. The building of monumental structures such as pyramids and ziggurats were manifestations of the new state system, as was an increase in warfare. In contrast to the preceding Neolithic period, there was considerable division of labor, including such specialists as metallurgists, potters, priests, weavers, goldsmiths, and peasants. In keeping with this specialization there was an increase in trade and communication. Writing systems appeared in all the Old World civilizations and among the Maya and Aztecs of the New World, although not among the Inca of Peru. In all these areas, moreover, there were developments in mathematics and in astronomical and calendrical calculations.

Writers such as Wittfogel, Carneiro, and Steward have pointed out apparent cross-cultural regularities in the development of civilizations. At the same time it seems that each of the Old World Bronze Age civilizations retained a distinctive culture.

Sir Leonard Woolley, *The Beginnings of Civilization; History of Mankind: Cultural and Scientific Development,* vol. 1, pt. 2 (New York: Mentor Books, 1965) is a learned, thick compendium of information, available as an inexpensive paperback.

Stuart Piggott, ed., *The Dawn of Civilization: The First World Survey of Human Cultures in Early Times* (New York: McGraw-Hill Book Co., 1961) is a beautifully illustrated collection of articles by authorities in the field.

For an attempt to analyze causal factors accounting for political centralization in "hydraulic societies," see Karl A. Wittfogel, *Oriental Despotism: A Comparative Study of Total Power* (New Haven, Conn.: Yale University Press, 1957).

The best guide to Sumerian culture is Samuel Noah Kramer, who has written several books and articles about Sumer. One of these is a popular, well-illustrated introduction, *Cradle of Civilization* (New York: Time, Inc., 1967). Kramer's list of Sumerian "firsts" appears in *History Begins at Sumer* (New York: Doubleday-Anchor Books, 1959). See also *The Sumerians: Their History, Culture, and Character* (Chicago: University of Chicago Press, 1963). All are well written.

An early, absorbing account of archaeological discovery is C. Leonard Woolley, *Ur of the Chaldees: A Record of Seven Years of Excavation* (Harmondsworth, Middlesex: Penguin Books, 1940); a later, more up-to-date version appears in *Excavations at Ur: A Record of Twelve Years' Work* (London: Ernest Benn, 1955). A learned work that deals more with the later Mesopotamian cultures (Babylonia, Assyria) than with Sumer is A. Leo Oppenheim, *Ancient Mesopotamia: Portrait of a Dead Civilization* (Chicago: University of Chicago Press, 1964). For an imaginative interpretation, contrasting the Egyptian and Mesopotamian civilizations, see Henri Frankfort, *The Birth of Civilization in the Near East* (New York: Doubleday & Co., Inc., Anchor Books, 1956).

For a brief, well-illustrated popular account, see Lionel Casson, *Ancient Egypt* (New York: Time, Inc., 1965).

A more advanced general survey is available in John A. Wilson, *The Culture of Ancient Egypt* (Chicago: University of Chicago Press, 1951).

A good general work on Indian prehistory is Stuart Piggott, *Prehistoric India to 1000 B.C.* (Harmondsworth, Middlesex: Penguin Books, 1950).

More recent surveys may be found in the following works by Mortimer Wheeler: *Early India and Pakistan, to Ashoka* (New York: Frederick A. Praeger, 1959), pp. 93–117; "Ancient India," in *The Dawn of Civilization: The First World Survey of Human Culture in Early Times,* ed. Stuart Piggott (New York: McGraw-Hill Book Co., 1961), pp. 229–52; and *Civilizations of the Indus Valley and Beyond* (New York: McGraw-Hill Book Co., 1966).

For both the Chinese Neolithic and Shang China, see Kwang-chih Chang, *The Archaeology of Ancient China* (New Haven, Conn.: Yale University Press, 1963).

For Mesoamerica, see Eric R. Wolf, *Sons of the Shaking Earth* (Chicago: University of Chicago Press, 1959).

For the Maya: Sylvanus Griswold Morley, *The Ancient Maya,* 3rd ed., rev. by George W. Brainerd (Stanford, Calif.: Stanford University Press, 1956); Michael D. Coe, *The Maya* (New York: Frederick A. Praeger, 1966).

For the Aztecs: George C. Vaillant, *The Aztecs of Mexico: Origin, Rise and Fall of the Aztec Nation* (Baltimore: Penguin Books, 1956). See also Michael D. Coe, *Mexico* (New York: Frederick A. Praeger, 1962).

For the Inca: J. Alden Mason, *The Ancient Civilizations of Peru* (Baltimore: Penguin Books, 1957); John H. Rowe, "Inca Culture at the Time of the Conquest," in *Handbook of South American Indians,* ed. Julian H. Steward, Smithsonian Institution, Bureau of American Ethnology Bulletin no. 143, vol. 2 (Washington, D.C., 1946), pp. 183–330.

Two early sources for our knowledge about the Aztecs and the Inca, respectively, that are well worth reading are: Albert Idell, ed. and trans., *The Bernal Díaz Chronicles: The True Story of the Conquest of Mexico* (New York: Doubleday & Co., Dolphin Books, 1956); *The Incas: The Royal Commentaries of the Inca, Garcilaso de la Vega,* trans. by Maria Jolas from the critical annotated French edition of Alain Gheerbrant (New York: Orion Press, 1962).

part three
The study of contemporary cultures

11

THE STUDY OF LANGUAGES

P art three deals with the varied cultures of the world today which have been described and analyzed by ethnologists. The term *culture* was discussed in chapter 1, where it was pointed out that the main medium for the transmission of culture is language. It is language that makes possible the universe of shared understanding and behavior patterns that we call culture. It is also part of culture, being transmitted from one generation to the next through learning and imitation, as are other aspects of culture. Part three, therefore, begins with a chapter on linguistics, the study of languages. But first, to get some perspective on our own complex system, let us briefly examine some aspects of communication in other animal species.

Animal communication

All animals communicate in some way in various social contexts: in mating, aggressive behavior, relations between parents and offspring, group movements, and other situations. Language is a form of communication that is uniquely human insofar as we can tell. Although the apes share our "organs of speech," as they are called, and although the apes make sounds with those organs, they do not have a language. But, like all the higher primates that live in social groups, they do communicate with one another. A special terminology has been developed for discussing communication processes, whether they be linguistic or nonlinguistic. An *addresser encodes* a *message* in a particular *code* directed through a particular channel to an *addressee* who is able to *decode* the message. The *signal* that is originated by the addresser may be distorted en route by intrusive factors, called *noise,* which the addressee must screen out sufficiently to understand the message.

Research in animal communication has been of relatively recent origin, but scientists have already learned how to at least partially break the codes

189

of several such systems. One of the best known is the way in which bees direct other members of their hive to a source of food through a circular dance. In the process, information is conveyed through various channels, not only visual but also olfactory and auditory. The duration of a whirring sound produced by the dancing bee gives information about the distance of the nectar supply, and the odor of the nectar on its wings can be smelled by the worker bees, who thus get an idea of its quality. There seem to be "dialect" differences among bees. Austrian and Italian bees can interbreed and work together if placed in the same colony, but they misinterpret one another's signals and either fly too far or not far enough in search of food.

Primates, even apart from humans, probably communicate more with one another than most animals do because of their year-round social life. Communication is involved in grooming, sexual interaction, play, and other activities carried out together.

Various channels of communication are used by the apes and monkeys. The tactile sense is important in juvenile play, in grooming, and in sexual and affectionate behavior. Sounds are produced not only by the vocal organs but also by other means, as in the chest thumping and ground slapping of the gorilla and in the tree drumming of the chimpanzee. Facial expressions, such as baring of teeth, and special postures also have communicative functions, as they do among ourselves.

The usual primate vocal repertoire of sounds seems to be limited, usually between ten and 15 sound-signal types. Ground-dwelling primates are often very quiet. Baboons make few vocal sounds, although they give warning barks in time of danger and emit various grunts, roars, and growls on occasion. But they may also remain silent for many hours at a time. Gorillas, when undisturbed, are strong, silent types. The chimpanzees, of course, are noisier.

Symbolic communication between humans and chimpanzees

Since chimpanzees are intelligent, relatively sociable, easy to work with, and vocal, some attempts have been made by human beings to teach young chimpanzees to talk, including chimps raised in a human household from an early age. These efforts have not been successful (see Hayes 1951).

There has been more success in teaching the deaf sign language in the case of a chimpanzee called Washoe to whom a husband-wife team of psychologists, Allen and Beatrice Gardner (1969), have taught a "vocabulary" of 160 items. This success is understandable, since chimpanzees use gestures in communicating with one another in their natural habitat, and they evidently find much less difficulty in comprehending and imitating human gestures than vocal sounds. The first gesture word learned by Washoe was not "mama" or "papa" but "more," a functionally useful term for a young chimp. This simian Oliver Twist often wanted to get into various closets and cupboards which were normally locked. Washoe learned to ask "open key food" to get into the refrigerator or "open key blanket" to get a blanket. Her teachers noted that she used a consistent word order when trying to get access to these places.

By using sign language with Washoe, the Gardners can compare the development of her communication with that of deaf children using sign language and with the language development of normal children. Washoe started her sign language training when she was 11 months old. The Gardners are now experimenting with younger chimpanzees who were exposed to sign language within one or two days after birth. Among those teaching these young chimps are persons who were born deaf and who can therefore use the sign language more fluently than could the Gardners at the outset of their work. Although she was a late starter, considering the rapid maturation of apes, Washoe showed linguistic productivity in combining signs in a creative fashion. Once, on seeing some swans, she named them "water birds." A similar feat by a seven-year-old female chimpanzee was to call a watermelon "drink fruit." These parallels to our own language are rather remarkable.

Washoe has now been moved to the Institute for Primate Studies in Oklahoma, where there are about a dozen chimps learning sign language. But before describing the work done there, let us consider another attempt to communicate with chimpanzees. David and Ann James Premack of the University of California at Santa Barbara have taught a young female chimpanzee, Sarah, to "read" and "write," using variously shaped and colored pieces of plastic, each of which stands for a particular word. These include not only nouns like "apple" but also verbs like "give" and abstract concepts such as "same," "different," and "name of." Incidentally, the symbol for apple is neither round nor colored red; it is represented by a blue triangle. This corresponds to the arbitrary nature of language, in which the sound of a word bears no direct relation to the named object. Although Sarah could not speak, she was able to symbolize if she accepted the convention that a blue triangle can stand for an apple. An interrogative symbol was included, so that Sarah could answer questions about whether two objects were the same or different. Sarah has a "vocabulary" of about 130 terms and uses them with a reliability of between 75 and 80 percent (Premack and Premack 1972). Although this experiment is a tribute to Sarah's intelligence, it does not permit much spontaneity or initiative on the part of the subject. Sarah could not communicate with other chimpanzees as readily as those who have learned sign language. She cannot lug around her language board and assorted plastic symbols from one chimp to another in the hope of striking up a conversation.

It is the potential spread of sign language among chimpanzees that gives significance to experiments now under way at the Institute for Primate Studies in Oklahoma. Some of the young chimpanzees who were born there have been "adopted" by human families who communicate with them through sign language. They are later introduced to others of their species on an island at the institute. The question now is how much use they will make of sign language in their mutual relations with one another.

Some interesting experiments are being planned. Some objects will be introduced to the island for which only Washoe knows the sign. The aim is to see if she teaches it to the others. Also, a mysterious new object will be brought in for which not even Washoe knows the sign. Will the chimps coin a name for it? If so, how will the new sign spread from one to another? It is hoped that Washoe will some day give birth to an infant. Then will she teach it sign language? These are among the intriguing questions for the future (Linden 1974:130–34; 151–52; 168–69).

The child's acquisition of language

Eric H. Lenneberg (1966, 1967) has argued that the basis for language capacity in human beings is probably transmitted genetically as a species-specific human ability. The development of language learning in children is a remarkably rapid and orderly process, which follows a regular sequence of events. In the second six months of life, a child begins learning words. By the age of three and a half to four years, it may be speaking 1,500 words and have an understanding of well over twice that number. But the child does not simply learn words; it also acquires a knowledge of syntax and learns to fit words into an appropriate sequence. When a child repeats its mother's sentences, it often leaves words out but retains the original word order. A careful study of the speech of two English-speaking children, aged 27 months and 18 months, showed that nouns and verbs were apt to be retained and, to a lesser degree, adjectives. The elements omitted included inflections, auxiliary verbs, articles, prepositions, and conjunctions (Brown and Bellugi 1966). There is something amazingly intelligent and creative in the child's acquistion of language. Grown-ups do not deliberately teach children rules of grammar and generally do not even have a conscious knowledge of them. But the child somehow figures out what these rules are, so that they soon become part of his or her own unconscious knowledge.

A language involves a semantic system, a phonological system, and a syntactic sytem. Perhaps the most mysterious of these is the first, the semantic system, which has to do with the essence of language: communication of meaning. How has meaning come to be associated with particular words? In general, the association between words and things seems to be arbitrary. We use the term *horse;* the French say *cheval* and the Germans *pferd.* It could hardly be argued that one of these terms is better or closer to the original than any of the others. It is true that there are onomatopoetic words like "twitter" and "moo" that seem to copy nature, but in most cases the relationship between word and meaning is arbitrary and conventional. Phonological and syntactic systems are dealt with in the field of descriptive linguistics, to which we turn next.

A basic branch of linguistics is *descriptive,* or *structural,* linguistics, which **Descriptive** analyzes the components of language. It deals with a language as a synchronic **linguistics** system, at one period of time. Descriptive linguistics is concerned with both phonology and grammar. *Historical* linguistics deals with changes in languages over time.

In analyzing a language, the linguist breaks it down into its component phonemes and morphemes.

Phonemes

A *phoneme* is a minimal sound unit that serves to distinguish one word or syllable from another for the speakers of a particular language. The English words *pit* and *bit* sound somewhat alike; the initial consonants are both bilabial stops produced with the lips, but we can tell these words apart, as we can with *pin* and *bin, pig* and *big,* and so on. English *p* and *b* are separate phonemes. But we cannot assume that they will be separate phonemes in another language, for different languages may make use of different significant sounds.

The number of phonemes in any language is limited. English contains 24 consonants, nine vowels, three semivowels, and some other features, including pitches and stresses, giving a total of 46 phonemes (Gleason 1955:50). Obviously the 26 standard letters of the English alphabet do not equate with the 46 phonemes of English speech, although some of the letters do reliably signal phonemic sound values. This is true of: *p b t d k g f v s z m n l r w y h.* Linguists have had to prepare phonetic alphabets to replace our traditional one, which is full of inconsistencies. We spell differently words that sound alike (*beat, beet; Beatle, beetle*) and spell alike words that sound differently, as in the verb and noun for *lead.* Some of our letters duplicate the work of others; *x* can be replaced by *ks* and *gz,* while the ambiguous *c* can be replaced by *k* (cat) and *s* (cent).

Linguists have devised new symbols or letters for some of our consonants, such as ð for *th* as in *then,* to be distinguished from θ for *th* as in *thin,* which is a different sound. Other symbols include: č for *ch* as in *chin,* ǰ for the initial sound in *gin;* ŋ for the terminal sound in *sing;* š for the *sh* sound in *shin,* and ž for the terminal sound in *rouge.* A system has also been developed for transcribing vowel sounds more consistently than is done in our alphabetic writing. This facilitates work in the recording, analysis, and comparison of the phonetic systems of different languages. Various schemes of phonetic transcription have been employed by linguists, but a commonly used one is the alphabet adopted by the International Phonetic Association, which makes use of the symbols given above.

There is variation in the pronunciation of the foregoing phonemes, not only on the part of different speakers but often by the same speaker as well. The *t* in *water* may be given slight emphasis in comparison to the *t* in *tin.* A *t* sound may be produced by application of the tongue tip to the ridge behind the upper gums, or it may be made with the tip of the tongue turned back, touching the palate further away from the front teeth. How the sound is made makes little difference in English, as long as a recognizable *t* sound results, and we pay little attention to such variations. But it does make a difference in Hindi, where a back *t* (which may be represented as *ṭ)* has a different phonemic significance from a front *t. Roṭi* "bread" is pronounced in this manner. Hindi also makes distinctions between front and back *d, k, n,* and *r.*

Different languages, then, may have different phonemes. English does not employ the German *ch* sound which appears in *Buch* (book). Yet English, German, and Hindi are all related languages belonging to the Indo-European language stock. Some African languages make use of suction sounds or clicks which are not found in English, German, or Hindi. So there is great variation in the phonemic systems of the languages of the world.

Phonemes do not consist of only vowel and consonant sounds but also of different kinds of pitch and stress. The Japanese word *hana* means "nose" if both syllables have the same normal pitch, but it means "beginning" if there is higher pitch on the first syllable and "flower" if there is higher pitch on the second syllable. Differences in stress in English indicate the

Side view of oral cavity, showing palate, tongue, teeth, and other organs involved in producing speech sounds.

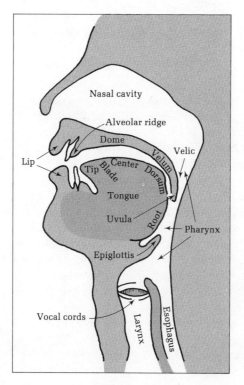

distinction between noun and verb in such words as *permit, pervert, conduct,* and *convict.*

Morphemes

While phonemes are significant units of sound, *morphemes* are significant units of meaning. A morpheme may be defined as the smallest unit that is grammatically significant. It may be a single syllable or phoneme or it may consist of several syllables.

In the sentence, "The dogs barked at the foolish clown," the words *the, at,* and *clown* are irreducible morphemes; they cannot be meaningfully subdivided. But *dogs* has two morphemes: *dog* and *-s;* the latter indicates plurality. *Barked* consists of *bark* and *-ed;* the suffix indicates past tense. The *-ish* in *foolish* is found in many adjectives like *mulish* and *boyish,* meaning to have the characteristics of a certain category. A morpheme that can stand alone, having meaning by itself, such as *dog* and *fool,* is said to be a *free morpheme,* while affixes like *-ed* and *-ish* that must be combined with a stem are said to be *bound morphemes.*

Languages differ in the extent to which words are inflected. In Chinese most words have one morpheme, while the Eskimo language makes use of many bound affixes, so that words may have ten or more morphemes. To the word *igdlo* (a house), about 80 suffixes can be added. *Igdlorssuaq* means "He builds a large house." There is one word for "When he bade him go to the place where the rather large house was to be built" (Birket-Smith 1959:62–63).

Languages may thus be analyzed with regard to the processes by which words are constructed, the morphology of the grammar.

Syntax

Languages may also be analyzed with regard to the order in which morphemes are arranged and sentences constructed. This is the study of *syntax.* In English, *Dog bites man* is different from *Man bites dog;* here the word order is crucial. It does not matter in Latin, which has different inflected forms for nominative and accusative cases, making possible either *Canis hominem mordet* or *Hominem canis mordet.* Either way, the meaning is clear. Since Chinese lacks inflection, word order is most important in that language. While this is less true of Latin, word order is still of significance in Latin and in all known languages.

As a way of discovering syntactical regularities, linguists break utterances down into *immediate constituents,* or IC's, dividing up sentences and phrases into progressively smaller units, like boxes within boxes. *The dog bit the man* is thus divided into two IC's: *The dog* and *bit the man.* The break is justified by the fact that we could substitute other phrases for *The dog* (for example, *The lion bit the man*) without changing the second segment of the sentence; we could similarly change the second segment without altering the first (*The dog barked*). Each segment may then be subdivided into its own IC's, so that the first has *The* and *dog,* while the second has *bit* and *the man,* with the latter phrase breaking up into *the* and *man.* If we analyze enough sentences in this way, we may find out what the typical constructions are in a particular language. These, of course, vary in different languages. In some, verbs come at the ends of sentences. In French, adjectives usually follow nouns rather than preceding them as in English. Some languages have articles like English *the* and *a,* while others lack them. Some languages have gender distinctions, with which the device of *concord* is associated; that is, words linked with others must have certain requisite forms. Thus, Latin *illa bella puella* (that pretty girl) or *puellarum bonarum* (of the good girls); here the adjectives agree in gender, number, and case.

Gender categories do not always concern sex. In Cree there is a distinction between animate and inanimate categories, and other sets of distinctions are made in other languages.

Transformational grammar

In 1957, Noam Chomsky, a linguist at M.I.T., published a book called *Syntactic Structures,* which has had a strong impact among linguists and has led to the formation of factions among them, including those for and against Chomsky's views. His work has been mainly in the field of syntax. He does not object to the procedures described above for analyzing syntax but holds that traditional grammars do not set forth all the laws that govern the production of utterances. There is a system in the grammar of any language that a child, simply from hearing people speak, is able to learn. His implicit grasp of the principles underlying the language is known as his *competence,* while his actual speech expression is known as his *performance.* People are not apt to be consciously aware of their linguistic competence; they speak correctly without knowing why or how. Working with a small, finite number of phonemes, a much larger but still finite number of morphemes, and some rules of syntax, the speaker of a language is able to produce an endless number of sentences, many of which may never have been spoken before. Because of his or her (largely unconscious) competence, the speaker is able to creatively generate new and varied statements, which can be understood by others with similar competence. It should be possible to specify all the rules concerning utterances in a particular language that make such communication possible. According to Chomsky, however, traditional grammars do not do this. Analyzing a language by means of the immediate constituent approach may give misleading results. For example, in the sentence "You can always tell a Harvard man, but you can't tell him much," the point of the joke lies in the ambiguity of the phrase "you can tell a Harvard man," which might mean either "You can identify a Harvard man" or "You can inform a Harvard man" (about something). IC analysis does not clarify such ambiguity. "The missionary was eaten" and "The missionary was drunk" have the same word order but carry different connotations. The first sentence is in the passive voice and could be restated in the active voice: "Someone ate the missionary." This is an example of what Chomsky calls a *transformation*. The same idea may be expressed in different ways by different grammatical means. Chomsky uses the terms *surface structure* and *deep structure*. The surface structure may be analyzed by the method of immediate constituents. To get to the deep structure one may have to make transformations, as from the passive to the active voice. The deep structure, which expresses the meaning, is common to all languages. The transformational rules that convert deep to surface structure may differ from one language to another.

Chomsky believes that children are born with a capacity to learn language, although not any particular one. Although languages differ greatly from one another, a normal child can learn any natural language to which it is exposed. Languages, then, despite their differences, share some universal features, and Chomsky believes there is such a thing as universal grammar.

There has been much debate about these ideas. How useful is the concept of deep structure? Can't we get along without it? What does it mean to say that children have a language-learning capacity? It must be so, in some sense, since they do learn to speak, but does this notion tell us anything new?

Chomsky believes his views show up the weakness of empiricist ideas in philosophy and behavioristic concepts in psychology about the acquisition of language. The empiricist and behaviorist traditions hold that the mind of a newborn child is a blank slate that has no knowledge before experience. Knowledge comes from experience, from stimulus-response conditioning, and from the association of ideas. Chomsky believes that the learning of language by children cannot adequately be explained along these lines. What children hear spoken around them consists of fragmentary bits of language, often incorrect. They learn to speak before their general intellectual faculties are developed. Besides, all children learn to speak, both the smart and the stupid ones. It cannot be, Chomsky asserts, that the mind is a blank slate at birth; the child's brain must be programmed for language-learning. These, at any rate, are some of the issues concerning transformational grammar, about which there is still a good deal of disagreement.

In the late 18th century, it was discovered that Sanskrit, the language brought into India by the Aryans around 1500 B.C., was related to Greek and Latin and to the Romance and Germanic languages of Europe. This was shown by many correspondences in grammar and vocabulary. The term *Indo-European* was applied to this widespread linguistic stock. A school of comparative philology that developed in the 19th century devised some methods of analysis of these Indo-European languages; these could later be applied to linguistic stocks in other parts of the world.

Historical linguistics

Some examples of *cognate* words, which have both phonemic and semantic correspondences in Sanskrit, Greek, and Latin, are shown in the accompanying table.

	Father sky god	Sheep	Foot
Sanskrit	Dyaus pitar	avis	pat
Greek	Zeus pater	ouis	pous
Latin	Jupiter	ovis	pes

These correspondences give us more than purely linguistic information; they also tell us something about the culture of early Indo-Europeans, suggesting that they believed in a male sky god and kept sheep. We will come back to such cultural implications later, but first let us consider some purely linguistic features.

Notice that the words for *foot* and *father* begin with *p* in all three languages, while in German and English they start with *f.* Similarly, Latin *piscis* has become English *fish.* In the course of time, the initial Indo-European *p* in these and several other words became *f* in Germanic languages. This sound shift, along with several others, was first discovered by Jakob Grimm in 1822. The shift from *p* to *f* occurred long ago, judging from the earliest available texts in Germanic languages. For example, a sixth-century Gothic manuscript has *fadar* for *father.* An Old English ninth-century text has *feder;* in an Old Saxon ninth-century manuscript we have *fader,* and an Old High German text from the ninth century yields *fater.* From the comparative analysis of these cognate forms, it has been deduced that the primitive Germanic prototype form was *fader* (Bloomfield 1933:303).

Through the same kind of analysis, the probable forms of much earlier Proto-Indo-European words have been ferreted out, giving us some of the vocabulary of the earliest common stock from which later Indo-European languages developed. A knowledge of the direction of sound shifts facilitates such analysis.

Reconstructions from linguistic data

Scholars have tried to figure out, from the vocabularies of Indo-European languages, where the speakers of the early common stock were located. The noun and verb for *snow* are found so often in Indo-European languages that it seems unlikely they came from India. Moreover, there are no Proto-Indo-European words for elephant, tiger, monkey, or fig tree. Nor are they likely to have originated in Iran or the Mediterranean region, since there are no Proto-Indo-European words for camel, donkey, lion, olive, vine, or cypress. There are, however, words for some domesticated animals: dog, cattle, sheep, horse, pig, goat; and for many wild ones: wolf, bear, fox, stag, hare, mouse, snake, hedgehog, turtle, otter, beaver, salmon, eagle, fal-

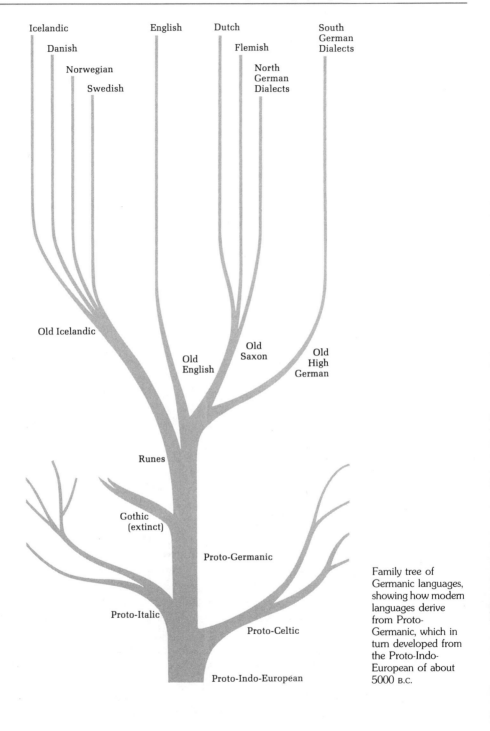

Family tree of Germanic languages, showing how modern languages derive from Proto-Germanic, which in turn developed from the Proto-Indo-European of about 5000 B.C.

con, owl, crane, thrush, goose, duck, fly, hornet, wasp, bee, louse, and flea. The fauna suggest a northerly area, which fits in with the words for plants and trees: barley, birch, beech, aspen, oak, yew, willow, fir, spruce, and alder.

Since turtles are not found in Scandinavia, that area can be ruled out. The homeland seems to have been south of the Baltic Sea. Salmon are found only in rivers that flow into the Baltic and North seas, including the Vistula, Oder, and Elbe. Hence, Paul Thieme (1964) has concluded that the early Indo-European homeland area was in the domain of the salmon rivers and their tributaries, west of the "beech line" outside of Scandinavia, south of the Baltic Sea.

Thieme's reconstruction sounds convincing and may be right, but it should be noted that some other scholars, reasoning along other lines, have located the homeland of the early Indo-Europeans in the steppes of southern Russia and the lands eastward to the Caspian Sea (Piggott 1950:248).

Bloomfield (1933:321) has deduced some residence and social patterns from the linguistic data. Indo-European languages have terms for a woman's relatives by marriage (husband's brother and sister) but not for a man's relatives by marriage. From this he concluded that patrilocal residence was customary, (the residence of a married couple with or near the husband's kinsmen).

Language and cognition

Comparisons have sometimes been made between language and culture. Both establish "rules" about how things should be done, but these rules are not always followed in practice. One may speak ungrammatically if one wishes, although it sometimes defeats one's own purpose in communicating to do so. Both language and culture are restricting in some ways and liberating in others. Each provides a map, a book of rules, and a shared understanding with others; each provides the individual with a particular set of lenses through which to see reality.

All languages classify the objects of the surrounding world in some way, but there are many possible ways in which that may be done. Several 19th-century theorists who were intrigued to learn that some "primitive" peoples lack distinguishing terms for green and blue or blue and black concluded from this that such people must be deficient in color vision. But in 1877 an investigation of some Nubians, who used the same word for both blue and black, showed that they were able to sort out blue and black yarn and blue and black pieces of paper. They could clearly tell the difference, although their language did not assign different words to these colors. The color spectrum has continuous gradations, and there are many ways of dividing it up. The Navaho have a word that covers a range from green through blue to purple, while the Zuñi have a term that includes both orange and yellow. Cultures differ in the numbers of colors differentiated. Our own language is rich in color terms, partly through the influence of the fashion business and traditions of the arts. The largest collection of English color terms has over 3,000 entries, although only about eight terms are commonly used. Some languages, on the other hand, have only three color terms, generally corresponding to our black, white, and red.

In all languages there are names for plants, animals, and other aspects of the environment, and different languages may have quite different ways of classifying them.

Cognitive anthropologists use the phrase *semantic domain* to refer to a class of objects that share some characteristic feature or features that differentiate them from other domains. For example, furniture is a domain that includes chairs, sofas, desks, and tables but not sandwiches or parakeets. Items of furniture can be classed in hierarchic fashion to form a *taxonomy,* so that tables, for example, may be subdivided into end tables, dining tables, and so on (Tyler 1969:7–8). Items in lower levels of this classification, such as end tables, are kinds of items in higher levels, such as tables and furniture. There are other kinds of semantic arrangements that do not follow a system of hierarchic ordering. Cognitive anthropologists investigate the principles of organization and classification in the languages they study. If the principles of classification in another language differ from those in our own, we cannot conclude, as some 19th-century writers did, that the language is inferior to ours. It is only recently that we have come to realize how complex some "primitive" classifications are. Claude Lévi-Strauss's work, *The Savage Mind,* documents this very well. With regard to plants, he writes (1966a:5):

A single Seminol informant could identify two hundred and fifty species and varieties of plants (Sturtevant). Three hundred and fifty plants known to the Hopi Indians and more than five hundred to the Navaho have been recorded. The botanical vocabulary of the Subanun of the Southern Philippines greatly exceeds a hundred terms (Frake) and that of the Hanunóo approaches two thousand.

Lévi-Strauss (1966a:5) quotes R. B. Fox to the effect that: "Most Negrito men can with ease enumerate the specific or descriptive names of at least four hundred and fifty plants, seventy-five birds, most of the snakes, fish, insects, and animals, and of even twenty species of ants. . . ."

Summary

All animals communicate in some way in the processes of mating, aggressive behavior, relations between parents and offspring, group movements, and other situations. Various channels of communication are used by our closest relatives, the apes, monkeys, and other primates—through the tactile sense (in grooming, sexual and affectionate behavior), through sounds (calls, cries, chest thumping, tree drumming), baring of teeth and other facial expressions, and special postures. The primate vocal repertoire is usually limited to between about ten and 15 sound-signal types.

Although we also use such channels of communication, human beings have added to them the unique symbolic communication of language which makes human culture possible. We can communicate about events and things not present or visible, including abstract concepts.

All languages are structured and contain phonemes, morphemes, and rules of syntax, features which are analyzed in the branch of linguistics known as descriptive or structural linguistics. Descriptive linguistics deals with languages as synchronic systems, at one period of time, in contrast to historical linguistics, which deals with changes in language over time.

Interest in the relationship between language and cognition has led to the development of a special field of research known as cognitive anthropology or ethnoscience. Its purpose is to uncover the taxonomic principles of particular languages. The investigator questions informants to find out what categories exist in their language. It is hoped that in this way the anthropological linguist acquires some sense of how the native speakers construe the world in which they live.

Suggestions for further reading

A classic work is Leonard Bloomfield, *Language* (New York: Henry Holt & Co., 1933). See also Charles F. Hockett, *A Course in Modern Linguistics* (New York: Macmillan Co., 1958); H. A. Gleason, Jr., *An Introduction to Descriptive Linguistics* (New York: Henry Holt & Co., 1955).

Good collections of readings are available in Dell Hymes, ed., *Language in Culture and Society: A Reader in Linguistics and Anthropology* (New York: Harper & Row, Publishers, Inc., 1964); and also in Eric H. Lenneberg, ed., *New Directions in the Study of Language* (Cambridge, Mass.: M.I.T. Press, 1966).

For Chomsky's views, see Noam Chomsky, *Syntactic Structures* (The Hague: Mouton, 1957), and *Chomsky: Selected Readings,* ed. J. P. B. Allen and Paul van Buren (London: Oxford University Press, 1971).

For a thoughtful essay, see John Searle, "Chomsky's Revolution in Linguistics," *The New York Review,* June 29, 1972, pp. 16–24.

On cognitive anthropology, see Stephen A. Tyler, ed., *Cognitive Anthropology* (New York: Holt, Rinehart & Winston, 1969).

On communication between chimpanzees and humans, see Eugene Linden, *Apes, Men, and Language* (New York: Saturday Review Press, E. P. Dutton and Co., Inc., 1974).

12

ENVIRONMENT, TECHNOLOGY, PRODUCTION, AND DISTRIBUTION

E cology is the study of the interrelationship of organisms and their environment, including both the physical environment and other living organisms. Human adaptation to the environment involves the sphere of culture, not only with regard to technology but also patterns of social organization that may facilitate or inhibit economic cooperation, community size, and the spacing of social units. Like other animals, human beings must adapt to their environments. Unlike most animals, however, humans also create new environments in which to live, although this is also true of some other creatures, such as bees, ants, termites, and also beavers and other animals that have self-constructed dwellings. The artificial environments humans have constructed have taken many forms, the most extraordinary being the modern megalopolis, the huge termitary of present-day *Homo sapiens.*

Being warm-blooded mammals, equipped with cultural means of coping with nature, human beings have been able to adjust to a great variety of environments, including even polar lands. The food resources available in these different regions show great variation. One aspect of human adaptability has been the accommodation of our intestinal tract to a wide range of foods. We can be either vegetarians or carnivores, or both.

Human communities must cope not only with nature in all its manifestations but also with other human communities that appear within their living space. There are various solutions to such encounters: mutual avoidance, reciprocal exchange, trade, and warfare.

The population size of a community is influenced by the nature of the terrain, level of subsistence, type of technology, and the population policy of its members. The latter may include such features as female infanticide, birth-control practices, and postpartum sex taboos, among others. If a group's adjustment to its environment is successful, population increase is apt to

203

result, although it may be held in check by the population policies just mentioned and by diseases, epidemics, wars, and other disasters.

Geographical environments

Let us now consider some of the kinds of environments in which human beings have lived and the different potentialities these environments may have for the development of human culture.

Preston E. James (1959) has drawn up a classification of environments based upon vegetation and surface features, which some anthropologists have found useful. In James's scheme there are eight general types: Dry Lands, Tropical Forest Lands, Mediterranean Scrub Forest Lands, Mid-Latitude Mixed Forest Lands, Grasslands, Boreal Forest Lands, Polar Lands, and Mountain Lands.

Dry Lands consist of the arid regions or deserts that occupy similar positions on all the continents, on the west coasts, roughly between 20 degrees and 30 degrees both north and south of the equator. Deserts occupy about 18 percent of the land surface of the earth but, due to shortage of water, hold only about 4 percent of the world's population. Completely waterless sections are unoccupied. Oasis regions in deserts, however, provide very favorable environments, permitting greater densities of population. The Nile Valley has more than 1,700 people per square mile. The Bronze Age civilizations of the Old World developed in such areas, in Egypt, Mesopotamia, and the Indus Valley.

Tropical Forest Lands consist of tropical, semideciduous forests, rainforests and scrub forests found in a belt within 20 degrees latitude on either side of the equator, generally extending toward the poles along the eastern sides of the continents. Tropical Forest Lands vary greatly in population density. The Amazon-Orinoco basin, which is the largest of the Tropical Forest Land areas, is very sparsely settled, but Java and other parts of Southeast Asia have some of the denser populations of the world. Tropical Forest Lands include about 15 percent of the world's land area and about 28 percent of the world's population. The tropical forests do not supply good food resources except for societies that have developed advanced techniques of food production. However, some advanced civilizations developed in Tropical Forest Lands regions, as in Cambodia, Indonesia, and in the lowland Maya area.

Mediterranean Scrub Forest Lands include not only the lands bordering on the Mediterranean Sea but also areas with similar climates elsewhere in mid-latitude regions on the west coasts of continents between about 30 degrees and 40 degrees north and south latitude. Parts of California, Chile, South Africa, and Australia are included.

These regions, which have mild, rainy winters and hot, dry summers, are usually hedged in between mountains and seacoast. They have broadleaf evergreen scrub forests; oaks and chestnuts are common. Only about 1 percent of the earth's land surface falls into this category, but it holds about 4 percent of the world's population.

Mediterranean Scrub Forest Lands are easy to live in for human beings at any level of culture. Many wild fruits and nuts and small game are available, and the weather is mild. California was densely populated by hunting-gathering tribes before the coming of Europeans. Early centers of civilization developed in Israel, Greece, and Italy. Evidently this kind of environment is very favorable for human occupation, although only a small percentage of the world's people inhabits such areas.

In contrast to the foregoing, two fifths of the world's population live in Mid-Latitude Mixed Forest Lands, which make up 7 percent of the world's land area. This is an environment containing mixed broadleaf and coniferous forests, with plenty of rain and seasonal alterations of winter and summer. Areas near the sea may have relatively mild climates; those in the centers of continents have stronger seasonal ups and downs in temperature.

One region embraces eastern North America, including Canada's Saint Lawrence Valley. Another includes most of Europe north of the Mediterranean zone and south of the boreal forests. Here the trees, climate, and other features have much in common with those of eastern North America. Most of China north of the tropical forests and south of the northern and western plains falls into the same category, as does much of Korea and Japan.

This kind of environment, although heavily populated now, was sparsely settled in earlier times. Its occupation depended upon the development of adequate technology for cutting down the forest cover for agriculture and for keeping warm in cold winters.

Grasslands, which occupy zones between forests and deserts, have the advantage of containing much game for hunters, and they also lend themselves to occupation by pastoral nomadic or seminomadic herdsmen. Like the Mid-Latitude Mixed Forest Lands, their occupation depends upon the introduction of advanced technology; they have only recently been invaded on a large scale in different parts of the world. Their present percentage of the world's population is still low, perhaps around 6 percent or more, although the Grasslands cover about 19 percent of the earth's surface.

Boreal Forest Lands stretch across the Northern Hemisphere north of the Mixed Forest Lands and Grasslands. This is an area of very cold winters and short, cool summers. Rainfall is sparse, but little evaporation takes place, and there are many lakes, rivers, and swamps. Such environments are found in large parts of Scandinavia, Siberia, Alaska, and Canada. Boreal Forest Lands provide a difficult environment for humans at any level of culture. They cover 10 percent of the earth's land area but have only 1 percent of the world's population.

Polar Lands are those that lie at the northern and southern axes of the earth, including glaciated regions, polar deserts, and tundras. Although flowers bloom during the short summer, the summer is too short to allow the growth of forests. Wood is in short supply. The absence of vegetables forces the Eskimos who inhabit the northern Polar Lands to rely largely on animal food, in contrast to most other hunting-gathering people for whom vegetable foods make up the bulk of the diet. This is obviously a very difficult environment for human beings to cope with. Polar Lands cover 16 percent of the earth's surface but hold only a handful of human beings.

Mountain Lands differ from the preceding categories that are distinguished by types of vegetation; here, the main criterion is surface configuration. Mountains have different types of vegetation and climate at different levels of altitude.

Mountains cover about 12 percent of the earth's land area and hold about 12 percent of its population. The suitability of mountains for occupation depends upon where they are located. Those in low or low-medium latitudes provide good opportunities for exploitation of the environment. Wood and minerals are apt to be available.

Mountains have often served an important role as barriers. For example, the high barrier of the Himalayas has served to wall off India from the cultures of the north and east to a considerable degree. For this reason, mountain passes are important strategic points, trade and fighting units making their way through pass routes. Some of the other types of environments we have examined, such as deserts and tropical forests, may also serve as barriers, as do oceans and other large bodies of water in the absence of adequate means of navigation.

It is evident from the foregoing survey that some environments are more favorable for the development of culture than others. Much of the earth's surface is not suitable for human occupation. One of the astronauts who returned from the third Skylab space mission in 1974 remarked that, when seen from outer space, much of the earth looks bare and empty and that human beings are crowded into quite small areas on its surface.

The way in which a human group adapts to a particular environment is not determined by its geographical features alone but is also influenced by the technology characteristic of the group and by the way in which the group is organized to exploit the environment. To illustrate this point with a particular region, the American Southwest was first occupied by sparse nomadic, hunting-gathering bands. Later, Pueblo Indians, such as the Hopi and Zuñi, developed an agricultural way of life living in permanent, closely packed communities. Still later, the Spaniards appeared on the scene with horses, guns, and metal tools. Each of these groups had its own particular equipment for coping with the environment and winning a livelihood from it. And the present-day inhabitants of the same region, with electricity, air-conditioning, automobiles, and other modern conveniences, lead a still different way of life.

Culture areas   The Preston James classification just reviewed is made up of large general types of environments. Somewhat similar were the ten or so *culture areas* into which anthropologists Clark Wissler (1926) and A. L. Kroeber (1939) divided aboriginal North America. Both noted that different cultural configu-

Culture area map of
North America.

rations were associated with particular geographical regions and food resources, such as the Northwest Coast salmon area, the California wild-seeds area, and the Plains bison area. Neither Wissler nor Kroeber were geographical or environmental determinists, but they saw environments as setting limits on cultural potentialities. Melville J. Herskovits (1962) also made use of the culture-area concept in describing the cultures of Africa.

In practice, particular human groups often adjust to environmental settings that cannot be characterized as broadly as "Grasslands" or "Desert." Fredrik Barth (1956) has shown that three ethnic groups in the small state of Swat in northwestern Pakistan have adjusted to different ecological *niches* within that area. One group consists of sedentary agriculturalists, another of nomadic herders, while a third combines both agriculture and pastoralism. Each group has an economic and political organization that helps it exploit

Culture areas of Africa, indicated by heavy lines. Broken lines show political frontiers established under European colonial control.

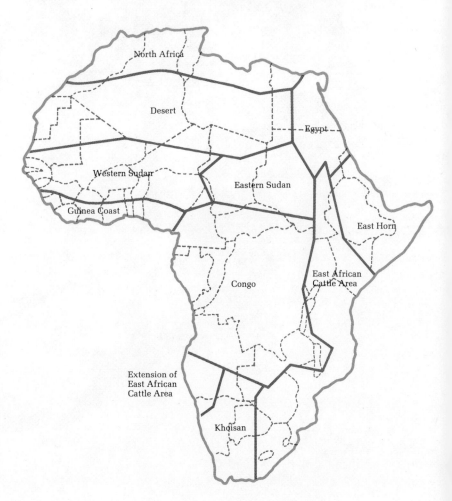

its particular niche; sometimes, there are also symbiotic relations between these groups.

Each human society, then, exploits a particular environment with a particular technological apparatus. Our early ancestors first lived in a tropical forest environment, later moving out into savannas, or tropical grasslands. About 700,000 years ago, humans explored Mediterranean Scrub Forests and the Mid-Latitude Mixed Forests of the Old World, having acquired fire and the use of tools, which helped them withstand the cold weather of the European forests and of northern China.

In the chapters that follow there will be frequent reference to four types of societies that appeared in evolutionary sequence: hunting-gathering, horticultural, agricultural, and industrial. In the present chapter we will consider the following questions with regard to each of these types of economy: How is food obtained and with what sort of technology? How are population size and density affected by this system? What is the composition of social groups engaged in food acquisition and production? How has the system affected the environment? What are the advantages and limitations of this system?

Hunting-gathering societies

Hunting-gathering groups usually have a limited inventory of tools. They often move from place to place, and it is incovenient to be burdened with possessions. There are exceptions among some hunting-gathering societies: the Indians of the northwest coast of North America, for example, had permanent village sites and a rather elaborate technology. But generally the technology is rather simple; tools can often be made on the spot, when required. Traps are used by many hunting people, although there are some, such as the Vedda of Sri Lanka and the Chenchu of southern India, who did not have any traps or snares at all.

In hunting-gathering societies the main division of labor is between the sexes. The men do the hunting, while the women do most of the gathering, which often means digging for roots and tubers with digging sticks. Such food, rather than meat, tends to make up the bulk of the diet in hunting-gathering societies. To collect seeds, nuts, or fruits, they also need some sort of container. Bags, baskets, and nets are made in many such societies. The Australian aborigines have shallow bark or wooden traylike devices for carrying. The Indians of the Great Basin had skin bags for storing grass seeds. The Bushmen use ostrich eggshells for carrying water. In some such societies good basketry is made, the most impressive being that of the Indians of California, who were able to make watertight baskets in which food could be cooked by dropping in hot stones. Plains Indians used folded leather containers (parfleches) to carry food and other things. Some hunting-gathering peoples, including Eskimos, have used pottery containers, but pottery does not lend itself well to a nomadic way of life.

Since hunting people often deal with skins, leather is often used for

Australian aborigines had a simple hunting-gathering technology, making use of spear, spear-thrower, and boomerang but lacking bow and arrow.

clothing and in making tents and boats. The buffalo hunters of the western Plains made great use of the buffalo's products, including the hide.

When collecting wild seeds and grains attains special importance, as it did in the broad-spectrum food exploitation of Mesolithic times, particular implements for reaping wild grains may be developed, such as the Natufian sickles of the Near East, along with grinding stones for crushing seeds and grain.

There is apt to be a relationship between the kinds of animals hunted and the social organization of hunting bands. Herding animals can be hunted communally, while solitary animals, like the moose, are best hunted by a single hunter. Buffalos were hunted communally by Plains Indians like the Cheyenne, who had rules against individual bison hunting during the summer-camp period.

Although bands that hunt herding animals like buffalo may become sizable, hunting societies usually do not maintain large year-round populations. Often there are seasonal splittings and later recombinations of bands, as occurred in both Plains and Woodland American Indian tribes. Among the Canadian Chippewa or Ojibwa there was a winter dispersal to take maximum advantage of food resources. It was the other way around among the Central

Eskimo. Winter, when seals were hunted, was the social time for congregation into groups of 100 to 150 persons. In summer they split up into groups of between 15 and 30 for fishing and hunting caribou.

The dry winter season is a time of congregation for South African Bushman groups, which sometimes number over 100. This coming-together involves more work and energy expenditure for the members. When they split up into smaller units of 20 or 30, less work is demanded. The excitement of social life and initiation ceremonies makes congregation into larger units worthwhile for the members, and yet new stresses are placed upon them at these times, for it is then that quarrels and murders most often take place. The break-up into quieter, smaller units also has its psychological rewards (Lee 1972). It used to be thought that hunting-gathering peoples were generally uncertain and anxious about the food supply, but more recent studies have shown that this is usually not the case. Two or three hours of work may produce enough food for a day, although there may also be difficult times in some such societies. Marshall Sahlins (1972) has gone so far as to call hunting-gathering groups "the original affluent society," because of their easily satisfied needs and abundant leisure. He claims that starvation is much more common in the world today than it was during the Stone Age. In recent times, at any rate, the hunting-gathering Chenchu of southern India were probably more secure and better fed than many of the agricultural villagers of India: "To wake in the morning with no food in the house does not disturb him in the least. He proceeds leisurely to the jungle to collect roots and fruits, . . . returns to the village in the evening to share with his family all that he has brought home" (von Fürer-Haimendorf 1943:57). No food is stored; all is eaten right away, as is often the case among hunting-gathering peoples. Richard B. Lee, who made a study of subsistence patterns in a Bushman group in South Africa, reports that food is almost always consumed within the local group and within 48 hours of its collection (Lee 1966).

It might seem that a hunting-gathering system is insecure, vulnerable to the disappearance of game and other resources; but human beings lived this way for more than 2 million years, and hunting-gathering is still a viable system in bleak marginal areas like the Kalahari Desert in South Africa. Within a particular region, however, the system may be threatened by population growth, requiring dispersal or adoption of a broad-spectrum exploitation of food resources.

It was noted earlier, in Chapter 8, that some anthropologists believe that over-hunting by North American big-game hunters resulted in the extinction of many species of mammals. It has also been suggested that early hunters encouraged the spread of grasslands and drove back forests through brush fires that were either set off accidentally or deliberately started in animal drives (Stewart 1956).[1]

---

[1] For a description of life in a particular hunting-gathering society, the Central Eskimo, see pages 267–68, below.

Horticultural societies

An early and still widespread form of food production is *swidden cultivation,* or slash-and-burn horticulture. This process involves clearing a patch of land by burning, planting crops and tending them for a year or more, and then abandoning the plot to lie fallow so that its fertility may be restored and the land used again later. Swidden cultivation is usually done on a small scale, often with plots of an acre or less.

In simple horticultural societies, sowing and planting are done with a digging stick used to punch a hole in the earth through the ashes to plant seeds. In forest conditions, with short periods of cultivation, there are not apt to be many weeds. Hence the main work involved is the initial clearing of the land. Not much time need be spent in preparing the soil, weeding, or manuring, as in more advanced forms of agriculture. Simple horticulturalists, like hunters, can enjoy ample leisure time—another version of the origi-

Woman planting taro in New Hebrides.

nal affluent society. Labor units need not be large when working the fields. A husband and wife can work together, or there can be other small working groups.

In different parts of the world, horticulture has facilitated permanent residence, even though fields have to be periodically abandoned to lie fallow when they become worn out. The population density in horticultural societies tends to be low, with settlements usually having less than 250 people. There is a centrifugal tendency in the need to clear new land and occasionally shift residence. However, chieftainships and kingdoms developed in many advanced horticultural societies, as among the lowland Maya, in Cambodia, Indonesia, and the African kingdoms of Uganda and Dahomey (see p. 305).

It is sometimes alleged that slash-and-burn horticulture is a wasteful form of cultivation, laying bare hillsides and destroying vegetation. While this may often be the case, it is not an inherent evil of the system. Von Fürer-Haimendorf has contrasted two neighboring tribes in India's North-East Frontier from this point of view: the Daflas and the Apa Tani. "Daflas will ruin a whole tract of country by the unregulated felling and burning of forest and then move on, leaving a treeless, desolate wilderness with the fertility of the soil exhausted and the hill slopes covered in useless grass too coarse even for fodder" (von Fürer-Haimendorf 1956:62). The Apa Tani, however, practice a form of conservation, introduce foreign plants into their valley, and have fenced-in groves in which they plant pines, bamboo, and fruit trees. No wasteful plants are allowed to grow. The Apa Tani valley is described as being a carefully tended garden.

A swidden system works well as long as there is plenty of forestland in relation to population; but, as population grows, pressure on the land resources is increased. One solution to this problem is to shorten the fallow period, but this may require more preparation of the soil before sowing. "Thus, the hoe is not introduced just as a technical perfection of the digging stick. It is introduced, typically, when an additional operation becomes necessary, i.e., when forest fallow is replaced by bush fallow" (Boserup 1965:24).

Advanced horticultural societies, then, have more efficient tools than simple horticultural societies, including hoes with separate handle and blade. Horticulture is still widely practiced in many parts of the world, in India, the Congo, the Amazon, Oceania, and among peasants in Mexico and Southeast Asia. It is clearly a viable system of food production; but, following Boserup's view, it is vulnerable to population increase, which leads to reduction of the fallow period and eventual adoption of intensive agriculture.[2]

As the period of fallow is reduced, with the increase of population, the introduction of a plow becomes useful in cutting through weed-infested, **Agricultural societies**

---

[2] For a description of a particular horticultural society, the Mundurucú of Brazil, see page 269.

grassy soil, which may also require the help of fertilizer, like manure, and the introduction of irrigation to remain productive.

The peasant is the food producer in this system. A peasant differs from a tribesman who raises crops in having a dependent relationship to the city and the state. "We see peasants as a peripheral but essential part of civilization, producing the food that makes urban life possible, supporting (and subject to) the specialized classes of political and religious rulers and other members of the educated elite" (Foster 1967:6). The peasant differs from a modern farmer in being less of a businessman concerned with profit, although peasants are often known to be shrewd in their transactions. According to the Russian economist A. V. Chayanov, the fundamental characteristic of a peasant economy is that it is a family economy; peasant food production is a family enterprise concerned with subsistence rather than profit and makes no use of hired labor. The peasant who switches to cash crops, employs hired labor, and seeks to expand through reinvestment ceases to be a peasant and becomes a farmer (Chayanov 1966; see also E. R. Wolf 1966).

The peasants' primary concern with their own families does not keep them from involvement with others, although a state of "amoral familism" has been described for some Italian peasant communities in which interfamily cooperation is rare and each family is concerned mainly with its own interests (Banfield 1958).

In societies having irrigation the agriculturalists who draw upon the same water resources are brought into a necessary relationship with one another, and the nature of their work is influenced by the irrigation process. "Irrigation agriculture requires a rowlike arrangement of the seeds not only for crops such as corn and potatoes but also for cereals. Plants can be watered by ditches only if proper space for the distributing furrows is provided" (Wittfogel 1956:158). An orderly system of this kind involves more work than the earlier form of horticulture. The soil may be plowed or harrowed several times before being sown. However, the result is a very productive form of food production. Induced by population increase, according to Boserup (1965), intensive agriculture encourages still further increase and greater population density.

Agricultural technology and sources of energy

Besides the plow, an important invention associated with agriculture in the Old World was the wheel, used in the peasant's cart and also the potter's wheel of Bronze Age times. Another early application of this principle, in the first millennium B.C., was the water-raising wheel, a vertical wheel equipped with buckets or pots that lifted water for irrigation purposes. Still another application of this basic invention was the spinning wheel. The useful potentialities of the wheel were not discovered in the New World, although small wheeled objects, evidently used as toys, have been found in Mexico.

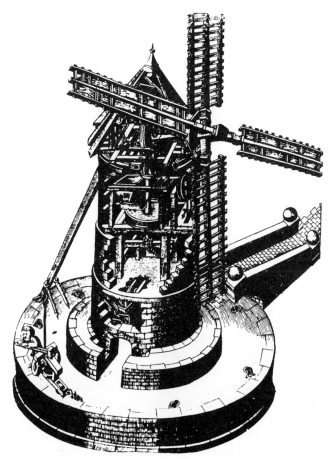

Corn-grinding tower
mill from a 16th
century drawing.

Another important feature of advanced agriculture in the Old World was
the exploitation of animal energy, which began in Neolithic times. This
was not limited to plowing, threshing, and pulling carts. Many peasants
and farmers make use of animal energy in drawing water for irrigation,
with camels, oxen, or donkeys going round and round or back and forth
on an inclined plane. Some time after 200 B.C. oxen were used to provide
the power for water-raising wheels by walking round and round a vertical
shaft. Donkeys were similarly employed even earlier to keep rotary querns
or mills in operation.[3]

Power was also derived from wind and water in the Old World. Windmills

---

[3] A significant improvement in the exploitation of animal power was the invention of the
modern harness which replaced the less efficient form known to the Romans. The improved
harness appeared first in China between the third and seventh centuries A.D. and in Europe
from the ninth century on. At about the same time, the practice of shoeing horses was introduced
in Europe. These two improvements together greatly increased the utility of horses and led
to their replacing oxen in agricultural work in Europe.

and waterwheels were used for irrigation and grinding grain. Windmills proliferated in Holland in the 16th century A.D. and thereafter, since the Low Countries are flat and their streams too sluggish to provide good waterpower. But windmills were also used in France and in Spain, where Don Quixote tilted against them. Their main function was to grind grain, but they were also used for sawing wood and raising water.

In Roman times the waterwheel was used only for grinding grain, but from the 11th century on it was also used for fulling cloth, making pulp for paper, raising water for irrigation, and other purposes. Waterwheels were not used much in Roman times, since the availability of slaves (an alternative source of power) made the laborsaving advantages of inanimate power unnecessary; there was large-scale unemployment in the Roman Empire, and laborsaving machinery would only have added to the difficulty. But during the Middle Ages, when the institution of slavery had declined, the advantages of waterwheels and windmills could be appreciated, and they came into their own. Thus, under advanced agriculture, much more energy became available to the food producer than was possible under previous systems.

Types of peasant communities

Peasant communities have assumed many forms in different parts of the world, and various ways of classifying subtypes have been suggested. Eric Wolf has made a distinction between closed corporate peasant communities and open peasant communities. In a closed community membership is restricted to people born and raised within it, and marriages usually take place within the group. There is corporate control over the land, which may not be sold to outsiders. Leveling mechanisms often exist to equalize conditions within the community, such as periodic reallotments of land. Open peasant communities are more involved in cash crops and marketing and the national culture. There is no communal jurisdiction over land in the open communities. In Latin America, closed corporate communities are found in marginal highland areas, while the open communities are located in the lowlands. The corporate communities make use of a traditional technology and tend to be poor. Wolf finds that closed corporate societies with features like those of Latin America are also found in central Java. While closed corporate communities may be seen as traditional holdovers, they also represent self-protective reactions on the part of peasants to outside pressure in colonial regions (E. R. Wolf 1955, 1957, 1966).

Patterns of exchange labor not involving money payments are common among peasants. Charles J. Erasmus (1956) has described two types: festive labor and exchange labor. The former type involves feasting a work crew assembled for a task, such as house building or harvesting, with perhaps more than ten workers, or even more than 100. Exchange labor is a simple matter of reciprocal exchange. A agrees to work for B, expecting that B will later work a roughly similar amount for him. Exchange labor involves

The major peasant regions of the world.

smaller work gangs than festive labor, seldom more than ten men. These patterns are not so popular as they once were, for the acquisition of farm machinery such as threshing machines obviates some of the need for collective work, while rising food prices tend to make wage labor cheaper than festive labor.

Like horticulture, intensive agriculture has sometimes had deleterious effects on the environment, particularly in the destruction of forests because of population increase, the need for more fields, and also because of demands for timber in house construction, fuel, and other purposes. The heavily populated Indo-Gangetic plain in northern India and Pakistan was once forested but is now relatively bare of trees. The same sort of deforestation occurred in ancient China and was responsible for the annual floods that have plagued northern China ever since. Parts of North Africa that supplied the ancient Romans with grain have become desiccated and semidesert. Central Italy itself lost its forests, which resulted in flooding, as in China.

Industrial societies with factory production are consequences of the Industrial Revolution, which developed in England during the last third of the 18th century. This was partly the result of tapping a new source of energy.

Waterpower was used in the early stages of the Industrial Revolution in England to provide the energy for cotton mills. This meant that these

Industrial societies

factories were not located in towns or cities but beside streams near hills in narrow valleys.

The disadvantage of the waterwheel was that it had to be located by a stream. In 18th-century England there was a search for new sources of power, largely to find ways of pumping water out of the deep coal mines that were then being exploited. Several attempts to build a workable steam engine were made before James Watt produced an improved model. This engine was used not only in the mines but later in railways and steamboats as well. Now factories could be built away from streams and near coal mines and also near the cities where a labor force and markets were available. Lewis Mumford (1934:161–62) has discussed some of the sociological consequences of this change:

Wind and water were free; but coal was expensive and the steam engine itself was a costly investment; so, too, were the machines that it turned. Twenty-four-hour operations, which characterized the mine and the blast furnace, now came into other industries which had hitherto respected the limitations of day and night.

The working day was often lengthened to 16 hours.

Manning Nash (1966:23) has written that in primitive and peasant societies, the

. . . social organization carrying out the making of goods or the tendering of services is dependent on and derived from other sets of social relations. Peasant and primitive societies do not have organizations whose only tasks are those of production, and there are no durable social units based solely on productive activities.

A peasant family household may be a unit of economic production. Among the Tiv of Nigeria a *kraal* is a basic unit of production, representing a local segment of a lineage. Such units do not exist for production alone but have many other functions and purposes.

In the cottage industry of 18th-century Yorkshire, woolen goods were sometimes produced by family units. Paul Mantoux (1961:58) writes: "If the weaver's family was large enough it did everything, its members dividing all the minor operations amongst themselves—the wife and daughters at the spinning wheel, the boys carding the wool, while the man worked the shuttle." Here, the workshop was the home, and the weaver owned both the means of production and the raw material he prepared.

But during the same period in England the factory system was changing the social organization of production. One consequence was a great increase in the size of the work force. This was not a completely new development. There was a shield factory during the period of the Roman Empire that employed 120 slaves. In the early 16th century, the weaving establishment of John Winchcombe, known as Jack of Newbury, was reported to have hired as many as 600 workers, although this may have been an exaggeration. But the first great increase in the size of industrial plants and labor force took place at the time of the Industrial Revolution, when power-driven machinery was applied on a large scale. This machinery was complicated and expensive; since it was worked from one power station, it had to be located in one main building. Such a factory represented a capital of several thousand pounds, and some industrialists owned several of them. In 1802 Peel employed more than 15,000 persons in the cotton industry. All this meant that some people had to be able to amass large sums of capital. In investing so much money they had to be confident of making a profit. Much larger, more distant markets had to be found than the local markets which had absorbed the products of previous means of production. Moreover, continuous supplies of raw materials had to be bought to feed into the machines, which were kept working from 12 to 14 or more hours a day.

The industrial system, born in the 18th century, grew rapidly in the 19th. It received further impetus from the development of electricity as a source of power.

The principle of the dynamo was discovered by Michael Faraday in 1831; generators were well developed by 1882. The new discoveries were first applied to lighting but soon to other fields as well, such as electric railways and power for factories. Although an electric fan was invented in 1889 and vacuum cleaners were sold in small quantities from around the turn of the century, Samuel Lilley (1966:123) writes that "electric power made

Workers coming out of Rouge Ford plant.

no serious impact on the domestic scene till after 1918." The recency of the use of electricity is thus rather astonishing.

Electricity can be developed by energy from many sources, including coal, waterfalls, tides, and windmills. It is easy to transmit and is readily convertible into various forms, in motors, lamps, X-ray tubes, and so forth. Because of the development of electricity, industry is much less dependent on the coal mine as a source of power; electricity thus facilitates some decentralization of population.

Today, the scale of some industrial organizations is enormous. General Motors, for example, has over 700,000 employees and over 1.3 million stockholders.

Not only has the labor force grown vastly in modern corporations, but it has become differentiated into all kinds of subdivisions. A large American corporation today has many stockholders, most of whom have no other connection with its business than owning a few shares. It has a board of directors, a president, an executive committee, and a finance committee. It is apt to have a sales division with an advertising staff, market analysts, and accountants; a manufacturing division with many further subdivisions; and auxiliary departments concerned with research, employee relations, legal advice, and so on. Below all these come the army of employees who operate the machines, supervise others, and turn out the product, whatever it is.

These people have nothing to do with food production but have to buy the food they eat. The farmers who provide it are businessmen rather than peasants and would not produce such food if there were no profit in it for them.

Agribusiness

Like industry, agriculture has also grown in scale and has benefited from technological development. By 1963 the top 3 percent of America's farms produced more than did the bottom 78 percent and had acquired nearly half the farmland with average-sized holdings of over 4,000 acres, more than six square miles apiece. The productivity of such large units is made possible by mechanization. Between 1917 and 1960 the number of tractors increased from 51,000 to nearly 5 million, while the number of horses and mules on American farms dropped from almost 27 million to 3 million (Higbee 1963:3, 10). Big farms hire airplanes to spread fertilizer and pesticides on their fields. Modern agriculture makes abundant use of nitrogen fertilizers, which are an important source of pollution of American lakes and streams.

The machinery and equipment needed to run such big farms are expensive. Hence, *agribusiness,* as it has been called, may have stockholders and management organization (Roy 1967). Canning, refrigeration, and transportation are also involved in food production. There is much regional specialization;

lettuce comes from California, wheat from the Dakotas, cheese from Wisconsin. On a family's breakfast table there may be orange juice from California or Florida, bacon and corn products from Iowa, sugar from Louisiana, and coffee from Brazil. So the food costs represent not only payment to the farmer but also costs for food processing, storage, transportation, and marketing. We are a long way from the hunting-gathering system of direct contact with the foods we eat.

The way in which food progresses from producer to consumer in this system is so complicated that it seems vulnerable to dislocation at any of the various steps between farm and supermarket. Another problem is that one needs money or food stamps to buy food, and when unemployment increases and food prices go up, many poor people are in trouble. A striking and hopeful aspect of the system, however, is that so few farmers are able to produce so much food for the predominantly nonfarming population.

Pollution

Much has been written about how modern industry and agriculture have damaged the environment. We have seen that this was true to some degree at each stage of food getting. Hunters probably killed off some species of game in Paleolithic times, horticulturalists denuded hills, and agriculturalists destroyed forests. But industrial societies have had more lethal effects upon the environment than all the earlier systems. With increasingly more people on our planet, there is less free space. In the United States and other advanced industrial nations, more people means more automobiles and more exhaust fumes. More factories belch pollutants into the air. Cities—Los Angeles, for example—are covered with smog, which may become dangerous in the case of temperature inversion, when hot air does not rise and blow pollutants away as it normally does. Because of inversion and air pollution, 12,000 people died in London in 1952; there were similar attacks there in 1956 and 1962. There has been a great increase in emphysema, lung cancer, and bronchitis in our cities. Our atmosphere has also been contaminated by fallout from nuclear explosions, although the number of detonations in the atmosphere has been reduced since the Test Ban Treaty of 1963.

The major rivers of the United States are heavily polluted, as are the Great Lakes, especially Lake Erie. Sewage and factory wastes pour into the rivers; oil slicks are washed ashore on the seacoasts, closing beaches and killing birds.

While demands for fresh water increase, less pure water is available. It has been estimated that an average American throws away eight pounds of refuse a day, making it increasingly difficult for municipalities to get rid of their mountains of trash and garbage. (Chase 1968:64–68). These problems affect not only the United States but the nations of western Europe, the USSR, Japan, and other countries as well.

Distribution of goods

Goods are not only produced in every society, but they must also be distributed in some way, and there are various ways in which that may be done. Let us take the example of a male factory worker in our society. Having cashed a paycheck, he hands some money over to his wife, who goes to the market or grocery store to buy food. But the members of her family do not have to pay her for her labor and skill in preparing meals. Not all transactions, then, are money transactions. We are also familiar with the custom of gift giving, such as occurs at Christmastime. Much of this, again, is within the family, but not exclusively so.

The significance for us here of such nonmonetary exchanges is that factories, money, and markets are relatively recent institutions; before money and markets came into being, goods and services had to be exchanged in some other way. The exchange of gifts may give us a clue to one form of precapitalistic distribution.

Reciprocity

The donation of a gift places the recipient under an obligation. That person may not actually want to have the present, but it would be difficult to refuse it, for in that case the insulted donor might become an enemy. To give and receive gifts is an age-old way of maintaining peace and friendship. The recipient is not only more or less obliged to receive the present but sooner or later is obligated to return it with a gift of about equal value. This is known as *reciprocity*. (These generalizations do not apply to gift-giving situations when there are marked disparities of status, such as a handout to a beggar or a present from an adult to a child.)

In many "primitive" societies there is much giving of presents and sharing of goods, and in such societies generosity is always admired. To freely give away a valued present brings prestige. At the same time, the stingy person evokes disapproval. Elizabeth Thomas (1959:22) writes:

A Bushman will go to any lengths to avoid making other Bushmen jealous of him, and for this reason the few possessions that Bushmen have are constantly circling among the members of their groups. No one cares to keep a particularly good knife too long, even though he may want it desperately, because it will become the object of envy. . . .

There are powerful sanctions, then, to encourage generosity.

Gifts may be given to members of other societies besides one's own, partly to maintain peace but also to acquire goods not locally obtainable. One kind of exchange, in which the partners never see each other, is known as *silent trade*. One person leaves some animal skins or other gift in a customary place. The person who collects it replaces it with an exchange gift. In this way, the Pygmies of the Congo trade with their Bantu neighbors without having to confront them.

Floating market
scene in Thailand.

The institution of the trading partner is found in many societies. Trading partners are people who count on a generally reciprocal pattern of exchange. There may be no immediate equivalent return for a gift, but over the course of time these people expect that their trading partners will even the balance.

Reciprocal exchanges may occur not only between individuals but also between groups, and this may help to strengthen their mutual interdependence. Marriages and gift exchanges establish close ties between neighboring groups.

The kula ring

Malinowski's description of the kula ring, (1922) is one of the classics of anthropology. It presents one of the first and most detailed accounts of economic exchanges in a non-Western society.

The area studied by Malinowski between 1914 and 1920 comprised the eastern mainland of New Guinea and the island archipelagoes to the east and northeast, particularly the Trobriand Islands. The inhabitants of these islands are horticulturalists who raise yams and catch fish in a tropical environment well supplied with palms, breadfruit, and mangoes. They have large, seagoing canoes, hollowed from logs and equipped with outriggers, in which they make expeditions to other islands. The expeditions that arouse their greatest interest and enthusiasm are those having to do with the kula.

The kula is a form of ceremonial trade, intertribal in scope, occurring in a wide range of islands. Within this ring two classes of valued objects are exchanged, red shell necklaces and white shell armbands. The necklaces travel in a clockwise direction along the ring, while the armbands move in a counterclockwise direction.

Those who engage in this trade are men, particularly those of higher status, who have learned the magic and etiquette connected with these transactions and who have been able to obtain one or more of the valued objects to trade with. A young man may learn the requisite magic and etiquette from either his father or his mother's brother, one of whom may also give him the trading item he needs to get started. He must then acquire some trading partners, perhaps from among those with whom his father previously exchanged. Chiefs may have hundreds of such partners; commoners, only a few. A partnership is a lifelong relationship, often binding together men of different tribes and different languages.

When a man receives a necklace or armband, he does not keep it long. Like the few possessions of the Bushmen, the armbands and necklaces keep passing from hand to hand, but in this case they pass along regular routes. Most of the armbands are too small to be worn, even by young children; those that can be put on are worn only at important ceremonial dances. The necklaces are also seldom worn, being considered too valuable for everyday use. While such objects are in a man's possession, they are much discussed; some of them are well known and have long histories, like famous diamonds in the Western world. But a man must soon relinquish this prize to a trading partner in the appropriate direction in the circle. Since the geographical expanse covered by this circle is wide, covering hundreds of miles, it may take from two to ten years for an armband or necklace to return to its starting point.

There is no haggling or discussion of price in kula transactions. The partners count on reciprocity, sooner or later. In addition to this ceremonial exchange of precious objects, there is also trade in other goods. When visiting a distant island, the Trobrianders have an opportunity to exchange some of their own special produce for goods that may not be available at home, including coconuts, sago, fish, baskets, mats, clubs, and stones. In this trade, bargaining does take place.

The kula ring illustrates the role of reciprocity in some primitive exchanges. It also shows that economic transactions may be tied up with all sorts of magical and ceremonial activities in a primitive society. Although the kula cycle may seem unusual from our point of view, it is not unique. Exchanges of valued goods following particular routes, similar to the kula, have also been reported for some of the tribes of Australia.

Redistribution

The Trobriand economy illustrates another principle besides reciprocity: that of *redistribution,* by which goods are funneled to a central place of storage and then redistributed by some central administrative authority.

A Trobriand man assumes the responsibility of providing his married sister and her family with a regular supply of yams, which are kept in a storehouse at her home. Most Trobriand Islanders are monogamous, but a chief may have as many as 60 wives coming from the different constituent communities of his area. Having so many wives, a chief has a correspondingly large number of brothers-in-law, all bringing him yams. One Trobriand chief was reported by Malinowski to receive from 300 to 350 tons of yams a year. This enables a chief to give tremendous feasts to entertain visitors and to be a paragon of generosity.

This system differs from reciprocity in the enhanced status of the chief through whom goods are distributed. The system allows the chief to appropriate some of the goods for his own purposes. As Gerhard E. Lenski has pointed out, in such societies there is usually no clear distinction between the chief's personal wealth and the people's surplus. The chief is a kind of symbol of his tribe; as its representative he is expected to be generous. While this may inhibit his acquisition of private wealth and power to some extent, the chief may be able to accumulate some private stores, particularly when the economy is expanding. The next step might be the creation of a retinue of dependent officials and retainers who will have a vested interest in the chief's power and be able to support him. This is how Lenski has accounted for the development of political power in advanced horticultural societies (Lenski 1966:164–68).

A similar argument has been made by Morton H. Fried, who believes that reciprocity is the mode of exchange associated with simple, egalitarian societies of the hunting-gathering level, while redistribution is found in what he calls "rank societies." These are societies that have reached a Neolithic level of food production and have experienced a growth of population and physical expansion beyond that of the hunting-gathering band. Redistribution may also be found in some favorably situated hunting-gathering societies such as those of the Northwest Coast of North America (Fried 1967:109–18).

Redistribution need not always work to promote chiefly power. In some Oceanic societies, according to Berndt Lambert (1966), redistribution may have more ritual than economic importance, serving to confirm a chief's authority rather than to establish an economic basis for it.

Polanyi (1957a:51) believes that the principle of redistribution was an important aspect of the large-scale economies of ancient times, including the Babylonian kingdom of Hammurabi and the New Kingdom of Egypt. Modern systems of taxation and the provision of government services may be seen as a form of redistribution.

The Kwakiutl potlatch

The Kwakiutl potlatch was a lavish, carefully staged feast in which much property was given away and sometimes destroyed. The Indians who occupied the coastal regions of British Columbia in aboriginal times depended on hunting, fishing, and gathering but were sufficiently well off to live in villages with large, plank-walled, gable-roofed houses. Many other tribes inhabited this area, including the Nootka, Bella Bella, Tsimshian, Haida, and Tlingit, but we will focus on one group, the Kwakiutl.

The Kwakiutl got much of their food from the streams and the sea: salmon, cod, herring, candlefish, halibut, flounder, and many other fishes, and such sea mammals as seals, porpoises, and occasional stranded whales. They also collected many kinds of berries and roots and hunted inland game. Some of their food was stored and preserved for winter, when conditions were less favorable.

In the late 18th century, the coming of whites and the fur trade enriched Northwest Coast culture. When iron knives and other cutting tools were

Two Kwakiutl women.

introduced, the Indians produced the splendid totem poles that are the hallmark of their culture. The idea of the totem pole was already present in that culture, but the improved knives greatly facilitated carpentry and wood carving, manifest also in finely made cedar boxes, masks, and other forms of woodwork. Another introduction of the fur trade was the Hudson Bay blanket, which became a form of currency, frequently changing hands, being borrowed and lent at high rates of interest. In Boas' day a cheap, white, woolen blanket was worth 50 cents. Highly valued objects were hammered and decorated sheets of copper, worth hundreds of blankets. Blankets, coppers, and canoes figured prominently in the gift distributions at a potlatch.

Potlatches were held on occasions marking changes of status: a girl's first menstruation, a wedding, a funeral, and various other occasions. A chief would give a potlatch to establish an heir. A potlatch could be given by one tribe to other tribes. The other basic potlatching unit was the *numaym,* a named landholding group, headed by a chief, whose members were related to the chief, usually by patrilineal descent (see p. 247), but sometimes through their mothers or wives.

A potlatch was a channel for redistribution. The male members of a *numaym* gave some of the game and fish they caught to their chief, while the women gave his wife some of their roots and berries. By accumulating such goods the chief was able to prepare for a feast and to pay for the building of canoes, a new house, or the carving of totem poles. He might also borrow blankets in order to have a big supply to give away.

The best potlatchers would be those who gave away so many gifts to their guests that they would never be able to repay. In this way they demonstrated their wealth and splendor. These giveaways were sometimes accompanied by boastful speeches by the hosts extolling their own greatness and deriding the poverty and inferiority of the guests. There was also destruction of property, the smashing and burning of canoes, and the pouring of buckets of candlefish oil into the flames. The climax might be the breaking of a copper, the pieces being thrown into the fire or into the sea. These extravagant features may have been late developments in the potlatch.

The potlatch served many functions: it announced and validated changes in rank and status, emphasized the solidarity of the *numaym* or tribe, and brought about much redistribution of goods, while providing a lot of drama and excitement in the process.

Markets

Many agricultural societies have been able to get along with little or no reliance on money or markets. If the typical family is largely self-sufficient, growing its own grain, raising livestock, spinning its own thread, and making its own clothing, it may not have to depend much on trade and can resort to barter for needed items. Early New England colonial families provide an illustration of such a state of affairs. Even in a society that has long had money and markets, rural people may be able to get along without handling much currency. An example will be given later, in Chapter 16, when we discuss the *jajmani* system by which goods and services are exchanged in rural villages in India, with little use of money involved. But with growing specialization and division of labor, a barter system is apt to become unwieldy. This may explain why market systems using a common medium of exchange have appeared in different parts of the world.

The term *market* is used in two senses: first, as a place where buyers and sellers meet to complete transactions and, second, as a state of affairs, as when we speak of there being a good market for men's shorts. Market systems have not developed in all horticultural and agricultural societies; they were not found, for example, in Polynesia, but they do have a wide distribution among peasant societies.

Market systems are greatly facilitated by the use of a common medium of exchange, whether it be shell money, as in parts of Micronesia, cacao beans among the Aztecs, or the coinage of advanced Old World civilizations.

It seems likely that, as a system of exchange, reciprocity preceded redistribution, while the latter antedated the development of market systems. But market systems are fairly old, nevertheless. One of the first known city markets was the *agora* of Athens of the fifth century B.C., which was associated with a coinage system. Markets and coinage may be even earlier in Sardis, the capital of Lydia. The Aztecs and Inca had market systems in the New World.

Market systems vary in the extent to which the market is *open,* that is,

Mexican market scene, 1937.

the extent to which buyers and sellers are free to enter the market. A market is *free* if the prices are determined by the interactions of buyers and sellers and not by rules and regulations.

Karl Polanyi, whose writings have had much influence in the field of economic anthropology, believed that the modern capitalist price-governed market system differs in kind rather than in degree from primitive exchange systems which utilize such mechanisms as reciprocity and redistribution. A primitive economy is embedded in social relations. In the modern world it is the other way around; social relations are embedded in an economic system that dominates all aspects of modern life. Polanyi believed that, since primitive and modern economic systems are so different, it would be impossible to apply economic theory, which was developed to analyze our own market system, to the understanding of primitive economies. This is the point of view of some workers in the field of economic anthropology who call themselves *substantivists.*[4]

Polanyi referred to the commercial revolution that accompanied the Industrial Revolution as "the great transformation." He pointed out that in a commercial-industrial system everything involved in production must be readily available for purchase. Otherwise production is too risky both for the capitalist who risks money and for the community which depends upon the enterprise for income and employment.

Now, in an agricultural society such conditions would not naturally be given; they would have to be created. That they would be created gradually in no way affects the startling nature of the changes involved. The transformation implies a change in the motive of action on the part of the members of society: for the motive of subsistence that of gain must be substituted (Polanyi 1957a:41).

An essential feature of this market system is that it be self-regulating, responsive to laws of supply and demand. Everyone in this system gets a livelihood from selling something; laborers sell their labor; landowners, their land or its produce; and farm and factory owners, their products. A new science, economics, developed as this market system expanded; it was geared to the analysis of this system, concerned with the forces that determine prices in a market economy.

Summary

The study of the adaptations of organisms to their environment is known as *ecology.* Mankind's adaptation involves the sphere of culture, including not only technology but also patterns of social organization which may facilitate or inhibit economic cooperation, community size, and the spacing of social units.

Some environments have been more favorable to human cultural develop-

---

[4] The opposing view, held by the so-called formalists, is that economic theory, utilizing such concepts as "maximizing" and "economizing" *can* be applied to the study of primitive economies.

ment than others. Seen from outer space, much of the earth is not suitable for human occupation. But technological development may make such areas habitable.

Four general types of economic systems may be distinguished: hunting-gathering, horticultural, agricultural, and industrial. Hunting-gathering groups usually have a limited inventory of tools, since they often move from place to place, although there are some exceptions to this generalization. In hunting-gathering societies the main division of labor is between the sexes, with men doing the hunting and women being occupied with gathering, cooking, child-rearing, and other tasks. The nature of the social organization may be influenced by the kinds of animals hunted. Herding animals like buffalo can be hunted communally, while moose are best pursued by single hunters. There is a tendency for hunting groups to have alternate periods of segregation and reassemblage, depending upon the possibilities of the food supply.

Horticultural societies vary in size and in the degree of political centralization. Labor units may be small in simple horticultural societies.

In agricultural societies, depending upon use of the plow, irrigation, and other techniques to increase food production, the peasant is the cultivator. Peasants are agriculturalists who are connected with a state or city life but who mainly engage in subsistence farming on a family basis and do not hire labor or specialize in cash crops.

In the Old World, various technological devices developed at the level of civilization to tap new sources of energy, such as the water wheel and wind mill.

Industrial societies with factory production resulted from the development of the Industrial Revolution in England during the last third of the 18th century. New sources of power were steam and, later, electricity, both of which permitted a lengthening of the working day. There was a change in the social organization of production, which was no longer based on a family unit or labor-exchange group but involved a much larger work force. The Industrial Revolution was accompanied and spurred by a commercial revolution involving a self-regulating market system responsive to laws of supply and demand.

In preindustrial times there were other ways in which goods and services were exchanged, notably reciprocity and redistribution. In the kula ring of the Trobriand Islanders and their neighbors, reciprocity became formalized, operating between trade partners, with valued goods passing along regular routes.

The system of redistribution involves the funneling of goods to a central place of storage and their redistribution by some central administrative authority, such as a headman or chief. The Kwakiutl potlatch was cited as an example.

Although reciprocity and redistribution still operate today, modern economy is prevailingly a market economy, which substantivists like Karl Polanyi believe is fundamentally different in nature from the primitive exchange systems that preceded it.

For a concise discussion of human ecology, see Richard A. Watson and Patty Jo Watson, *Man and Nature: An Anthropological Essay in Human Ecology* (New York: Harcourt, Brace, and World, 1969). See also Julian H. Steward, *Theory of Culture Change: The Methodology of Multilinear Evolution* (Urbana: University of Illinois Press, 1955), especially Chapters 2, 6, 10, 11, and 12.

For geographical environments, see Preston E. James, with the collaboration of Hibberd V. B. Kline, Jr., *A Geography of Man,* 2nd. ed. (Boston: Ginn and Co., 1959).

For the human hunting-gathering stage, see Richard B. Lee and Irven De Vore, eds., *Man the Hunter* (Chicago: Aldine Publishing Co., 1968).

For a detailed discussion of the ecology of a particular horticultural tribe in New Guinea, see Roy A. Rappaport, *Pigs for the Ancestors: Ritual in the Ecology of a New Guinea People* (New Haven, Conn.: Yale University Press, 1967).

An explanation for the shift to intensive agriculture is provided by Ester Boserup, *The Conditions of Agricultural Growth: The Economics of Agrarian Change Under Population Pressure* (Chicago: Aldine Publishing Co., 1965).

For a concise analysis of peasant societies, see Eric R. Wolf, *Peasants* (Englewood Cliffs, N.J.: Prentice-Hall, Inc., 1966). See also Jack M. Potter, May N. Diaz, and George M. Foster, *Peasant Society: A Reader* (Boston: Little, Brown & Co., 1967).

Two books that deal not only with technology but also with some of the sociological aspects are Lewis Mumford, *Technics and Civilization* (New York: Harcourt, Brace & Co., 1934); Samuel Lilley, *Men, Machines, and History: The Story of Tools and Machines in Relation to Social Progress,* rev. ed. (New York: International Publishers, 1966). See also Lynn White, *Medieval Technology and Social Change* (Oxford: Oxford University Press, 1962).

The consequences of the commercial revolution that accompanied the Industrial Revolution are set forth by Karl Polanyi in *The Great Transformation* (Boston: Beacon Press, 1957). For the consequences of the introduction of the new system into the world's colonial areas, see Eric R. Wolf, *Peasant Wars of the Twentieth Century* (New York: Harper & Row, 1969).

Two short general works on economic anthropology are recommended: Cyril S. Belshaw, *Traditional Exchange and Modern Markets* (Englewood Cliffs, N.J.: Prentice-Hall, Inc., 1965); Manning Nash, *Primitive and Peasant Economic Systems* (San Francisco: Chandler Publishing Co., 1966). There are also two readers: George Dalton, ed., *Tribal and Peasant Economics: Readings in Economic Anthropology* (New York: Natural History Press, 1967); Edward E. LeClair, Jr., and Harold K. Schneider, eds., *Economic Anthropology: Readings in Theory and Analysis* (New York: Holt, Rinehart, & Winston, 1968).

For a classic study of reciprocity, see Marcel Mauss, *The Gift: Forms and Functions of Exchange in Archaic Societies* (Glencoe, Ill.: Free Press, 1954).

For a series of essays on economic anthropology, see Marshall Sahlins, *Stone Age Economics* (Chicago: Aldine-Atherton, Inc., 1972).

Suggestions for further reading

13

MARRIAGE, FAMILY ORGANIZATION, AND KINSHIP

We have seen that all primates, including humans, live in social groups. Every human society, whatever its size, has some kind of social structure or organization. The social relations within a human group are much more complex than in the groups of nonhuman primates, since humans have a language that adds new dimensions to their communication with one another. Thus we have terms like *mother, father, brother, sister, uncle, aunt,* and *cousin* to designate kin, and in many societies there are also terms corresponding to *chief* and *boss* which reflect political authority. Associated with such terms are concepts of status and role.

A *status* is a person's position in relation to others. An individual occupies many statuses. In our society a man may be a son to his parents, a brother to his sister, a husband to his wife, a father to his children, a foreman in relation to factory workers, a subordinate to higher officials, and maybe also the head of a glee club. A person's overall social status is derived from these composite statuses, giving some general idea of the position occupied in society. Status may be ascribed or achieved. An *ascribed status* is one assigned to an individual because of some biological characteristic such as sex or through birth into a particular family. One cannot usually do much about an ascribed status. An *achieved status,* however, is brought about through effort and competition. A *role* is the behavior associated with a status, through which it is maintained.

When analyzing a particular society, an anthropologist or sociologist looks for the social units that comprise it. Very often such units are families. A *family* is a social group whose members usually live together and engage in economic cooperation; it normally includes two or more adults of both sexes responsible for rearing and educating the children who have been born to the female or females of the group or who have been adopted.

A family is a sexual unit in the sense that husband and wife may have sexual relations that cannot be regarded as illegal or cannot be socially disapproved. But in many societies both premarital and extramarital sexual liaisons are permitted; sexual behavior is not meant to be confined to the family, as in the United States. This shows that satisfaction of the sex drive is not the only reason for establishment and maintenance of a family.

Functions of the family

We do not usually think of a family as being engaged in economic cooperation, but families do have economic functions, which are of particular importance in societies where the main division of labor is that between the sexes.

Marriage also conveys status. Lévi-Strauss (1960:269) speaks of the "true feeling of repulsion which most societies have toward bachelorhood." In most societies a bachelor is felt to be an incomplete person. A similar, though milder, attitude is directed toward childless couples. Marriage and the birth of children are everywhere occasions for congratulations and festivity. A groom or a new father has, in a sense, "arrived."

The family may provide basic security and emotional satisfaction for its members, although it does not always do so. It is within the family that children are socialized and receive at least their earliest education.

The various functions of the family—sexual, reproductive, economic, status enhancing, emotional, and educational—may, of course, all be fulfilled outside the family unit, and sometimes more successfully than within it. It has already been noted that many societies permit premarital and extramarital affairs. Illegitimate children and orphans are often brought up in institutions. Friendships and other emotionally rewarding social ties are formed outside of the family. There are many other sources of status and prestige than being a spouse or parent. Certainly most of the economic cooperation in our society takes place outside the family unit, and children receive most of their education at school. Nevertheless, we still have families.

It is evident that families are quite successful social institutions, despite the fact that they often generate much tension, frustration, and hostility. One reason for the persistence and virtual universality of family groups is that children need the close care, attention, and companionship of adults. Families generally provide for these needs more successfully than larger, more impersonal institutions do. Not only is the adult-to-child ratio usually more satisfactory in the family, allowing for better care, but the parents of a child are more likely to feel some personal involvement with it than a hired nurse is apt to do. Of course, some institutions may be well staffed and well run, while some families may contain neurotic or psychotic parents. For these reasons young children may sometimes be better off in an orphanage than in a home, but, by and large, it seems that they are not. In fact, infants raised in institutions often show apathy and retardation and have a high death rate when adequate mother surrogates are not available.

In view of their virtual universality and the relative success with which family units manage to fulfill their functions, it seems likely that families will continue to exist in the future, although their disappearance has some-times been predicted by social prophets.

The simplest complete family unit, and a very widespread form, is the nuclear family consisting of husband, wife, and children. Yet there is an even simpler unit, that of mother and child, which is also very common. It is often regarded as a manifestation of breakdown or social disorganization, but in several Latin American countries such units represent one fourth or more of all the households (R. N. Adams 1960).

Exogamy and the incest taboo

In social science parlance it is customary to distinguish between a person's *family of orientation,* into which that person has been born, and *the family of procreation,* established when he or she gets married. Normally one cannot marry into one's family of orientation. A marriage thus brings together people from two different families. In all societies there are rules of exogamy affecting marriage. *Exogamy* is a general term for the requirement to marry outside of a particular group. (For the opposite principle of *endogamy,* see p. 285). There are different forms of exogamy. In northern India one must marry outside of one's village and sometimes outside of a complex of about 20 villages. One could call this "village exogamy." Unilineal kinship groups such as clans, which will be discussed later, are generally exogamous. In this case, we speak of "clan exogamy." We have no clans in the United States. Our exogamous units are small in comparison with those of most societies. A person in our society must at least marry outside of the family of orientation; many would also taboo marriage with a first cousin and various other relatives, such as uncle or aunt. Not only is it forbidden to marry within it but it is also considered very wrong to have sexual relations with a member of one's family of orientation. Incest taboos are present in all societies, particularly with respect to mother-son, father-daughter, and brother-sister relations.

Incest taboos and rules of exogamy are not the same thing. The former concerns sex relations; the latter has to do with marriage. Of course, one cannot marry a person with whom one cannot have sexual relations, but the two concepts should be kept distinct. Understandably, most societies disapprove of sexual relations between persons who are forbidden to marry, although there are some exceptions; in some African tribes a man may have intercourse with women of a lineage into which he may not marry.

The inbreeding theory of incest taboos

Anthropologists have wondered why incest taboos are so important and have offered various explanations to account for their origin. Two theories, which were suggested long ago, are usually rejected as inadequate but have recently found some partial support. One of these is the notion that primitive people somehow discovered that inbreeding has deleterious biological effects. A common response to this suggestion has been that close inbreeding is not necessarily damaging unless there are harmful recessive traits in the genotypes of the persons involved. Cleopatra came of a long line of brother-sister marriages. Brother-sister marriage was also practiced by ruling families in Hawaii and by the Inca of Peru without noticeable harmful effects. (Such marriages were generally forbidden to the rest of the population in these societies, although brother-sister marriages seem to have been allowed in Egypt during the period of Roman rule.) In some cases, inbreeding may be positively advantageous, which is why it is deliberately brought about by animal breeders. Thus, it has been argued, favorable cases should offset negative ones.

Until recently this seemed to be a good criticism of the inbreeding theory, but studies in population genetics have shown it to be invalid, for the ratio of deleterious and lethal recessive genes to selectively advantageous genes turns out to be high. Close inbreeding over many generations is possible in lower mammals, such as rats, but not in more advanced, slow-maturing mammals that produce only one or two offspring at a time, with widely spaced births. Thus, close inbreeding in humans would have biological disadvantages after all, particularly in the mating of primary relatives (Aberle et al. 1963; Parker 1976:287).

While this strengthens the case for the inbreeding argument, it seems unlikely that primitive humans could have figured it out, particularly since some nonliterate peoples such as the Arunta of Australia and the Trobriand Islanders of Melanesia do not fully understand the connection between sexual intercourse and pregnancy and have quite different explanations for conception. If we adhere to the inbreeding explanation for the incest taboos, we have to resort to an argument in terms of natural selection: those societies that developed incest taboos were more likely to survive than those that did not.

The childhood association theory

The other usually rejected theory explains the development of incest taboos on the grounds that people who have been brought up together from childhood, like brother and sister, are not apt to feel erotic attraction toward one another. The theory seems to be disqualified by the fact that cases of brother-sister incest do come to the attention of social workers. One may also cite the brother-sister marriages in the ruling families of Egypt, Hawaii, and Peru.

There may be some basis for the argument, nevertheless. Arthur P. Wolf has described a form of marriage among Chinese in northern Taiwan in which a girl is adopted by a boy's parents at often less than a year and seldom more than three years of age. They grow up together like brother and sister but marry when the girl becomes old enough. In the same community the more traditional form of arranged Chinese marriage is also found, in which the bride and groom are often strangers when they meet on the wedding day. Wolf presents evidence that the former type of marriage works out much less successfully than the latter and that much distaste is expressed for it. He also cites the Israeli *kibbutz*, in which children who have been raised together from infancy claim to feel like brothers and sisters and to feel no erotic attraction for one another. Love affairs within such a group are very rare (A. P. Wolf 1966).

One difficulty in applying such findings to the problem of the origin of incest taboos is that, if lack of erotic feeling resulted from siblings growing up together, there would seem to be no reason for any society to have brother-sister incest taboos since there would be no need to proscribe behavior that was unlikely to occur.

Freud's theory

Sigmund Freud made the opposite assumption, that strong erotic impulses are experienced within the family circle, primarily by a boy toward his mother. This is the basis for the *Oedipus complex* postulated by Freud: an erotic attachment to the mother accompanied by feelings of hostility toward the father. (In the case of a girl, the attachment is to the father.) These feelings and impulses have to be renounced or repressed but may continue to exist in the individual's unconscious. The horror generally shown at the idea of incest is interpreted, in this view, as an unconscious defense against temptation. Incest taboos, then, are regarded as reactions to the existence of incestuous desires. One advantage of this theory, in contrast to the one previously discussed, is that it does offer an explanation for the taboos.

A weakness of the theory is that among nonhuman primates that have been closely observed over long periods, mother-son sexual relations do not seem to take place, although there may be frequent grooming behavior between mother and son (Parker 1976:290).

Life-span considerations

Mariam Slater has made calculations of the possibilities of incestuous relations in family groups living under primitive conditions. The life span is generally short in hunting-gathering societies. If the life span is from 25 to 35 years and if puberty starts from 13 to 16, there is not much likelihood of a boy having sexual relations with his mother. If a woman has five children and lives to be 35, only an oldest male child who lives to maturity could become the father of one of her children—the last one. By the time most of the children are old enough to mate, their parents are dead; so they have to seek mates outside the family if they are going to mate at all. According to Slater, these patterns of mating out existed before (and became the basis of) the development of incest taboos (Slater 1959). This seems convincing, although some of the assumptions about the life span and length of breeding periods of early humans may be incorrect. The analysis shows why early human beings had to find mates outside the family unit, but it does not exactly explain why incest taboos were subsequently formulated.

Functional interpretations

There are some interpretations which do not suggest any mechanism whereby incest taboos were brought about in the first place but which do try to show that incest taboos had to be established if human society was to endure. If there were no incest taboos, it has been argued, there would be such disruptive sexual rivalry and tension within the family that it could no longer function as a family unit. This view has been countered by the argument that the sharing of sexual partners does not necessarily lead to conflict. Some forms of polygamous marriage will be discussed later in which there does not usually seem to be marked rivalry or tension, although sexual partners are shared. However, none of these marriage forms involve families in which both father and son have sexual access to the son's own mother or sister.

Another functional argument is that incest taboos are required to maintain roles in the family appropriate to the socialization process (Coult 1963). Still another interpretation is that incestuous family units would become isolated and culturally stagnant, while marriage into other social groups provides social contacts, allies, and channels for cultural diffusion. Groups developing such extrafamilial bonds would thus be more apt to survive than those without them. This explanation really has to do with exogamy, rather than with incest. Robin Fox has commented on this point:

In some societies fathers are allowed sexual intercourse with their daughters, and the daughters subsequently marry other men without, seemingly, any problems arising. . . . If, then, it is possible to have incestuous relationships and still marry out, the advantages of marrying out do not explain the prohibition on sex (Fox 1967:57; Fox does not specify which societies allow father-daughter incest).

In different societies, families vary greatly in size and composition. There are monogamous families and polygamous ones, small conjugal units and large consanguine family households. One way of classifying forms of family is in terms of the numbers of spouses involved. There are four general possibilities: (1) *monogamy,* a form of marriage involving one man and one woman; (2) *polygyny,* a form of marriage involving one man and more than one woman; (3) *polyandry,* a form of marriage involving one woman and more than one man; and (4) *group marriage,* involving more than one man and more than one woman. It must be emphasized that these are all socially recognized forms of marriage in the societies where they occur, in contrast to adulterous, bigamous, or temporary "illicit" relationships. The term *polygamy,* a general term for marriage with plural spouses, is

Forms of marriage

more widely known than *polygyny* and *polyandry,* but the latter are more specific in meaning.

	Males	Females
Monogamy	1	1
Polygyny	1	X
Polyandry	X	1
Group marriage	X	X

Note: X stands for more than one.

Monogamy and polygyny are the two most common forms of marriage, both having had a wide distribution among the societies of the world. Even in polygynous societies most marriages must be monogamous, for there are not enough women to go around. Since the sex ratio tends to be about even, it would not be possible for every man to have two or three wives; so, in polygynous societies, it is usually the wealthier or more powerful men of high status who can afford additional wives, while the common man must be satisfied with one.

Monogamy

Monogamy is the form of marriage with which the reader will be most familiar, since it is the form characteristic of the Western world. However, in Murdock's "World Ethnographic Sample" only about 24 percent of the 565 societies listed were described as monogamous (Murdock 1957:686). This form, which seems so natural to us, is thus relatively rare if one considers societies as wholes. Monogamy is found not only in advanced civilized societies but also occurs as the preferred form in such hunting-gathering groups as the Semang, the Veddas, and the Andamanese. Agricultural southwestern Pueblo Indians such as the Hopi have monogamous families, as did the aboriginal Iroquois of New York. This form of marriage, therefore, occurs at different levels of socioeconomic development. Since the sex ratio is about the same in most human groups, monogamy is an understandable development, particularly in rather egalitarian societies.

Murdock has suggested that "Where the productive accomplishment of the two sexes is approximately equal, and a small unit is as efficient as a larger one, monogamy may be economically advantageous" (Murdock 1949:36). This hypothesis seems reasonable, although it cannot always be easy to judge how nearly equal the productive accomplishments of the two sexes may be in particular societies, or in which cases small units are as efficient as larger ones, particularly when there are seasonal variations involving different kinds of activities in the course of a year.

Polygyny

Polygyny (meaning "many women" in Greek) involves a recognized marriage between a man and two or more women. It would not be considered polygyny if a man has a secret mistress or a concubine not recognized as a spouse, or if, in our society, a man is guilty of bigamy, supporting two separate wives who are not known to one another. Polygyny has been a favored form of marriage in most parts of the world: in Africa, the Near East, formerly in India and China, Melanesia, Polynesia, and among various aboriginal tribes of North and South America.

We have seen that monogamy is characteristic of many egalitarian hunting-gathering societies. While polygyny may also be found in such societies, as among the Eskimos, Ojibwa, and Sirionó, it seems to be generally related to a more advanced, productive type of economy. Remi Clignet has suggested that in Africa general polygyny tends to prevail in societies with a subsistence basis depending on roots, tubers, and aboriculture, which encourages the maintenance of large households. He concludes: "Rare among societies characterized by a lack of social stratification or, alternatively, by a large number of social levels, plural marriage is most frequent among societies divided into age grades or in which a hereditary aristocracy is separated from the bulk of the population . . ." (Clignet 1970:21). Clignet claims that polygynous societies are characterized by a division of labor in which women carry out much of the agricultural production. The economic advantages of plural wives will be discussed further later.

A polygynous family. A Bakhtiari man with three wives.

In view of the roughly equal sex ratio in most societies, how are enough females made available so that most of the less-fortunate males in a polygynous society are able to have at least one wife? This may be explained by the fact that girls tend to be married when they are quite young, while the men marry at a later age. Younger husbands may be monogamous, older ones polygynous. In a survey of a Gusii community in Kenya, Robert and Barbara LeVine found that the number of monogamous and polygynous adults was about the same. However, more than two thirds of the community's children had polygynous parents, since many monogamous men were young husbands whose wives had not yet given birth or had done so only once. As these young men get older and have more children, they take on additional wives (LeVine and LeVine 1963:39).

Tax registers for the Nyakyusa of Tanzania (then Tanganyika) in the 1930s showed that in parts of the district, in a population of 3,000 men of 18 years of age or older, 34 percent were bachelors, 37 percent monogamists, and 29 percent polygynists. It was the young men who proved to be bachelors and monogamists, while men over 45 were polygynists. There was a difference of ten years or more in the average marriage age of women and men (Wilson 1950:112).

It is very common for the first wife to have the highest status in a polygynous household. Linton says that secondary wives are drawn from women who are not attractive enough to be chosen as first wives and from widows and divorcees (Linton 1936:185). However, secondary wives tend to be younger than the first one and are often preferred by the husband. Wife Number One at least has the compensation of her higher status.

Different strategies are possible in the organization of a multiwife menage. A man may either live in one household with all of his wives together, or else he may set up separate households, one for each wife. The Sirionó who live in the forests of eastern Bolivia follow the first system. Each wife occupies a separate hammock in a communal dwelling, placed with reference to the husband's hammock in order of status; so that Wife Number One has her hammock to the husband's right; Wife Number Two, to his left; Wife Number Three, at his head; and Wife Number Four, at his feet. In a more advanced kind of dwelling, a Yoruba male in Nigeria may have three or four wives living in a house containing about a dozen rooms.

On the other hand, in many African tribes a man sets up a separate household for each wife, sometimes located within a walled compound. Each wife has her own collection of pots and cooking vessels and brings up her own children. She may have her own field, separate from those of her co-wives, and a granary of her own. In such circumstances a dutiful husband follows a rotation system, perhaps spending Monday nights with one wife, Tuesday nights with another, Wednesday nights with a third, and so on. The Fon of Bafut in Cameroon, West Africa, had too many wives to follow such a system. In his case the Fon's two top-ranking wives made out a schedule for him, allotting different wives for different nights. It was

not up to the Fon but up to these social secretaries to handle the arrangements (Ritzenthaler 1966:171). Some such rotation system reduces friction
and disputes among the wives. But it is not simply a matter of tact on
the part of the husband; the rights of the wives are often supported by
local law. In Madagascar, if the husband spends one wife's day with another
wife, it constitutes adultery under native law. The injured wife may demand
a divorce with alimony amounting to one third of the husband's property
(Linton 1936:186).

The women in a polygynous household are not necessarily browbeaten
creatures, although they sometimes are. They often seem to be self-confident
and self-assertive. There is frequently strong rivalry and jealousy among
co-wives, but this is not invariable, for they may share a cooperative relationship. From the point of view of the women involved, there are various
advantages in having co-wives. Many hands make light work. The co-wives
may form an efficient working team. As a collective union they may face
their husband with a set of joint demands. In the Western world a man
can be henpecked by only one wife; in Africa, by five or more. As Elenore
Smith Bowen (1964:128) wrote, concerning a West African family:

. . . what man can stand up against five united women? If Ava's husband raised
his voice to any one of his wives, all of them refused to cook for him. If he bought
one of them a cloth, he had to buy four other identical cloths. Discipline of the
wives was in Ava's hands, and stayed there. When the poor man got drunk one
day and struck one wife for nagging—well, until he had given many and expensive
presents to all his wives, the five of them slept barricaded in one hut.

From the man's point of view there are sexual advantages, not only in
the sense of variety but also in the fact that sexual intercourse is often
tabooed during pregnancy, for a year or two after childbirth, or during
menstrual periods. If Wife Number One is thus disqualified, the husband
can turn to Wife Number Two or Three. The husband in a monogamous
family in the Western world has no legal alternatives in such cases.

Polygyny makes possible the production of many children, and both
children and wives are sources of prestige. In some cases, extra wives provide
clear economic advantages as well. Mention was made in Chapter 12 of
the Trobriand chief who might have 60 wives drawn from different villages.
Since it was customary for brothers to provide their sisters with yams and
other garden produce, the chief was continually supplied with a food surplus
by his brothers-in-law, and he was able to give lavish feasts. Another Melanesian tribe, the Siwai, have feasts involving pigs. Pigs are a source of prestige
in this society—the more pigs you have, the higher your reputation. But
women are needed to raise pigs, so the more wives you have, the more
pigs you can raise, and the larger your gardens will be. A great increase
in polygyny took place among the Blackfoot Indians of the Western Plains
when the fur traders began to buy tanned hides. Since women did the
tanning, they were in great demand. The more wives a man had, the more

hides he could sell, and the richer he became. In some societies, therefore, there have been definite economic advantages in polygyny for the men, as well as the advantages of prestige and sexual satisfaction.

One form of polygyny that has had a wide distribution is *sororal polygyny,* a form of marriage in which a man marries two or more women who are sisters. It seems that in such cases there is a greater likelihood for the co-wives to share the same dwelling than in families where the wives are unrelated to one another. Some statistical support for this generalization has been provided by Murdock (1949:31). Among the Crow Indians, the wives lived in one tepee if they were sisters but had separate tepees if they were not.

As we have seen in the foregoing pages, polygyny may have various advantages both for the man and the women involved in such a union. Nevertheless, despite these benefits and the wide distribution of polygyny, this system of marriage seems to be on its way out in many parts of the world. The most influential industrialized nations of Europe, the United States, the USSR, the People's Republic of China, and Japan all require monogamous marriage. In societies now becoming more industrialized and influenced by Western culture, there are often feminist movements on behalf of monogamy. It is true that the Islamic religion supports polygyny, but it limits the permissible number of wives to four, and most Muslims can afford only one. In 1937, when Egypt was more traditional than today, only 0.02 percent of Egyptian marriages involved four wives, while 96.86 percent of the marriages were monogamous (Ammar 1966:201).

Polyandry

Polyandry (from a Greek term meaning "many men") is a form of marriage in which one woman lives with two or more husbands. It is generally said to be a rare form of marriage, but Prince Peter of Greece and Denmark (1963) has listed a fairly sizable number of societies that practice it, including some tribes in the former Belgian Congo and northern Nigeria, the Paviotso Indians of North America, the Marquesans, the Kandyans of Ceylon, the Da-La of Indochina, and various peoples in India, Tibet, Kashmir, and Sikkim. Just as there are many monogamous families in societies that favor polygyny, so monogamy is also apt to be found in societies having polyandry. In Tibet and in the adjoining areas influenced by Tibetan culture, which make up the largest single continuous area where polyandry has flourished in recent times, cases of group marriage and polygyny may also be found.

Two types of polyandry may be distinguished: fraternal and nonfraternal. *Fraternal polyandry* is a marriage relationship in which a woman has two or more husbands who are brothers, the converse of sororal polygyny. In the second type of polyandry, the husbands are not related. Tibetans who practice fraternal polyandry sometimes explain it in terms of land inheritance. If two or more brothers share their land and share a wife there is no need for division of property and land fragmentation, such as has plagued India,

A "polygynandrous"
family,
Jaunsar-Bawar.

where holdings become progressively smaller whenever sons divide land inherited from their father. In western Tibet, where fraternal polyandry is common, there has been an impressive stability in the number and size of landholdings over many generations (Carrasco 1959:30). We cannot say that this explains why fraternal polyandry developed in Tibet, but one function of the system has been to preserve landholdings intact from one generation to the next.

In Jaunsar-Bawar in the state of Uttar Pradesh in northern India, the oldest brother in a fraternal polyandrous household has a definite priority over the others. It is he who goes through the marriage ceremony; his brothers then automatically become cohusbands. But, whenever the oldest brother is in the house, the younger ones may not have intercourse with the wife (Saksena 1962:20).

In Jaunsar-Bawar all the brothers of a polyandrous household are called "Father" by their children; they are not distinguished by separate kinship terms, despite the priority of the oldest brother. Among the Todas of the Nilgiri Hills in southern India, a child has a socially designated father. Social anthropologists use the term *pater* to designate a socially recognized father as distinguished from the *genitor,* or biological father. In our society the genitor and pater are expected to be the same person, except in the case of stepfathers. The Todas are not concerned with identifying the genitor of a child—something that would be hard to determine, in any case, in a polyandrous household. In the seventh month of pregnancy, a Toda woman goes through a ceremony with a man that makes him the *pater* of her forthcoming child and also of her succeeding children until such time as she decides to go through the ritual with another man, who then becomes the pater of those who follow.

Group marriage

Group marriages occur only rarely; they sometimes develop from polyandrous households in Tibet, among the Todas, the Marquesans, and the Kandyans of Ceylon. To illustrate one way in which this might occur, let us say that the wife of three brothers from western Tibet fails to give birth to a child. If they suspect she is barren, they may add another wife to the household. The two wives are not divided among the brothers but are the common wives of all.

If a man and his brothers have in common three living wives and yet no child they may not marry another wife but may call in to their family circle another man as an additional husband. If he too begets no child still another man may be called in. If he too is childless the original husband and wife must resort to adoption (Carrasco 1959:36).

Group marriages may also develop if one of the husbands in a polyandrous family takes a fancy to a girl and asks his brothers to bring her into the family circle. It is possible that special alliances and preferences form in such a setting, but they must not become too marked if the group marriage is to remain intact. Group marriage occurred among the Todas during the period of British rule in India. In former times the Todas practiced female infanticide, which kept down the female population and thus helped to perpetuate polyandry. The British took strong measures to discourage infanticide. When the Todas gave it up, the number of women increased, which is said to have led to a rise in group marriages.

Levirate and sororate

There are some kinds of secondary marriage reminiscent of fraternal polyandry and sororal polygyny. The *levirate,* as it is usually defined, is the custom whereby, when a man dies, his widow is expected to marry one of her dead husband's brothers. There is, however, another meaning for the term *levirate,* which Radcliffe-Brown refers to as the "true levirate." This is the custom, followed by the Hebrews of biblical times and by the present-day Nuer and Zulu tribes of Africa, whereby a man is required to cohabit with a dead brother's widow so that she may have children who are counted as children of the deceased. In this system the surviving brother is not considered to be the husband of the woman or the father of her children (Radcliffe-Brown 1950:64).

The sororate is the custom whereby, when a woman dies, her husband is expected to marry one of his dead wife's sisters. Thus, the terms *levirate* and *sororate* are used for secondary marriage with a sibling of a deceased spouse. The question may be raised, What if the deceased spouse has no sibling? The answer is that there may be a general sense of obligation on the part of the lineage or clan of the deceased to provide a substitute—if not an actual sibling, then some other appropriate member of the kinship line. For example, in some African tribes a man is given a wife's brother's daughter as a wife. Such customs show that, in societies where they occur, a marriage is not just a bond between individuals but serves to link two lineages or clans. The relationship is not terminated by the death of a spouse; a substitute is supplied to maintain the linkage.

The levirate and sororate are widespread institutions. Of the 250 societies studied by Murdock in his *Social Structure* (1949:29), 127 were reported to have the levirate and 100 to have the sororate.[1]

We are all related to some other persons through descent, marriage, or adoption, and we use kinship terms to designate these relationships. Persons related to us through birth or descent are *consanguine* or "blood" relatives; those related to us through marriage ("in-laws") are *affinal* relatives. Although all societies have terms for different kinds of relatives, like mother, father, and uncle, societies differ in the relationships they distinguish and the ways in which relatives are lumped together or separated. There are some common basic principles, however, that are used to distinguish between different categories of relatives. These principles are set forth below (Kroeber 1909):

Kinship relations

1. Generation. Most English kinship terms make use of the criterion of generation. Father, mother, uncle, and aunt belong to the parental generation. Grandfather and grandmother are in the generation before that. Brother and sister are in Ego's generation. Son, daughter, nephew, and niece are of the generation below Ego, the person from whom the relationships are reckoned.

2. Relative age. A criterion we do not use in our system but which is employed in some other kinship systems is distinction of age levels within a generation. Different terms are used for one's older and younger siblings or for one's father's or mother's older and younger siblings.

3. Lineality versus collaterality. Lineal kin are related in a single line, as grandfather-father-son, while collateral kin are related through a linking relative, such as father's brother or mother's brother. In some kinship systems, known as *merging,* such distinctions are not made. Father's brother may be addressed by the term for father, and father's brother's sons may be equated with siblings and addressed as "brother" in such a system.

4. Sex of relative. The English terms for mother, father, brother, sister, uncle, aunt, nephew, and niece all make distinctions in the sex of the relative, but our term for cousin does not.

5. Consanguine versus affinal kin. Kinship based on descent (mother, sister) is contrasted with relationship through marriage (mother-in-law, sister-in-law).

---

[1] The numbers should probably be higher, since relevant data were not available for many societies.

Except for the second criterion of relative age, our system makes use of the above principles. But there are some other widely used principles not employed in our system:

6. *Sex of speaker.* In some societies different kinship terms are used by males and females.

7. *Sex of linking relative.* Distinctions between collateral relatives may be made on the basis of the sex of the connecting relative. This serves to distinguish cross cousins from parallel cousins (see p. 252).

8. *Status or life condition.* Distinctions may be made between relatives on the basis of whether a linking relative is alive or dead, married or single.

Bilateral descent

In our society we have what is called *bilateral descent,* that is, we feel we are equally related to the mother's and father's people, although there is a unilineal principle in the passing-down of the family name through males. Our society is not alone in having bilateral descent, nor is this principle limited to the more advanced civilizations of the world. It is also found among some of the technologically simplest hunting-gathering societies. About 60 percent of the hunting-gathering societies listed in Murdock's "World Ethnographic Sample" have bilateral descent. But bilateral descent also occurs among agricultural societies at different levels of technological advance.

Why should it be that both the most and least technologically advanced societies so often have this kind of descent-reckoning rather than unilineal clans and lineages? The answer seems to be that flexibility and mobility are required in both hunting-gathering societies and modern industrial societies. In both cases it is adaptive for nuclear families to be able to move in search of game resources or new job opportunities without first getting clearance from large family councils.

Unilineal descent

A *clan* is a unilineal descent group, the members of which believe that they are related to one another through descent from a common ancestor or ancestress. The same definitions could be given for a *lineage,* except that in a lineage the members are able to trace their descent to known forebears, while in a clan the common ancestor is more distant and usually mythical. A clan may contain many lineages.[2] Unilineal descent means that kin relationship is traced through one line, either through males, in which case we speak of *patrilineal* descent, or else through females, in which case we speak of *matrilineal* descent. In a society with unilineal descent, one is either a member of one's father's lineage or clan, or a member of one's mother's lineage or clan, but not of both, although there are some exceptions

---

[2] In his *Social Structure,* Murdock used the word *clan* for quite a different social unit and uses the word *sib* for what is here called clan. The usage followed here is a traditional one in British and American social anthropology.

in cases of "double descent," which is discussed later in this chapter. In societies having patrilineal descent, property and titles are passed from father to son; in matrilineal societies, they are handed down from a man to his sister's son. Thus, property remains within the lineage or clan.

In clan societies a husband and wife almost always belong to different clans. This is due to the rule of clan *exogamy,* the requirement to marry outside one's clan. Clans can be identified by the fact that they have names. Very often they are named after animals such as Bear, Wolf, or Fox, or after plants or other aspects of the environment. If a man belonging to the Bear clan meets a girl who says that she is a Bear, he knows that he cannot marry her, even though they may be unable to trace their genealogical relationship to one another.

A clan, a subclan, or a lineage may be a landowning unit. As a group it can be responsible for blood vengeance, if a member has been killed, and may demand indemnity. Religious cults may be associated with the unilineal group, such as the ancestor worship of traditional Chinese culture. Sacred objects or places of worship may be in charge of a particular clan, as among the Hopi. A named social unit that has a certain unity and special identity, which may own land, and may serve as a focus for collective economic or religious activity can be called a *corporate* group. Members of such a group show their solidarity by coming together on ceremonial occasions such as initiations, weddings, and funerals. They often have the obligation to extend hospitality or financial aid to other members of the group. Myths are sometimes told about the origin of the kinship group, serving to reinforce its corporate character and identify it as a unit set apart from others. Sometimes members of a lineage group occupy a single, large dwelling, as in the Iroquois longhouse or the large communal dwellings of the Tupinambá of the tropical forests of eastern Brazil. Or they may live in several homes grouped closely together. Unilineal systems are common among the societies of the world, numbering about 60 percent of the societies in Murdock's "World Ethnographic Sample." Unilineal systems are often found in horticultural and agricultural societies in which land rights are held by kin groups.

Patrilineal descent

When unilineal descent is traced in the male line, we speak of patriliny, or patrilineal descent. In this case, one belongs to one's father's clan, not to one's mother's clan. This is illustrated in the accompanying diagram. In kinship charts like the one presented here, a triangle designates a male and a circle represents a female. An equal sign indicates a marriage. Siblings, brothers and sisters, are linked by a bar. *Ego,* from the Latin word for "I," is the person from whom the relationships are reckoned.

One's patrilineal kin include one's father's father and his siblings (brothers and sisters), one's father and his siblings, the children of father's brothers,

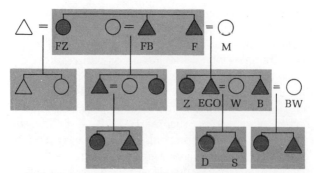

Diagram showing
persons related
through patrilineal
descent.

Note: B is Ego's brother; Z his sister. F is Ego's father; FB is his father's
brother; FZ is his father's sister. M is Ego's mother. S and D are son and
daughter.

one's own brothers and sisters, and the children of one's brothers. Patriliny
affiliates a person with kin related through males only.

The majority of societies having unilineal descent are patrilineal. They
range from hunting-gathering societies, such as the Chippewa, to advanced
civilizations, like that of traditional China. Most of India, except for parts
of the south, has patrilineal descent. Patrilineal American Indians included
both some Siouan-speaking and Alonquian-speaking tribes. There are many
patrilineal tribes in East Africa, among the Nagas of Nagaland in India,
and among tribes in New Guinea.

Incidentally, it may be noted that there is another way of diagramming
kinship relations. Another system is shown below. Students are likely to
encounter both of these kinds of diagrams in works on anthropology. In
the second system a husband and wife are connected by a bar beneath
the symbols, while brother and sister are linked by a bar above them.

This diagram shows Ego's relationship to parents and sister. In this chapter

Diagram of a
nuclear family.

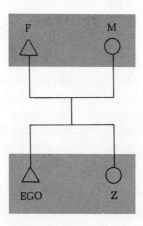

the first system of diagramming kinship relations will be used henceforth, rather than the latter.

Matrilineal descent

Matriliny, or matrilineal descent, affiliates a person with kin related through females only. In this case, one belongs to one's mother's, not one's father's, clan. One's matrilineal relatives include one's mother's mother and her siblings, one's mother and her siblings, the children of mother's sisters, one's own brothers and sisters, and the children of one's sisters.

This system of descent is relatively restricted in range. Only about 15 percent of the societies in Murdock's "World Ethnographic Sample" are matrilineal. Among American Indians, the Navaho, Hopi, Zuñi, Hidatsa, Crow, Cherokee, Iroquois, Tlingit, and Haida were matrilineal. So are the people of Truk and the Trobriand Islands. The Nayar, Tiyyar, and Mappilla of Kerala in southwestern India follow matrilineal descent, as do the Minangkabau of Indonesia. In Africa the Ashanti, the Plateau Tonga, the Bemba, and the Yao have matrilineal descent.

Another possible way of tracing descent is through double descent, a combination of the patrilineal and matrilineal principles. In this system the individual belongs to both the father's patrilineal group and the mother's matrilineal group.

Phratries and moieties

In some societies two or more clans are linked together to form a *phratry*. The member clans may feel that they have particularly close ties with the other clan or clans of the phratry. They may perform reciprocal services on ceremonial occasions. Sometimes, as among the Hopi of Arizona, the phratry is an exogamous unit, so that one may not marry members of the other clans within the phratry.

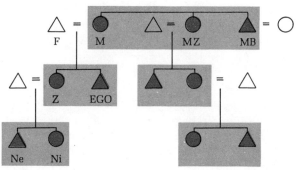

Diagram showing persons related through matrilineal descent.

Note: Ne is nephew; Ni is niece.

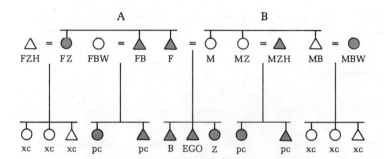

Two exogamous
moieties, A and B.

In some societies the clans form two groups in which each half is called a *moiety*. These are usually exogamous; a man must marry a woman of the opposite moiety. Sometimes the moieties are associated with contrasting abstract concepts or different phenomena of nature. The conceptual universe of the Murngin, a hunting-gathering society in northeastern Arnhem Land in Australia, is divided into a dual system in which plants, animals, stars, and people belong to either one moiety or the other. Myths and folklore supply rationalizations for the allocation of objects to particular moieties, explaining why a spear, for example, belongs to one moiety while a spear-thrower belongs to the other (Warner 1958:30).

Elaborate systems of contrasting associations are found in many exogamous groups in Indonesia, so that one side, for example, may be associated with such symbolic features as Right, Male, Land or Mountainside, Above, Heaven, In Front, East, and Old; the other side is associated with Left, Female, Coast or Seaside, Below, Earth, Behind, West, and New (van der Kroef 1954:852). Bororo villages in eastern Brazil are divided into exogamous matrilineal moieties known as Weak and Strong. In some communities these moieties are crosscut by moieties called Upstream and Downstream (Steward and Faron 1959:386).

Dual divisions like these facilitate patterns of reciprocity, not only in relation to marriage but also in the exchange of special services. For example, members of one moiety among the Seneca performed mourning services for those of the other. Such symbolic contrasts as Right and Left and North and South serve to emphasize the complementary roles played by the two divisions.

Totemism

Similar ideas may be associated with clans or other unilineal units in some societies. Among central Australian aborigines, members of the Kangaroo clan have the idea that the remote ancestor of their clan was a kangaroo and that they have a special affinity with kangaroos. Where beliefs of this kind exist, there may be a taboo on eating the meat of the clan animal. A complex of beliefs and customs relating to such ideas is called *totemism*.

The Bondo, a hill tribe in the state of Orissa in eastern India, have totemistic concepts relating to their moieties, Cobra and Tiger. Members of the Cobra moiety cannot kill a cobra, "for it is our brother." Similarly, members of the Tiger moiety never kill a tiger. They say, "When we go out hunting, we feel very embarrassed if we meet a tiger; we just don't know what to do and our weapons fall of their own accord from our hands. The tiger also feels awkward and goes away." Verrier Elwin, who recorded this statement, adds, "But I suspect a certain apprehension on the part of the Bondo that, while he himself may be strictly orthodox, the tiger may not be equally observant of the rules" (Elwin 1950:29).

Segmentary lineage systems

Unilineal descent is of particular importance in societies with *segmentary lineage systems,* such as the Tiv of Nigeria, the Nuer of the Sudan, and the Bedouins of Cyrenaica. These are patrilineal tribes lacking centralized political organization. The segments that make up the society are not ranked in a hierarchy but are roughly equivalent duplicates of one another. In these "tribes without rulers," as they have been called, the lineage is a political unit, having collective responsibility in blood vengeance; a good deal of feuding goes on between lineage groups.

Unilineal systems are normally in process of segmentation. Two brothers of one family may become the heads of two new lineages. They usually remain close allies, however, and one will come to the aid of the other if he is attacked. Usually, one's sense of loyalty is greatest to those kin most closely related, although one may also acknowledge ties to more distant kin. Feuds are more common and more bitterly fought with more remote kin, but, in case of attack from without the tribe, feuding kinsmen will unite against the outsiders. When a quarrel breaks out between two segments, closely related groups are apt to be drawn into the affair on both sides, for there is no organized political machinery for dealing with internal conflicts. The normal tendency in these societies is toward a kind of social atomism. Political consolidation occurs only to meet a threat from outside the tribe, and, once that danger is over, the atomistic condition is resumed.

The Tiv are conscious of their tribal unity through descent from a common ancestor, and this awareness enables them to make common cause against another tribe, when that is necessary.

In societies of this type, the lineages should have roughly equal status, but there are also societies with more political centralization in which one lineage, that of the king or chief, is more important than the others.

So far we have dealt with kinship ties determined by consanguinity. But kinship ties are also achieved through marriage. Indeed, for Claude Lévi-Strauss (1969a) these are the most significant relations in human societies.

Affinal ties

According to Lévi-Strauss, men in primitive societies brought about alliances through marrying their daughters or sisters to other men. The resulting network established social cohesion, tying families or bands more closely together. This was probably a necessary stratagem in hunting-gathering days, when the use of weapons, unknown to nonhuman primates, heightened the potential dangers of strange groups. In a pioneer discussion of exogamy in 1888, E. B. Tylor wrote that savage tribes faced the alternatives of marrying out or being killed out, and he quoted these lines from Genesis 34:16: "Then will we give our daughters unto you, and we will take your daughters to us, and we will dwell with you, and we will become one people." This biblical passage illustrates the process of establishing peace and broadening social bonds through intermarriage.

Cross-cousin marriage

A widespread form of marriage which links small family groups together is cross-cousin marriage. It is found among many peoples in southern India, parts of China and Melanesia, and among many tribes of Australian aborigines, African tribal groups, and North American Indians.

The kinship system of the Western world does not distinguish between cross cousins and parallel cousins, but the distinction is important in many of the world's kinship systems since it may designate which cousins are marriageable and which are not. In defining these types of cousins it is useful to use the word *sibling,* which is a general term for brother or sister, without specifying the sex. Parallel cousins, then, are children of siblings of the same sex, while cross cousins are children of siblings of opposite sex. In other words, a man's parallel cousins are his father's brother's children and his mother's sister's children; they are children of siblings of the same sex. A man's cross cousins are his father's sister's children or his mother's brother's children; they are children of siblings of opposite sex.

It is quite common for parallel cousins, such as father's brother's children, to be equated with siblings and termed brother and sister, while quite different terms are employed for cross cousins.

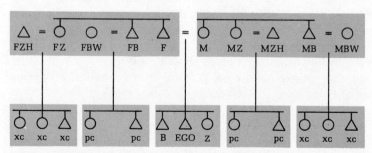

Note: In this chart xc stands for cross cousin; pc stands for parallel cousin.

The Tswana of South Africa practice cross-cousin marriage. They regard marriage with a mother's brother's daughter as the preferred form, while marriage with a father's sister's daughter is a second choice. But the Tswana are unusual in also practicing marriage with a father's brother's daughter or mother's sister's daughter. Members of this tribe are divided into nobles and commoners. I. Schapera has pointed out that there is a difference in the incidence of marriage types in these two social strata. Fifty percent of the commoners practice matrilateral cross-cousin marriage, with roughly equal distributions in the other three brackets. But nearly 48 percent of the nobles have father's brother's daughter marriage. The Tswana have a proverb, "Child of my father's younger brother, marry me, so that the (*bogadi*) cattle may return to our kraal." This suggests an economic motivation in such marriages. Schapera, however, believes that the main motive in the upper class is not the acquisition of cattle but maintenance of status and political advantages within the family (Schapera 1950:151, 157, 163).

Parallel-cousin marriage

Marriage with a father's brother's daughter is a widespread form of alliance among Muslims in North Africa, the Near East, Pakistan, and India, having Islamic religious support. Among some Arab peoples, if a family wishes to marry their daughter to someone other than her father's brother's son, the cousin must be handsomely paid for his permission. Among the Arabs, as among the Tswana, marrying among close kin may serve to conserve property and status, and it may also maintain family solidarity among members of pastoral tribes such as the Bedouins, who have to be ready to defend themselves against sudden attacks from other groups.

We have considered kinship relations through birth (consanguine) and through marriage (affinal). There is another way in which persons may be related—through adoption or fictive kinship.

Fictive kinship

The godparent is an important figure in many societies. In Latin America the institution of *compadrazgo* not only provides a child with a godparent but also establishes mutual ties between the coparents, or *compadres.*

Patterns of "blood brotherhood" or institutionalized friendship are found in some societies. Among the Jimdars of eastern Nepal two men or two women may go through a simple ceremony that commits the partners to a quasifamilial relationship. This brings about incest barriers between a man and members of his friend's family, and an avoidance relationship develops between the man and his friend's wife.

All human societies are structured in more complex ways than the societies of nonhuman primates, since human groups have languages which include kinship terms for particular relatives and terms for different grades of age and status.

Summary

The basic social units in most societies are families. A family is a social group whose members usually live together and engage in economic cooperation; it normally includes two or more adults of both sexes responsible for rearing and educating the children of the group. The family has various functions—as a sexual and reproductive unit and as a source of status, security, and emotional satisfaction for its members. Incest taboos forbid sexual relations within the family between parents and children or between siblings. Some such taboos are found in all societies.

There are four types of family in terms of the numbers of spouses involved: *monogamy,* with one man and one woman; *polygyny,* with one man and more than one woman; *polyandry,* with one woman and more than one man; and *group marriage,* involving more than one man and more than one woman. Monogamy and polygyny are the two most common forms of marriage.

Two kinds of secondary marriage are the *levirate,* in which a widow is expected to marry one of her dead husband's brothers, and the *sororate,* in which a widower is expected to marry one of his dead wife's sisters. Both are widespread institutions, found in many societies.

Persons related through birth or descent are *consanguine* relatives; those related through marriage are *affinal* relatives. In our society we have *bilateral* descent, meaning that we are equally related to the mother's and father's people. This is a widespread pattern in many societies at different levels of technology. *Unilineal* descent relates members through descent from a common ancestor or ancestress, as in a lineage or clan. If the line is traced through males, we speak of *patrilineal* descent. If it is traced through females, we speak of *matrilineal* descent. Unilineal systems are often found in horticultural and agricultural societies in which land rights are held by kin groups. The majority of societies having unilineal descent are patrilineal; only a minority have matrilineal descent.

Some societies are divided into two exogamous groups known as *moieties.* It is very common for such groups to have contrasting symbolic associations such as Right versus Left, Sky versus Land, and so forth. In some societies *totemistic* ideas are related to clans, involving beliefs in a spiritual relationship with the animal from whom the clan is descended, sometimes including a taboo on eating the flesh of the totem animal.

A widespread form of marriage which links small family groups together is *cross-cousin* marriage, a system in which a man should marry a father's sister's daughter or a mother's brother's daughter but not a *parallel cousin* such as a mother's sister's daughter or a father's brother's daughter. A preference for parallel-cousin marriage (with a father's brother's daughter) exists among Muslims in North Africa, the Near East, Pakistan, and India.

Kinship relations are not always based on biological relationship or on marriage. There is also adoptive or *fictive* kinship, which incorporates an outsider into a kinship network.

Three good books on the family, each having much cross-cultural data are: Ruth Nanda Anshen, ed., *The Family: Its Function and Destiny* (New York: Harper & Bros., 1959); Stuart A. Queen, Robert W. Habenstein, and John B. Adams, eds., *The Family in Various Cultures* (Philadelphia: J. B. Lippincott Co., 1961); William N. Stephens, *The Family in Cross-Cultural Perspective* (New York: Holt, Rinehart & Winston, 1963).

A good analysis of polygynous family systems in Africa is Remi Clignet, *Many Wives, Many Powers: Authority and Power in Polygynous Families* (Evanston, Ill.: Northwestern University Press, 1970).

An insight into the workings of a polygynous household may be obtained from a collection of life histories in Edward H. Winter, *Beyond the Mountains of the Moon: The Lives of Four Africans* (Urbana: The University of Illinois Press, 1959). Also recommended is the novel by anthropologist Elenore Smith Bowen, *Return to Laughter* (New York: Doubleday & Co., Inc., 1964). The best general survey of polyandry is that by H. R. H. Prince Peter of Greece and Denmark, *A Study of Polyandry* (The Hague: Mouton & Co., 1963). A classic early ethnographic account of a particular polyandrous society is W. H. R. Rivers, *The Todas* (London: Macmillan & Co., 1906).

Two paperback books provide brief introductions to the study of kinship: Roger M. Keesing, *Kin Groups and Social Structure* (New York: Holt, Rinehart & Winston, 1975), and Burton Pasternak, *Introduction to Kinship and Social Organization* (Englewood Cliffs, N.J.: Prentice-Hall, Inc., 1976).

A good general work is Robin Fox, *Kinship and Marriage: An Anthropological Perspective* (Baltimore: Penguin Books, 1967).

14

MARITAL RESIDENCE AND MALE-FEMALE RELATIONS

A newly married couple has to set up residence somewhere. There are different customs concerning this in different societies, which may be influenced by whether the kinship system is patrilineal, matrilineal, or bilateral. Marriage involves relationships with affinal relatives or in-laws. Especially in patrilineal societies, payment may have to be made to members of the wife's lineage to compensate for her loss. Some matrilineal societies have this custom, too—for example, the Trobriand Islanders. Various ways of handling these matters have been developed in different societies.

Economic exchanges in relation to marriage

In many societies a girl leaves her own community when she gets married and goes to live with her husband's people. Her own lineage group thus loses a useful worker. The groom's lineage may make up this deficiency by marrying one of its daughters into the other group, thus evening matters and further strengthening mutual ties.

Sometimes payment is made by the groom or by his family to the girl's family at the time of marriage. Although this is called *bride price,* it is not purchase; the girl is not considered a slave or marketable commodity. (For this reason the term *bridewealth* is sometimes used instead in ethnographic accounts.) Rather, the payment is a kind of restitution to the girl's family for the loss they have incurred. The payment is also a kind of insurance that the girl will be well treated. If she is not, she may return to her parents, and her husband is often unable to get the bride price back, especially if it is felt that he is to blame for the breakup.

In many African tribes that have cattle, the traditional medium of payment is cows. The cows are used by the girl's family to finance the marriage of one of their sons. A boy who wants to marry may have to wait until his sister's bride price has been paid and the cattle driven into the kraal.

256

Sometimes a man cannot acquire enough wealth to pay the bride price. In some societies where such problems have come up, an institutionalized solution is at hand, namely, bride service or suitor service. The young man goes to the home of the girl and works for her parents, as Jacob worked for Rachel in the Old Testament. This practice is found in many societies, for example among the Reindeer Chukchee of Siberia and the Kaska Indians of British Columbia. Since the young man lives with the girl's family in such cases, he is more or less her husband from the beginning.

In some societies, payments go the other way—from the bride's family to the groom's. In present-day India, the bride's parents pay a sum of money to the groom, despite the fact that their daughter leaves her community and moves to her husband's paternal residence. The dowry is particularly high in the case of young men who have studied in England and who are therefore thought to have promising futures. Even in small rural villages the dowry paid by the bride's parents may represent the savings of many years. Families often go in debt on this account.

The possible forms of postmarital residence are rather limited; a newly married couple can live alone, with the man's relatives, with the woman's relatives, or they can shuttle back and forth between her family and his. There are some other possible arrangements and combinations, but there is a limitation of possibilities for the options.

In many societies there is a dominant or usual form of marital residence, as in some examples that follow. But there may be differences in residence in different segments of a population, as in a heterogeneous, modern, industrial society. And there may be different patterns for older and younger sons.

Neolocal residence

The custom we are familiar with in the United States is for the newly married couple to set up a separate home, living with neither the husband's nor the wife's parents. This is called *neolocal* residence. It is consistent with the bilateral emphasis in American kinship and with our traditions of individualism, romantic love, and individual choice in the selection of a mate. It is a useful pattern in a highly industrialized society like ours, since it permits of much individual mobility. This form of residence is associated with a small conjugal family having rather weak ties to the relatives of either husband or wife. It is a rare form of residence among the societies of the world, being found in only 27 of the 565 societies in Murdock's "World Ethnographic Sample."

Patrilocal residence

The custom whereby a bride goes to live with or near her husband's patrilineal kinsmen is called *patrilocal* residence. This is far more common than neolocal residence, being found in 314 societies in Murdock's "World Ethnographic Sample." It is also more common than *matrilocal* residence, to be described later, which is found in 84 societies, and *avunculocal* residence, which is found in only 18 societies (Stephens 1963:133).

To give an example of arrangements relating to patrilocal residence, let us consider conditions in northern India, where patrilineal descent is followed. In northern India, marriages are arranged by parents. The bride and groom usually have not met before the first wedding ceremonies, for the bride does not come from the same village as the groom. A man must marry a woman from another village. Indeed, in some parts of northern India one must marry outside of a complex of about 20 villages. Marriage is not completed all at once, in one ceremony, but involves various stages drawn out over a period of about three years. In the first years of marriage, the bride still spends a lot of time in her native village, but, as time goes on, she comes to spend more and more time in her husband's community, which before long becomes her main place of residence. There, she lives with her husband in his parents' home. If he has married brothers, they and their wives and children all share the same joint household. A young bride in such a household must show great respect to her father-in-law and to her husband's older brothers, covering her face with her veil in their presence. They rarely exchange conversation. She is freer in the presence of her husband's younger brothers. Among the Jats, who allow leviratic marriages, a joking relationship exists between a man and his older brothers' wives.

Young Indian mother.

Matrilocal residence involves residence of the married couple with or near the wife's female matrilineal kinsmen. This is the custom among the Hopi Indians of Arizona who have matrilineal clans. The Hopi have individual courtship before marriage, and there is a good deal of premarital intercourse. The boys visit girls at night in their homes but leave before dawn. If a girl becomes pregnant, she names the boy she wants to marry, and a match is arranged. Marriages are monogamous. The Hopi girl continues to live in the household into which she was born. This household includes her parents, her unmarried brothers, her sisters, and their husbands and children. In the north Indian household it is the bride who must adjust to her in-laws; among the Hopi it is the groom who must adapt himself. However, their situations are not the same. The Indian bride is a stranger in her husband's village, while the Hopi groom normally comes from the same community. He courted his wife and knew her and her relatives before marriage. His mother's home, which he continues to visit, is apt to be in the same village; so he is less isolated than the bride in north India, and he enjoys a higher status.

Matrilocal residence

The Hopi woman's status is also high, however, since she, or her clan, owns the house and fields where the men work. In his autobiography, Don Talayesva thus describes his wife's situation:

She owned the house and all the property that her relatives gave her, including orchards, stock, water holes, land, and personal possessions. She also owned any property she made with her hands, such as pots, baskets, milling stones, and clothes, or anything that she earned for work or purchased with our money. She owned the fuel and the foodstuffs that I brought into her house, as well as all household equipment and utensils (Simmons 1942:272).

The husband's status in this home is weakened by the fact that his wife's brothers and other maternal kinsmen have important roles in authority and decision making.

Residence of a married couple with or near the husband's male matrilineal kinsmen, particularly his mother's brother, is called *avunculocal* residence. The Trobriand Islanders of Melanesia provide an example. Most Trobriand Islanders are monogamous. Descent is traced matrilineally. There is individual courtship and much premarital intercourse, although some of the higher-status families arrange patrilateral cross-cousin marriages for their sons, marriage with a father's sister's daughter. Such marriages, arranged in infancy, are considered binding. Otherwise, most Trobriand marriages are the outcome of courtship. At the time of marriage, or soon thereafter, the husband leaves the village of his father, where he has grown up, and moves to a village owned by his mother's subclan, where his mother's brother lives. From the point of view of the bride, Trobriand postmarital residence may be said to be *virilocal,* residence at the husband's home, or community.

Avunculocal residence

But it is classed as avunculocal because of the husband's shift to his maternal uncle's village.

In a matrilineal society the mother's brother is an important figure, since he belongs to Ego's lineage or clan. Property and titles are inherited from him rather than from the father, who does not belong to Ego's lineage or clan. Among the Trobriand Islanders the maternal uncle is the principal authority figure, a source of discipline. It is the maternal uncle who teaches his nephew the traditions of his clan.

We find residential customs like those of the Trobriand Islanders among the matrilineal Tlingit of the American Northwest Coast. Among the Tlingit a boy left his home at around the age of eight to ten and moved to the house of his maternal uncle, who was responsible for the boy's training. This type of residence resembles the patrilocal residence of patrilineal societies in the sense that it maintains in association some male kinsmen who belong to the same unilineal group. Avunculocal residence would seem to give the husband a stronger position in the household than is the case in matrilocal residence.

Bilocal residence involves either patrilocal or matrilocal residence with about equal frequency. In some societies a married couple starts off living with the bride's parents or in their community and later moves to live permanently in the home or community of the husband.

Many societies cannot be said to have any one particular type of marital residence. For example, the Dogrib Indians, hunting people in northwestern Canada, have many options, marrying either within or without the band, living with the parents of either husband or wife or with a brother of the husband, and so on. Many changes in residence may occur over a period of time. June Helm, who has described this fluid pattern, states that it also occurs in other hunting societies such as the Nambikwara of the Matto Grosso of Brazil, the !Kung Bushmen, and some Australian tribes (Helm 1968).

Determinants of marital residence

Why does a society come to prefer one form of residence over others? Many considerations must be involved. It has been argued that there is a stress on patrilocal residence in the case of hunting-gathering band societies where there is a premium on a man's knowing his hunting area where he, his father, and his brothers have hunted. Patrilocal residence also keeps together males who have grown up together and learned to defend themselves against outside attack. For reasons such as these, the claim has been made that all hunting-gathering societies in the past were patrilocal (Service 1962). This view is no longer generally held. As we have seen, there are hunting societies like the Dogrib and !Kung Bushmen that have no one consistent pattern of marital residence. This does not seem to be an aberrant modern development; the flexibility of such a system would have had advantages in the past as well as now (Lee and DeVore 1968:7–8).

Any aspect of a society's economy that enhances male status or favors male cooperation would seem, nevertheless, to strengthen the chances of patrilocal residence. Thus, pastoralism favors patrilocality; so does plough agriculture. Conditions favoring matrilocal residence would be those that foster cooperative work among women in gathering, fishing, or horticulture. Absence of herds and other forms of property associated with males and a low degree of political organization also seem to give weight to the matrilocal side. According to Kathleen Gough (1961:560) ". . . avunculocal residence seems most likely to occur where the descent group jointly owns an estate of relatively high productivity, in relation to which the products of the men require redistribution, and their labor, regular coordination, on the part of an authority." Neolocal residence seems to be favored by factors that result in the isolation of the conjugal family and strengthen monogamy. An emphasis on individual private property and personal freedom would have the same result. Bilocal residence may be favored by migratory habits and appear in societies where the sexes have relatively equal status. The foregoing suggestions are largely hypothetical, since residence rules in most societies are very old and one cannot see them in process of formation.

It seems reasonable to suppose that kinship systems with patrilineal descent developed as a result of patrilocal residence. In such cases, the men form a permanent corporate group; the women are marrying-in outsiders. Pastoralism, warfare, and political centralization have probably contributed to patrilineality as well as to patrilocality.

Some possible determinants of kinship forms

Matriliny, on the other hand, has probably developed from matrilocal residence. Matriliny often seems to be related to horticulture at a low level of productivity. Except in the case of some groups in southern India, the Minangkabau of Indonesia, and a few other societies, matriliny is not found in areas having plough agriculture and extensive agricultural works.

Since patriliny and patrilocality have a much higher incidence than matriliny and matrilocality, there seem to be some inherent disadvantages in the latter institutions. Perhaps marrying-in males who are outsiders from different communities form a less effective team for cooperation and defense than members of a patrilineal lineage who have grown up together. On the other hand, Kalervo Oberg (1955:481) has argued that matrilocality provides for effective mobilization of manpower among lowland tribes in South America. A man gets economic assistance from his sons-in-law; but his sons, who marry into nearby villages, can also be called upon for help when needed. If the sons remained at home and the daughters married out, the sons-in-law could be called upon for help, but their ties to him would be weaker. Of course, the advantages of the matrilocal system depend upon the villages being rather close to one another.

Authority is usually in the hands of males. In patrilineal societies, there is consistency in the tracing of descent and exercise of authority by men.

Hopi women. The
Hopi have matrilocal
residence and
matrilineal descent.

In matrilineal societies, however, there is some discontinuity. Marrying-in males do not have much authority in the wife's lineage, and initially, at any rate, are placed in a position of relative inferiority. But a woman in northern India, trained to be submissive, is more easily kept in her inferior status than a marrying-in male in a matrilineal society. This creates some strain and tension for men in the latter case. Perhaps it is not surprising that a high rate of divorce has been reported for some matrilineal, matrilocal societies, such as the Hopi and Minangkabau. Max Gluckman (1950:190) has suggested that patrilineal tribes in Africa tend to have lower divorce rates than matrilineal or bilateral tribes.[1] Strong conjugal ties between husband and wife are probably more compatible with patrilineal than matrilineal systems.

Matrilineal societies face other problems. If a woman gets married and

---

[1] The same point has been made for Indonesia (Loeb 1935:68 ff). David M. Schneider (1961:16) has observed: "The institutionalizing of very strong, lasting or intense solidarities between husband and wife is not compatible with the maintenance of matrilineal descent groups."

moves to her husband's community, her kinfolk have to find ways to maintain control over her children. Authority is divided between her brothers and her husband. But if there is matrilocal residence and her husband moves to her community, her brothers move out upon their marriages. Either way, it is difficult to secure discipline for the children from the maternal uncles (A. I. Richards 1950:246). If the clans have political functions, it may be harder for the male members of the clan to get together. These dilemmas are less pressing if the husband's and wife's families live near one another, as among the Hopi. The problem facing a matrilineal family group or lineage is how to maintain control over both its male and female members. In patrilineal, patrilocal societies, females are lost to the group, but this is less of a disadvantage since they are not needed to fill authority roles, while men must fill such roles in matrilineal societies.

The various forms of family organization and residence which have been reviewed represent different ways of combining males and females, parents and children. In many of these systems men seem to have higher status than women, while women have higher status in some arrangements than in others.

Male-female relations

In most societies men carry out occupational and political roles which are conceived to be more important than those of women. At present there are women's movements which protest against the condition of male dominance. Others defend male dominance as a natural state of affairs resulting from the biological differences between men and women. A variant of this viewpoint is that male dominance stems from the long period during which human beings lived by hunting and gathering. It is argued that the greater strength of males gave them leadership positions in hunting and defense of the group. Women were tied to the home base by the demands of childbirth, suckling, and child rearing. They consequently engaged in such domestic tasks as cooking, fetching food and water, making clothing, and bringing up children. Although this was clearly essential work, women's tasks carried less prestige than the activities of men. Our culture today seemingly retains traces of our long hunting-gathering heritage in these respects.

While there are myths in some societies about a former state of matriarchy, in which women were dominant and held political power, anthropologists have found no society in which women actually control the political system. (Perhaps the nearest approach to such a state of affairs is the former society of the Iroquois, to be discussed later.) Men seem to have always been dominant in the political sphere, despite the occasional appearance of a Golda Meir or Indira Gandhi. Although queens have reigned, their advisors have usually been male councillors; their generals and soldiers were males.

In opposition to those who hold male dominance to be natural and inevitable are those who consider it to be essentially arbitrary, not supportable by the biological distinctions between the sexes or past cultural conditions.

Indira Gandhi.

One way to approach this subject is through a comparison with other primate species.

Primate comparisons: Dominance and aggression

Some primate species, particularly terrestrial ones, are marked by *sexual dimorphism,* differences in size and strength between males and females. In such species males are generally dominant over females, and generally show more aggression than females.

Juvenile male primates engage in more rough-and-tumble play than do juvenile females. The sexual distinction in such behavior is probably influenced, though not completely determined, by the action of endocrine glands. This is suggested by laboratory experiments in which the male sex hormone testosterone was administered to pregnant female rhesus monkeys. Their "masculinized" female offspring showed more threatening behavior and rough-and-tumble play than did an untreated control group of females (Young, Goy, and Phoenix 1964). Experiments have been carried out in various animal species to change the structure of a group's dominance hierarchy by administering male hormones to its more submissive members.

Both men and women have both male and female hormones in their systems, but a man secretes 2–2.5 times as much of the male hormone as a woman does. Women have a more variable endocrine balance. "At times, a normal woman may produce even less of the female hormone than an average man does, but at other times her production shoots up to much more than ten times as much" (Scheinfeld 1947:134). Since the endocrine glands form an interconnected system, it would be oversimplified to relate the male hormone directly to aggression. Besides, the term *aggression* is often used loosely, sometimes to cover all expressions of self-assertion.

On the basis of observation of children's behavior in seven cultures, Whiting and Edwards (1973) stated that boys aged three to six generally engage in more rough-and-tumble play than girls. Insulting and dominating egoistically are also common male traits in this age group. Girls, on the other hand, exhibited more passive, dependent, and nurturant behavior than boys. These observations are in accord with the usual stereotyped expectations about boys and girls. That, indeed, is what Whiting and Edwards believe is responsible for their findings. They attribute the contrasts in behavior not to any inborn predispositions but, rather, to early training for the expected roles of males and females.

Cross-cultural studies of aggression in children

Another cross-cultural study by Barry, Bacon, and Child (1957) which examined data from 110 societies, found a widespread pattern of stressing nurturance, obedience, and responsibility in girls, while emphasizing self-reliance and achievement motivation in boys.

In all these cross-cultural studies the emphasis of the authors is on socialization and training for adult life rather than on the influence of biological factors in causing contrasting patterns in the behavior of boys and girls. But if socialization is all that is involved, one wonders why parallel contrasts appear in so many species of higher primates as well as in so many human societies. It must be that biological reasons underlie the divergent training patterns that direct boys and girls toward different goals. There should be good reasons why boys and girls receive the contrasting kinds of socialization they do.

In still another cross-cultural study, Ronald P. Rohner examined data from 101 societies and found, as usual, that boys were invariably more aggressive than girls. In none of the societies were girls said to be more aggressive than boys. However, Rohner also found that the amount of aggression varied considerably from one society to another and that the level of aggression in one sex within a society tended to approximate that of the other sex, although boys always showed at least slightly more aggression than girls. Among the Chenchu of southern India, for example, the ethnographer never saw any quarrels or show of bad temper among the children within a six-week period. In a Colombian village in South America, on the other hand, constant displays of aggression among both boys and girls were observed. The level of aggression, then, is obviously influenced by general sociocultural conditions (Rohner 1976).

Rohner cites an unpublished cross-cultural study of 125 societies by Herbert Barry III and associates in which it is claimed that in only 20 percent of the societies were young boys *encouraged* to be more aggressive than girls. There would seem, then, to be some natural predisposition toward greater aggression on the part of boys, which, again, is apt to be considerably modified by sociocultural conditions and by particular child-rearing practices.

There are some societies where differences between males and females are not greatly emphasized; there are others in which they are stressed. In the latter group fall societies in which large animals are hunted and pastoral societies in which large animals are herded. In both cases male roles must be distinguished from female ones; correspondingly different training practices are therefore developed for boys and girls.

The following sections of this chapter present features of societies having different patterns of subsistence: hunting-gathering, horticultural, agricultural, and industrial societies.

Hunting-gathering societies

The argument that male dominance stems from our long hunting past has been advanced by such male writers as Lionel Tiger, Robin Fox, and Robert Ardrey. Tiger and Fox believe that there is a natural and universal tendency, which they call *male bonding,* for men to form cooperative groups that exclude women. Male bonding first developed during mankind's hunting phase, during which territoriality and defense of the group became vital concerns (Tiger and Fox 1971; Ardrey 1976).

A contrasting view of human evolution has been offered by two female anthropologists, M. Kay Martin and Barbara Voorhies (1975), who claim that in foraging (hunting-gathering) societies women are economically dominant and have a status equal to that of males. The basis for this contention is that in over two thirds of the foraging societies in a sample of 90, hunting provides only 30–40 percent of the diet. Gathering by women is therefore the mainstay of such a society. The authors admit that the recently studied groups that make up their sample are marginal peoples who do not have the rich game resources enjoyed by our Paleolithic forebears, but they claim that there is no evidence that the hunting-to-gathering ratio has been significantly altered. Naturally, no evidence for that is available from the remote past. Martin and Voorhies fail to mention an important consideration: the likelihood that there was much less gathering of plant foods in the days before cooking was developed. Plant foods of any caloric value generally need to be cooked before they can be digested by human beings, and many plants are poisonous in the raw state (Leopold and Ardrey 1972).

A few million years of foraging preceded the human use of fire for cooking. Early humans must have collected fruits, nuts, seeds, and edible roots and shoots, but much of the plant food now consumed by marginal foragers was not yet utilizable. This is not to deny the claim that the sexes generally have an egalitarian, complementary relationship in hunting-gathering societies. Ernestine Friedl has noted that in such societies each sex controls resources and services required by the other, and both men and women enjoy a good deal of autonomy. On the other hand, male hunters often control extradomestic exchanges of meat, which gives them some additional authority and prestige. According to Friedl (1975:31–32), dominance is least and equality between the two sexes is greatest in societies, such as the Washo of the Great Basin of North America, where men and women share the same subsistence tasks. Male dominance is greatest in societies, such as the Eskimo, where hunting is almost the sole source of food. Yet even in traditional Eskimo society there seems to have been a complementary, mutually dependent relationship between the sexes. A quotation from Franz Boas' early ethnographic work, *The Central Eskimo,* gives a vivid picture of what that relationship was like and what work was expected of the two sexes. Boas (1884:561–65) describes a typical day in wintertime:

At this time of year it is necessary to make use of the short daylight and twilight for hunting. Long before the day begins to dawn the Eskimo prepares for hunting. He rouses his housemates; his wife supplies the lamp with a new wick and fresh blubber and the dim light which has been kept burning during the night quickly brightens up and warms the hut. While the woman is busy preparing breakfast the man fits up his sledge for hunting. He takes the stone block which closes the entrance of the dwelling room during the night out of the doorway and passes through the low passages. Within the passage the dogs are sleeping, tired by the fatigues of the day before. . . . The sledge is iced, the harnesses are taken out of the storeroom by the door, and the dogs are harnessed by the sledge. Breakfast is now ready and after having taken a hearty meal of seal soup and frozen and cooked seal

Eskimo hunter.

meat the hunter lashes the spear that stands outside of the hut upon the sledge, hangs the harpoon line, some toggles, and his knife over the antlers, and starts for the hunting ground. Here he waits patiently for the blowing seal, sometimes until late in the evening. . . .

Meanwhile the women, who stay at home, are engaged in their domestic occupations, mending boots and making new clothing, or they visit one another, taking some work with them, or pass their time with games or in playing with the children. While sitting at their sewing and at the same time watching their lamps and cooking the meat, they incessantly hum their favorite tunes. About noon they cook their dinner and usually prepare at the same time the meal for the returning hunters. As soon as the first sledge is heard approaching, the pots, which have been pushed back during the afternoon, are placed over the fire, and when the hungry men enter the hut their dinner is ready. While hunting they usually open the seals caught early in the morning, to take out a piece of the flesh or liver, which they eat raw, for lunch. . . .

After the hunters reach home, they first unharness their dogs and unstring the traces, which are carefully arranged, coiled up, and put away in the store room. Then the sledge is unloaded and the spoils are dragged through the entrance into the hut. A religious custom commands the women to leave off working, and not until the seal is cut up, are they allowed to resume their sewing and the preparation of skins. . . .

When the men have finished their meal the women take their share, and then all attack the frozen meat which is kept in the store rooms. The women are allowed to participate in this part of the meal. . . .

All the work being finished, boots and stockings are changed, as they must be dried and mended. The men visit one another and spend the night in talking, singing, gambling, and telling stories. The events of the day are talked over, success in hunting is compared, the hunting tools requiring mending are set in order, and the lines are dried and softened.

Here there seems to be a rather egalitarian relationship between men and women, although the men are the focus of more attention. But we will see later in Chapter 18 that Central Eskimo myths and tales often depict women as negative and dangerous beings. A devaluation of women is also suggested by the formerly common Eskimo practice of female infanticide. On the other hand, Jean L. Briggs (1974), who spent 30 months in the Central Arctic, saw no conscious, institutionalized conflict between the two sexes.

Horticultural societies

The difficulty of generalizing about horticultural societies, which show much variability, is stressed both by Friedl and by Martin and Voorhies, but both studies make some general statements. In a worldwide sample of 515 horticultural societies, Martin and Voorhies (1975) claim that women dominate cultivation activities in about 41 percent of the cases. In only 22 percent of the societies are men the exclusive cultivators. In societies where the two sexes contribute equally (37 percent), the men usually have the responsibility of clearing the garden plots, while the women tend and harvest the crops. As dependency on crops increases, so does the role of men in cultivation.

Although the range is great, most horticultural societies are small; in about 79 percent of the sample the populations are less than 400. In societies with larger populations than that, there is an increased male share in cultivation.

Despite the important economic roles of women, patrilineal kinship systems predominate in horticultural societies. Matrilineal societies make up only one quarter of the sample. Ernestine Friedl notes that warfare is endemic in many horticultural societies. That would tend to strengthen male status. Men also engage in extrafamilial food distributions, a source of prestige. Separate men's houses are found in many horticultural societies. Furthermore, polygyny occurs in 55 percent of the Martin and Voorhies sample. If several wives are busy cultivating plants, a man's wealth and prestige multiply. Hence there are many factors that bolster the status of males in horticultural societies. On the other hand, women also have certain advantages. They often engage in trade in such societies and enjoy a good deal of autonomy and influence, particularly in matrilineal and matrilocal systems.

Yolanda Murphy and Robert F. Murphy (1974) have focused on women's roles in a study of the Mundurucú, a South American Indian horticultural tribe located east of the upper Tapajós River in Brazil. A Mundurucú village contains from 50 to 100 persons. The men occupy a men's house, and there are three to five dwellings where the women and children live. Houses are set in a circle grouped around a village plaza. There are two moieties, subdivided into clans; extended cross-cousin marriage is practiced. Descent is patrilineal, but residence is usually matrilocal, which results in a scattered dispersal of clansmen. Women, on the other hand, form compact, continuing groups held together by collective labor. Men's work—hunting, fishing, and formerly warfare—takes them outside the village; women's work is done within it. Although men clear the fields, women do most of the horticultural work.

A group of village women—mothers, daughters, sisters, and others— makes up a collective team for processing manioc and controls its distribution. Moreover, a woman distributes the game brought back by her husband. Women seem to have a secure position in village life. A senior woman is the acknowledged head of her dwelling. Men do not challenge her authority; they live in their separate men's house and play no role in women's domestic activities. There is little economic cooperation between husband and wife; the nuclear family is not a productive unit in this society. It is the cooperative women's group that controls production.

However, in Mundurucú ideology women are considered inferior to men. A myth recounts that women were formerly dominant and played sacred trumpets which men took away from them and now store in the men's house. The Murphys suggest that the myth expresses the men's insecurity about their own current dominance. Women are supposed to be passive and submissive; those who violate the standards are subject to mass rape by the men. The women resent this practice and do not acknowledge the male claims of superiority. Under the circumstances it is hard to define the status of women in Mundurucú society. The men judge it to be low, but the women do not accept the males' definition of the situation.

Another horticultural society, in which women had a more acknowledged high status, was that of the Iroquois in the 18th century. Descent was matrilineal; residence was matrilocal in longhouses which contained several family units in separate compartments. An elder woman in charge of a longhouse could evict a man for misbehavior. As among the Mundurucú, women had control over the production, storage, and distribution of food. Communally owned land, inherited matrilineally, was held by the women, who also owned the farming implements and seeds. Horticultural work was organized under the supervision of an elected female leader chosen by the women who worked together.

A council of chiefs headed the confederacy or League of the Iroquois. Selection of these chiefs was determined by matrons of the matrilineal clans, who could also impeach a chief whose actions met with their disapproval. Iroquois matrons had a role in council deliberations and veto power in declarations of war, for since men could not hunt while on a war party they had to depend on dried rations provided by the women. Women also controlled such assets as wampum. Moreover, in contrast to the Mundurucú, they played important roles in the religious life. Iroquois ideology does not seem to have pictured women as inferior. The high status of Iroquois women may be attributed to the combination of matrilineal descent, matrilocal residence, and women's control of both production and distribution (Martin and Voorhies 1975:225–28; J. K. Brown 1970).

Agricultural societies

In agricultural societies, including peasant societies, male authority is heightened and female status is often considerably depressed. Men are usually the main cultivators, since the ploughing and irrigation connected with agriculture involve strenuous work in which male strength is clearly advantageous. Since farming is mainly men's work, polygyny ceases to be adaptive as it was under horticulture, and this type of family becomes much less common (Martin and Voorhies 1975:288).

In a review of 46 peasant community studies, Evalyn J. Michaelson and Walter Goldschmidt (1971) found that economic control and authority are in the hands of men. Fathers tend to be authoritative and mothers indulgent. In patrilineal families, which are common, marriages are usually arranged, and there are weak affective ties between husband and wife; although strong bonds usually develop between mother and son. A common feature of peasant life is social segregation of the sexes.

The custom of *purdah,* or seclusion of women, is found in Muslim households, primarily in cities, in Pakistan and northern India and also among many Hindus in northern India. According to the purdah system a woman generally stays within special women's quarters in the home. If she leaves its confines, she must cover her face with a veil or part of her sari. The Rājpūts in northern India have separate houses or sleeping quarters for men and women. Husbands may visit their wives in the women's courtyard at night. Patrilocal residence is practiced. A married woman covers her face in the presence of her husband's older male relatives and other visitors and she sits at a lower level than her in-laws. Strictly speaking, she should cover her face in front of her mother-in-law and older sisters-in-law until the birth of her first child, but since this custom involves so much inconvenience, it is often omitted. Ideally, a man and his wife should not talk to one another in the presence of older members of his family—who are usually present (Minturn and Hitchcock 1963:240–41, 266).

Sexual segregation is also practiced in rural Egyptian towns. In Silwa, in upper Egypt, women are expected to stay within the home. A woman who often leaves her house is called a "strayer." Women keep to the wall when walking down the street, while men walk down the middle. If she should meet a man, a woman turns her head away or pulls her head covering over her face (Ammar 1966).

This kind of sexual segregation finds support in the Koran, where it says of women: "They should not go out of the house lest they commit a grave sin." Therefore a pious woman should first get her husband's consent before leaving the house. Urban Egyptian women were generally veiled until the 1920s, when that custom was ended by a liberalizing feminist

Veiled women in Morocco.

movement, but until then veiling was common in much of North Africa and the Near East.

Veiling and purdah were not practiced in precommunist China, but the position of women was comparable in many ways to that of northern Indian women, since arranged marriages, patrilineal descent, and patrilocal residence were customary. As in India, a young bride was under the domination of her mother-in-law and had to be on her best behavior in her husband's family. The low status of women was expressed by the high incidence of female infanticide in traditional China. However, it seems that accounts about submissive daughters-in-law in the literature about China have given Westerners an oversimplified conception of the Chinese woman. That is suggested by the work of Margery Wolf, who gives an intimate picture of women's life in rural Taiwan. She shows that women were not just passive pawns at the mercy of a stern mother-in-law. They were not confined to walled courtyards, but spent much time washing clothes by the river, cleaning vegetables at a pump, or sewing under a tree in the company of other women. These groups formed gossip centers where a bride had an opportunity to complain about her mother-in-law's behavior. Since a mother-in-law knows about the force of local gossip, that should act as a check on her behavior. From Margery Wolf's account we learn that the women in rural Taiwan do not fit the usual stereotype. "A truly successful Taiwanese woman is a rugged individualist who has learned to depend largely on herself while appearing to lean on her father, her husband, and her son" (Wolf 1972:41).

Industrial societies

If agricultural societies emphasize that women's place is in the home, industrialism brought women out of the home, first into factories as machine workers and later into offices as typists and stenographers. The greater strength of males was of less significance in a factory where muscle was provided by machines; and since women's labor was cheaper than men's, it was in great demand. By 1860 one third of all factory workers in New England were women. During the Civil War, women not only became nurses and took factory jobs but also got clerical work in business offices which had formerly employed only men. After the war, women became the dominant sex in teaching.

The factories that employed women often produced goods that replaced the traditional kinds of work women had done in earlier agricultural times, such as prepared cereals, canned vegetables, and factory-made clothing. The new kinds of work ultimately affected women's dress too. Long skirts were dangerous in a factory; skirts became shorter and dresses simpler after 1890 (Degler 1964).

There were over 1 million female factory workers by the 1890s, most of whom were young and unmarried. But married women, including those with children, increasingly sought employment, particularly during and after World War II. Between 1948 and 1967 the rate of employment for mothers of young children nearly doubled. In 1969 a government publication stated that women made up 37 percent of the work force in the United States; more than one third of the working women had dependent children.

Accompanying the changes in women's roles were demands for equal treatment with men. American women got the right to vote in 1920. Since then demands have been made for equal pay and equal employment opportunities with men. Although many women are not satisfied with the advances made so far, there have been remarkable changes in these respects since World War I.

This brief review has dealt with the United States as an example of an industrial society, but comparable developments have taken place in the other industrial societies of the world. The sex ratio is in favor of women in the Soviet Union, since so many men were killed in World War II. Fifteen years after the war there were 20 million more women than men in the Soviet population. There are proportionately even more female school teachers in the USSR than in the United States, and the elected leaders of peer collectives in schools are likely to be girls (Bronfenbrenner 1970:73). However, women do not hold prominent administrative posts in either the government or the Communist Party. Apart from education, they figure prominently in the field of medicine, making up 75 percent of the total, but 92 percent of the women hold lower-ranking positions. In education, too, women teachers are mainly found in the lower grades (Martin and Voorhies 1975:379).

Despite the very different political systems and ideologies of Russia and the United States, there has been a good deal of convergence in the experiences of women in moving from a mainly domestic realm into factories, hospitals, schools, and other contemporary spheres of occupation.

Summary

The possible forms of post-marital residence are rather limited. A newly married couple can set up an independent (*neolocal*) residence; they can live with or near the husband's patrilineal kinsmen (*patrilocal* residence); with or near the wife's female matrilineal kin (*matrilocal* residence); with or near the husband's male matrilineal kinsmen (*avunculocal* residence); or they may alternate between patrilocal and matrilocal residence with about equal frequency (*bilocal* residence).

Since patriliny and patrilocality have a much higher incidence than matriliny and matrilocality, there may be some inherent disadvantages in the latter institutions. Perhaps marrying-in males form a less effective team for cooperation and defense than members of a patrilineal lineage who have grown up together. High rates of divorce have also been reported for a number of matrilineal, matrilocal societies. Moreover, it is difficult to secure discipline of children by their maternal uncles, since married brothers and sisters often live in different communities.

In human societies there is a general tendency for males to have higher status than females, and in most societies men carry out occupational and political roles which are considered to be more important than those of women. One explanation for this state of affairs attributes it to the long period during which human beings lived by hunting and gathering. As hunters and defenders of the group, it is held, males acquired positions of leadership.

Comparisons with nonhuman primate groups show that males are generally more aggressive and that juvenile males engage in more rough-and-tumble play than females. The same impression is gained from cross-cultural studies of aggression among human children. In the case of humans, the contrast may either be attributed to hormonal and other biological differences between the sexes, to contrasting patterns of socialization for boys and girls, or to some synthesis of biological and sociocultural factors. In some societies differences between males and females are not greatly emphasized; in others they are stressed, as in many hunting and pastoral societies. Among hunting-gathering societies male dominance is greatest in societies, as among the Eskimo, in which hunting is almost the sole source of food. There is greatest equality between the sexes in societies where men and women contribute about equally to subsistence. This kind of equality is also found in many horticultural societies, but female status tends to be depressed in agricultural societies in which men are the main cultivators. Male strength is advantageous in ploughing and irrigation. Seclusion of women, such as the Indian custom of purdah, is found in many agricultural societies. Industrialization, however, opened up new opportunities for work and education for women, leading to feminist demands for equal treatment with men.

Suggestions for further reading

Good studies of matriliny and matrilocality are available in A. I. Richards, "Some Types of Family Structure among the Central Bantu," in *African Systems of Kinship and Marriage,* ed. A. R. Radcliffe-Brown and Daryll Forde (London: Oxford University Press, 1950), pp. 207–51; and in the more comprehensive survey of matrilineal societies, David M. Schneider and Kathleen Gough, eds., *Matrilineal Kinship* (Berkeley and Los Angeles: University of California Press, 1961).

The question of how or to what extent males and females differ in personality is discussed in two collections of articles: Dirk L. Schaffer, ed., *Sex Differences in Personality: Readings* (Belmont, Calif.: Brooks/Cole, 1971), and Eleanor E. Maccoby, ed., *The Development of Sex Differences* (Stanford, Calif.: Stanford University Press, 1966).

The view that male dominance stems from the hunting tradition is presented in Lionel Tiger and Robin Fox, *The Imperial Animal* (New York: Holt, Rinehart, & Winston, 1971) and also in Robert Ardrey's books, the latest of which is *The Hunting Hypothesis* (New York: Atheneum, Publishers, 1976).

A more feminist approach to the evolution of culture is expressed in M. Kay Martin and Barbara Voorhies, *Female of the Species* (New York: Columbia University Press, 1975) and in Ernestine Friedl, *Women and Men: An Anthropologist's View* (New York: Holt, Rinehart, & Winston, 1975).

Some interesting reading is provided in two collections of articles by female anthropologists: Michelle Zimbalist Rosaldo and Louise Lamphere eds., *Woman, Culture, and Society* (Stanford, Calif.: Stanford University Press, 1974), and Carolyn J. Matthiasson, ed., *Many Sisters: Women in Cross-Cultural Perspective* (New York: The Free Press, 1974).

15

AGE GRADES AND VOLUNTARY ASSOCIATIONS

A s we have seen, kinship is an important organizing principle not only in tribal societies but also at higher levels of socioeconomic integration. However, it is not the only organizing principle. Societies are knit together in other ways than through kinship.

Just as all societies have kinship terms for different relatives, they also have terms for persons of different age levels, corresponding roughly to our words: infant, baby, child, boy, girl, adolescent, young man, young girl, man, woman, old man, old woman—to which various other terms could be added. These refer to different *age grades*.

Age grades and age sets

The term *age set* is used for a group of persons of the same sex who are of about the same age, such as the members of a particular class in school. Together they advance from one grade to another. Members of an age set may develop strong bonds of solidarity, supporting one another in everyday activities and in marriage and other ceremonies. Like kinship units, they may be corporate groups, although they do not usually own property or have special religious cults or shrines.

Initiation ceremonies

In some societies, movement from one age grade to another is celebrated by elaborate rituals, especially at puberty. Indeed, boys' initiation ceremonies at puberty receive far more emphasis in some societies than do marriage ceremonies.

This is the case among the Arunta of central Australia, whose initiation ceremonies go on for weeks or months and are marked by various stages. The boys are first segregated from the women and children and are made

Boys' initiation
ceremony, Xavante
tribe, South America.

to fast and stay awake at night. Then the old men throw the boys up in the air and beat them when they come down. The men sit around an initiate and bite his scalp and chin until they bleed (which makes the hair grow and is good for the scalp, they say). Then the boys are circumcised and subincised. In a final ordeal they have to lie on some leaves over a smoldering fire. A boy who has gone through all that is surely entitled to feel that he is now a man.

Circumcision and other genital operations have a wide distribution in the puberty ceremonies of Africa, Melanesia, and Australia. In some Australian societies, a tooth gets knocked out instead. In the tropical forest area of South America, youths are often tested by fasting, exposure to ant bites, scarification, and whipping. A girl may be hoisted in a hammock up to the ceiling of the large communal house in which she lives, where she is exposed to smoke from fires within the house.

These ordeals are reminiscent of the hazing that accompanies initiation into secret societies, and, in a sense, that is what is involved. The boys who are admitted into the ranks of the older males are often given instruction about matters hitherto kept from them, and they may be warned on pain of death or severe punishment never to reveal these secrets to the women or uninitiated children.

Arunta men have sacred objects of stone or wood, decorated with simple designs, called *churingas*. These are kept in secret storage places and taken out on solemn occasions, passed from hand to hand among the men, and sometimes rubbed on their bodies. These *churingas* must never be seen by women or children, but, after a boy has been initiated, he may be shown them and told something about the mysteries associated with them.

In the Chaga tribe in East Africa, the adult men are not supposed to defecate. At least, that is the impression they try to give to the women. They say that at the time of initiation a man's anus is stopped up by a plug, which he retains until old age. Defecation must be done very secretly, and severe punishments are threatened to any man who should be so disloyal as to spill the secret. However, the women know what is going on. In *their* initiation ceremonies, the older women tell the young girls that the men pretend not to defecate, and they are warned not to laugh about the matter.

So, initiation into adulthood involves learning all kinds of things one did not know before. For the boys, initiation involves separation from their mothers and closer association with the adult men. Such ceremonies celebrate and reinforce male social solidarity. They often occur in warring polygynous societies in which male solidarity is an important desideratum. Upon initia-

Initiation among the Iatmul of New Guinea. The boy, clasped and comforted by his mother's brother, is cut by a member of the moiety opposite to that of the boy.

tion the boy may be given a new name, new accouterments, and new privileges that designate his enhanced status.

Some different explanations have been offered by anthropologists to account for why there are initiation ceremonies in some societies and not in others. In some Pacific islands there are no such transition rites; so socialization of the young can take place without them. Explanations for this range from psychological to sociological in nature. John W. M. Whiting and some of his colleagues have offered a series of interpretations based on cross-cultural correlations in 56 societies. It was hypothesized that societies likely to have initiation ceremonies for boys at puberty are those in which mother and child sleep exclusively together for at least a year after the birth and which have a taboo on sexual relations between husband and wife during that period. The reason first put forward for this hypothesis was that the mother-son sleeping arrangement establishes a strong, dependent relationship of the boy upon the mother and Oedipal hostility toward the father, both of which need to be counteracted by the time of puberty. An initiation ceremony serves these functions by separating the boys from their mothers and bringing them into the ranks of the adult males. A later interpretation by Whiting, which was felt to be more satisfactory than the earlier one, was that one consequence of exclusive mother-child sleeping arrangements is a boy's cross-sex identification with his mother that needs to be overcome and replaced by male identification through the drama of the initiation ceremony. Whiting and his colleagues found correlations in support of their hypotheses linking exclusive mother-child sleeping arrangements and postpartum sex taboos with initiation ceremonies. Of 20 societies where both antecedent variables were found, 14 had initiation ceremonies and 6 did not. Where both of the antecedent variables were absent, only 2 of the 25 societies had the ceremonies (Whiting, Kluckhohn, and Anthony 1958; Burton and Whiting 1961).

Interpretations of a more sociological, less psychological sort have been offered by Yehudi A. Cohen and Frank W. Young, both of whom have also made use of the cross-cultural correlation approach. In a sample of 65 societies, Cohen distinguished between those in which socialization is directed toward establishing the individual in a larger kin group stressing interdependence (28 societies) and those in which socialization is directed toward independence anchored in a nuclear family (37 societies). Initiation ceremonies were found in 18 of the 28 societies of the first type (about 65 percent) but in only 1 of the second type. This suggests that initiation ceremonies are more apt to occur in societies in which the interdependent action of clan or lineage members is important (Cohen 1964:113).

Frank W. Young claims that initiation ceremonies serve to dramatize and reinforce male solidarity in "middle-level" societies "where the variety of food exploitation patterns is limited and where the resources may be exploited by cooperative groups. Moreover, it is among such societies that intergroup hostilities conducive to male solidarity are possible" (Young 1962:380).

In another cross-cultural study, Judith K. Brown finds that no initiation ceremony takes place for girls in societies where they leave home upon marriage since the act of leaving marks that change. But, in societies where the girl remains in the same social setting after marriage, a ceremony may be performed to mark her change of status, especially in societies in which women make a notable contribution to subsistence (J. K. Brown 1963).

Men's houses

Many societies have a special men's house where unmarried men sleep. It also frequently serves as a ceremonial center and military stronghold. Among the Rengma Naga of northeastern India, boys move to the men's house when they are six or seven years old and sleep there until they get married. Older men come there to sit and gossip and to instruct the young boys. In former days, when fighting was frequent, men kept their knives, spears, and shields in the men's house. This place was regarded as a sanctuary. No fugitive criminal could be harmed if he sought protection there. Corresponding to the men's house there was a "dormitory" for unmarried women, which girls entered at the age of six or seven and left at marriage.

Men's houses are found in various societies in Africa, Indonesia, Melane-

Men's house in New Guinea.

sia, Micronesia, Polynesia, and South America. The character and functions of such houses differ in different cultures, but their existence in any society serves to symbolize and strengthen male solidarity. The bonds among the adult men crosscut kinship lines, enabling the men of a society to act in concert, whether they are related by kinship ties or not.

Nyakyusa age-set villages

An unusual arrangement emphasizing age sets has been worked out by the Nyakyusa, a Bantu-speaking tribe in East Africa. Until around ten years of age, boys live in their fathers' homes, but, after that, they leave and start a new village with other boys of their age set and build little huts of reeds in which they sleep. Later, when they are older, the boys build more substantial houses with better thatch. At first, two or three friends share a hut, but, eventually, each builds his own house. Unmarried youths continue to eat at their fathers' houses, which they visit in small groups in turn.

When a young man of about 25 gets married, he brings his wife to his village. Then, for the first time, he is able to have fields of his own and eat his own produce, for cultivation requires the cooperation of a man and a woman, and cooking is women's work.

Eight or ten years after the young men from the chief's village have begun to marry, their fathers hand over the government of the country to them, following an elaborate series of ceremonies.

This system should lead to considerable autonomy and independence on the part of young men. Although bonds with age mates are emphasized, kinship ties are still important, for property, such as cattle, circulates within the kinship group rather than within the age-set village (Wilson 1951).

The solidarity of an age set may be brought about by other means, such as membership in school classes or fighting groups. In these systems the age grades crosscut kinship lines and provide for wider social ties.

Voluntary associations

So far we have been dealing with society-wide categories according to age. Some societies also have voluntary associations not joined by all members of the society, although they are not limited by kinship. These include people of different age sets and different kin groups. Some societies may have several parallel, roughly equivalent social units of this kind, which are competitive in some respects. An example is provided by the military societies of Plains Indian tribes such as the Cheyenne.

Cheyenne military societies

The equestrian, buffalo-hunting Cheyenne Indians of the early 19th century on the Great Plains had six military societies: Fox, Elk, Shield, Bowstring, Dog, and Northern Crazy Dogs. The members in each of these came from all the bands that made up the summer-camp circle, with the exception of the Dog soldiers, who were from a single band. Except for the latter, the military societies could function only during the summer months when all the Cheyenne bands came together. In wintertime the camp circle was dispersed and the component bands hunted in separate territories.

It was an honor to belong to a military society, and each claimed to be the best and bravest. Each society had special ways of painting the body and personal possessions and maintained some special traditions. The military societies had the responsibility of keeping order when the tribe was on the march, during communal buffalo hunts, and on tribal ritual occasions. They represented a kind of police force under the authority of the tribal council of 44 chiefs and could punish persons who violated the rule against unauthorized hunting of the buffalo and broke other tribal laws. These social units obviously had much political importance in regulating social order among the Cheyennes. They crosscut kinship, age, and band divisions.

Secret societies

In some societies there are voluntary associations whose membership is secret. Some American Indian tribes, including the Hopi, Kwakiutl, and Iroquois, have had such societies; they are also important in West Africa and the Congo. Sometimes, as among the Hopi, the Iroquois, and the Mende of Sierra Leone, secret societies are associated with the curing of particular ailments. Sometimes they have political functions. African secret societies help to maintain social order, backed by strong religious sanctions. Since secret societies sometimes perform in public dances or rituals, it is not surprising that many have developed the use of masks or other forms of disguise, like the Ku Klux Klan.

Among the Mende, secret societies play roles in the education of the young, regulation of sexual conduct, supervision of political and economic affairs, and the operation of various social services, including medical treatment, entertainment, and recreation. In the Poro society, boys undergo a long initiation which involves both ordeals and instruction. They learn something about native law, crafts, agricultural techniques, drumming and singing, bridge building, and the setting of traps. There is a parallel society for girls, who receive training in housework and child care and are given sex instruction. The Humoi society is concerned with the regulation of sexual conduct. The Mende have many taboos concerning sex, and there are many relatives with whom sexual intercourse is forbidden; it is believed that transgression of such rules results in sickness. Persons must be treated by the society concerned with the taboos they have broken; so those who violate sexual regulations report to the Humoi society. Illness may also be explained as being due to a person's having entered that part of the bush where secret society meetings have been held. Confession to the society is required, followed by medical treatment and purification. Those who have been so treated become members of the secret society, since they have learned something about the society's operations in the process.

The Poro society has important political functions. No one can hold office among the Mende without being a Poro member; no chief can be appointed without its approval. There are dangers of autocracy here, but the Poro may, at the same time, act as a check on the autocracy of rulers. The Poro society also has economic functions in fixing prices for certain commodities and regulating trade (Little 1949).

Secret societies have sometimes played political and economic roles in the Western world as well—witness the Ku Klux Klan and the Mafia. Anthropologists have not done much work on secret societies, but that is understandable, for if an anthropologist can learn the secrets of such a society, it's not a very secret society.

Religious cults

Religious cults that require periodic ceremonies bring members together and emphasize their common ties. Among many possible examples, let us consider the Drum Dance, or Dream Dance, of the Chippewa Indians in northern Wisconsin. This dance was borrowed from the Sioux in the 1870s, after peace was made between these Indian groups. It is said to have originated from the vision of a young Sioux Indian girl who was instructed by the Great Spirit to spread the dance as a means of reconciling the Chippewa, Sioux, and other Indian groups. Not all Chippewa Indians are members of this cult. In the 1940s (the period for which the following description applies), there were three drum groups at the Lac Court Oreilles reservation, each consisting of about 30 people. Such a group tries to meet at least once every season to drum, sing, and pray. Members also assemble on various emergency occasions—to remove mourning from a person who is initiated into the group, to install new members, or to effect curing through the presence of certain powerful individuals who relate dreams of their buffalo or grizzly-bear spirits.

The drum groups also visit other communities and act as hosts to visiting drum groups from outside. Not only do the Chippewa Indians from different reservations pay mutual four-day visits to each other but the Drum Dance network also includes Menomini, Potawatomi, and Winnebago Indians, for the Drum Dance aims to cut across local and tribal ties and to establish friendly relations everywhere. This intercommunication is fostered by the practice of giving drums away every few years. Such a cult provides an in-group for its members, taking on some of the attributes and functions of a kinship unit.

Voluntary associations in the United States

The United States is a nation in which all kinds of voluntary associations flourish—clubs, including women's clubs (unheard of in some nations), learned societies, Rotarians, Lions, Moose, Elk, nudist groups, bird-watching societies, veterans' associations, alumni, chess players, societies for helping the American Indian or Negro Americans, associations for aiding museums, conserving nature, and many other causes. This aspect of American life must have developed early in our history, for it was commented upon, with his usual penetrating attention, by Alexis de Tocqueville in the 1830s.

Tocqueville (1954:117–18) found that voluntary associations were much more numerous here than in other countries, and he related this to the democratic traditions of the United States:

As soon as several of the inhabitants of the United States have taken up an opinion or a feeling which they wish to promote in the world, they look out for mutual assistance; and as soon as they have found one another out, they combine. From that moment on they are no longer isolated men, but a power seen from afar, whose actions serve for an example and whose language is listened to.

Impressed by this phenomenon, Tocqueville (1954:118) concluded, "If men are to remain civilized or to become so, the art of associating together must grow and improve in the same ratio in which the equality of conditions is increased."

Summary

An *age grade* includes members of a society who belong to a particular age bracket, while an *age set* is a group of persons of the same sex and about the same age who advance from one age grade to another. In some societies the passage from one age grade to the next is marked by initiation ceremonies, especially at around the time of puberty. Distinctions between the sexes and age grades are emphasized in societies that have special men's houses, where adult men congregate and where unmarried men sleep.

Some societies have voluntary associations that include people of different age sets and kin groups. The Cheyenne military societies of the early 19th century provide an example. In some societies, such as the Hopi, Iroquois, and Kwakiutl, there are voluntary associations whose membership is secret. Masks may be used by such groups in public dances and ceremonies.

The United States is particularly rich in voluntary associations. Tocqueville, who noted this abundance early in the 19th century, related it to the democratic traditions of the United States.

Suggestions for further reading

Puberty ceremonies, especially those involving genital operations such as circumcision and subincision, have lent themselves to various Freudian and sociological analyses, of which the following references provide a variety of interpretations: Theodor Reik, *Ritual: Psychoanalytic Studies* (New York: International Universities Press, 1958), pp. 99 ff.; Bruno Bettelheim, *Symbolic Wounds: Puberty Rites and the Envious Male* (Glencoe, Ill.: Free Press, 1954); John W. M. Whiting, Richard Kluckhohn, and Albert Anthony, "The Function of Male Initiation Ceremonies at Puberty," in *Readings in Social Psychology,* ed. Eleanor E. Maccoby, Theodore M. Newcomb, and Eugene L. Hartley, 3d ed. (New York: Henry Holt & Co., 1958), pp. 359–70; William N. Stephens, *The Oedipus Complex: Cross-Cultural Evidence* (Glencoe, Ill.:

Free Press, 1962); Yehudi A. Cohen, *The Transition From Childhood to Adolescence: Cross-Cultural Studies of Initiation Ceremonies, Legal Systems, and Incest Taboos* (Chicago: Aldine Publishing Co., 1964); Frank W. Young, *Initiation Ceremonies: A Cross-Cultural Study of Status Dramatization* (Indianapolis: Bobbs-Merrill Co., Inc., 1965).

16

CASTES AND CLASSES

C aste and class stratification are found mainly in advanced civilizations. Although some exceptions can be cited, there is usually not much internal ranking in hunting-gathering bands. Hereditary social classes appear in many advanced horticultural and agricultural societies. In this chapter we shall consider some aspects of the caste system in India and similar features in some other societies. After that, concepts of class and class stratification will be discussed.

A Hindu caste is an endogamous, hierarchically ranked social group, which is sometimes associated with a particular occupation. Rules determine whether or not one may accept food or water from persons of different caste. Usually, one may accept food from one's own and from higher, but not lower, castes. Concepts of pollution are associated with the lowest-ranking castes, termed *untouchables,* who often have separate wells and live in separate quarters in a town or village.

Hindu castes

Endogamy

Endogamy is the requirement to marry within a particular group. Like the opposite rule of exogamy, it may apply to different kinds of social units. Among the Inca of Peru there was a requirement to marry a person of one's own village or community; this could be called village or local endogamy. In the Hindu caste system one must marry within the caste or subcaste. A caste resembles a clan in that membership is determined by birth. However, clans are exogamous; husband and wife are members of different clans but must always belong to the same caste.

Hierarchical ranking

Castes in India are ranked. Some castes are considered to be purer and higher than others. The Brahmans, associated with the priesthood and with education, are accorded the highest rank, while Chamars (leatherworkers) and Bhangis (sweepers) are the lowest. In some of the intermediate ranks, there may be disagreement about relative position in the system, but there is a rough consensus about the structure of the hierarchy and placement of castes within it.

The relative rank of a caste group is related to its traditional occupation. Those engaged in work that is considered defiling, such as handling leather or cleaning latrines, are low in the social order. Some low-caste groups have tried to raise their collective status by refusing to follow traditional occupations, tabooing the eating of meat, and being meticulous in the observance of orthodox Hindu rituals.

Because of the stratification in the caste system, some people have regarded castes as frozen classes. One theory about the origin of the caste system is that it resulted from efforts of the light-skinned Aryan invaders after 1500 B.C. to maintain social distance between themselves and the dark-skinned peoples they conquered. Yet another equally plausible view is that a caste system was already in operation in India before the arrival of the Aryans. Contrary to the usual assumptions, a caste system does not preclude social mobility. The hierarchy is not absolutely frozen. Some Hindu untouchables are wealthy; many Brahmans are poor. An untouchable, B. R. Ambedkar, was India's first minister of law. Status in India is affected by criteria other than caste membership alone.

Traditional occupation

Not all Hindu castes are associated with particular occupations. Exceptions occur in the case of some groups, such as the Jats of northern India, that originated as tribal groups. Many hill tribes, which formerly constituted separate social units with distinctive cultures, have become absorbed into the Hindu caste system, often, though not always, with low rank.

To give an example of a particular Indian village, let us consider the caste composition of the village of Rampur, 15 miles west of Delhi, with a population of about 1,100. This village, like many in northern India, has a "dominant caste"—a caste that not only has numerical superiority but also owns all the land in the village. In Rampur the dominant caste is that of the Jats, who number 78 families. They have the reputation of being hard-working farmers.

There are 15 Brahman families in Rampur. The men of these families are farmers, whose actual status is no higher than that of the Jat landlords. None of them are priests.

Not far below the Jats in status are the four Khati (carpenter) families and one Lohar (blacksmith). There is one Baniya (merchant) family. There are three Nai (barber), two Chipi (tailor), seven Kumhar (potter), five Jhinvar (water carrier), and four Dhobi (washerman) families. At the bottom of the hierarchy are the 20 Chamar (leatherworker) and 10 Bhangi (sweeper) families.

Most of the houses of the Jats are clustered in the center of the village, along with some Brahmans, the Nais, and the Baniya families. Most of the other castes are on the outskirts of the village.

Not all persons carry on the traditional occupation associated with the caste. Many Chamars refuse to do so because of their desire for higher status. But many persons do follow the traditional work (Lewis with Barnouw 1958: chaps. 1, 2).

The jajmani system

In villages like Rampur there is a system whereby goods and services are exchanged that has come to be known as the *jajmani* system. It is helpful to understand how this system works in a rural Indian village, since it serves to make the caste system more comprehensible to a person from the Western world.

To contrast jajmani practices with our own, let us consider the problem of getting a haircut. In the United States a man who wants to get a haircut goes to a barbershop, waits for his turn, has his hair cut, pays for it, and gives the barber a tip. If he lives in a city, he may go to many different barbershops in the course of a year, not being obliged to patronize the same one all the time. In Rampur, however, there are no barbershops. If you are a Jat, a barber comes to your home or visits you in the fields. Payment is made, not when the job is finished but later, at harvest time. You can expect the barber to come around in about a month to cut your hair and give you a shave once more. It is always the same barber or a close relative, a brother or son, who cuts your hair. Maybe that person is not a very good barber and you would rather have another one, but the rules do not permit it.

Barbers have hereditary ties with certain Jat families whose hair they cut. They do not serve all Jat families, for the barbers of a particular area have to divide up the clientele. The client who is served in this system is called a *jajman;* the person performing the service is termed a *kamin*. A particular kamin family may have served a jajman family for many generations. The barber's father cut the hair of the jajman's father, and the barber's son will cut the hair of the jajman's son or grandson. At harvest times, when the kamins present themselves at the fields, stipulated amounts of grain are handed out by the jajmans to their kamins. There may be many of the latter, for the jajman has similar relations with families of other castes. A particular potter family provides clay vessels when needed during the year. Members of a particular Chamar family drag off the jajman's dead cows, skin them, and make sandals and other leather objects. A particular Bhangi family sweeps the jajman's courtyard and cleans the latrine. Thus, many goods and services are exchanged with little exchange of money.

Besides grain, kamins receive various other benefits from the system: a virtually free house site; some free food, fodder, and timber; and credit facilities and legal advice and aid from their jajmans. They are tied to their client families in various ways. Nais (barbers), for example, used to be marriage go-betweens and helped to arrange the marriages of their jajman's children. Chamars did various kinds of fieldwork, repaired roofs, and dug wells, among other things. Each caste has a particular role to play at a wedding and may expect to receive some food and other handouts on the occasion. Lower castes exchange some goods and services among themselves.

The jajmani system is now breaking up in Rampur and in many other villages through an increasing involvement with the money economy from outside the village and because of the refusal of some lower caste groups, particularly Chamars, to perform their traditional services (Lewis with Barnouw 1958).

One might suppose that if the jajmani system is breaking up, the caste system itself might be disappearing in India, especially since the government has passed much legislation against the observance of untouchability and caste discrimination. However, that is not the case. Caste endogamy is still

Hindu barber shaving customer in Rampur.

the rule. A small minority of well-to-do westernized persons are willing to marry across caste lines, but, otherwise, this is seldom done. In elections, castes tend to vote in blocs. There has probably been an increase in caste solidarity in recent years among low-caste groups, such as the Chamars, who are campaigning for better treatment. Caste journals are published. There are caste hostels, banks, hospitals, and cooperatives. Separate seats are set aside for "Ex-Untouchables" in Parliament and state legislatures, and there are separate scholarships for them in schools and universities. These institutions paradoxically emphasize and perpetuate caste distinctions.

Many societies, as in Egypt, Iran, Europe, and Japan, have at various times developed rules confining certain occupations to particular social groups. In itself this regulation does not bring about a caste system, but it does combine the rule of endogamy with a traditional hereditary occupation.

Castelike systems outside of India

From the 12th to the middle of the 19th century A.D., Japan had a system of five ranked social groups headed by the military Samurai. At the bottom of the social order were groups like the Eta, leatherworkers, whose position was remarkably like that of the Hindu Chamars of India.

The Eta of Japan

Like the Chamars and similar groups in Tibet and Korea, the Eta traditionally work with dead animals in removing carcasses, butchering, and shoemaking and other leatherwork. The Hindu notion that work with dead animals and hides is defiling was evidently diffused along with Buddhism to Tibet, Korea, and Japan. In the seventh, eighth, and subsequent centuries in Japan, legislation was passed forbidding hunting and slaughtering, and Shinto notions of uncleanness became associated with meat eating; but it was apparently not until the Tokugawa period (1603–1868) that the Eta became distinguished as a kind of untouchable caste, required to marry within their own group and to live in separate Eta villages. They were sometimes obliged to wear a patch of leather sewn on the kimono, to walk on one side of the street, and to observe various other restrictions like those affecting the Chamars in India.

The Eta were officially emancipated by government edict in 1871, but their lot has not greatly improved, and they still live in ghettos. Like Chamars in northern India, many Eta have refused to remove the carcasses of dead animals and to continue leatherwork. Self-improvement and protest movements and demands for integration provide parallels with such developments in India and the United States. Although the Eta are racially indistinguishable from other Japanese and hence "invisible," they are not unidentifiable. Since their homes are restricted to Eta neighborhoods, their addresses give them away, and "passing" is very difficult (De Vos and Wagatsuma 1966).

Castelike groups in Africa

The term *caste system* has been applied to the African kingdom of Ruanda, which has a population of nearly 2 million. The situation is different from that of India with its thousands of caste groups, for in Ruanda there are only three main castes: (1) the Tutsi, who are the wealthiest and who own most of the cattle in the country; (2) the Hutu, the agriculturalists; and (3) the Twa, who are hunters and potters. The Hutu make up 85 percent of the population, the Tutsi 10 percent, and the Twa 5 percent. The three groups have somewhat different physical appearance, the Tutsi being Nilotic, while the Hutu are of Forest Negro type and the Twa are pygmylike, although taller than the Pygmies.

The term *caste* seems justifiable here, since these groups are mainly endogamous, hierarchically ranked, and associated with different occupations. The Tutsi constitute the dominant group, exerting political control over the larger Hutu caste (Maquet 1960).

In Somalia some groups are treated in ways reminiscent of untouchability in India. Tanners and hunters, known as Midgan, are regarded as unclean and are tabooed in marriage. Similar attitudes are held concerning blacksmiths, who are considered inferior and defiling by the Masai.

Black-white relations in the United States

In the 1940s some writers compared black-white relations in the Deep South of the United States with caste relations (Davis, Gardner, and Gardner 1941; Dollard 1949; Myrdal 1944). Although ideals of racial endogamy were upheld by both blacks and whites, the frequency of interbreeding shows that this particular criterion of caste was rather weak. The authors, however, pointed out that black-white marriages were not recognized in the South at the time of their research and that illegitimate offspring of a white man and a black woman were always classed as black.

Differences in occupation held to some extent between blacks and whites, and this is still much the same today, since many blacks are of low socioeconomic class, poorly educated, and face barriers of prejudice (H. P. Miller 1964:90, 94, 95).

Emphases on endogamy and hierarchy are castelike features of a society. Orthodox Hindu religious traditions about the inherent inferiority of low castes find their American parallels in biblical texts that have sometimes been cited to support segregation. There is even a concept of untouchability or pollution, suggested by the separate washrooms and drinking fountains formerly characteristic of the South.

Although the application of the concept of caste to black-white relations is loose in some respects, there seem to be striking parallels with Hindu caste attitudes and practices and with Japanese-Eta relations, suggesting regularities in social and psychological patterns in hierarchically structured

Entrance to waiting room, train station, Atlanta, Georgia.

societies.[1] It was the coexistence of this tendency toward hierarchic attitudes with American democratic traditions that led Gunnar Myrdal to term this problem an "American dilemma."

With the development of castes and classes, the vertical axis acquired an interesting symbolic significance in human thought. Certain attitudes are built into some Indo-European languages and are expressed in several English words used in preceding pages, such as *super*ordinate and *sub*ordinate, *upper* class and *lower* class. We distinguish between *high-* and *low*-ranking persons, *over*lords and *under*lings, *top* dog, and *low* man on the totem pole. This kind of hierarchy is often expressed in myths and religious traditions. For example, according to one of the hymns of the Rig-Veda of the Aryans, the four *varna,* or social divisions of India, sprang from different parts of a primeval man, the Brahmans (priests) from his mouth, the Kshatriya (warriors) from his arms, the Vaishya (peasants) from his thighs, and the Shudra (serfs) from his feet. (Basham 1954:35). Here, the ranking of the *varna* corresponds with the vertical order.

Differences between castes in India are symbolized by sitting arrange-

Cognitive aspects of hierarchy

---

[1] Another somewhat parallel situation is to be found in Ladino-Indian relationships in Guatemalan communities (Tumin 1952).

ments. In a north Indian village, if a low-caste man, such as a potter or water carrier, approaches a group of higher-ranking Rājpūts who are sitting on string cots, he should not sit at their level but should squat on the ground some distance away. Similar practices are followed on the Indonesian island of Bali, where there are caste divisions based on the Hindu *varna.* A low-caste person should never be at a higher level than a high-caste person. Note how this "vertical" symbolism contrasts with the more "horizontal" and reciprocal symbolism concerning moieties discussed on page 250.

Class

Class differs from caste in lacking a kinship basis. Since a child is usually assigned to the class of its parents, and since persons often marry within their own class, the distinction may not seem clear. But in societies with class stratification it is possible for a person to move either up or down the class hierarchy and to marry someone of a different class. In India, Chamars are always Chamars, even if they change their occupation and become well-to-do; Brahmans always remain Brahmans. Caste membership is more explicit and unalterable than class membership, although, in some societies, classes may be distinguished by different speech patterns and clothing and may thus seem quite distinct from one another and separated by marked social distance.

Class has been variously defined or determined by different writers. Some have used income or occupation for assigning class membership, while others have made use of additional criteria, such as type of housing, residence area, and prestige rating. Karl Marx, whose system of ideas made such important use of the concept of class, defined class in terms of relationship to the means of production. The bourgeoisie are owners of the means of production, such as factories. Members of the proletariat, or working class, have no such ownership and must work for the bourgeoisie to earn a living. Although Marx also referred to other class groups in his writings, these two were the crucial ones from his point of view, for he believed that the future conflict between the workers of the world and the bourgeoisie would ultimately usher in the communist society.

Classes in Middletown

In their well-known study *Middletown,* Robert and Helen Lynd presented a view of class membership that was similar, if not identical, to the bourgeois-proletarian dichotomy. Middletown (a pseudonym) in Indiana was considered to be a typical U.S. community, with about 36,500 inhabitants, when it was studied by the Lynds in the 1920s. They saw Middletown, then, as being made up of two groups: the Working Class and the Business Class. The workers made things and performed services, while those in business sold and promoted things, services, and ideas. There were two and a half times as many people in the Working Class as in the Business Class. To quote the Lynds (1929:23–24):

The mere fact of being born upon one or the other side of the watershed roughly formed by these two groups is the most significant cultural factor tending to influence what one does all day long throughout one's life; whom one marries; when one gets up in the morning; whether one belongs to the Holy Roller or Presbyterian church; or drives a Ford or a Buick; whether or not one's daughter makes the desirable high school Violet Club; or one's wife meets with the Sew We Do Club or with the Art Students' League . . . .

In 1937 the Lynds published the results of a restudy of Middletown, whose population had since increased to almost 50,000. They found that conditions, including the class structure, had changed somewhat. Without altogether giving up their former two-class division, they now set forth a series of six occupational groups, which in some ways resemble the six classes based on prestige rating, style of living, and other factors that W. L. Warner described for the New England town of "Yankee City" (Lynd and Lynd 1937:443–61). If both Middletown studies are valid, it seems that classes can change or differentiate rapidly within a ten-year period, at least in some parts of the United States.

Defining class membership

Analyses like those of the Lynds raise the question: Is a class something that exists in the minds of members of the society or something that exists in the mind of the sociologist? Middletowners often denied the reality or significance of class differences; nevertheless, according to the Lynds, their whole lives were being shaped by them. In this case, then, classes were distinguished by the observer rather than by the people themselves.

This is not always the case in class-stratified societies. Reporting on a questionnaire given to large numbers of persons in England, Geoffrey Gorer writes: "Nine out of ten English people feel no hesitation in assigning themselves to a social class. Five of them call themselves working class and three middle class. . . ." (Gorer 1955:34).[2]

Self-assignments to class groups are not always determined by income or occupation; subjective factors are often involved. Thus, one woman wrote: "I was born in the slums of London of working class parents and although I have attained a higher standard of living I still maintain I am working class" (Gorer 1955:34). Conversely, people who consider themselves to be middle class sometimes live in the slums and have low incomes. Identification

---

[2] Here we note a contrast with the United States, where public opinion polls (like the *Fortune* magazine poll in 1940) have found that about 80 percent of Americans describe themselves as "middle class."

with a particular class stems from family background as well as from occupation and income.

Warner took such subjective factors into account in drawing up a sixfold prestige-rank classification of 99 percent of the families in Yankee City, the name he gave a New England town with a population of about 17,000. His classifications were as follows:

1. Upper-upper. Wealthy old families who have lived in the best neighborhoods for several generations; 1.4 percent of the population.

2. Lower-upper. Slightly richer in average income than the upper-upper but with less prestige, because they are relative newcomers or because their wealth has been recently acquired; their manners are held to be less polished and their families less well established; 1.6 percent.

3. Upper-middle. Families of moderately successful business and professional people; 10.2 percent.

4. Lower-middle. Families of clerks, skilled and semiskilled workers, and wholesale and retail dealers; 28 percent.

5. Upper-lower. "Respectable" working-class families, 32.6 percent.

6. Lower-lower. Low-prestige working-class families; 25.2 percent (Warner and Lunt 1941).

This, then, is a partly subjective ordering of social classes, in contrast to Marx's distinction of classes in terms of relationship to the means of production. However, Warner's six groupings seem to correspond to social realities. This is suggested by another study made by Warner et al. (1949), that of a Midwestern town he called Jonesville, with a population of about 6,000. The same town was studied by August B. Hollingshead (1949), who named it Elmtown. Both sociologists, using different procedures, made prestige ratings of the community's families and came out with very similar results. Each distinguished five social classes. Since a number of such studies have yielded similar results, it seems that at least some U.S. cities and towns are stratified along some such lines.

Warner's system of classification would not seem to be applicable cross-culturally in non-Western stratified societies, where other models would have to be devised. Nor would it apply to the Soviet Union, which also has class stratification, though of a different order.[3]

The power elite

One potential way of studying stratified systems cross-culturally would be to determine which people within a particular society make the important decisions. Except for atomistic societies in which there is little political centralization, most societies have people in positions of authority whose decisions

---

[3] One interpretation distinguished eight social classes in the Soviet Union in rank order as follows: the ruling elite, the superior intelligentsia, the general intelligentsia, the working-class aristocracy, the white-collar workers, the well-to-do peasants, the disadvantaged workers, and the forced-labor group (Inkeles 1950).

affect many other persons. These are not exclusively political or governmental leaders; in the United States, for example, leaders of large corporations form part of the power elite. An upper class may be much larger than the core of leading decision makers, but it may be assumed that there is some sort of relationship between the core and the broader upper class; this relationship may be examined in any particular society.

In an effort to identify the power elite in the United States, G. William Domhoff has used both social and economic criteria, such as listing in the *Social Register,* attendance at one of a select group of prep schools such as Choate, membership in one of a select group of men's clubs, and substantial family wealth. Although friendships and marriages are apt to occur within this social level, it is an open class into which newcomers keep being admitted. The problem is to show that members of this wealthy class make important political decisions. Domhoff points out the predominant representation of its members in the universities, the big foundations, the Council on Foreign Affairs, the Foreign Policy Association, and the National Association of Manufacturers. This upper class, according to Domhoff, provides the main financial support for both the Republican and Democratic parties, and from its ranks often come those who fill cabinet posts and act as presidential advisers. But there are many other sources of power on the American scene (labor unions, local politicians), and the upper class obviously does not control all aspects of American life. Moreover, it does not seem to share a unified viewpoint; one could not predict how "it" would act in any given situation (Domhoff 1967).

Despite the differences in economic and political systems in the Soviet Union and the United States, there are special rewards in both nations for people with advanced, specialized education and those in managerial positions. Such persons receive much higher salaries in the Soviet Union than do common laborers. The top elite level consists of *apparatchiki,* full-time Communist Party functionaries and their families. H. Gordon Skilling (1971:379–80) roughly estimates the numbers of the Soviet elite as follows: ". . . 100,000 to 200,000 *apparatchiki,* 100,000 managers in heavy industry, several 100,000 military officers, perhaps the same number of military police, 100,000 lawyers, 300,000 economists (including planners and statisticians), and 6,000 writers (members of the Writer's Union)." Like the American power elite, these groups do not share a unified viewpoint but often have conflicting interests and goals.

Poverty

There are different ways of defining poverty or deciding which persons make up "the poor." One way is to establish a particular income level. One writer, for example (Gallaway 1973), uses a salary of $3,000 per year per family as a standard, below which families are said to be poor. That is close to the poverty income line of $3,335 for a nonfarm family of four,

East Harlem.

established in the late sixties by the Social Security Administration. Another way of defining poverty is to arbitrarily take the families in the bottom fifth of the income distribution. In 1958 the lowest fifth of U.S. families had 4.7 percent of total personal income, while the highest fifth had 45.5 percent. One might also gauge poverty in terms of the presence or absence of certain goods or facilities, such as baths and inside toilets, but this may give conflicting evidence since there are families that lack baths and inside toilets but nevertheless have automobiles or TV sets.

Whatever index is used to define poverty, the poor must be considered numerous. In *The Other America* (1964), Michael Harrington estimates that the poor make up about one fourth of our population, somewhere between 40 million and 50 million people. If such a high estimate surprises the reader, it may be because much present-day poverty is invisible, at least to some of the population. As Harrington put it, poverty is often off the beaten track, away from the freeways, hidden in rural areas like Appalachia; and urban slums may be bypassed or only briefly glimpsed by suburban dwellers.

Although there are traditions that idealize poverty, most people seem to regard it with disfavor. Several books and articles have presented evidence that there is more mental disorder among the poor than among higher classes. Best known among these studies is one by August Hollingshead and Fredrick Redlich (1958), who divided the population of New Haven into five socioeconomic classes. They found that in the lowest class (Class V) the incidence of psychoses was almost three times greater than in the two highest classes (I and II) and twice the rate for Class IV.

Summary

Caste and class stratification are found mainly in advanced civilizations. There is usually not much internal ranking in hunting-gathering societies or simple horticultural societies.

A Hindu caste is an endogamous, hierarchically ranked social group, which is sometimes associated with a particular occupation. Concepts of pollution are associated with the lowest-ranking castes, such as sweepers and leatherworkers, who often live in segregated quarters and use separate wells. In Indian villages there are exchanges of goods and services between occupational caste groups involving little use of money. Although the jajmani system, as this system is known, is now breaking up, that has not led to a decline in the caste system itself. Caste endogamy is still the rule.

Caste-like groups have been reported for some societies outside of India, such as the African kingdom of Ruanda. Relations between higher castes and untouchables have found some parallels in white-black relations in the United States and in the position of the Eta, a leatherworking group in Japan.

Class differs from caste in lacking a kinship base. Karl Marx defined class according to the ownership of means of production, resulting in the two-fold class division of the bourgeoisie and the proletariat, or working class. W. L. Warner took subjective factors into account in drawing up a six-fold division of the classes in a New England town. Some other American sociologists have found similar divisions in other American communities.

There are different ways of defining poverty. One way is to establish a particular income level as designating the poor. Another way is to take the families in the bottom fifth of the income distribution. Or one may determine poverty in terms of the presence or absence of certain goods or facilities, such as baths and inside toilets. Whichever index is used, the poor must be considered numerous in the United States.

Suggestions for further reading

A standard work on caste is J. H. Hutton, *Caste in India: Its Nature, Function, and Origins,* 3d ed. (Bombay: Oxford University Press, 1961). For comparisons between India's untouchables, the Eta of Japan, and American Negroes, see George De Vos and Hiroshi Wagatsuma, eds., *Japan's Invisible Race: Caste in Culture and Personality* (Berkeley: University of California Press, 1966).

For cross-cultural studies of class stratification, see Gerhard E. Lenski, *Power and Privilege: A Theory of Social Stratification* (New York: McGraw-Hill Book Co., 1966); Joseph A. Kahl, ed., *Comparative Perspectives on Stratification: Mexico, Great Britain, Japan* (Boston: Little, Brown & Co., 1968). For class stratification in the

United States, see the studies by the Lynds, Warner, and others cited in the chapter, and Joseph A. Kahl's *The American Class Structure* (New York: Rinehart & Co., 1957).

See also Charles A. Valentine, *Culture and Poverty: Critique and Counter-Proposals* (Chicago: University of Chicago Press, 1968).

17

POLITICAL ORGANIZATION, LAW, AND WARFARE

A political unit occupying a particular territory is faced with two require-
ments: to preserve order within its ranks and to regulate relations
with outside groups. All societies have rules of conduct, but rules
are not automatically obeyed. They have to be enforced in some way by
someone or other, if the rules are held to be important for the society's
continuance and well-being.

Societies are also characterized by internal conflict and competition between persons and groups, which need to be worked out or controlled in
some way.

Conflicts occur in all societies, and this is not necessarily unfortunate
or harmful. In some cases, conflict within a group may help to establish,
or reestablish, unity. Indeed, Lewis A. Coser (1956:151) has argued that
such conflicts may be positively functional for the social structure when
they concern goals, values, or interests that do not contradict the basic
assumptions on which the relationship is founded. However, conflict may
be experienced as stressful and dangerous by members of a society, especially
by supporters of the status quo. It is to their interest, and often to the
interests of most members of the society, to resolve conflicts and prevent
their further spread. Whether we label it as law or not, some means of
conflict resolution must exist. This is another function of political authority.

Social control and conflict resolution concern internal order. But a political
community must also deal with outside groups and may engage in warfare,
which may strengthen the authority of the political leadership, at least temporarily. Some societies have developed different leadership offices for the
two spheres of internal and external relations, having both a "peace chief"
and a "war chief"; but more often the political locus of authority deals
with both internal control and external affairs.

In this chapter we will examine how these issues are handled in societies with different bases of subsistence. Following a general approach employed earlier, we will deal in turn with (1) hunting-gathering societies, (2) simple horticultural societies, (3) pastoralists, (4) advanced horticultural societies, (5) agricultural societies, and (6) industrial societies. While these categories do not always permit neat generalizations, they do provide a rough evolutionary framework that can help us to look for possible cross-cultural regularities. We will begin with societies in which there is little political authority, in which headmen have little power. Yet these societies are viable systems. One reason for this is that proper behavior on the part of a society's members is not determined by fear of punishment alone. There are other deterrents to antisocial behavior.

According to Radcliffe-Brown (1952:205), "A sanction is a reaction on the part of a society or of a considerable number of its members to a mode of behavior which is thereby approved (positive sanctions) or disapproved (negative sanctions)." Praise is a positive sanction: applause, awards, medals, the good opinion of one's neighbors. Disapproval is a negative sanction: ostracism, blacklisting, unpopularity. Fear of sorcery is a negative sanction which may serve to inhibit aggression. Fear of ghosts, punitive ancestors, or eternal damnation after death may also contribute to good behavior during this life in different societies. Laws that punish offenders are negative sanctions, but sanctions are a more inclusive category, found in all societies, whether they have law courts and prisons or not. These sanctions are learned in the process of socialization as one grows up.

Hunting-gathering societies

Hunting-gathering societies usually have little political organization. Bands may have headmen or chiefs, but they do not normally exercise much authority over its members. The term *atomistic* has sometimes been used to describe groups such as the Canadian Ojibwa (or Chippewa), the Great Basin Shoshones, and the Central Eskimos. These peoples lived under ecological conditions that favored dispersal at certain seasons; their groups were small and scattered. It was not difficult for the component units, such as families, to break away from the larger group. Hence, it would often be hard for a headman to apply social sanctions against an errant band member.

Among the Canadian Ojibwa there was village life during the summer months when between three and 15 families came together; during the winter months these families broke up to take maximum advantage of the game resources. The families did not always return to the same village sites. Villages were not stable in numbers or location over any considerable period of time.

Pygmy bands in the Congo have been described as frequently breaking up and regrouping in different patterns. This fission and fusion has the function of maintaining peace; if a quarrel threatens, the band may split. This shifting band composition would make it difficult for a headman to wield much authority.

Headmen among the Bushmen of Botswana have responsibilities such as planning the band's movements, but their authority is relatively weak. Lorna Marshall (1967:38) writes: "Headmanship is not especially advantageous to the individual. Among the !Kung, each person does his own work, carries his own load, and shares meat. Headmen are as thin as the rest. No regalia, special honours, or tributes mark them out."

According to Allan Holmberg (1950:59), among the Sirionó of eastern Bolivia ". . . there is no obligation to obey the orders of a chief, no punishment for nonfulfillment. Indeed, little attention is paid to what is said by a chief unless he is a member of one's immediate family."

Under such circumstances, informal sanctions must operate to control aggression. There seems to have been little murder, theft, or open show of hostility among the Canadian Ojibwa. A. Irving Hallowell (1955:278) attributed this to a widespread fear of sorcery, which served to check the expression of aggression. Some Eskimo bands, on the other hand, had high rates of homicide. Knud Rasmussen reported of one Eskimo band that all the adult males of its 15 families had been involved in a homicide, either as principals or accessories; usually this was due to quarrels over women. Female infanticide was common among the Eskimos, but this was not considered a crime by them; nor was the killing of old people who were unable to keep up with the rest of the band when it moved from place to place. If a person is murdered, a kinsman may kill the murderer. A danger here is that a blood feud may develop between the two families.

Among the Eskimos an alternative to murder and the inception of a blood feud is a challenge to a singing contest. Two enemies face one another in a circle of onlookers and alternately sing songs of derision in which each insults the other with such charges as stinginess, incest, cannibalism, or murder. Public opinion has a chance to express itself in the responses of the surrounding crowd, whose applause or jeers help to elect the winner. At the end of the song duel, the enemies are supposed to put aside their quarrel and resume normal relations.

Not all hunting-gathering societies lacked political organization. With the emphasis on relative rank in Northwest Coast Indian tribes, high-ranking chiefs seem to have had more political power than in most hunting societies.

Simple horticultural societies are those in which the digging stick is the chief farming tool. Such societies have been found in parts of North and South America and the Pacific islands, including New Guinea but not Australia. Simple horticultural societies are not very different from hunting-gathering societies in community size and other features, but they are sometimes larger and less egalitarian. Gerhard E. Lenski (1966:139) has argued that, in simple horticultural societies, headmen have more prerogatives than they do in hunting-gathering bands. They may wear special clothes or insignia and may be addressed in a more formal manner than others. In some

Simple horticultural societies

cases such headmen practice polygyny or have larger garden plots. This increase in power may sometimes be due to the chief's role as an agent in the redistribution of goods. Horticultural societies in South America, Polynesia, and New Guinea frequently engage in warfare, which may contribute to the relatively high status of the headman or chief. This warfare is sometimes over land resources, but this is not always the reason for such fighting (Vayda 1961; Chagnon 1968). A chief in such societies, as among hunting-gatherers, is often expected to be generous, an expectation that should serve to restrain exploitative tendencies to some extent. Moreover, slash-and-burn (or swidden) horticulture has a centrifugal influence on settlement patterns, which should discourage political centralization and the influence of chiefs (Sahlins 1968:31).

Pastoralists   Since societies classified as pastoral live in different kinds of environments (grasslands, deserts, steppes) and herd different kinds of animals (cattle, camels, sheep, goats, horses, reindeer, yak), this forms a heterogeneous category difficult to generalize about. Moreover, pastoral societies differ

A Samoan chief.

widely in population density, and it seems likely that there would be more political centralization in pastoral groups which have the greater density (Krader 1965). Some pastoralists are mounted horsemen; other are not. Despite this heterogeneity, many pastoral societies in both Asia and Africa have segmentary lineage systems with little political organization.

Most pastoralists are forced to be mobile, since their herds eat grass and must move on to new pasture grounds as the area becomes overgrazed. Moreover, the herds need water, and as they trample and spoil water courses, they must be moved to unspoiled areas. The nomadic way of life of pastoralists often has atomistic tendencies, making it possible for groups to segment and split off. Fredrik Barth (1961:25–26) has described the situation among the Basseri tribe of South Persia, in which camp members are faced with daily decisions about whether to move or stay put, and which routes to follow next:

These decisions are the very stuff of a pastoral nomad existence; they spell the difference between growth and prosperity of the herds, or loss and poverty. Every household head has an opinion, and the prosperity of his household is dependent on the wisdom of his decision. Yet a single disagreement on this question between members of the camp leads to fission of the camp as a group—by next evening they will be separated by perhaps 20 km of open steppe and by numerous other camps, and it will have become quite complicated to arrange for a reunion.

On the other hand, a factor leading to political centralization in pastoral societies is organization for warfare. Cattle-herding pastoralists often engage in fighting and raiding. In such societies, the main form of wealth is cattle, and cattle are easy to steal. If herds become depleted by disease or enemy raids, they must be replenished. So pastoral societies, such as the Karimojong and the Nuer of the Nilotic Sudan, go in for much fighting over cattle. As far as the Nuer are concerned, there is almost no political centralization. There are other pastoral tribes, however, in which a militant ruling group has developed aristocratic traditions and established itself as a political elite.

The Bahima of Uganda are a pastoral people who have overpowered and dominate the Bairu, who are farmers. The Bahima have become a ruling class, the Bairu are serfs. The Bahima developed some feudal tendencies; thus they swear loyalty to their king and promise to follow him in war, when called upon. They are also obliged to hand over some of the cattle acquired in a private raid. In return, the king protects his subjects' cattle from outside raiders, and he would help them start new herds if all of their cattle were stolen or died of disease. Only the Bahima were allowed to own productive cows; Bairu could own only barren cows. These two groups were endogamous and could not intermarry. Hence they had a kind of caste system, to which was added a still lower class or caste of slaves; they thus formed a stratified society comparable to that of the Tutsi, Hutu, and Twa of Ruanda, discussed in the preceding chapter.

The Bahima king was believed to be sacred, the supreme authority. He had a chief military adviser and an entourage of warriors. Subordinate chiefs carried out his orders and supervised the collection of tribute. A Bahima chief acted as a redistributive agent, giving to his followers articles made for him by Bairu craftsmen as well as some of the beer and millet porridge which came to him as tribute (Oberg 1940).

A parallel to some of these features may be seen in the ancient Aryans, who also had hard-fighting aristocratic traditions, and who conquered and dominated the agricultural peoples of northern India from around 1500 B.C.

Something like a state system exists in some pastoral tribes, while others have little political centralization. At the more advanced level there may be formal court procedures and the announcement of decisions by a judge or judges. In societies which lack such features there must be some other means of conflict resolution, such as resort to blood feuds, payment of compensation, and employment of a go-between.

Blood feud and compensation

The Tiv of Nigeria and the Nuer and Dinka of the Nilotic Sudan have segmentary lineage systems. As mentioned in Chapter 13, the lineage is a political unit, having collective responsibility in blood vengeance in these societies; much feuding goes on between lineage groups. A murder is not punished by a superordinate state; instead, there is retaliation by members of the dead person's lineage. If, in such a society, a member of lineage A kills a member of lineage B, someone of lineage B is likely to kill either the murderer or some other member of that lineage. This retaliation need not be seen as punishment; rather, in some societies, it restores balance between lineages that should have equal status. John Beattie (1964:175) has written:

Only one life should be taken for one life, and in some societies, such as that of the Berbers of North Africa, the requirement of exact equivalence demands that the person killed in revenge must be of the same standing as the original victim. So if a man in one group kills a woman in another, the object of the injured group will be not to kill the murderer, but to kill a woman on their opponent's side.

The very existence of the institution of blood feud must serve to restrain aggression to some extent, since a potential murderer knows that either he or a relative will die if the victim dies.

To prevent a blood feud from developing, a murderer may try to offer compensation to the offended lineage. Among the Nuer, who are horticulturalists as well as pastoral people, a murderer goes to the home of an official called leopard skin chief. Since the latter is believed to have some sanctity, his home is a haven for the murderer; the dead person's kin cannot attack the guilty there. After performing some sacrifices and purification rites for the murderer, the leopard skin chief may act as a go-between or mediator between the two lineages. He will find out how much cattle the murderer's kin possess, what they are willing to pay in compensation, and whether the murdered person's relatives will accept it. The leopard skin chief has no judicial or executive authority and cannot compel anyone to accept a settlement.

In some African societies where cattle are accepted in compensation, they serve the role of replacement. The cattle may be used to acquire a wife who will bear children for the lineage.

The Nuer leopard skin chief is an example of the go-between, an institution which is often found in societies that are politically decentralized. Another example is afforded by the Ifugao of the Philippines, who also lack political organization. They do not have clans but have close-knit bilateral groups of kinsmen who support one another in quarrels with other groups. When seeking compensation for a wrong or an insult, a person asks a member of the Ifugao upper class to act as go-between. If he agrees, the mediator goes back and forth with claims, proposals, counterclaims and counterproposals. Like the Nuer leopard skin chief, the mediator has no authority to impose a settlement but is more like the arbitrator in a labor dispute who tries to get both parties to agree on a compromise. If the go-between fails, a feud develops—a serious matter, for the Ifugao of former times were headhunters. In the cases of the Nuer and Ifugao, there are no courts of law, but there are methods of conflict resolution.   **Go-betweens**

In societies with more advanced political organization, the state may insist upon the right to punish murderers, and the institution of blood feud declines. The degree of political centralization may be gauged by this factor. The Shilluk of the Nilotic Sudan had a "divine king" who was an important symbol of unity for the tribe but who otherwise was no more than a figurehead, having no real political authority. This is expressed in the fact that blood feud flourished among the Shilluk. This "kingdom" was more like a segmentary lineage system with a symbolic but powerless ruler at its head.

Advanced horticultural societies in Africa often had a high degree of political organization. Both Ralph Linton and George P. Murdock have stressed the autocratic aspects of such African kingdoms as Uganda and Dahomey. Some of these were large states numbering hundreds of thousands of persons. The king was often believed to be divine and had the power of life and death over his subjects. He lived in ritual isolation, held court, surrounded by attendants, officials, and symbols of office, and maintained a harem. He dispensed justice and was the court of last appeal. Under the king there was a bureaucracy that collected taxes and supervised corvée labor. The leading ministers formed a council to advise the king (Linton 1955:463; Murdock 1959:37–39). This political centralization may perhaps be interpreted in terms of the chief's or king's exploitation of his control over redistribution. It may be, however, that some aspects of African kingdoms were influenced by 19th-century contacts with European and Arab traders relating to the slave trade (Service 1968:164–65).   **Advanced horticultural societies**

When a kingdom becomes established, it is likely that the king's lineage will come to be seen as more important than other lineages. In such cases,   **Royal lineages**

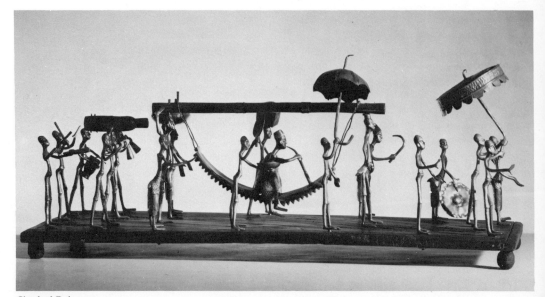

Chief of Dahomey and entourage. Bronze casting from Benin, West Africa, showing symbolic attributes of high status—litter, umbrellas, and attendants.

measures may be taken by the royal lineage to retain its power and authority.

Among the Swazi of southeastern Africa there is a royal couple who act as the symbolic parents of the people. They appeal to their royal ancestors to help the nation, just as ordinary Swazi household heads appeal to their own ancestors to aid their families. Although clan exogamy is normally practiced in this society, the royal clan is segmented into subclans, which enables the king to marry closely related women and which keeps the ruling line restricted in numbers. Sisters and daughters of the king are sent as wives to important chiefs, to spread the influence of the royal family (Kuper 1950:86–87,110).

The development of a royal lineage is one way for a ruler to establish a group of persons on whom he can count for support. Another way of achieving the same goal would be to forge bonds with unrelated persons, a body of retainers who owe loyalty to their ruler. Since closely related kinsmen may become rivals to the throne, more trust has sometimes been placed in dependent, unrelated henchmen.

An important way of resolving conflicts in advanced horticultural societies in Africa is the court system, with a judge, such as a chief or king, witness, the hearing of testimony, and the announcement of decisions. A common aspect of court procedure is taking oaths to ensure truthfulness. Ordeals are sometimes administered to test the honesty of the accused.

Agricultural societies

As we have seen, agricultural societies with more advanced farming techniques than horticulture developed in Mesopotamia, Egypt, the Indus Valley,

Shang China, Southeast Asia, Peru, and Mexico. In such societies, as in some advanced horticultural ones, we find court systems.

Court systems developed in advanced urban centers in both the Old **Court systems** World and the New. In Mexico, Aztec courts adjudicated market disputes. There were local courts in each quarter of the city and one for each district outside the city, all in session daily. The ruler's palace was a court of appeals and for the commoners a court of last resort. Nobles could appeal to a supreme court consisting of a war leader and a council of 13 elders. This system resembled that of modern states in several ways but lacked professional lawyers and trial by jury.

With court systems we have the development of a systematic body of law.

In Bronze Age Mesopotamia, when political centralization in city-states **Law** exerted control over progressively larger populations, the invention of writing made possible the first written codifications of laws, culminating in the Code of Hammurabi. Written laws increased the stability of the legal system and provided for a quick examination of precedents and previous rulings in any contingency. In later periods, after the diffusion of the alphabet, when a larger percentage of the population became literate, public tabulation of the laws had a democratizing influence. This happened in Greece in the seventh century B.C., when the open publicizing of the laws served as a check on the arbitrary authority of the ruling class.

A law differs from a custom in the quality of obligation. A person who deviates from custom may be considered eccentric but cannot be punished for an infraction. I may not approve of a young man who has long hair down to his shoulders and who walks about barefoot, but he is not doing anything against the law. But, if the young man rides his motorcycle beyond the prescribed speed limit or if he decides to undress in front of a policeman, he is liable to arrest. These distinctions may seem arbitrary, since some societies allow what others do not, and a society may change its laws over a period of time. But laws are customs that persons *must* abide by. This means that laws must somehow be enforced; they are enforced by an agency that is recognized as having political authority within the society.

Some anthropologists hold that law is universal, found in all societies, while others say that law is associated only with state societies. Law can be defined to suit either view.

Donald Black (1976:2–3) defines law as governmental social control and contrasts it with other kinds of social control such as were discussed in reference to sanctions (p. 300). Black (1976:6) has advanced the proposition: "Law varies inversely with other social control." This means that there is more law in societies where other forms of social control are relatively weak. Within a society, too, law fills a vacuum when other forms of social control are lacking. There is more juvenile law, for example, in societies where family discipline is weak.

Ruling elites

Estimates for the size of ruling groups in preindustrial agrarian societies have indicated very small minorities. The governing class in the last days of the Roman republic is estimated to have been about 1 percent of the capital's population. During the first half of the 19th century the Chinese gentry who made up the ruling class constituted about 1.3 percent of the population. A similar figure is given for Russia of the mid-19th century (Lenski 1966:219). How could such a small ruling class dominate such a large population? One explanation is that a ruling elite is apt to be highly organized, while the majority is not. The elite in an agrarian society is usually supported by a somewhat larger retainer class consisting of army officials, soldiers, servants, and others close to the ruling elite. Another reason for the continuing authority of the small ruling group is that it has many sources of power and influence. As an example, let us consider the sources of wealth of the 19th-century Chinese gentry.

The Chinese gentry were not engaged solely in political activity. It is estimated that in 19th-century China only 1.6 percent of the gentry held office in the central government at any given time, while about two thirds of the gentry got some of their income from holding governmental positions at the local level. Another large source of income was land ownership. In the late 19th century, about one quarter of all arable land in China was owned by the gentry. They also received some income from mercantile activity and moneylending (Lenski 1966:225–27; Fei 1953:98–99). The gentry thus occupied strategic positions both in government and in the economic system of the country.

The concentration of power and wealth in a small ruling class has been characteristic of many agrarian societies. In Mexico, before the revolution, 1 percent of the population owned 97 percent of the land, while 96 percent of the people owned only 1 percent of the land (Stern and Kahl 1968:6).

Feudalism

Feudalism is one of those vague but useful terms which have been defined in various ways. Here we will follow the view of Rushton Coulborn (1965:4–8,364), who sees feudalism as primarily a method of government, not an economic or social system; a method of government in which the essential relationship is between lord and vassal and in which the agreements between leaders and followers usually emphasize military service. Feudal tendencies are apt to develop in prevailingly agricultural societies, not in societies with highly organized commerce. Coulborn also sees feudalism as a mode of revival of a society that has experienced disintegration.

We know that in western Europe feudalism developed after the collapse of the Roman Empire and the subsequent failure of Charlemagne's heirs to keep western Europe united in a new empire. Coulborn suggests that

Marksburg castle in the Rhine Valley, begun in the 11th century.

similar feudal revivals, building on a contracted local scale, may have taken place in other societies that formerly controlled wider areas but suffered dismemberment and collapse. Here we have another hypothesis about cross-cultural regularities.

The best parallel with western European feudalism is provided by Japan in the period between the 14th and 19th centuries A.D. During this time, effective government was on a local basis. Feudal lords (*daimyō*) commanded the services of armed knights (*samurai*) to defend and control a particular area. The imperial family and court nobility had little real political power, but, as in Europe, the concept of a larger centralized state was remembered from the past. In both areas an earlier, wider polity had become weakened, and local magnates—landlords, fighting men, clan or tribal chiefs—had assumed responsibility for local control and defense. Both Europe and Japan had its "barbarians" who influenced the character of the feudal period. In the case of Japan, the barbarians occupied the northeastern half of the central island of Honshu.

The true period of feudalism in Japan is said to date from the collapse

Hirosaki castle,
Aomori, Japan.

of the Kamakura regime in A.D. 1333. The era of "high feudalism" runs
from the 14th to the 16th century A.D., corresponding to the period in
France between the later 10th to the 12th centuries. During the second
half of the 16th century in Japan there was a rash of castle building, in
which there appeared many similarities to the architecture of Europe. Castles
were defended by masonry-faced earthworks and surrounded by moats. Parallel to the medieval European code of chivalry, there were strong traditions
of feudal loyalty and a code of honor among samurai. Religion played an
important role in both feudal regimes, and it is a curious parallel that a
"universal" church with a monastic order was present in both. Buddhist
monasteries owned much land and controlled large groups of warriors in
Japan.[1]

The many parallels indicate that some cross-cultural regularities were at
work in these two widely separated regions. Coulborn has suggested that
two other areas exemplify a similar feudal development, although not in
so clear-cut and striking a fashion: Chou China to about 700 B.C. and Mesopotamia in the 500 or 600 years after Hammurabi.

Not all disintegrating empires give birth to feudal regimes. In many cases,
successful attempts are made to restructure the old political order. Feudalism
cannot be seen as an inevitable stage of development in the evolution of
human culture. It is one possibility, which seems to have occurred in a
number of different times and places.

---

[1] Some qualifications about the classification of feudalism in relation to Japan are given
in John W. Hall (1968).

The great increase in business enterprise of the 19th century associated with the Industrial Revolution was followed by a corresponding expansion of the state in the 20th century. In 1901 there were fewer than 240,000 employees of the U.S. federal government, but by 1975 there were 2,882,000, while the number of employees of state and local governments increased by 200 percent between 1940 and 1970. Much of the federal bureaucracy is concerned with military affairs, related to which, too, is the space program. About half the federal civilian employees are connected with defense. Much of the bureaucracy is also involved in control and regulation of trade, transportation, and communication, and the fields of education, job training, and social security.

Industrial societies

Consider our relationship to the state in connection with just one aspect of our culture, the automobile. The automobile has become so much a part of our lives that Americans can hardly imagine life without it. It has transformed the appearance of the country, which is now crisscrossed with highways that have gasoline stations and motels strung along at intervals. These highways are built and kept in repair by the state or federal government, which establishes laws about speed limits.

In order to drive an automobile, one must pass a test, buy and renew a driver's license, and yearly license the car one has bought. One must drive on the prescribed side of the street, stop at red lights, and obey other traffic signals. If one drives through a red light, exceeds the speed limit, or otherwise breaks the law, one may be arrested by a police officer and be given a fine or a jail sentence, depending on the nature of the offense. The police officer is a recognized agent of government, identifiable by badge and uniform. Police have legitimate power, acknowledged by members of the society, whether they like it or not.

What applies to the automobile applies to many other aspects of our lives. If we transgress our nation's laws, a host of legal institutions may be brought into play: police officers, law courts, judges, prisons, and parole boards. Legal machinery is also resorted to in conflict resolution, in the adjustment of disputes, and in arguments over property or contracts. The agencies that deal with these matters have to do with the nation's internal law, the regulation of its own affairs. But a modern state also deals with other nations and has institutions for dealing with them: ambassadors, consuls, state departments, agents of espionage, and the armed forces.

The expansion of the modern state in the past century came on the heels of the expansion of industry, and there has been some mutual influence in these two spheres of action. A large industry like General Motors is itself a kind of political system, but it must work in harmony with the larger political system of the United States, in accord with the prevailing legal code. A corporation may also derive advantages from the state in the form of mineral depletion allowances, tax benefits, large defense contracts, tariff and quota considerations, and so forth.

Since a modern state is such a powerful institution, with nuclear bombs at its disposal in many cases, the state has often been regarded with fear and apprehension, as in George Orwell's novel *1984*.

There are potential dangers of dictatorship and authoritarianism in the state. At the same time, the incorporation of so many people within the ranks of modern government may have a democratizing tendency. We have seen that preindustrial agrarian societies were ruled by very small elites, which were often authoritarian. By comparison, many modern industrial nations are more democratic. All have elaborate codes of written laws that are meant to apply impartially to all citizens, although this often does not work out in practice. Modern industrial nations tend to have high rates of literacy and well-developed media of communication, which at least have the potentialities for making citizens well informed. Of course, the same instruments can also be used for propaganda. At the time of Hitler's rise to power, Germany was the best-educated nation in Europe. The Soviet Union emphasizes education but also maintains the harsh labor camps described by Alexander Solzhenitsyn in *The Gulag Archipelago*. Even so, there seem to be grounds for optimism in the presence of a high literacy rate and good educational facilities, features that were generally lacking in preindustrial agrarian societies.

Politics

This chapter has been about political organization rather than about politics. That is to say, it concerns institutions or systems for dealing with social control and conflict resolution, such as go-betweens and courts. Politics, on the other hand, deals with the analysis of competitive political processes rather than with structural analysis. Following Swartz, Turner, and Tuden (1966:4–7), we may say that politics concerns public goals desired by members of a group or faction relating to the allocation of power. These authors describe some political processes as follows: During a preliminary phase of organization, competing groups try to win support and allies through persuasion and influence, promising rewards for support and spreading adverse gossip about the opposing faction or factions. Attempts may be made to win over or bribe members of an opposing group and to split it. This preliminary phase is succeeded by an open encounter or showdown which precipitates a crisis, signaled by violating a norm of usual ethical behavior. The crisis is apt to produce countervailing tendencies toward restoration of harmony. After resolution of the conflict, there must be some restoration of peace. Swartz, Turner, and Tuden refer to such sequences as "political phase developments." They have stimulated cross-cultural processual studies of politics along these lines (Swartz, Turner, and Tuden 1966:32–39). Detailed studies of factional struggles involve a multiplicity of factors and relationships. It may be necessary, for example, to sketch the personalities of particular leaders and their sources of influence. Such studies become, in effect, essays in history (e.g., Turner 1957).

A society must not only preserve order within its borders but must also regulate relations with other social groups, making treaties or agreements about boundaries and spheres of influence, acting as host to visiting strangers, carrying on trade, and so forth. Failure to regulate such matters adequately may result in warfare.

Warfare

Warfare has been reported for societies at all levels of cultural evolution. Some tribes, such as the Jivaro of Ecuador, live in a state of endemic warfare. In some societies, for example the former Plains Indian tribes, warfare was a seasonal matter, taking place in summer. In some societies, warfare has acquired ritualized aspects, with some of the qualities of a game.

Warfare may claim many lives in societies at all levels of technological development. Among the hunting-gathering Murngin of Australia, there was an estimate of 200 deaths from fighting in a population of 700 adult males. About 25 percent of adult males died in warfare among the Enga of New Guinea and about 24 percent among the Yanomamö of Venezuela, both horticultural societies. A similar percentage has been recorded for the Piegan of the northern Plains. For the more advanced civilization of the Valley of

Warfare scene, highlands of New Guinea.

Mexico before the Spanish conquest, there were estimated to have been about 15,000 deaths a year due to warfare and human sacrifice.[2]

The scale of warfare has, of course, increased in the course of cultural evolution as population density became greater, state control wider, and weapons more efficient.

Some writers, like Konrad Lorenz (1967) and Robert Ardrey (1966) believe that humans are inherently aggressive creatures with inborn urges to defend the territories in which they live. But our instinctual nature is probably not the best explanation for the long record of warfare and aggression of the human species. Our actions are determined more by learned behavior, by culture, than by instincts or drives. And this is a source of hope, if not of actual optimism, for culture and cultural traditions can change. Since Lorenz puts the emphasis on instinct, he recommends ways of sublimating aggression in order to avoid war: more Olympic games, competitive sports, and the competition of the space race. But it seems unlikely that such maneuvers could prevent war as long as there are powerful governments that see some advantage in it. Our problems lie not in the genes of the common man but in the ambitions of those with power.

Summary

A political unit must preserve internal order and also regulate external relations with other groups. Internal order is not solely due to the presence of laws and fear of punishment. It is also supported by informal sanctions such as the opinions of neighbors and fears of sorcery, ghosts, gods, and punitive ancestors.

Hunting-gathering societies usually have little political organization. Chiefs or headmen may not be able to exercise much authority, especially in cases where groups easily break up. In some simple horticultural societies the authority of a headman is greater; he may be distinguished by special insignia and enjoy extra prerogatives, which may be due to his role in redistributing goods or to the presence of warfare.

Pastoralists tend to be mobile and may have an atomistic social structure with little political centralization. On the other hand, cattle raiding and warfare may encourage centralization and the formation of a ruling elite. In pastoral tribes with segmentary lineage systems there are often blood feuds between lineages and the consequent employment of a go-between, like the Nuer leopard skin chief, to resolve such conflicts.

Advanced horticultural societies in Africa often had a high degree of political organization, with kings, royal lineages, and court systems. This is also true of agricultural societies. Court systems developed in advanced urban centers in both the Old World and New World.

Industrial societies are marked by an expansion of the state and a great increase in political bureaucracy. This has unfortunately been accompanied by a parallel increase in the scale of warfare.

---

[2] These figures are drawn from Livingstone (1968).

This chapter has been influenced by Gerhard E. Lenski, *Power and Privilege: A Theory of Social Stratification* (New York: McGraw-Hill Book Co., 1966).

A well-written general essay on the development of political organization in human societies is Morton H. Fried's *The Evolution of Political Society: An Essay in Political Anthropology* (New York: Random House, 1967). Another thoughtful work on the subject is Georges Balandier, *Political Anthropology,* trans. from the French by A. M. Sheridan Smith (New York: Pantheon Books, Random House, 1970).

For the hunting-gathering stage, see Richard B. Lee and Irven De Vore, eds., *Man the Hunter* (Chicago: Aldine Publishing Co., 1968).

For horticulture, see Marshall D. Sahlins, *Tribesmen* (Englewood Cliffs, N.J.: Prentice-Hall, Inc., 1968). For the African scene, see Meyer Fortes and E. E. Evans-Pritchard, eds., *African Political Systems* (London: Oxford University Press, 1940); Lucy Mair, *Primitive Government* (Baltimore: Penguin Books, 1964).

The best work on the cross-cultural study of law is E. Adamson Hoebel, *The Law of Primitive Man: A Study in Comparative Legal Dynamics* (Cambridge, Mass.: Harvard University Press, 1954). See also Laura Nader, ed., *The Ethnography of Law,* Special Publication, *American Anthropologist,* vol. 67, pt. 2 (1965); Paul Bohannan, ed., *Law and Warfare: Studies in the Anthropology of Conflict* (New York: Natural History Press, 1967), and Laura Nader, ed., *Law in Culture and Society* (Chicago: Aldine Publishing Co., 1969).

The processual approach to the study of politics is exemplified in two readers: Marc J. Swartz, Victor W. Turner, and Arthur Tuden, eds., *Political Anthropology* (Chicago: Aldine Publishing Co., 1966); and Marc J. Swartz, ed., *Local Level Politics: Social and Cultural Perspectives* (Chicago: Aldine Publishing Co., 1968).

Anthropologists have not paid much attention to the cross-cultural study of warfare, but a special symposium has been devoted to the subject: Morton H. Fried, Marvin Harris, and Robert Murphy, eds., *War: The Anthropology of Armed Conflict and Aggression* (New York: Natural History Press, 1968).

Suggestions for further reading

18

RELIGIOUS IDEOLOGY AND RITUAL

In George P. Murdock's list of universal aspects of culture that have been reported for all societies for which we have ethnographic descriptions, there are several items that concern religion. According to Murdock (1945:124), all societies have the custom of propitiating supernatural beings and have religious rituals. All known cultures contain beliefs of some sort about the soul and life after death. Funeral rites and mourning customs are universal. Divination is practiced in all cultures, according to Murdock, and belief in magic is also found everywhere.

These universals apply to cultures rather than to individuals. There are, of course, many persons in the United States, Europe, the Soviet Union, and elsewhere who do not believe in spirits, gods, or life after death; but these ideas are part of the cultural tradition and are accepted by great numbers of people, even in the Soviet Union, where the favored official view on religion is atheistic.

Culture patterns that are so widespread, found in all parts of the world and among societies at different levels of technology, must be very old.

Nineteenth-century writers who wrote about "primitive religion" hoped to figure out how religious beliefs originated in the first place and what the characteristics of the earliest primordial religion were. This was part of the general 19th-century interest in origins and evolution, applied also to the origin of the family, the state, and other institutions. The problem as they saw it was to find out how the institution got started and then to trace it through different stages of cultural evolution to the present. These 19th-century writers tended to be rationalists, with an optimistic faith in reason, science, and the future of mankind. They often regarded religion as the product of erroneous reasoning. In some cases, there was an implication that, as society advanced and people learned to reason more effectively, religious faiths would be supplanted by a more rational outlook.

The chief representative of 19th-century rationalism in this field was Edward B. Tylor. About half of his two-volume work *Primitive Culture* (1877) is devoted to religion. Later writers who concerned themselves with religion generally felt obliged to either agree or disagree with Tylor's views. It is convenient, therefore, to start our discussion of religion with an examination of his theories.

Tylor wanted to find a "minimum definition" of religion which would **Animism** apply to all religions in different parts of the world and different stages of development. He ruled out certain features that are not universal, such as belief in a supreme being, the notion of reward and punishment after death, worship of idols, and the practice of sacrifice. These are found in many societies but not in all, Tylor observed. What he chose as his minimum definition was "the belief in spiritual beings," to which he gave the name *animism*. It encompasses belief in souls, ghosts, gods, demons, and other supernaturals. For Tylor, animism was the core of religion from which all of its other aspects sprang. Once this idea was implanted in people's minds, various other beliefs and practices followed as a rather logical consequence.

But how did the belief in spirits arise in the first place? Theologians would answer that it stemmed from revelation, a view Tylor rejected. His own way of accounting for the origin of animism was in the experiences, shared by humans everywhere, of having dreams and reflecting about such phenomena as trance states, disease, and death. When waking up, a person remembers having had various experiences during the night, traveling about and having conversations with others. Yet companions will confirm that the person has been asleep all night and has not moved. Reflecting about this paradox, humans would reach the dualistic conclusion that there is a soul that inhabits the body and animates it but is able to leave the body at night and communicate with other souls. When the soul returns to the body, the person wakes up again and is reanimated. But, when the person dies, it is because the soul has left the body for good. Tylor argued that these beliefs need not be derived from revelation but are more likely to have arisen from the natural process of reasoning about universal experiences.

There are further natural consequences that follow upon a belief in spiritual beings. One conclusion would be that, once the soul has left the body, it may continue an existence after death or may be reborn in another bodily form. It was only natural to assume that other animals and plants also had souls. A cult of ancestor worship was still another likely consequence; this is not universal, but such cults could easily arise on the basis of animistic assumptions.

The belief in *possession* is another possible consequence, which is not universal, being not much developed among American Indian tribes although widespread in the Old World. This is the idea that a discarnate entity, spirit or soul, can take possession of a living body, temporarily dislodging its rightful occupant. In societies that have such beliefs, where people become "possessed," it is understandable that rites of *exorcism* have often developed to drive out invading spirits. But, often, as among spiritualist mediums and Siberian shamans, possession is voluntary, sought after. In other cases, as in devil possession in medieval Europe, it is considered evil, involuntary, requiring exorcism.

If a spirit can invade a living organism, then perhaps it can also take up lodgment in an object such as a piece of wood. This idea Tylor termed *fetishism* (not to be confused with sexual fetishism), the fetish being an object that is worshiped because it is conceived to be inhabited by or associated with a spirit.

Nature worship may also stem from animistic beliefs. Trees, rivers, animals, and plants may all be seen as having souls and may be worshiped. From this pattern arose the polytheistic pantheons of civilized and near-civilized peoples in which different gods were believed to control different aspects of nature: rain, thunder, earth, sea, sun, and moon.

Tylor saw *monotheism* as being a late development in the evolution of religion, which could arise in various ways. One god might be elevated to dominance over the others. In a society having a king and aristocracy, it might be assumed that the supernatural realm had the same political organization as the known earthly world. A supreme deity, supported by an aristocracy of lesser gods, might then be assumed to rule the universe.

Tylor's work had great influence; it is still considered a classic in anthropology, but in time his views about religion attracted criticism from various angles. Tylor's explanation of the origin of animistic beliefs has the weakness that it cannot be proven. Other, perhaps equally plausible, explanations for the origin of religion were offered by some of his contemporaries. How can one choose between these alternatives? It becomes a matter of personal taste. This is part of the reason why later anthropological works on religion turned from speculation about origins to a study of the functions of religions in living cultures.

One criticism of Tylor's theories about the origin and development of animism was that they overemphasized the role of reason and the conceptual side of religion. R. R. Marett (1914:xxxi) argued that ". . . savage religion is something not so much thought out as danced out." It involves awe and other emotions as well as thought.

Animatism

Marett pointed to a widespread religious concept that could not logically be derived from belief in spirits and might be just as old as, or older than, animism. This is belief in an impersonal supernatural power.

Mana is a word used in both Melanesia and Polynesia for impersonal supernatural power. Marett gave the term *animatism* to belief in such a power, which is conceived to pervade the universe but is stored up more in some objects or persons than in others. Chiefs, priests, people of high status, have more mana than ordinary folk. An odd-shaped stone may be thought to have mana. If someone plants such a stone in the garden and if the yield of yams subsequently increases, the person may become convinced that there is mana in it. Such ways of thinking are not foreign to the conceptions of the Western world. We regard the altar of a church as being somehow qualitatively different from a lamppost on the corner; it is more "sacred," just as holy water is thought to be different from ordinary water.

Like electricity, mana may be dangerous as well as beneficial. An object handled by a Polynesian chief may be considered perilous for a commoner to touch. Hence, the concept of *taboo* in Polynesia was closely associated with that of mana. The word *taboo* has implications of sacredness as well as the forbidden. Idols, temples, members of the ruling family, priests, canoes of the gods, and many other objects were taboo to commoners, a practice that served to widen social distance between the ruling family and the common people.

As Ruth Benedict (1938a) pointed out, conceptions about the supernatural may be based on two kinds of contrasting assumptions. On the one hand, one may conceive of supernatural things as having the attributes of objects, such as color and weight. On the other hand, one may attribute personality to all segments of the universe, to stars, plants, animals, storms, and other aspects of nature. To attribute mana to a stone, seeing it as being full of power, would be the first alternative, that of animatism. To assume that a spirit lives within the stone would be the second alternative, that of animism. Benedict made a distinction between an *amulet,* an object that is believed to automatically radiate supernatural power or good luck but is not personified, and a *fetish,* an object that is worshiped because of its indwelling spirit. Both objects are regarded as sacred but for different reasons. In Africa the fetish is talked to, cajoled or pleaded with, and otherwise addressed as a person. This is not done with an amulet. If the emphasis in a religious system is on animatism, people try to tap, build up and increase supernatural power. If the emphasis is on animism, people try to establish contact with the gods and offer petitions and sacrifice. The former system tends more in the direction of manipulation and magic; it operates with cause and effect sequences and, in that respect, is similar to science. The second system tends more in the direction of personal religion involving interpersonal relationships with gods and spirits. In practice, however, most religious systems represent a complex mixture of animism and animatism, religion and magic.

Magic

There have been different ways of distinguishing between magic and religion. One has just been referred to; Ruth Benedict, following James G. Frazer, saw magic as being manipulative, while religion is supplicative. Frazer regarded magic as "primitive man's science," although it is based on two erroneous principles which Frazer called the "Law of Similarity" and the "Law of Contact." The former is the belief that like produces like, while the latter is the notion that things that have once been in contact continue to act on each other at a distance. According to the first principle, the magician imitates the effects desired, such as jabbing pins into a doll and thus wounding the enemy. According to the second principle, the magician assumes that what is done to a material object will affect the person with whom it was once associated. Thus, sorcery can be worked against someone if one has acquired some of the person's fingernail parings, feces, teeth, or clothing (Frazer 1943:11–45). In either case, the effect is conceived to be brought about more or less automatically through the will and ritual actions of the magician, who does not appeal to a higher authority for help.

Émile Durkheim, who emphasized the social, collective nature of religion in his book, *The Elementary Forms of the Religious Life,* claimed that magic is mainly an individual affair in which no lasting social bonds are established, while religion is a collective enterprise that involves a church or community of fellow believers.

Bronislaw Malinowski (1954:17–90) made a series of distinctions between magic and religion: magic is a means to an end, while religion is an end in itself; belief in magic is simple and its aim is straightforward and definite, while religious belief is more complex, involving pantheons of supernatural

Hindu ritual.

beings. He argued that humans resort to magic when faced with the possibility of failure. A hunter cannot find game; a lover cannot win over the beloved. Despite one's best efforts, one cannot attain the valued goal through normal, rational means. A natural recourse in such blocked circumstances, according to Malinowski, is resort to magic. Moreover, this has an effect, for it gives the magician confidence. Feeling that something has been done to bring the goal closer, the hunter or lover perseveres with renewed effort. Religion also gives humans the confidence to carry on, but on a more long-range basis, establishing positive attitudes and values.

Although much of this seems convincing, Francis L. K. Hsu (1952) has subjected Malinowski's contrast between magic and religion to severe criticism and has shown that in practice, when dealing with a particular religious system, it is very difficult to separate magic and religion from one another or even sometimes to say which is which. Perhaps it is useful for analytical purposes to distinguish between magic and religion, as Frazer, Durkheim, and Malinowski have done in their different ways, but magicians may make use of religious practices and appeal to spirits for help, while religious bodies may make use of magical techniques, as in sprinkling holy water, and in pursuit of immediate practical ends, as in a prayer meeting for rain. Magic is not always individual, nor religion always collective; the young Ojibwa Indian, fasting alone in the woods, is engaged in a religious quest.

Unusual psychological states

In visions, dreams, states of trance, and "possession," human beings receive convincing support for the existence of the gods and spirits in which they believe.

Visions may sometimes be induced by lack of food. Early humans must often have gone hungry and then experienced unusual psychological states. Young men among the Ojibwa and other American Indian tribes deliberately fasted in order to have visions of their guardian spirits. We may assume that hunting-gathering people who ate a wide variety of vegetable foods must occasionally have swallowed hallucinogenic plants. After the discovery of their properties, these were often eaten deliberately for their effects. This is the case, at any rate, among some Siberian tribes of the Kamchatka Peninsula, some Mount Hagen natives of Northeast New Guinea, and some of the peoples of Mexico. In each of these areas, hallucinogenic mushrooms are eaten for their visionary effects. It is very likely that the intoxicating *soma* juice often referred to in the Vedas of the ancient Aryans was derived from hallucinogenic mushrooms. In northern Mexico and the southwestern United States, the peyote "button" was consumed for the same purpose. In South America, datura was used; in wide areas of the Old World, opium, *bhang,* or hashish have been smoked, with similar effects. In recent years in the United States, there has been a vogue for experimenting with LSD and other "mind-changing" drugs. Besides fasting and drugs, there are other methods used in various parts of the world to induce states of dissociation, including the repetition of rhythmic motor activities, drumming, singing, or dancing to the point of exhaustion.

The purposes of seeking visionary experiences are many, but one of them is to learn about matters not accessible to the normal conscious mind. A shaman goes into trance to find where game is located or to find the whereabouts of a missing person. Whether or not this can be done, the belief in such faculties is widespread. The pattern of crystal gazing or of staring at a flame or into water or some other liquid to gain information about unknown matters is almost universal. It has been reported among Canadian Indians, Iroquois, Apaches, Polynesians, Maoris, the Malagasy of Madagascar, the Zulus, and the Inca of Peru, as well as among the peoples of modern Europe (Lang 1909:83–87).

Tylor referred to the experience of visions and hallucinations as being a contributory factor in the development of animistic beliefs. He also briefly alluded to the belief in "second sight," or what we now call extrasensory perception. Andrew Lang took Tylor to task for not inquiring into the possible validity of such experiences:

> . . . it might seem to be the business of Anthropology, the Science of Man, to examine, among other things, the evidence for the actual existence of those alleged and supernormal phenomena. . . . About the psychical condition of the savages who worked out the theory of souls and founded religion we necessarily know nothing. If there be such experiences as clairvoyance, telepathy, and so on, these unknown ancestors of ours may (for all that we can tell) have been peculiarly open to them, and therefore peculiarly apt to believe in separable souls (Lang 1909:44, 56).

Lang presented some anecdotes to show that telepathy is widely believed in by primitive peoples. Lang's plea that anthropologists undertake cross-cultural psychical research has been largely ignored since his day, perhaps because most anthropologists, like most psychologists, do not believe in extrasensory perception and therefore do not think there is anything to investigate. The writer made a small attempt in this direction, giving a series of 48 runs of Rhine's ESP (extrasensory perception) card-guessing test to an old Chippewa religious leader in the summer of 1944. The Rhine test makes use of a pack of cards with five symbols, each card having one of five: circle, star, wave, cross, and square. The subject, often seated in a separate room from the examiner, is asked to guess the order in which the symbols appear after the pack has been shuffled. The old Chippewa, who certainly believed in telepathy, did not score significantly above chance. The most ambitious attempt along these lines has been Ronald Rose's administration of ESP test to Australian aborigines, who did score better than chance. Rose and his wife recorded 16,625 guesses; chance would have been 3,325 "hits," but they recorded 3,870 correct hits (Rose 1956:227).

Rose thought this was evidence that Australian aborigines had ESP abilities, but most psychologists would probably not agree.

The *shaman,*[1] or medicine man, is mankind's first specialist, although not on a full-time basis. In a hunting band he is a hunter like anyone else. In most hunting-gathering societies and among many simple horticulturalists, there are religious practitioners of this sort. They are also to be found in advanced civilizations, but then they coexist with another type of religious specialist, the priest, who will be discussed later. The shaman is an intermediary between the members of his society and the supernatural world, with which he communicates either by talking to the spirits and listening to their replies or through possession. Edwin M. Loeb (1929) has made a distinction, on this basis, between *seers* and shamans. The seers have visions of spirits, who talk to them, but true shamans are possessed; the spirits speak *through* them. Loeb believes the seer is the older type of religious specialist, being found among American Indian tribes and among the more primitive and isolated peoples of the Old World, such as the Australian aborigines and Andaman Islanders. Possession shamanism is widespread in the Old World. Another writer, Mircea Eliade (1950:299), makes a distinction between shaman and medicine man, restricting the term *shaman* to those who make "an ecstatic trip to Heaven, to the Lower World, or to the depths of the ocean." Most anthropologists, however, use the terms *shaman* and *medicine man* interchangeably; there seems to be no harm in doing so.

Medicine men fill various functions; they "communicate" with spirits and learn about hidden matters, and they are sometimes believed to influence the weather and to make the rain fall or stop. As the term implies, a medicine man is also concerned with curing. Various medical techniques are used by shamans in different societies, including the administration of herbs, roots, brews, poultices, salves, ointments, enemas, massage, and sweat baths. Many of these are valid curative practices, but even when that is not the case, the curing process itself provides reassurance to the patients and often helps them get well, especially if the ailment is of psychosomatic origin. The cure may be helped along by drum-beating, singing, dancing, and impressive, dramatic behavior on the part of the medicine man, which assures the patients that they are in good hands.

A widespread, probably ancient technique is the sucking cure, in which the shaman goes through the motions of sucking a disease from the patient's body. Usually he "extracts" something, which he shows to the patient and other persons present as proof that the sickness has been removed. This, again, must have a reassuring, sometimes therapeutic, effect upon the patient. Of course, it does not always work, just as modern medical practices some-

Shamanism

---

[1] Although in some groups a shaman can be either a man or a woman, for convenience we will refer to a shaman as a male.

times do not work. But even if the patient dies, that does not necessarily lead to a loss of faith in this curing method, for the shaman may have a ready explanation, such as, for example, that a powerful sorcerer was responsible for the death and that he was summoned too late to prevent it. Some variant of the sucking cure is found among the Jivaro Indians of Ecuador, the Ojibwa of the Great Lakes region in North America, the Cochiti Indians of New Mexico, the Kwakiutl Indians of the Northwest Coast, the St. Lawrence Island Eskimos, and the Arunta of Australia.

The objects "extracted" from the patient's body may be stones, pieces of wood, and other objects that the shaman has probably kept in his mouth, although it is sometimes difficult to see how he has managed to do that. Harry B. Wright (1957:14–15), a dentist and explorer from Philadelphia, recorded that a Jivaro medicine man spat out the following objects in succession during the course of a cure: a splinter of wood, a mouthful of ants, a grasshopper, and a lizard. (Both the grasshopper and the lizard were dead). This cure, incidentally, was for a toothache and was a complete success.

The term *magic* has more than one meaning. In previous pages it has referred to supernatural manipulation, as in love magic, hunting magic, garden magic, or sorcery. But the term has another, colloquial meaning, referring to sleight of hand, the magic of performers like Houdini. It is interesting that medicine men have often been magicians in both senses of the word. The sucking-out of objects is itself quite a good trick, but shamans have often performed other marvels, sometimes as a prelude to a cure, as a way of establishing a receptive, trusting attitude on the part of the patient. By demonstrating that they can perform miracles, the shamans shows their credentials, demonstrate their power, and win assent from the clientele. Many such performances must have been very crude, but some that have been described by travelers are impressive.

An Ojibwa sucking doctor at work.

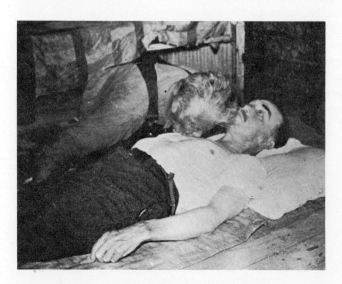

Becoming a shaman in three cultures

Let us see how one becomes a shaman in three hunting-gathering societies for which there are good ethnographic data: the Eskimos, the Ojibwa, and the Arunta. As will be seen, there are many similarities in the shamanism of these three groups.

Both men and women can become shamans among the Eskimos, but most of them are men. Among the Central Eskimos, a candidate who wishes to study under a shaman must present him with something valuable, perhaps some wood, which is scarce. Then the candidate and his parents must confess to all the breaches of taboo they have committed. The training period involves exposure to cold and fasting. A Caribou Eskimo gave Knud Rasmussen a doubtless exaggerated account of having fasted for five days; then being allowed a mouthful of warm water and then going another 15 days without food. Again he was given a mouthful of warm water; then he fasted for ten days more, after which he was allowed to eat but had to avoid entrails and other tabooed foods. The informant claimed that he sat alone in a cold snow hut in wintertime for 30 days; then, he finally had visions of the spirit he sought (Rasmussen 1930:51–54).

In East Greenland, candidates started training at the early age of seven or eight. They had to sit for hours in a deserted place rubbing one stone against another. It is believed that if the boy keeps this up long enough, a bear will come up from the lake and swallow him. Then, the bear will spit him out again, and the novice's body parts will become reassembled. After this experience, the young man can declare that he is a shaman and may start to practice, but the novitiate usually lasts from five to ten years (Thalbitzer 1931:430–36).

Among the Central Eskimos, as soon as young persons have become shamans, they are given a special shaman's belt, to which are attached various bone carvings of human figures, fishes, and harpoons. These are presents from people who hope to thereby be protected or, at least, not harmed by the shaman's helping spirits (Rasmussen 1929:111–14).

Among the Ojibwa, or Chippewa, there was no training for novices. The power to become a shaman came from a dream or vision of a guardian spirit. All Ojibwa children fasted in former days, beginning from between four and six years of age. In the morning a parent smeared some charcoal over the child's face; seeing this, a neighbor would know that the child should not be given food. A boy was sent out to play in the woods without breakfast; he might be given some food during the day, but not much. He could, however, break his fast at nightfall. Fasting of this kind might continue for a few days and then stop, to be resumed later. Thus it was kept up sporadically throughout childhood until the sacred dream finally came. This dream or vision should come before puberty. Sometimes, eager for the dream experience, boys fasted for as much as ten days or more on a kind of platform built high in the treetops, where they sometimes chewed on a piece of lead or deer fat to keep their mouths from getting dry.

Girls also fasted and might get a dream or vision, but it was much more important for boys to succeed in this quest since their lives involved the risks and uncertainties of hunting and warfare, while women's work was more routine and dependable. Shamanism was men's work, although women sometimes became shamans, particularly after the menopause. Not all dreams or visions were sacred. A sacred dream had to have some rather stereotyped elements, mainly a meeting with a guardian spirit that could assume either human or animal form. In the case of boys destined to be shamans, the guardian spirit gave instruction about their practice. Usually, they were not supposed to embark upon their shamanistic careers until many years after the vision.

There were two kinds of medicine men: sucking doctors and tent shakers. Some shamans were both. The sucking cure has already been briefly described. Tent shaking was a specialty, also known as conjuring, which involved the construction of a barrel-shaped lodge, which was entered by the medicine man. It was put up on occasions when people needed information about something not accessible to their normal conscious minds: the whereabouts of a lost person, the location of game or, in former days, the enemy. It could also be used for diagnosis of an ailment or the identification of a sorcerer. The conjuring lodge is called a shaking tent because, after the medicine man gets into it, it starts to vibrate. It probably does so because the shaman is shaking it, but the Indians believe that the vibration is caused by a strong wind inside the structure. Voices issue from the tent, doubtless produced by the shaman but attributed by the Indians to the various spirits that enter the lodge. Since the power of conjuring supposedly comes from a fasting vision, there could be no instruction in this technique, or at least it could not be admitted that there had been any. It is not known how the knowledge was passed on from one generation to the next (Hallowell 1942; Landes 1968).

Among the Arunta of central Australia, a man who wants to become a medicine man wanders away from his camp until he comes to a cave, in front of which he goes to sleep. At daybreak a spirit is supposed to come from the cave and throw an invisible lance through his head, making a hole in his tongue. This hole is the badge of shamanhood, and it should remain open as long as the shaman practices. It is probably made by the shaman himself, but he would never admit that. The spirit that spears him is believed to take the novice into the cave, remove his entrails, and replace them with a new set. The spirit also places some magic stones in the novice's body, which are later used in shamanistic practices.

There is another way to become a medicine man and to acquire the sacred stones and the requisite hole in the tongue. A novice may be initiated by some medicine men who perform the tongue operation for him and press rock crystals into his skin, supposedly forcing them into his body (Spencer and Gillen 1927).

Some parallels may be noted in these three societies. Women could be-

Ojibwa shaman beside conjuring lodge. During a seance the framework is covered by hides, cloth, or blankets.

come shamans in all three cultures, but most shamans were men. Fasting was an important approach to shamanism among the Eskimos and Ojibwa. Ojibwa and some Arunta novices purportedly received no training or instruction from shamans, while Eskimos and some Arunta did receive training. The novitiate generally involves the inducement of dissociated states. The Greenland Eskimo novice is swallowed by a bear and his body parts are reassembled; the Arunta has his entrails removed and gets a new set. The idea of dying and being reborn with a somewhat different body is implicit in these ways of acquiring shamanistic power.

The sucking cure is practiced by the Ojibwa, Arunta, and the Eskimos of St. Lawrence Island. Clairvoyant and telepathic abilities are attributed to shamans in all three societies. Arunta and Ojibwa shamans are feared as sorcerers and are believed to be able to assume the forms of birds or animals. It is evident that shamans are regarded with some ambivalence. Since they cure the sick and help the members of their society in various ways, their services are naturally valued. But the very fact that the shamans are believed to have so much supernatural power makes them potentially dangerous, capable of killing others through sorcery, if they are so inclined.

Mythology   Even though it may contain internal contradictions and inconsistencies, the mythology of a society expresses a kind of world view and presents a set of answers for some of the riddles of life—such as why people have to die or why hunters sometimes cannot find game. In ceremonies, the gods and spirits may be appealed to or their roles may be enacted. Ceremonies may, in part, be dramatizations of myths.

Let us consider a crucial part of Central Eskimo mythology, which also finds expression in some of their ceremonies. This myth answers the question of why hunters sometimes cannot find game. This is certainly a vital matter for the Eskimos in wintertime, when they largely depend upon sea mammals for food, especially upon the seals, whom they harpoon through blowholes in the ice when the seals come up to breathe.

Sedna

The Central Eskimos formerly believed in the existence of a woman at the bottom of the sea, often known as Sedna. Her story is told with local variations, but goes roughly like this: Sedna was once an Eskimo girl; she married a bird and went to an island to live with her husband. Her father and brothers did not approve of this match, so they went to the island in a boat and rowed away with Sedna. Angered, the bird called up a storm and great waves on the sea. Sedna's father threw his daughter overboard, but she clung to the side of the boat. Her father then chopped off the first segments of her fingers, but she hung on. Father next chopped off the second segments; Sedna still hung on. After one more blow of the knife, Sedna sank to the bottom of the sea, where she remains to this day. The different segments of her fingers turned into different sea mammals, seals and walrus.

Sedna sometimes gets angry at human beings for breaking taboos. Eskimo life is hedged about by so many taboos that it is difficult not to break some of them. There are more taboos affecting women than men, especially concerning menstruation, stillbirths, and food. When a woman breaks a taboo, a kind of smoke or vapor rises up from her body, sinks through the sea, and settles in Sedna's hair in the form of dirt or maggots, which Sedna cannot comb from her hair since she has no fingers. Angered at human beings, she calls down all the sea mammals, former segments of herself, to the bottom of the sea. The Eskimos then face the possibility of starvation.

Here we see an explanation for the hunters' failure to kill game. They have been out by the blowholes, on the ice, all day but have had no luck. The story tells us that it is not their fault; it is their wives who are to blame for breaking taboos. We will never know whether it was men or women who made up this story, but one would suspect that the men would find it a satisfactory explanation, providing for displacement of possible feelings of guilt or failure. Apart from this, any explanation is better than none, especially when a course of action is made available once the cause of failure is known.

The person who comes to the rescue in this case is the medicine man; he arranges a seance and the lights are put out. The shaman's voice in the darkness gets fainter as he sinks to the bottom of the sea. Some Eskimos believe that the shaman goes to the bottom of the sea in his bodily form, while others hold that only his spirit travels there. At any rate, when he reaches Sedna's home, he appeases her, combs her hair for her, and persuades her to release the sea mammals. Then he surfaces, returning to the Eskimo dwelling from whence he came.

Upon his return, all the persons in the dwelling must confess the taboos they have broken. They may be reluctant to admit them, of course, but fear of famine and of Sedna's anger forces them to confess. In this way, everyone learns about everyone else's secrets. Women may be sent for who are not present; the young wives who come in, crying and penitent, also confess. After this, the men return to their blowholes with renewed confidence (Rasmussen 1929:123–29).

Sedna is not a very benevolent deity; she has to be placated and coaxed to help mankind and not bring on starvation; and the Eskimos seem to feel some hostility toward her. Boas described a ceremony in which Sedna was harpooned by two shamans who stood on either side of a coil of rope, which represented a seal's breathing hole. The shamans proudly displayed the blood-sprinkled harpoon to their audience (Boas 1884:604).

In the seance, when the shaman dives to the bottom of the sea, the people present are made aware of the reality of Sedna, who, in the absence of such dramatizations, might seem to be a rather abstract concept. Similarly, when the Ojibwa shaman brings spirits into the shaking tent, one can hear their voices, and their immediate reality is brought home to the onlooker.

Anthony F. C. Wallace (1966:84–88) has drawn up a typology of cult institutions as follows: (1) individualistic, (2) shamanic, (3) communal, and (4) ecclesiastical.

A typology of cult institutions

The individualistic type refers to rituals performed by persons who are not specialists, such as an Ojibwa boy's vision quest or a person's private prayer at a family shrine.

The second category refers to shamanism, in which distinction is made between the magico-religious specialist and ordinary laymen.

Communal cults are performed by groups of laymen in rites of transition, calendrical ceremonies, ancestor cults, or other ceremonies. No full-time priesthood is involved.

Ecclesiastical cult institutions, however, do have priests, professional religious specialists who are neither shamans nor lay officials.

There is an implicit evolutionary progression in Wallace's scheme:

In societies containing an ecclesiastical cult institution, there will also be communal, shamanic, and individualistic institutions. Where there is no ecclesiastical institution, but a communal one, there will be also shamanic and individualistic varieties. And when there is neither ecclesiastical nor communal, there will be shamanic and individualistic (Wallace 1966:88).

The presumably earlier forms are retained in the later. There seem to be no societies that have only individualistic cult institutions, but there are some, such as the Eskimos, that have both individualistic and shamanic types.

Rites of transition

Rites of transition, or rites of passage, are ceremonies performed at certain stages in the life cycle of an individual when he or she moves from one status to another. A ceremony may be performed at birth to greet the new baby and welcome it into the world of the living. This ceremony also involves a change of status for the married couple, especially if it is their first child—they now become parents.

Initiation ceremonies mark the transition from childhood to adulthood at puberty. Some societies lack puberty ceremonies. Margaret Mead explained the absence of female initiation in Samoa in terms of the smooth transition from childhood to womanhood with little change in roles.

The Arunta initiation of young boys is under the supervision of the older men, who also go through ceremonies involving the *churingas* and totemic rites.

In societies that have ecclesiastical cults, rites of transition may be presided over by priests, rather than a group of laymen.

Marriage is an important transition point, although it does not involve ceremonial behavior in all societies. Among the Kaingang, Murngin, Papago, and Sirionó, there are no marriage ceremonies, and there is very little ceremony at the time of marriage among the Ifaluk, Kwoma, and Trobriand Islanders (Stephens 1963:221). At the other extreme, in northern India, the marriage cycle is drawn out over a period of two years or more, with various ritual stages before the final consummation of the marriage.

Death is another occasion for rites of transition, usually accompanied by mourning. This reaches an acute pitch among the Arunta, who gash themselves with knives and sharp, pointed digging sticks at a funeral, the women "battering one another's heads with fighting clubs," as Spencer and Gillen reported. Among the Arunta there is not only sadness at a death but also a kind of rage or anger, probably because deaths are seen as being due to sorcery.

Why do people mourn and weep at a funeral? The answer seems simple: because they have lost a loved friend, spouse, or relative. Durkheim, in analyzing Spencer and Gillen's data, rejected this apparently obvious explanation. He pointed out that in the midst of mourning, if someone speaks of some temporal interest, the mourners' expressions may suddenly change and the people may assume a laughing tone before going back to their weeping. "Mourning is not a natural movement of private feelings wounded by a cruel loss; it is a duty imposed by the group," concluded Durkheim (1965:443). No member of the group is allowed to be indifferent; by collectively mourning, the members express their solidarity, and in doing so they overcome and repair the loss that has befallen them. Durkheim's view seems a bit cynical in denying to the mourners spontaneity of feeling, which must often be real enough, but he is no doubt right about the function of mourning in unifying the group.

Freud also had a theory about mourning. It was his belief that people are invariably ambivalent in their emotions, particularly among neurotic individuals. One does not only love one's wife or husband; one also hates him or her, although the hatred may be repressed and only partially conscious. At one point or other, according to Freud, one has wished for the death of one's spouse. Thus, when the death actually occurs, it may trigger a sense of guilt in the survivor. Freud accounted in this way for the deep depression and self-blame that sometimes follows a death. The survivors may accuse themselves of not having been attentive enough to the deceased, even though their records on that score may have been excellent. Freud explained in these terms the fact that recently deceased persons, in many non-Western societies, are often regarded as malevolent spirits, hostile to the living; for the survivors, plagued with feelings of guilt, project their own aggressions onto the ghost. Freud noted that modern humans no longer fear the recent dead. His explanation for this was that primitive peoples must have been more ambivalent in their emotions than modern humans (Freud 1938:852–58; see also Opler 1936).

Calendrical rites

Calendrical rites are found in relatively advanced agricultural societies that have developed sufficient knowledge about the sun, moon, and stars to have an idea of the yearly cycle and its different seasons. The Hopi Indians of Arizona have a communal cult of the *katcinas,* which involves both a calendrical cycle and initiation ceremonies for the young. The katcinas are ancestral spirits, believed in by the Hopi, who are also spirits of the rain clouds. They are said to spend half the year in the San Francisco Mountains and the other half among the Hopi. During the latter period they are impersonated by men who wear large masks.

According to Hopi mythology, friendly katcinas accompanied the Hopi in their emergence from the underworld and helped them with rain dances when the Hopi began to plant crops. They left the Hopi to go and live in the San Francisco Mountains but left behind their masks, rattles, and other paraphernalia. Since then, the Hopi have impersonated the katcinas and worn their masks in order to bring rain and fertility to their fields.

The masked impersonations are held between the winter and summer

Hopi Snake Dance at Walpi, Arizona. From mural by George Peters, Milwaukee Public Museum.

solstices, beginning late in November. Dances are performed in *kivas,* underground chambers. At the Powamu ceremony in February, beans are grown in heated kivas, a seemingly miraculous event in the middle of winter, and the bean sprouts are distributed among the people. When the weather gets warmer, katcina dances are held outside in the plaza. These are impressive, well-rehearsed performances. At the end of their half-year's stay, there is a final ceremony to bid goodbye to the departing katcinas.

Adults, of course, know that the masked beings are Hopi men in disguise, but children think that the katcinas are real spirits, and they do not discover the true identity of the men in disguise until their initiation into the katcina cult. The katcinas sometimes give presents—rattles or bows and arrows to boys and katcina dolls to girls. If a boy has been unruly, his parents may decide to frighten him into better behavior by calling in a giant katcina impersonator. The masked man enters the house saying he wants to carry off the little boy and eat him since he has been behaving badly. The parents offer the katcina some meat as an alternative, but he rejects it and chases after the little boy. After having thoroughly frightened him, the katcina grudgingly accepts the substitute meat but warns that he will be back again if the boy continues to act badly.

The katcina initiation, held every fourth year, is for boys and girls between the ages of six and ten. On this occasion the boys are naked, but girls wear dresses. They are taken into a kiva, the underground ceremonial chamber, which becomes filled with masked katcinas. A boy, held by a ceremonial godfather, is whipped by one of the katcinas. The children are thus whipped in turn, the girls receiving gentler treatment than the boys. If a boy has been unruly, as Don Talayesva, the author of *Sun Chief* was, he may get a severe flogging; indeed, Don received permanent scars from his whipping.

Four days later, in another ceremony in the kiva, the boys and girls see the katcinas without their masks and discover that they are their older brothers, fathers, uncles, and neighbors. The children are then warned never to tell this secret to uninitiated children lest they be flogged more severely than before—perhaps even to death. This experience has been described by some Hopi informants as extremely disillusioning. Nevertheless, it seems to have the intended effect, for Don Talayesva writes in his autobiography, "I thought of the flogging and the initiation as an important turning point in my life, and I felt ready at last to listen to my elders and to live right" (Simmons 1942:87).

The katcina cult is a very complex institution and serves many functions. Children are taught to be obedient by live, masked bogeymen, perhaps more effectively than by purely imaginary ones. The carrot is offered as well as the stick; the katcinas bring presents and reward good children, like benevolent Santa Clauses. The whipping at initiation is a powerful incentive to obedience and cooperation with the village elders in community enterprises. The katcina dances unite the community and provide much color and entertainment. Of course, they probably have some negative, dysfunctional consequences as well.

One might think that the disillusionment of the initiation and the new knowledge that the masked gods are only men would lead to an agnostic, skeptical attitude among the young adults, but this does not seem to happen. They continue to believe in the katcinas. After his second initiation, into the Wowochim society, Don Talayesva wrote that he had learned a great lesson, that the ceremonies handed down among the Hopi meant life and security, and that ". . . the Hopi gods had brought success to us in the desert ever since the world began" (Simmons 1942:178).

Priesthood

Priests are religious specialists who are found in relatively advanced agricultural societies, including the Bronze Age civilizations of the Old World, and the Inca, Aztec, and Maya Indians of the New. Priesthood depends upon the existence of an organized cult worshiping a god or pantheon of gods and having definite doctrines and rituals. The job of the priest is to learn the rituals properly; as a novice he undergoes training in this and other matters until he is declared by his superiors to be a qualified priest. The priest differs from the shaman in various ways. He does not have to see spirits or be possessed by them or have any particular dreams or visions. He succeeds to an office, while the shaman is more of a self-made man, or one who has acquired spirit helpers. The priest does not depend upon spirit helpers. His authority comes from the religious order of which he is a part; he is an organization man. He is also more apt to be a full-time specialist than the shaman.

In societies where priests and shamans coexist, there may be rivalry between them, with the shaman as a freewheeling individualist trying to bypass the authority of the cult organization, while the latter tries to monopolize religious activities under its own control.

The foregoing generalizations about shamans and priests do not always hold. Although the Ojibwa were hunting-gathering people, they had a kind of priest, the Mide priest, or priest of the Medicine Dance. He was often a shaman as well, but he did not need to be, and he was not required to have had a fasting dream or vision. A man who became a Mide priest learned ritual and Mide lore as an assistant and understudy to a Mide priest.

Wallace, whose typology of religious cults we have been following, distinguishes between two kinds of ecclesiastical institutions in which priests officiate: *Olympian,* which recognizes a pantheon of gods; and *monotheistic,* in which there is worship of one supreme being. As an example of Olympian religion, he cites precolonial Dahomey, a west coast African kingdom based on advanced horticulture. In the Dahomean Great Gods cult, each deity was responsible for a particular aspect of nature; each had its own temple, priests, ritual, and mythology. Similar Olympian cults existed in the American Indian civilizations of the Inca, Maya, and Aztecs, and in such East Asian societies as Burma, Indonesia, Korea, and Japan.

As examples of monotheistic, ecclesiastical cults, Wallace lists Hindu-Buddhist, Judeo-Christian, Islamic, and Chinese monotheism. But the characterization of Hinduism as monotheistic is questionable; insofar as traditional village practices are concerned it is better characterized as Olympian. Monotheism seems to be associated with political complexity. Guy E. Swanson (1969), at any rate, found this association in a cross-cultural study of 50 societies, as well as an association between monotheism and food production rather than food collection.

Bellah's evolutionary scheme

An evolutionary sequence of forms of religion, different from Wallace's, has been proposed by Robert N. Bellah (1964). This has five stages: Primitive religion, Archaic religion, Historic religion, Early modern religion, and Modern religion.

The first stage, *Primitive religion,* is based on data about the Australian aborigines, since Australia was the only major culture area that was largely unaffected by the cultural developments of the Neolithic period. According to Bellah, this kind of religion has two main features: (1) the high degree to which the mythical world is related to features of the actual world, and (2) the fluidity of organization. Rather than worshiping supernaturals, people identify with them and participate with them. Ritual involves acting out

Australian
aborigines in
religious ritual.

rather than praying or sacrificing, and there is little distance between humans and the supernatural beings. There are no priests as mediators, and there is no religious organization.

In the second stage, *Archaic religion,* there is a more definite distinction between humans and gods and more distance between them. Worship and sacrifice are now offered, and there are many different cults. Much of what is usually called primitive religion falls under this heading.

The third category, *Historic religion,* is relatively recent and found in more or less literate societies. Historic religions stress the theme of world rejection; they are dualistic and transcendental and have a pessimistic view of the human condition but a potentially better (or worse) conception of the afterlife. Salvation is now regarded as the main purpose of life, and a religious elite, a priesthood, is committed to helping people attain it.

The main example Bellah offers for the fourth category, *Early modern religion,* is the Protestant Reformation. At this stage, salvation no longer needs to be mediated but is potentially open to anyone. There is a stress on faith rather than on ritual behavior, and there is more individualism.

Finally, in *Modern religion,* the tendencies set in motion during the preceding stage are carried further. There is a collapse of orthodoxy, and there is still more individualism. Indeed, freedom increases at each of these five stages.

It would be difficult to synthesize Wallace's and Bellah's schemes, since they emphasize different things. Because the religious system of the Australian aborigines is both shamanic and communal, it appears relatively late in Wallace's scheme, but it represents the earliest stage of religion in Bellah's outline, earlier than the development of shamanism, which presumably developed as part of the Archaic religion.

Religion and projection

Sigmund Freud, the founder of psychoanalysis, suggested that concepts about gods may be modeled after a child's relationships with its parents. We are relatively defenseless creatures who need reassurance against anxiety. Freud has written (1957:39–40):

> Now when the child grows up and finds that he is destined to remain a child for ever, and that he can never do without protection against unknown and mighty powers, he invests these with the traits of the father-figure; he creates for himself the gods, of whom he is afraid, whom he seeks to propitiate, and to whom he nevertheless entrusts the task of protecting him.

Abram Kardiner, a later psychoanalyst, carried this notion further. He believed that in societies with good parental care, idealized deities will appear in the pantheon, modeled after the benevolent parents. But in societies where the parental care is poor and where children are neglected, it will be difficult for the members of the society to idealize their gods. A case in point is Alor, an Indonesian society studied by Cora DuBois, where children suffer much maternal neglect and where little is expected of the deities, whose effigies are carelessly made and soon discarded. In the Western world, on the other hand, we have long traditions of good parental care and also belief in an idealized, loving God the Father, from whom all blessings flow (Kardiner 1945).

In some societies there are beliefs in gods who are hostile and threaten human beings. This is hard to account for in terms of the familiar notion that religion is a solace, a source of reassurance. While it may supply reassurance, religion also often adds to human fears and anxieties. Christianity gives people belief in a loving God and the hope of Heaven but also a Devil, Hell, and the prospect of eternal damnation. Thus, religions sometimes seem to take away with one hand what they give with the other.

The religious pantheons of some societies contain more frightening gods and spirits than benevolent ones. Jules Henry (1944:95) writes of the Kaingang of the jungles of Brazil that ". . . the emphasis in the supernaturalism is not on the beneficence of the supernaturals but on their vindictiveness if thwarted and on the danger inherent in any contact with them." Similarly for the Aymara of Peru: ". . . the great majority of supernatural beings are at best ambivalent toward mortals, if, indeed they are not actively malevolent" (Tschopik 1951:190). In the list of deities believed in by the Ifugao of the Philippines, R. F. Barton gives the names of 31 gods who send dysentery, 21 "boil and abscess producers," 20 "liver-attacking deities," 4 "headache deities," 14 that cause wounds, 5 that send arthritis, 50 "harpies," and 10 "spitters" (Barton 1946:62–74).

An attempt has been made to relate such fears to patterns of socialization in a cross-cultural survey undertaken by William W. Lambert, Leigh Minturn Triandis, and Margery Wolf. The authors rated 62 societies described in ethnographic accounts in terms of (1) general benevolence or aggressiveness attributed to supernaturals, and (2) children's experience of pain or relative lack of pain from their nurturing agents. Their statistical analysis showed that in societies where infants were treated punitively, there tended to be beliefs in aggressive supernaturals. This would be in harmony with the Freud-Kardiner theory of projection. Lambert, Triandis, and Wolf (1959), however, have a somewhat different interpretation of their correlations. They reason that anxiety is produced in a child through its conflicting anticipations of pain and nurture. This conflict is reduced by conceiving of a god or gods as aggressive, which is in keeping with the anticipation of harm. Their findings must be considered as only preliminary. More investigations should be made into the contrasting belief systems in different societies about benevolent and malevolent supernaturals.

Religious movements

Religious movements of great dynamism have often swept quickly over large populations, sometimes crossing national and linguistic borders. Very often they are started by visionary prophets. They may be a response to contact with peoples having a more advanced culture, and the religion may then represent a kind of nationalistic protest, as in the Shawano cult of the Woodland Indians in 1808, the Ghost Dance of the Plains in the 1870s and again in 1890, and the Cargo cults of Melanesia from 1913 to recent years. Let us consider these three movements briefly.

The prophet of the Shawano cult was the brother of the Indian leader Tecumseh, and his religion was related to the latter's struggle against the whites. The prophet called for a return to Indian ways and a boycott of the trader's goods—beef and pork, flint and steel, guns and traps. The Indians were urged to give up sorcery, to throw away their medicine bags, and to stop drinking liquor. We see here something reminiscent of India's anti-British, noncooperation movement under Gandhi's leadership, an effort to break away from dependence on the enemy through boycott and to return to some earlier, simpler conditions of life during the struggle. Although it did not succeed, since the whites were already so well entrenched, the Shawano cult was a practical, realistic movement, in contrast to the Ghost Dance, which relied more heavily on magic.

The Ghost Dance found many converts among the Paiute and some tribes in California and Oregon in the early 1870s, since it promised that adherents to the cult would be reunited with their dead parents and other relatives and that the whites would disappear and the Indians become rich. There was some disillusionment when these prophecies did not come true, but in 1889 and 1890, there was a revival of the Ghost Dance, which this time affected the Indians of the Great Plains. The culture of these Indians was being destroyed by the disappearance of the buffalo herds on which they had depended. Added to the earlier prophecies of the white man's extinction and the return of the Indian dead, there was also included the return of the buffalo. The religion involved prolonged dancing, until some members fell into trance states. Members wore supposedly bullet-proof "ghost shirts," some of which (sometimes with bullet holes in them) are now on display in our museums. The ghost shirt exemplifies the magical, unrealistic nature of this cult, which quickly died out, although there is still an Indian group in Canada that adheres to a Ghost Dance cult.

Many Cargo cults, as they have been called, have flourished in Melanesia at different times and places. The most common element is a prediction that ships or airplanes will soon appear, bringing all kinds of valued goods to the natives, including refrigerators and other things possessed by the whites. Sometimes the cultists are enjoined to throw away their old belongings, otherwise the new goods will not come. These movements sometimes have antiwhite predictions, like those of the Ghost Dance.

The Melanesians have seen Europeans enjoying the use of all kinds of equipment that have come by ship; they have no idea of how or where they are made. It is apparently a kind of magic, which some Melanesians have tried to divert to themselves by engaging in cult activities that imitate magical European behavior, such as marching, drilling, and performing rituals with flagpoles. In the Vailala movement of Papua from 1919 to 1929, it was thought that flagpoles were the media through which messages came from the dead. These heavily magical cults usually have a short life, since the promised cargoes do not materialize; their ship does not come in.

These three examples of religious movements show that religion does not necessarily remain stable and may be affected by economic crises, contacts with other cultures, a sense of relative deprivation and resentment and of nationalistic feelings.

Summary

Various aspects of religion, including animistic beliefs and religious rituals, are manifest in all societies, if not in all individuals. E. B. Tylor argued that *animism* (belief in spiritual beings) is the core of religion, from which all other aspects of religion sprang, including concepts of possession and fetishism, beliefs in an afterlife, ancestor worship, and the worship of nature gods. According to Tylor, the basic belief in spirits developed naturally from people's experiences of dreaming and reflections about dreams, trance states, illness, and death. In his view, monotheism was a late development in the evolution of religion.

Animatism, an aspect of religious thought not discussed by Tylor, is belief in an impersonal supernatural power, like *mana.* Religion may emphasize either the personal, animistic aspects of the supernatural world or else its impersonal animatistic aspects. The former approach is supplicative in nature, while the latter is magical and manipulative.

Émile Durkheim claimed that magic is mainly an individual affair, while religion is a collective enterprise involving a community or congregation. Malinowski saw magic as a relatively simple means to an end, while religion is an end in itself, involving a more complex ideology. According to Malinowski, human beings turn to magic when they encounter an impasse in their efforts to achieve a goal. Under such blocked circumstances it is natural for people to resort to magic, which has the function of reassuring them and giving them the confidence to persevere. Despite the plausibility of Malinowski's thesis, it is often difficult in practice to distinguish between magic and religion in particular cases.

The shaman or medicine man is a magico-religious specialist who acts as an intermediary between the members of the society and the supernatural world in which they believe. Shamans generally acquire the necessary skills and powers through their own efforts, in contrast to priests, whose authority comes from religious orders or cults in which they are ordained. Techniques for acquiring shamanistic power involve, among others, fasting in solitude to induce visionary experiences. Priests, who do not have to seek such experiences, are specialists in performing rituals and prayers which they learned as novices in their orders.

From a psychoanalytic point of view, religions are projective systems; beliefs about gods are modeled after children's ideas about their parents. Thus, in a society with good parental care one would expect to find an idealization of supernatural beings, who are conceived as being helpful to humans. However, religious systems do not remain stable. They have often been affected by economic crises and contacts with other cultures, sometimes precipitating nativistic, messianic, and nationalistic cults of considerable dynamism.

Suggestions for further reading

A very good source is William A. Lessa and Evon Z. Vogt, eds., *Reader in Comparative Religion: An Anthropological Approach,* 3d ed. (New York: Harper & Row, 1972). It contains well-chosen selections from the writings of Tylor, Frazer, Durkheim, Malinowski, Radcliffe-Brown, Rasmussen, Linton, Kluckhohn, Opler, and many others.

Bronislaw Malinowski's *Magic, Science and Religion and Other Essays* (New York: Doubleday-Anchor Books, 1954) is recommended.

An outstanding work is Victor W. Turner, *The Ritual Process* (Chicago: Aldine Publishing Co., 1969).

An interesting collection of readings is available in Ari Kiev, ed., *Magic, Faith, and Healing: Studies in Primitive Psychiatry Today* (London: Free Press of Glencoe, 1964).

Two good readers on the effects of hallucinogenic drugs and their relation to religion are also recommended: Peter T. Furst, ed., *Flesh of the Gods: The Ritual Use of Hallucinogens* (New York: Praeger Publishers, 1972); and Michael J. Harner, ed., *Hallucinogens and Shamanism* (New York: Oxford University Press, 1973).

19

THE ENJOYMENT OF LIFE: SIMPLE PLEASURES AND THE ARTS

L ife brings much disappointment, frustration, and tragedy. This may seem like an odd way to start a chapter entitled "The Enjoyment of Life," but the point is that there are usually sufficient incentives to go on living, in spite of sickness, deformity, debts, taxes, loneliness, boring work, unhappy marriage, feuds with neighbors, military service, and all the other miseries that may assail us. Religion and other compensations give some people the strength to carry on, but many others break down, fall ill, go mad, or commit suicide. Even so, most people seem to find life worth living. "Life can be beautiful," the saying goes. In this chapter, we shall briefly examine some of the pleasures of life that men and women have enjoyed in different times, places and cultures, ranging from the more biological satisfactions of food and sex and such simple pleasures as games and joking to the enjoyment of the arts: story-telling, decorative art, and music.

Food

Eating is something we have to do to stay alive. Most people find it enjoyable, too, although there are children with feeding problems and some persons who do not seem to get much pleasure from it. Cultures vary, as individuals do. The French and Chinese are noted for their cuisine, the variety of their dishes, and their interest in food, whereas English cooking has a low reputation. Oscar Lewis (1951:187–91) writes that the basic diet of the people of Tepoztlán, Mexico, is corn, beans, and chile. Corn provides from 10 to 70 percent of the family diet. For most people, breakfast consists of black coffee and tortillas; the midday dinner generally features tortillas and chile, and sometimes, on good days, there is meat and vegetables and rice or noodles cooked in broth. For supper there are tortillas or bread, with perhaps some cheese. This sounds like a monotonous diet to a middle-

VICTOR BARNOUW

Hindu woman
cooking.

class American. But Lin Yutang (1937:253–54), the Chinese writer, in turn, finds American cuisine "dull and insipid and extremely limited in variety," especially in its treatment of vegetables and soups.

Lin Yutang, who holds eating to be "one of the very few solid joys of human life," remarks that it is fortunate that it is less hedged about with taboos than sex, and that "generally speaking, no question of morality arises in connection with food" (Yutang 1937:48). Here, he seems to forget that food taboos of one kind or another are universal. There are millions of Hindus and Jains in India who, for religious reasons, will not eat meat. The idea of eating beef is particularly abhorrent to them, as is the eating of pork to Muslims and Jews. The Apache Indians will not eat fish, although edible trout are available in their streams.

Lin Yutang lists with evident gusto some dishes he particularly enjoys, including carp's head, pig's tripe, ox's tripe, and large snails, which pious Hindus, and perhaps many Americans, would not dream of eating.

The pleasure of eating is surely enhanced or diminished by the nature of the social setting in which it takes place and by cultural traditions about food. In Europe, the United States, China, Japan, and many other regions, there is a tradition of the family meal, where all the family members eat together. When men are away all day at work and the children have lunch at school, this is not always feasible, but the tradition is still maintained, when possible. This custom strengthens the sense of family unity and may be (although it often is not) an occasion for pleasant conversation and relaxed enjoyment. While the tradition of the family meal may seem to be a natural, almost inevitable, invention, it is not found in all societies. Among the Rājpūts of Khalapur in northern India the men eat separately from the women and children. Minturn and Hitchcock write (1963:244):

Each man eats either at his own hearth or men's quarters. Each woman takes her food into her own room or into a corner of the courtyard where she can turn her back toward the other women. Children are fed when they demand food and may eat together or separately. . . .

There is no set dining hour. The custom of turning one's back to others while eating, sometimes associated with feelings of embarrassment or uneasiness about food, is found in some other cultures, including those of Bali and the Trobriand Islands.

The Sirionó of eastern Bolivia do much of their eating individually, late at night. This is partly because they spend most of the day hunting and gathering, but also because they do not want to be forced to share food with others who come around begging for scraps. So they have furtive late-night snacks while others are asleep (Holmberg 1950:36).

One cannot be sure that individualistic eating patterns such as those of the Rājpūts of Khalapur and the Sirionó diminish the enjoyment of food; perhaps, instead, they enhance it. But they would seem, at least, to shorten the meal and to lessen opportunity for relaxed sociability in connection with it. Like the hurried chompers of frankfurters at a quick-lunch counter, they may be missing something.

The Chinese are notable not only for the variety of their food and their

Japanese tea ceremony.

interest in eating but also for the development of aesthetic attitudes about it. Lin Yutang devotes many pages to the pleasures of drinking tea, which has been popular in China since at least the fourth century A.D. and perhaps earlier. The Japanese have developed an elaborate ceremony around tea drinking. In both China and Japan, the sipping of tea is associated with quietness, reflection, and aesthetic contemplation. Where such aesthetic and gastronomic traditions are present, the satisfactions of food and drink are probably much increased. It would seem that if food is one of the main pleasures of life, some societies allow greater scope for such enjoyment than others.

Desmond Morris has stated that man is "the sexiest primate alive"; in **Sex** this case, "man" embraces woman, as the proverbial professor of anthropology told his class. "Sexiest" does not refer to physical appeal; Morris means that humans have a stronger sexual drive than other primates. He notes that copulation in apes and monkeys is often very brief, lasting only a few seconds in baboons. Morris (1969:53) writes: ". . . we can see that there is much more intense sexual activity in our own species than any other primates, including our closest relations. For them, the lengthy courtship phase is missing. Hardly any of the monkeys and apes develop a prolonged pair-bond relationship." If the human sexual drive is so strong, its satisfaction must be correspondingly intense, although the intensity varies from one individual to another.

One of the surprising discoveries of the first Kinsey report was the great variability in the number of orgasms experienced by males. One man was reported to have had over 30 orgasms a week for over 30 years, while another said that he had had only one ejaculation in 30 years. The mean frequency for white American males under 30 years of age is reported to be about 3.3 per week (Kinsey, Pomeroy, and Martin 1948:195). Great variability is also reported for women in the second Kinsey report: ". . . 22 percent of the married females between the ages of sixteen and twenty and 12 percent of the married females between the ages of twenty-one and twenty-five, had never experienced any orgasm from any source . . ." (Kinsey, Pomeroy, Martin, and Gebhard 1953:532). On the other hand, about 14 percent of the females in the married sample regularly had multiple orgasms during coitus (Kinsey, Pomeroy, Martin, and Gebhard 1953:375). It is evident that the satisfactions derived from sex vary enormously among individuals.

The Kinsey report on American males also showed that sexual behavior is influenced by economic class membership and by the extent of education. Hence it is affected by cultural conditions.

There are great differences in lovemaking among the various cultures of the world. If love is a universal language, it has many dialects. Kissing, so important in American lovemaking, is not a trait of nonhuman primates and is not found in all human groups. Clellan Ford and Frank Beach list the following societies where kissing is said to be unknown: Bali, Chamorro, Lepcha, Manus, Sirionó, and Thonga (Ford and Beach 1951:58). The position assumed in intercourse is often culturally determined. Kinsey, Pomeroy, and Martin estimated that 70 percent of American couples have never experimented with any other position than the most common one, in which the woman lies on her back and the man lies above her. Among the Trobriand Islanders, on the other hand, the man is usually in a squatting position, while among the Murngin the woman lies on her side with her back to the man.

Attitudes about sex also differ greatly in different societies, ranging from great permissiveness and acceptance to feelings of guilt and disapproval. As in the idea of Original Sin, such attitudes may be associated with religion. Many Hindus, for example, believe that semen is stored in the head and that to accumulate the supply leads to physical and spiritual power; so there is reluctance to lose semen.

The setting and circumstances in which sexual behavior occurs also affect the nature and degree of sexual satisfaction. In many villages in northern India the men sleep in a separate men's quarters. If a man wants to have intercourse with his wife, he gets up during the night and goes to the women's quarters, where many women and children may be sleeping. These arrangements do not allow for much privacy. Privacy is lacking in many societies where a family shares a single-room dwelling, such as a wigwam, tepee, igloo, mud hut, or log cabin. Under such circumstances it is difficult to keep children from observing adult intercourse. It may be partly for this reason that in many such societies no effort is made to prolong the sex act or to delay orgasm. The Berens River Ojibwa, for example, make no effort of this sort. They engage in little or no foreplay or petting, little kissing, and no manipulation of breasts. Oral-genital contacts are taboo. The couples seldom undress to the point of nudity. The man's aim is to achieve orgasm as quickly as possible, and the woman's role is purely passive. A. Irving Hallowell (1949), who provides this information, points to the similarity of these patterns to those of lower-class Americans, as described in the Kinsey report.

As in the case with food, we may conclude that the enjoyment of sexual experience is much affected by attitudes and values, and that some societies allow much greater possibilities for such enjoyment than others.

Play

A general primate trait, play is, of course, a very important activity among human beings, not limited to childhood. The most frequent social activity among young apes and monkeys is play fighting, which finds especially elaborate expression among chimpanzees. Young monkeys may spend four or five hours a day playing in groups. Play is inhibited by some factors and facilitated by others. Exposure to unfamiliar objects or conditions may depress play, while moderate novelty encourages it. The amount of play activity varies in different primate species; the chimpanzee seems to be one of the most playful primates and the gorilla one of the least (De Vore 1965:528–30, 619). It seems likely that humans evolved from a more playful and imaginative chimpanzee-like ancestor, rather than from a forerunner like the dull, businesslike gorilla.

Athletic sports and games both appear in Murdock's list of universal aspects of culture, found in all cultures about which there is adequate information (Murdock 1945:124).[1] Simple athletic sports, such as chasing and wrestling, seem to be carry-overs from the social play of young primates; it is easy to understand their universality. Games may be more complex phenomena and more remote from bodily activities, as are checkers or chess. Both sports and games involve traditional rules, unlike the spontaneous play of children who are involved in a world of make-believe.

Johan Huizinga, who has discussed the importance of play in the development of human culture, describes some of the characteristics of play as follows (1955:13):

. . . we might call it a free activity standing quite consciously outside "ordinary" life as being "not serious," but at the same time absorbing the player intensely and utterly. It is an activity connected with no material interest, and no profit can be gained by it.

Huizinga does not distinguish between play, sports, and games. He regards play (or a game) as having a definite beginning and end and as taking place within a circumscribed area. For Huizinga, the play-area boundary forms a magic circle, within which a different order of reality exists and where special rules apply. The squares for marbles or hopscotch, the tennis court, and the chessboard all have their separate kinds of order.

Games

Societies differ not only in the kinds of games that are played but also in the degree of involvement in games. Roberts et al (1959, 1962) define games as recreational activities characterized by organized play, competition between two or more sides with agreed-upon rules and criteria for determining the winner. In these respects games are distinguished from unorganized amusements, such as swimming or making string figures. The authors subdivide games into three main types: (1) physical skill (races, boxing, hockey); (2) strategy (chess, checkers); and (3) chance (dice, roulette). Games of physical skill may be subdivided into those in which physical skill is the only relevant attribute, as in weight lifting, and those in which strategy is also involved, such as fencing or football. Other combinations of types are

---

[1] According to Roberts and Sutton-Smith (1962:169), there are some societies, such as the Murngin of Australia, that do not have games. There may be gaps in the ethnographic reporting on such societies, although the authors report "complete information" for the Murngin.

also possible, but the above are the classifications of games used by the authors in their cross-cultural surveys of games.

In the first study, 43 societies were rated on the basis of the ethnographic literature as having either low political integration or high political integration and as having games of strategy or not having them. In the statistical analysis it was found that games of strategy tend to be associated with high political integration; they are more apt to be found in societies having complex social organization:

. . . among the adequately-covered tribes, the four hunting and gathering groups lacked games of strategy, only one out of five fishing groups had such a game, and only one out of three pastoral groups. On the other hand, no truly complex society appears to have lacked them (Roberts and Sutton-Smith 1962:601).

We see here an implication of cultural evolution. Games of physical skill are found in societies at all levels of social organization, but games of strategy appear mainly where political integration is more advanced. There may be significance in the fact that symbolism of royalty and relative rank is evident in the king, queen, bishop, knight, and pawn of the strategic game of chess and in the king, queen, and jack of the card deck.

Team sports

Team sports are so familiar to us in the United States that we might assume they are universal, but such is not the case. The Olympic games of the ancient Greeks seem to have emphasized individual athletic competition rather than teams. In Europe, before the 16th century, there were semi-ritualistic team games symbolizing the conflict between darkness and light, winter and spring, but these do not seem to have involved much cooperative team play.

In the pre-Columbian New World, team games were widespread, and it seems likely that the idea of team sports was carried to Europe after the discovery of America. Shinny and hockey were played over a wide area in eastern North America; hockey was also played in central Mexico and in the Gran Chaco area of South America. Lacrosse also had a wide distribution in central and eastern North America. But the most interesting of American Indian team sports was the rubber ball game, which had a distribution from Arizona in the north, through Mesoamerica and the Circum-Caribbean area to as far south as San Salvador. This game involved something unknown in Europe before the discovery of America: the bouncing rubber ball. The game was played in a ball court flanked by sloping walls. The two opposing teams varied in composition from two or three members to 10 or 11. The players were not allowed to touch the ball with hands or feet but could bounce the ball from elbows, knees, or hips, all of which were padded. Points were made when the ball touched the opponents'

Maya ball court,
Zaculeu, Guatemala.

end zone, but the climax of a game, outscoring all other points, came if a player sent the ball through a vertical stone ring affixed in the center of either side wall. That brought the game to an end and entitled the scorer to collect jewels and clothing from the audience. There was betting for high stakes among the spectators. This was a very violent game in which the participants often died; moreover, the captain of a losing team was sometimes sacrificed to the gods. On the other hand, a winning captain was greatly honored. Religion and sport were closely intermingled in the rubber ball game.

In 1528, Hernando Cortés brought some Aztec ballplayers to the court of Charles V in Spain, where they staged several demonstration games. The use of rubber balls considerably influenced European sports, and the team principle may also have been copied, leading to the present forms of some of the sports we know today, such as volleyball, soccer, and football. In basketball we also have the idea of sending a ball through a ring or hoop, although the basketball hoop is horizontal and much wider than the narrow, vertical ball court ring (Borhegyi and Borhegyi 1963; T. Stern 1948).

The diffusion of team sports throughout the world in recent years shows how readily they appeal to people of different cultures. Perhaps, on a small scale, they represent a moral equivalent of war, a relatively safe arena for the expression of competition and aggression.

Gambling

Gambling is a widespread activity among the societies of the world, but it is not universal. A. L. Kroeber (1948:552–53) lists among nongambling peoples the Australian aborigines, Papuo-Melanesians, most Polynesians and Micronesians, and many Indonesians. In the pre-Columbian Americas, most of the northern continent gambled, while most of the southern did not. Gambling takes place in most of Asia, except some marginal fringes. Nongamblers are found in East Africa, while many tribes in West Africa and the Congo Basin gamble. Kroeber finds no consistent, worldwide correlation of gambling with subsistence economy, wealth system, or type of religion.

Joking

Joking appears on Murdock's list of universals (1945). It is nice to know that people joke in all societies. In some societies there are structured joking relationships, so that people are expected to joke with persons related to them in a particular way, as in the bawdy badinage that used to take place between cross cousins of opposite sex among the Ojibwa Indians.

There are many theories about the nature of humor and why some things are considered funny while others are not. The problem is made more difficult by the relativistic nature of humor. What is held to be funny at one time or place may not draw a smile in another. It is often impossible to translate a joke from one language to another, especially, of course, in the case of puns. Well known is the story about how Abraham Lincoln, at a tense moment during the Civil War, took time out to read aloud to the members of his cabinet a passage from the writings of Artemus Ward. The President evidently thought the passage was very funny, and it was probably so regarded by his listeners. Both Stephen Leacock and Max Eastman quote the passage in their books on humor; as they point out, it is hard to see how anyone could find the passage funny today.

One of the efforts made to explain the nature of humor is Eastman's analysis. He believes that one must be in a playful spirit to perceive something as funny and that anything seen as funny would have an unpleasant aspect if one were not in a playful state. A joke, then, contains potentially unpleasant experiences playfully enjoyed. Eastman asks what most jokes have been about through the ages in Western culture, and his answer is: "Mothers-in-law, unpaid bills, drunks, taxes, tramps, corpses, excretory functions, politicians, vermin, bad taste, bad breaks, sexual ineptitudes, pomp, egotism, stinginess and stupidity!" (Eastman 1936:25). It would be interesting to have a cross-cultural survey of humor in different societies to see if such topics form the subject matter of joking in other cultures. Oddly enough, anthropologists have not investigated this question.

Another view of humor, not at odds with Eastman's, would see it as a form of one-upmanship, a way of feeling superior to others. This is true of at least some humor. The ancient Greeks had "dumb peasant" jokes like this one quoted by Stephen Leacock (1935:221): "A peasant, having heard that parrots live for a hundred years, bought one to see if it was true." Another example is of a peasant who wanted to see if his horse could live without food. A while after he stopped feeding him, the horse died. "Alas," said the peasant, "just as he was learning to live without food, he died." We feel superior to the peasant; so we smile. Similar "Polish" jokes are told today in Milwaukee and other cities that have Polish minorities. (Poles tell them, too.)

Minority groups form the subject matter of much joking in our own society. We have jokes about the irrationality of Irishmen ("Lucky are the parents who have no children"), the stinginess of Scots, and the wiliness of Jews. Such jokes help to reinforce group stereotypes and perhaps make the narrator and hearers feel comfortably superior for a moment. It would be interesting to know whether similar jokes are current in other societies that have minority groups.

In all known societies, people have told stories to one another. There **Story telling** may be some peoples, like the nomadic Sirionó of eastern Bolivia, who are reported not to tell many stories, but all societies have at least some traditional tales. Such stories are often referred to as *folklore,* although this term is sometimes given a much wider scope to include such matters as costume and dance (Dundes 1965:3).

Story telling differs from written literature in various ways. The writer does not directly confront an audience. He or she writes a work that is, or should be, original; and, when it is published, it appears in a fixed, usually unalterable form, unless and until it is reprinted with minor corrections or issued in a revised edition. Storytellers on the other hand, face an audience, even though it may consist of only one or two persons. They usually did not invent the story and are often telling a tale which the hearers have heard many times and may know very well. Among the Central Eskimos, the audience is quick to correct a narrator who makes a mistake in what should be a perfectly memorized, stylized account. In this case, exact repetition is valued, but in some societies there is more room for improvisation, and, over a period of time, the story may change markedly in character. An example is provided by the Italian story of "The Cock and the Mouse," which Frank H. Cushing (1965) told to a group of Zuñi Indians. A year later, Cushing revisited Zuñi and heard the story, which had now become transformed and adapted to the Zuñi scene and Zuñi traditions.

The narrator in a non-Western culture does not simply tell a story, but may also enact it, dramatize it, and even dance it. Moreover, members of the audience often participate by giving responses, promptings, or encouragement. The more isolated writer does not experience this kind of direct feedback, although he or she may receive comments in reviews and letters from readers.

A classification of folktales has been made by a Finnish folklorist, Antti

Bushman story teller,
Botswana.

Aarne, with revisions by Stith Thompson, the latest appearing in 1961 with
the title *The Types of the Folktale: A Classification and Bibliography*. But
these deal with only Indo-European tales; 2,000 synopses are given, with
a code number for each. Stith Thompson has also compiled a six-volume
Motif-Index of Folk Literature (1955–58), which has worldwide coverage.

Folktales may be combed by ethnologists for historical clues—for evidence
of past migrations and contact with other cultures. Tales and motifs may
be mapped and their areas of diffusion traced. Some myths and folktales
have an almost worldwide distribution. The story of a flood is one example;
it is often associated with the motif of a diving animal that brings up some
grains of soil from the bottom of the sea, from which the earth is made.
Various explanations have been put forth to account for the wide distribution
of flood myths. It used to be argued that once there must have been a
great flood or several floods, the memory of which has been preserved in
the myths. A psychoanalytic view would be that water has an unconscious
symbolic meaning for all peoples and, hence, is apt to appear in dreams
and become embodied in myths. Flood myths probably diffused from one
or more centers, from one society to another.

A widespread but not universal story is the Magic Flight. A hero who is pursued by some kind of ogre magically causes obstacles to form behind himself by throwing three objects in turn: a stone, which causes a mountain to rise; a comb, which creates a forest; and a liquid, which forms a lake or river. This story has probably spread by diffusion, being told in a continuous area from Europe, through northern Asia, to North America.

Otto Rank (1956), Lord Raglan (1937), and Joseph Campbell (1949) have all been struck by certain recurrent themes in the lives of legendary heroes, some of which are as follows. The hero is the son of a king and queen. Before his birth a prophecy is made about him, which leads to an attempt, often initiated by his father, to have him killed. Instead, the child is spirited away and reared by foster parents. When he reaches manhood, the hero goes to his future kingdom, where he wins a victory over the king or else over a giant, dragon, or wild beast. He then marries a princess and becomes king.

Lord Raglan made a list of 22 items, including most of the themes just mentioned, together with several others. He then found that 20 of the items applied to the story of Oedipus, 20 to that of Theseus, 17 to Romulus and Heracles, 16 to Perseus, Bellerophon, and King Arthur, and 21 to Moses. Other heroes who were scored included Jason, Pelops, Asclepius, Dionysus, Apollo, Zeus, Joseph, Elijah, Siegfried, and Nyikang, a Shilluk hero. Raglan concluded that the lives of the various heroes could not be historical but must reflect a bygone ritual involving birth, initiation, and death. Rank, on the other hand, saw the stories as reflecting the Oedipus complex posited by Freud, in which a young man unconsciously wishes to marry his mother and do away with his father. The area dealt with by Raglan consisted mainly of western Europe and the Near East, but it has been shown that essentially similar hero myths are found in the Far East. Roughly analogous tales are told by the Navaho, where the parallels are less close (Kluckhohn 1965).

Functions of myths

It was characteristic of Malinowski's functionalist approach that he rejected the effort to find origins of myths but emphasized, instead, the functions they serve. The most obvious, immediate function of all oral literature is entertainment. People enjoy hearing stories, and the narrator, who becomes the center of attention, gets satisfaction from the telling. But Malinowski pointed out that myths also provide a "charter" of belief, explaining how things came to be as they are. Unacculturated Ojibwa, for example, believe that their myths are true—that they are not just entertaining tales. Myths provide an explanation of, and support for, traditional customs and correct behavior. On the other hand, some characters in myths do shocking things that are normally taboo, such as committing murder and incest. There is some inconsistency here, but it can be argued that even these immoral episodes serve useful functions in letting off steam and bringing normally repressed material into the open.

How well does the oral literature of a society reflect its culture? Certainly, it is never a complete mirror image. Folklore is selective; important aspects of the culture may not appear in the narratives at all. For example, the pig, which plays so important a role in Melanesian culture, does not figure in Melanesian mythology. W. H. R. Rivers (1968), who drew attention to this fact, suggested that familiar and uniform aspects of culture are less likely to be dealt with in mythology than elements that have some variety and inconstancy. If the moon inspires more mythological elaboration than the sun, it is because it undergoes more changes of appearance, while the sun, especially in tropical countries, is much the same from day to day, year after year.

But the element of variety is not enough, in itself, to account for the presence of an item in folklore. Among the Clackamas Chinook Indians, there was much interest in girls' puberty ceremonies, marriage negotiations, sorcery, and shamanistic cures, but there were few stories dealing with these topics. Melville Jacobs (1959:130) has explained this by saying that these were conscious concerns that were much discussed and also resolved in ritual performances. It was the repressed tensions that became expressed in Clackamas Chinook mythology, including tension about women, in-laws, and other relatives.

Recurrent themes in Central Eskimo folklore

In Chapter 18, the story of Sedna was presented, the woman who sits at the bottom of the sea and controls the movements of the sea mammals which came into being when the segments of her fingers were chopped off. She is sometimes called by a name that means Meat Dish, since she is the ultimate source of the Eskimos' principal food. In some versions of the Sedna myth, she is said to be living with her father at the bottom of the sea. Sedna is large and tall, but her father, who is crippled, with only one arm, is no larger than a ten-year-old boy. In some versions, Sedna is said to have been blinded in one eye by her father. She has, of course, no fingers, and she can barely move. As a nutritive Meat Dish and in her large size, Sedna seems to be a Magna Mater figure, although she is not always generous and nurturant.

According to Rasmussen (1929:66, 98), Sedna's father is described as being habitually ill-tempered. After death, people who have committed sexual sins have to pay penance by living in his place for one year or more before they can go on to the land of the dead. They have to lie beside him and let themselves be pinched or beaten by him. In the case of persons who have committed bestiality, Sedna's father strikes them continually on the genitals for a year or more. According to Boas, who describes him in more favorable terms, Sedna's father is called "the man with something to cut (with a knife) . . ." (Boas 1884:583 ff).

This suggests fear of castration; note, too, that Sedna's fingers have been chopped off, and her father has only one arm. If this interpretation seems fanciful, consider another prominent female supernatural being, the woman who lives in the moon. She is called "the one with the *ulo,*" a knife used by women. When men visit the moon, she tries to make them laugh by dancing in a ludicrous, sensual manner. If a man so much as smiles, she immediately slits his belly, tears out his entrails, and dumps them into a dish. Behind her hover a crowd of pale men whom she has disemboweled but who laugh at everything she does (Rasmussen 1929:76).

Here we have two instances of supernatural beings with knives. In an analysis of Nunivak Island Eskimo folklore, far to the west, Margaret Lantis (1953:131) noted that the most frequently mentioned physical dangers were cutting and stabbing, biting, and eating. When supernaturals are involved, it is the spirits who cut and bite the protagonist, not the other way around. Among the Central Eskimos, however, human beings may stab supernaturals. The harpooning of Sedna by a shaman was described earlier (p. 329). Of course, the Eskimos are always using knives to cut up the animals on which they depend for food. Eskimos have sometimes expressed guilt about living at the expense of animals, which they believe have souls, just as humans do. The fear of cutting may thus represent fear of retaliation. But there may also be a sexual element involved. The woman in the moon disembowels a man only when she has forced him to laugh or smile. There is one other reference to a taboo on smiling among the Central Eskimos. This occurs at a festival, described by Rasmussen (1929:241–43), at which men and women are paired for sexual relations. Two masked figures preside, one a woman with a snowbeating stick, the other a man with a huge artificial penis. Each paired couple has to pass by these masked beings who make all kinds of grotesque, lascivious gestures, trying to make them laugh. The couples have to keep their faces set and stiff, while the onlookers roar with laughter and try to get them to smile. Perhaps the taboo has something to do with the close quarters in which Eskimos sleep, sharing a sleeping platform, huddled close together. The same close proximity may also provide temptation for incest, which might in turn lead to castration anxiety.

Rasmussen (1929:300–301) tells one incest story about some women whose husbands had been murdered and who lived alone with their little sons, whom they carried in their *amauts,* the hoods in back of their jackets. The women had such a need for men that they had sexual relations with their sons. As a result, the latter never grew. The women did the hunting but were instructed by their sons from the *amauts.*

Another fearsome female supernatural being is the *Amaut* witch, a great ogress whose *amaut* is filled with old, rotten seaweed and the human beings whom she has captured (Rasmussen 1929:212).

Eskimo folklore seems to express a bias against women. Sedna, the moon woman, and the *Amaut* witch are all rather unpleasant. Of course, so is Sedna's father, but the moon woman is paired with a moon man who has benevolent traits. He helps young men hunt and protects those who die in accidents or commit suicide. If a woman is barren, she lets the light of the full moon shine on her bare lap, and he thus helps her have children. The moon man warns people about the moon woman and turns her out of his house when she tries to do harm (Rasmussen 1929:76). It will be recalled that, when men fail to kill seals, it is not their fault but the fault of women who have broken taboos. Women, then, seem to be seen as dangerous troublemakers.

The Caribou Eskimos have a story about a man named Kivioq who was carried out to sea on the ice and reached a strange land, where he met an old woman and her daughter. He married the girl, but, one day, while Kivioq was out hunting, the old woman killed her daughter, flayed her, and pulled the skin over herself. This disguise did not fool Kivioq when he returned, for he could see the black, wrinkled legs of the old woman; so he ran away.

The old hag caused obstacles to rise in front of him. First, he came to two bears fighting. He slipped through them. Then, there were two hilltops that opened and closed. Although he passed safely between them, the tail of his coat was cut off. Then, Kivioq came to a boiling cooking pot, which he also got by.

Freudians might point out that both the cooking pot and the hilltops that open and close sound like vagina symbols. If so, the symbolism becomes more explicit in the next episode, when the road is barred by the huge underpart of a woman. After Kivioq "lay with the thing," he was able to continue. Another obstacle was some sealhide thongs in his path.

Then Kivioq came to the house of an old woman who had a tail made of iron. When he lay down to sleep, he was careful to place a flat stone on his chest. Laughing, the old woman jumped up in the air to land on top of Kivioq and pierce him with her iron tail. But it struck the stone, was driven into her inner parts, and she died.

Kivioq went on from there, cruising in a kayak. A huge mussel shell almost cut him in two, but he escaped, with only the stern of his kayak cut off. Kivioq finally managed to return to his own country, and he was so happy to see it again that he sang for joy. His mother said, "That sounds like Kivioq's voice." Then, when his parents caught sight of Kivioq, they were so overjoyed that they fell over and died (Rasmussen 1930:97–99).

A remarkable aspect of this story is the applicability of Freudian symbolism, not only in the vagina symbols already referred to but also in the castration motifs. The tail of Kivioq's coat is cut off by the clashing hilltops, and the stern of his kayak is clipped off by the huge mussel shell. Kivioq is in flight from female sexuality; he tries to return to his parents, but that is forbidden, and they die. More examples could be given of Eskimo stories

Elderly Eskimo couple.

dealing with tension between men and women (Rasmussen 1929:221–22,287–90; 1921:52–55,90–92).

There seems to be no easy way to account for this emphasis, but some possibilities may be suggested. In wintertime, particularly, the Eskimos are cooped up for long periods of time in close quarters and probably get on one another's nerves, although they seem to be very sociable and philosophical about hardships. Perhaps the men, hunched over the blowholes all day on the ice in winter, resent the fact that the women at home are warm, comfortable, and out of danger, just as soldiers in combat resent the safety of those at bases behind the lines. The temptations and taboos of incest may also contribute to the male-female conflict expressed in these narratives.

However, it must be admitted that these are only guesses. The difficulty with such analyses has been well stated by Lévi-Strauss (1967:203):

If a given mythology confers prominence on a certain figure, let us say an evil grandmother, it will be claimed that in such a society grandmothers are actually evil and that mythology reflects the social structure and social relations; but should the actual data be conflicting, it would be readily claimed that the purpose of mythology is to provide an outlet for repressed feelings. Whatever the situation, a clever dialectic will always find a way to pretend that a meaning has been found.

Some approaches to the study of folklore

One approach to the study of folktales is the intensive examination of the oral literature of a single society, as we have done to some extent in reviewing Central Eskimo folktales above and as Margaret Lantis (1953) did in much more detail in an analysis of Nunivak Eskimo mythology. In such a study the aim is to see if there are any recurring themes and emphases which may differ from those in other bodies of folklore and to provide an explanation for their presence.

Still another approach to the study of folktales is the cross-cultural survey method, making use of the ethnographic data in the Human Relations Area Files (see p. 418), applying scoring systems and looking for statistical correlations. For example, the folktales of a number of societies may be scored for the degree of achievement motivation (*n* achievement) evidenced in the tales. Then one can see if there is any correlation between *n* achievement and certain features in the child-training patterns in the societies selected for investigation (McClelland and Friedman 1952; Child, Storm, and Veroff 1958).

The foregoing approaches involve analyses of *themes*. Studies have also been made of the *structure* of folktales. A Russian folklorist, Vladimir Propp, claimed that most Russian fairy tales follow a standard pattern, divided into a series of what he called *functions,* or components of the tale. Propp (1968) has listed these functions and provided a brief definition and a conventional sign for each, so it is possible to diagram the structure of a tale with his symbols. Since some European fairy tales are similar to Russian ones, it would be possible to apply Propp's system to them but not to most other bodies of folklore, which have different structures.

A structural analysis has been applied to Cinderella stories of Northwest Coast Indian tribes, which have been compared to European Cinderella tales. Betty Uchitelle Randall (1949) distinguishes four basic steps common to both Old World and New World Cinderella tales: (1) *The need for change.* Recognition of an inferior status or situation by a mistreated stepdaughter or younger son. (2) *The reason for change.* Behavior of others makes the situation worse: rejection, abandonment. (3) *The process of change.* The means by which the hero attains the goal. (4) *The result of change.* The fulfillment of the goal. (5) A fifth step, *Retribution,* is sometimes added: punishment of those who made the hero or heroine suffer. This last step is more common in European than in American Indian stories, since an ethical dualism of good and bad is prominent in European but not in Indian tales. Another contrast is that the emotions of the hero are given full expression in the Indian stories, while Grimm's Cinderella expresses no feelings. The only outspoken emotion in the story is the hatred of the wicked stepmother.

The most ambitious attempt to analyze folklore in recent years is the four-volume *Mythologiques* of Claude Lévi-Strauss. Whereas Propp's structural approach has been called *syntagmatic* (concerned with the linear sequence of episodes, as in the analysis of a sentence's syntax), Lévi-Strauss's approach has been termed *paradigmatic,* in search of patterns. He always looks for binary oppositions that he assumes underlie myths, such as the contrasts of raw and cooked, nature and culture. Lévi-Strauss claims that the function of a myth is to provide a resolution or mediation of a conflict.

Dancing, music, and decorative art are all listed in Murdock's catalog **Decorative art** of universal aspects of culture (1945:124). Adumbrations of such activities may be seen in some of the behavior of nonhuman primates, particularly among chimpanzees. Man's pleasure in rhythmic movement and rhythmic sound must be a heritage from a prehominid level.

Drawing and painting among apes in captivity

Nonhuman primates, however, do not seem to produce decorative art; its universality may thus be somewhat less understandable than that of dancing and music. But it is interesting that some apes and monkeys in captivity have learned to scribble with pencil on paper and to make fingerpaintings and paint with a brush. When an ape is given a pencil and makes a mark with it, it is very interested in seeing what it has produced, and it continues to make marks. These scribbles are not purely random; they are, first of all, confined to the page and seldom spill over. Desmond Morris presented his chimpanzee subject, Congo, with a sheet of paper on which a large rectangle had been drawn, leaving a one-inch margin; Congo's scribbles remained within this rectangle. Alpha, a young female chimpanzee, always marked the four corners of a blank sheet of paper before scribbling in the center; but she ignored the corners if there was a square, circle, or other form on the page. Then, she placed almost all of her marks within the square or circle, with only a few spots outside. If the square or circle was small, she scribbled over it instead of within. If there was a small, solid figure on the page in an off-center position, Alpha did not mark it but scribbled in the open space in such a way as to balance the figure. Congo did the same. These apes had their individual differences. Congo did not mark all four corners as Alpha did, and he favored a fan-shaped type of composition which Alpha did not produce, although other primates have done so.

A striking aspect of ape art production is the intense interest and motivation shown by the ape while drawing or painting. This work was not rewarded by food or other awards; it was done for its own sake. Indeed, at such times, food was ignored. An interruption could cause a temper tantrum. A female chimpanzee, interrupted in the middle of a drawing, bit her keeper, although she did not usually do such a thing, even when the keeper took attractive food away from her. Congo's drawing sessions usually lasted between 15 and 30 minutes, with between five and ten drawings being produced, but on one occasion he worked without stopping for nearly an hour and turned out 23 drawings and paintings.

If decorative art is a universal feature of human cultures, it may be that

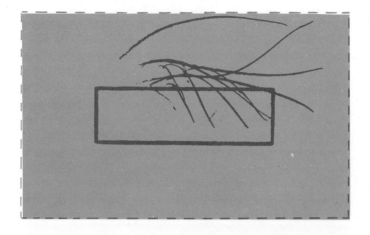

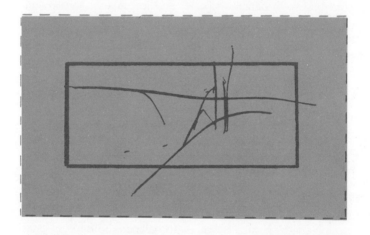

A chimpanzee's reaction to rectangles. (*Top*) all marks are made within the rectangle and none in the one-inch margin. (*Center and bottom*) the rectangles are smaller—with some markings made outside the rectangle (*center*) and markings under rather than inside the rectangle (*bottom*).

a feeling for balance, symmetry, and rhythm was inherited from our prehominid ancestors (Morris 1962).

Design forms

The feeling for balance and regularity may find expression in designs
characterized by bilateral symmetry. Franz Boas pointed out that such designs
are found even in the simplest forms of decorative art, including Paleolithic
geometrical figures and the body paintings of Andaman Islanders and of
natives in Tierra del Fuego. Perhaps the stress on bilateral symmetry is
ultimately based on the bilateral symmetry of the human body itself. Boas

Greek key designs.
(*Left*) two pieces of
mammoth ivory from
the Ukraine, about
15,000 years old,
engraved with Greek
key design. (*Right*) a
Greek key pattern in
matwork made by
Indians of the Rio
Branco in
northwestern Brazil.

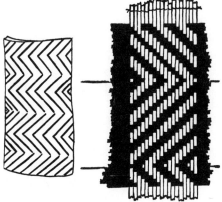

Zigzag herringbone
designs. (*Left*)
engraved mammoth
ivory from the
Ukraine, probably
15,000 years old.
(*Right*) woven textile
made by Bakairi
Indians of the
Amazon jungle.

(1955:33) suggested that the sensation of the motions of right and left might lead to the feeling of symmetry. At any rate, such patterning is widespread in the decorative arts of the world.

Rhythmic repetition is another fundamental aspect of design. We see it in the regular flaking of a Solutrean flint blade and in the adzing of a Haida canoe, where the adze marks were purposely left unsmoothed for the sake of their texture and patterned effect. Rhythmic repetition often appears in the decoration of pottery, baskets, and textiles.

In some cases, particular design patterns have been imposed or suggested by a process of manufacture. Checkerwork basketry presents a chessboard pattern, especially if the two sets of interlacing strands have different colors or shades. Twilling produces diagonal strips, which may also be combined into diamond forms. The coiling of a basket may suggest a spiral (Lowie 1940:182).

A design form known as the Greek key, fret, or meander, has a very wide distribution, partly because of its association with a particular weaving technique. Its oldest known appearance is on an engraving on mammoth ivory from a site in the Ukraine dating from about 15,000 years ago. On a second piece of such ivory a zigzag herringbone design was engraved. Gene Weltfish has shown that both of these designs develop naturally from the twill-plaited weaving of basketry and matting, such as is made by some Amazon Indians today. On this basis, Weltfish argues convincingly that this weaving technique must have been known 15,000 years ago.

Once a design like the Greek key has come into circulation, it may be transferred from one medium to another, as seems to have been the case in the mammoth-ivory engravings. It may also be diffused from one society to another.

The diffusion of art motifs

Like folklore motifs, design forms can be mapped, and efforts may be made to trace their diffusion. It seems likely that designs that have been imposed or suggested by processes of manufacture have appeared independently in many different times and places. The same is probably true of relatively simple forms, such as crosses, spirals, and swastikas. But, when design motifs become more complex, and when their component parts do not seem to be obviously related to one another, the possibility of diffusion presents itself whenever similar motifs appear in different culture areas.

Trans-Pacific diffusionists, who believe that much of the advanced culture in the New World was affected by Asian influence, base much of their argument on the similarities of design motifs in Asia and the Americas. Consider, for example, what has been called the *Hocker* motif: a figure with bent arms and legs extended on either side of the body, with dots or disks appearing between the knees and elbows. Similar figures appear in Shang or early Chou China, in Malaysia, Melanesia, Polynesia, Mexico,

(*Top*) two hockers carved on stone slabs, Ecuador. (*Bottom left*) hocker from Dyak woodcarving, Borneo. (*Below right*) clay stamp from Guerrero, Mexico. (*Bottom right*) painted pottery from Puerto Rico.

Peru, Ecuador, Brazil, and on the Northwest Coast of North America. In some of these figures, eyes and faces appear on the joints and hands. This pattern is found in the Northwest Coast, in Aztec reliefs, in the Mississippi Basin, and in parts of Melanesia.

There are many parallel features in the architecture of Mexico, Guatemala, India, Java, and Indochina, including pyramids with stairways and sometimes serpent columns and balustrades. Serpent balustrades appear at Chichén Itzá of the Mexican period and at Tula in Mexico; they are also found in the Borobudur in Indonesia. Not all anthropologists would agree that these features diffused across the Pacific; many would insist that the similarities are simply due to independent invention in the two hemispheres.

Music

Music is an expressive form of communication found in all societies. Like decorative and plastic art, music is culturally patterned and differs from one society to another. Just as it is often difficult (despite the influence of Picasso and modern art) for an American to appreciate the aesthetic qualities of an African statue or Melanesian mask, it is also difficult to enjoy the music of a Chinese opera as much as we enjoy more familiar Western music. In all societies there are traditions about the patterns of art production with which persons are familiar from an early age. The symbolic meanings attached to particular aspects of art in one society may not be at all understood in another. This was shown in an experiment undertaken by Robert Morey (1940). Pieces by Schubert, Handel, and Wagner that were meant to express such emotions as fear, reverence, rage, and love were played to members of a Liberian tribe, who did not make the emotional associations one would expect of a European or American audience.

This does not mean that we cannot enjoy another style of music. Some styles are sufficiently similar to our own to be easy to assimilate. Music developed by New World Negroes is said to represent a syncretism or blending of African and European-American music. According to Richard A. Waterman (1952), this syncretism was made possible because there is enough similarity between African and European music. But European music is quite different from North American Indian music, making syncretism more difficult. Alan P. Merriam, who has studied music among the Flathead Indians of Montana, writes that a Flathead child may learn to play the clarinet in a marching band at school while at the same time learning traditional Indian music at home. Here, the result is not syncretism but compartmentalization. The two kinds of music are kept separate for different occasions. Aspects of the traditional music do not appear in a Western performance, nor are aspects of European music introduced into an American Indian performance (Merriam 1964). Of course, some syncretism may develop in time, but it has not done so yet.

Persons who are familiar with a particular style of music may feel a heightened sense of solidarity when they either perform together or collectively listen to music they enjoy, as in the case of a hymn-singing church congregation or a large audience of young Americans at a rock festival. Such occasions may be very important in some societies, as they were among the Plains Indians. It has been estimated that about a third or more of a Ponca's year was devoted to preparing for or participating in dancing and ceremonial activity that involved music (Howard and Kurath 1959:1).

Cultures vary widely in the number and kinds of musical instruments present. Musical instruments have been divided into idiophones (rattles,

Bushman playing musical bow.

marimbas, gongs, bells), membranophones (skin instruments, such as drums), cordophones (stringed instruments), and aerophones (wind instruments). Rhythmic instruments such as rattles and drums seem to be the oldest, judging by their wide distribution and presence among many hunting-gathering societies, but flutes are also ancient and widespread. Stringed instruments are more limited; they did not occur in pre-Columbian America.

Fine museum displays and beautifully illustrated books have made people familiar in recent years with some of the arts of non-Western societies. At the same time, the influence of abstract and expressionist art has, to some extent, modified earlier aesthetic attitudes and made it possible for many people to now see beauty in African sculpture and other artworks they might formerly have dismissed as barbarous and grotesque. Non-Western art has thus become more acceptable and familiar. However, the context in which we see African masks, Kwakiutl shamans' rattles, and other such objects is very different from those in which they once functioned. We see them atomistically arranged on a wall, in a display case, or on the pages of a book. They have been recreated as something new in their new setting. While it is good that we can appreciate these objects, it is worth keeping in mind that they are quite removed from the world in which they once had a very different function and significance.

Integration of the arts

The arts are often interrelated and integrated. Consider, for example, a Kwakiutl winter ceremonial, held at night in a huge, dark, gable-roofed, plank-walled house in the light of a crackling fire. Architecture, costumes, masks, music, singing, dancing, pageantry, and oral literature were all combined on such occasions. The costumes were magnificent, including dark mantles of Hudson's Bay blankets bordered with scarlet flannel and sewn with buttons or dentalium shells. The masks, beautifully carved and painted, represented the spirits that were believed to possess the dancers. Some of the masks were huge composite structures with movable parts operated by weights, pulleys, and strings, so that beaks could snap and bite, or so that the mask could split in two and widen to display another mask within. The bodies of the dancers were often hidden under long fringes of cedar bark. These impressive figures danced about the flickering fire to the accompaniment of singing. The men who did this dancing, acting, and singing were also the carvers of the masks. Although some artists were known to be outstanding, most men did some carving. This widespread familiarity with the arts made possible a high level of sophistication and art criticism that maintained or raised local standards.

Similarly impressive are the masked dances of the Zuñi Shalako ceremony,

Balinese play scene.

where, again, there is a combination of impressive setting, colorful costumes, ingenious masks, and well-rehearsed dancing.

One more example of integration in the arts is the Balinese drama, usually enacted in front of an elaborately carved temple with magnificently costumed players, some of whom may be masked, to the accompaniment of a *gamelan* orchestra. The performances are done with such professional skill that it is hard to remember that these dancers, actors, and musicians are peasant farmers who spend much of the day in their rice fields and who meet at night to rehearse and perform their dazzling dramas. The travelers from Europe and the United States who witness such performances realize what we may have lost, in our modern world, in the course of economic specialization and industrial progress.

The artist in social context

In modern industrial society the artist is often considered to be an aberrant individual who may be highly talented but who is somehow set apart from the more practical world of the majority. This is not the case in many non-Western societies, where the practice of art is not held to be either deviant or limited to talented persons. The Anang of Nigeria believe that all people are equal in their innate artistic potentialities; ability is simply a matter of training and practice. "Once an individual commits himself to this occupation by paying the fee and participating in a religious ritual, he almost never fails to develop the skills which will enable him to enjoy success as a professional." (Messenger 1958:22). This applies to all the arts among the Anang: carving, dancing, singing, and weaving.

In such a society a person does not create art for the purpose of self-expression or aesthetic satisfaction alone. The work is more apt to be intended for some general social purpose, such as ceremonial activity, and the artist may work in collaboration with others, so that the finished object is the work of several persons. Since so many people are producers of artwork in such a society, there are commonly shared standards of craftsmanship, and there are apt to be expressions of criticism or admiration of particular products, which help to maintain or improve the level of artistic production.

In some societies where high standards of workmanship prevail, there may be some specialization. Although carving techniques were generally known in the Northwest Coast of North America, some men specialized in carving and were held to be better at it than others. But they engaged in hunting and fishing and other everyday activities like anyone else.

In Bali, where everyone seems to be an artist, according to the gifted artist and ethnographer Miguel Covarrubias (1937:163), wealth and fame were not important considerations. "The artist in Bali is essentially a craftsman and at the same time an amateur, casual and anonymous, who uses his talent knowing that no one will care to record his name for posterity.

His only aim is to serve his community . . ." There are constant demands on artists in Bali, since the soft sandstone used in temple sculpture crumbles after a few years and the sculpture must be renewed. The same is true of wooden sculpture, often eaten by ants, while paper and cloth rot from the humidity.

The motives that lead people to engage in art are various. A distinction should first be made between the process of art production and contemplation of the finished product. We have seen how intent and absorbed chimpanzees are when engaged in drawing and painting, but they seem to have little interest in the work of art when it is done. They do not try to hoard it or put it up on the wall. Instead, they may crumple it up or try to eat it. At the opposite extreme are modern collectors of art who do nothing whatever to produce an *objet d'art* but are proud and pleased to have artworks on display in their homes.

Part of the motivation for engaging in art production is the sense of mastery and control, the satisfaction of successfully coping with a challenge. Even when making an arrowhead, basket, or pot, the workmen are usually not satisfied with a product that simply does the job. They want it, of course, to be utilitarian, but they are apt to lavish more attention on the object than purely utilitarian considerations would demand. Vanity and prestige may also motivate art production. Painting the face and body, tattooing, scarification, and elaborate headdress, ornaments, and clothing all draw attention to the self, and so do special clubs, maces, stools, and other objects that may be the prerogatives of kings, chiefs, or other persons of high status. Another motivation in art production has been in connection with religion, in the search for security. Masks that represent the ancestors or the gods must be well made to ensure supernatural aid. Shrines or temples are beautified to enhance the holiness of the place. There is also the pleasure of being surrounded by beautiful things, as in the decoration of a home, its embellishment with objects of beauty. Finally, there is patronage, artwork done upon commission for a king or wealthy person, who may thus employ several artists.

Societies like the Kwakiutl and the Balinese represent a high level of art production and keen interest in the arts. Not all societies reach such high levels of aesthetic interest. Although the arts are universal, there is much more art in some societies than in others. In some societies, certain fields of artistic expression remain unexplored. The Ona of Tierra del Fuego did not model or carve, although they did paint their bodies and perform elaborate dances. The California seed gatherers made no pottery, but they produced very beautiful, intricately woven baskets. These variations may sometimes be due to the level of technology of the society or to the presence or absence of certain materials or resources in the local environment, but such explanations do not always apply. It still remains a problem why artistic expression is much more developed in some societies than in others.

Most of the pleasures of life discussed in this chapter are enjoyed in all known cultures: eating, sex, athletic sports, games, joking, storytelling, decorative art, and music. Societies differ, however, in the emphasis given to these enjoyments. Some societies have much more varied menus or a greater development of the arts than others. Games, stories, music, and art motifs may diffuse from one society to another, which is an important source of cultural enrichment. For example, Europe does not seem to have had team sports before the rubber ball game was introduced from the New World. But the members of a society can only accept what is congenial and sufficiently familiar to be acceptable; hence many Americans find difficulty in appreciating African masks or Chinese music.

Although the artist is often considered to be an aberrant or unusual person in our society, that is not the case in many non-Western societies where the artists work with others in a social enterprise. They are often anonymous creators, who expect no lasting fame from their contributions.

Summary

A good, brief introduction to the field of folklore studies is Alan Dundes, "Oral Literature," in *Introduction to Cultural Anthropology: Essays in the Scope and Methods of the Science of Man,* ed. James A. Clifton (Boston: Houghton Mifflin Co., 1968), pp. 117–29.

A classic work is Stith Thompson, *The Folktale* (New York: Dryden Press, 1946).

Valuable for providing insight into the historical development of approaches to oral literature is Robert A. Georges. ed., *Studies on Mythology* (Homewood, Ill.: The Dorsey Press, 1968). It contains articles by Boas, Rivers, Radcliffe-Brown, Malinowski, Benedict, Kluckhohn, Firth, Leach, and Lévi-Strauss. Two other anthologies are also recommended: Alan Dundes, ed., *The Study of Folklore* (Englewood Cliffs, N.J.: Prentice-Hall, Inc., 1965); John Middleton, ed., *Myth and Cosmos: Readings in Mythology and Symbolism* (New York: Natural History Press, 1967).

A good introduction to the cross-cultural study of art is provided by Erna Gunther, "Art in the Life of Primitive Peoples," in *Introduction to Cultural Anthropology: Essays in the Scope and Methods of the Science of Man,* ed. James A. Clifton (Boston: Houghton Mifflin Co., 1968), pp. 76–114. Another is Ruth Bunzel, "Art," in *General Anthropology,* ed. Franz Boas (New York: D. C. Heath & Co., 1938), pp. 535–88.

A classic work is Franz Boas, *Primitive Art* (New York: Dover Publications, 1955). (First published in 1927.) See also Paul S. Wingert, *Primitive Art: Its Traditions and Styles* (New York: Oxford University Press, 1962); Gene Weltfish, *The Origins of Art* (Indianapolis: Bobbs-Merrill Co., 1953).

For ethnomusicology see Alan P. Merriam, *The Anthropology of Music* (Evanston, Ill.: Northwestern University Press, 1964).

Suggestions for further reading

20

CULTURE
AND PERSONALITY:
GROWING UP IN
DIFFERENT SOCIETIES

In previous chapters we have seen that human sociocultural systems may differ greatly from one another in subsistence basis, forms of marriage, postmarital residence, social and political organization, and other respects. Children born into these different systems must adjust to them and learn the rules and values of the culture, whatever they may be. The adults of each society teach their own conceptions of reality to the young. Since they generally have no alternative models to follow, the young accept these teachings, identify with their parents, and strive, with varying degrees of effort and success, to approximate the ideal type of their society.

Psychological schools as different as those of behaviorism and psychoanalysis place a central emphasis on the childhood years. From their points of view, the adult personality is formed mainly in childhood. The behaviorists believe that so-called instincts and emotions are largely learned reactions. Freud, on the other hand, believed that humans, even as children, have to cope with strong instincts or drives. The ways in which these instincts are thwarted or find expression in the childhood years determine what kind of personality will develop. Behaviorism and psychoanalysis, then, have different assumptions about human nature, but they both agree on the great importance of the early years, an emphasis shared by still other psychological schools. This consideration underlies the work that has been done in the cross-cultural study of child development.[1]

Maternal deprivation

Normal human development depends upon an adequate amount of maternal care. Among human beings the absence of such a relationship, without

---

[1] For two books which marshall evidence against the view that the early childhood years are crucially formative in human psychological development, see Morgan (1975) and Clarke and Clarke (1976).

adequate substitutes, may have very severe effects upon the development of the individual. It has been argued by several writers that children suffering from maternal deprivation fail to develop normally in later years. The evidence for this, however, is conflicting, and there are differences of opinion as to what constitutes the essential deprivation from which the children suffer.

Soon after birth all primates, except for humans, cling to their mothers; they remain in close contact with them throughout infancy. Harry Harlow (1962) showed that when rhesus monkeys were deprived of their mothers, they did not develop normal patterns of heterosexual behavior in later years. When deprived female rhesus monkeys were impregnated by normal male monkeys, they failed to develop maternal feelings toward their offspring and treated them with indifference or hostility. However, Harlow also found that infant monkeys who had been deprived of their mothers but allowed to play with other young members of their species for 20 minutes a day seemed to develop normally with regard to social and sexual interaction.

Such experiments in deprivation, fortunately, are not made with human beings, but a roughly analogous trauma may be seen in cases of children who have been separated from their mothers and placed in institutions. If such a child is between 15 and 20 months old and has had an adequate relationship with the mother before separation, it will react in a predictable manner, which John Bowlby (1969:27) has broken down into the successive, overlapping stages of protest, despair, and detachment. If the separation is sufficiently prolonged, the child will show no relief or satisfaction when the mother returns but will seem apathetic and disinterested, a condition that may persist into later years. In cases of briefer separation, a period of detachment may be succeeded by ambivalent phases of alternate rejection and demands for parental attention.

René Spitz (1945) contrasted the development of infants living in a foundling home with those reared in a prison nursery. Although physical care was good in the foundling home, the infants had no opportunity to have closer contacts with adults. The infants in the prison nursery, however, had daily sessions with their mothers. The foundling-home infants showed various emotional disturbances, states of depression, and actual physical deterioration, sometimes even leading to death. However, institutionalization does not always have such negative results. No doubt the age of the child at the time of institutionalization, the nature of the institution, and the number and character of the caretakers all make a difference.

As was mentioned earlier, there is a difference of opinion as to what constitutes the basic deprivation from which institutionalized children suffer. Spitz believed that it is lack of mother love. Other writers, however, have argued that the basic problem is lack of stimulation. When there are many children and few caretakers, the latter do not have the time to give much personal attention or stimulation to their charges. Wayne Dennis (1960) studied the behavioral development of children in three institutions in Iran.

Maternally deprived, young rhesus monkeys huddle together for compensatory close contact.

In two of these institutions, the children were greatly retarded in many respects, including the ability to sit alone, to stand, and to walk. In the third institution, the children were not retarded in these respects. Dennis believes that the differences were due to the fact that in the first two institutions, there was not enough handling of the children by their attendants, who did not place them in the sitting and prone positions. The children were thus not able to learn to sit up and look around but spent most of their time lying on their backs. Lack of experience in the prone position led to failure to learn to creep and to a general retardation of locomotion.

Freudian theory

Erik Homburger Erikson, a modified Freudian, believes that experiences in the first year of life, especially in relation to the mother, establish a sense of basic trust or else basic mistrust. This period corresponds to Freud's oral stage, when much of the child's contact with the outside world, including its mother, is channeled through the mouth and lips. If sufficient trust is acquired during the first year of life, the child moves on to a succeeding stage when, according to Erikson (1963: Chap. 7), there is a conflict between the sense of autonomy and feelings of shame and doubt. This period (the second year) corresponds to Freud's anal stage, when toilet training is initiated in many societies. During this period the child develops a sense of control over itself and its environment and learns both literally and figuratively to stand on its own two feet, although it is still dependent on its parents. The years from three to five are a period of rapid physical development and locomotion, awareness of genital sensations, and the appearance of the Freudian Oedipus complex, in which the boy's attachment to the mother is combined with jealous hostility toward the father. Freud calls this period the phallic stage, which is followed by a latency period of sexual quiescence until the coming of puberty and the attainment of genital primacy. From Freud's point of view, traumas and disappointments during this developmental sequence may lead to fixation at a particular stage or regression to an earlier one, if the trauma is sufficiently severe, thus forming neurotic or psychotic personality patterns. The child's ego is vulnerable to traumatic experiences because it is still in the process of development, not yet ready to cope with crises which it could handle easily at a later stage of maturity. Freudian interpretations of childhood psychosexual development are not accepted by everyone, but they have influenced many anthropologists in the field of culture-and-personality.

Maturation and development

Stages of motor development in childhood may vary somewhat because of cultural factors. Thus, Balinese children do not go through a crawling phase, as American children do, because they are habitually carried about by the mother and other persons during the first year of life. Creeping on all fours is disapproved of as animal-like. Hence, Balinese children are less active than American children of that age (Mead and MacGregor 1951:42 ff).

The tempo of maturation in some respects may be affected by cultural patterns. The development of infants in Uganda is a case in point. When compared with the stage of development of European infants of the same age, all aspects of development among Uganda children during their first two years have been reported to be precocious, including prehension, manipulation, adaptivity, and language development. It has been stated that Uganda children can sit alone a couple of months before English children, and the same is reported of crawling, standing, and walking. There may be a problem here as to whether observers of children in different countries have used the same definitions or criteria of such acts as sitting, crawling, and standing. However, Marcelle Géber, who examined 252 Uganda infants and young children in or near Kampala, believes they manifest precocity in these respects, and she attributes it to close mother-child relationship,

Uganda baby with mother.

demand feeding, and intimate physical contact. Géber suggests that the way the child is carried on the mother's back may strengthen its ability to hold the head steady and may help the child to sit alone earlier (Ainsworth 1967). If so, this shows the importance of stimulating experience and close maternal contact in the child's first year of life, just as the studies of institution-alized children reveal the consequences of their absence or scarcity.

The precocity of Uganda children is less marked in their second year of life, and, after three years of age, Uganda children are less advanced than European children. This decline is thought to be due to the traumatic abruptness of the weaning process in Uganda and to a subsequent diminution of mother-child interaction. When another baby is born, the mother gives her full attention to the new infant and pays little attention to older children, who have few toys and playthings and engage in few organized activities. There is reported to be relatively little stimulation for them after the first year (Ainsworth 1967). Claims of precocity have been made for the children of other sub-Saharan nations besides Uganda.[2]

---

[2] For a critical review of this literature, see Warren (1972).

In some societies the amount of mother-child contact and interaction is greater than in our own. This is true, for example, in Japan, where there is more continuous sleeping together of mother and child and more closeness in back-carrying and bathing patterns (Barnouw 1973:223–27). Comparable patterns occur in some other societies. There are societies that have a postpartum sex taboo for a year or more after the child is born; the parents then have no sexual relations, and throughout this period the child sleeps with its mother. Some writers have argued that this must establish strong dependent ties on the mother or an identification with her on the part of the child. A long suckling period is believed to have the same result, although that may be countered by later experiences. Societies differ greatly in the length of the suckling period. In the United States it is generally very brief, in comparison to most other societies. In one of the earliest studies to make use of the Human Relations Area Files, John W. M. Whiting and Irvin L. Child found that in 75 societies the median age of weaning was two and a half years old.

Like the satisfaction of oral needs, the manner of toilet training is also held to influence personality, whether it is instituted early or late in life and the extent to which lapses are punished. In the study just mentioned, Whiting and Child (1953) drew attention to the fact that anal training is stricter in the United States than in most other societies studied. Slightly over half of the primitive societies begin toilet training somewhere between the ages of one and a half and two and a half years old.

It is understandable that nomadic people would be less fussy about toilet training than middle-class Americans who have wall-to-wall carpeting. The nomadic Sirionó of Bolivia, for example, make little effort to teach sphincter control to their children and do not punish them for soiling. These differences in child-training patterns in different societies must have consequences for personality formation, although this has not been well documented by anthropologists. Severe toilet training in early childhood is believed to generate compulsive tendencies involving such personality traits as fussiness, pedantry, obstinacy, self-righteousness, and suspicion of others. Belief that severe toilet training leads to such traits rests on clinical evidence, which some writers have rejected (Orlansky 1949) and others have supported (Axelrad 1962).

Sexual disciplines vary considerably in different societies, as was noted in Chapter 19, and this too must have different consequences in personality formation. The latency period, which Freud distinguished as a phase of childhood in which there is a loss of interest in sex, was declared by Malinowski (1953) to be missing among the Trobriand Islanders, who are very permissive in their acceptance of sex play among children. Adolescence is traditionally a time of "storm and stress" in the Western World, but Margaret Mead (1928) found this was not the case among Samoan girls, where, again, there are permissive attitudes toward premarital lovemaking. Although culture impinges at every phase in the developmental cycle, this is not, of course, to deny the importance of biological or biochemical factors. The cultural context may, however, place them in a different configuration in one society than in another.

The Alor study   An outstanding work in culture-and-personality is *The People of Alor* (1944) by Cora DuBois. This study not only relied upon the observation of behavior and interviews with informants but also made use of some psychological tests, particularly the Rorschach (ink blot) Test, which was given to 37 subjects. This test consists of ten bilaterally symmetrical inkblots which are always shown to test subjects in the same order. The subject is required to tell what he or she sees in the blots. Although the blots are objectively the same for all subjects, the responses given to them vary enormously. This shows that the persons taking the test project something into the blots, which is why the Rorschach is called a *projective* test. Analysis of the nature of the subjects' responses provides clues to their personality organization. DuBois also collected children's drawings from 33 boys and 22 girls and recorded eight rather long life histories.

One innovation of this project was the procedure of "blind analysis," submitting the projective materials to different specialists who were given no information about the culture. The Rorschachs were analyzed by a Rorschach analyst, the drawings by a drawing analyst, and the life histories were analyzed by Abram Kardiner. Each specialist was required to give a general personality description of the Alorese on the basis of the material submitted. If these descriptions had turned out to differ quite a bit from one another, one would have been inclined to doubt the validity of the methods employed. As it turned out, however, there was a good deal of congruence among the reports and agreement with the impressions of the ethnographer. This method minimized the possibility of bias and subjectivity in the personality description of the Alorese.

Emil Oberholzer, the Rorschach analyst, remarked that the Alorese were suspicious and mistrustful of one another. He concluded that they were passive and uncreative, lacking in goals that involved sustained effort. He assumed that the Alorese readily gave way to emotional outbursts, rage, and temper and that they did not have close friendships.

The drawing analyst remarked that the children had a feeling of aloneness and lacked creativity.

Kardiner observed that parental figures were not idealized and that superego formation was weak.

What aspects of life are responsible for this depressing picture? Kardiner and DuBois believe that it is largely due to maternal neglect in infancy. This is a society in which the women play the main role in subsistence; they are the agriculturalists, while the men busy themselves with the financial exchanges of pigs, gongs, and kettledrums. Between ten days and two weeks after the birth of a child, the mother returns to the fields to resume regular agricultural work. She does not take the baby with her to the fields, as is done in some societies, but leaves it in the care of its father, brother, sister, or grandparents. She is gone most of the day. A child may sometimes be nursed by another woman, but, since such substitutes are not consistently available, the child suffers from oral deprivation. When the mother comes home in late afternoon, she offers her child the breast. According to DuBois, frustrations become worse after the walking stage is reached. The child is no longer carried about and thus loses the constant skin contacts and support previously experienced. It is fed irregularly by older siblings and others. Teasing of the child and provoking jealousy, as in Bali, is practiced by mothers. Youngsters are playfully menaced by adults with knives and threats of cutting off their hands or ears.

Temper trantrums are a common aspect of Alorese childhood. They occur when the mother sets off for the fields in the morning. A child may then go into a rage and beat its head on the ground. These tantrums begin to cease around the age of five or six.

Kardiner and DuBois find the explanation for Alorese personality traits in these childhood frustrations. Relations between men and women in adult life are strained; they average two divorces apiece. It is interpreted that male-female tensions develop from the child's original ambivalence toward the mother and the male's continuing search for a nurturing mother. Since the wife cannot adequately fill this nurturant role, the frustrations persist.

Although criticisms have been made of some aspects of this study, *The People of Alor* remains an impressive accomplishment. If skeptical of some of the analytic interpretations, the reader can examine the data on which they are based. The life histories make up about half the book. Many of the children's drawings are reproduced. Some of the Rorschach records are presented, together with Oberholzer's detailed analysis of the records.

The Six Cultures project

The fullest and most ambitious investigation in the cross-cultural study of childhood was undertaken by a group of scholars from Cornell, Harvard, and Yale under the direction of William W. Lambert, Irvin L. Child, and John W. M. Whiting (Whiting 1963; Minturn and Lambert 1964; Whiting and Whiting 1975). An effort was made to bring about comparability in the ethnographic reports of the six teams of investigators involved in this project. Each team spent from six to 14 months in the field. The six communities studied were: a Gusii community in Kenya, East Africa; a Rājpūt community in northern India; a village on Okinawa; a town in Mexico; a barrio in the Philippines; and a New England town in the United States. Each field team, usually consisting of a husband and a wife, worked in a community of between 50 and 100 families and with a sample of 24 mothers, each of whom had at least one child aged three to ten years. The mothers were interviewed on a standard schedule, and the children were systematically observed and interviewed. Each team was provided with a guide (John W. M. Whiting et al., *Field Guide for a Study of Socialization* 1966).

The last production of the Six Cultures project was a review by Whiting and Whiting (1975), in which the authors found some consistent differences between the three culturally more complex groups (in India, Okinawa, and the United States) and the three simpler ones (in Africa, Mexico, and the Philippines). Cultural complexity was determined by such factors as the degree of occupational and religious specialization, differentiation of settlement patterns, social stratification and political centralization. In the simpler group, children were on the whole more nurturant and responsible, in keeping with demands for cooperation and performance of chores within the family and community. In the more complex societies there was more schooling and also evidence of some egoism and competitiveness among the children. The simpler societies assigned more chores to children and assigned them at an earlier age. This is a general feature in many tribal and peasant societies. Bringing firewood and water, taking care of animals, farm work, running errands, and looking after junior siblings are common experiences in many parts of the world. Since this work represents a real contribution, the regular performance of such tasks must give many of these children feelings of worth, responsibility, and competence, although they must also often resent these obligations.

In societies with formal education, children cannot be saddled with so many chores, since they must attend school for part of the day. The more complex societies are hierarchically organized, which may encourage competitiveness and orientation toward achievement. Whiting and Whiting (1975:128) found that "Children brought up in complex cultures tended to be more dependent-dominant and less nurturant-responsible than children brought up in simpler cultures."

The Six Cultures project has provided detailed information about how children are brought up in six different sociocultural worlds and should be amenable to analysis from various theoretical points of view. Whiting's *Field Guide* has been used by other ethnologists in the organization of their fieldwork and will undoubtedly be so used in the future, which will provide more comparable accounts of different cultures.

Culture, cognition, and perception

Not only is personality directed along somewhat different lines in different cultural settings, but the same is true of cognition and perception. Consider, for example, the Müller-Lyer illusion (see Figure A). The Müller-Lyer illusion is that the horizontal line to the left in Figure A looks longer than the one on the right, but it is the same length. Non-Western subjects in parts of Melanesia, South India, and Africa are less susceptible to this illusion than are Europeans and Americans. Segall, Campbell, and Herskovits (1966), who tested 1,878 persons in 14 non-European areas and in the United States, suggest that people who live in a "carpentered world" and have an "experience with two-dimensional representation of reality," as Western peoples do, are more susceptible to the Müller-Lyer illusion than are non-Western peoples. They also suggest that people who inhabit areas with broad horizon-

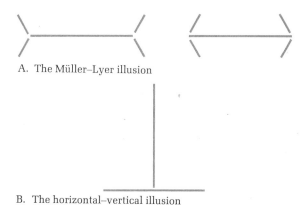

A. The Müller–Lyer illusion

B. The horizontal–vertical illusion

The Müller-Lyer and
the horizontal-vertical
illusions.

tal vistas are more likely to be subject to the horizontal-vertical illusion
(Figure B) than are persons who live in restricted environments such as
forests. The illusion in the latter figure is that the vertical line is longer,
although both lines are equal. While the data amassed by Segall, Campbell,
and Herskovits fit their hypotheses, there are other studies which do not
confirm or only partially confirm their findings (Price-Williams 1975: 11–
14). Still, it does seem to have been shown that the nature of one's culture
and environment influences some aspects of visual perception.

To consider another aspect of perception, individuals differ in the speed
with which they can find a hidden figure embedded in a picture. Herman
A. Witkin and his associates (1962) use the term "field independent" for
those who are quick to do so, while "field dependent" persons have difficulty
in separating the figure from the organized ground. Persons respond consistently in three different kinds of tests for these differences in cognitive style
(Witkin 1967). Field independence is seen to represent a tendency toward
psychological differentiation; it increases with age, although children who
are more "field dependent" than their age mates tend to have similar positions as young adults. Field-dependent persons are said to have a less differentiated body image than field-independent persons and tend to repress
their feelings. The tests for field dependence have been given in some different cultures, and contrasting results have been found in some cases. For
example, the Temne of Sierra Leone rated high on field dependence, while
the Eskimo of Baffin Island proved to be much more field independent
(J. W. Berry 1966). Much work has been done recently in the cross-cultural
study of perception and cognition, including attempts to test the degree
of uniformity in different cultures of the sequence of stages in cognitive
development during childhood, which have been distinguished by Jean
Piaget (see Dasen 1972). The article by Dasen just cited appears in a new
journal devoted to such issues: *Journal of Cross-Cultural Psychology*.

Summary

Many psychologists and psychiatrists of both Freudian and behaviorist schools emphasize the importance of the early childhood years in the formation of personality. It should make some difference, then, whether a child is born into a large extended family or a small nuclear one, or into a monogamous, polygynous, or polyandrous household. Societies differ in the extent of maternal care a child receives. It has been shown that maternal deprivation may be a very traumatic experience for an infant, resulting in the formation of such personality traits as hostility, dependency, and low self-esteem. According to DuBois' study, such traits developed among Alorese children due to the maternal neglect caused by a typical mother's day-long work in the fields.

The ways in which children are brought up in different cultures vary greatly. The suckling period may be quite short, as in the United States, or over three years in some societies. Toilet training may be begun early or late, and sexual disciplines vary from very lenient to very strict. In some societies infants are tightly swaddled or placed on a cradleboard during the first year. In Bali, children are carried about during the first year of life and not allowed to crawl. Many peasant societies assign children tasks and chores from an early age, while in other societies they have a great deal of freedom until puberty. These varying gamuts of childhood experience must have correspondingly different effects in personality formation.

Different societies also hold up contrasting ideals for the growing child, ranging from the proud self-assertive warrior to the mild, self-effacing citizen. The prevalent world view of a society must shape the personalities of its members. These are among the variables studied by anthropologists in the field of culture-and-personality. Their field work has involved observation of behavior, interviews with informants, collection of life-history material, and the administration of tests such as the Rorschach Test. The study of perception and cognition in different cultures makes use, among other methods, of such standardized figures as the Müller-Lyer illusion, the horizontal-vertical illusion, and Witkin's embedded figures test.

Suggestions
for further
reading

Some of the material in this chapter has been drawn from Victor Barnouw, *Culture and Personality,* rev. ed. (Homewood, Ill.: The Dorsey Press, 1973).

Several good readers are available: Clyde Kluckhohn, Henry A. Murray, and David M. Schneider, eds., *Personality in Nature, Society, and Culture* (New York: Alfred A. Knopf, 1953); Douglas C. Haring, ed., *Personal Character and Cultural Milieu,* 3d ed. (Syracuse, N.Y.: Syracuse University Press, 1956); Bert Kaplan, ed., *Studying Personality Cross-Culturally* (Evanston, Ill.: Row, Peterson & Co., 1961); Francis L. K. Hsu, ed., *Psychological Anthropology* (Cambridge, Mass.: Schenkman, 1972); Robert Hunt, ed., *Personalities and Cultures: Readings in Psychological Anthropology* (New York: Natural History Press, 1967).

Three studies which can be recommended are: Erich Fromm and Michael Maccoby, *Social Character in a Mexican Village: A Sociopsychoanalytic Study* (Englewood Cliffs, N.J.: Prentice-Hall, Inc., 1970); Robert B. Edgerton, *The Individual in Cultural*

Adaptation. A Study of Four East African Peoples (Berkeley: University of California Press, 1971); and George A. De Vos, with contributions by Hiroshi Wagatsuma, William Caudill, and Keichi Mizhuma, *Socialization for Achievement: Essays on the Cultural Psychology of the Japanese* (Berkeley: University of California Press, 1973).

For a recent reader on cognition and perception, see J. W. Berry and P. R. Dasen, eds., *Culture and Cognition: Readings in Cross-Cultural Psychology* (London: Methuen and Co., 1974). See also Robert L. Munroe and Ruth H. Munroe, *Cross-Cultural Human Development* (Monterey, Calif.: Brooks/Cole Publishing Co., 1975).

21

CULTURE CHANGE

O ur present age is a time of rapid culture change. The cultures of the world have always undergone alterations, but the tempo of such change has varied in different times and places. When Europeans first landed in Australia, they found people who had no agriculture, weaving, or pottery, no clothing, no bow and arrows. This does not mean that the Australian aborigines had experienced no culture change before the coming of Europeans, but, at least in the realm of technology, their hunting-gathering way of life had changed relatively little for thousands of years. An advanced civilization may also have long periods of stability, as was true of Egypt between around 2700 and 1700 B.C. However, change is more likely to take place in a complex society than in a simple one. The more complex a culture is, the more likely it will be to produce innovations, which depend upon combinations of previously existent patterns. Invention of the lost-wax process of casting, for example, was made possible by the prior existence of several inventions (knowledge of the properties of wax, fired clay, and molten metal), just as the development of the atomic bomb depended upon a particular level of knowledge about physics, chemistry, mathematics, and industrial technology. Cultural evolution is cumulative; it has involved an advance through progressively higher plateaus of cultural complexity. The more material there is to work with in the shape of tools, patterns, and ideas, the more possible combinations may be made.

Culture change within a society may be brought about either by internal invention and development or through contact with other societies. New ideas may spread through diffusion, not only between two societies, A and B, which are in contact, but also between societies A and E through intervening societies B, C, and D, which may have trade or other relations with one another. A new item, such as the practice of smoking tobacco, may be passed on directly from one society to another, or else there may be

Taos pueblo, New Mexico.

stimulus diffusion, in which a foreign notion stimulates the development of a local innovation, as in the case of the invention of a successful Cherokee syllabary by an Indian who was illiterate but who grasped the basic *principle* of writing (not the system itself) by watching white people read and write.

The term *acculturation* has been given to phenomena involving culture changes that occur when two formerly distinct cultures come into contact with one another. Relations between societies that have different cultural traditions vary in many respects. One variable concerns the extent to which such societies may be said to be permeable, flexible, and open, rather than rigid and closed. Using such terminology, Homer Barnett and his associates (1954) have suggested that "hard-shelled vertebrate" cultural systems, which have many boundary-maintaining mechanisms and rigid internal structures, may be less susceptible to change in acculturation than "soft-shelled inverte-brate" cultural systems, which are more open and flexible.

Societies are apt to be selective in what innovations they accept from others. Ruth Benedict (1934) showed that, although the Hopi, Zuñi, and other Pueblo Indians of the Southwest had long been in contact with non-Pueblo tribes, such as the Apache and Navaho, they did not accept from other tribes various cultural patterns that ran counter to their own values, such as the use of drugs, self-torture, or ecstatic religious practices.

Even when an alien culture pattern is accepted by members of a receiving society, they may consciously or unconsciously change the innovation so that it will fit into their own cultural framework.

Integration versus change

The Hopi and Zuñi had highly integrated cultures. If a sufficiently isolated society like that of the Hopi has time to develop an internally consistent way of life, lacking in conflicts and contradictions, we speak of its culture as being *integrated*. This is a relative term, since there are always some internal conflicts in any sociocultural system, but some cultures appear to be more highly integrated than others. This tendency should foster stability; the members of such a society have a similar outlook and a shared set of values.

Contact with another society may serve to jolt a highly integrated society, however, leading either to a change of values or to reaffirmation of traditional ones. Around 1900 the U.S. government ordered the Hopi of Oraibi to send their children to a government boarding school away from the reservation. This led to a split between the "Friendlies," who favored cooperation with the whites, and the "Hostiles," who opposed it. Since unity of sentiment within a community was important to the Hopi, it was decided that one of the two factions should leave the pueblo. The issue was decided in 1906 by a tug-of-war in the plaza. The Hostiles lost and left Oraibi to found a new settlement. This episode expresses both continuity and change. There was internal conflict, in opposition to Hopi ideals, but it was peacefully resolved by the tug-of-war and the departure of the losing faction. Hopi children did go away to the government school, but this did not dissolve the integration of Hopi culture, as may be seen in the strong affirmation of Hopi values by one of the school graduates from Oraibi who wrote the best autobiography we have by an American Indian (Simmons 1942).

In some cases, an integrated culture may break up quickly under the impact of outside forces. This seems to have happened on the small island of Tikopia in western Polynesia, whose population was 1,281 in 1929. There were four clans, each associated with the magical control of aspects of nature. One clan had control over yams, another over taro, a third over breadfruit, and a fourth over coconuts. Each clan was also associated with one of the wind points or directions from which rains and storms came. Elaborate religious rituals involving mutual reciprocal behavior between the clans, headed by their chiefs, who acted as priests, served to promote the growth of crops and success of fishing expeditions.

Despite all this reciprocity and interdependence, there was also rivalry between the clans and districts of the island, which may have contributed to the breakup of the system. In 1923 the chief of one of the four clans became converted to Christianity and ordered the people of his district to do the same. Before this time there had been a drought and poor crops for about eight months. Since the weather got better after the conversion, it was taken as a sign that the new religion was effective. The defecting clan chief no longer took part in the traditional crop-promoting rituals, leaving a gap in the religious fabric. By 1929 half of the island had become Christian. A final blow to the old system came in 1955, when 200 people died in an epidemic, including two of the clan chiefs. One of these was succeeded by a Christian, which left only two non-Christian chiefs. These men then decided to convert to the new religion, and most of their clan members followed suit. A highly elaborate, integrated religious system thus dissolved within a generation, to be replaced by a foreign one imported by missionaries.[1]

It has been argued that culture patterns learned early in life are more resistant to change than those acquired at later age levels. Edward M. Bruner (1956) has made a case for this hypothesis in explaining why the Mandan-Hidatsa Indians have preserved some aspects of their traditional culture (such as the kinship system, role conceptions, and values), while others, such as the age-grade-society system and the religious complex, have disappeared. The former patterns were learned early in life from members of Ego's lineage, while the latter patterns were learned late from persons who were not members of Ego's lineage. It would be interesting to see how well this hypothesis is supported in studies of other cultures in contact situations.

Early learning versus change

In some integrated cultures, innovations are resisted because of ideological traditions. On religious grounds, the more conservative members of the Old Order Amish of Pennsylvania will not use such modern contraptions as automobiles, telephones, and radios; they will not even use buttons on their clothes but have hooks and eyes instead.

Efforts to resist change

In some cases an ideology favoring conservatism affects outsiders. The anthropologist Verrier Elwin (1943) strongly opposed contacts between aboriginal hill tribes in India and the outside world. It was his belief that the hill tribes had a vigorous, creative way of life that would be spoiled by the growing influence of village India. Elwin's campaign to isolate the hill tribes was attacked by Indian nationalists who wanted to develop a unified, modern nation.

Vested interests may oppose culture change, such as a doctor's opposition to Medicare or socialized medicine, or the rejection by 17th-century theologians of Galileo's assertion that the earth revolved around the sun. Factory workers may oppose automation, which deprives them of jobs.

For ideological reasons, certain agents seek to induce culture change, such as the missionaries of proselytizing sects or the members of revolutionary movements. An agriculture extension agent tries to persuade farmers to plant a new type of corn or use a new farming technique.

Efforts to induce change

Culture change in regard to industrialization and modernization is deliberately planned by modern governments, such as in the five-year plans of

---

[1] This process has been traced in detail in a series of books by Raymond Firth, beginning with *We, The Tikopia* (1936).

the Soviet Union, India, and other nations. The space program and moon explorations of the United States provide another example. Deliberate planning for change in some aspects is carried out by modern industrial corporations as well.

Reform movements are also agents of change. Abolition of slavery, women's suffrage, the black-power movement, and antiwar protests are all attempts to bring about changes in public opinion and the laws of the land.

Different segments of the population respond differently to such campaigns and to culture change in general. Being more flexible and less committed to tradition, young people are often more receptive to new alternatives than are members of older age brackets. According to Everett E. Hagen (1962), members of groups that have lost status are more eager for culture change than are members of the establishment in an agrarian or developing society.

As the world becomes smaller, the technologically advanced societies come into ever closer contact with less advanced ones. When new gadgets such as electric ranges and refrigerators first appear in a new setting, as in New Guinea, it is usually only a small minority of well-to-do, non-native people who can afford to get them. Feelings of relative deprivation consequently develop among the natives, who did not have such feelings before. They may resent and envy the possessors of such goods, the higher standard of living they enjoy, and the attitude of superiority they may express. The sense of relative deprivation may in time lead to the development of nationalistic or revolutionary political movements, or else to nativistic religious cults, such as the Cargo cults of Melanesia (*see* p. 338). In either case, changes in culture follow, involving changes in attitudes, values, and feelings of group solidarity and poilitical cohesion among the rebels or the cultists.

Internal causes of change

A distinction may be made between internal and external causes of culture change. The former have to do with human motivation, while the latter concern environmental or situational factors.

Great man theory

To emphasize the role of the inventor or innovator is to invoke the internal principle. A person of inventive mind or genius makes a new discovery, which is transmitted to others and thus becomes part of the now-modified culture. This is sometimes called the great man theory. A. L. Kroeber and Leslie A. White both criticized this notion by pointing to simultaneous discoveries of the same invention by different people. Their point is that, when culture has reached a certain level, some particular inventions are inevitable and will be made sooner or later by somebody. Moreover, to become part of culture, a new invention must be shared with others. Geniuses may make discoveries that are ahead of their times; if they cannot convey their meanings,

Gregor Mendel.

those discoveries will not be incorporated into the culture. Leonardo da Vinci made sketches of airplanes in his notebooks, but the technology of his age was not ready for further advances in this field; his sketches remained confined to his notes. It may be that other brilliant people of Leonardo's period made similar sketches and speculations, but nothing could come of them then.

Isaac Newton and G. W. Leibniz both invented the infinitesimal calculus. Anticipating the views of Kroeber and White, Thomas Babington Macaulay wrote in 1828: ". . . mathematical science, indeed, had then reached such a point that, if neither of them had ever existed, the principle must inevitably have occurred to some person within a few years" (Macaulay 1877:324).

Gregor Mendel gave two reports on his discoveries in genetics before the Brünn Society for the Study of Natural Science in 1865, and he published a paper on his findings in that society's proceedings in 1866. But Mendel apparently spoke to deaf ears; no attention was given to his work until the simultaneous rediscovery of his principles by three men in 1900: W. O. Focke, Hugo de Vries, and Karl Correns. These cases seem to illustrate the "inevitability" argument.

However, some support for the great man theory has come from Tertius Chandler, who claims that in these cases the people did not work independently. Newton and Leibniz corresponded with each other, and Mendel's work was not altogether forgotten, for Correns knew of it by 1897. Chandler reviews a series of alleged parallel discoveries and in most cases is able to single out an originator who preceded the others. His conclusion (1960:497) is: "Where originality is needed, one man of keen mind is required. If he fail, the job may well stay undone forever." However, it is necessary to remember the point made earlier: a certain level of cultural evolution may be necessary before a new invention or pattern can be assimilated in a society.

It may be noted that the argument about parallel discoveries concerns inventions but could not be applied so well to the arts. Could we say that if Beethoven had not lived, someone else would have written his Fifth Symphony?

Protestant ethic and achievement motivation

Apart from the great man theory, there have been other "internal" explanations for culture change that emphasize the role of motivation. Some related examples are Max Weber's notion of the Protestant ethic, David Riesman's theory of inner direction, and David C. McClelland's concept of achievement motivation.

The sociologist Max Weber noted that the great economic advance in Europe after the Industrial Revolution was associated with Protestant rather than Catholic countries, and he concluded that this was due to the greater Protestant stress on independence, asceticism, and hard work.

David Riesman coined the phrase "inner direction" for a means of ensuring conformity in a society undergoing population growth and economic expansion. This is a time of opening frontiers, economic opportunities, and greater individualism than in a traditional society with a stable population. Wealth, fame, and achievement are goals toward which people strive through hard work and determination. At a later period, when a modern, industrialized state has developed and population growth has slackened off, a new mode of conformity develops, which Riesman calls "other direction." The production system now demands harmonious working within an established organization and a personality that is adaptable to the moods and feelings of others (Riesman 1950).

David C. McClelland's work (1961) is related to the ideas of Weber and Riesman. For McClelland, the Protestant ethic is only a special case of a more general phenomenon, since there are non-Protestant countries, such as modern Japan and the Soviet Union, that have a similar stress on hard work. McClelland sees the key psychological factor as being a high need for achievement, which he believes precedes economic growth, and he has found some ingenious ways to demonstrate this point. He cites some studies which indicate that parental attitudes in childhood may stimu-

late a need for achievement by setting high standards while granting autonomy to the children, so that they can work things out for themselves.

Studies in Japan have indicated that personality tendencies analogous
to the Protestant ethic, with a high need for achievement, help to account
for the remarkable economic development of that nation (Bellah 1957; De
Vos 1973).

There are various external sources of culture change, such as population
increase, wars, and economic dislocation, among others. Only a few examples
will be cited here.

External causes of change

Population increase

Population increase as "prime mover" forms the basis for various theories
about cultural evolution. According to Lewis R. Binford (1968) and Kent
V. Flannery (1969), population increase in sedentary Mesolithic communities
in the Old World led to a budding off of daughter groups which impinged
on surrounding marginal populations. Groups in the marginal zone were
forced to adopt a broad-spectrum pattern of food exploitation, including
wild grains and cereals, from which the domestication of plants ultimately
developed.

According to Ester Boserup (1965), population increase in horticultural
societies leads to a shortening of the fallow period and the adoption of
more intensive advanced forms of agriculture. As we saw in Chapter 10,
population increase in a circumscribed setting provides the basis for Robert
L. Carneiro's explanation for the origin of the state.

Economic dislocation

The Industrial Revolution and its accompanying commercial revolution
not only shook up the European nations, where they originated, but also
were exported abroad, introducing the standards of a money economy into
societies that had not formerly known them. In colonial countries, peasants
were under pressure to switch from subsistence farming to cash crops. Toward the end of the 18th century in India, the British East India company
demanded that revenue be paid in cash instead of in crops, as formerly,
which forced peasants to turn to cash crops, such as cotton, indigo, and
opium, in order to pay their taxes. The rise in rural indebtedness led to a
rise of moneylenders and the spread of Marwaris, who specialized in this
field, to all parts of India. The hand of the moneylender was strengthened
by new laws introduced in the courts, under which land could be attached
and sold for nonpayment of revenue, a new state of affairs for the peasant.
At the same time, many artisans like weavers were losing their markets,
since England imported cheap factory-made goods into India.

In all colonial areas the world of the peasant was thrown into upheaval. In *Peasant Wars of the Twentieth Century* (1969), Eric R. Wolf documented the similar dislocations, problems, and responses of the peasants in six countries: Mexico, Russia, China, Vietnam, Algeria, and Cuba.

The colonial system also introduced new inventions into these countries, the products of Europe's Industrial Revolution, which, of course, brought many more changes. To use India again in illustration: In 1817 a line of telegraphs was installed between Calcutta and Nagpur. Steam navigation on the Ganges River began in 1828, and the first railway started in 1853.

Summary

Societies vary considerably in rates of culture change. Cultural complexity favors culture change, since there is more material to work with and more possible combinations to be made. Change may come about either through internal invention or else through contact with other societies. Such contacts need not be direct but may be mediated through intervening societies.

Societies are apt to be selective in what new culture patterns they accept from others. They also often bring about changes in the innovations that are accepted, so that they will be in keeping with the society's particular cultural configuration. A highly integrated culture may resist change. On the other hand, once new patterns are accepted in such a society, culture change may rapidly take place, with factional splits developing in the process. Vested interests and ideological traditions may either resist or encourage such changes.

A distinction may be made between internal causes (involving human motivation) and external (environmental) causes of culture change. The great man theory emphasizes the role of the inventor or innovator, while cultural evolutionists of the Leslie White school play down this role by pointing to the frequency of independent parallel inventions. The role of individual motivation is emphasized in such concepts as Weber's Protestant ethic, Riesman's inner direction, and McClelland's need for achievement. Among the external causes of culture change to which analysts have drawn attention are such factors as population increase and the economic dislocations brought about by the great transformations of the industrial and commercial revolutions and by colonialism.

Suggestions for further reading

Still a good source for the discussion of culture change is A. L. Kroeber, *Anthropology* (New York: Harcourt, Brace & Co., 1948), especially Chapters 9–12. A work often cited is Homer G. Barnett, *Innovation: The Basis of Cultural Change* (New York: McGraw-Hill Book Co., 1953). See also Homer G. Barnett et al., "Acculturation: An Exploratory Formulation," *American Anthropologist*, vol. 56 (1954), pp. 973–1002; Godfrey Wilson and Monica Wilson, *The Analysis of Social Change* (Cambridge, England: Cambridge University Press, 1945).

On cultural evolution, see Leslie A. White, *The Evolution of Culture* (New York: McGraw-Hill Book Co., 1959); Julian H. Steward, *Theory of Culture Change: The Methodology of Multilinear Evolution* (Urbana: University of Illinois Press, 1955).

22

APPLIED ANTHROPOLOGY

T he world's population of about 3 billion is expected to double within the next 35 years. The doubling will occur sooner in the so-called developing nations than in the industrially more advanced ones. Before World War II, developing nations such as those of Latin America were exporters of grain, but now they must import grain to feed their people. The world's food resources are not increasing sufficiently to keep up with the rise in population; hence, many demographers and agronomists warn that widespread famines will strike the world before long. Famines were already reported during 1974 for parts of North Africa, India, and Bangladesh. A so-called green revolution, involving the use of new seeds, has improved matters in parts of Southeast Asia and India, but population increase still poses a threat in those regions.

To cope with these problems, many countries have instituted village development programs. For example, in its first Five-Year Plan, in 1951, India launched a Community Development Movement that had multiple aims, including the following: land reclamation and increased irrigation; development of rural electrification; provision of fertilizers and improved seeds; spreading of agricultural information; introduction of better agricultural implements and practices; provision of marketing and credit facilities; improvement of roads and transportation; increase of education; public health work in sanitation, drainage, waste disposal, control of malaria, and other diseases; provision of medical care and midwife services; and many other programs.

The U.S. government has given aid in such enterprises in Point Four agricultural programs and through the Agency for International Development. Private foundations, such as the Ford Foundation, and churches, missions, and other agencies have all tried in various ways to help increase the agricultural productivity of less-developed nations and improve their conditions of health.

Resistance to innovations

Much good work has, of course, been accomplished along these lines. But observers have often been surprised that agricultural improvements are sometimes not welcomed by the farmers; improved seeds are rejected and health facilities not used. There are many reasons for such failures. Sometimes it is necessary to study the culture of the community in question to understand why a particular project failed. This is one of the roles of the applied anthropologist, or action anthropologist, who sometimes may also be able to suggest ways of overcoming the difficulty, whatever it is, although this is not always possible. Let us consider some examples of resistance to or rejection of innovations.

Improved seeds

If an agricultural extension worker tries to persuade a group of farmers to use a new type of seed, one might expect that they would be willing to try it, since, after all, that person is one of authority. But farmers are often reluctant to do so. This is true not only of peasants in India or Latin America but also of farmers in Texas, who, in the 1930s, were very disinclined to try the new hybrid corn then being introduced. One farmer jokingly offered to plant some of the new seed if the extension worker would promise to pay the difference in profit if the new seed produced less than the old. The extension worker decided to take the chance; so half of a field was planted with the old seed and half with the new. The hybrid variety was drought resistant, and during that summer there was little rain. The old seeds thus fared poorly, while the hybrid corn grew up bright green. All the farmers round about came to look at the field and became convinced, but it required this demonstration to turn the tide of public opinion (Arensberg and Niehoff 1964:84–85).

Although new seeds may be introduced in this way, farmers sometimes reject them after a trial. Hybrid corn was introduced into a Spanish-American community in New Mexico in 1946. A demonstration plot yielded a harvest three times the normal one. By 1947 about three fourths of the farmers were using the hybrid seed, but two years later almost all of them had reverted to the former variety. The reason was that the women of the community did not like the hybrid corn; it did not hang together well in the making of tortillas, and they did not care for the taste (Apadaca 1952). A similar response has been reported for some villages in India where new seeds have been introduced. In one community the villagers acknowledged the superiority of the new seed with regard to yield, disease resistance, and other qualities, but they preferred their old variety on grounds of taste and amenability in food preparation (Dube 1958:133). In another Indian village it was found that the cows and bullocks did not like the straw of the new wheat, and it did not make good thatching for roofs. The old wheat was not used just for food but served multiple purposes (Marriott 1952).

It may sound strange, but taste preferences have had a conservative effect in Indian villages with regard to the use of cow dung for fuel. The villagers realize that manure would be more valuable as fertilizer than as fuel, but they find that burning cow dung is the best way to slowly heat milk in preparing ghee, or clarified butter, an essential part of their diet. It is also the most satisfactory fuel to use in smoking water pipes; the use of other fuel reduces the pleasure (Dube 1958:134).

Consumption of milk among Zulus

The Zulus of southwestern Natal had bad health conditions in 1940; their infant mortality rate was very high, and more than 80 percent of the people showed signs of malnutrition. Pellagra and kwashiorkor, a disease afflicting severely malnourished infants and children, were common; there was much tuberculosis, venereal disease, and dysentery. One of the efforts made by members of a health center was to urge the Zulus to consume more eggs and milk. For various reasons, eggs were not commonly eaten, it was thought uneconomical to eat an egg that might later hatch, and eating eggs was considered a sign of greed and a source of licentiousness among girls. However, these ideas were not strongly held, and the members of the health center, through an educational campaign, were able to increase egg consumption considerably.

Milk proved to be more of a problem. The Zulus raise cattle and are much attached to them. Milk was thus available and was consumed by the men, but a complex of beliefs restricted milk consumption by women. The milk produced by a man's cattle can only be consumed by members of his kin group. One cannot get milk from another family. Moreover, once women have started to menstruate, they must not pass near cattle or drink milk. A married woman who lives with her husband's people is under a double restriction, being in a different kin group. Hence, married women were the persons least likely to drink milk. Members of the health center could not challenge this deep-seated belief system. At the same time, they wanted to provide better nutrition, including milk, for expectant and lactating mothers. This problem seemed insuperable, but there turned out to be a surprisingly easy partial solution: introduction of powdered milk. The Zulus knew that this was milk, but it was different, not subject to the taboos and restrictions of "real" milk, and milk consumption rapidly rose.

The workers at the health center were also able to increase the growing and consumption of green vegetables. Through their efforts, there was a marked decrease in malnutrition within a ten-year period. The incidence of kwashiorkor fell from 12 or more cases a week to less than 12 cases a year (Cassell 1955).

Compost pits in an Indian village

In the villages of northern India, women pile cow dung in a corner of the courtyard or in an open space near the house. Village-level workers engaged in India's community development program tried to persuade the

Indian village with dung pile.

villagers to place refuse and dung in compost pits outside the village. This could be more sanitary; it would help clean up the village and preserve manure more effectively. However, in some villages, although compost pits were dug, they remained unused.

Although women of high caste may handle cow dung and stack it up near their homes, they do not want to be seen carrying dung to the edge of the village. Very few families have servants to do such work, and men cannot do it because it is considered to be women's work. So the traditional practices continued (Dube 1958:68, 71, 135).

Introducing latrines

In community development programs in different parts of the world, efforts have often been made to introduce latrines, for obvious hygienic reasons. Such efforts have been resisted for various reasons. In Uganda, people believe that one should never let enemies know where one defecates, since feces are used in sorcery. Under such circumstances latrines would hardly be popular.

A different consideration underlay opposition to latrines in an Indian village where women were accustomed to going out into the fields to defecate. This gave them an opportunity to meet and talk with women friends, an occasion particularly valued by high-caste women who were generally confined to their homes (Foster 1969:11).

New appliances may be introduced into a community and become accepted by the people, but they may later be abandoned, not because the people resist them or fail to appreciate their benefits but simply because they lack the technical knowledge to repair the new gadgets and keep them in good working order. An example is provided by the wells that were installed in Laos by an American drilling company. The local people were glad to have some good sources of water available, but, within two years, almost three fourths of the wells were out of commission because the people did not know how to repair the pumps. It happened that some of the wells had been drilled in Buddhist temple grounds, and these were kept in good repair by the monks. If the drilling company had given the Laotian villagers some instructions about maintenance, and if they had drilled more wells in temple grounds, there might have been better success with this innovation (Arensberg and Niehoff 1964:4–5).

Maintenance of innovations

Some innovations brought about by a community development project may differentially affect segments of the community; some people may benefit by the innovations, while others may resent them. For example, communal road building was encouraged by village-level workers in India. The idea was to get a whole village to cooperate in an undertaking which was conceived to benefit everyone. At the same time, such activity dramatized the dignity of labor. The more well-to-do people of higher caste welcomed these work drives, for the new roads made it possible for them to transport more grain and sugarcane to markets outside the village. The poorer people of lower caste did not have large crops of sugarcane or wheat, nor did they own bullock carts to transport such goods; hence, they did not feel the same enthusiasm for the roads. To add insult to injury, those of higher caste assumed supervisory roles in the communal work drives, and it was those of lower caste who had to do most of the manual work, for which they received no wages (Dube 1958:80–82).

Innovations and the social order

Sometimes it is the well-do-do members of a community who resist innovations, regarding them as a threat to the status quo. This was the case in the Vicos Project supported by Cornell University and directed by anthropologist Allan Holmberg (1960) in Peru. The purpose was to modernize and democratize a large hacienda. The project was successful enough to arouse fears of revolution among the landowning classes, not only in the Vicos Valley but throughout Peru.

A medical clinic established in the Mexican town of Tepoztlán was seen as a threat by an influential local *curandero,* or healer, who campaigned against it by spreading various false charges and rumors. Some local political officials joined in the criticism, and the clinic was ultimately abandoned (Lewis 1955). Thus, considerations of class and politics may affect the fate of innovations designed to help the community at large.

This chapter has perhaps given an unduly negative impression of efforts in directed culture change. It is true that much of the literature of applied anthropology has to do with failures, such as the inadequacy of a program to persuade Peruvians to boil their drinking water, the failure of the Tepoztlán clinic, and the lack of success of many village development projects in India. But much can be learned from these failures, and later efforts along similar lines can thus be better prepared. Anthropologists may learn to anticipate some of the side effects of culture patterns undergoing change.

Formerly, ethnologists did not try to change the culture of the society in which they did their fieldwork. Sometimes they even hoped it would be preserved as it was, as much as possible. The anthropologists took field notes and described what they saw. On their return to civilization, they hoped to publish their findings. These publications might or might not have some influence on the community where they had worked. In this respect the applied anthropologists differ, for they no longer simply describe the culture and go home; they try to bring about deliberate changes in the society they study.

There are dangers in this, and the anthropologist may make mistakes. But culture change is inevitable in the less-developed countries of the world today, and, if the anthropologist is hesitant about becoming involved in such activities, there are plenty of people—often with less knowledge and goodwill—who are ready enough to influence the course of events in one way or another. The goals discussed in this chapter are purposes of which no one need be ashamed: increased food production, sanitation, and public health.

Criticisms of applied anthropology

Nevertheless, serious criticisms have been made of the work of applied anthropologists. Guillermo B. Batalla has made the following charges (1966:89–92):

1. There has been too much emphasis on psychological factors, such as native concepts of disease and health, and not enough examination of the basic causes of sickness and malnutrition.

2. The applied anthropologists are anxious to avoid rapid changes that may lead to social and cultural disorganization; hence, they are essentially conservative.

3. The anthropological tradition of cultural relativism makes anthropolo-

gists hesitate to pronounce value judgments about cultures and institutions. But, if one cannot say that one culture or institution is better than another, there is no point in doing work in applied anthropology.

4. Anthropologists tend to believe in multiple causation and hold that it is impossible to know all the causes of a given phenomenon. General social laws are hard to formulate, since no two groups have the same needs or problems. In each case, therefore, a detailed study of the local community is required. This often results in a monograph about a particular community without consideration of its ties with the larger world. There is an implicit conservative bias in this approach.

5. Most social problems in developing countries are related to low income levels and an unequal distribution of wealth. Most anthropologists, however, seem to believe that income levels can change only very slowly. They do not wish to challenge the social system that causes and perpetuates poverty.

6. Anthropologists seem to think that diffusion is the most important process in bringing about change. They rarely establish goals to accelerate change in internal institutions. Applied anthropologists change what is necessary so that things can stay as they are, and so they have allied themselves with the conservative elements of the society.

Glynn Cochrane (1971) has also criticized applied anthropologists for concerning themselves with only small community studies. He claims that anthropologists do not know the contributions of other disciplines and professions in development work and cannot collaborate well with them. According to Cochrane, applied anthropologists should become familiar with the practical aspects of bureaucratic administration and should specialize in economic or legal anthropology in order to be more effective in their work.

Summary

Applied anthropologists have worked in community development projects in developing nations. Knowledge of the sociocultural milieu in a particular region often helps to account for the lack of success of a particular project, for which applied anthropologists may suggest solutions. An example was the difficulty of getting married Zulu women to drink milk, despite its availability. The problem stemmed from a complex of beliefs which were resistant to arguments by members of the health center. The successful solution to this particular issue was the introduction of powdered milk, which was not subject to the traditional taboos.

Introduced innovations sometimes fail because of conflicts with local beliefs and customs or due to the difficulty of maintaining new technological items, as in the case of the well pumps in Laos. Innovations may differentially affect segments of the community, adversely affecting the richer or poorer members, which may trigger resistance from the one group or the other. Technology is not the issue in such cases; the problem concerns social structure and local beliefs and attitudes. That makes it an appropriate sphere of investigation for sociocultural anthropologists.

Suggestions for further reading

For someone who wishes to read more about applied anthropology, it might be best to begin with two readers referred to in this chapter. Each presents a series of cases; both are well written. The first is Edward H. Spicer, ed., *Human Problems in Technological Change: A Casebook* (New York: Russell Sage Foundation, 1952). The second is Benjamin D. Paul, ed., *Health, Culture, and Community: Case Studies of Public Reactions to Health Programs* (New York: Russell Sage Foundation, 1955).

Four general works may be recommended: George M. Foster, *Applied Anthropology* (Boston: Little, Brown & Co., 1969); Conrad M. Arensberg and Arthur H. Niehoff, *Introducing Social Change: A Manual for Americans Overseas* (Chicago: Aldine Publishing Co., 1964); Ward Hunt Goodenough, *Cooperation in Change* (New York: Russell Sage Foundation, 1963); Charles J. Erasmus, *Man Takes Control: Cultural Development and American Aid* (Minneapolis: University of Minnesota Press, 1961).

The Vicos Project supported by Cornell University is described in Allan R. Holmberg, "Changing Community Attitudes and Values in Peru: A Case Study in Guided Change," in *Social Change in Latin America Today: Its Implications for United States Policy,* ed. Richard N. Adams et al. (New York: Harper & Brothers, 1960), pp. 63–107.

Batalla's criticisms and other articles on applied anthropology may be found in James A. Clifton, ed., *Applied Anthropology: Readings in the Uses of the Science of Man* (Boston: Houghton Mifflin Co., 1970).

23

CITY LIFE

O ur man-made urban environment progressively covers more of the earth. In 1800 there were only 50 cities in the world with a population of over 100,000; today there are more than 1,400 such cities. By 1969 there were over 140 cities that had 1 million or more inhabitants and contained 11 percent of the world's population (Ferkiss 1969:114). In 1790, 95 percent of Americans lived in rural areas; by 1960, 70 percent lived in urban areas.

In the early development of the world's big cities, the population increase was largely due to migration from the countryside, where birth rates were higher than in the cities. The cities also had higher death rates related to their overcrowding and poor sanitary conditions. But with better medical facilities now available and more public health funds going to cities, the people in the world's cities are now multiplying more rapidly, and rural-urban migration is a less significant factor in urban population increase.

The first cities came into being in Bronze Age times. Harappa and Mohenjo-daro, which flourished around 2000 B.C. in the Indus Valley region of Pakistan, show evidence of city planning, having housefronts lined up in straight lines and streets intersecting at right angles. Sewers ran along beneath the street level, with pipes emptying into them from the houses. The *Arthashastra,* composed around 300 B.C., describes how an Indian royal city should be laid out, with the four *varna*—Brahman, Kshatriya, Vaishya, and Shudra (see p. 291)—being assigned to different quarters of the city, as were followers of different occupations. A similar segregation existed in some Arab cities, such as Fez in Morocco and Aleppo in Syria. Occupational and ethnic groups occupied different wards closed in by walls, the gates to which were locked at night. In both Near Eastern and Indian cities it

Preindustrial cities

was customary to have special streets occupied by members of a particular trade, such as goldsmiths.

There was planning in the organization of cities of the Roman Empire. The forum, where public affairs were transacted, was surrounded by law courts, offices, temples, and baths. Aqueducts brought water into the city; sewers and roads also give evidence of city planning. Yet these large urban centers disintegrated in Europe in the eighth century A.D., and western Europe reverted to an agrarian economy with very little trade or urban settlement.

As Basil Davidson has shown (1959), there were preindustrial cities in Africa, south of the Sahara, before the European colonial period began. Yoruba cities in West Africa were inhabited by many farmers who, in contrast with modern suburban commuters, left the city every morning for their farms on the outskirts. William Bascom (1963) has pointed out how these preindustrial cities differed from the modern African cities that developed as a result of European contact. Most inhabitants spent their lives in the city from birth, whereas in modern African cities there are many recent migrants who live in the city only temporarily and hope to return to their villages before they die. In the traditional Yoruba city, husbands lived with their wives and children, and family and lineage ties remained intact. There was little social disorganization or crime, in comparison with modern cities. This suggests that city life need not of itself lead to rootlessness, anomie, and crime, as some writers have asserted; the circumstances of urbanization must be taken into account.

Two special types of preindustrial cities include political centers (Delhi in India, Peking in China) and religious centers of pilgrimage (Banaras in India, Karbala in Iraq).

Colonial cities   A particular type of political center developed in colonial regions dominated by European powers. The Spaniards in Mexico and Peru established capital cities on the sites of former native centers of power (Tenochtitlán, Cuzco). Hugo G. Nuttini (1972) has noted that the Spaniards and Portuguese, who aimed to Catholicize as well as dominate the native peoples, located their cities in inland regions, in contrast to the British, French, and Dutch in North America who established coastal towns linked to Europe by trade across the sea.

Spanish colonial cities have an imposing square in the center where the government buildings and cathedral are located. This is the case, for example, in Mexico City, where the conqueror Cortés forced the Indians to move out of the central area. The finest homes, including that of Cortés, were located near the center. Mexico City today has a residence pattern which differs from that of many North American cities, where it is common to find deteriorating slum areas near the central business district. In Mexico City the worst slums are on the outer edge of the metropolitan area, a condition that has persisted for more than 440 years (Hayner 1966). Mexico

Slum area on the outskirts of Madras, south India. In the background is a laundry-drying area used by people of Dhobi (laundryman) caste.

City may be called a *primate* city, that is, a city that dominates a surrounding area and is much larger than the other urban centers. It is the center of transportation, manufactures, and political and intellectual life for the nation. A difference between most Latin-American cities and the cities of North America is that industrialization developed slowly in Latin America. At the same time, the population of large cities in Latin America is now doubling every 14 years (L. R. Brown 1972:78).

British colonial cities in India have a character somewhat similar to the Spanish colonial ones. In cities where troops were stationed, there is a modern section known as the *cantonment,* which has straight, broad streets, in contrast to the narrow, jumbled alleys of the old preindustrial city. The cantonment contains offices of government, law courts, churches, clubs, banks, and stores with European goods. As in Mexico City and many other Latin-American cities, the poor tend to be located in slums on the city's outskirts, rather than near the central business district, while the well-to-do tend to live fairly close to the center. The lowest castes are often grouped on the outskirts of India's cities, as they are in many Indian villages. There are caste neighborhoods in some Indian cities, where one may find, for example, a high percentage of Brahmans.

A striking feature of Indian cities is the number of homeless persons who sleep on the streets. Estimates of their number in Calcutta have ranged between 100,000 and 300,000. In an article in the *New York Times* of September 8, 1967, Joseph Lelyveld described a young Calcutta couple with two children who share the same patch of sidewalk every night; they have never lived indoors. They do, however, rent a stall about five-feet square in a shanty across the street, where they eat and where the woman gave birth to the two children. But the stall is less comfortable to sleep in than the pavement outside. Most of Calcutta's sidewalk dwellers, says Lelyveld, have such a stall, which gives them a legal existence, an address to qualify for a ration card or a place in school for their children. The homeless inhabitants of Calcutta illustrate the problems faced by industrializing countries in which urbanization is developing rapidly, while job opportunities remain insufficient for the growing population. India's urban growth had a slow start but is now increasing rapidly. In 1951 there were only two cities in India with a population of over 1 million, but now there are seven such cities.

Industrial cities

Industrial cities differ from preindustrial ones by the presence of industries that rely on inanimate sources of power, such as steam and electricity. This system, which originated in Europe, is now in operation to a greater or lesser degree in all nations. Development of the railroad accompanied industrialization. In the United States there are key railroad and port centers, like Chicago and Buffalo, that are centers of both industry and transportation.

Studies made by sociologists Robert E. Park, Ernest W. Burgess, and others in the 1920s and 1930s showed that there was a concentric zonal pattern in Chicago. Zone I was the central business district, containing the department stores, office buildings, and centers of economic, political, and social life. Zone II was a transitional zone, including the factory district and a rundown roominghouse area. Zone III was a zone of workingmen's homes: Zone IV, a better residential area; and Zone V, a commuters' zone. Thus there was seen to be a series of concentric circles, with better residential areas toward the periphery (Burgess 1961). A similar pattern has been described for other U.S. cities, although not all fit the scheme so well. We have noted that Latin-American and Indian cities do not have this particular zonal plan and their slums are located on the peripheries rather than near the central business districts.

Early urban studies by sociologists such as Louis Wirth emphasized the anonymity and impersonality of life in a modern city. Anthropologist Robert Redfield echoed this view in his concept of the folk-urban continuum, in which homogeneous folk society was contrasted with heterogeneous city life. In the small, face-to-face folk society, according to Redfield, kin relationships are important, and religion is incorporated into other aspects of the culture; but, in the more secular city, kin ties lose their importance and the individual is more isolated from others. Redfield (1941) tried to document these generalizations by comparing four communities in Yucatán, from the modern city of Merida to a small, unacculturated tribal village, with two intermediate communities in between.

The central slum areas of modern cities were thought to be particularly disorganized and conducive to anomie and schizophrenia (Faris and Dunham 1939). The absence of close personal relationships and rarity of voluntary associations were cited as causative factors. Such views were commonly expressed in the 1930s and 1940s, particularly by writers dealing with the city of Chicago.

More recently it has been realized that city dwellers are not deprived of close friendships and associations, even in rundown slum areas. William F. Whyte (1943) wrote a detailed study of Italian-American street-corner life in Boston, in which he showed that close personal ties often extend beyond adolescence. Herbert J. Gans (1962) and Marc Fried (1963) have also written about the sense of community experienced in an Italian Boston slum. Voluntary associations do exist in such slum areas, and informal opportunities for social contact are also present (e.g., C. E. Richards 1963–64).

Ethnic grouping

Cities are heterogeneous centers with immigrants from many countries and regions. This is less true of a more racially and culturally homogeneous nation like Japan, although Japan has Chinese and Korean minority groups and localized diversities in culture. But the cities of Africa contain persons from many tribes, and the cities of India have migrants from different parts of the subcontinent who speak various languages. Adjustment to city life forces some degree of "melting pot" accommodation to the dominant urban culture. On the other hand, strangers to a city tend to seek out relatives and friends from their own region, and thus one often finds ethnic clustering—a Chinatown, a German Yorkville in New York, a Polish or Italian neighborhood. When Italian immigrants poured into New York in the 19th and early 20th centuries, they clustered in specific neighborhoods: those from Naples settling in the Mulberry Bend area, those from Genoa on Baxter Street, those from Sicily on Elizabeth Street, and those from North Italy in the Eighth and Fifteenth wards west of Broadway (Jones 1960). Such centers of common origin formed the basis for voluntary associations and provided an in-group with some sense of social solidarity, mutual aid, and a center for learning about sources of employment and other useful information. Similar developments took place in other American cities. Particular national groups sometimes specialized in certain occupations. In Chicago in the late 19th century sailors in Great Lakes shipping tended to be Scandinavians, apartment janitors were often Flemish, while eastern European Jews went into the garment industry (Pelling 1960).

Since newly arriving immigrants were often poor, they tended to accept low-paid unskilled work and to live in slum areas. These circumstances fostered the development of stereotyped attitudes toward these minorities by higher-status, longer-established Americans. Many of the opinions which are now held by well-to-do whites about American urban blacks were also held about the Irish in the 19th century. A book entitled *The Dangerous*

Classes of New York, published in 1872, dealt mainly with the Irish (Kristol 1970).

The experience of prejudice may lead to some closing of ranks and attempts toward solidarity within the disadvantaged group. Thus, blacks are urged in the black press and churches to patronize black business firms when there is competition with white-owned firms. Most of the basis for black capitalism is within the black community itself (Hannerz 1974:55).

While ethnicity may provide a basis for support within the in-group, it may also create obstacles to economic and social advancement for individuals. Hence immigrants with higher status often look down upon later arrivals with whom they do not wish to be identified.

Despite the melting-pot tendencies of American life, ethnic groups are still identifiable and are often a source of pride and self-identity. Thus efforts are made to retain or reestablish old ethnic patterns. The Irish march on St. Patrick's day. German and Polish groups in Milwaukee practice traditional folk dances from the old country. Urban American Indians from different tribes try to find a new or old identity in the Pan-Indian movement. Blacks speak about soul and wear their hair in Afro style. These varied activities, whether traditional or synthetic, provide some heterogeneity and color in American life, as do the various kinds of ethnic foods—Jewish delicatessen, Italian pasta, and Chinese chop suey, to mention only a few.

Cities were in existence as far back as 3000 B.C. or earlier, but their
proliferation and increase in size have been recent, dating from the advent
of the Industrial Revolution. Preindustrial cities included centers of government and pilgrimage. Such cities were often compartmentalized into separate
walled wards for different occupational and ethnic groups.

Summary

Colonial cities were established by European powers during the period
of their expansion. Spanish colonial cities in the New World have a central
square where government buildings and cathedral are located. Slums are
found on the outskirts rather than near the center of the city, as in many
cities in the United States. British colonial cities in India had a modern
cantonment area with broad streets, where there were government buildings,
banks, churches, clubs, and stores. This area was quite separate from the
old city. Indian cities often have caste neighborhoods, with separate sections
on the outskirts for the lowest castes.

Industrial cities rely on steam, gas, and electricity for power, and are
related to the development of the railroad. American cities like Buffalo
and Chicago are both railroad and port centers. Many such cities have a
more or less concentric plan, with a central business district containing department stores, banks, hotels, restaurants, and office buildings, with a nearby
factory district and rundown roominghouse area. Better homes are located
on outer zones, particularly in the commuters' suburbs. Such cities have
heterogeneous populations which cluster in separate ethnic neighborhoods,
often having some specialization in occupations.

A reader on urbanism with a cross-cultural emphasis is Sylvia Fleis Fava, ed.,
Urbanization in World Perspective: A Reader (New York: Thomas Y. Crowell Co.,
1968). A good reader on U.S. urban life is Joe R. Feagan, *The Urban Scene: Myths
and Realities* (New York: Random House, 1973).

**Suggestions
for further
reading**

Works by anthropologists about non-Western cities include the following: John
Gulick, *Tripoli: A Modern Arab City* (Cambridge, Mass.: Harvard University Press,
1967); Hortense Powdermaker, *Copper Town: Changing Africa: The Human Situa-
tion on the Rhodesian Copperbelt* (New York: Harper & Row, 1962); Andrew H.
Whiteford, *Two Cities of Latin America: A Comparative Description of Social Classes*
(New York: Doubleday Anchor Books, 1964).

On ethnic groups, see Abner Cohen, ed., *Urban Ethnicity* (London: Tavistock
Publications, 1974), particularly the chapter by Ulf Hannerz, "Ethnicity and Opportu-
nity in Urban America," pp. 37–76. See also Nathan Glazer and Daniel Patrick
Moynihan, *Beyond the Melting Pot* (Cambridge, Mass.: MIT Press, 1963).

Two studies of American urban life are recommended: William F. Whyte, *Street
Corner Society: The Social Structure of an Italian Slum* (Chicago: University of
Chicago Press, 1943); Elliot Liebow, *Tally's Corner: A Study of Negro Streetcorner
Men* (Boston: Little, Brown & Co., 1967). See also William Mangin, ed., *Peasants
in Cities: Readings in the Anthropology of Urbanization* (Boston: Houghton Mifflin
Co., 1970); Joseph G. Jorgensen and Marcello Truzzi, ed., *Anthropology and Ameri-
can Life* (Englewood Cliffs, N.J.: Prentice-Hall, Inc., 1974).

24

ANTHROPOLOGICAL THEORY: A HISTORICAL REVIEW

I n the section on the historical background of anthropology in Chapter 1, attention was drawn to the developing interest in questions about human physical and cultural evolution during the 19th century. But this interest had to contend with challenge and opposition; modern anthropological theory began in an atmosphere of controversy.

In the early 19th century in England and France, there was a conservative, indeed reactionary, school of thought that attacked romantic Rousseauist doctrines and upheld biblical traditions. Its chief representative, Comte Joseph de Maistre (1753–1821), argued that the American Indian savages had degenerated from a formerly higher condition:

Savage races came later than civilized races and represent their disintegration. . . . One thing is sure, the savage is necessarily later in time than civilized man. For example, let us examine America. This country has every characteristic of a new land. But since civilization is of great antiquity in the old countries, it follows that the savages who inhabited America at the time of the discovery descended from civilized man (quoted in Hays 1958:54).

Edward B. Tylor

The English anthropologist Edward B. Tylor (1832–1917) argued that, on the contrary, all the evidence showed that mankind's earliest tools were simpler than later ones and that there had been a cultural evolution from simple to complex forms running through the three stages of savagery, barbarism, and civilization.

Tylor was the man who introduced the term *culture,* in its modern anthropological sense, to the English reading public, defining it as "that complex whole which includes knowledge, belief, art, morals, law, custom, and any other capabilities and habits acquired by man as a member of society" (Tylor 1877:I, 1).

404

Tylor thus provided a new label, a new definition of culture, and, in defining it, set forth the subject matter of a new science, cultural anthropology.

One of the first problems dealt with by late 19th-century writers on anthropology was how to explain similarities of culture in widely separated societies. Edward B. Tylor argued that cultural evolution had often progressed along similar lines in different parts of the world.

Parallel inventions versus diffusion

Tylor believed that cultural similarities in different regions are due to the "like working of men's minds under like conditions." There is, in other words, a psychic unity of mankind, independent of race or language, so that people in different societies, when faced with similar problems, have come up with similar solutions to them.

Tylor was aware that there is another explanation for similarities of culture in different parts of the world, namely *diffusion,* the spread of a culture trait from one society to another. Indeed, he wrote that civilization is a plant much more often propagated than independently developed. Both parallel invention and diffusion contribute to the content of a culture, and it is not always easy to be sure which process has been responsible for the presence of a particular culture pattern.

A problem that intrigued Tylor (1896) was whether the Aztec game of patolli was related to the game of pachisi, which originated in India and later spread to Europe and America; some readers of this book will recognize it as the game of Parcheesi. Both patolli and pachisi involve the movement of counters along spaces on a cruciform board according to the throw of dice (although the Aztec dice were flat, not cubical, and more than just two were thrown). In both games there were penalty or safety stations and the rule that a person can "kill" an opponent's counter if he or she lands on the same space, forcing that counter to go back to the starting point. Since there were so many rules common to both games, Tylor concluded that the games must be related; so perhaps pachisi diffused from Asia to Mexico. He was, thus, perfectly aware of the importance of diffusion, but he was more interested in parallel cultural evolution in different parts of the world.

In Chapter 18, Tylor's theory of animism was set forth. Tylor saw religious concepts as being based on ideas about spiritual beings which understandably developed from human speculations about dreams, trance states, and death. Here, again, was another illustration of the psychic unity of mankind, resulting in the development of similar ideas and practices in different parts of the world.

Another key figure in the development of anthropology in the 19th century was Lewis Henry Morgan (1818–81). A lawyer in upstate New York, Morgan developed an interest in the local Iroquois Indians and became the friend of an educated Seneca Indian, Ely Parker, who later became Commissioner

Morgan and the study of kinship

of Indian Affairs during Grant's administration. With Parker, Morgan visited the Tonawanda reservation and became fascinated by the still-living traditions and customs of the Iroquois. After he had defended the Seneca in a land-grant case, Morgan was adopted into the Tonawanda band by the grateful Indians. This gave him a further entrée into the Indian community and a familiarity with it that led to the publication of *League of the Ho-dé-no-sau-nee or Iroquois* in 1851, the first full field study of an American Indian tribe. In the course of learning about Iroquois life, Morgan was surprised to discover that they had different kinship institutions and terminology from those of the Western world.

They had what Morgan terms a *classificatory* kinship system in contrast to the Euro-American *descriptive* system. In our descriptive system, terms applied to lineal kin are not applied to collateral relatives, but in the classificatory system, such terms as *father, mother, brother, sister, son,* and *daughter* are extended to many persons who are not lineal kin.

In connection with a financial interest in railway construction, Morgan made some trips to Wisconsin in the 1850s. While there, he visited a Chippewa Indian reservation and inquired into their kinship system. Chippewa kinship is quite different from Iroquois; the Chippewa have clans with patrilineal rather than matrilineal descent. But Morgan was more struck by the similarities than the differences. He wondered whether clans and classificatory systems were characteristic of American Indian societies in general. To find out, Morgan sent a questionnaire to missions and federal agencies west of the Mississippi. Morgan had the idea that if all American Indian tribes turned out to have classificatory kinship systems, and if such systems were also found in Asia, that would prove the Asiatic origin of the Indians. Morgan himself traveled to Kansas and Nebraska to collect information at Indian reservations. One of the persons to whom Morgan sent a questionnaire was an American missionary in southern India. Upon receipt of the missionary's Tamil kinship chart, Morgan burst excitedly into a friend's office to show him its close similarities to the Iroquois system. Morgan decided that the next problem was to find out in which areas of the world descriptive systems existed—how widespread classificatory systems were. He now sent out questionnaires on a worldwide scale in the hope of covering other parts of India, Mongolia, Siberia, China, Japan, Australia, the islands of the Pacific, Africa, and South America. These questionnaires were sent to consular and diplomatic representatives of the United States under the auspices of the Smithsonian Institution. The resulting tables, together with Morgan's analysis, were published as *Systems of Consanguinity and Affinity of the Human Family* by the Smithsonian Institution in 1870.

Morgan assumed that the widespread classificatory system was the earlier form, from which a descriptive system developed among the Aryans and Semites. But why did that change take place? Morgan thought that such a transition could develop only through "great reformatory movements"; but another catalytic influence was the idea of property. Morgan began to speculate about the relationships between kinship and economic and political institutions, and this resulted in the publication of *Ancient Society* (1877), his best-known work. *Ancient Society* presented a scheme of cultural evolution, showing that technology, government, and family organization had passed through different stages of Savagery, Barbarism, and Civilization. These stages were the same as Tylor's, but Morgan subdivided the first two stages into Lower, Middle, and Upper. During the Lower Savagery stage, humans lived on fruits and nuts, without the use of fire. They had fire and added fish to their diet in the Middle phase and acquired bows and arrows in the Upper. Pottery was made in the Lower Barbarism phase. In the Middle phase, humans domesticated animals in the Old World and cultivated maize in the New. Iron tools came in with Upper Barbarism, alphabet and writing with Civilization.

How did 19th-century writers like Morgan draw up their stages of cultural evolution? What sort of information was at their disposal? In those days archaeological evidence was still limited, although it did suggest that there had been a general development from simpler to more complex cultures. Written history provided fuller documentation but was also quite limited, dealing mainly with relatively late civilizations of the Western world. This left one important source of information: reports about non-Western societies at different levels of subsistence: hunting-gathering, horticulture, and agriculture. Such societies could be seen as having remained arrested at a level of cultural evolution that others had transcended. So one could get an idea of what the Paleolithic was like by studying the Australian aborigines and learn about the Neolithic from the Pueblo Indians. There are many different societies at a hunting-gathering level and their cultures are not all alike, but one can get a general idea of this stage of cultural evolution from the elements that they have in common. In this way Morgan reconstructed stages of cultural evolution from ethnographic accounts, supplemented by some guesswork. There were many weaknesses in Morgan's scheme. Humans have been hunters for millions of years; neither a nuts-and-fruit stage nor a subsequent fishing stage seems plausible. If we were to follow Morgan's scheme, the Polynesians would appear at the same cultural evolutionary level as the Australian aborigines, while the Inca and Maya would rank below African tribes that have acquired iron. These and many other criticisms have been made of Morgan's outline, but at least it had the advantage of setting forth a provisional plan of evolutionary development.

The comparative method

Different stages were characterized, according to Morgan, by different forms of family and kinship organization. Morgan's ideas on this subject were influenced by (and contributed to) the thinking of other 19th-century writers. There were strong differences of opinion among some of these.

Cultural evolution

Tylor, John F. McLennan (1827–81), and John Lubbock (1834–1913) severely criticized Morgan's work. But there were also some widespread ideas shared by many of the late 19th-century writers, including, for example, Johann Jacob Bachofen (1815–87). It was generally believed that the first human beings lived in a state of sexual promiscuity and later in a somewhat more controlled form of group marriage. Since a child would never know who its father was under such a system, the term *father* would be extended to all males of the first ascending generation. The term *mother* would also be extended to all women of the first ascending generation who were potential stepmothers.

When unilineal kinship systems came into being, they were first matrilineal, since at least a child would know who its mother was; but, in the course of time, it was held, matrilineal clans gave way to patrilineal ones as the married pair became a more stable unit and as a sense of private property developed. For Morgan and most other 19th-century writers, the monogamous family of the Western world was the supreme development in the evolution of the family.

The concept of *survivals* was used in reconstructing aspects of cultural evolution. Tylor used this term to refer to culture patterns that have been carried from an earlier into a later stage of culture through force of habit, with the result that their original significance has been forgotten. The presence of such a pattern provides a clue to past practices. Tylor made use of this concept in a statistical exercise in which he tried to show that matrilineal descent and matrilocal residence must have preceded patrilineal descent and patrilocal residence. This study is important as a pioneer cross-cultural survey like those used later with the resources of the Human Relations Area Files. Tylor (1889) collected data about 350 peoples "ranging from insignificant savage hordes to great cultured nations." Unfortunately, he did not list them, and there is no way of knowing now who his 350 peoples were or where they were located. Tylor presented a series of tables showing correlations among certain institutions. When he found a greater than chance coexistence of two or more institutions, he concluded that there was some inherent connection between them. He found, for example, that there was a relationship between matrilocal residence and mother-in-law avoidance by a man. Tylor concluded that in such households marrying-in men are formally treated as strangers. There was also a relationship between matrilocal residence and *teknonymy,* the practice of naming the parents, usually the father, from the child, so that a man is called "Father of So-and-So." In a matrilocal household, reasoned Tylor, the husband would acquire status as a father; hence the correlation. Tylor also considered correlations with the customs of levirate, couvade, and bride-capture and concluded from all this that matrilineal descent generally preceded patrilineal. The presence of survivals from an earlier period indicated to him that a particular stage was later than one in which such survivals were absent. Patrilineal cultures would retain some matrilineal survivals but not the other way around.

In the discussion that followed Tylor's presentation of this paper at the Royal Anthropological Institute in 1889, Francis Galton pointed out that some of the tribes in question might have borrowed their practices from neighboring peoples and that Tylor had not taken diffusion into account. If the different societies could not be counted as separate units, the chance-probability statistics would then become rather meaningless.

Cultural evolution was a lively field of speculation in the late 19th century, stimulated by the Darwinian concepts about biological evolution which were then being debated. Although their views challenged traditional ones, men like Tylor and Morgan were not radicals. Indeed, Morgan asserted that the dominance of the concept of property over the other passions marked the commencement of civilization.

Under the circumstances, it seems odd that Morgan was taken up by the Marxists and eventually became a hero in the Soviet Union. Karl Marx claimed that Morgan had independently discovered the materialist conception of history. Friedrich Engels, who collaborated with Marx in writing the *Communist Manifesto,* wrote *The Origin of the Family, Private Property and the State* (1884) as a leftwing *Reader's Digest* version of Morgan's *Ancient Society.*

The Marxists gave a new twist to Morgan's ideas. Just as capitalism and private property, from their point of view, do not represent the final stage of economic development, in the same way monogamy will be superseded with a change in social conditions. Primitive bands were communistic; their cohesion gave way with the development of the idea of private property. But the society of the future will once again become communist, and the isolation of the bourgeois family will then disappear. This view conjured up visions of a "return" to conditions of sexual promiscuity. In practice, the Soviet Union has supported the integrity of the individual family; if Engels predicted its withering away under communism, it has not yet done so there.

The Marxist canonization of Morgan has led to many of his doctrines being accepted as virtual laws, including the universal priority of matriliny before patriliny. Much of Soviet archaeology has been dominated by Morgan's conceptions. As we shall see, Morgan's ideas met with a different, more fluctuating, reception in the United States.

Diffusionism

In addition to cultural evolutionist schemes, the later 19th and early 20th centuries also produced schools that emphasized the role of diffusion. There were two main schools, one British, the other German and Austrian. The leading spokesmen of the British school were G. Elliot Smith, William J. Perry, and W. H. R. Rivers. It was their belief that most aspects of higher civilization first developed in Egypt and then diffused to other parts of the world. If agriculture, pottery making, weaving, pyramid building, and various other features were to be found in the Americas and elsewhere, it was due to the explorations of Egyptians or of people who had been in contact with Egyptian civilization. These notions were based upon the assumptions that most people are uninventive and that parallel cultural evolution is rare. American anthropologists were hostile to this school of thought, which seems by now to have become extinct.

The German and Austrian *Kulturkreis* (culture circle) school was represented by Fritz Graebner and Father Wilhelm Schmidt, among others. Their reconstructions represent an amalgam of cultural evolution and diffusion, sharing with the pan-Egyptian school some skepticism about alleged cases of parallel evolution, since they too believed that human beings are generally uninventive. Members of this school held that diffusion of culture traits may take place over great distances and that they may diffuse in great complexes of traits. For example, Graebner related the "Melanesian bow culture" to the Neolithic culture of central Europe, since both had pile dwellings with rectangular ground plans, coiled pottery, a special way of hafting adzes, and spoons.

Father Schmidt isolated a group of what he considered to be the "ethnologically oldest" peoples. These consisted of hunting-gathering bands which were remnants of societies that had diverged from the world's oldest culture without having since added many new cultural trappings, since they had made their ways into marginal areas of the world—in the Arctic, Tierra del Fuego, deep jungles, deserts, and other isolated regions. This early horizon is represented by the Pygmies, Semang, Andamanese, Australian aborigines, Tasmanians, Eskimos, Algonkian Indians, Indians of central California, and some of the tribes of Tierra del Fuego. By studying the common characteristics of these cultures, Father Schmidt suggested, we may be able to reconstruct characteristics of the oldest culture of the world.

One of the later cultural strata (of which there are several) was a matrilineal horticultural type of society in which women gained prestige through their association with tillage and hence developed matrilocality, matrilineal descent, female puberty ceremonies, and worship of female deities. Men reacted against this domination by developing masked secret societies which aimed to replace the worship of goddesses with that of male ancestors.

While the posited functional relationships may be plausible, not much documentation was provided for the existence of these *Kulturkreise* and their influences upon one another. As Robert Lowie remarked (1937:190), "Until these events are actually documented somewhere on the globe we must reject the scheme as not a whit more empirical than Morgan's." The *Kulturkreis* doctrine is more complex and hydra-headed than that of the pan-Egyptian school and hence harder to refute. While no American anthropologists seem to have supported the pan-Egyptian dogma, there was some support for the *Kulturkreis* school (e.g., Kluckhohn 1936).

Anthropology as an academic discipline came into being in an age of imperialism. Racist beliefs and ideas about the uninventiveness of nonwhite peoples were part of the ideology of imperialism and colonialism. The concept of the white man's burden, with its theme of *noblesse oblige,* was a more benevolent aspect of the same outlook, assuming the superior ability and motivation of white people.

Three influential figures ushered in the modern phase of anthropology: Franz Boas (1858–1942), Bronislaw Malinowski (1884–1942), and A. R. Radcliffe-Brown (1881–1955). They were professional, academic anthropologists who taught and trained others in their discipline.

Field research: A new emphasis

Both Boas and Malinowski started out in other fields, in the physical sciences. Boas got a doctoral degree in physics at Kiel, Germany, with a dissertation written on the color of seawater. Malinowski got a Ph.D. in physics and mathematics at the University of Cracow. Although they had grown up and been educated in Germany and Poland, respectively, both of these men wrote most of their anthropological works in English and made their greatest influence felt in the United States and England.

These men also differed from their predecessors in doing more fieldwork. It is true that Morgan visited the Iroquois reservation, but he did not live there as Malinowski lived among the Trobriand Islanders in Melanesia. As a young man, Tylor traveled in Mexico, but that was not the same thing as doing ethnographic research. Most of the 19th-century writers on anthropology were indefatigable readers and compilers of data from books. One thinks of James G. Frazer, who never saw a living "savage" but whose massive work, *The Golden Bough,* ran to 12 volumes. Father Schmidt, who also did no fieldwork, wrote *The Origin of the Idea of God* in 11

Franz Boas.

volumes. Tylor, Morgan, Frazer, Schmidt, and other 19th-century theorists built up their compilations from reports of early travelers, sea captains, missionaries, and other commentators.

Boas, Malinowski, and Radcliffe-Brown were charismatic teachers who aroused great loyalty and admiration among the students whom they sent out to do fieldwork. Boas warned that primitive cultures all over the world were disappearing under the impact of Western civilization. He pointed out that time was short and that anthropologists should go out to record the facts of native life before these cultures vanished.

Malinowski was a prime exponent of the method of *participant observation,* in which ethnographers immerse themselves in the everyday life of the people whom they study. That is what Malinowski did in the Trobriand Islands where he lived during World War I. Both Boas and Malinowski stressed the value of learning the native language as a way of understanding the culture as experienced by its participants.

Franz Boas

A reaction against 19th-century cultural evolutionism and diffusionism came from the work of Franz Boas and his students. Born in 1858, Boas was reared and educated in Germany.

Boas' first fieldwork was among the Central Eskimos from 1883 to 1884. He had been influenced by the concept of geographical determinism and wanted to see to what extent the culture of the Eskimos was shaped by their environment. His experience in Baffinland led Boas to conclude that geography plays a mainly limiting rather than creative role. The Eskimos did things in spite of their environment, not just because of it; they had a particular history and set of traditions behind them that were different from those of other northerly peoples, such as the Siberian Chukchee, who lived in a similar environment. A culture is shaped by many historical forces, including contacts with other societies.

This awareness of the complexity of determinants led Boas to be skeptical of universal laws such as those set forth by the cultural evolutionists. He thought that broad generalizations might perhaps be arrived at; but, if so, these might turn out to be only commonplace truisms. Rather than announcing any new doctrine, Boas attacked the works of previous writers, and his students followed this critical bent. For example, John Swanton showed that the tribes of North America did not show the progression of kinship organization postulated by Morgan and others. Hunting bands with bilateral or patrilineal descent lived at a simpler level of culture than the more advanced Hopi, Zuñi, Creek, and Natchez Indians who had matrilineal descent.

Boas thought that the global generalizations about cultural evolution made by 19th-century writers were premature, based on inadequate information about primitive cultures collected from the writings of traders, sea captains, and missionaries, who often had only a biased, superficial understanding of the people whom they observed. Boas declared for a moratorium on theorizing. He recommended that we first get the facts and build up a body of ethnographic data from which more reliable generalizations can later be made.

Boas followed his own prescription. From 1886 to 1931, he made 13 field trips to the Northwest Coast of North America. He trained himself to learn the languages of Indians of the area, as he had earlier learned Eskimo. Boas was a leader in the development of American linguistics. One reason for this emphasis was that he believed a culture should be understood in terms of the categories of the natives themselves, not in those imposed by an outside observer. The purpose should be to see how the world looks to a member of that culture. Folktales were recorded by Boas in the native language and later translated. The recording of texts was one of his main activities in the field. Some understanding of the language was necessary, he believed, when dealing with complex sets of ideas, such as those concerning religion, which may be distorted when translated by an interpreter.

Boas' students worked in this tradition. Hence, we have today an impressive body of field reports on American Indian cultures, on the Winnebago, Crow, Arapaho, and the tribes of the Pueblo area and California. Boas' students were often interested in different topics and problems; hence it is often asserted that there was no "Boas school." Marian Smith has suggested that Boas wanted the data collected to be as free of bias as possible; interpretations should be made only after the ethnography has been recorded. Smith (1959:53) noted, "It therefore followed that information gathered for a particular purpose became suspect, for selection in itself suggested distortion."

Boas trained his students to be camera eyes, recording everything and anything. Smith (1959:54) has characterized this as a "natural history" approach and describes it as follows:

Interest lies not mainly in systems per se, but in "the surrounding world." There is a fascination in following the details of a subject just for its intrinsic interest, and there is also the knowledge that, once accumulated, such systematic data will have value—sometimes in wholly unexpected directions.

This fascination for details may lead to a lack of focus. For example, Boas recorded page after page of blueberry-pie recipes in the Kwakiutl language, with the English translation on facing pages. We still do not know to what use they may ultimately be put.

Boas' effort to learn as much as possible about a particular culture in all of its minutiae is an *idiographic* approach to culture, as opposed to a *nomothetic* approach, which involves a search for general laws or regularities. As has been mentioned, he was skeptical about the possibility of finding cultural laws and suggested that it would be better to reconstruct the historical development of particular cultures. If this were done on a sufficiently large scale, it might become possible to compare histories of cultural development and see if regularities were discernible.

By 1930, however, Boas was skeptical of such an outcome:

An error of modern anthropology, as I see it, lies in the overemphasis on historical reconstruction, the importance of which should not be minimized, as against a penetrating study of the individual under the stress of the culture in which he lives (quoted in Harris 1968:281).

Boas thus advocated a turn to the field of culture-and-personality, in which his students Ruth Benedict and Margaret Mead distinguished themselves.

The idiographic approach of Boas and many of his followers, with its mistrust of laws and generalities, led finally to critical attacks by Leslie White and others who wanted to make anthropology more of a generalizing science.

Bronislaw Malinowski

After studying anthropology in England for four years, just before World War I, Malinowski set out to do fieldwork in Melanesia and Australia, where he was interned as an enemy alien but allowed to continue his work from 1915 to 1918. Malinowski's prolonged stay in the Trobriand Islands formed the basis for a series of ethnographic works that have become classics in anthropology. He was attracted to the social life of Europeans in the islands, but he determined to cut himself off from these contacts and to live among the Trobriand people, whose language he learned. Like Boas, Malinowski took down texts in the native tongue and tried to find the natives' own terms of classification for their institutions and practices in an effort to "get inside the native's skin." Also like Boas, he was interested in the many interrelated aspects of the total culture and in what he called "the imponderabilia of actual life." He was not, however, concerned with trying to reconstruct the antecedents of Trobriand culture, about which he thought little could be learned. Malinowski promoted an approach he called "functionalism," seeing the culture of a society as providing various means for satisfying the needs of its members. He wrote (1926b:132):

The functional view of culture insists upon the principle that every type of civilization, every custom, material object, idea, and belief fulfills some vital function, has some task to accomplish, represents an indispensable part within a working whole.

This view was partly in reaction to the attitude that the customs of non-Western societies are often bizarre, irrational, or represent survivals from earlier stages of cultural development; earlier in the same passage Malinowski wrote:

The field worker who lives among savages soon discards the antiquarian outlook. He sees every implement constantly used; every custom backed up by strong feeling and cogent ideas; every detail of social organization active and effective.

There is a danger, however, in characterizing certain institutions or culture patterns as "indispensable" in meeting human needs, for those needs may

Bronislaw
Malinowski.

be met by other means. Malinowski's view implies a somewhat rigid and static concept of culture (see Merton 1949:28–79). At the same time, however, Malinowski did not see individuals as being dominated by their culture. He suggested that perhaps "the heathen can be as self-seeking and self-interested as any Christian" (Malinowski 1926a:ix). Whenever a Trobriand native can escape his obligations without losing prestige, he is likely to do so.

In his work Malinowski's focus was on a particular society at a given moment in time. He was interested in seeing how food is acquired from the environment and distributed within the society, how social conflicts are handled and adjusted, and how social cohesion and cooperation are insured. This involves a study of the interrelations between economics, social organization, religion, and other institutions, for Malinowski saw all aspects of culture as being closely interwoven. This integration was exemplified in Malinowski's discussion of the kula trade ring, presented in Chapter 12.

Malinowski's interest in the functions of magic and religion in meeting human psychological needs was touched on in Chapter 18. Magic, said Malinowski, comes into play when normal, rational means to an end meet with failure. People may then resort to magic, which has the effect of giving them confidence to persevere toward their goal.

As his interpretation of magic indicates, Malinowski was always interested in the individual member of society. Although he referred to Trobriand natives as "savages" in the 19th-century fashion, and although he sometimes wrote of them contemptuously in the day-by-day journal which he kept, Malinowski described the Trobrianders in his books and articles as reasonable, pragmatic persons, whose behavior is altogether understandable when one knows their cultural premises.

**A. R.
Radcliffe-
Brown**

Alfred Reginald Radcliffe-Brown was born and educated in England and studied anthropology under W. H. R. Rivers and A. C. Haddon. He did ethnological fieldwork in the Andaman Islands from 1906 to 1908, providing the material for his book *The Andaman Islanders.* From 1910 to 1912 he did fieldwork in Australia, and in subsequent years taught anthropology in universities in many parts of the world, including Capetown, Sydney, Chicago, and Oxford.

Like Malinowski, Radcliffe-Brown was interested in the synchronic study of a particular society at one period of time and was not concerned with historical reconstruction. He sometimes called himself a functionalist and wrote about the concept of function, stating that the function of an institution is the contribution it makes to the maintenance of structural continuity in the society. Radcliffe-Brown's view of functionalism was not allied to Malinowski's notion about cultural institutions satisfying human needs. Rather, he placed the emphasis on the maintenance of social structures. Hence, his approach has sometimes been called "structural-functional." It is largely through his influence that British social anthropologists, and many Americans as well, have focused their attention on the kinship systems of different societies.

The proper focus for investigation, for Radcliffe-Brown, was not the culture of a society—too vague and broad a concept for him—but its social

A. R. Radcliffe-
Brown.

structure, the network of social relations. Kinship ties are always important in the tribal societies studied by Radcliffe-Brown and his students. The emphasis on social structure made Radcliffe-Brown a kind of sociologist, as he himself declared. Radcliffe-Brown saw himself as a social scientist seeking nomothetic social laws, but the laws he claimed to have discovered are usually rather vague and do not seem to add a great deal to our understanding of social issues. Nevertheless, he was an extremely influential teacher, commanding great loyalty among his students.

We have seen that by 1930 Franz Boas was advocating "a penetrating study of the individual under the stress of the culture in which he lives." *Patterns of Culture* (1934) written by Boas' student, Ruth Benedict, was an effort in that direction; in this popular work Benedict contrasted three cultures, Pueblo, Dobu, and Kwakiutl. She emphasized the differences in values and world view characterizing these three cultural worlds. A child born into the Kwakiutl society is destined to have very different experiences and to be driven toward different goals and underlying assumptions about life from those of a child born among the Hopi or Zuñi.

Culture-and-personality

Margaret Mead's early studies (1939) also drew attention to the importance of cultural milieu in shaping personality. She contrasted the easygoing adolescence of Samoan girls with the tenser coming-of-age of American youngsters. Mead also observed and recorded the typical childhood experiences of the Manus of New Guinea and pointed out ways in which these experiences resembled and differed from those of American children.

The cross-cultural study of childhood has been a relatively recent develop-

Margaret Mead.

ment in anthropology, which was originally concerned with adult culture. If any attention was paid to child training in the earlier ethnography, it was usually a secondary matter, a side issue. An interest in child training among anthropologists was brought about partly by the influence of Freudian theory and also by the influence of John Dewey in education. Both of these currents may be seen in the work of Margaret Mead. Bronislaw Malinowski (1953) was also one of the first to concern himself with childhood experience and the relevance of psychoanalytic theory in a non-Western society.

In the late 1930s and 1940s, a seminar in culture-and-personality was given at Columbia University by Ralph Linton, an anthropologist, and Abram Kardiner, a psychoanalyst. In this seminar a series of nonliterate cultures were analyzed with regard to the relationship between childhood training practices and other aspects of the culture. Kardiner developed the concept of "basic personality structure," referring to the common aspects of personality shared by the members of a particular society. He noted that child-training methods, such as those involving suckling and toilet training, tend to be fairly standardized within a particular society, so that women tend to suckle their children for about the same length of time as their neighbors do, feed them the same foods, and apply the same kinds of toilet training and other disciplines. Therefore, the children who grow up within a particular society pass through the same general gamut of childhood experiences. They are apt to react to such experiences in much the same ways and therefore develop many personality traits in common. As Linton has put it: "The *basic personality type* for any society is that personality configuration which is shared by the bulk of the society's members as a result of the early experiences which they have in common" (Kardiner et al. 1945:viii).

This school emphasized the need for getting more data on child-training practices in different societies. Two outstanding field studies influenced by this school of thought are *The People of Alor* by Cora DuBois (1944) and *Truk: Man in Paradise* by Thomas Gladwin and Seymour B. Sarason (1953). DuBois' work was discussed in Chapter 20.

Cross-cultural surveys

Another kind of research was made possible in the 1940s with the development of the Yale Cross-Cultural Survey, which later became known as the Human Relations Area Files (HRAF). These files contain ethnographic data about a few hundred societies from the various culture areas of the world. A simple coding system makes it possible for someone to quickly find the information sought about cultural practices in different societies, whether they be fishing techniques or toilet-training practices. The leading figure in organizing the Yale files was George P. Murdock.

One advantage of this method of data organization is that it facilitates the discovery of correlations of culture patterns. For example, we may ask, as Tylor did: With which forms of postmarital residence is the custom of mother-in-law avoidance most often found? With which forms is it negatively correlated? The files readily provide answers to such questions. The files also permit the testing of hypotheses. One may predict that certain correlations will appear under particular conditions. On the other hand, correlations do not speak for themselves; when they do appear there may be conflicting explanations for them, with inconclusive results.

A common criticism of studies based on the HRAF files is that the method involves pulling items out of context for comparative, quantitative puposes. But perhaps that is necessary if comparisons are to be made. Indeed, if they are not made, how can anthropology claim to be a scientific discipline?

Broad cross-cultural surveys, like those making use of the HRAF files, are quite different in nature from the intensive description of a single culture, like that of Malinowski. The former studies tend to be nomothetic, the latter idiographic and relativistic. Malinowski's desire to "get inside the native's skin" and see the world as a Trobriander sees it has been called an *emic* approach to the study of culture, in contrast to an *etic* approach which relies upon classifications and judgments agreed upon by outside "scientific" observers. These terms, *emic* and *etic,* were coined by the linguist Kenneth Pike on the analogy of the terms *phonemic* and *phonetic.* An etic analysis may consist of observation of behavior that does not involve learning the viewpoints of those involved. The categories of the Human Relations Area Files provide an etic grid which may be applied to the cultures of the world.

Many problems are involved in the use of the cross-cultural survey method. One is Galton's problem, referred to in relation to Tylor's pioneer statistical study, concerning the role of diffusion as a "contaminating" factor. However, various attempts have been made to control for the factor of diffusion (Naroll 1961, 1964; Naroll and D'Andrade 1963). Despite the many difficulties, an extensive collection of books and articles has appeared, making use of the HRAF files.

One of Murdock's chief colleagues in developing the files was John W. M. Whiting, who has made use of HRAF cross-cultural data in many articles on child-training practices. In coauthorship with Irvin L. Child, Whiting produced an influential book, *Child Training and Personality: A Cross-Cultural Study* (1953). One weakness of this work, and of other early HRAF cross-cultural studies of childhood, was that the information about childhood was very uneven in the Human Relations Area Files. For some societies there were abundant data, for others almost none. It was clear that more complete descriptions were needed of childhood experience in different societies. Whiting and his associates extended their cross-cultural investigations of childhood experience in the Six Cultures project, which is discussed in Chapter 20.

We have seen that Boas and his followers were often critical of the works of 19th-century cultural evolutionists, including Morgan and Tylor, and that they were skeptical of the value of making broad cross-cultural generalizations. Beginning in the 1930s, the Boasian emphasis on historical

The return to cultural evolution

particularism came in for a series of polemic attacks by Leslie A. White. White became an ardent champion of Morgan and Tylor and a proponent for the study of cultural evolution. In time, he acquired a band of enthusiastic disciples, while another constellation of disciples (some of whom were also followers of White) formed about another prominent student of cultural evolution, Julian H. Steward. White and Steward have sometimes been referred to as *neoevolutionists,* a term rejected by White, who claimed that he was simply carrying on the 19th-century traditions of Tylor and had added nothing new.

White did, however, add something new; for one thing, he propounded a "Basic Law of Evolution," which read as follows: "Other factors remaining constant, culture evolves as the amount of energy harnessed per capita per year is increased or as the efficiency of the means of putting the energy to work is increased" (White 1959:368–69). What distinguishes a stage of evolution from a preceding stage is the increase in available energy. For White, adaptation and culture change are not synonymous with evolution; history is not evolution. Cultural evolution occurs when more energy is made available to humans, this tends to be associated with increased complexity of social organization and social differentiation.

White claims that Steward has sometimes failed to make a proper distinction between mere culture change and evolution. A case in point is a comparison Steward made between two groups adapting to European contact— the horticultural Mundurucú of Brazil and the hunting-gathering Algonquin Indians of North America. Although the two ecological and cultural settings were very different, both groups became similarly dependent upon European trading posts. Steward saw this as a convergent evolutionary development, but to White these adaptations had nothing to do with evolution. It is evident that different interpretations may be made as to what constitutes cultural evolution.

Steward (1955:14–15) has made a distinction between three schools of evolutionary thought:

First, *unilinear evolution,* the classical nineteenth-century formulation, dealt with particular cultures, placing them in stages of a universal sequence. Second, *universal evolution*—a rather arbitrary label to designate the modern revamping of unilinear evolution—is concerned with culture rather than with cultures. Third, *multilinear evolution,* a somewhat less ambitious approach than the other two, is like unilinear evolution in dealing with developmental sequences, but is distinctive in searching for parallels of limited occurrence instead of universals.

Morgan and Tylor, then, would be unilinear evolutionists, White a universal evolutionist, and Steward a multilinear evolutionist.

Steward has been concerned with discovering cross-cultural regularities, similar patterns in cultural development such as occurred in the Bronze Age Old World civilizations, on the one hand, and the New World civilizations of Mexico and Peru, on the other. Analysis of such regularities may reveal underlying processes that have led to the appearance of similar institutions. For this reason, Steward was attracted to Wittfogel's theory about the role of irrigation in the formation of despotic societies.

Human adaptation to the environment involves culture; hence, Steward used the term *cultural ecology* for the study of human adjustment to particular geographical settings. He followed three basic procedures, involving analyses of: (1) the relationship between technology and environment, (2) behavior patterns involved in exploiting a particular area with a particular technology, and (3) the extent to which these behavior patterns affect other aspects of culture.

Human ecology

Steward noted that hunting-gathering bands varied in size and composition, depending on local resources and circumstances. Some had large, composite bands, while others had small family units, like the Shoshone Indians. Steward's interests were not limited to the hunting-gathering level of sociocultural integration but extended to large hydraulic civilizations and modern nations as well. Thus there is a close relationship between Steward's work in cultural ecology and his outline of cultural evolution.

There have been other approaches besides Steward's to the study of human ecology. Andrew P. Vayda and Roy A. Rappaport (1968) have a more biological and functional orientation, hoping to bring ecological studies in anthropology within the theoretical framework of general ecology. This is evidenced in Rappaport's study (1967) of the Tsembaga of New Guinea, who periodically slaughter large numbers of pigs. He argues that these ritual slaughters keep the land from being overrun with pigs and maintain balances between the people and their sweet-potato crops and fauna. This is a form of functionalist analysis, with an ecological emphasis.

Claude Lévi-Strauss, who seems to be presently the leading figure in anthropology in continental Europe, is the exponent of what he calls *structural anthropology,* the title of a collection of his papers published in 1963. One might think that structural anthropology has to do with the analysis of social structure in the manner of Radcliffe-Brown and his followers. Indeed, Lévi-Strauss is the author of an influential paper on "Social Structure" (1953), and his book *The Elementary Structures of Kinship,* first published in 1949, has to do with kinship organization. Nevertheless, despite his close familiarity with this field, Lévi-Strauss's interests are more psychological than sociological. He has stated that "ethnology is first of all psychology," and it is significant that the comment appears in a work entitled *La Pensée Sauvage,* which has been translated into English as *The Savage Mind* (1966a:131).

Claude Lévi-Strauss

This interest in psychology does not concern the emotional aspects of personality that have been investigated by some workers in the field of culture-and-personality; rather, Lévi-Strauss's concern is with cognitive proc-

Claude Lévi-Strauss.

esses very much along the lines of the school of cognitive anthropology. Early in *The Elementary Structures of Kinship* the author devotes a chapter to studies of child psychology in order to clarify the psychological basis for the idea of reciprocity. Ways in which people classify things and make order of the world around them is a matter of particular fascination to Lévi-Strauss and forms the main theme of *The Savage Mind.*

An important point made by the author is that the mental abilities of "primitive" peoples have long been greatly underrated. He presents a good deal of evidence that peoples with a relatively simple technological culture often have highly elaborate systems for classifying plants and animals, involving much accurate knowledge. This close observation is not limited to species that are edible or useful in other ways. The classifications seem to be generated by sheer intellectual curiosity and by a desire to impose order on the world. This concern is also devoted to making distinctions between moieties, clans, and other social units.

Structuralism is an approach that is not limited to anthropology. Persons who call themselves structuralists are also found in the fields of mathematics, psychology, and philosophy (Lane 1970). But the main source of structuralism has been linguistics. Lévi-Strauss has compared his approach to ethnological data with the methods of structural linguistics which stress the study of the unconscious infrastructure that underlies linguistic phenomena. Similarly, Lévi-Strauss tries to reveal the "mental structures" that underlie human behavior. According to him, these usually take the form of binary contrasts or oppositions. Hence the frequency with which moieties or other forms of dual organization are associated with contrasting qualities, such as left and right, low and high, cold and warm, earth and sky, north and south, white and black, and so forth.

It must be admitted that some of Lévi-Strauss's theories seem bizarre. For example, in an article entitled "The Culinary Triangle" (1966b), Lévi-Strauss states that the cooking practices of a society may be analyzed in the same way as a language; like a language, they contain certain structural oppositions. He finds a significant contrast between roasting and boiling. The former is more primitive, involving direct exposure of food to the fire, whereas boiling makes use of a container. The author hypothesizes that boiling is associated with in-group solidarity, while roasted food is served to guests. He then extends this discussion to cannibalism, with the suggestion that boiling may be used when eating either relatives or enemies, but roasting would more frequently be used with enemies.

Not many of Lévi-Strauss's theories are open to testing, but this one is, and it has fared poorly under investigation (Shankman 1969).

On the other hand, Lévi-Strauss has written much that is thoughtful and stimulating, particularly in *The Savage Mind.*

In this chapter, some current schools of thought in ethnology have been briefly presented, but this survey is by no means complete. Many anthropologists cannot be fitted into particular pigeonholes, such as "functionalism," "structural anthropology," or whatnot. Present-day anthropology is characterized by remarkable diversity; it is like Stephen Leacock's knight who jumped on his horse and rode off in all directions. Perhaps the best way to get an idea of the variety of interests, aims, and methods in anthropology is to look through a list of the titles of papers given at one of the recent annual meetings of the American Anthropological Association. This diversity gives reason to believe that the younger generation of anthropologists is not likely to become brainwashed by any one ethnological doctrine or school of thought.

Summary

Our review of modern anthropological theory started with the work of Edward B. Tylor, who insisted that cultural evolution had taken place despite conservative arguments to the contrary. It was Tylor who first used the word *culture* in the sense now accepted by anthropologists. Although Tylor was aware of the role of cultural diffusion, he was more interested in parallelism or independent invention. Tylor tended to attribute similarities in widely separated cultures to the "like working of men's minds under like conditions," in other words to the psychic unity of mankind. Widespread similarities in religious beliefs and customs could be attributed to this source.

Both Tylor and Lewis H. Morgan drew up schemes of cultural evolution which included the stages of savagery, barbarism, and civilization. Morgan, who initiated the cross-cultural study of kinship organization, provided subdivisions of lower, middle, and upper for the first two stages. He used information about contemporary hunting and horticultural tribes in setting forth the salient characteristics of these early stages.

It was generally believed by 19th-century cultural evolutionists like Tylor and Morgan that matrilineal descent preceded patrilineal descent in the evolution of the world's kinship systems. Tylor tried to demonstrate this priority in a pioneer cross-cultural correlational study, which had the weakness, common to many such studies, of not controlling for the influence of diffusion.

The British pan-Egyptian school of G. Elliot Smith, William J. Perry, and W. H. R. Rivers exaggerated the role of diffusion, attributing most aspects of civilization in the New World to Egyptian origins. The German-Austrian *Kulturkreis* school combined cultural evolution with diffusionism in an ambitious attempt to reconstruct the culture history of the world.

Franz Boas criticized both the cultural evolutionary and diffusionist schools of the 19th century as being premature formulations based on inadequate data. He urged his students to do ethnographic field work in the non-Western societies of the world before their cultures disappeared under the impact of Western civilization. Meanwhile, some of Boas' students cast doubt on the notion that matriliny had always preceded patriliny, and similarly questioned other cultural evolutionary dogmas.

Like Boas, Bronislaw Malinowski emphasized the value of intensive field work. He declared himself to be a functionalist, holding every custom and tradition in a society to have a vital function. Culture, he claimed, is instrumental in serving human needs. Radcliffe-Brown, who has also been labeled a functionalist, saw the function of an institution as the contribution it makes to the maintenance of structural continuity in the society. A kind of sociologist, Radcliffe-Brown sought to formulate nomothetic social laws.

In the 1930's the field of culture-and-personality came into being with the pioneer studies by Ruth Benedict, Margaret Mead, and others. The concept of basic personality structure was propounded by Abram Kardiner and Ralph Linton and that of modal personality by Cora Du Bois. Projective tests began to be used in field work, together with the recording of life history material, and the technique of blind analysis of projective tests was followed, notably in Du Bois' Alor study and in the study of Truk by Gladwin and Sarason.

Projects of this kind involve the intensive study of a single culture. A quite different kind of research is the cross-cultural survey employing the Human Relations Area Files, which provide an etic grid for classifying ethnological data. By examining information from a large number of societies one may formulate and test hypotheses concerning correlations that may appear between particular institutions.

The search for cross-cultural regularities is also a prominent feature of the work of Julian H. Steward, who along with Leslie A. White, brought about a revival of cultural evolutionary theory. Steward was also a pioneer in the field of cultural ecology concerning sociocultural adaptations of human groups to their environments.

Two surveys of the history of anthropological theory are Marvin Harris, *The Rise of Anthropological Theory: A History of Theories of Culture* (New York: Thomas Y. Crowell Co., 1968), and John J. Honigmann, *The Development of Anthropological Ideas* (Homewood, Ill.: The Dorsey Press, 1976). For a collection of essays on the history of anthropology, see George W. Stocking, *Race, Culture, and Evolution: Essays in the History of Anthropology* (New York: Free Press, 1968).

The best approach to the authors cited in this chapter would be to read some of their original writings. For example, the articles by A. R. Radcliffe-Brown, collected in *Structure and Function in Primitive Society: Essays and Addresses* (Glencoe, Ill.: The Free Press, 1952), are written with economy and elegance. Also worth reading is Malinowski's "Introduction" to his *Argonauts of the Western Pacific* (New York: E. P. Dutton, 1961), pp. 1–26; it gives a good account of his fieldwork methods. Margaret Mead's early books are very readable, especially *Coming of Age in Samoa* (1928) and *Growing Up in New Guinea* (1930). Together with *Sex and Temperament in Three Primitive Societies* (1935), these books are collected in one volume in Margaret Mead, *From the South Seas: Studies of Adolescence and Sex in Primitive Societies* (New York: William Morrow & Co., 1939). The most readable of Lévi-Strauss's books is *The Savage Mind* (Chicago: University of Chicago Press, 1966).

Brief biographies and commentaries on such figures as Edward Tylor, Franz Boas, Bronislaw Malinowski, Ruth Benedict, and others are available in Abram Kardiner and Edward Preble, *They Studied Man* (Cleveland: World Publishing Co., 1961). Nineteenth-century cultural evolutionism is discussed in Robert L. Carneiro, "Classical Evolution," in Raoul Naroll and Frada Naroll, eds., *Main Currents in Cultural Anthropology* (New York: Appleton-Century-Crofts, 1973), pp. 57–121.

The career and ideas of Lewis Henry Morgan are presented in Carl Resek, *Lewis Henry Morgan. American Scholar* (Chicago: University of Chicago Press, 1960).

A series of articles about Franz Boas and his work is available in *The Anthropology of Franz Boas: Essays on the Centennial of His Birth,* ed. Walter Goldschmidt, American Anthropological Association Memoir no. 89, 1959. For a critical assessment of both Boas and Radcliffe-Brown, see Leslie A. White, *The Social Organization of Ethnological Theory* (Houston, Texas: Rice University Studies, vol. 52, 1966), pp. 1–66.

Adam Kuper's *Anthropologists and Anthropology: The British School: 1922–1972* (New York: Pica Press, 1973) deals with the works of Malinowski, Radcliffe-Brown, Lévi-Strauss, and their followers in England. On Lévi-Strauss, see Edmund Leach, *Claude Lévi-Strauss* (New York: Viking Press, 1970). For two critical assessments, see Francis Korn, *Elementary Structures Reconsidered: Lévi-Strauss on Kinship* (Berkeley: University of California Press, 1973), and Philip Pettit, *The Concept of Structuralism: A Critical Analysis* (Berkeley: University of California Press, 1975).

Suggestions for further reading

25

THE FUTURES OF MANKIND

Mankind has many futures, not only in the sense that the future of India, let us say, will be somewhat different from that of the United States, but also in the sense that the cultures of the world will, no doubt, be quite different at different points in time, from century to century, assuming that we still have some centuries ahead of us. Some prophets, like Jacques Ellul in *The Technological Society* (1964), disapprove of the future and do not want to go there. (Ellul's counterparts in fiction are the grim anti-Utopias of Aldous Huxley's *Brave New World* and George Orwell's *1984.*) On the other hand, there are also enthusiasts of the future, writers like Arthur C. Clarke and Richard Landers, who are fascinated by the marvels of 21st-century technology. It is possible that both the pessimists and optimists are right. Many futurists are agreed that the next two decades or so will bring hard times for the human species. If we can navigate and survive the near future, the distant shores of the technological society may indeed be bright. Our problem is how to get there from here, if that is where we want to go.

We cannot know the future, although remarkable prophecies have sometimes been made. Ten years before the event, Arthur C. Clarke made a bet that the first man to land on the moon would do so by June 1969. He was only a month off (Bernstein 1969:40). Clarke, who invented the idea of a communications satellite and coauthored the film *2001: A Space Odyssey,* has a good record for such forecasts, but some of his predictions may prove to be quite wrong.

If we had a battery of reliable cultural or social laws, predictions might perhaps be made with more confidence. Charles Issawi has offered some tongue-in-cheek "laws of social motion," which seem to be just about as acceptable as more solemnly proposed social laws. His "Law of Conservation of Evil" runs: "The total amount of evil in any system remains constant.

426

Hence any diminution in one direction—for instance a reduction in poverty or unemployment—is accompanied by an increase in another, e.g., crime or air pollution." Issawi's second law is, "Most things get steadily worse." He points out that this does not contradict his first law, for a few things have become much better, such as surgery, economic theory, and long-playing records (Issawi 1970:42).

Since we cannot know the future, it is surprising, at first glance, that the literature about it is so enormous. Mankind has always been interested in speculating about the future and planning for it, but this interest has greatly increased in recent years. There are committees and "think tanks" dedicated to this cause. The World Futures Society, founded in 1965 in Washington, publishes a journal called *The Futurist.* The first International Congress of Futures Research was held in Oslo in 1968.

Much of the planning and forecasting in the United States has to do with the needs of the military-industrial complex. The RAND Corporation, the Hudson Institute, and the Institute of Defense Analysis are examples. In 1965 the American Academy of Arts and Sciences created the Commission on the Year 2000. Its leader, sociologist Daniel Bell (1967:xxvi), has explained that the commission's effort is not ". . . to 'predict' the future, as if this were some far-flung rug of time unrolled to some distant point, but the effort to sketch 'alternative futures'—in other words, the likely results of different choices, so that the polity can understand the costs and consequences of different desires." Organizations similar to the Commission on the Year 2000 exist in England, France, and other countries. In the Soviet Union (where science fiction is as popular as in the United States), futures planning has long been related to government five- and ten-year plans. In this chapter, we shall briefly review some of the topics that are prominent in publications about the future. Needless to say, there are often differences of opinion among the authorities.

Except for warfare, the most immediate problem facing the world is the population explosion. One authority states: "The present rate of world population increase—20 per 1,000—is almost certainly without precedent, and it is hundreds of times greater than the rate that has been the norm for most of man's history" (Coale 1974:51). Our species reached its first billion mark in 1850, its second in 1930, its third in 1960, and its fourth in 1976. This population boom may bring in its train a host of calamities, including widespread famine. The world's population is now doubling within a period of 35 years, but the rate is faster in the less-developed nations. The population of India may double within 28 years. In 1971 India's population was about 548 million; it adds 13 million a year, and may reach 1 billion by A.D. 2000. There have been predictions that 75 percent of the world's population by then will be living in Africa, Asia, and Latin America. China should have over 1 billion people by A.D. 2000.

Population increase

In former periods, population increased most in the more successful, expanding economies, but now it is the poor, less-developed nations that are seeing the greatest increase. This boom is not due to higher birth rates but, rather, to lower death rates resulting from the introduction of better sanitary and medical practices. Even the introduction and greater use of soap have made a difference, and there has been a drop in malaria and other diseases due to DDT-spraying campaigns. Vaccination, inoculation, use of penicillin, and improved medical facilities have led to a reduction in smallpox, typhoid, plague, cholera, tuberculosis, and other ailments, in spite of the low number of doctors in relation to the population in the less-developed nations.

Another reason for further population growth in such countries is that nearly half the people in them are under 15 years of age, and they will soon have families of their own. In India almost everyone gets married, marries early, and brides have many reproductive years ahead of them. Nowadays, they live longer; in India the expectation of life at birth rose from 23 years in 1931 to 46 years in 1961. But while, in the last six decades of British rule, the population of India increased over 50 percent, the increase of cultivable land in that time was only 1.5 percent. Similarly, between 1960 and 1965, the production of food went up by 6 percent in Latin America, but the population increased by 11 percent.

In 1965 the Director General of the Food and Agriculture Organization (FAO) announced that there had been no appreciable increase in food production per head of the world's population in the past seven years. In the following year, the FAO stated there had been no increase in agricultural production in 1966, although the world's population had grown that year by 70 million (Paddock and Paddock 1967:45).

It has been estimated that the countries of eastern and southern Asia, Africa, and Latin America must increase their food production within ten years by 26 percent just to maintain their present inadequate dietary levels. It seems unlikely they will be able to do so (Paddock and Paddock 1965:55). Consequently, some demographers and agronomists have warned that famines will occur before long. In 1966 the then Secretary of Agriculture Orville L. Freeman estimated that the United States could continue to export wheat to the hungry nations of the world until 1984; but, after that year, the total agricultural productivity of the United States will no longer be enough to avert famines.

To be sure, other estimates are more optimistic. Donald Bogue (1968) believes that the population explosion has been exaggerated and that the gloomy prophecies are based on the premise, "If recent trends continue . . .," whereas recent trends are not continuing. In their generally optimistic forecast of the future, Kahn, Brown, and Martel (1976:34, 212) predict that 200 years from now the earth's population will be about 15 billion, give or take a factor of two, and that this population will be rather stable. The authors claim that the rate of population growth is now declining in

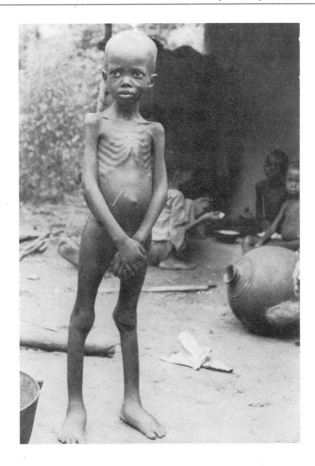

Famine victim.

almost all developed countries. Hence there may be no need for alarm about world population growth in the long run.

The problem, however, is that meanwhile population is still increasing, while food resources are uncertain. In recent years there have been widespread famines in the Sahel area south of the Sahara and in parts of South Asia. A World Food Conference study estimates that half of all child deaths are "in some way attributable to malnutrition" and that 200 million living children are undernourished (Rothschild 1974:30–31).

Food resources

One problem, not always remembered, is that there must also be enough food resources for our domesticated animals, as well as for humans. John McHale (1969:79) writes:

Recent calculations . . . suggest that the present maintenance of three billion humans in the biosphere requires a plant yield sufficient to accommodate 14.5 billion other consumers. These others, the animal populations, are an essential element in maintaining the humans by acting as intermediate processors for many plant products indigestible by man. Pigs, for example, consume as much food as 1,600 million people, when measured on a global scale; the world horse population has a protein intake corresponding to that of 650 million humans—almost the population of China.

In 1968 and 1969, there were reports of a "green revolution" in India, with such improved agricultural productivity that India expected to achieve self-sufficiency in food production within four years. This hope was based upon the introduction of new high-yield strains of rice and wheat, chemical fertilizers, and advanced irrigation techniques. It was reported that the 1968 wheat crop had topped India's previous record harvest by 35 percent, or by 4.3 million tons. Between 1967 and 1970 Pakistan increased its wheat harvest by over 70 percent. But the green revolution is vulnerable. It depends upon the free use of fertilizers, including petroleum-based chemical fertilizers, the prices of which went up sharply in 1974 at the time of the fuel crisis. Moreover, the new grains planted on a wide scale are susceptible to pests and rust and may require the development of pesticides which do not, at the same time, otherwise damage the environment. Water scarcity is another problem. So it remains to be seen whether this agricultural boom can be sustained and whether it will keep pace with the population increase. Similar booms have been reported for Pakistan, Sri Lanka, the Philippines, China, Turkey, and Mexico, but all these countries are also experiencing population explosions.

Birth control   India and some of the other less-developed countries have embarked on birth-control programs. By 1968, 4.2 million persons in India had been sterilized. Ninety percent of these sterilizations were vasectomies; the rest were tubectomies. By 1968, 2.4 million IUD "loops" (intrauterine devices) were in use, and about 100,000 women were taking contraceptive pills under medical supervision. Other methods of contraception were also being advanced by offices of family planning. It has been estimated that through these methods India has prevented the arrival of some 10 million to 15 million babies (Chandrasekhar 1968). The sterilization campaign was intensified in the year preceding Indira Gandhi's ouster in the elections of 1977; between April 1976 and January 1977, 7.8 million persons were sterilized. But it remains to be seen how this program will affect India's population increase in the long run. Most men in India who submit to sterilization already have a few children, at least one or two sons, and many of them have large families.

In any case, it seems likely that many other nations will have to engage in programs like India's if they hope to curb the population boom. Attitudes and values concerning optimum family size will undergo change. Conservative religious opposition to birth control, whether it be Hindu, Islamic, Christian, or whatever, will be challenged in different parts of the world as the numbers of people increase and reserves of food diminish.

Related to the problems of food resources and population increase is the fact that the world seems to be dividing into two unequal blocs: a poor, largely southern area (Latin America, Africa, Asia) and a better-off northern area (North America, Europe, the Soviet Union, and Japan). The disparity may be seen in the fact that in the 1970s, income per person in the United States was more than $4,000, and in India, less than $100. The rich-poor gap is widening, rather than narrowing, largely because of the poorer countries' population increase, which is double that of the richer group. The enormous energy consumption of the United States underlines the present gap in wealth: with 6 percent of the world's population, the United States uses one third of the world's energy and consumes between one fourth and one half of most minerals.

The poorer countries are also the nations with the lowest rates of literacy. Adult illiteracy occurs mainly in Asia, Africa, and Latin America. Despite a worldwide increase in education, there are more illiterate persons today than there were 20 years ago because of the growth in population. About two fifths of the world's adults cannot read and write. The countries with the least to spend on education are those with the highest birth rates (L. R. Brown 1972:116, 127).

The poorer countries are dependent on the richer ones for capital and technology, but the rich ones are dependent on the poor countries for essential minerals. The United States must import aluminum, manganese, nickel, tin, zinc, and chromium. Unfortunately, however, the rich countries tend to trade more with one another than with the poorer countries.

Poor and rich nations

In the course of evolution, human beings have considerably increased in body size from that of the prosimian stage of 50 million years ago. This increase may be seen as an indication of adaptive success. Such increases have occurred in different classes of animals in the course of evolution. But large size is not always adaptive; indeed it has sometimes presaged extinction. And increase in body size is reversible. Mammals, especially some of the larger forms, tended to decrease in size after the Pleistocene.

In recent years, especially since World War II, there is no doubt that an increase in stature has taken place in both Europe and the United States. In 1960, 13-year-old boys in Glasgow, Scotland, were found to be 4 inches taller than 13-year-olds had been 40 years before, and they weighed 14½ pounds more, while girls were 3¼ inches taller and weighed 16½ pounds more (Dubos 1965:78).

In the past 30 years Americans have been getting taller and taller. Children tend to be taller than their parents. This development has had all kinds of repercussions in the field of business. Shoe companies have been making more shoes of larger size. Hotels have been installing more longer-sized beds. Movie theaters have been installing wider seats to fit the broadening American posterior. This increasing size is probably due to improvements

Body size and environmental conditions

in nutrition—vitamin-enriched breads, cereals, and other foods. The mixing-up of populations attendant upon industrialization may also have led to genetic diversity and hybrid vigor, leading to taller stature. This suggestion was made by Harry L. Shapiro (1974:63–66), who notes that inbreeding, which was common in medieval European populations, tends to reduce stature, whereas population mixture and gene flow may lead to taller stature. The tendency to grow taller is not limited to Caucasoids, for since World War II, the same thing has been happening in Japan where, again, children are often taller than their parents. If this tendency persists, it may work a revolution in the architecture of the low-ceilinged Japanese home.

But the trend toward larger size will not be worldwide. In many parts of the world large size would be disadvantageous under present conditions. In the underdeveloped and overpopulated countries of Asia, people are often undernourished. Large body size with its demands for larger food intake would be an unfortunate development in these areas. The advent of economic prosperity in such regions, however, might well be accompanied by an increase in body size, like that now seen in the United States, Europe, and Japan. However, if worldwide population increase continues, it may ultimately be of selective advantage for our species to become smaller again, to reduce competition for the available food resources of our planet—unless, of course, scientists find the means to greatly increase those resources.

Rate of maturation

Another current change, concomitant with size increase, is that boys and girls now reach sexual maturity much earlier than they did a generation or two ago. In the United States the average age at *menarche,* or first menstruation, is now 12.9 years, with much individual variation. A generation ago the mothers of these girls began to menstruate a year or half a year later than their daughters do now. As in the case of height, better nutrition may be involved in this change, for girls of lower socioeconomic groups tend to mature later. The amount of hard work required in childhood may also be a factor. That is suggested by a study of height and age at menarche among girls in rural Poland. Farming girls, required to do more manual work, were found to begin menstruation later (a little over age 14) than girls of nonagricultural groups, who menstruated earliest, before age 14; while girls of a farmer-worker category were intermediate in that respect. The girls of the agricultural group were also a little shorter and lighter than those of the farmer-worker and nonagricultural groups (Laska-Mierze-jewska 1970).

A problem facing us today is that while individuals reach sexual maturity earlier, the educational process and the period of adolescent dependency are lengthening. There is something wrong with this situation, as the tension among so many adolescents in our society attests. Societies of the future will have to work out some solutions to these difficulties.

Longevity

What about longevity? Will people of the future live to be 100 or 200 years old? That seems possible in view of mankind's increasing knowledge about biology and medicine. Looking back at our evolutionary record, it seems that the human life span has increased over time. Based on a study of skeletal material it has been estimated that the average age at death for the australopithecines was 18.0 for *A. robustus* and 22.9 for *A. africanus.* During Paleolithic and Mesolithic times the average life span was around 30 years. As late as 1931 India had an average length of life of less than 27 years, but by 1900–1902 the United States already had an average life span of 61.5 years, and it is now more than 70 years. Thus environmental conditions clearly influence longevity.

One would expect, then, that at least some groups of *Homo sapiens* of the future will have a good chance for a longer life, especially considering the increased knowledge of medicine and biology. Permanent immunization against most diseases is now considered possible, and it is thought that the human life span could be lengthened by 50 years. Rejuvenation of the brain by injections of DNA is also contemplated (McHale 1969:109). Organ transplants are among the manifestations of increasing medical skill, and artificial organs may be developed in the future. Heart, kidney, spleen, pancreas, and duodenum have all been successfully transplanted. Organ and tissue banks, blood banks, have also been started. Artificial kidney machines are in use. Pacesetters operating on small mercury batteries have a wide distribution (McHale 1969:103–4). Lasers have been used in hundreds of operations to repair defects in the retina. Great advances have taken place in ear surgery to correct hearing loss, and electronic hearing aids have been greatly improved. Medical aid to embryos, as in cases of Rh-positive babies with Rh-negative mothers, is being rapidly advanced. All these relatively recent developments should add to human effectiveness and longevity, while some of the debilitating effects of old age will be simultaneously reduced.

There is a problem, however, in relation to world population increase. A longer life span will add to the general overcrowding of our planet.

Megalopolis

It has been estimated that by 1980 there may be between 55 million and 60 million *more* persons in metropolitan areas than there were in 1960. Population increase is apt to affect all the world's city populations.

Kahn and Wiener (1967:61–62) predict that the United States will have three giant megalopolitan areas in A.D. 2000, to which they give the picturesque names of Boswash, Chipitts, and Sansan. Boswash will extend from Boston to Washington and may contain almost one fourth of the U.S. population. Chipitts, concentrated around the Great Lakes, will stretch from Chicago to Pittsburgh and may extend north to Detroit, Toledo, Cleveland, Akron, Buffalo, and Rochester. Sansan would stretch initially from San Diego to Santa Barbara and ultimately from Santa Barbara to San Francisco. The three megalopolitan areas are expected to include about half the U.S. population in the year 2000. It is predicted that similar megalopolitan areas will develop in other parts of the world—in southeastern England, in the Tokyo-Osaka strip in Japan, and elsewhere.

The potentialities for further air and water pollution in such massed agglomerations are obviously immense, particularly if the present form of automobile continues to be used.

Energy
sources

The world now depends on energy from fossil fuels, supplies of which are finite, but within the next 50 years it will have to rely increasingly on alternate sources such as solar, wind, geothermal energy, and nuclear power. During the transition period there will probably be heavy dependence on coal and shale to supplement resources of oil and natural gas. The Energy Research and Development Administration projects that by the end of the century the percentage of our country's energy needs supplied by oil and gas will be down to 45–50 percent, although it is now about 75 percent.

Solar energy has been used to provide heat and hot water (with backup systems of electricity or gas for sunless periods) and could also be used to generate electricity, although the methods now devised would be expensive and require large tracts of land. In 1977 the federal government was spending just less than $300 million on solar energy; it might supply as much as one fourth of our energy needs in the next century.

Large modern windmills, strategically located, could be in operation by the 1980s, and ocean tides could be tapped for power. Geothermal energy, heat within the earth, may also be tapped through deep-drilling operations. Some pilot projects are underway to develop energy systems along new lines. A team from Oklahoma State University, under contract from the United Nations, will design an energy center for a village in Sri Lanka (Ceylon) which will make use of solar energy, wind power, and energy from agricultural wastes.

A few years ago optimistic expectations were expressed about the future uses of nuclear power. In a fact sheet issued by the Federal Energy Administration in 1975 it was estimated that atomic power would account for about 15 percent of demand by 1985 and between 30 and 40 percent by the year 2000. But since then more attention has been paid to the drawbacks, expenses, and dangers of radioactivity and the possibility of explosions, leakage, and sabotage in nuclear fission plants. Some hope, however, has been placed in the future development of nuclear fusion, in which these dangers would be much reduced.

Fuels require engines built of iron, copper, zinc, and other metals. Although copper is now abundant, it may be in short supply 200 years from now, and there may also be shortages of mercury, gold, silver, lead, and other metals (Skinner 1976). Even if recycling methods improve in the future, the rate of use of recycled metals will decline, requiring an increased dependence on iron and other abundant metals.

Much social unrest is expected to occur all over the world between now and the year 2000. One of the reasons for this will be unemployment. In the developing countries of the world, industrialization provides many new jobs, but, at the same time, the population, as we have seen, is increasing. There were three times as many unemployed in India in 1961 (9 million) as in 1951 (3 million). In 1965 there were 15 million totally unemployed. If the "underemployed" were counted, the figure would be much higher. College graduates in India are often unable to find jobs. It is not surprising that many turn to extremist left-wing or right-wing movements and sometimes engage in rioting. Political unrest and clashes between different linguistic and religious groups, such as Hindu and Muslim, may be expected to continue in the future.

Similar conditions exist in some of the more industrially advanced nations, where automation (to be discussed further below) adds to the ranks of the unemployed. In the United States mechanical farm equipment and factory automation have reduced opportunities for unskilled labor, leading to a cityward migration of southern blacks. During the last 60 years the rundown central areas of many American cities have become increasingly populated by Negroes from the south, while whites have been moving out to the suburbs, an exodus that has been more difficult for nonwhites. Between 1940 and 1950 the white population in America's largest cities increased 3.7 percent, while the Negro population rose 67.8 percent. (Grodzins 1970:293). Since much of this population is concentrated in the central areas, a kind of racial segregation has in effect come about, which raises problems concerning educational facilities and related issues.This is a potentially dangerous situation, especially since inflation and widespread unemployment have made the problems of urban blacks worse than ever.

Social unrest is widespread throughout the world: tribalism and nationalism in Africa, racial tensions in South Africa and Rhodesia, conflicts between regional and linguistic groups and between high and low castes in India, between political factions in China, between social classes in Latin America, and so forth. Moreover, judging from past experience, it seems likely that wars will continue to break out in different parts of the world during the next two decades.

Such hazards, of course, are not new, but relatively new are the enhanced potentialities of terrorism. The high level of the world's technology and the complex interdependence of our institutions make for great vulnerability to terrorist activity, including bombing, kidnapping, hijacking, and seizure of hostages. A small number of terrorists can wreak a great deal of damage in a short time, and since it is difficult to adequately forestall such assaults, we may expect to see more of them in the coming decades.

So far, our survey of possible future developments has drawn a bleak and depressing picture. When it comes to the advance of human knowledge and technology, the outlook seems more encouraging, although it is just this aspect of the future that alarms Jacques Ellul, as he has indicated in his *The Technological Society*. The problem, of course, is: How will people use the new knowledge at their disposal? Will a totalitarian superstate emerge to manipulate vast subservient populations, as in the nightmare worlds of Aldous Huxley and George Orwell? That is a possibility, but we need not assume it will happen.

Some scientists are quite confident about the future. Here is a statement by Emmanuel Mesthene, director of the Harvard Program in Science and Technology:

We have now, or know how to acquire, the technical capacity to do very nearly everything we want. Can we transplant human hearts, control personality, order the weather that suits us, travel to Mars or Venus? Of course we can, if not now or in five or ten years, then certainly in 25 or in 50 or 100 (quoted in Sullivan 1967).

The idea that anything is possible for science is expressed in what Arthur C. Clarke has called Clarke's Law:

If a distinguished but elderly scientist says that something is possible he is almost certainly correct. If he says something is impossible he is very probably wrong.

Clarke adds, "By elderly scientist I mean anyone over thirty" (Clarke 1968:247).

Twice in 1969 men were sent to the moon, landed safely, and returned to earth. These dramatic events made it seem that, indeed, scientists can accomplish anything they put their minds to. However, scientific projects like the moon landing require funding, and this has been made difficult recently by economic problems, the energy crisis, and inflation.

While astronauts have been exploring outer space, aquanauts have been probing the "inner space" of the world's oceans. Not only are the oceans rich in untapped plant and animal food resources but they are also rich in minerals, including manganese, cobalt, nickel, and copper. Special underwater vehicles, living quarters, and laboratories have been designed. The first manned undersea work station was established off Marseilles in 1962 by Jacques-Yves Cousteau; two men stayed underwater for a week at a depth of 33 feet, daily exploring outside to a depth of 85 feet. A later undersea work station was inhabited by six men for 30 days (McHale 1969:203). Four American scientists spent 60 days on the ocean floor in February–April of 1969.

Another remarkable scientific development has been the orbiting of a series of communications satellites, one over the Pacific Ocean, one over the Indian Ocean, and two over the Atlantic. These form a global communications link, making it possible to communicate between any two parts on earth through a single electronic system. The space shuttle is another new device, scheduled to start operations in 1979.

With these accomplishments on record, it is understandable that we are

Astronaut James B.
Irwin on the moon.

now trying to chart new pathways in space. The moon is seen by some as a prospective site for colonies equipped with strategic telescopes, a source for valuable minerals, and a sanitarium for earthly patients who will benefit from the weak lunar gravity. Adrian Berry (1974), who discusses these possibilities, goes on to visualize some more ambitious probes into the universe, such as to Venus, whose impossible "hellish" climate will, he believes (following a suggestion by Carl Sagan), undergo far-reaching man-made changes. Berry shrugs off cutbacks in space budgets as mere temporary deterrents in the exploration of space, for he is thinking in terms of thousands of years, not just decades or centuries.

Automation and computers

Although the word *automation* has come to refer to laborsaving machinery in general, it also has a more precise meaning, referring to machines with a feedback system, so they can control their own operations. If something goes wrong, the machine corrects itself, thus obviating the human attendant. A thermostat governing an oil burner provides an example of feedback; when temperature in the room reaches a predetermined level, the thermostat turns off the burner, but turns it back on again if the temperature drops below this level.

A computer is a self-regulating machine, which has been characterized as a complex, fast-operating sort of abacus. Computers regulate the sequences in automated machinery. They can provide an integrated data-processing system for businesses, replacing older, slower manual methods. Computers have enabled banks to dispense with manual operations and provide their customers with improved services. Information about patients in hospitals, tax data, and crime records may all be made available very quickly by computers. They are widely employed in scientific work and research. We could not have landed men on the moon without computers.

The computer industry is expected to multiply in the near future. According to a House of Commons Select Committee in 1971, it will be the world's third largest industry in the 1980s, after automobiles and oil (A. Berry 1974:144).

A combination of inventions involving computers, satellites, and other devices has made possible new systems of telecommunication which will make it as simple to communicate with Peking as to complete a local call. Scientists visualize two-way communication instead of the one-way television reception we have now, allowing for conversations and conferences among widely separated persons who will appear on one another's screens.

Education

If automation makes more leisure possible, more time could be given to education by young people. In 1971 half of the U.S. population was under 15 years of age, and 40 percent of those of college age were in college. Since then there has been some falling off in college enrollments, partly because of inflation, high tuition costs, and the end of the post-World War II "baby boom." The number of college-educated people in the United States remains impressive, however, especially when compared with conditions only 50 years ago. According to U.S. Bureau of the Census statistics, 50,000 students were enrolled in colleges and universities in 1871, or 0.3 percent of the American population. By 1930 the figure had climbed to 1,100,000, or 4.4 percent, and by 1971 to 8,090,000, or 10.1 percent (Lenski and Lenski 1974:405).

Education of the present generation prepares the groundwork for education of the next generation. Well-educated parents want their children to be well educated too. A child grows up with a better start for learning in such a setting. By itself, education is no panacea, but it does develop critical skills and judgment to some degree. The steady and rather remarkable increase in higher education is therefore a promising sign. We may hope for a more open-minded and better-educated generation, able to cope with the strange transformations of the world today. We depend upon these young men and women to help bring our world humanely and adventuresomely into the 21st century.

Summary

Population growth and the greatly increased urbanization of recent years raise the spectres of future famine, disease, and pollution. Solutions to these problems lie partly in increased scientific knowledge about food production and medicine. Government policies concerning health, agriculture, and birth control are also important means for coping with these issues.

The world seems to be dividing into two unequal blocs of rich and poor nations. The latter group has seen the greatest population increase and also has the lowest rates of literacy. In such a situation, wars and social unrest seem to be likely prospects for the rest of the 20th century. At the same time, there is much promise in the remarkable expansion of knowledge and the growth of higher education in the United States.

Herman Kahn and his associates have been the most persistent American futurologists, responsible for the following books: Herman Kahn and Anthony J. Wiener, eds., *The Year 2000: A Framework for Speculation on the Next Thirty-Three Years* (New York: Macmillan Co., 1967); Herman Kahn and B. Bruce-Briggs, *Things to Come: Thinking About the Seventies and Eighties* (New York: Macmillan Co., 1972); Herman Kahn, William Brown, and Leon Martel, *The Next Two Hundred Years: A Scenario for America and the World* (New York: William Morrow and Co., 1976). Kahn has been concerned with relatively short-range projections of the future. Stimulating for its more long-range forecasts is Adrian Berry, *The Next Ten Thousand Years: A Vision of Man's Future in the Universe* (New York: E. P. Dutton and Co., Inc. 1974). For a variety of viewpoints, see Alvin Toffler, ed., *The Futurists* (New York: Random House, 1972). On computers, robots, and cyborgs, see David M. Rorvik, *As Man Becomes Machine: The Evolution of the Cyborg* (New York: Doubleday & Co., 1971). See also: Stuart Chase, *The Most Probable World* (New York: Harper & Row, 1968); John McHale, *The Future of the Future* (New York: George Braziller, 1969); Victor C. Ferkiss, *Technological Man: The Myth and the Reality* (New York: George Braziller, 1969); Lester R. Brown, *World Without Borders* (New York: Random House, 1972).

Many of the foregoing works have an optimistic bias. For a less hopeful view, see Gordon Rattray Taylor, *How to Avoid the Future* (London: Secker and Warburg, 1975).

Suggestions for further reading

Peoples and tribes
Glossary
References cited
Illustrations
Index

PEOPLES AND TRIBES: IDENTIFICATION AND GEOGRAPHICAL LOCATIONS

A

Alorese. Agricultural people on the island of Alor in Indonesia, about halfway between Java and New Guinea

Anang. Bantoid-speaking horticultural people of southern Nigeria.

Andaman Islanders. Negrito hunting-gathering people in islands in the Bay of Bengal south of Burma.

Apa Tani. Advanced sedentary horticultural tribe inhabiting the Subansiri Valley in Arunachal Pradesh (formerly the Northeast Frontier Agency) in northeastern India.

Apache. Athapaskan-speaking hunting-gathering tribes of the American Southwest.

Arunta. Hunting-gathering tribe in central Australia.

Aymara. Large group of Indians, mostly peasants, in Boliva and Peru.

Aztecs. Dominant ruling tribe in the Valley of Mexico at the time of the Spanish conquest.

B

Balinese. Inhabitants of the island of Bali in Indonesia east of Java.

Berbers. Hamitic-speaking Caucasoid peoples of North Africa, most of whom are agriculturists.

Blackfoot. Algonkian-speaking Indians of Montana who were Plains Indian mounted hunters during the early 19th century.

Bondo. Highland people of Orissa in central east India who practice horticulture and agriculture.

Bororo. A sedentary horticultural tribe in Central Brazil.

Bushman. Short-statured hunting-gathering people of Kalahari Desert region of South Africa.

C

Chaga, or Chagga. Bantu-speaking agriculturalists who occupy the slopes of Mt. Kilimanjaro and Mt. Meru in Kenya, East Africa.

Cheyenne. An Algonkian-speaking tribe of the western Plains of North America.

Chippewa. See **Ojibwa Indians.**

Creek.   A confederacy of mostly Muskoghean-speaking Indians formerly inhabiting Alabama, Georgia, and Florida.

Crow.   A Siouan-speaking Plains tribe inhabiting the region between the Platte and Yellowstone Rivers.

D

Dafla.   Seminomadic pastoral and horticultural tribe in the Subansiri Valley of Arunachal Pradesh (formerly the Northeast Frontier Agency) in northeastern India.

Dahomey.   West African kingdom on the gulf of Guinea during the 19th century.

Dinka.   Tribe in the Nilotic Sudan which combines pastoralism and horticulture.

Dobu.   Melanesian tribe on an island near the Trobriand Islands.

E

Eskimo.   Hunting people scattered mainly along the coastal regions of Arctic North America from Alaska to Greenland.

F

Flathead Indians.   Tribe in Montana formerly having a Plains Indian culture.

G

Gusii.   A pastoral and agricultural Bantu-speaking tribe in Kenya, East Africa.

H

Hopi.   A sedentary Shoshonean-speaking agricultural Pueblo tribe in northeastern Arizona.

I

Iatmul.   A formerly head-hunting Melanesian tribe in the Sepik River region of New Guinea.

Ifugao.   A hill people in northern Luzon in the Philippines who cultivate rice on terraced hillsides.

Inca.   Ruling tribe in Peru and adjacent regions of South America at the time of the Spanish conquest.

Iroquois.   Confederacy of tribes in the region of present-day New York state who combined maize-growing with hunting and gathering in pre-Columbian and early contact times.

J

Jats.   Farming people in the region of Delhi in North India.

K

Kutchin.   Athapaskan-speaking tribe in the Yukon territory of Alaska.

Kwakiutl.   Northwest Coast American Indian hunting-gathering tribe on Vancouver Island and British Columbia which had permanent settlements due to relative abundance of food resources.

M

Mandan-Hidatsa.   The lumping together of two Siouan-speaking sedentary tribes located on the upper Missouri River.

Manus.   Trading and fishing people of the Admiralty Islands north of New Guinea, who before World War II lived in houses raised on stilts above the waters of a lagoon. They now live on the mainland.

Marquesans.   Polynesians of the Marquesas Islands.

Marri Baluch.   Pastoral tribe in Baluchistan in western Pakistan.

Maya. Advanced horticultural people of Mexico, Guatemala, and Honduras, who had one of the highest civilizations of the pre-Columbian New World.

Minangkabau. Matrilineal agricultural people in the high valleys in interior Sumatra in Indonesia, having both wet-rice and swidden cultivation.

Mundurucú. A horticultural tribe located east of the upper Tapajós River in Brazil.

Murngin. A hunting-gathering tribe in northeastern Arnhem Land in northern Australia.

N

Navaho. Athapaskan-speaking tribe in Arizona, New Mexico, and Utah, formerly hunting-gathering but now with a farming and pastoral basis of subsistence.

Nayar. A formerly martial caste located in Kerala on the Malabar coast of South India.

Nyakyusa. An agricultural Bantu-speaking tribe in Tanzania, East Africa.

O

Ojibwa Indians. Algonkian-speaking, formerly mainly hunting-gathering peoples located in the Great Lakes region of North America.

Omaha. A Siouan-speaking tribe now located in northeastern Nebraska.

Ona. Hunting-gathering tribe of Tierra del Fuego near the southernmost tip of South America.

P

Pilagá. A hunting-gathering, fishing, and horticultural tribe living near the Pilcomayo River in the Argentine Gran Chaco.

R

Rājpūts. A tribal group in North India which prides itself on its martial traditions.

S

Samoans. Polynesians of the Samoan Islands.

Shilluk. Pastoral-horticultural tribe of the Nilotic Sudan.

Sirionó. Nomadic hunting-gathering tribe of Bolivia

Siwai. Melanesian horticultural tribe.

Swazi. Bantu-speaking sedentary agricultural and pastoral tribe in South Africa.

T

Tikopia. Small island in western Polynesia whose inhabitants are dependent on horticulture and fishing.

Tiv. Mainly horticultural tribe of the Nigerian plateau in West Africa, having many domesticated animals.

Tlingit. Northwest Coast American Indian hunting-gathering tribe, whose northernmost representatives live on the coast of Alaska and who had permanent settlements due to relative abundance of food resources.

Toda. Pastoral tribe in the Nilgiri Hills of South India.

Trobriand Islanders. Horticultural and fishing Melanesian people of the Trobriand Islands off the southeast end of New Guinea, located mainly on the island of Kiriwina.

Trukese. Inhabitants of the island of Truk in Micronesia.

Tsembaga. A Maring-speaking horticultural tribe in the Australian-administered Territory of New Guinea.

Tswana. A Bantu-speaking tribe in Botswana, formerly Bechuanaland, South Africa.

U

Uganda. East African nation north of Lake Victoria, formerly a kingdom during the 19th century.

V

Vedda. Hunting-gathering tribe in Śri Lanka or Ceylon.

Y

Yako. Bantoid-speaking horticultural tribe in southern Nigeria.

Yokuts. Hunting-gathering tribe in San Joaquin Valley and adjacent regions of California in pre-Columbian times.

Z

Zulu. Bantu-speaking people in South Africa who developed a centralized political system under a king in the late 18th and early 19th centuries.

Zuñi. A sedentary agricultural Pueblo tribe in New Mexico.

GLOSSARY

A

Absolute dating.   Giving a date in terms of specific years.

Acculturation.   Phenomena involving culture change when two formerly distinct cultures come into contact with one another.

Acheulean.   Lower Paleolithic tool tradition containing hand axes, cleavers, and flakes produced by the Levallois technique.

Adolescence.   Period between puberty and adulthood.

Adze.   A cutting tool with the blade set at right angles to the handle.

Aegytopithecus zeuxis.   A fossil hominoid primate from the Egyptian Fayum dating from the Oligocene period.

Aerophone.   Air or wind musical instrument.

Affinal.   Related by marriage.

Age grade.   Members of a society who belong to a particular age bracket for which there is usually a separate term.

Age set.   A group of persons of the same sex and about the same age who advance from one age grade to another.

Agglutination.   Clumping of blood cells.

Agribusiness.   The organization along business lines of advanced, modern, large-scale agriculture.

Agriculture.   A system of food production that makes use of plow and draft animals (Old World) or fertilizing, terracing, irrigation, or use of *chinampas* (pre-Columbian New World).

Alleles.   Partner genes at the same locus on a pair of chromosomes.

Amphibians.   A class of cold-blooded vertebrates intermediate in some respects between fishes and reptiles.

Anemia.   A deficiency of red blood cells or hemoglobin.

Animatism.   Belief in impersonal supernatural power such as *mana*.

Animism. Belief in spiritual beings.

Anthropoidea. The suborder of Primates containing the higher primates, such as monkeys, apes, and human beings.

Antibody. A protein substance that attacks invading foreign proteins within the body.

Ape. Member of the family Pongidae within the superfamily Hominoidea, including chimpanzees, gorillas, orangutans, gibbons, and siamangs.

Apparatchiki. Full-time Communist Party functionaries in the Soviet Union.

Applied anthropology. A branch of anthropology concerned with directed culture change.

Arboreal. Tree-dwelling.

Archaeology. A main division of cultural anthropology that deals with past cultures through excavation and analysis of their remains.

Archaic tradition. North American Indian way of life dating from around 8000 B.C. depending on a broad-spectrum food exploitation, including the use of shellfish, hunting, and collecting.

Artifact. A worked or man-made object.

Assemblage. The material, including artifacts, found in an archaeological site.

Atlatl. See **Spear-thrower.**

Aurochs. Wild cattle ancestral to modern domesticated cattle.

Australopithecines. Hominids of the late Pliocene and early Pleistocene epochs with small cranial capacity and upright posture.

Australopithecus. A hominid genus of the late Pliocene and early Pleistocene epochs, divided by some authorities into two species: *africanus* and *robustus*.

Avunculocal residence. Residence of a married couple with or near the husband's male matrilineal kinsmen, particularly the mother's brother.

Azilian. A European Mesolithic culture.

B

Basic personality structure. The common aspects of personality shared by the members of a particular society.

Bâton de commandement. Name given to Upper Paleolithic objects of bone and horn that may have been used for straightening arrows or spears.

Bergmann's rule. An assertion that the smaller-sized races of a species are found in the warmer parts of its range, while the larger races are found in the cooler zones.

Bifurcate merging. A form of kinship system that merges father and father's brother, while distinguishing them from mother's brother, and that merges mother and mother's sister, while distinguishing them from father's sister. Related to this is a distinction between cross and parallel cousins, with the latter being equated with Ego's siblings.

Big-Game Hunting tradition. The first clearly distinguishable culture in the New World, associated with the hunting of bison, mastodon, camel, and horse.

Bilateral descent. Reckoning of kinship equally through both parents.

Bilocal residence. Either patrilocal or matrilocal residence for a married couple, with about equal frequency of each.

Bipedalism. Upright locomotion on two feet.

Blade. A sharp-edged flake with long, parallel sides, at least twice as long as they are wide. A characteristic stone tool of the Upper Paleolithic period in the Old World.

Blade core. A piece of flaked stone from which blades are struck off.

Blind analysis. The submission of materials such as the Rorschach Test, Thematic Apperception Test, or drawings to analysts who know nothing about the culture from which the materials were collected and who must make an analysis without access to other information.

Blood group. A classification of types of red blood cells, determined by their reactions to particular antibodies.

Bola. Round stone balls connected with cords, thrown to entangle an animal.

Boomerang. Australian throwing stick used in hunting.

B.P. Before the present.

Brachiation. A means of locomotion through trees by arm swinging from branch to branch, practiced especially by gibbons and siamangs.

Broad-spectrum food exploitation. The practice of exploiting a great range of different plant and animal food resources within a particular environment.

Bronze Age. A period of advanced civilization and urban life in parts of the Old World from around 3500 to 1500 B.C..

Burin. A chisel-like stone tool used in the Upper Paleolithic period for working bone, ivory, antler, and wood.

C

Calendrical rite. A ritual performed at a regular point in the yearly cycle.

Calibration. Rectification.

Canine fossa. A hollow in the cheekbones on either side of the nose in modern humans.

Carbon-14. See **Radioactive carbon dating.**

Cargo cult of Melanesia. Magico-religious movement in which predictions are made about the future advent of ships or planes bringing cargo to the Melanesians.

Carnivorous. Meat-eating.

Caste. An endogamous, hierarchically ranked social group that is sometimes associated with a particular occupation.

Catarrhine. Old World anthropoid, having a dental formula that includes only two premolars in each jaw on either side, as opposed to the platyrrhine New World monkeys which have three premolars in each jaw on either side.

Caucasoid. A term for the "white" race.

Ceboidea. The Primate superfamily containing the New World monkeys.

Ceropithecoidea. The Primate superfamily containing the Old World monkeys.

Chinampa. A man-made islet, anchored by willow trees, constructed by pre-Columbian Aztecs of Mexico to support topsoil for growing crops.

Chopper.   Earliest type of stone tool, with a jagged cutting edge formed by striking off a few flakes.

Chromosome.   A structure in the nucleus of a cell containing the genes.

Churinga.   Wooden or stone slab carved with totemic designs by male Australian aborigines, regarded as a sacred object not to be seen by women or children.

Civilization.   Advanced form of culture associated with agriculture, metallurgy, division of labor, class stratification, formation of a state, and city life.

Clan.   A unilineal descent group whose members believe they are related to one another through descent from a common ancestor or ancestress.

Class.   A division of social stratification determined by economic factors and relationship to strategic resources.

"Classical" Neanderthal.   A type of Neanderthal having a thick skull, heavy brow ridges, low elevation of the skull, and not much of a chin.

Classificatory system.   A form of kinship system in which merging is often employed, so that terms such as father, mother, brother, sister, son, and daughter are extended to persons who are not lineal kinsmen.

Cline.   A gradient in the frequency of a biological trait over a geographical range.

Codex (plural, **codices**).   An ancient manuscript. The codices of pre-Columbian Mesoamerica were made of folded strips of beaten bark paper.

Cognate words.   Words that have both semantic and phonemic correspondence in two or more related languages.

Cognition.   The process of knowing.

Cognitive anthropology.   A branch of anthropology, more particularly of anthropological linguistics, that is concerned with the ways in which the speakers of particular languages classify and conceptualize phenomena. Sometimes known as ethnoscience.

Collateral relative.   A relative related indirectly through a linking relative.

Communal cult.   A collective religious performance, not requiring a magico-religious specialist.

Comparative method.   The method used by 19th-century cultural evolutionists to reconstruct stages of cultural evolution on the basis of ethnographic descriptions of different cultures ranging from those of hunting-gathering societies to advanced civilizations.

Competence.   In linguistics, refers to an individual's grasp of the principles underlying his or her language; knowledge of the rules needed to speak it.

Competitive exclusion principle.   The proposition that two species with similar food habits cannot long occupy the same ecological niche.

Composite tool.   A tool consisting of different parts and made with different materials.

Conflict resolution.   The process of finding a settlement between parties in a dispute.

Consanguine.   Related through descent.

Cordophone.   Stringed musical instrument.

Core tool.   A flaked stone tool making use of the original core of stone from which flakes have been struck.

Corvée labor. Forced unpaid labor exacted by the state.

Coup de poing. See **Hand axe.**

Court. An assembly for the transaction of judicial business.

Couvade. The practice of a husband resting up and observing taboos after his wife has given birth.

Cranial capacity. The volume of the cranial vault, which gives an idea of brain size. Measured in cubic centimeters.

Cross cousins. Children of siblings of opposite sex.

Cross-cultural survey. A comparison of data from a group of societies, such as those described in the Human Relations Area Files, for the purpose of finding correlations between particular institutions and practices.

Cultural anthropology. With physical anthropology, one of the two main divisions of anthropology; it includes the fields of linguistics, ethnology, and archaeology, all of which have to do with the study of human cultures.

Cultural diffusion. The spreading of a culture trait from one society to another.

Cultural ecology. The study of human sociocultural adaptation to our environments.

Cultural evolution. The development of culture through progessively more complex stages, with increases in the energy available to humans.

Cultural integration. The tendency of a culture to reconcile or overcome internal conflicts or inconsistencies.

Cultural relativism. The idea that a practice or institution must be understood in the context of its culture, thus tending to an abstention from critical value judgments.

Culture. The shared behavior learned by members of a society, the way of life of a group of people. (For other definitions, see pages 1–2.)

D

Datum point. A fixed point established at an archaeological site as a reference point for excavations.

Deep structure. In linguistics, the underlying meaning of an utterance.

Dendrochonology. An absolute dating technique involving the analysis of annual growth layers or rings of trees in a particular area.

Descriptive linguistics. A branch of linguistics concerned with the analysis of a language as a synchronic system, its phonemes, morphemes, and rules of syntax. Also called structural linguistics.

Descriptive system. As opposed to classificatory system, a kinship system in which merging is not employed and in which terms such as father, mother, brother, sister, son, and daughter are not extended to other relatives.

Determinative. A marker or sign used to clarify ambiguities in an ideographic system of writing.

Diachronic study. A study (of a culture or language) involving the time dimension.

Diastema. A gap in a tooth series for admission of the canine tooth from the other jaw.

Diffusion.   See **Cultural diffusion.**

Digging stick.   An implement used by food gatherers to dig up roots and tubers; the main tool used in simple horticulture for making a hole in the ground to deposit seeds.

Diurnal.   Active during the daytime, in contrast to nocturnal.

DNA.   Deoxyribonucleic acid, made of sugar-phosphate chains, capable of self-replication.

Dominant.   Referring to an allele that is expressed phylogenetically even if the alleles are heterozygous.

Double descent.   A kinship system in which a person belongs to both the father's parilineal group and the mother's matrilineal group.

Dryopithecines.   Apes of the Miocene epoch dating from around 15 million years ago.

Dryopithecus.   Genus of Miocene apes.

Dryopithecus (or Y-5) pattern.   A tooth pattern having five cusps with a Y-shaped groove running between them, found in the lower molars of dryopithecine apes and modern chimpanzees, gorillas, and humans.

E

Ecclesiastical cult institution.   A religious organization involving a priesthood.

Ecological niche.   The particular environment to which a population adjusts itself.

Ecology.   The study of the interrelationship of organisms and their environment, including both the physical environment and other living organisms.

Ego.   In kinship diagrams, the person from whom relationships are reckoned.

Emic.   Referring to interpretations in terms of distinctions made by the members of a particular society under investigation.

Endogamy.   The requirement to marry within a particular group.

Eocene epoch.   A geological period between approximately 58 and 35 million years ago.

Epicanthic fold.   A fold of skin covering the lower margin of the eye near the nose, often found in Mongoloids.

Ethnocentrism.   The tendency to negatively evaluate other ways of life in terms of one's own culture.

Ethnography.   *a.* A detailed written description of a particular culture.
                        b. The general body of such literature.

Ethnology.   A main division of cultural anthropology which deals with the study of living cultures.

Ethnoscience.   See **Cognitive anthropology.**

Etic.   Referring to interpretations in terms of distinctions made by a community of outside observers, not in terms of distinctions made by members of the society under investigation.

Eutherian mammals.   Mammals that have a placenta for nourishment of the embryo during the intrauterine period.

Evolution. The development of more complex forms of life from simpler forms. Descent with modification.

Exogamy. The requirement to marry outside of a particular group.

F

Family. In biology: a classification more inclusive than a genus and less inclusive than an order. Sociologically: a social group whose members usually live together and engage in economic cooperation, normally including two or more adults of both sexes responsible for rearing and educating the children born or adopted into the group.

Femur. Thighbone.

Fetish. In religion, an object considered sacred because it is believed to be inhabited by or associated with a spirit. To be contrasted with an amulet, an object considered sacred because it is believed to contain some inherent power.

Fetus. The developing organism within the maternal uterus, especially after attaining the basic structural plan of the species, from the second or third month after conception until birth.

Feudalism. A method of government involving relationships between a lord and vassals, which usually include military service.

Fictive kinship. The incorporation of an outsider into a kin network.

Flake tool. A tool made from a flake struck from a core of stone.

Folklore. Defined in narrow terms: oral literature, consisting of stories, myths, folktales, legends, riddles, and proverbs. Defined in broader terms, it also includes costume, dance, games, and other aspects of culture.

Folk society. A term used by Robert Redfield for homogeneous tribal and peasant societies having close face-to-face relations, with kinship and religious practices playing important roles.

Folktale. An oral narrative dealing with the adventures of a hero or trickster.

Folk-urban continuum. Robert Redfield's bipolar contrast of large, heterogeneous modern city and small, face-to-face homogeneous folk society, with intermediate communities ranged in between.

Folsom point. A fluted stone projectile point made by big-game hunters in North America around 10,000 B.C.

Foramen magnum. A hole in the base of the skull through which the spinal cord connects with the brain.

Formalism. In anthropological economics, a view that economic theory, using such concepts as "maximizing" and "economizing" can be applied to the study of primitive or non-Western economic systems.

Fossil. The remains of an ancient form of life, often mineralized.

Founder effect. The establishment of a new breeding population by a small group which is unrepresentative of its parental stock in genetic features.

Fraternal polyandry. A form of marriage in which a woman is married to two or more men who are brothers.

Functionalism. A school of thought or approach in anthropology that attempts to determine the functions fulfilled by the institutions of a society under investigation.

G

Gene. A unit of heredity, in a particular position on a chromosome.

Gene flow. The exchange of genes between populations.

Gene frequency. Relative incidence of an allele in a population.

Gene pool. The sum total of the genes in a breeding population.

Generative grammar. See **Transformational grammar.**

Genetic drift. Changes in allele frequency through isolation of a group from its larger population.

Genetics. The study of biological heredity and variation.

Genotype. The genetic makeup of an organism, the complete set of genes inherited from parents.

Genus. A classification within and less inclusive than a family, more inclusive than a species. Human beings belong to the genus *Homo* and to the species *sapiens.*

Geographical determinism. The notion that geographical environment is a prime determinant of the characteristics of a culture.

Geology. The study of the earth and its changes over time through the analysis of its different layers and their fossil contents.

Gloger's rule. Races of birds and mammals living in warm, humid regions have more melanin pigmentation than races living in cooler, drier regions.

Go-between. An intermediary in a dispute.

Grammar. The body of rules that governs the arrangement of words and morphemes in a language.

Great man theory. The idea that changes in culture are due to the inventions and new ideas of exceptional men.

Grooming. The practice among primates of combing through fur with hands and teeth.

Group marriage. A form of marriage in which more than one man are married to more than one woman.

H

Hand axe. A pear-shaped unshafted stone core tool widely used in the Lower Paleolithic period.

Heterodont. Having different kinds of teeth for different functions, as among mammals, in contrast to the homodont tooth pattern of reptiles.

Heterosis. See **Hybrid vigor.**

Heterozygous. Having alleles of different types.

Hieroglyphic. A form of writing in which ideograms are combined with phonetic elements.

Historical linguistics. The diachronic study of languages over time.

Hominid. A member of the family Hominidae, or used as an adjective referring to that family.

Hominidae. The family that includes human beings and their precursors, such as *Homo erectus* and the australopithecines.

Hominoid. A member of the superfamily of Hominoidea, or used as an adjective referring to that superfamily.

Hominoidea. The Primate superfamily that includes both apes and human beings.

Homo africanus. Term used by John T. Robinson for *Australopithecus africanus.*

Homodont. Having teeth of the same type, as among reptiles, in contrast to the heterodont tooth pattern of mammals.

Homo erectus. A form of hominid that lived between 1 million and 300,000 years ago, represented by such examples as Java man and Peking man.

Homo sapiens (sapiens). Modern human.

Homozygous. Having alleles of the same type.

Horticulture. A system of food production lacking the use of plow and draft animals and utilizing a simple technology, principally a digging stick.

Human ecology. The study of human adaptation to environment.

Human Relations Area Files (HRAF). An extensive file of ethnographic data.

Hunting-gathering. A means of subsistence without horticulture or agriculture, dependent upon the collecting of plants, nuts, and fruits and the hunting of animals.

Hybridization. See **Gene flow.**

Hybrid vigor, or **heterosis.** A condition of Darwinian fitness manifest by a plant or animal, resulting from the cross-breeding of distinct varieties, in which the organism proves to be superior to either parental strain.

Hydraulic society. An advanced agricultural society making use of irrigation and tending to have a high degree of political centralization.

I

Ideogram. An individual symbol in an ideographic system of writing.

Ideographic writing system. A form of writing in which the symbols or ideograms may stand for various concepts.

Idiographic approach. An ethnographic approach that aims at a thorough and objective documentation of a culture in all its unique features without involving a search for general principles or laws.

Idiophone. A musical instrument that produces sounds through vibrations, such as rattles, gongs, and bells.

Immediate constituent (IC). In linguistics, a subdivision of an utterance.

Incest taboos. Taboos on sexual relations between members of a designated kin group, such as a nuclear family.

Independent invention. The discovery of the same invention by two or more different persons or in two or more different cultures.

Individualistic cult institution. A solitary ritual performed by someone who is not a religious specialist.

Indo-European languages. A family of languages found in most of Europe and parts of the Middle East and South Asia.

Industrial Revolution. The development of the factory system and associated phenomena that began in England in the 18th century.

Industrial society. A society making use of a factory system and a money economy.

Industry. In archaeology, the artifacts of a particular kind made by the same people at the same time, found at an archaeological site.

Initiation ceremony. A rite of passage to signal a change of status in the initiated person, such as the transition from childhood to a more adult status in puberty ceremonies.

Inner direction. David Riesman's term for a mode of conformity associated with a period of population growth, opening frontiers, and expanding economic opportunities, involving an emphasis on hard work, discipline, and achievement.

Insectivorous. Insect-eating.

Interglacial. A period between glaciations.

Ischial callosities. Calloused areas on the buttocks of Old World monkeys and some apes.

Isolating mechanism. Any circumstance that prevents reproduction or an exchange of genes.

J

Jajmani system. A system by which members of different castes in rural villages in India exchange goods and services with little exchange of money.

K

Kamin. A person who performs services for a client in the jajmani system.

Katcina, or **kachina.** Among the Hopi and Zuñi, ancestors and rain gods enacted by masked men in rituals.

Kindred. A person's bilateral relatives on both the maternal and paternal sides.

Kingdom. In biology, the primary division of living forms into animals and plants.

Kinship. The classification of persons on the basis of relationship through descent or marriage.

Kitchen midden. A refuse heap, often consisting largely of shells.

Kiva. An underground chamber where rituals are performed among the Hopi and Zuñi.

Knuckle-walking. Means of locomotion in gorillas and chimpanzees in which the long arms bear the weight of the animal in quadrupedal locomotion.

Kula ring. An intertribal cycle of ceremonial exchanges among the Trobriand Islanders and their neighbors in Melanesia.

Kuru. A degenerative disease affecting the nervous system carried by a latent virus among the Fore of New Guinea. It was probably spread by cannibalism involving the consumption of brains infected by the virus.

L

Law. A body of social norms in a society, which its members must abide by and which may be enforced by an agency recognized as having political authority in that society.

Leister. A trident-shaped spear with a point flanked by two prongs, used for spearing fish in the Upper Paleolithic period in Europe.

Levallois technique. A way of making flake tools by first trimming and preparing the core from which they are detached.

Levirate. A custom whereby, when a man dies, his widow is expected to marry a brother of the deceased.

Lineage. A unilineal descent group whose members believe they are related to one another through descent from a common ancestor or ancestress and who are able to trace their descent to known forebears.

Lineal kin. Persons related in a single line, as grandfather-father-son.

Linguistics. The study of languages.

Living floor. Area of former human activity at an archaeological site.

Locus. The position of a gene on a chromosome.

Loess. Wind-blown dust from glaciers.

Lost-wax process (or cire perdu method). Method of casting metal objects in molds shaped of wax, coated with clay.

Lumbar curve. Curve in the lumbar region of the spine, characteristic of human beings but not of apes.

M

Magic. The use of rituals to direct and control supernatural forces.

Maglemosian. A coastal culture in northern Europe during the Mesolithic period.

Mammals. A class of warm-blooded vertebrates to which human beings belong.

Mana. Melanesian and Polynesian concept of impersonal supernatural power.

Mandible. The lower jaw.

Market. A place where goods are regularly bought and sold.

Marriage. A socially recognized union of husband and wife.

Matrilineal descent. The tracing of descent in the female line, from mother through daughter.

Matrilocal residence. Residence of a married couple with or near the wife's female matrilineal kin.

Medicine man. See **Shaman.**

Meganthropus palaeojavanicus. A hominid, possibly australopithecine, from Java, dated at nearly 2 million years ago.

Melanin. Pigmentation in the skin of human beings.

Membranophone. Skin musical instrument, such as a drum.

Meoisis. The cell-division process of reproductive cells.

Merging. The practice of using the same kinship terms for lineal and collateral relatives.

Mesoamerica. The area between northern Mexico and Costa Rica.

Mesolithic. The period between the Paleolithic and Neolithic dated in Europe between 11,000 and 5000 B.C.

Mesopotamia. The area of the Tigris and Euphrates Rivers, extending from the mountains of Asia Minor to the Persian Gulf.

Metallurgy.   The technology and process of making metal objects.

Microlith.   A small stone tool made from a blade which has been snapped into fragments, including arrowheads and scraping, cutting, and boring tools, often hafted to handles of bone or antler.

Miocene epoch.   A geological period between approximately 23.5 million and 5 million years ago.

Mitosis.   The process of division in cells other than reproductive cells.

Moiety.   One half of a dual division of a society divided into two exogamous groups.

Mongoloid.   Racial classification including Chinese, Japanese, and American Indians, peoples grouped around the Pacific Ocean.

Monkey.   A member of the suborder Anthropoidea, or higher primates, distinguished from the apes and humans and divided into two subfamilies, one of Old World and one of New World monkeys.

Monogamy.   A form of marriage in which one man is married to one woman.

Monotheism.   Belief in a single God or supreme being.

Morpheme.   A unit of meaning in a language, the smallest unit that is grammatically significant.

Mousterian.   A Middle Paleolithic industry associated with Neanderthals.

Multilinear evolution.   A school of ethnology associated with Julian H. Steward, which is concerned with the analysis of cross-cultural regularities in culture change.

Mutation.   A change in the structure or the chemistry of a gene.

Myth.   A sacred story that is believed to be true in the society in which it is told.

N

Natufian.   Mesolithic culture in Israel.

Natural selection.   A process of selection that takes place in nature without anyone's intentional control (as opposed to artificial selection by breeders); the mechanism of evolution suggested by Darwin whereby organisms with adaptive advantages tend to survive and reproduce their kind more successfully than those that lack such adaptations.

Neanderthal.   A late Pleistocene type of *Homo sapiens* that preceded modern humans.

Negrito.   Short-statured Negroid peoples, such as the Andaman Islanders and the Semang of the Malay Peninsula.

Negroid.   Racial grouping of dark-skinned African and Melanesian peoples.

Neo-evolutionism.   A school of ethnology that, while admitting the weaknesses in the works of Tylor and Morgan, reaffirms the importance of studying the evolution of human culture.

Neolithic.   The New Stone Age period in which plants and animals were domesticated in the Old World, dated between around 8000 and 3500 B.C in the Near East.

Neolocal residence.   The practice of a married couple to set up a separate residence, living with neither the husband's nor the wife's parents.

New archaeology. An approach in modern archaeology that emphasizes the study of process and culture change, associated with Lewis R. Binford, Kent V. Flannery, and others.

Nocturnal. Active at night, as opposed to diurnal.

Nomadism. Movement from place to place without fixed residence.

Nomothetic approach. An approach in ethnology that seeks to establish general laws or regularities.

Nucleus. The central part of a cell containing the chromosomes.

Numaym. A named landholding kinship group among the Kwakiutl Indians.

O

Obsidian. Volcanic glass.

Ocher, or **ochre.** An earthy iron ore, usually red or yellow, used as a pigment and often found in prehistoric graves both in the Old World (as in the Upper Paleolithic) and in the New.

Oldowan tool. See **Chopper.**

Olfactory. Referring to the sense of smell.

Oligocene epoch. A geological period between approximately 23.5 million and 35 million years ago.

Oligopithecus. An Oligocene primate found in the Fayum, Egypt.

Olympian ecclesiastical cult. A religious cult involving a priesthood that worships a pantheon of gods.

Omnivorous. Eating a diversified, unspecialized diet.

Onager. A wild ass, domesticated by the Sumerians in the Bronze Age.

Opposable thumb. A thumb that can touch the other digits of the hand.

Oral literature. See **Folklore.**

Order. A classification less inclusive than a class and more inclusive than a family. Human beings belong to the order of Primates in the class of mammals.

Osteology. The study of bones.

Other direction. David Riesman's term for a mode of ensuring conformity in a modern industrial society in which there is an emphasis on sensitivity to the needs and feelings of others.

P

Paleocene. A geological period dating between approximately 65 million and 58 million years ago.

Paleolithic. The Old Stone Age, dating from the first use of tools to around 11,000 B.C. in Europe.

Paleontology. The study of the forms of life of past geological periods from their fossil remains.

Paradigmatic approach. In folklore, an analytic approach involving a search for significant patterns.

Parallel cousins. Children of siblings of the same sex.

Participant observation. A method of ethnological fieldwork that involves participation in community activities and informal conversations with its members.

Passage grave. A collective megalithic burial chamber characteristic of Europe from Mesolithic to Bronze Age times.

Pastoralism. A means of subsistence relying heavily on domesticated herding animals.

Peasants. Agriculturalists who are connected with a state or city life but who mainly engage in subsistence farming on a family basis and do not hire labor or specialize in cash crops.

Pelvis. The hip bones and sacrum.

Pemmican. Dried meat used by North American Indians, made of pounded dried meat mixed with melted tallow and sometimes seasoned with berries.

Peppercorn hair. Hair clustered in clumps on the skull, as among the Bushmen of South Africa.

Performance. In linguistics, actual speech.

Phenotype. The observable appearance of an organism.

Philtrum. A median groove in the upper lip in human beings.

Phoneme. A minimal significant sound unit in a language which serves to distinguish one word or syllable from another for the speakers of that language.

Phonetics. The study and classification by linguists of the different sounds made in speech utterances.

Phratry. A group of two or more closely associated clans which may become an exogamous unit.

Phylum. A major subdivision of a kingdom, more inclusive than a class.

Physical anthropology. A field that deals with humans as physical organisms and with human evolution and variation; with cultural anthropology, one of the two main divisions of anthropology.

Pictographic writing. The earliest kind of writing system, consisting of pictures that stand for concepts.

Pithecanthropus erectus. The designation given by Eugène Dubois to the first find of *Homo erectus* remains, discovered in Java in 1891.

Placenta. An organ in the maternal uterus from which embryos of eutherian mammals get nourishment and oxygen.

Pleistocene epoch. A geological period between approximately 1.8 million and 10,000 years ago.

Pliocene epoch. A geological period between approximately 5 million and 1.8 million years ago.

Political organization. The aspects of social organization related to the management of public policy.

Pollen analysis. Analysis of pollen from an archaeological site to reconstruct ecological conditions of that time.

Polyandry. A form of marriage in which one woman is married to more than one man.

Polygamy. A general term for plural marriage, including both polyandry and polygyny.

Polygyny. A form of marriage in which one man is married to more than one woman.

Polytheism. A belief in many gods.

Pongids. Apes, members of the family Pongidae within the superfamily Hominoidea, including the chimpanzee, gorilla, orangutan, gibbon, and siamang.

Population genetics. A branch of genetics concerned with calculating the gene frequencies of breeding populations.

Possession. A belief that a spirit may temporarily occupy a person's body.

Postpartum sex taboo. Abstention from sexual relations by a husband and wife for a year or two after childbirth.

Potassium-argon dating. A dating technique for determining the age of rocks in volcanic areas from the ratio of radioactive potassium to argon.

Potlatch. A feast among the Indians of the Northwest Coast of North America at which gifts were distributed.

Predator. An animal that lives by eating other animals.

Prehensile. Grasping. A characteristic of the primate hand and foot. Some South American monkeys have prehensile tails.

Prehistory. The period before the advent of writing systems.

Priest. A religious specialist who performs rituals and who is elected or appointed to office within a cult organization, in contrast to the more individualistic shamans, who are believed to communicate directly with the supernatural world through their own abilities.

Primate city. A city that dominates its surrounding area and is much larger than the other urban centers in the nation.

Primates. The order of mammals that includes lemurs, tarsiers, monkeys, apes, and human beings.

Prognathism. Forward protrusion of the facial region and jaws.

Projection. Apperceptive distortion, in which inner concepts are attributed to the outer world.

Pronograde. Locomotion on all fours, with trunk in horizontal position.

Propliopithecus. A hominoid fossil of the Oligocene epoch in the Fayum, Egypt.

Prosimian. A member of the suborder Prosimii, containing the lower primates.

Protestant ethic. A set of attitudes and values that emphasizes the virtues of asceticism, hard work, and responsibility, advocated in the teachings of the Protestant Reformation.

Psychic unity of mankind. The assumption that all human beings, regardless of race or level of cultural development, share the same mental attributes and capacities.

Pueblo Indians. American Indians of the southwestern United States, including the Hopi and Zuñi among others, who raise crops and live in communities with houses made of adobe mud, wood, and stone.

Q

Quadrupedal. Locomotion on all fours.

Quern. A milling stone for grinding grain.

Quipu. A collection of knotted strings used by the Inca of Peru for keeping records. .

R

Race. A human population whose members have in common some hereditary biological characteristics that distinguish them from others.

Racism. The explanation of a people's behavior in terms of genetic endowment, usually associated with a belief in the innate superiority and inferiority of particular groups.

Radioactive carbon dating. A dating technique to determine the approximate age of organic material from the amount of carbon-14 (C^{14}) it contains.

Ramapithecine. A member of the genus *Ramapithecus.*

Ramapithecus. A possible hominid, or a hominoid having hominid-like dental features, dated between 8 and 14 million years ago.

Ramus. Ascending portion of the lower jaw.

Random mating. Mating resulting purely from chance without any bias due to selection.

Recessive. Referring to a gene that is not expressed phenotypically, except when the alleles are homozygous.

Reciprocity. The giving of goods or services with an expectation of a roughly equivalent return.

Redistribution. A system of economic exchange in which goods are funneled to a central place of storage and then distributed by some central administrative authority.

Relative dating. A form of dating that does not give an absolute date but establishes a chronological sequence in placing some items later or earlier than others.

Religion. Beliefs and practices related to the supernatural world.

Rorschach Test. A projective personality test in which the subjects are asked to give responses about what they see in a series of ten standardized ink blots.

S

Sacrum. Group of fused vertebrae at the bottom of the vertebral column that joins with the pelvis to form the pelvic girdle in human beings.

Sagittal crest. Crest on top of the skull from front to back for the attachment of muscles that move the jaw; found in male gorillas and chimpanzees.

Sanction. A reaction by members of a society to show approval or disapproval of certain behavior as a way of bringing about conformity in social norms.

Savanna. A tropical or subtropical grassland zone, between forests and deserts, containing scattered trees.

Secret society. A voluntary association whose membership is secret.

Sedentism. Pattern of settled residence.

Semantic. Related to meaning in a language.

Semantic domain. A class of objects that share some characteristic feature or features which differentiate them from other domains.

Sexual dimorphism. Contrasts in size and strength between males and females.

Shaman, or medicine man. A magico-religious specialist who acts as an intermediary between the members of his society and the supernatural world on the basis of self-acquired powers, in contrast to a priest, who is an appointed member of a cult organization.

Sibling. General term for brother or sister without specifying sex.

Sickle-cell anemia, or **sicklemia.** A form of anemia caused by inheritance of the sickling gene.

Simian shelf. A bar of bone that binds together the lower jawbones of apes.

Slash-and-burn horticulture. See **Swidden cultivation.**

Social anthropology. A branch of anthropology concerned with analyzing networks of social relations.

Social stratification. Social organization involving hierarchical distinctions of caste or class.

Society. A more or less organized group of people of both sexes who share a common culture.

Sororal polygyny. A form of marriage in which a man is married to two or more women who are sisters.

Sororate. The custom whereby, when a woman dies, her husband is expected to marry one of her sisters.

Spear-thrower. A grooved board used for propelling a spear; an invention that appeared in the Upper Paleolithic period in the Old World.

Species. An interbreeding population of organisms reproductively isolated from other such groups.

Steatopygia. Enlargement of buttocks with fat deposits, sometimes found among Bushman women in South Africa.

Stela. Sculptured stone slab or column, such as those found in Maya areas.

Stereoscopic vision. Depth perception made possible by having both eyes on the frontal plane with an overlapping field of vision.

Structural anthropology. A school of ethnology, of which Claude Lévi-Strauss is the leading exponent, that seeks to uncover the "mental structures" which are believed to underlie human behavior.

Structural-functionalism. A functional approach in social anthropology that is concerned with how social structures are maintained.

Structural linguistics. See **Descriptive linguistics.**

Substantivism. In anthropological economics, the view that economic theory, using such concepts as "maximization" and "economizing," cannot be meaningfully applied to the study of primitive or non-Western economic systems.

Superposition, law of. In geology, the lower strata of earth are generally older than those above them.

Surface structure. In linguistics, the organization of spoken utterances, which may be analyzed through the method of immediate constituents, in contrast to the underlying deep structure.

Swidden cultivation, or **slash-and-burn horticulture.** A method of food production that involves clearing a patch of land by burning, planting crops, and tending them until the fertility of the soil begins to be exhausted; the land is then allowed to lie fallow.

Synchronic study. The study (of a language or culture) at one time period.

Syncretism. A blending of two or more different forms, as in religion or musical styles.

Syntagmatic approach. A structural approach in folklore that analyzes the linear sequence of episodes.

Syntax. The branch of grammar concerned with the order in which morphemes are arranged and sentences constructed.

T

Taurodontism. Enlargement of the pulp cavities in molar and premolar teeth.

Teknonymy. The custom of naming a parent after his or her child such as "Father (or Mother) of So-and-So."

Terrestrial. Ground-dwelling.

Territoriality. An organism's practice of defending a particular stretch of territory.

Thalassemia. A form of anemia caused by hereditary genetic factors.

Thematic Apperception Test. A projective personality test in which the subject is asked to tell stories in response to a series of standardized pictures.

Throwing board. See **Spear-thrower.**

Totemism. A set of beliefs concerning the relationship of clan members to the totemic animal from which the clan gets its name and from which the members are often believed to be descended. In some cases this may involve a taboo on eating the flesh of the totem animal.

Transformational grammar. A way of analyzing grammar developed by Noam Chomsky and his followers that makes a distinction between deep structures and surface structures.

Trans-Pacific diffusion. The notion that some American Indian culture patterns, including some art motifs, reached the New World by diffusion across the Pacific in pre-Columbian times.

U

Uniformitarianism. The doctrine that the same natural agencies that help shape the earth today, such as wind, water, heating, cooling, erosion, and so forth, have always done so in the past.

Unilineal descent. The tracing of descent in a single line, either through males or through females.

Unilinear evolution. The conception of cultural evolution held by 19th-century writers involving human progression through the stages of savagery, barbarism, and civilization.

Universal aspects of culture. Aspects of culture found in all known societies but not necessarily among all individuals.

Universal evolution. The view of the general evolution of culture held by Leslie A. White.

Universal grammar. Features of grammar that Noam Chomsky believes to be characteristic of all languages.

Untouchability. The belief that it is polluting for persons of higher caste to be touched by low-caste persons.

Uxorilocal residence. Residence of a married couple at the wife's residence; the wife is not necessarily living matrilocally.

V

Vertebrates. Bilaterally symmetrical animals with segmented backbones.

Virilocal residence. Residence of a married couple at the husband's residence; the husband is not necessarily living patrilocally.

Voluntary association. A group open to members of different age sets and kin groups, entrance to which is voluntary.

Y

Y-5 pattern. See **Dryopithecus pattern.**

Z

Ziggurat. A large pyramidal mound in Bronze Age Mesopotamia having a shrine at the top.

REFERENCES CITED

Aarne, Antti A.
1961 The Types of the Folktale, a Classification and Bibliography. Second revision. Stith Thompson, ed and trans. Helsinki: Suomaleinen Tiedeakatemia.

Aberle, David F., et al.
1963 The Incest Taboo and the Mating Patterns of Animals. American Anthropologist 65:253–65.

Adams, Richard N.
1960 An Inquiry Into the Nature of the Family. *In* Essays in the Science of Culture. Gertrude E. Dole and Robert Cameiro, eds. Pp. 30–49. New York: Thomas Y. Crowell.

Adams, Robert McCormick
1966 The Evolution of Urban Society: Early Mesopotamia and Prehistoric Mexico. Chicago: Aldine Publishing Co.

Ainsworth, Mary D. Salter
1967 Infancy in Uganda: Infant Care and the Growth of Love. Baltimore: Johns Hopkins Press.

Ammar, Hamed
1966 Growing up in an Egyptian Village. New York: Octagon Books.

Andrews, Peter, and Alan Walker
1976 The Primate and Other Fauna from Fort Ternan, Kenya. *In* Human Origins: Louis Leakey and the East African Evidence. Glynn Ll. Isaac and Elizabeth R. McCown, eds. Pp. 279–304. Menlo Park, Calif.: W. A. Benjamin, Inc.

Apadaca, Anacleto
1952 Corn and Custom: Introduction of Hybrid Corn to Spanish American Farmers in New Mexico. *In* Human Problems in Technological Change: A Casebook. Edward H. Spicer, ed. Pp. 35–39. New York: Russell Sage Foundation.

Ardrey, Robert
1966 The Territorial Imperative. New York: Atheneum.
1976 The Hunting Hypothesis. New York: Atheneum.

Arensberg, Conrad M., and Arthur H. Niehoff
1964 Introducing Social Change: A Manual for Americans Overseas. Chicago: Aldine Publishing Co.

467

Axelrad, Sidney
1962 Infant Care and Personality Reconsidered: A Rejoinder to Orlansky. *In* The Psychoanalytic Study of Society. Warner Muensterberger and Sidney Axelrad, eds. Vol. 2, pp. 75–132. New York: International Universities Press.

Banfield, Edward C.
1958 The Moral Basis of a Backward Society. Glencoe, Ill.: The Free Press.

Barber, Richard J.
1970 The American Corporation: Its Power, Its Money, Its Politics. New York: E. P. Dutton & Co.

Barnett, Homer G., et al.
1954 Acculturation: An Exploratory Formulation. American Anthropologist, 56:975–79.

Barnouw, Victor
1973 Culture and Personality. Rev. ed. Homewood, Ill.: Dorsey Press.

Barry, Herbert, III, Margaret K. Bacon, and Irvin L. Child
1957 A Cross-Cultural Survey of Some Sex Differences in Socialization. Journal of Abnormal and Social Psychology 55:327–32.

Barth, Fredrik
1956 Ecological Relationships of Ethnic Groups in Swat, North Pakistan. American Anthropologist 58:1079–89.
1961 Nomads of South Persia: The Basseri Tribe of the Khamsheh Confederacy. Boston: Little, Brown & Co.

Barton, R. F.
1946 The Religion of the Ifugao. American Anthropological Association Memoir no. 65.

Bascom, William
1963 The Urban African and His World. Cahiers D'Etudes Africaines 164–83.

Basham, A. L.
1954 The Wonder That Was India. New York: Grove Press.

Batalla, Guillermo Bonfil
1966 Conservative Thought in Applied Anthropology: A Critique. Human Organization 25:89–92.

Beals, Ralph L., and Harry Hoijer
1965 An Introduction to Anthropology. Third ed. New York: Macmillan Co.

Beattie, John
1964 Other Cultures: Aims, Methods, and Achievements in Social Anthropology. New York: The Free Press.

Bell, Daniel
1967 Introduction. *In* Kahn and Wiener 1967.

Bellah, Robert N.
1957 Tokugawa Religion: The Values of Pre-Industrial Japan. Glencoe, Ill.: The Free Press.
1964 Religious Evolution. American Sociological Review 29:358–74.

Benedict, Ruth
1934 Patterns of Culture. Boston: Houghton Mifflin Co.
1938a Religion. *In* General Anthropology. Franz Boas, ed. Pp. 627–64. New York: D. C. Heath & Co.
1938b Continuities and Discontinuities in Cultural Conditioning. Psychiatry 1:161–67.

Bernstein, Jeremy
1969 Out of the Ego Chamber. The New Yorker. August 9, pp. 40–65.

Berry, Adrian
1974 The Next Ten Thousand Years: A Vision of Man's Future in the Universe. New York: Saturday Review Press/E. P. Dutton and Co., Inc.

Berry, J. W.
  1966   Temne and Eskimo Perceptual Skills. International Journal of Psychology 1:207–29.

Binford, Lewis R.
  1968   Post-Pleistocene Adaptations. *In* New Perspectives in Archaeology. Sally R. Binford and Lewis R. Binford, eds. Pp. 313–41. Chicago: Aldine Publishing Co.

Birdsell, J. B.
  1972   Human Evolution: An Introduction to the New Physical Anthropology. Chicago: Rand McNally and Co.

Birket-Smith, Kaj
  1959   The Eskimos. London: Methuen & Co.

Black, Donald
  1976   The Behavior of Law. New York: Academic Press.

Blakeney, E. H., ed.
  1936   The History of Herodotus. George Rawlinson, trans. Vol. 1. London: J. M. Dent & Sons.

Bloomfield, Leonard
  1933   Language. New York: Henry Holt & Co.

Boas, Franz
  1884   The Central Eskimo. Bureau of American Ethnology Annual Report no. 6. Pp. 399–664. Washington, D.C.: Smithsonian Institution.
  1938   The Mind of Primitive Man. Rev. ed. New York: Macmillan Co.
  1955   Primitive Art. New York: Dover Publications. (First published in 1927.)

Bogue, Donald
  1968   End of the Population Explosion? U.S. News and World Report 64 (March 11):59–61.

Bordes, François
  1968   The Old Stone Age. J. E. Anderson, trans. New York: McGraw-Hill Book Co.

Borhegyi, Stephan de, and Suzanne de Borhegyi
  1963   The Rubber Ball Game of Ancient America. Lore 13:44–53.

Boserup, Ester
  1965   The Conditions of Agricultural Growth: The Economics of Agrarian Change Under Population Pressure. Chicago: Aldine Publishing Co.

Bowen, Elenore Smith
  1964   Return to Laughter. New York: Doubleday & Co., Inc.

Bowlby, John
  1969   Attachment and Loss. Vol. I, Attachment. New York: Basic Books, Inc.

Brace, C. Loring
  1962a   Refocusing on the Neanderthal Problem. American Anthropologist. 64:729–41.
  1962b   Cultural Factors in the Evolution of the Human Dentition. *In* Culture and the Evolution of Man. M. F. Ashley Montagu, ed. Pp. 343–54. New York: Oxford University Press.
  1964   A Nonracial Approach towards the Understanding of Human Diversity. *In* Montagu 1964, pp. 103–52.

Braidwood, Robert J.
  1975   Prehistoric Men. Eighth ed. Glenview, Ill.: Scott, Foresman & Co.

Briggs, Jean L.
  1974   Eskimo Women: Makers of Men. *In* Many Sisters: Women in Cross-Cultural Perspective. Carolyn J. Matthieson, ed. Pp. 261–304. New York: The Free Press.

Bronfenbrenner, Urie
  1970 Two Worlds of Childhood: U.S. and U.S.S.R. New York: Russell Sage Foundation.
Brose, David S., and Milford H. Wolpoff
  1971 Early Upper Paleolithic Man and Late Middle Paleolithic Tools. American Anthropologist 73:1156–94.
Brown, Judith K.
  1963 A Cross-Cultural Study of Female Initiation Rites. American Anthropologist 65:837–53.
  1970 Economic Organization Among the Iroquois. Ethnohistory 17:151–67.
Brown, Lester R.
  1972 World Without Borders. New York: Random House.
Brown, Roger, and Ursula Bellugi
  1966 Three Processes in the Child's Acquisition of Syntax. *In* New Directions in the Study of Language. Eric H. Lenneberg, ed. Pp. 131–61. Cambridge, Mass.: MIT Press.
Bruner, Edward M.
  1956 Cultural Transmission and Cultural Change. Southwestern Journal of Anthropology 12:191–99.
Burgess, Ernest W.
  1961 The Growth of the City: An Introduction to a Research Project. *In* Studies in Human Ecology. George A. Theodorson, ed. Pp. 37–44. New York: Harper & Row.
Burton, Roger V., and John W. M. Whiting
  1961 The Absent Father and Cross-Sex Identity. Merrill-Palmer Quarterly of Behavior and Development 7:85–95.
Bygott, J. D.
  1972 Cannibalism Among Wild Chimpanzees. Nature 238:410–11.
Campbell, Bernard G.
  1974 Human Evolution: An Introduction to Man's Adaptations. Second ed. Chicago: Aldine Publishing Co.
Campbell, Joseph
  1949 The Hero With a Thousand Faces. Bollingen Series no. 17. Princeton, N.J.: Princeton University Press.
Carneiro, Robert L.
  1970 A Theory of the Origin of the State. Science 169:733–38.
Carrasco, Pedro
  1959 Land and Polity in Tibet. Seattle: University of Washington Press.
Carrighar, Sally
  1968 War is Not in Our Genes. *In* Man and Aggression. M. F. Ashley Montagu, ed. Pp. 37–50. London: Oxford University Press.
Cassell, John
  1955 A Comprehensive Health Program Among South African Zulus. *In* Health, Culture, and Community: Case Studies of Public Reactions to Health Programs. Benjamin D. Paul, ed. Pp. 15–41. New York: Russell Sage Foundation.
Chagnon, Napoleon
  1968 Yanomamö Social Organization and Warfare. *In* Fried, Harris, and Murphy 1968:109–59.
Chandler, Tertius
  1960 Duplicate Inventions? American Anthropologist 62:495–98.
Chandrasekhar, S.
  1968 How India is Tackling Her Population Problem. Foreign Affairs 7:138–50.
Chang, Kwang-chih
  1968 The Archaeology of Ancient China, Rev. ed. New Haven, Conn.: Yale University Press.

1970   The Beginning of Agriculture in the Far East. Antiquity 44:178–85.

Chase, Stuart
1968   The Most Probable World. New York: Harper & Row.

Chayanov, A. V.
1966   The Theory of Peasant Economy. Daniel Thorner, Basile Kerblay, and R. E. F. Smith, eds. Homewood, Ill.: Richard D. Irwin, Inc.

Child, Irvin L., Thomas Storm, and Joseph Veroff
1958   Achievement Themes in Folk Tales Related to Socialization Practice. *In* Motives in Fantasy, Action, and Society. John W. Atkinson, ed. Pp. 479–92. Princeton, N.J.: D. Van Nostrand Co.

Childe, V. Gordon
1953   Man Makes Himself. New York: Mentor Books.

Chomsky, Noam
1957   Syntactic Structures. The Hague: Mouton and Co.

Clark, J. Desmond
1971   A Re-Examination of the Evidence for Agricultural Origins in the Nile Valley. Proceedings of the Prehistoric Society 37:34–79.

Clarke, Ann M., and A. D. B. Clarke
1976   Early Experience: Myth and Evidence. New York: The Free Press.

Clarke, Arthur C.
1968   Explorations in Tomorrow. *In* Man and the Future. James E. Gunn, ed. Pp. 246–77. Lawrence University Press of Kansas.

Clignet, Remi
1970   Many Wives, Many Powers: Authority and Power in Polygynous Families. Evanston, Ill.: Northwestern University Press.

Coale, Ansley J.
1974   The History of the Human Population. Scientific American 231:41–51.

Cochrane, Glynn
1971   Developmental Anthropology. New York: Oxford University Press.

Cohen, Yehudi A.
1964   The Transition from Childhood to Adolescence: Cross-Cultural Studies of Initiation Ceremonies, Legal Systems, and Incest Taboos. Chicago: Aldine Publishing Co.

Coon, Carleton S.
1954   Climate and Race. *In* Climatic Change. Harlow Shapley, ed. Cambridge, Mass.: Harvard University Press.
1962   The Origin of Races. New York: Alfred A. Knopf.

Coon, Carleton S., Stanley M. Garn, and Joseph B. Birdsell
1950   Races: A Study of the Problem of Race Formation in Man. Springfield, Ill.: Charles C Thomas, Publisher.

Coser, Lewis A.
1956   The Functions of Social Conflict. Glencoe, Ill.: The Free Press.

Coulborn, Rushton, ed.
1965   Feudalism in History. Hamden, Conn.: Archon Books.

Coult, Allan D.
1963   Causality and Cross-Sex Prohibitions. American Anthropologist 66:266–77.

Covarrubias, Miguel
1937   The Island of Bali. New York: Alfred A. Knopf.

Cushing, Frank Hamilton
1965   The Cock and the Mouse. *In* Dundes 1965:269–76.

Darwin, Charles
  1859 The Origin of Species by Means of Natural Selection or the Preservation of Favored Races in the Struggle for Life. New York: Modern Library.
Dasen, Pierre R.
  1972 Cross-Cultural Piagetian Research: A Summary. Journal of Cross-Cultural Psychology 1:23–39.
Davenport, William
  1959 Nonunilinear Descent and Descent Groups. American Anthropologist 61:557–72.
Davidson, Basil
  1959 The Lost Cities of Africa. Boston: Little, Brown & Co.
Davis, Allison, Burleigh B. Gardner, and Mary R. Gardner
  1941 Deep South: A Social Anthropological Study of Caste and Class. Chicago: University of Chicago Press.
Degler, Carl N.
  1964 Revolution Without Ideology: The Changing Place of Women in America. Daedalus: Journal of the American Academy of Arts and Sciences 93:653–70.
De la Vega, Garcilaso
  1962 The Incas. The Royal Commentaries of the Inca, Garcilaso de la Vega, 1539–1616. Maria Jolas, trans. New York: Orion Press.
Dennis, Wayne
  1960 Causes of Retardation Among Institutionalized Children: Iran. Journal of Genetic Psychology 90:47–59,
De Vore, Irven, ed.
  1965 Primate Behavior. Field Studies of Monkeys and Apes. New York: Holt, Rinehart & Winston.
De Vos, George A., ed.
  1973 Socialization for Achievement: Essays on the Cultural Psychology of the Japanese. Berkeley: University of California Press.
De Vos, George A., and Hiroshi Wagatsuma, eds.
  1966 Japan's Invisible Race: Caste in Culture and Personality. Berkeley: University of California Press.
Dollard, John
  1949 Class and Caste in a Southern Town. Second ed. New York: Harper & Row.
Domhoff, William
  1967 Who Rules America? Englewood Cliffs, N.J.: Prentice-Hall, Inc.
Dube, S. C.
  1958 India's Changing Villages: Human Factors in Community Development. Ithaca, N.Y.: Cornell University Press.
Du Bois, Cora
  1944 The People of Alor: A Socio-Psychological Study of an East Indian Island. Minneapolis: University of Minnesota Press.
Dubos, René
  1965 Man Adapting. New Haven, Conn.: Yale University Press.
Dumond, D. E.
  1965 Population Growth and Cultural Change. Southwestern Journal of Anthropology 21:302–24.
Dundes, Alan
  1965 The Study of Folklore. Englewood Cliffs, N.J.: Prentice-Hall, Inc.
Durkheim, Émile
  1965 The Elementary Forms of the Religious Life. Joseph Ward Swain, trans. New York: The Free Press. (First published in 1915.)

Eastman, Max
 1936   Enjoyment of Laughter. New York: Simon and Schuster.

Eberhard, Wolfram
 1958   Review of Oriental Despotism by Karl A. Wittfogel. American Sociological Review 23:446–48.
 1965   Conquerors and Rulers: Social Forces in Medieval China. Leiden, Netherlands: E. J. Brill.

Eliade, Mircea
 1950   Shamanism. *In* Ancient Religions. Vergilius Ferm, ed. Pp. 297–308. New York: Philosophical Library.

Ellefson, John O.
 1968   Personality and the Biological Nature of Man. *In* The Study of Personality: An Interdisciplinary Approach. Edward Norbeck, Douglass Price-Williams, and William McCord, eds. Pp. 137–49. New York: Holt, Rinehart & Winston.

Elwin, Verrier
 1943   The Aboriginals. Oxford University Pamphlets on Indian Affairs.
 1950   Bondo Highlander. Bombay: Oxford University Press.

Ember, Carol R.
 1973   Feminine Task Assignment and the Social Behavior of Boys. Ethos 1:424–39.

Erasmus, Charles J.
 1956   Culture Structure and Process: The Occurrence and Disappearance of Reciprocal Farm Labor. Southwestern Journal of Anthropology 12:444–69.

Erikson, Erik Homburger
 1963   Childhood and Society. Second ed. New York: W. W. Norton & Co., Inc.

Faris, Robert E. L., and H. Warren Dunham
 1939   Mental Disorders in Urban Areas. Chicago: University of Chicago Press.

Fei, Hsiao-Tung
 1953   China's Gentry: Essays in Rural-Urban Relations. Chicago: University of Chicago Press.

Ferkiss, Victor C.
 1969   Technological Man: The Myth and the Reality. New York: George Braziller.

Firth, Raymond
 1936   We, the Tikopia. London: George Allen and Unwin.

Flannery, Kent V.
 1965   The Ecology of Early Food Production in Mesopotamia. Science 147:1247–56.
 1969   Origins and Ecological Effects of Early Domestication in Iran and the Near East. *In* The Domestication and Exploitation of Plants and Animals. Peter J. Ucko and G. W. Dimbleby, eds. Pp. 73–100. Chicago: Aldine Publishing Co.

Ford, Clellan S., and Frank A. Beach
 1951   Patterns of Sexual Behavior. New York: Harper & Brothers.

Foster, George M.
 1965   Peasant Society and the Image of Limited Good. American Anthropologist 67:293–315.
 1967   Introduction: What is a Peasant? *In* Peasant Society: A Reader. Jack M. Potter, May N. Diaz, and George M. Foster, eds. Pp. 2–14. Boston: Little, Brown & Co.
 1969   Applied Anthropology. Boston: Little, Brown & Co.

Fox, Robin
 1967   Kinship and Marriage: An Anthropological Perspective. Baltimore: Penguin Books.

Frazer, James George
 1943   The Golden Bough: A Study in Magic and Religion. 1 vol. abridged ed. New York: Macmillan Co. (First published in 1890. Revised 12-vol. edition published in 1911–15.)

Freud, Sigmund
  1938 Totem and Taboo. *In* The Basic Writings of Sigmund Freud. New York: Modern Library.
  1957 The Future of an Illusion. New York: Doubleday & Co., Inc., (First published in 1927.)

Fried, Marc
  1963 Grieving for a Lost Home. *In* The Urban Condition. Leonard J. Duhl, ed. Pp. 151–70. New York: Basic Books.

Fried, Morton H.
  1967 The Evolution of Political Society: An Essay In Political Anthropology. New York: Random House.

Fried, Morton H., Marvin Harris, and Robert Murphy, eds.
  1968 War: The Anthropology of Armed Conflict and Aggression. New York: Natural History Press.

Friedl, Ernestine
  1975 Women and Men: An Anthropologist's View. New York: Holt, Rinehart & Winston.

Gallaway, Lowell Eugene
  1973 Poverty in America. Columbus, Ohio: Grid, Inc.

Gans, Herbert J.
  1962 The Urban Villagers. New York: The Free Press of Glencoe.

Gardner, R. Allen, and Beatrice T. Gardner
  1969 Teaching Sign Language to a Chimpanzee. Science 165:644–72.

Georges, Robert A., ed.
  1968 Studies on Mythology. Homewood, Ill.: The Dorsey Press.

Giles, Eugene
  1973 Culture and Genetics. *In* Human Evolution: Readings in Physical Anthropology. Third ed. Noel Korn, ed. Pp. 234–47. New York: Holt, Rinehart & Winston.

Glass, Bentley
  1955 On the Unlikelihood of Significant Admixture of Genes from the North American Indians in the Present Composition of Negroes in the United States. American Journal of Human Genetics 7:368–85.

Glass, Bentley, and C. C. Li
  1953 The Dynamics of Racial Intermixture—an Analysis Based on the American Negro. American Journal of Human Genetics 5:1–20.

Gleason, H. A., Jr.
  1955 An Introduction to Descriptive Linguistics. New York: Henry Holt & Co.

Gluckman, Max
  1950 Kinship and Marriage among the Lozi of Northern Rhodesia and the Zulu of Natal. *In* Radcliffe-Brown and Forde 1950:166–206.

Gorer, Geoffrey
  1955 Exploring English Character. New York: Criterion Books

Gough, E. Kathleen
  1961 Variation in Residence. *In* Schneider and Gough 1961:545–76.

Grodzins, Martin
  1970 The Metropolitan Area as a Racial Problem. *In* Urban Man and Society: A Reader in Urban Sociology. Albert N. Cousins and Hans Nagpaul, eds. Pp. 293–99. New York: Alfred A. Knopf.

Hagen, Everett E.
  1962 On the Theory of Social Change: How Economic Growth Begins. Homewood, Ill.: The Dorsey Press.

Hall, John W.
  1968 Feudalism in Japan—A Reassessment. *In* Studies in the Institutional History of Early Modern Japan. John W. Hall and Marius B. Jansen, eds. Princeton, N.J.: Princeton University Press.

Hallowell, A. Irving
  1942 The Role of Conjuring in Saulteaux Society. Philadelphia: University of Pennsylvania Press.
  1949 Psychosexual Adjustment, Personality, and the Good Life in a Nonliterate Culture. *In* Psychosexual Development in Health and Disease. Paul H. Hoch and Joseph Zubin, eds. Pp. 102–23. New York: Grune & Stratton.
  1955 Culture and Experience. Philadelphia: University of Pennsylvania Press.

Hannerz, Ulf
  1974 Ethnicity and Opportunity in Urban America. *In* Urban Ethnicity. Abner Cohen, ed. Pp. 37–76. London: Tavistock Publications.

Harlow, Harry
  1962 The Heterosexual Affectional System in Monkeys. American Psychologist 17:1–9.

Harrington, Michael
  1962 The Other America: Poverty in the United States. New York: Macmillan Co.

Harris, Marvin
  1968 The Rise of Anthropological Theory: A History of Theories of Culture. New York: Thomas Y. Crowell Co.

Hayes, Cathy
  1951 The Ape in Our House. New York: Harper & Row.

Hayner, Norman S., in collaboration with Una Middleton Hayner
  1966 New Patterns in Old Mexico. New Haven, Conn.: College and University Press.

Hays, H. R.
  1958 From Ape to Angel. New York: Alfred A. Knopf.

Helm, June
  1968 The Nature of Dogrib Socioterritorial Groups. *In* Lee and DeVore 1968:118–25.

Henry, Jules
  1944 Jungle People. New York: J. J. Augustin.

Herre, Wolf
  1963 The Science and History of Domesticated Animals. *In* Science and Archaeology: A Comprehensive Survey of Progress and Research. Don Brothwell and Eric Higgs, eds. Pp. 235–49. New York: Basic Books.

Herskovits, Melville J.
  1962 The Human Factor in Changing Africa. New York: Alfred A. Knopf.

Higbee, Edward
  1963 Farms and Farmers in an Urban Age. New York: The Twentieth Century Fund.

Hollingshead, August B.
  1949 Elmtown's Youth. New York: John Wiley & Sons.

Hollingshead, August B., and Fredrick C. Redlich
  1958 Social Class and Mental Illness: A Community Study. New York: John Wiley & Sons.

Holmberg, Allan R.
  1950 Nomads of the Long Bow: The Sirionó of Eastern Bolivia. Institute of Social Anthropology Publication no. 10. Washington, D.C.: Smithsonian Institution.
  1960 Changing Community Attitudes and Values in Peru: A Case Study in Guided Change. *In* Social Change in Latin America Today: Its Implications for United States Policy. Richard N. Adams, ed. Pp. 63–107. New York: Harper & Brothers.

Howard, James H., and Gertrude P. Kurath
1959 Ponca Dances, Ceremonies, and Music. Ethnomusicology 3:1–14.

Howell, F. Clark, and the Editors of Life
1965 Early Man. New York: Life Nature Library.

Howells, William
1973 Evolution of the Genus Homo. Reading, Mass.: Addison-Wesley Publishing Co.

Hsu, Francis L. K.
1952 Religion, Science, and Human Crises. London: Routledge and Kegan Paul

Huizinga, Johan
1955 Homo Ludens: A Study of the Play-Element in Culture. Boston: Beacon Press.

Huxley, Julian
1957 Evolution in Action. New York: Mentor Books.

Ibn-Khaldun
1967 An Introduction to History: The Muqaddimah. N.J. Dawood, ed. Franz Rosenthal, trans. London: Routledge and Kegan Paul.

Inkeles, Alex
1950 Stratification and Mobility in the Soviet Union. American Sociological Review 15: 465–79.

Issawi, Charles
1970 Issawi's Laws of Social Motion. Columbia Forum 13:42–43.

Jacobs, Melville
1959 The Content and Style of an Oral Literature: Clackamas Chinook Myths and Tales. New York: Viking Fund Publications in Anthropology no. 26.

James, Preston E., with the collaboration of Hibberd V. B. Kline, Jr.
1959 A Geography of Man. Boston: Ginn & Co.

Jensen, Arthur R.
1969 How Much Can We Boost I.Q. and Scholastic Achievement? Harvard Educational Review 39:1–123.

Jones, Maldwyn Allen
1960 American Immigration. Chicago: University of Chicago Press.

Kahn, Herman, William Brown, and Leon Martel
1976 The Next Two Hundred Years: A Scenario for America and the World. New York: William Morrow and Co.

Kahn, Herman, and Anthony J. Wiener, eds.
1967 The Year 2000: A Framework for Speculation on the Next Thirty-Three Years. New York: Macmillan Co.

Kardiner, Abram, et al.
1945 The Psychological Frontiers of Society. New York: Columbia University Press.

Kardiner, Abram, and Ralph Linton
1939 The Individual and His Society: The Psychodynamics of Primitive Social Organization. New York: Columbia University Press.

Kinsey, Alfred C., Wardell B. Pomeroy, and Clyde E. Martin
1948 Sexual Behavior in the Human Male. Philadelphia: W. B. Saunders Co.

Kinsey, Alfred C., Wardell B. Pomeroy, Clyde E. Martin, and Paul H. Gebhard
1953 Sexual Behavior in the Human Female. Philadelphia: W. B. Saunders Co.

Klein, Richard G.
1973 Geological Antiquity of Rhodesian Man. Nature 244:311–12.

Kluckhohn, Clyde
1936 Some Reflections on the Method and Theory of the Kulturkreis Lehre. American Anthropologist 38:157–96.
1965 Recurrent Themes in Myths and Mythmaking. In Dundes 1965:158–68.

Krader, Lawrence
    1965   Ecology of Central Asian Pastoralism. Southwestern Journal of Anthropology 11: 301–26.

Kramer, Samuel Noah
    1959   History Begins at Sumer. New York: Doubleday-Anchor Books.
    1963   The Sumerians: Their History, Culture, and Character. Chicago: University of Chicago Press.

Kretschmer, Norman
    1972   Lactose and Lactase. Scientific American 227:70–78.

Kristol, Irving
    1970   The Negro Today is Like the Immigrant Yesterday. *In* Cities in Trouble. Nathan Glazer, ed. Pp. 139–57. Chicago: Quadrangle Books.

Kroeber, A. L.
    1909   Classificatory Systems of Relationship. Journal of the Royal Anthropological Institute 39:77–84.
    1939   Cultural and Natural Areas of Native North America. University of California Publications in American Archaeology and Ethnology, Vol. 38.
    1948   Anthropology. New York: Harcourt, Brace & Co.

Kuper, Hilda
    1950   Kinship Among the Swazi. *In* Radcliffe-Brown and Forde 1950:86–110.

Lambert, Berndt
    1966   The Economic Activities of a Gilbertese Chief. *In* Swartz, Turner, and Tuden 1966:155–72.

Lambert, William W., Leigh Minturn Triandis, and Margery Wolf
    1959   Some Correlates of Beliefs in the Malevolence and Benevolence of Supernatural Beings: A Cross-Societal Study. Journal of Abnormal and Social Psychology 58: 162–69.

Landes, Ruth
    1968   Ojibwa Religion and the Midéwiwin. Madison: University of Wisconsin Press.

Lane, Michael, ed.
    1970   Introduction to Structuralism. New York: Basic Books.

Lang, Andrew
    1909   The Making of Religion. London: Longmans, Green & Co.

Lantis, Margaret
    1953   Nunivak Eskimo Personality as Revealed in the Mythology. Anthropological Papers of the University of Alaska, Vol. 2. no 1.

Laska-Mierzejewska, Teresa
    1970   Effects of Ecological and Socio-economic Factors on the Age at Menarche, Body Height and Weight of Rural Girls in Poland. Human Biology 42:284–92.

Leacock, Stephen
    1935   Humor: Its Theory and Technique. New York: Dodd, Mead & Co.

Lee, Richard B.
    1966   !Kung Bushman Subsistence: An Input-Output Analysis. *In* Ecological Essays. David Damas, ed. Proceedings of the Conference on Cultural Ecology. Ottawa: National Museum of Canada Bulletin no. 230. Reprinted with minor revisions in Environment and Cultural Behavior. Andrew P. Vayda, ed. Pp. 47–79. New York: Natural History Press, 1969.
    1972   Work Effort, Group Structure, and Land-Use in Contemporary Hunter-Gatherers. *In* Man, Settlement, and Urbanism. Peter J. Ucko, Ruth Tringham, and G. W. Dimbleby, eds. Pp. 177–85. Cambridge, Mass.: Schenkman Publishing Co.

Lee, Richard B., and Irven DeVore, eds.
    1968   Man the Hunter. Chicago: Aldine Publishing Co.

Lenneberg, Eric H.
1966   A Biological Perspective of Language. *In* New Directions in the Study of Language. Eric H. Lenneberg, ed. Pp. 65–88. Cambridge, Mass.: MIT Press.
1967   Biological Foundations of Language. New York: John Wiley & Sons

Lenski, Gerhard E.
1966   Power and Privilege: A Theory of Social Stratification. New York: McGraw-Hill Book Co.

Lenski, Gerhard, and Jean Lenski
1974   Human Societies: An Introduction to Macrosociology. Second ed. New York: McGraw-Hill Book Co.

Leopold, A. Carl, and Robert Ardrey
1972   Toxic Substances in Plants and the Food Habits of Early Man. Science 176: 512–14.

LeVine, Robert A.
1961   Africa. *In* Psychological Anthropology: Approaches to Culture and Personality. Francis L. K. Hsu, ed. Pp. 48–92. Homewood, Ill.: The Dorsey Press.

LeVine, Robert A., and Barbara B. LeVine
1963   Nyansongo: A Gusli Community in Kenya. *In* Whiting 1963:15–202.

Lévi-Strauss, Claude
1953   Social Structure. *In* Anthropology Today: An Encyclopedic Inventory. A. L. Kroeber, ed. Pp. 524–53. Chicago: University of Chicago Press.
1960   The Family. *In* Man, Culture, and Society. Harry L. Shapiro, ed. Pp. 261–85. New York: Oxford University Press.
1966a   The Savage Mind. Chicago: University of Chicago Press.
1966b   The Culinary Triangle. Partisan Review 33:586–95.
1967   The Structural Study of Myth. *In* Claude Lévi-Strauss. Structural Anthropology. Claire Jacobson and Brooke Grundfest Schoepf, trans, Pp. 202–28. New York: Doubleday Anchor Books.
1969   The Elementary Structures of Kinship. James H. Bell, John R. von Sturmer, and Rodney Needham, trans. Boston: Beacon Press.

Lewis, Oscar
1951   Life in a Mexican Village: Tepoztlán Restudied. Urbana: University of Illinois Press.
1955   Medicine and Politics in a Mexican Village. *In* Health, Culture, and Community: Case Studies of Public Reactions to Health Programs. Benjamin D. Paul, ed. Pp. 403–34. New York: Russell Sage Foundation.

Lewis, Oscar, with the assistance of Victor Barnouw
1958   Village Life in Northern India: Studies in a Delhi Village. Urbana: University of Illinois Press.

Lewis, Thomas M. N., and Madeline Kneberg
1958   Tribes that Slumber: Indian Times in the Tennessee Region. Knoxville: University of Tennessee Press.

Lilley, Samuel
1966   Men, Machines, and History: The Story of Tools and Machines in Relation to Social Progress. Rev. ed. New York: International Publishers.

Linden, Eugene
1974   Apes, Men, and Language. New York: Saturday Review Press/E. P. Dutton and Co., Inc.

Linton, Ralph
1936   The Study of Man. New York: D. Appleton-Century Co.
1945   The Cultural Background of Personality. New York: Appleton-Century Co.
1955   The Tree of Culture. New York: Alfred A. Knopf.

Little, Kenneth L.
  1949 The Role of the Secret Society in Cultural Specialization. American Anthropologist 51:199–212.

Livingstone, Frank B.
  1958 Anthropological Implications of Sickle Cell Gene Distribution in West Africa. American Anthropologist 60:533–62.
  1964 On the Nonexistence of Human Races. *In* Montagu 1964, pp. 46–60.
  1968 The Effects of War on the Biology of the Human Species. *In* Fried, Harris, and Murphy 1968:3–15.

Loeb, Edwin M.
  1929 Shaman and Seer. American Anthropologist 31:60–84.
  1935 Sumatra: Its History and People. Vienna.

Loomis, W. Farnsworth
  1973 Skin-Pigment Regulation of Vitamin-D Biosynthesis in Man. *In* Human Evolution: Readings in Physical Anthropology. Third ed., Noel Korn, ed. Pp. 248–61. New York: Holt, Rinehart & Winston.

Lorenz, Konrad
  1967 On Aggression. New York: Bantam Books.

Lovejoy, C. Owen, K. G. Heiple, and A. H. Burstein
  1973 The Gait of Australopithecus. American Journal of Physical Anthropology 38: 757–79.

Lowie, Robert H.
  1937 The History of Ethnological Theory. New York: Farrar and Rinehart.
  1940 An Introduction to Cultural Anthropology. New York: Rinehart & Co.
  1967 Some Aspects of Political Organization Among the American Indians. *In* Comparative Political Systems: Studies in the Politics of Pre-Industrial Societies. Ronald Cohen and John Middleton, eds. Pp. 63–87. New York: Natural History Press.

Lynd, Robert S., and Helen Merrell Lynd
  1929 Middletown: A Study in American Culture. New York: Harcourt, Brace & Co.
  1937 Middletown in Transition: A Study in Cultural Conflicts. New York: Harcourt, Brace & Co.

Macaulay, Thomas Babington
  1877 Critical, Historical and Miscellaneous Essays. Vol 1. New York: Hurd and Houghton.

MacNeish, Richard S.
  1976 Early Man in the New World. American Scientist 64:316–27.

Malinowski, Bronislaw
  1922 Argonauts of the Western Pacific: An Account of Native Enterprise and Adventure in the Archipelagoes of Melanesian New Guinea. London: George Routledge and Sons.
  1926a Crime and Custom in Savage Society. New York: Harcourt, Brace & Co.
  1926b Anthropology. Encyclopaedia Britannica. First supplementary volume; 132.
  1929 The Sexual Life of Savages in North-Western Melanesia. New York: Harcourt, Brace & Co.
  1953 Sex and Repression in Savage Society. London: Routledge & Kegan Paul. (First published in 1927).
  1954 Magic, Science and Religion and Other Essays. New York: Doubleday-Anchor Books.

Mantoux, Paul
  1961 The Industrial Revolution in the Eighteenth Century. London: Jonathan Cape.

Maquet, J. J.
  1960 The Problem of Tutsi Domination. *In* Cultures and Societies of Africa. Simon Ottenberg and Phoebe Ottenberg, eds. New York: Random House.

Marett, R. R.
1914 The Threshold of Religion. London: Methuen & Co.

Marriott, McKim
1952 Technological Change in Overdeveloped Rural Areas. Economic Development and Cultural Change 1:261–72.

Marshack, Alexander
1976 Implications of the Paleolithic Symbolic Evidence for the Origin of Language. American Scientist 64:134–45.

Marshall, Lorna
1967 !Kung Bushman Bands. *In* Comparative Political Systems: Studies in the Politics of Pre-Industrial Societies. Ronald Cohen and John Middleton, eds. Pp. 15–43. New York: Natural History Press.

Martin, M. Kay, and Barbara Voorhies
1975 Female of the Species. New York: Columbia University Press.

McClelland, David C.
1961 The Achieving Society. Princeton, N.J.: D. Van Nostrand Co.

McClelland, David C., and G. A. Friedman
1952 A Cross-Cultural Study of the Relationship Between Child Training Practices and Achievement Motivation Appearing in Folk Tales. *In* Readings in Social Psychology. Rev. ed. Guy E. Swanson, Theodore M. Newcomb, and Eugene L. Hartley, eds. Pp. 243–49. New York: Henry Holt & Co.

McCracken, Robert D.
1971 Lactase Deficiency. An Example of Dietary Evolution. Current Anthropology 12:479–517.

McHale, John
1969 The Future of the Future. New York: George Braziller.

Mead, Margaret
1928 Coming of Age in Samoa. New York: William Morrow & Co.
1939 From the South Seas: Studies of Adolescence and Sex in Primitive Societies. New York: William Morrow & Co.

Mead, Margaret, and Frances Cooke MacGregor
1951 Growth and Culture: A Photographic Analysis. New York: G. P. Putnam's Sons.

Mellaart, James
1967 Çatal Hüyük: A Neolithic Town in Anatolia. New York: McGraw-Hill Book Co.

Merriam, Alan P.
1964 The Anthropology of Music. Evanston, Ill.: Northwestern University Press.

Merton, Robert K.
1949 Social Theory and Social Structure. Glencoe, Ill.: The Free Press.

Messenger, John C.
1958 Reflections on Aesthetic Talent. Basic College Quarterly. Vol. 4. East Lansing: Michigan State University.

Michaelson, Evalyn J., and Walter Goldschmidt
1971 Female Roles and Male Dominance Among Peasants. Southwestern Journal of Anthropology 27:330–53.

Miller, Herman P.
1964 Rich Man, Poor Man. New York: Thomas Y. Crowell Co.

Minturn, Leigh, and John T. Hitchcock
1963 The Rājpūts of Khalapur, India. *In* Whiting 1963:203–361.

Minturn, Leigh, and William W. Lambert
    1964   Mothers of Six Cultures: Antecedents of Child Rearing. New York: John Wiley and Sons.

Montagu, Ashley, ed.
    1963   Race, Science, and Humanity. Princeton, N.J. D. Van Nostrand Co.
    1964   The Concept of Race. London: Free Press of Glencoe, Collier-Macmillan, Ltd.

Morey, Robert
    1940   Upset in Emotions. Journal of Social Psychology 12:333–56.

Morgan, Patricia
    1975   Child Care: Sense and Fable. London: Temple Smith.

Morley, Sylvanus Griswold
    1956   The Ancient Maya. Third ed. Rev. by George W. Brainerd. Stanford, Calif.: Stanford University Press.

Morris, Desmond
    1962   The Biology of Art: A Study in the Picture-Making Behavior of the Great Apes and Its Relationship to Human Art New York: Alfred A. Knopf.
    1969   The Naked Ape. New York: Dell Publishing Co.

Mumford, Lewis
    1934   Technics and Civilization. New York: Harcourt, Brace & Co.

Murdock, George Peter
    1945   The Common Denominator of Cultures. *In* The Science of Man in the World Crisis. Ralph Linton, ed. New York: Columbia University Press.
    1949   Social Structure. New York: The Free Press.
    1957   World Ethnographic Sample. American Anthropologist 59:664–87.
    1959   Africa: Its Peoples and Their Culture History. New York: McGraw-Hill Book Co.

Murphy, Jane M.
    1964   Psychotherapeutic Aspects of Shamanism on St. Lawrence Island. *In* Magic, Faith and Healing: Studies in Primitive Psychiatry Today. Ari Kiev, ed. Pp. 53–83. London: Free Press of Glencoe.

Murphy, Yolanda, and Robert F. Murphy
    1974   Women of the Forest. New York: Columbia University Press.

Myrdal, Gunnar, with the assistance of Richard Sterne and Arnold Rose
    1944   An American Dilemma: The Negro Problem and Modern Democracy. New York: Harper & Brothers.

Naroll, Raoul
    1961   Two Solutions to Galton's Problem. Philosophy of Science 28:15–39.
    1964   A Fifth Solution to Galton's Problem. American Anthropologist 66:863–67.

Naroll, Raoul, and Roy G. D'Andrade
    1963   Two Further Solutions to Galton's Problem. American Anthropologist 65:1053–67.

Nash, Manning
    1966   Primitive and Peasant Economic Systems. San Francisco: Chandler Publishing Co.

Nuttini, Hugo G.
    1972   A Latin American City: A Cultural-Historical Approach. *In* The Anthropology of Urban Environments. Thomas Weaver and Douglas White, eds. Society for Applied Anthropology Monograph no. 11.

Oakley, Kenneth P.
    1964   Man the Tool-Maker. Chicago: University of Chicago Press, Phoenix Books.

Oberg, Kalervo
    1940   The Kingdom of Ankole in Uganda. *In* Fortes and Evans-Pritchard 1940:121–62.

1955   Types of Social Structure Among the Lowland Tribes of South and Central America. American Anthropologist 57:472–87.

Opler, Morris E.
1936   An Interpretation of Ambivalence in Two American Indian Tribes. Journal of Social Psychology 7:82–115.

Orlansky, Harold
1949   Infant Care and Personality. Psychological Bulletin 46:1–48.

Oxnard, Charles E.
1975   Uniqueness and Diversity in Human Evolution: Morphometric Studies of Australopithecines. Chicago: University of Chicago Press.

Paddock, William, and Paul Paddock
1967   Famine—1975! America's Decision: Who Will Survive? Boston: Little, Brown & Co.

Parker, Seymour
1976   The Precultural Basis of the Incest Taboo: Toward a Biosocial Theory. American Anthropologist 78:285–305.

Pehrson, Robert N.
1966   The Social Organization of the Marri Baluch. New York: Viking Fund Publications in Anthropology no. 43.

Pelling, Henry
1960   American Labor. Chicago: University of Chicago Press.

Peter, Prince of Greece and Denmark
1963   A Study of Polyandry. The Hague: Mouton & Co.

Pfeiffer, John E.
1969   The Emergence of Man. New York: Harper & Row.

Piggott, Stuart
1950   Prehistoric India to 1000 B.C. Harmondsworth: Penguin Books.

Polanyi, Karl
1957a   The Great Transformation. Boston: Beacon Press.
1957b   The Economy as Instituted Process. *In* Trade and Market in the Early Empires, Economies in History and Theory. Karl Polanyi, Conrad M. Arensberg, and Harry W. Pearson, eds. Pp. 243–70. New York: The Free Press.
1957c   Marketless Trading in Hammurabi's Time. *In* Trade and Market in the Early Empires, Economies in History and Theory. Karl Polanyi, Conrad M. Arensberg, and Henry W. Pearson, eds. Pp. 12–26. New York: The Free Press.

Polgar, Steven
1964   Evolution and the Ills of Mankind. *In* Horizons of Anthropology. Sol Tax, ed. Pp. 200–211. Chicago: Aldine Publishing Co.

Premack, Ann James, and David Premack
1972   Teaching Language to an Ape. Scientific American 227:92–99.

Price-Williams, Douglass R.
1975   Explorations in Cross-Cultural Psychology. San Francisco: Chandler & Sharp.

Propp, Vladimir
1968   The Morphology of the Folktale. Second ed. Publications of the American Folklore Society, Bibliographical and Special Series. Rev. ed. Vol. 9. (First published in Russian in 1928.)

Protsch, Reiner, and Rainer Berger
1973   Earliest Radiocarbon Dates for Domesticated Animals. Science 179:235–39.

Radcliffe-Brown, A. R.
  1924 The Mother's Brother in South Africa. South African Journal of Science 21:542–55. Reprinted in Radcliffe-Brown 1952:15–31.
  1950 Introduction. *In* Radcliffe-Brown and Forde 1950:1–85.
  1952 Structure and Function in Primitive Society: Essays and Addresses. Glencoe, Ill.: The Free Press.

Radcliffe-Brown, A. R., and Daryll Forde, eds.
  1950 African Systems of Kinship and Marriage. London: Oxford University Press.

Raglan, Lord
  1937 The Hero: A Study in Tradition, Myth and Drama. New York: Oxford University Press.

Randall, Betty Uchitelle
  1949 The Cinderella Theme in Northwest Coast Folklore. *In* Indians of the Urban Northwest. Marian W. Smith, ed. Pp. 243–85. New York: Columbia University Press.

Rank, Otto
  1956 The Myth of the Birth of the Hero. New York: Random House, Inc.

Rappaport, Roy A.
  1967 Pigs for the Ancestors: Ritual in the Ecology of a New Guinea People. New Haven, Conn.: Yale University Press.

Rasmussen, Knud
  1921 Eskimo Folk Tales. W. Worster, trans. Copenhagen: Gyldendal.
  1929 Intellectual Culture of the Iglulik Eskimos: Report of the Fifth Thule Expedition, 1921–24. Vol. 7, no. 1. Copenhagen: Gyldendalske Boghandel, Nordisk Forlag.
  1930 Observations on the Intellectual Culture of the Caribou Eskimos: Report of the Fifth Thule Expedition, 1921–24. Vol. 7, no. 2. Copenhagen: Gyldendalske Boghandel, Nordisk Forlag.

Redfield, Robert
  1941 The Folk Culture of Yucatan. Chicago: University of Chicago Press.

Richards, A. I.
  1950 Some Types of Family Structure Among the Central Bantu. *In* Radcliffe-Brown and Forde 1950:207–51.

Richards, Cara E.
  1963–64 City Taverns. Human Organization 22:260–68.

Riesman, David, with Reuel Denney and Nathan Glazer
  1950 The Lonely Crowd: A Study of the Changing American Character. New Haven, Conn.: Yale University Press.

Ritzenthaler, Pat
  1966 The Fon of Bafut. New York: Thomas Y. Crowell Co.

Rivers, W. H. R.
  1968 The Sociological Significance of Myth. *In* Georges 1968:27–45.

Roberts, John M., Malcolm J. Arth, and Robert R. Bush
  1959 Games in Culture. American Anthropologist 61:597–605.

Roberts, John M., and Brian Sutton-Smith
  1962 Child Training and Game Involvement. Ethnology 1:166–85.

Rohner, Ronald P.
  1975 They Love Me, They Love Me Not. HRAF Press.
  1976 Sex Differences in Aggression: Phylogenetic and Enculturation Perspectives. Ethos 4:57–72.

Robinson, John T.
  1963 Adaptive Radiation in the Australopithecines and the Origin of Man. *In* African

Ecology and Human Evolution. F. Clark Howell and François Bourliére, eds. Pp. 385–416. Viking Fund Publications in Anthropology no. 36. Chicago: Aldine Publishing Co.

1972   Early Hominid Posture and Locomotion. Chicago: University of Chicago Press.

Rose, Ronald
1956   Living Magic: The Realities Underlying the Psychical Practices and Beliefs of Australian Aborigines. Skokie, Ill.: Rand McNally & Co.

Rothschild, Emma
1974   Running out of Food. The New York Review. September 19, pp. 30–32.

Rowe, John Howland
1965   The Renaissance Foundations of Anthropology. American Anthropologist 67:1–20.

Roy, Paul Ewell
1967   Exploring Agribusiness. Danville, Ill.: Interstate Printers and Publishers.

Sahlins, Marshall
1968   Tribesmen. Englewood Cliffs, N. J.: Prentice-Hall, Inc.
1972   Stone Age Economics. Chicago: Aldine-Atherton, Inc.

Saksena, R. N.
1962   Social Economy of a Polyandrous People. Bombay: Asia Publishing House.

Sanders, William, and Barbara J. Price
1968   Mesoamerica: The Evolution of a Civilization. New York: Random House.

Schapera, I.
1950   Kinship and Marriage Among the Tswana. *In* Radcliffe-Brown and Forde 1950: 140–65.

Scheinfeld, Amram
1947   Women and Men. London: Chatto and Windus.

Schneider, David M.
1961   Introduction: The Distinctive Features of Matrilineal Descent Groups. *In* Matrilineal Kinship. David M. Schneider and Kathleen Gough, eds. Berkeley and Los Angeles: University of California Press.

Segall, Marshall H., Donald T. Campbell, and Melville J. Herskovits
1966   The Influence of Culture on Visual Perception. Indianapolis: Bobbs-Merrill Co.

Service, Elman R.
1962   Primitive Social Organization: An Evolutionary Perspective. New York: Random House.
1968   War and Our Contemporary Ancestors. *In* Fried, Harris, and Murphy 1968: 160–67.

Shankman, Paul
1969   Le Rôti et le Bouilli: Lévi-Strauss's Theory of Cannibalism. American Anthropologist 71:54–69.

Shapiro, Harry L.
1974   Peking Man. New York: Simon and Schuster.

Sharp, Andrew
1957   Ancient Voyages in the Pacific. Harmondsworth, Middlesex: Penguin Books.

Simmons, Leo, ed.
1942   Sun Chief: The Autobiography of a Hopi Indian. New Haven, Conn.: Yale University Press.

Simonds, Paul E.
1974   The Social Primates. New York: Harper & Row.

Skilling, H. Gordon, and Franklyn Griffiths, eds.
1971   Interest Groups in Soviet Politics. Princeton, N.J.: Princeton University Press.

Skinner, Brian J.
  1976 A Second Iron Age Ahead? American Scientist 64:258–69.

Slater, Mariam Kreiselman
  1959 Ecological Factors in the Origin of Incest. American Anthropologist 61:1042–59.

Slotkin, J. S., ed.
  1965 Readings in Early Anthropology. Viking Fund Publications in Anthropology no. 40. Chicago: Aldine Publishing Co.

Smith, Marian W.
  1959 Boas' "Natural History" Approach to Field Material. *In* The Anthropology of Franz Boas: Essays on the Centennial of his Birth. Walter Goldschmidt, ed. American Anthropological Association Memoir no. 89.

Spencer, Baldwin, and F. J. Gillen
  1927 The Arunta: A Study of a Stone Age People. 2 vols. London: Macmillan & Co., Ltd.

Spitz, René A.
  1945 Hospitalism: An Inquiry into the Genesis of Psychiatric Conditions in Early Childhood. *In* The Psychoanalytic Study of the Child. Vol. 1. Pp. 53–74. New York: International Universities Press.

Stephens, William N.
  1963 The Family in Cross-Cultural Perspective. New York: Holt, Rinehart & Winston.

Stern, Claudio, and Joseph A. Kahl
  1968 Stratification Since the Revolution. *In* Comparative Perspectives on Stratification: Mexico, Great Britain, Japan. Joseph A. Kahl, ed. Boston: Little, Brown & Co.

Stern, Theodore
  1948 The Rubber Ball Games of the Americas. Monographs of the American Ethnological Society no. 17. New York: J. J. Augustin.

Steward, Julian H.
  1955a Theory of Culture Change: The Methodology of Multilinear Evolution. Urbana: University of Illinois Press.
  1955b Development of Complex Societies: Cultural Causality and Law: A Trial Formulation of the Development of Early Civilizations. *In* Steward 1955a, pp. 178–209.

Steward, Julian, and Louis C. Faron
  1959 Native Peoples of South America. New York: McGraw-Hill Book Co.

Stewart, Omer C.
  1956 Fire as the First Great Force Employed by Man. *In* Man's Role in Changing the Face of the Earth. William I. Thomas, ed. Pp. 115–33. Chicago: University of Chicago Press.

Stuckert, Robert P.
  1976 Race Mixture: The Black Ancestry of White Americans. *In* Physical Anthropology and Archaeology: Introductory Readings. Second ed. Peter B. Hammond, ed. Pp. 135–39. New York: Macmillan Co.

Suggs, Robert C.
  1960 . The Island Civilizations of Polynesia. New York: Mentor Books.

Sullivan, Walter
  1967 Our Future is Incomputable. New York Times. March 26

Swanson, Guy E.
  1969 The Birth of the Gods. Ann Arbor: University of Michigan Press.

Swartz, Marc J., Victor W. Turner, and Arthur Tuden, eds.
  1966 Political Anthropology. Chicago: Aldine Publishing Co.

Teleki, Geza
  1975   The Omnivorous Chimpanzee. *In* Biological Anthropology. Solomon H. Katz, ed. Pp. 91–102. San Francisco: W. H. Freeman & Co.

Thalbitzer, W.
  1931   Shamans of the East Greenland Eskimo. *In* Sourcebook in Anthropology. A. L. Kroeber and T. T. Waterman, eds. Pp. 430–36. New York: Harcourt, Brace and Co.

Thieme, Paul
  1964   The Comparative Method of Reconstruction in Linguistics. *In* Language in Culture and Society: A Reader in Linguistics and Anthropology. Dell Hymes, ed. Pp. 585–97. New York: Harper & Row.

Thomas, Elizabeth Marshall
  1959   The Harmless People. New York: Alfred A. Knopf.

Thompson, Stith
  1955–58 Motif-Index of Folk Literature. Rev. and enlarged ed., 6 vols. Copenhagen: Rosenkilde and Bagger.

Tiger, Lionel, and Robin Fox
  1971   The Imperial Animal. New York: Holt, Rinehart & Winston.

Tocqueville, Alexis de
  1954   Democracy in America. 2 vols. New York: Alfred A. Knopf, Vintage Books.

Treistman, Judith M.
  1972   The Prehistory of China: An Archaeological Exploration. New York: Natural History Press.

Tschopik, Harry, Jr.
  1951   The Aymara of Chucuito, Peru; I, Magic. New York: American Museum of Natural History Anthropological Papers no. 44.

Tumin, Melvin M.
  1952   Caste in a Peasant Society: A Case Study in the Dynamics of Caste. Princeton, N.J.: Princeton University Press.

Turner, Victor W.
  1957   Schism and Continuity in an African Society: A Study of Ndembu Village Life. Manchester, England: Manchester University Press.

Tyler, Stephen A.
  1969   Introduction. *In* Cognitive Anthropology. Stephen A. Tyler, ed. Pp. 1–23. New York: Holt, Rinehart & Winston.

Tylor, Edward B.
  1877   Primitive Culture: Researches Into the Development of Mythology, Philosophy, Religion, Language, Art, and Customs. 2 vols. New York: Henry Holt & Co. (First published in 1871.)
  1889   On a Method of Investigating the Development of Institutions Applied to Laws of Marriage and Descent. Journal of the Royal Anthropological Institute of Great Britain and Ireland 18:245–69.
  1896   On American Lot-Games as Evidence of Asiatic Intercourse Before the Time of Columbus. Ethnographische Beitrage. Supplement to Internationales Archiv für Ethnographie 9:55–67.

Vaillant, George C.
  1956   The Aztecs of Mexico: Origin, Rise and Fall of the Aztec Nation. Baltimore: Penguin Books.

Van der Kroef, Justus
  1954   Dualism and Symbolic Antithesis in Indonesian Societies. American Anthropologist 56:847–62.

Van Lawick-Goodall, Jane
1971   In the Shadow of Man. Boston: Houghton Mifflin Co.

Vayda, Andrew P.
1961   Expansion and Warfare Among Swidden Agriculturists. American Anthropologist 63:346–58.

Vayda, Andrew P., and Roy A. Rappaport
1968   Ecology: Cultural and Non-cultural. *In* Introduction to Cultural Anthropology: Essays in the Scope and Methods of the Science of Man. James A. Clifton, ed. Pp. 476–97. Boston: Houghton Mifflin Co.

von Fürer-Haimendorf, Christoph
1943   The Chenchus: Jungle Folk of the Deccan: The Aboriginal Tribes of Hyderabad. Vol. 1. London: Macmillan.
1956   Himalayan Barbary. New York: Abelard-Schuman.

Wallace, Anthony F. C.
1966   Religion: An Anthropological View. New York: Random House.

Warner, W. Lloyd
1958   A Black Civilization: A Social Study of an Australian Tribe. Rev. ed. New York: Harper & Row.

Warner, W. Lloyd, et al.
1949   Democracy in Jonesville. New York: Harper & Brothers.

Warner, W. Lloyd, and Paul S. Lunt
1941   The Social Life of a Modern Community. New Haven, Conn.: Yale University Press.

Warren, N.
1972   African Infant Precocity. Psychological Bulletin 78:353–67.

Washburn, Sherwood L., and Ruth Moore
1974   Ape Into Man: A Study of Human Evolution. Boston: Little, Brown & Co.

Waterman, Richard A.
1952   African Influence on the Music of the Americas. *In* Acculturation in the Americas. Sol Tax, ed. Vol. 2. Pp. 207–18. Chicago: Proceedings of the 29th International Congress of Americanists.

Weltfish, Gene
1953   The Origins of Art. Indianapolis: Bobbs-Merrill Co.

Weyer, Edward
1932   The Eskimos. New Haven, Conn.: Yale University Press.

Wheat, Joe Ben
1972   The Olsen-Chubbuck Site: A Paleo-Indian Bison Kill. Memoirs of the Society for American Archaeology 26.

White, Leslie A.
1959   The Evolution of Culture. New York: McGraw-Hill Book Co.

Whiting, Beatrice B., ed.
1963   Six Cultures: Studies of Child Rearing. New York: John Wiley & Sons.

Whiting, Beatrice, and Carolyn Pope Edwards
1973   A Cross-Cultural Analysis of Sex Differences in the Behavior of Children Aged Three Through Eleven. Journal of Social Psychology 91:171–88.

Whiting, Beatrice B., and John W. M. Whiting
1975   Children of Six Cultures: A Psycho-Cultural Analysis. Cambridge: Harvard University Press.

Whiting, John W. M., and Irvin L. Child
1953   Child Training and Personality: A Cross-Cultural Study. New Haven, Conn.: Yale University Press.

Whiting, John W. M., Richard Kluckhohn, and Albert Anthony
  1958   The Function of Male Initiation Ceremonies at Puberty. *In* Readings in Social Psychology. Third ed. Eleanor E. Maccoby, Theodore M. Newcomb, and Eugene L. Hartley, eds. Pp. 359–70. New York: Henry Holt & Co.

Whiting, John W. M. et al.
  1966   Field Guide for a Study of Socialization. New York: John Wiley & Sons.

Whyte, William F.
  1943   Street Corner Society: The Social Structure of an Italian Slum. Chicago: University of Chicago Press.

Wilber, Charles C.
  1960   Physiological Regulations and the Origins of Human Types. *In* Readings on Race. Stanley M. Garn, ed. Pp. 107–15. Springfield, Ill.: Charles C Thomas, Publisher.

Willey, Gordon R.
  1966   An Introduction to American Archaeology. Vol. I, North and Middle America. Englewood Cliffs, N. J.: Prentice-Hall, Inc.

Wilson, John A.
  1951   The Culture of Ancient Egypt. Chicago: University of Chicago Press.

Wilson, Monica
  1950   Nyakyusa Kinship. *In* Radcliffe-Brown and Forde 1950:111–39.
  1951   Good Company: A Study of Nyakyusa Age-Villages. London: Oxford University Press.

Wissler, Clark
  1926   The Relation of Man to Nature in Aboriginal North America. New York: D. Appleton.

Witkin, Herman A.
  1967   A Cognitive-Style Approach to Cross-Cultural Research. International Journal of Psychology 2:233–50.

Witkin, Herman A., R. B. Dyk, H. F. Faterson, D. R. Goodenough, and S. A. Karp
  1962   Psychological Differentiation: Studies of Development. New York: John Wiley & Sons.

Wittfogel, Karl A.
  1956   The Hydraulic Civilizations. *In* Man's Role in Changing the Face of the Earth. William I. Thomas, Jr., ed. Pp. 152–64. Chicago: University of Chicago Press.
  1957   Oriental Despotism: A Comparative Study of Total Power. New Haven, Conn.: Yale University Press.

Wolf, Arthur P.
  1966   Childhood Association, Sexual Attraction, and the Incest Taboo: A Chinese Case. American Anthropologist 68:883–98.

Wolf, Eric R.
  1955   Types of Latin American Peasantry: A Preliminary Discussion. American Anthropologist 57:452–71.
  1957   Closed Corporate Peasant Communities in Mesoamerica and Central Java. Southwestern Journal of Anthropology 13:7–12.
  1966   Peasants. Englewood Cliffs, N.J.: Prentice-Hall, Inc.
  1969   Peasant Wars of the Twentieth Century. New York: Harper & Row.

Wolf, Margery
  1972   Women and the Family in Rural Taiwan. Stanford, Calif.: Stanford University Press.

Wolpoff, Milford H.
  1971a   Vértesszöllös and the Presapiens Theory. American Journal of Physical Anthropology 35:209–15.
  1971b   Competitive Exclusion Among Lower Pleistocene Hominids: The Single Species Hypothesis. Man 6:601–14.

1973 Posterior Tooth Size, Body Size, and Diet in South African Gracile Australopithecines. American Journal of Physical Anthropology 39:375–91.

Woolley, Leonard
1965 The Beginnings of Civilization: History of Mankind, Cultural and Scientific Development. Vol. I. Part 2. New York: Mentor Books.

Wright, Harry B.
1957 Witness to Witchcraft. New York: Funk & Wagnalls.

Young, Frank W.
1962 The Function of Male Initiation Ceremonies: A Cross-Cultural Test of an Alternative Hypothesis. American Journal of Sociology 67:379–91.

Young, William C., Robert W. Goy, and Charles H. Phoenix
1964 Hormones and Sexual Behavior. Science 143:212–18.

Yutang, Lin
1937 The Importance of Living. New York: Reynal & Hitchcock.

ILLUSTRATIONS

part three

INDEX

This book has been set in 10 and 9 point Souvenir Light, leaded 2 points. Part numbers are 48 point Souvenir Demi-Bold and part titles are 24 point Souvenir Demi-Bold. Chapter numbers are 72 point Caslon Old Style No. 540 and chapter titles are 16 point Souvenir Light. The size of the overall type area is 33½ picas by 47 picas.